MY

COLLECTED LETTERS OF
Samuel Taylor Coleridge

COLLECTED LETTERS OF
# Samuel Taylor Coleridge

EDITED BY
EARL LESLIE GRIGGS

VOLUME II

1801–1806

OXFORD
AT THE CLARENDON PRESS
1956

*Oxford University Press, Amen House, London E.C.4*
GLASGOW NEW YORK TORONTO MELBOURNE WELLINGTON
BOMBAY CALCUTTA MADRAS KARACHI CAPE TOWN IBADAN
*Geoffrey Cumberlege, Publisher to the University*

PRINTED IN GREAT BRITAIN

# CONTENTS

ABBREVIATIONS AND PRINCIPAL
   REFERENCES                vii

TEXT OF THE LETTERS 1801-1806   661

INDEX                                    1207

# ILLUSTRATION

SAMUEL TAYLOR COLERIDGE, from a painting by James Northcote    *facing page* 1101

# ABBREVIATIONS AND PRINCIPAL REFERENCES

*Abbreviations*

| | |
|---|---|
| Biog. Lit. | Coleridge, S. T.: *Biographia Literaria*, . . . 2 vols., 1817; ed. by H. N. Coleridge, 2 vols., 1847; ed. by J. Shawcross, 2 vols., 1907. (When necessary the edition is indicated.) |
| Campbell, *Life* | Campbell, J. D.: *Samuel Taylor Coleridge, a Narrative of the Events of His Life*, 1894 |
| Campbell, *Poetical Works* | Campbell, J. D., ed.: *The Poetical Works of Samuel Taylor Coleridge*, 1893 |
| Chambers, *Life* | Chambers, E. K.: *Samuel Taylor Coleridge: A Biographical Study*, 1938 |
| *Charles Lamb and the Lloyds* | Lucas, E. V.: *Charles Lamb and the Lloyds*, 1898 |
| *Coleridge* | Blunden, E., and Griggs, E. L., editors: *Coleridge: Studies by Several Hands*, . . . 1934 |
| E. L. G. | Griggs, E. L., ed.: *Unpublished Letters of Samuel Taylor Coleridge*, . . . 2 vols., 1932 |
| *Early Letters* | De Selincourt, E., ed.: *The Early Letters of William and Dorothy Wordsworth (1787–1805)*, 1935 |
| *Early Rec.* | Cottle, Joseph: *Early Recollections; chiefly relating to the late Samuel Taylor Coleridge*, . . . 2 vols., 1837 |
| *Essays on His Own Times* | Coleridge, Sara, ed.: *Essays on His Own Times*, . . . *By S. T. Coleridge*, 3 vols., 1850 |
| *Frag. Remains* | Davy, John: *Fragmentary Remains, Literary and Scientific, of Sir Humphry Davy*, . . . 1858 |
| *John Rickman* | Williams, Orlo: *Life and Letters of John Rickman*, 1912 |
| *Journals* | De Selincourt, E., ed.: *Journals of Dorothy Wordsworth*, 2 vols., 1952 |
| *Lamb Letters* | Lucas, E. V., ed.: *The Letters of Charles Lamb, to which are added those of His Sister, Mary Lamb*, 3 vols., 1935 |
| *Later Years* | De Selincourt, E., ed.: *The Letters of William and Dorothy Wordsworth: the Later Years*, 3 vols., 1939 |
| *Letters* | Coleridge, E. H., ed.: *Letters of Samuel Taylor Coleridge*, 2 vols., 1895 |
| *Letters from the Lake Poets* | [Coleridge, E. H., ed.] *Letters from the Lake Poets . . . to Daniel Stuart*, 1889 |
| *Letters to Estlin* | Bright, H. A., ed.: *Unpublished Letters from Samuel Taylor Coleridge to the Rev. John Prior Estlin* (Philobiblon Society, *Miscellanies*, xv, 1877–84) |
| *Life and Corres.* | Southey, C. C., ed.: *The Life and Correspondence of the late Robert Southey*, 6 vols., 1849–50 |

## Abbreviations and Principal References

### Abbreviations

| | |
|---|---|
| *Memoir of William Taylor* | Robberds, J. W., ed.: *A Memoir of the Life and Writings of the late William Taylor of Norwich,* . . . 2 vols., 1843 |
| *Memoirs of Wordsworth* | Wordsworth, Christopher: *Memoirs of William Wordsworth,* 2 vols., 1851 |
| *Memorials of Coleorton* | Knight, Wm., ed.: *Memorials of Coleorton, being Letters . . . to Sir George and Lady Beaumont,* . . . 2 vols., 1887 |
| *Middle Years* | De Selincourt, E., ed.: *The Letters of William and Dorothy Wordsworth: the Middle Years,* 2 vols., 1937 |
| *Poems* | Coleridge, E. H., ed.: *The Complete Poetical Works of Samuel Taylor Coleridge,* . . . 2 vols., 1912 |
| *Rem.* | Cottle, Joseph: *Reminiscences of Samuel Taylor Coleridge and Robert Southey,* 1847 |
| *Southey Letters* | Warter, J. W., ed.: *Selections from the Letters of Robert Southey,* 4 vols., 1856 |
| *Southey's Poet. Works* | *The Poetical Works of Robert Southey,* 10 vols., 1838. (The engraved title-pages of vols. i–iii are dated 1837.) |
| *Thomas Poole* | Sandford, Mrs. Henry: *Thomas Poole and His Friends,* 2 vols., 1888 |
| *Tom Wedgwood* | Litchfield, R. B.: *Tom Wedgwood the First Photographer,* . . . 1903 |
| *William Godwin* | Paul, C. Kegan: *William Godwin: His Friends and Contemporaries,* 2 vols., 1876 |
| Wise, *Bibliography* | Wise, T. J., *A Bibliography of . . . Samuel Taylor Coleridge,* 1913 |
| *Wordsworth* | Dunklin, G. T., ed.: *Wordsworth: Centenary Studies,* . . . 1951 |
| *Wordsworth and Coleridge* | Griggs, E. L., ed.: *Wordsworth and Coleridge: Studies in Honor of George McLean Harper,* 1939 |
| *Wordsworth, Poet. Works* | De Selincourt, E., and Darbishire, Helen, editors: *The Poetical Works of William Wordsworth,* 5 vols., 1940–9 |

### 373. *To Thomas Poole*

*Address*: Mr T. Poole | N. Stowey | Bridgewater | Somerset
*MS. British Museum. Pub. with omis. E. L. G. i. 166.*
*Postmark*: 9 January 1801. *Stamped*: Keswick.

Tuesday Night, Jan. 7. [6] 1801

My dear Poole

I write, alas! from my bed, to which I have been confined for almost the whole of the last three weeks with a Rheumatic Fever—which has now left me, I trust—but the pain has fixed itself in my hip, & in consequence, as I believe, of the torture I have sustained in that part, & the general feverous state of my body, my left testicle has swoln to more than three times it's natural size, so that I can only lie on my back, and am now sitting wide astraddle on this wearisome Bed. O me, my dear fellow! the notion of a Soul is a comfortable one to a poor fellow, who is beginning to be ashamed of his Body. For the last four months I have not had a fortnight of continuous health / bad eyes, swoln Eyelids, Boils behind my ears, & heaven knows what!—From this year I commence a Liver by Rule—the most degrading, perhaps, of all occupations, & which, were I not a Husband & Father, I should reject, as thinking human Life not worth it.—

My visit to the South I must defer to the warm weather—the remaining months of the winter & the Spring I must give totis viribus to Health & Money—. But for my illness I should have been so far beforehand with the world, that I should in all probability have been able to have maintained myself all this year without drawing on [the] Mr Wedgewoods, which I wished with a very fever of earnestness: for indeed it is gall to me to receive any more money from them, till I can point to something which I have done with an inward consciousness, that therein I have exerted the whole of my mind.—As soon as my poor Head can endure the intellectual & mechanical part of composition, I must immediately *finish* a volume which has been long due—this will cost me a month, for I must not attempt to work hard. When this is finished, I shall receive 70£ clear—which will not be sufficient by some pounds to liquidate my debts: for I owe 20£ to Wordsworth, 25£ to Shopkeepers & my Landlord in Keswick, & 25£ to Phillips, the Bookseller (moneys received on the score of a work to be done for him which I could do indeed in a fortnight & receive 25£ more; but the fellow's name is become so infamous, that it would be worse than any thing I have yet done to appear in public as his Hack.)—Besides these I owe about 30£, 17£ of it to you, & the remainder to Lamb—but these are of no pressing nature, whereas the above mentioned are imperious.——After this work I shall publish my Tragedy, which I have greatly added to, & altered, under the title of a Poem—& likewise, & by itself, Christabel. These will fetch me 60£—& here end the List of my immediate & certain Resources.—— I have by me a Drama, and a sort of Farce—written wholly *for* the Theatre, & which I should be ashamed of in any other view—works written purposely vile—if aught good *should* come of them, it would set me at ease at once; but that is but a Dream.—The result of all this is (I am so dizzy in consequence of so long lying a bed that I do not know whether I write legibly in manner or intelligibly in matter) that much as it may distress me, I must draw on Mr Wedgewood—I do not know how much of this year's money I have anticipated—I hope, not more than 40£—if so, I have 110 coming.— One thing I must request of you, that you will desire Mr King to pay 15£ to Mrs Fricker on my account—and *I have written* to Mr Wedgewood to repay that sum to you. I have done this, because she is in immediate want of the money, & it saves the circuit of Letters, & it would have been gross to have had the money sent to her immediately from Mr Wedgewood.—My Wife & Children are well—Derwent is a fine fat little fellow, that very often looks just like your dear Mother. Hartley is a universal Darling—he seems to have administered Love Philtres to the whole Town.— God bless you, my dearest Poole!—I have scarce strength left to fold up the Letter—

S. T. Coleridge

## 374. To Humphry Davy

*Address*: Mr Davy | Pneumatic Institution | Hotwells | Bristol
MS. Royal Institution. *Pub. with omis.* E. L. G. *i. 168.*
*Postmark*: 14 January 1801. *Stamped*: Keswick.

Jan. 11. 1801

My dear Davy

With legs astraddle & bebolster'd back,<br>Alack! alack!

I received your letter just in time to break up some speculations on the Hernia Humoralis, degenerating into Sarcocele, 'in which (after a long paragraph of Horrors) the Patient is at last carried off in great misery.'——From the week that Stoddart left me to the present I have been harrassed by a succession of Indispositions, inflamed eyes, swoln eyelids, boils behind my ear, &c &c—Somewhat more than 3 weeks ago I walked to Grasmere, & was wet thro'—I changed immediately—but still the next day I was taken

## 11 January 1801

ill, & by the Lettre de cachet of a Rheumatic Fever sentenced me to the Bed-bastille—the Fever left me, and on the Friday before last I was well enough to be conveyed home in a chaise—but immediately took to my bed again—a most excruc[ia]ting pain on the least motion, but not without motion, playing Robespierre & Marat in my left Hip & the small of my back—but alas! worse than all, my left Testicle swelled, without pain indeed, but distressing from it's weight; from a foolish shamefacedness almost peculiar to Englishmen I did [not] shew it to our doctor till last Tuesday night. On examination it appeared that a Fluid had collected between the Epididymis & the Body of the Testicle (*how* learned a Misfortune of this kind makes one)—Fomentations & fumigations of Vinegar having no effect, I applied Sal ammoniac dissolved in verjuice, & to considerable purpose; but the smart was followed by such a frantic & intolerable *Itching* over the whole surface of the Scrotum, that I am convinced it is the identical Torment which the Damned suffer in Hell, & that Jesus, the good-natured one of the Trinity, had it built of Brimstone, in a pang of pity for the poor Devils.—In all the parts thro' which the Spermatic Chord passes, I have dull & obtuse pains—and on removing the suspensory Bandage the sense of weight is terrible.—I never knew before what it was to be truly weak in body—I h[av]e such pains in the Calves of my Legs— / yet still [m]y animal spirits bear me up—tho' I am so weak, that even from sitting up to write this note to you I seem to sink in upon myself in a ruin, like a Column of Sand informed & animated only by a Whirl-blast of the Desart.[1] Pray, my dear Davy! did you rectify the red oil which rises over after the Spirit of Hartshorn is gotten from the Horns, so as to make that animal oil of Diphelius?[2] And is it true what Hoffman[3] asserts, that 15 or 20 drops will exert many times the power of opium both in degree & duration, without inducing any after fatigue?—

You say W.'s 'last poem is full of jus[t] pictures of what human life ought to be'—believe me, that such scenes & such char[acters]

---

[1] Cf. the following lines from *The Triumph of Loyalty*:

> The Whirl-blast comes, the desert-sands rise up
> And shape themselves; from Heaven to Earth they stand,
> As though they were the Pillars of a Temple,
> Built by Omnipotence in its own honour!
> But the Blast pauses, and their shaping spirit
> Is fled: the mighty Columns were but sand.

*Poems*, ii. 1072, and also i. 423.

[2] Presumably Coleridge refers to the animal oil invented by J. K. Dippel, 1673–1734.

[3] Probably Friedrich Hoffmann (1660–1742), the celebrated German physician.

374]                *To Humphry Davy*

really exist in this county—the superiority [of] the small Estatesman, such as W. pain[ts in] old Michael, is a God compared to our Peasants & small Farmers in the South: & furnishes important documents of the kindly ministrations of local attachment & hereditary descent—

Success, my dear Davy! to Galvanism & every other ism & schism that you are about. Perge, dilectissime! et quantum p[otes] (potes autem plurimùm) rempublicam hu[ma]ni generis juva. Videtur mihi salte[m a]lios velle—te vero posse. Interea a Deo [optimo] maximo iterum atque iterum precor, ut Davy meus, Davy, meum cor, meum cap[ut,] mea spes altera, vivat, ut vivat diu et feliciter!——Tui amantissimus

S. T. Coleridge

Raptum properante Γραμματαφόρῳ

## 375. To Thomas Poole

*Address*: Mr T. Poole | N. Stowey | Bridgewater | Somerset    *Single Sheet*
MS. British Museum. *Partly pub*. Thomas Poole, ii. 27.

On 19 January 1801 Coleridge sent Poole a sheet containing (1) a copy of a letter from Wordsworth to Charles James Fox, in Dorothy Wordsworth's handwriting (see *Early Letters*, 259), (2) a copy of a letter from Wordsworth to William Wilberforce in Dorothy Wordsworth's handwriting but dictated to her by Coleridge, and (3) a personal letter from Coleridge to Poole. At the top of the manuscript Coleridge wrote: 'Dear Poole Turn to the Back of the Letter before you read this. S. T. C.' Since the letter to Wilberforce is unpublished and is Coleridge's own composition, it is added as an addendum to the letter to Poole.
*Postmark*: 22 January 1801.    *Stamped*: Keswick.

Monday Night, Jan. 19, 1801

My dearest Poole

Since I last wrote, I have had a sad time & a painful—a fluid, it seems, had collected between the tunica vaginalis & the left Testicle—in short, 'twas an hydrocele. By the increased weight the spermatic cord was affected, and in consequence the hip & the back, & where ever the spermatic cord passed, were troubled constantly by a *dull* pain and frequently by sharp & shooting Pains—& towards night I had regularly feverish Symptoms. But the sense of Lassitude, if I only sate up in bed, was worst of all— I seem'd to fall in upon myself in ruin, like a column of sand, that had been informed & animated only by a whirl blast of the desart— such & so treacherous were my animal spirits to me.—The Vinegar fomentations & fumigations, &c producing no effect, we had recourse to an application of Sal Ammoniac dissolved in verjuice—

this promised well at first, but it soon by the extreme irritation brought on over the whole surface of the scrotum such a *frantic* Itching, that I have no doubt but that this & no other is the Torment in Hell, & that Brimstone was given not [as] a producer, but as a merciful Palliative, of the Punishment.—This Itching was succeeded by the appearance of five small but angry Ulcers on the Scrotum / on Wednesday morning I had *three* Leeches applied, & the wounds by means of hot cloaths were kept bleeding the whole day—& after this I applied poultices, of bread grated & mixed up with a strong solution of Lead.—Since that day I have been (not indeed without sorrowful Relapses at Evening) mending fast—the fever toward night is almost gone—& the Fluid has been absorbed & is absorbing apace—and all seems doing well. This day for the first time I sate up for an hour or two, & do not find myself the worse.—Our Surgeon & apothecary is an excellent, modest, truly intelligent man.—

The Lyrical Ballads will be published by the time this Letter reaches you—for my sake, & Wordsworth's, & your own, you will purchase not only the new Volume, but likewise the second Edition of the First Volume, on account of the valuable Preface. By my advice, & at Longman's expence, copies with appropriate Letters were sent to the Dutchess of Devonshire, Sir Bland Burgess,[1] Mrs Jordan, Mr Fox, Mr Wilberforce, & 2 or 3 others— I dictated all the other Letters while W. wrote one to Mr Fox.[2] I have had that letter transcribed for you, for it's excellence—& mine to Wilberforce, because the two contain a good view of our notions & motives, poetical & political.—I *had written* to Mr Wedgewood to repay you. I rejoice at your dear Mothe[r's heal]th. Love to Ward, & congrat. on his Sister's account. God love you, *dear* Friend—S. T. Coleridge. *Write.*

I have not heard from Mr Wedgewood since I wrote—& am not a little pinched for money. Last week I payed 25£ to Phillips, in consequence of an attorney's Letter,[3] the first I ever received &

---

[1] Sir James Bland Burges (1752–1824), politician and man of letters.
[2] For note concerning Fox's reply see Letter 380.
[3] This 'attorney's Letter' has been preserved:

London 9 Jany 1801

Sir

I have been applyd to by Mr Rd Phillips of this City Bookseller who directs me to inform You that unless your engagemt. with him is forthwith completed I have his instructions to commence an Action against You without further Notice

I am Sir | Your most Obt Servt
D. Abbott.

Rolls Yard Chancery Lane / .

which amused me infinitely.—I felt like a man of this World. I had irritated P. by an exceedingly humorous Letter, which I will send you.

Wordsworths left me this morning.—

### To William Wilberforce Esqr. M.P.
### [Composed by Coleridge for Wordsworth]

Sir,

I composed the accompanying poems under the persuasion, that all which is usually included under the name of action bears the same pro[por]tion (in respect of worth) to the affections, as a language to the thing sign[ified.] When the material forms or intellectual ideas which should be employed to [rep]resent the internal state of feeling, are made to claim attention for their own sake, then commences Lip-worship, or superstition, or disputatiousness, in religion; a passion for gaudy ornament & violent stimulants in morals; & in our literature bombast and vicious refinements, an aversion to the common conversational language of our Countrymen, with an extravagant preference given to *Wit* by some, and to outrageous *incident* by others; while the most sacred affections of the human race seem to lay no hold on our sympathies unless we can contemplate them in the train of some circumstances that excite *curiosity*, or unriddle them from some gaudy phrases that are to attract our wonder for themselves. It was the excellence of our elder Poets to write in such a language as should the *most* rapidly convey their mean[ing,] but the pleasure which I am persuaded the greater number of Read[ers re]ceive from our modern writers in verse & prose, arises from the sense of having overcome a difficulty, of having made a series of lucky guesses, & perhaps, in some degree, of understanding what they are conscious the lower Classes of their Countrymen would not be able to understand. The poems which accompany this letter were written with no idle expectation of the Author's immediate fame or their rapid circulation: had my predominant influences been either the love of praise or the desire of profit, I should have held out to myself other subjects than the affections which walk 'in silence and in a veil' and other rules of poetic diction than the determination to prefer passion to imagery, & (except when the contrary was chosen for dramatic purposes) to express what I meant to express with all possible regard to precision and propriety but with very little attention to what is called *dignity*. In thus stating my opinions I state at the same time my reasons for soliciting your acceptance of these Volumes. In your religious treatise[1] these truths are developed, & applied to the present state of our religion; I have acted on them in a less awful department, but not I trust with less serious convictions. Indeed had I not persuaded myself that in the composition of them I had been a Fellow-labourer with you in the same Vineyard, acting under the perception of some one common truth & attributing to that truth the same importance & necessity;[2] if I had not appeared to myself to have discovered (in my intentions at least) some bond of connection between us; I could not without self-reproof have taken this opportunity of &c &c

W. Wordsworth.

### 376. To John Thelwall

*Address*: Mr John Thelwall | Hereford | Herefordshire
*MS. Pierpont Morgan Lib. Hitherto unpublished.*
*Postmark*: 26 January 1801.   *Stamped*: Keswick.

Jan. 23. 1801   Keswick, Cumberland

Dear Thelwall

Shortly after I wrote to you, I was seized with a Rheumatic Fever, & after that with an Hydrocele—I have been now for more than 5 weeks confined to my bed, and at the time your Letter arrived too ill to read it—& *Now* I can only write merely but to inclose the note—a blank half-sheet—for as a supersacramentary penance to my other grievous ones my right eye is inflamed & the Lid prodigiously swollen. But I am weary of writing of this I—I—I—I—so bepatched & bescented with Sal Ammoniac & Diaculum, Pain & Infirmity. My own Moans are grown stupid to my own ears.

I rejoice sincerely that you have left a situation wholly unfit for you—doubtless, by your Talents you will always be able to earn sufficient for the Day at least. I wish for your sake that so many foolish Epic Poems had not been published lately, or on the eve of Publication. You entirely misunderstood me as to religious matters.—You love your wife, children, & friends, you worship nature, and you dare hope, nay, have faith in, the future improvement of the human Race——this is true Religion / your notions about the historical credibility or non-credibility of a sacred Book, your assent to or dissent from the existence of a supramundane Deity, or personal God, are absolutely indifferent to me / mere figures of a magic Lanthern. I hold my faith—you keep your's.

[1] William Wilberforce, *A Practical View of the Prevailing Religious System of Professed Christians*, 1797.
[2] The remainder of this letter is in Coleridge's handwriting; all that precedes is in Dorothy Wordsworth's.

Write to inform me, that you have received the note—for your address—Hereford—is a very brief one indeed.

The account I gave you is the true one—had I been able to send 10£ or 100£ on my own account, I would do it with eagerness—but without any *gravities* concerning your injuries or your merits— / these speculations are superseded in me by plain simple affection.

My love to your dear Wife. Derwent, my youngest, is a fat healthy hungry pretty creature—the abstract idea of a Baby— a fit Representative of Babe-borough. Hartley is quite the contrary—a fairy elf—all life, all motion—indefatigable in joy—a spirit of Joy dancing on an Aspen Leaf. From morning to night he whirls about and about, whisks, whirls, and eddies, like a blossom in a May-breeze.—

Sara desires to be kindly remembered to you—& your's.

God bless you | &
S. T. Coleridge

I have not seen your Novel—nor knew that you had written one.[1] Any thing left for me at Mr Longman's, Paternoster Row, will find it's way to me sometime or other.

P.S. By all means procure a sight of the 2nd Volume of the Lyrical Ballads, and of the second Edition of the first Volume— the Preface is invaluable.

### 377. To Thomas Poole

*Address*: Mr T. Poole | N. Stowey | Bridgewater | Somerset.
*MS. British Museum. Pub. E. L. G. i. 170.*
*Postmark*: 4 February 1801.   *Stamped*: Keswick.

My dear Poole    Sunday Night. Feb. I. 1801

It mingles with the pleasures of convalescence, with the breeze that trembles on my nerves, the thought how glad you will be to hear that I am striding back to my former health with such manful paces. The Fluid is nearly, indeed almost wholly absorbed, and though I cannot sit up very long without lassitude & pains in my back, yet I can sit up every day longer than the Day before. I have begun to take Bark, and I hope, that shortly I shall look back on my long & painful Illness only as a Storehouse of wild Dreams for Poems, or intellectual Facts for metaphysical Speculation. Davy in the kindness of his heart calls me the Poet-philosopher—I hope, Philosophy & Poetry will not neutralize each

---

[1] In 1801 Thelwall published a novel, *The Daughter of Adoption*, 4 vols., under the pseudonym, John Beaufort, LL.D.

other, & leave me an inert mass. But I talk idly—I feel, that I have power within me: and I humbly pray to the Great Being, the God & Father who has bidden me 'rise & walk' that he will grant me a steady mind to employ the health of my youth and manhood in the manifestation of that power. One week more of Repose I am enjoined to grant myself: & then I gird up my Loins, first, to disembarrass my circumstances by fulfilling all my engagements / & then to a Work—O my dear dear Friend! that you were with me by the fireside of my Study here, that I might talk it over with you to the Tune of this Night Wind that pipes it's thin doleful climbing sinking Notes like a child that has lost it's way and is crying aloud, half in grief and half in the hope to be heard by it's Mother.[1] But when your Ripping is over, you will come, or at farthest immediately after your Hay Harvest.—Believe me, often and often in my walks amid these sublime Landscapes I have trod the ground impatiently, *irritated* that you were not with me.—Poor dear Mrs Robinson! you have heard of her Death. She wrote me a most affecting, heart-rending Letter a few weeks before she died, to express what she called her death bed affection & esteem for me—the very last Lines of her Letter are indeed sublime—

'My little Cottage is retired and comfortable. There I mean to remain (if indeed I live so long) till Christmas. But it is not surrounded with the romantic Scenery of your chosen retreat: it is not, my dear Sir! the nursery of sublime Thoughts—the abode of Peace—the solitude of Nature's Wonders. O! Skiddaw!—I think, if I could but once contemplate thy Summit, I should never quit the Prospect it would present till my eyes were closed for ever!'

O Poole! that that Woman had but been married to a noble Being, what a noble Being she herself would have been. Latterly, she felt this with a poignant anguish.—Well!—

> O'er her pil'd grave the gale of evening sighs;
> And flowers will grow upon it's grassy Slope.
> I wipe the dimming Water from mine eyes—
> Ev'n in the cold Grave dwells the Cherub Hope![2]

Our children are well—twenty times a week I see in little Derwent such a striking *Look* of your dear Mother!——My love to Ward.—I congratulate him on his Brother's Marriage.——Have you received the 15£ from Mr Wedgewood? he informed me that he would send it to you speedily. I received 25£ from him, which I payed off immediately—and now that I am so near to Health, & shall be soon able to finish my engagements with Longman, I feel

---

[1] Cf. *Dejection; an Ode,* lines 121–5; *Poems,* i. 368; and Letter 438, p. 795.
[2] *Poems,* ii. 996.

377]       *To Thomas Poole*

a repugnance at sending to him again for more money immediately. If it would [be] no inconvenience to you to let me have 20£ for six weeks, you would make my mind easy—at that time I will either send you back the Money myself, or write to Mr Wedgewood to do so. But if it be inconvenient to you, feel no pain in telling me so—only write to me. I have paid Phillips, *as* I told you, I believe; & that the Fellow sent me an Attorney's Letter——it amused me exceedingly at first—but afterwards it made my very heart ache, thinking of poor Cruckshank——God bless you, my dear
                  Friend! & S. T. Coleridge.—

### 378. *To Humphry Davy*

*Address*: Mr Davy | Pneumatic Institution | Hot Wells | Bristol    Single
MS. *Royal Institution*. *Pub*. Letters, *i*. 345.
*Postmark*: 6 February 1801.   *Stamped*: Keswick.

                                Tuesday, Feb. 3. 1801
My dear Davy

I can scarcely reconcile it to my Conscience to make you pay postage for another Letter. O what a fine Unveiling of modern Politics it would be, if there were published a minute Detail of all the sums received by Government from the Post Establishment, and of all the outlets, in which the sums so received, flowed out again—and on the other hand all the domestic affections that had been stifled, all the intellectual progress that would have been, but is not, on account of this heavy Tax, &c &c——The *Letters* of a nation ought to be payed for, as an article of national expence.——Well—but I did not take up this paper to flourish away in splenetic Politics.——

A Gentleman resident here, his name Calvert,[1] an idle, goodhearted, and ingenious man, has a great desire to commence fellow-student with me & Wordsworth in Chemistry.—He is an intimate friend of Wordsworth's—& he has proposed to Wordsworth to take a house which he (Calvert) has nearly built, called Windy Brow, in a delicious situation, scarce half a mile from Grieta Hall, the residence of S. T. Coleridge Esq. / and so for him (Calvert) to live with them, i.e. Wordsworth & his Sister.—In this case he means to build a little Laboratory &c.—Wordsworth has not quite decided, but is strongly inclined to adopt the scheme, because he and his Sister have before lived with Calvert on the same footing, and are much attached to him; because my Health is so precarious, and so much injured by Wet, and his health too is, like

[1] William Calvert, whose brother, Raisley Calvert, had left a legacy to Wordsworth.

little potatoes, no great things, and therefore Grasmere (13 miles from Keswick) is too great a distance for us to enjoy each other's Society without inconvenience as much as it would be profitable for us both; & likewise because he feels it more & more necessary for him to have some intellectual pursuit less closely connected with deep passion, than Poetry, & is of course desirous too not to be so wholly ignorant of knowleges so exceedingly important—. However whether Wordsworth come or no, Calvert & I have determined to begin & go on. Calvert is a man of sense, and some originality / and is besides what is well called a *handy* man. He is a good practical mechanic &c—and is desirous to lay out any sum of money that may be necessary. You know how long, how ardently I have wished to initiate myself in Chemical science—both for it's own sake, and in no small degree likewise, my beloved friend!—that I may be able to sympathize with *all*, that you do and think.—Sympathize blindly with it all I do even *now*, God knows! from the very middle of my heart's heart—; but I would fain sympathize with you in the Light of Knowlege.—This opportunity therefore is exceedingly precious to me—as on my own account I could not afford any the least additional expence, having been already by long & successive Illnesses thrown behind hand so much, that for the next 4 or five months, I fear, let me work as hard as I can, I shall not be able to do what my heart within me *burns* to do—that is, *concenter* my free mind to the affinities of the Feelings with Words & Ideas under the title of 'Concerning Poetry & the nature of the Pleasures derived from it.'——I have faith, that I do understand this subject / and I am sure, that if I write what I ought to do on it, the Work would supersede all the Books of Metaphysics hitherto written / and all the Books of Morals too.—To whom shall a young man utter *his Pride*, if not to a young man whom he loves?——

I beg you therefore, my dear Davy! to write to me a long Letter when you are at leisure, informing me I What Books it will be well for Mr Calvert to purchase. 2. Directions for a convenient little Laboratory—and 3rdly—to what amount the apparatus would run in expence, and whether or no you would be so good as to superintend it's making at Bristol.—Fourthly, give me your advice how to *begin*——and fifthly & lastly & mostly do send a *drop* of hope to my parched Tongue, that you will, if you can, come & visit me in the Spring.—Indeed, indeed, you ought to see this Country, this divine Country—and then the Joy you would send into *me*!

The Shape of this paper will convince you with what eagerness I began this Letter—I really did not see that it was not a Sheet.

I have been *thinking* vigorously during my Illness—so that I

( 671 )

cannot say, that my long long wakeful nights have been all lost to me. The subject of my meditations ha[s] been the Relations of Thoughts to Things, in the language of Hume, of Ideas to Impressions: I may be truly described in the words of Descartes. I have been 'res cogitans, id est, dubitans, affirmans, negans, p[auca] intelligens, multa ignorans, volens, nolens, imaginans etia[m,] et sentiens[1]—' & I please myself with believing, that [you] will receive no small pleasure from the result of [my] broodings, altho' I expect in you (in some points) [a] determined opponent—but I say of my mind, in this respect,

'Manet imperterritus ille
Hostem magnanimum opperiens, et mole suâ stat.'[2]

Every poor fellow has his proud hour sometimes—& this, I suppose, is mine.—

I am better in every respect than I was; but am still *very feeble*. The Weather has been woefully against me for the last fortnight, it having rained here almost incessantly—I take large quantities of Bark, but the effect is (to express myself with the dignity of Science) $X = 0\ 0\ 0\ 0\ 0\ 0\ 0$: and I shall not gather strength or t[hat] suffusion of bloom which belongs to my healthy state, till I can walk out.

God bless you, my dear Davy! & your ever affectionate Friend,
S. T. Coleridge.

P.S. An electrical machine & a number of little nick nacks connected with it Mr Calvert has.——*Write*.

### 379. To Dorothy Wordsworth

*Address*: Mr Clarkson | Euse hill by Pooley Bridge | near | Penrith    for | Miss Wordsworth
*MS. Lord Latymer. Hitherto unpublished.*
*Stamped*: Keswick.

Monday, Feb. 9.   1801

My dearest Rotha

The Hack, Mr Calvert was so kind as to borrow for me, carried me home as pleasantly as the extreme Soreness of my whole frame admitted. I was indeed in the language of Shakespere, not a Man but a Bruise—I went to bed immediately, & rose on Sunday quite restored.—If I do not hear from you any thing to the contrary, I shall walk half way to Grasmere, on Friday Morning—leaving Keswick at ten o'clock precisely—in the hopes of meeting Sara[3]—

---

[1] *Meditatio Tertia.*          [2] *Aeneid*, x. 770–1.
[3] Sara Hutchinson had arrived on 18 Nov. 1800 for a visit to the Wordsworths lasting for several months. *Journals*, i. 73.

## 9 February 1801

partly to prevent the necessity of William's walking so far, just as he will have begun to tranquillize, & partly to remove from Mrs Coleridge's mind all uncertainty as to the time of her coming, which if it depended on William's mood of Body, might (unless he went to the injury of his health) be a week, or a fortnight hence—— But if Sara should have been so fatigued, as not to be able to take so long a walk without discomfort, on Friday / I shall walk on to Grasmere, & return with her the next day—all this however to be understood with the usual Deo Volente of Health & Weather. The Small Pox is in Keswick—& we are anxious, and eddy-minded about Derwent— /

I had a very long conversation with Hartley about Life, Reality, Pictures, & Thinking, this evening. He sate on my knee for half an hour at least, & was exceedingly serious. I wish to God, you had been with us. Much as you would desire to believe me, I cannot expect that I could communicate to you all that Mrs C. & I felt from his answers—they were so very sensible, accurate, & well worded. I am convinced, that we are under great obligations to Mr Jackson, who, I have no doubt, takes every opportunity of making him observe the differences of Things: for he pointed out without difficulty that there might be five Hartleys, Real Hartley, Shadow Hartley, Picture Hartley, Looking Glass Hartley, and Echo Hartley / and as to the difference between his Shadow & the Reflection in the Looking Glass, he said, the Shadow was black, and he could not see his *eyes* in it. One thing, he said, was very curious—I asked him what he did when he thought of any thing— he answered—I look at it, and then go to sleep. To sleep?—said I— you mean, that you *shut your eyes*. Yes, he replied—I shut my eyes, & put my hands so (covering his eyes) and go to sleep—then I wake again, and away I run.——That of shutting his eyes, & covering them was a Recipe I had given him some time ago / but the notion of that state of mind being Sleep is very striking, & he meant more, I suspect, than that People when asleep have their eyes shut—indeed I *know* it from the tone & *leap up* of Voice with which he uttered the word 'wake.' To morrow I am to exert my genius in making a paper-balloon / the idea of carrying up a bit of lighted Candle into the clouds makes him almost insane with Pleasure. As I have given you Hartley's Metaphysics I will now give you a literal Translation of page 49 of the celebrated Fichte's Uber den Begriff der Wissenschaftslehre [1794]—if any of *you*, or if either your Host or Hostess, have any propensity to *Doubts*, it will cure them for ever / for the object of the author is to attain absolute certainty. So read it aloud. (N.B. the 'I' means poor Gilbert's *I—das 'Ich'—*)——'Suppose, that A in the proposition

( 673 )

A = A stands not for the I, but for something or other different, then from this proposition you may deduce the condition under which it may be affirmed, that it is established, and *how* we are authorized to conclude, that If A is established, then it is established. Namely: the Proposition, A = A, holds good originally only of the I: it is abstracted from the Proposition in the Science of absolute Knowlege, I am I—the substance therefore or sum total of every Thing, to which it may be legitimately applied, must lie in the I, and be comprehended under it. No A therefore can be aught else than something established in the I, and now therefore the Proposition may stand thus: What is established in the I, is established—if therefore A is established in the I, then it is established (that is to say in so far as it is established, whether as only possible, or as real, or necessary) and then the Proposition is true without possibility of contradiction, if the I is to be I.—Farther, if the I be established, because it is established, then all, that is established in the I, is established because it is established; and provided only, that A is indeed a something established in the I, then it is established, if it is established; and the second Question likewise is solved.'——Here's a numerous Establishment for you / nothing in Touchstone ever equalled this—it is not even surpassed by Creech's account of Space in his notes to Lucretius.[1]—

Remember me & my wife kindly to Mr & Mrs Clarkson[2]—& give a kiss for me to dear little Tom—God love him!—I gave H. pictures, nuts, & mince pie, all as a Present from Tommy.—— Heaven bless you, my dear friends!   S. T. C.—

### 380. *To Thomas Poole*

*Address*: Mr T. Poole | Nether Stowey | Bridgewater | Somerset
*MS. British Museum, Pub. E. L. G. i. 172.*
*Postmark*: 16 February 1801.   *Stamped*: Keswick.

Friday, Feb. 13. 1801

My dearest Friend

I received your Letter with the Bill inclosed this evening.—If you come in the beginning of May, you will make it joyous as an Italian Month to me.—Only let it be in the middle of May, that the Leaves may be all out.—I shall begin to look at the Lake, and the

---

[1] Thomas Creech (1659–1700) published his translation of Lucretius in 1682.

[2] Thomas Clarkson (1760–1846), after several years of strenuous activity on behalf of the abolition of the slave trade, had retired to Eusemere Hill in the Lake Country. Mrs. Clarkson, *née* Catherine Buck, became one of Dorothy Wordsworth's most intimate friends.

encamped Host of mountains with a new Interest—'*that* will delight him!'—God ever bless you, my dear dear Friend!—

I received from J. W. the same account as your's nearly in the same words[1]—*Inter nos*, I believe Mr Sharpe[2] to be a very shallow man, & as to Mackintosh—Lord have pity upon those Metaphysics, of which he is a competent Judge. I attended 5 of his Lectures— such a wretched patch work of plagiarisms from Condilliac[3]—of contradictions, and blunders in matter of fact, I never heard from any man's mouth before. *Their* opinion weighs as nothing with me.—But *I* take T. Wedgewood's own opinion, his own convictions, as STRONG presumptions that he has fallen upon some very valuable Truths—some he stated but only in short hints to me / & I *guess* from these, that they have been noticed before, & set forth by Kant in part & in part by Lambert.[4]—I *guess*, that it will be so / yet I wish, they may not be, both for the sake of the Truth, & because if they should be, it would damp his spirits.——I have been myself *thinking* with the most intense energy on similar subjects / I shall shortly communicate the result of my Thoughts to the Wedgewoods / but previously shall send off some Letters which I have only to copy out fair to J. Wedgewood respecting Locke & Des Cartes, & likewise concerning the supposed Discovery of the Law of Association by Hobbes.—Since I have been at Keswick, I have read a great deal / and my Reading has furnished me with many reasons for being exceedingly suspicious of *supposed Discoveries* in Metaphysics. My dear dear Poole! Plato, and Aristotle were great & astonishing Geniuses, and yet there is not a Presbyterian Candidate for a Conventicle but believes that they were mere children in Knowlege compared with himself & Drs Priestly & Rees,[5] &c——

My *Letters* to the Wedgewoods shall be copied out & sent you, in the course of the next week.[6] I do not think, they will entertain you very much, those already written, I mean / for they are

---

[1] On 8 Feb. Poole wrote to Coleridge that he had heard from Josiah Wedgwood as follows: '*When* Tom *was here he enjoyed a high satisfaction in explaining to* Mackintosh *the result of his metaphysical speculations, and in finding M. concur with him in his opinions.* . . . *He has also convinced Sharpe, as far as he has opened the business to him. The subjects he has cleared are no less than* Time, Space, *and* Motion; *and Mackintosh and Sharpe think a metaphysical revolution likely to follow.*' Thomas Poole, ii. 28.

[2] Richard, 'Conversation', Sharp (1759–1835), man of business, Member of Parliament, and critic.

[3] Étienne Bonnot de Condillac (1715–80), the French philosopher, whose name Coleridge consistently misspelled.

[4] Johann H. Lambert (1728–77), German physicist and mathematician.

[5] Dr. Abraham Rees (1743–1825), cyclopaedist and presbyterian divine.

[6] See headnote to Letter 381 and Letters 381–3.

crowded with Latin Quotations, & relate chiefly to the character of Mr Locke, whom I think I have *proved* to have gained a reputation to which he had no honest claim / and Hobbes as little to the reputation, to which T. Wedgewood & *after* him Mackintosh have laboured to raise him. But all this *inter nos*.

Wordsworth has received answers from all but Mr Fox[1]—all respectful & polite, but all written *immediately* on the receipt of the Poems, & consequently expressing no Opinion. His reputation as a Poet is high indeed in London.

Mr Sharpe told me of his Friend Rogers, the drivelling Booby that *let* the Pleasures of Memory—'I look upon him, Mr Coleridge! as a sweet *Enamel* Poet.'

Change of Ministry interests *me* not—I turn at times half reluctantly from Leibnitz or Kant even to read a smoking new newspaper / such a purus putus Metaphysicus am I become. Mrs Coleridge has been ill with an ulcerated Sore throat; but is bettering.—I am feebler far, than I could wish to be / but the weather is against me. Mrs C. desires her kindest, very kindest Love to your Mother—she sends her Love to Ward, & begs & intreats of him (if your Mother is not disposed to write) that he will immediately write *her* a Letter, full of news, Stowey news— of Mr & Mrs Rich, of the Chesters, of every body, & every thing— she hates the sight of your nasty Letters, with not a word for *a woman* to read in them.—But Ward is a bad hand—do get your dear Mother to write.

O May! best month of all the Year!

Derwent is going to be inoculated with the Cow Pox—he is a beautiful Boy. And Hartley I could fill Sheets about him.—God love my dearest Friend

&

S. T. Coleridge

[1] Fox answered on 25 May 1801. He said that the poems had given him the greatest pleasure and that *Harry Gill*, *We are Seven*, *The Mad Mother*, and *The Idiot* were his favourites. Of *The Brothers* and *Michael*, which Wordsworth had especially singled out, Fox could only say: 'I am no great friend to blank verse for subjects which are to be treated of with simplicity.' Concerning Coleridge's share in the first volume he wrote: 'Of the poems which you state not to be yours, that entitled "Love" appears to me to be the best, and I do not know who is the author. "The Nightingale" I understand to be Mr. Coleridge's, who combats, I think, very successfully, the mistaken prejudice of the nightingale's note being melancholy.' *The Prose Works of William Wordsworth*, ed. by A. B. Grosart, 3 vols., 1876, ii. 205–6.

*18 February 1801*

### 381. *To Josiah Wedgwood*

*Address*: Mr T. Poole | N. Stowey | Bridgewater | Somerset    *Single Sheet*
MS. British Museum. *Hitherto unpublished. A second and briefer holograph of this letter is among the MSS. of Lord Latymer.*

Early in 1801 Coleridge embarked upon a serious study of philosophy, and at the onset he determined to examine the bases of Locke's position. During February he composed a series of letters dealing mainly with Locke and Descartes (see Letter 380). On 18 February he sent the first of these letters to Josiah Wedgwood, and at the same time sent a copy to Poole (see Letter 381). Chagrined at not receiving any acknowledgement of this letter from Wedgwood, he delayed sending the remaining letters for more than a month (see Letter 388). On 24 March, however, he posted Letters 382 and 383 to Wedgwood and sent copies of them to Poole the same day (see Letter 389). Josiah Wedgwood received these letters, for on 31 March 1801 he wrote to Poole: 'As to metaphysics I know little about them, and my head is at present so full of various affairs that I have not even read the letters Coleridge has written on those subjects, as I have honestly told him. From the cursory view I took of them he seems to have plucked the principal feathers out of Locke's wings. Tom is with us . . . but not well enough to pursue his own speculations or to attend to those of others' (MS. British Museum). Poole acknowledged Letter 381 on 14 March and Letters 382 and 383 on 9 April (*Thomas Poole*, ii. 32 and 42).

The philosophical letters sent to Josiah Wedgwood (Letters 381–3) have disappeared, but the manuscript copies Coleridge prepared for Poole survive and furnish the present text.

The fourth philosophical letter (384) is only an incomplete rough draft, containing neither salutation nor conclusion. There is no evidence that it was sent either to Wedgwood or to Poole. It is among the Coleridge manuscripts acquired by the British Museum from E. H. Coleridge (Egerton MS. 2801).

Since Coleridge's four philosophical letters (381–4) were written in the face of a long-established tradition that Locke was entirely the critic of Descartes, and since Coleridge attempted to prove that 'Locke's *System* existed in the writings of Descartes', it will be well, perhaps, to examine briefly the reasons for the traditional view of Locke and to glance at one or two twentieth-century estimates of Locke's relation to Descartes.

James Gibson declares that 'without the influence of the Cartesian view of knowledge and the Cartesian conception of self-consciousness, it is not too much to say that the *Essay*, as we know it, would never have been written'. He insists, nevertheless, that 'the way in which Locke develops the view of knowledge which he found in Descartes, and the very different use to which he puts the conception of self-consciousness, suffice to negative at once the suggestion of any want of originality in his fundamental positions'; and he concludes that Locke so freely transforms the Cartesian principles 'that the existence of any positive relation of dependence upon them has frequently been ignored by the historian of philosophy, and the positions of Descartes and Locke have been set in antithetical opposition to each other'. (*Locke's Theory of Knowledge and its Historical Relations*, 1917, p. 207.)

Professor R. I. Aaron says that Leibnitz at the turn of the eighteenth century considered Locke as the protagonist of the Gassendists and as an opponent of Descartes. Subsequently, Aaron points out, Voltaire and the Encyclopaedists acknowledged Locke as the critic of Cartesianism, 'hailed him as the founder of the empirical school . . . [and] created . . . the erroneous view that the two schools had nothing in common', a view persisting until late in the nineteenth century, when Locke's indebtedness to Descartes was realized. 'In our own day,' Aaron continues, 'Locke is talked of as if he were a mere rationalist, owing everything to Descartes. This view is equally untrue and needs to be corrected. Locke accepted much that Descartes taught. Nevertheless, he was his constant critic, criticizing him in the light of empiricism, that of Bacon and of Boyle on the one hand, and of the Gassendists on the other.' (*John Locke*, 1937, pp. 10, 33–34, and 77.)

These philosophical letters, then, attack the view of Locke current in the early nineteenth century, but Coleridge overstated Locke's dependence upon Descartes and failed to recognize the fundamental differences between the two philosophers. Professor R. I. Aaron, who has examined these letters, says that Coleridge was among the first, if he was not the first, to realize Locke's debt to Descartes, but that in emphasizing only the indebtedness to Descartes he stated a half-truth. Professor Aaron agrees that Coleridge rightly identified Locke as a conceptualist, but suggests that while Coleridge gives evidence of having studied Book I and the opening chapters of Book II of the *Essay*, he does not seem to have read the rest of the work with much care. Nevertheless, Coleridge's letters are important in pointing out Locke's dependence upon Descartes half a century before such writers as Edward Tagart and T. E. Webb 'discovered once again the rationalist elements in Locke's thought', and as evidence of Coleridge's own rejection of British empiricism.

*Stamped*: Kendal.

Copy of a Letter sent to Mr Wedgewood. Feb. 18. 1801

My dear Sir

It gives me a pleasure not wholly self-respective, that I am able to inform you of my almost compleat Recovery.—May God grant me Hope, and a steady Mind! & I trust, I shall soon make up for the time, I have lost in Sickness. I wrote to you my intention of communicating to your Brother the result of *my* meditations on the relations of Thoughts to Things; but I will rather, with your permission, throw the burthen of reading them upon you—because you will of course shew them to Tom if they give you pleasure, & if they prove trifling & all awry, you are less likely, than he, to receive Pain from Disgust. (Believe me, my dear Sir! I scarcely half express the diffidence, I feel.)—But I shall previously make you pay post for a Letter or two respecting some *errors*, as I believe, in the generally received *History* of metaphysical opinions. I was led to this subject by a late Perusal of Locke's Essay on the Human Understanding. I had read, & I think, mentioned to you, a very small book, attacking the Essay, & was rather pleased with it, tho' it was but a superficial affair;[1] but after this it occurred to

[1] Since Coleridge is known to have annotated Henry Lee's *Anti-Scepticism*, 1702, which criticized Locke's *Essay*, chapter by chapter, it has been suggested that he refers to Lee here. Such an assumption is erroneous. Coleridge would not refer to Lee's large folio volume as 'a very small book' and 'a superficial affair'. The book could have been any one of a number of attacks on Locke.

*18 February 1801*

me, that Mr Locke's Essay was a Book which I had really never *read*, but only *looked thro'*—I felt, of course, that I had been guilty of *petulance*, and began to wonder at my long want of curiosity concerning the writings of a philosopher (our countryman), whose Name runs in a collar with Newton's, as naturally as Milton's name with that of Shakespere. I had read a multitude of out of the way Books, Greek, Latin, & German, & groped my way thro' the French of Malbranche;[1] & there are men, who gain the reputation of a wide erudition by consuming that Time in reading Books obsolete & of no character, which other men employ in reading those which every Body reads; but I should be sorry to detect in myself this silly vanity, & so, as aforesaid, I took Locke from my Landlord's Shelf, & read it attentively.—

In my Biographical Dictionary the writer introduces Locke as 'one of the greatest men that England ever produced.['] Mr Hume, a much more competent Judge, declares that he was 'really a great Philosopher.' Wolf, Feder, & Platner,[2] three Germans, the fathers or favourers of three different Systems, concur in pronouncing him to be 'a truly original Genius.' And Mr Locke himself has made it sufficiently clear both in his Essay, and in his Letters to the Bishop of Worcester,[3] that he did not regard himself as a Reformer, but as a Discoverer; not as an opposer of a newly introduced Heresy in Metaphysics but as an Innovator upon ancient and generally received Opinions. In his dedicatory Epistle speaking of those who are likely to condemn his Essay as opposite to the received Doctrines, 'Truth' (says he) 'scarce ever yet carried it by Vote any where at *it's first appearance. New* Opinions are always suspected, and usually opposed without any other reason but because they are not already common. But Truth, like Gold, is not the less so, for being *newly brought out of the mine.*'[4]—It would have been well, if Mr Locke had stated the Doctrines which he considered as Errors in the very words of some of the most celebrated Teachers of those Doctrines & enumerated the Truths of which he considered himself as the Discoverer. A short Postscript to this purpose would have brought to an easy determination the opinions of those, who (as Harris & Monboddo,[5] for instance) believe that Mr Locke has grossly misrepresented the ancient & received opinions, and that the Doctrines which he holds for Truths of his own Discovery are

[1] Nicolas Malebranche (1638–1715).
[2] C. F. von Wolf (1679–1754), J. G. H. Feder (1740–1821), and Ernst Platner (1744–1818).
[3] Edward Stillingfleet (1635–99). A copy of his *Origines Sacrae*, 1675, containing Coleridge's annotations is in the British Museum.
[4] *Human Understanding*, 1798, Epistle Dedicatory, xviii.
[5] James Harris (1709–80) and James Burnett, Lord Monboddo (1714–99).

many of them erroneous & none original. Exempli gratiâ—in the very commencement of the work he says 'It is an established opinion amongst some men, that there are in the Understanding certain Innate Principles, some primary notions, Κοιναὶ ἔννοιαι, characters as it were stamped upon the mind of Man, which the Soul receives in it's very first being, and brings into the World with it.'[1] His own opinion on the contrary is that there are but two sorts of ideas and both acquired by Experience, namely, 'external Objects furnish the mind with ideas of sensible Qualities, which are all those different Perceptions they produce in us: and the Mind furnishes the Understanding with ideas of it's own operations.'[2] Of course, as Locke teaches that the Understanding is but a Term signifying the Mind in a particular state of action, he means that the mind furnishes itself; and so he himself expresses the Thought in the preceding Paragraph, defining Ideas of Reflection by 'those, which the mind gets by reflecting on it's own operations within itself.'[3] Now, it would have been well if Locke had named those who held the former Doctrines, and shewn from their own Words that the two opinions (his and their's) were opposite or at least different.[4] More especially, he should have given his Readers the Definition of the obscure Word 'innate' in the very Language of the most accurate of such Writers as had used the Word. Pythagoras, it is said, and Plato, it is known, held the preexistence of human Souls, and that the most valuable Part of our knowlege was Recollection. The earliest of these Recollections Plato calls Ζώπυρα, living Sparks, & Ἐναύσματα, Kindle-fuel. These notions he enforces in the Theaetetus, and the Phaedon, and still more at large in the Menon; but neither in these nor elsewhere asserts, that any Ideas (in the present sense of the word) could be furnished originally or recollectively otherwise than by the mind itself or by things external to the Mind, i.e. by Reflection or Sensation.—The nihil in intellectu quod non prius in sensu of the Peripatetics is notorious, and that Aristotle speaks of the mind in it's first state ὥσπερ γραμματεῖον, ᾧ μηδὲν ὑπάρχει ἐντελεχείᾳ γεγραμμένον—the original of Gassendi's and Hobbes's tabula rasa, and Mr Locke's unwritten sheet of Paper. Of Aristotle's complete coincidence in this point with Mr Locke vide Cap. 18 (of the Anal. Poster. Lib. I.) entitled De ignorantia secundum negationem, but

[1] *Human Understanding*, Bk. I, ch. ii, § 1.
[2] Ibid., Bk. II, ch.i, § 5.
[3] Ibid., Bk. II, ch. i, § 4.
[4] Professor Aaron believes that Locke's polemic against innate knowledge 'was meant for the Cartesians, for the schoolmen, for certain members of the Cambridge Platonists, and for those others, Herbert and the rest, who advocated the theory of innate ideas in any way'. *John Locke*, 82.

*18 February 1801* [381

above all Cap XIX (of the Anal. Poster. Lib. II) entitled De cognitione Primorum Principiorum. The Stoics used the phrase κοιναὶ ἔννοιαι indeed; but that they meant nothing opposite to Mr Locke's opinions is made evident by a passage in the work (attributed to Plutarch) De Plac. Philos. 4. 11., in which are these words 'The Stoics regarded the Soul when it came into the World as an unwritten Tablet.['] The Realists among the Schoolmen held a Doctrine strangely compounded of the Peripatetic & Plotinian School, that universal Ideas are the Souls of all things. I have never read Aquinas or Scotus, the two great Defenders of this System;[1] but it is certain, it was a question of Psychogony not Psychology; the Soul, whatever it was, could only derive it's thoughts from itself or things external to itself. The nominalists taught that these abstract Ideas were mere names; the Conceptualists who *moderated* between these & the Realists coincided with Mr Locke fully & absolutely. (Of their party were Abelard & Heloisa.)—Mr Hume with his wonted sagacity has given an able statement of the utter unmeaningness of the assertion which Mr Locke had made. 'For what is meant by *Innate*? If innate be equivalent to Natural, then all the Perceptions and Ideas of the Mind must be allowed to be innate or natural, in whatever sense we take the latter word whether in opposition to what is uncommon, artificial, or miraculous. If by innate be meant, contemporary to our birth, the Dispute seems to be frivolous; nor is it worth while to inquire, at what time Thinking begins, whether before, at or after our Birth. Again the word Idea seems to be commonly taken in a very loose sense, even by Mr Locke himself, as standing for any of our Perceptions, our sensations, & Passions, as well as Thoughts. Now in this sense I should desire to know what can be meant by asserting that Self-love, or Resentment of Injuries, or the Passion betwixt the Sexes is not *innate*?'[2] Note at the end of Essay II.——I had not read this note of Mr Hume's when I had written the former part of this sheet; & having read it I should have desisted from the Subject altogether, had I not heard Mr Mackintosh affirm in his Lectures, that 'the Doctrine of Innate Ideas (a doctrine unknown to the ancients) was first introduced by Des Cartes, & fully overthrown by Locke.' Mr M. must have made a mistake—for Lord Herbert's Work De Veritate

[1] The Lord Latymer MS. contains the following addition: 'but I can easily conceive that the difference between their opinions & those of many Hyper-Berkleian Idealists in the present Day are not essentially Different.' Five months later Coleridge was reading Duns Scotus in the Durham Library. See Letter 405.
[2] David Hume, *Philosophical Essays concerning Human Understanding*, Essay II, 'Of the Origin of Ideas'.

### To Josiah Wedgwood

(which Mr Locke himself refers to in the third Chapter of his first book, § 15, as that which he had consulted, and in which these innate Principles were assigned) was published in 1624, whereas Des Cartes' Metaphysical Books did not appear till 1641. But laying this aside, yet in what sense can Des Cartes be called the introducer of the Doctrine? The Phrase 'innate Ideas' is surely not of Des Cartes' Invention—'ἔννοια ἔμφυτος'—πᾶσι τοῖς ζώοις ἔμφυτός ἐστιν ἡ τῆς Ὁμοιότητος θεωρία—(Diog. Laer. in the Life of Plato). A pueris tot rerum atque tantarum *insitas* et quasi consignatas notiones quas ἐννοίας vocant—Cic. Tusc. Quaest.[1]—Omnibus cognitio, Deum existere, naturaliter inserta est. Damascenus.— Deus attigitur notione innatâ. Ficinus in versione Iamblichi de Myst.[2] Des Cartes' Heresy therefore must have consisted in the new meaning he gave to the Word[s—] in something or other Mr Locke must have conceived [Des] Cartes's opinions as opposite to his own, for he never loses an opportunity of a sneer or sarcasm at the French Philosopher—and what if it were nevertheless true, that Mr Locke's whole System, as far as it is a system, pre-existed in Des Cartes? In order to shew this permit me to trace back the meaning of the word Ideas.

By *Ideas* Plato, notwithstanding his fantastic expressions respecting them, meant what Mr Locke calls the original Faculties & Tendencies of the mind, the internal Organs, as it were, and *Laws* of human Thinking: and the word should be translated '*Moulds*' and not '*Forms*'. (Cicero assures us, that Aristotle's Metaphysical Opinions differ from Plato's only as a Thing said in plain prose, i.e. worn out metaphors, differs from the same thing said in new & striking Metaphors—Aristotle affirms to the same purpose Δυνάμει πώς ἐστι τὰ νοητὰ ὁ Νοῦς, ἀλλ' ἐντελεχείᾳ οὐδὲν πρὶν ἂν μὴ νοῇ[3]—in respect of *Faculty* the Thought [Mind] *is* the Thoughts, but *actually* it is nothing previous to Thinking.) By the usual Process of language Ideas came to signify not only these original *moulds* of the mind, but likewise all that was cast in these moulds, as in our language the Seal & the Impression it leaves are both called Seals. Latterly, it wholly lost it's original meaning, and became synonimous sometimes with *Images* simply (whether Impressions or Ideas) and sometimes with Images in the memory; and by Des Cartes it is used for whatever is immediately perceived

[1] I. xxiv. 57.
[2] Marsilio Ficino, *Iamblichus de Mysteriis Ægyptiorum*, 1497.
[3] In the Lord Latymer MS. Coleridge, after this quotation from Aristotle, added: 'that is, in respect of Faculty the Mind *is* it's intellectual Thoughts. Plato's reasonings against Particulars &c probably meant little more than Lord Bacon's admonitions against the making of Experiments without some preconceived Generalization.'

*18 February 1801*

by the mind. Thus in Meditatione Tertiâ Des Cartes had said 'Quaedam ex his (scilicet cogitationibus humanis) tanquam rerum imagines sunt, quibus solis proprie convenit ideae nomen, ut cum hominem vel chimaeram vel caelum vel angelum vel Deum cogito.['] In the Objectiones Tertiae, which were undoubtedly written by Hobbes, the word Idea is obstinately taken for Image, and it is objected to the passage '*nullam* Dei habemus imaginem sive ideam.' To which Des Cartes answers 'Hîc nomine ideae vult tantum intelligi imagines rerum materialium in phantasiâ corporeâ depictas, quo posito facile illi est probare, nullam Angeli nec Dei propriam ideam esse posse; atqui ego passim ubique, ac praecipue hoc ipso in loco ostendo me nomen ideae sumere *pro omni eo quod immediate a mente percipitur*, adeo ut cum volo et timeo, quia simul percipio me velle et timere, ipsa Volitio et Timor inter Ideas a me numerentur, ususque sum hoc verbo, quia jam tritum erat a Philosophis &c; et nullum aptius habebam[']. Locke in his second Letter to the B. of Worcester gives the same definition and assigns the same Reason; he would willingly change the Term 'Idea' for a Better, if any one could help him to it. But he finds none that stands so well '*for every immediate object of the mind in thinking, as Idea does.*' As Des Cartes & Locke perfectly coincide in the meaning of the *Term* Ideas, so likewise do they equally agree as to their Sorts and Sources. I have read Mr Locke's Book with care, and I cannot suppress my feelings of unpleasant doubt & wonder, which his frequent claims to originality raised in me; his apologies for new words as necessary in a system deviating so widely, as his, from the hitherto received Opinions; and his repeated Triumphs over his nameless Adversaries for their incapability of instancing any one idea not derived from one or other of the two Sources, which he, Mr Locke, had pointed out.—I will give 4 quotations from 4 very different Authors—I Φασὶν οἱ Σοφοί τὴν Ψυχὴν τὰ μὲν διὰ τοῦ σώματος αἰσθάνεσθαι, οἷον ἀκούουσαν, βλέπουσαν, τὰ δὲ αὐτὴν καθ' αὑτὴν ἐνθυμεῖσθαι.[1] (All Philosophers say, that the Soul perceives some things thro' the Body, as when she hears or sees; and some things she herself notices in herself.) 2. Intellectio autem dividitur vulgo in Rectam et Reflexam. Recta dicitur quando tantum aliquid cognoscimus, ut in prima apprehensione Hominis, Bovis, Equi, &c. Reflexa autem, quâ mens seipsam cognoscit, scilicet se cognoscere et cognoscendi habere potestates.[2] 3. The mind receiving certain ideas from without, when it turns it's view inward upon itself and observes it's own actions about those Ideas,

---

[1] Diogenes Laërtius, *Life of Plato*, III. 12.
[2] Daniel Sennertus, *Opera omnia*, 3 vols., 1641, i. 117. For *potestates* read *potestatem*.

it has, takes from thence other ideas, which are as capable to be the Objects of it's Contemplation as any of those, it derives from foreign Things.—Likewise the Mind often exercises an active power in making several combinations: for it being furnished with simple Ideas, it can put them together in several compositions, and so make variety of complex ideas without examining whether they exist so together in nature.[1] 4 Ex ideis aliae *cogitativae*, aliae adventitiae, aliae a mente factae videntur: nam quod intelligam quid sit res, quid sit veritas, quid sit cogitatio, haec non aliunde habere videor quam ab ipsâmet meâ natura; quod autem nunc strepitum audiam, solem videam, ignem sentiam, a rebus quibusdam extra me positis procedere hactenus judicavi: ac denique Sirenes, Hippogryphes, et similia a me ipso finguntur, *diversas nempe ideas adventitias vi propriâ permiscente.*—These four quotations were evidently written by four men teaching precisely the same doctrine; but of the third and fourth one might almost suspect that the one was a free translation of the other. The first I extracted from Diog. Laert. in the Life of PLATO; the second from Daniel Sennertus, an adherent of the Aristotelian Philosophy who wrote the passage about the year 1620; the third you will know to be from Mr Locke, & the fourth is extracted from the Med. Tert. of Descartes; save only that instead of (*cogitativae*) the word in the original is *innatae* (cogitativae in the principia of Descartes being used instead of innatae) and the last sentence, *marked with Italics*, & crotchets / I have inserted into the text from one of Des Cartes' own explanatory notes. Here then we come at Locke's Innate Ideas, and find that the Author defines them not in relation to *Time* but merely in relation to their source, and that they are neither more nor less than Mr Locke's own Ideas of Reflection[2]— the intellectio reflexa of the Peripatetics, the αὐτὴ καθ' αὑτήν of Plato.—But to place this beyond the possibility of Doubt I will add another quotation to this Letter of Quotations. At the close of the year 1647 there was published in Belgium a Programma entitled Explicatio mentis humanae, &c, levelled at Descartes tho' his name is no where mentioned in it. The 12th Article of this Programma is as follows.[3] XII. Mens non indiget ideis vel notionibus innatis: sed sola ejus facultas cogitandi, ipsi, ad notiones suas peragendas, sufficit.—To this Des Cartes answers—In articulo XII non videtur nisi solis verbis a me dissentire. Cum enim ait, mentem

---

[1] *Human Understanding*, Bk. II, ch. vi, § 1, and ch. xxii, § 2.

[2] Professor Aaron suggests that by 'reflection' Locke meant what we call 'introspection'. 'Most of our information about the mind comes through reflection, that is, introspection' (*John Locke*, 120 and n. 3).

[3] See ibid., 78 f., for Professor Aaron's discussion of this quotation.

## 18 February 1801

non indigere ideis innatis, et interim ei facultatem cogitandi concedit (puta naturalem sive innatam) re affirmat plane idem, quod ego, sed verbo negat. Non enim unquam scripsi vel judicavi, mentem indigere ideis innatis, quae sint aliquid diversum ab ejus facultate cogitandi; sed cum adverterem, quasdam in me esse cogitationes, quae non objectis externis, nec a voluntatis meae determinatione procedebant, sed a solâ cogitandi facultate, quae in me est—ut ideas sive notiones, quae sint istarum cogitationum formae, ut [ab] aliis *adventitiis* aut *factis* distinguerem, *illas innatas vocavi, eodem sensu, quo dicimus generositatem esse quibusdam familiis innatam, aliis vero quosdam morbos, ut podagram vel calculum—non quod ideo istarum familiarum infantes morbis istis in utero matris laborent, sed quod nascantur cum quâdam dispositione sive facultate ad illos contrahendos.*

Good-night, my dear Sir!—Your's with grateful affection

S. T. Coleridge

P.S.—Hobbes objected to Des Cartes—'Praeterea, ubi dicit ideam Dei et animae nostrae nobis innatam esse, velim scire, si animae dormientium profunde sine insomnis cogitent. Si non, non habent eo tempore ideas ullas: quare nulla idea est innata: nam quod est innatum, semper adest.[']¹ Des Cartes answers:—Cum dicimus ideam aliquam nobis esse innatam, non intelligimus illam nobis semper obversari; sed tantum nos habere in nobis ipsis facultatem, illam eliciendi.²

P.S. Des Cartes took his divisions from Lord Bacon, who uses the words notiones nativae et adventitiae.—Nativae = innatae, & frequently Lord Bacon uses the very word *innatae* in the same sense with Des Cartes.

### 382. To Josiah Wedgwood

*Address*: T. Poole | N. Stowey | Bridgewater | Somerset   Single Sheet
*MS*. British Museum. *Hitherto unpublished.*
*Postmark*: 27 March 1801. *Stamped*: Keswick.

Tuesday, Feb. 24, 1801

My dear Sir

Ecce iterum Crispinus!³—It has been made appear then, I think, that Des Cartes & Locke held precisely the same opinions concerning the original Sources of our Ideas. They both taught, nearly in the same words and wholly to the same Purpose, that the Objects of human Knowledge are either Ideas imprinted on the

---

¹ *Objectiones Tertiae*, 'Objectio' X.
² 'Responsio' to 'Objectio' X.
³ Juvenal, iv. 1.

Senses, or else such as are perceived by attending to the passions and operations of the mind, or lastly Ideas formed by Help of Memory and Imagination, either compounding, dividing, or barely representing those originally perceived in the aforesaid Ways. This proves no more, I allow, than that Mr Locke's first Book is founded on a blunder in the History of Opinions, and that Des Cartes and Locke agreed with each other in a Tenet, common to all the Philosophers before them; but it is far enough from proving the assertion I made in my first Letter, that the whole System of Locke, as far [as] it was a System (i.e. made up of cohering Parts) was to be found in the writings of Des Cartes. But even that, which I have proved, trifling as it may seem, has led me to Reflections on the Rise & Growth of literary Reputation, that have both interested & edified me; nor can it, I suppose, be wholly without effect on the minds of any, who know or remember how much of Locke's Fame rests on the common Belief, that in overthrowing the Doctrine of Innate Ideas he had overthrown some ancient, general, & uncouth Superstition, which had been as a pillar to all other Superstitions. If you ask a person, what Sir Isaac Newton did—the answer would probably be, he discovered the universal action of Gravity, and applied it to the Solution of all the Phaenomena of the Universe. Ask what Locke did, & you will be told if I mistake not, that he overthrew the Notion, generally held before his time, of innate Ideas, and deduced all our knowledge from experience. Were it generally known, that these Innate Ideas were Men of Straw, or scarcely so much as that—and that the whole of Mr Locke's first Book is a jumble of Truisms, Calumnies, and Misrepresentations, I suspect, that we should give the name of Newton a more worthy associate—& instead of Locke & Newton, we should say, BACON & NEWTON, or still better perhaps, Newton and Hartley. Neither N. nor H. discovered the *Law*, nor that it was a Law; but both taught & *first* taught, the way to *apply* it universally. Kepler (aye, and Des Cartes too) had done much more for Newton, than Hobbes had done for Hartley / even were it all true which it has been fashionable of late to believe of Hobbes.

But I recur to my assertion, that Locke's *System* existed in the writings of Descartes; not merely that it is deducible from them, but that it *exists* in them, *actually, explicitly*. Do me the kindness to believe, my dear Sir! that I am sensible how exceedingly *dull* these Letters must needs be; but if the Facts, which they contain, have not been noticed to you, or by you, they can scarcely be so worthless, as to be *overpaid for* by the Reading of a long Letter in close handwriting: tho' this be no trifle to eyes like your's & mine. Without more apology then I proceed to detail my Proofs.—In the

*Meditations* and the Treatise De Methodo Descartes gives a little History of the rise & growth of his opinions. When he first began to *think* himself from out of that state in which he, like every body else, suppose themselves to perceive objects *immediately* without reflecting at all either on their minds or their senses, he saw that those Ideas, which referred him to Objects as externally present, were more vivid & definite than those of memory or imagination, & were not connected with volition. 'Experiebar enim, illas absque ullo meo consensu mihi advenire, et quum multo magis *vividae et expressae* essent quam ullae ex iis quas ipse prudens et sciens meditando effingebam, vel memoriae meae impressas advertebam, fieri non posse videbatur ut a meipso procederent: ideoque supererat, ut ab aliis quibusdam Rebus advenirent, quarum Rerum cum nullam aliunde Notitiam haberem, quam ex istis ipsis Ideis, non poterat aliud mihi venire in mentem, quàm illas iis similes esse['];[1] & seeing that his other Ideas were less vivid than those which referred him to Objects as externally present, et ex earum partibus componi, he was led to believe that his mind did nothing more than passively represent the Objects which were within the reach of the Senses. But afterwards, the Differences made by Distance in the Shape of Objects, and his often Detecting of himself in such Speeches as these 'Yonder is a man coming', when in truth he saw only a Red or Blue Coat, & perhaps only the Glimmer even of that, forced him to consider that this seemingly intuitive Faith was made up of *Judgements* passed by the Mind in consequence of repeated Experiences, that such Appearances in the Distance would form that other appearance which we call a man, when he came close to it; and that from hence he had been caused to judge, both that the appearance was a man, and that the Man was at a Distance. These Judgements too were often found to have been wrong; he often misunderstood the meaning of these appearances, and he saw clearly that if any one phaenomenon, however different, were connected with another sufficiently long & sufficiently often, they would be identified in the mind so as to pass for intuitions. This he illustrates by the common phrases, I have a pain in my Limbs, &c. He was led to consider the vast power of association chiefly by having his curiosity excited concerning the causes that determined the *place* of Pain, and relates in the fourth Part of his Principia the fact to which he had before alluded in his sixth meditation. Cum puellae cuidam, manum gravi morbo affectam habenti, velarentur Oculi quoties Chirurgus accedebat, ne curationis apparatu turbaretur, eique post aliquot dies brachium ad cubitum usque, ob gangraenam in eo serpentem, fuisset ampu-

[1] *Meditatio Sexta.*

tatum, et panni in ejus locum ita substituti ut plane ignoraret se brachio suo privatam fuisse, ipsa interim varios dolores, nunc in uno ejus manus, quae abscissa erat, Digito, nunc in alio se sentire querebatur[1]. To these he added the old crambe bis cocta of the Pyrrhonists, of the ordinary Phaenomena of Dreams and Deliria, in which Ideas became so vivid as to be undistinguishable from Impressions; but he observes in his own defence, 'Nec tamen in eo Scepticos imitabar, qui dubitant tantùm ut dubitent, et praeter incertitudinem ipsam nihil quaerunt. Nam contra totus in eo eram ut aliquid certi reperirem.'[2]—In consequence of his reflection on these and similar facts he informs us that he found himself compelled to turn his view inward upon his own frame and faculties in order to determine what share they had in the making up both of his Ideas and of his Judgements on them. He now saw clearly, that the objects, which he had hitherto supposed to have been intromitted into his mind by his senses, must be the joint production of his Mind, his Senses, and an unknown Tertium Aliquid / all which might possibly be developements of his own Nature, in a way unknown to him. The existence of archetypes to his Ideas was not therefore proveable either by the vividness of any Impression nor by it's disconnection from the Will. Et quamvis sensuum perceptiones a voluntate meâ non penderent, non ideo concludendum esse putabam illas a rebus a me diversis procedere, quia forte aliqua esse potest in me ipso facultas, etsi mihi nondum cognita, illarum effectrix.[3] All such ideas however, as arose in him without his will, & referred him to something separate from himself, or were *recollected* as such, he termed *adventitious*: and *factitious* when the parts only of any Shape were remembered by him, but the disposition, or number, of these parts were *imagined* either actively or passively by him, i.e. awake or in dreams. But besides these he found in himself certain Ideas of *Relation*, certain Ideas, or rather modes of contemplating Ideas, of which he had acquired the knowlege by attending to the operations of his own Thoughts, and which did not depend in any degree on his Will. In these he recognized the fountains of Truth, and of Truth immutable, because it did not depend upon the existence of any Archetypes. These Truths in his early works he called Innate Ideas, but in his Principia he dropped this name, & adopted that of res cogitativae, or experiences acquired by Reflection. By these, according to him, we may acquire the knowlege, that there is a God, and from the Veracity implied in the Idea of an absolutely perfect Being deduce a complete Assurance, that all these Things are real to the belief of the

[1] *Principia*, Pt. IV, Sect. cxcvi.    [2] *De Methodo*, Pt. III.
[3] *Meditatio Sexta*.

*24 February 1801*

Reality of which our Reason doth truly & irresistably compel us. A clear and distinct Perception therefore of any thing warrants it's Truth & Reality in the relation, in which it is clearly & distinctly perceived. On these grounds he builds the certainty of an external World— / in what *sense* he uses these words, I may have occasion to shew hereafter / and to consider his Ideas in reference to it. Accordingly he divides his Ideas, precisely as Mr Locke has done, into simple ideas, of one sense, of more than one sense, of Reflexion, & both of Reflexion & Sensation / and states the distinction of primary & secondary Qualities, or of Qualities & Powers, in words so exactly corresponding to Mr Locke's, that they might be deemed a free Translation, one of the other—save only that Solidity which Mr Locke distinguishes from Hardness, & affirms to be a primary Quality of Matter, Des Cartes considers only as a secondary Quality, a mode of Hardness, a mere sensation of Resistance, of course a power not a quality, that same Somewhat, which Mr Locke calls *Motivity* (& with Thinking form[s] according to him the primary Ideas of Spirit,) & which Des Cartes therefore very consistently excluded from his Idea of Matter: as Mr Locke *ought* to have done, unless he had been able to shew the difference between Resistance & Impulse, or power of *originating* motion, which last he expressly confines to the Idea of Spirit. The subjects of Perception, Retention, and Discerning which Locke has skimmed over so superficially & yet not without admixture of error in his 9th, 10th, & 11th Chapters, Des Cartes, in his Dissertatio De Methodo, in the fourth Book of his Dioptrics, & in the Pars Prima of his Work De Passionibus, has treated in a manner worthy of the Predecessor of Hartley. In these & the first Book of his Principia you find likewise the whole substance of Locke's 12, 14, 15, 16, 18, 20, 29, 30, 31, 32 & 33rd Chapters.—Mr Locke has given 25 folio pages to the explanation of Clear, Distinct, obscure, confused, real, fantastical, adequate, inadequate, true & false Ideas; and if I mistake not has exhibited throughout the whole a curious specimen of *dim* writing. Good heavens! twenty five folio pages to define half a dozen plain words; and yet I hazard the assertion, that the greater number of these words are explained falsely. Des Cartes took the words from the Schools, and defined them only as they occurred. I have taken the trouble to collect & arrange his Definitions / Read them, and when you have a leisure half hour glance your eye over Mr Locke's four Chapters on the meaning of these Words, & compare.—Our Ideas, says Descartes, are classed & distinguished, not in & for themselves, but in reference to the Judgements of the mind respecting their Relations to each other, to their supposed external Archetypes or Causes, and to Language.

Accordingly, Ideas may be divided into simple and complex—that is, into those which we cannot and those which we can analyse. Again, complex Ideas may be subdivided into complex ideas of memory, as a man, a horse, & complex Ideas of Imagination, as a Centaur, a Chimaera. Simple Ideas are said to be CLEAR, when they recur with such steadiness that we can use names intelligibly. James's Ideas of Red & Yellow are two clear Ideas / let a Red and a Yellow Thing be brought before him, & he will say, this is Red & this Yellow, in the same Instance in which others would say it— But his Ideas of Green & Blue are said to be OBSCURE (not that they are not clear in each particular instance in & for themselves, but) because they are so unsteady in relation to their supposed external Cause, that he *sometimes* mistakes Blue for Green, & Green for Blue—not *always*, for then his Ideas would be *steady*, consequently, his mistake undiscoverable, or more properly, no mistake at all. Again, a man may have an idea that is clear & steady, yet unintelligible because ANOMALOUS. James's Brother cannot distinguish Purple from Violet—two different external Objects produce uniformly *one* effect on *him*, that produce two on his neighbours. When he tells them, he has seen a man in a purple Coat, they know only that he means either Purple or Violet. Simple Ideas can be called neither distinct nor confused. (Mr Locke instead of saying 'the Smell of a Rose & that of a Violet are clear & distinct Ideas' need only have said, they are *two Ideas*. Distinct does not mean, in accurate language, difference merely, but such difference as can be stated in words.—When in his preface he says, he has ordinarily preferred the word determinate, & used it instead of clear & distinct, and used it in one sense for simple Ideas, & in another sense for complex Ideas, I may [be] allowed to say without petulance that his word is idly chosen / it means too many things to mean any thing *determinately*.) A complex idea may be either DISTINCT or CONFUSED. It is said to be distinct, when we distinguish all it's component parts—that is, when we see the Relations which the Ideas, it may be analysed into, bear to each other. An anatomist has a distinct Idea of the Eye; but I have only a CONFUSED one. I do not know all it's component parts, or I have not arranged them in my mind so as to enable me to pass from one to another, still perceiving their Relations as Parts to the Whole, and as Coparts to each other. When a Complex idea passes on the mind for a simple Idea, for instance, when a plain Man thinks, he has a *Pain* in his *Limbs*, this is said to be a clear but not a distinct Idea: in other words, it is to *him* a simple idea. Light to my child is a *clear* but not *distinct* idea, to me a complex but confused one, to Newton it was a distinct complex idea.—We are likewise said to have sufficient & insufficient, adequate & inadequate Ideas. (For sufficient & insufficient Mr Locke uses True & False Ideas, which I think injudicious.) I have a sufficient Idea of Winter Cole so far as it enables me to distinguish it from Savoy Cabbage; but insufficient inasmuch as I cannot distinguish it from Brocoli. The Botanist's Ideas of Plants may be sufficient to distinguish the Genera & Species; but insufficient to distinguish the Individuals of the same Species from each other. Adequate, that is, perfectly sufficient Ideas, belong only to the Supreme Being. To say with Mr Locke that all simple Ideas are adequate is an error in language. A simple Idea, as a simple Idea, cannot refer to any external Substance, representatively: for as Pythagoras said, nothing *exists* but in complexity. A simple Idea can be adequate therefore only in reference to itself; and this is merely affirming that this particular Idea is this same particular Idea, that is, if A be A, then A is A.—nor is it a whit more proper to say, that a Mathematician's Idea of a Triangle is adequate; for this is likewise to say, if A is A, then A is A. Adequate is not synonymous with 'complete', but with 'perfectly coincident': which is absurd to affirm of an Idea with itself.

S. T. Coleridge.

[A] Mathematician's Idea *of* a Triangle is falsel[y stated]—it should be, his Idea, Triangle.—

## 383. To Josiah Wedgwood

*Address*: Mr T. Poole | N. Stowey | Bridgewater | Somerset    Single Sheet
*MS. British Museum. Hitherto unpublished.*
*Postmark*: 27 March 1801.  *Stamped*: Keswick.

[February 1801]
My dear Sir

This letter I intend for a miscellaneous Postscript to my last / or if you like, a sort of sermon on a text from Hobbes 'Animadverte quam sit ab improprietate verborum pronum hominibus prolabi in errores circa res.' Mr Locke would have never disgraced his Essay with the first Book, if he had not mistaken innasci for synonymous with connasci, whereas to be 'born *in*', and to be 'born *at the same time with*', are phrases of very different import. My mind is, for aught I know to the contrary, *connate* with my brain / but a staunch materialist would perhaps deny this, and affirm that the Brain was the elder of the two, and that the mind is *innate in* the brain. Des Cartes chose the word 'innascor' because it implied Birth & of course *Subsequence*, & at the same time pointed out the *place* of Birth.—He confined it to what Locke calls Ideas of Reflection, merely because he did not wish to innovate on the established Language of metaphysics. But he expressly affirms, that in more accurate Language all ideas are *innate*, 'ipsas motuum et figurarum Ideas esse innatas'; the mind is both their Birth-place and their manufacturer; and we use the term '*adventitious*' [']quando *judicemus*, has vel illas Ideas, quas nunc habemus cogitationi nostrae praesentes, ad res quasdam extra nos positas referri—non quia res extra nos menti nostrae per organa sensuum illas ipsas Ideas immiserunt; sed quia *aliquid* tamen immittitur, quod menti occasionem dedit ad ipsas per innatam sibi facultatem hoc tempore potius quam alio efformandas.'[1] *Innate* therefore is inaccurately *opposed* to adventitious; but as the word had been in common use, he had adopted it to express those cognitions which the mind gains by attending to it's own passions & operations. These cognitions he elsewhere calls in the language of his age communes notiones and eternae veritates, the same which Mr Locke calls intuitive Knowlege,[2] & they are explained by Descartes to the same purport as these Intuitions are explained by Mr Locke to be those Laws in the conformation of the mind by which all men *necessarily* perceive ideas in certain *Relations* to each other. These Laws Aristotle calls Δύναμιν σύμφυτον κριτικήν, (φαίνεται δὲ τοῦτο ὑπάρχον πᾶσι τοῖς ζώοις) a power inherent in all living Beings determining the manner in which external objects must act upon them.—It is observable, that Des Cartes finding that he had been misunderstood both in the word 'innatae' and in the word 'Ideae', entirely dismissed them from his Principia / for innatae he uses cogitativae or intellectualis, and for Ideae he uses sometimes notiones, sometimes cognitiones, sometimes motus percepti, & when he wishes to express himself generally he resigns the *convenience* of a single Word, which was his first motive for using it, & expresses himself by a paraphrase 'Quaecunque sub perceptionem nostram cadunt.' The word Idea occurs but twice in the first book of the Principia, and then he uses it only in *reference* to his Meditations. It is a proof to me of Mr Locke's having never *read* the works of Des Cartes, that he adopted the word Idea / he would never have used this word, if he had seen the disputes in which it involved the French Philosopher, the anxious Warding-off of misinterpretation, which he never fails to manifest when he uses it, by repeated Definitions, & sometimes by marginal Nota benes: and in his Principia he wisely desisted from the use of the word altogether.

[1] *Notae in Programma quoddam, Explicatio*.
[2] Locke does not call *communes notiones* and *eternae veritates* 'intuitive knowledge'. For Locke on intuitive knowledge, see *Essay* IV, ii.

It is likewise to be observed that he uses it steadily in one sense, & never dreamt of introducing such a phrase as '*abstract Ideas.*['] Having thus seen how grossly Mr Locke has misunderstood Descartes, or perhaps how gossip-like he has taken up upon hearsay a rabble of silly calumnies respecting him, we shall be the less surprized at the 23rd Paragraph of the fourth chapter of his first Book, in which he implies that Aristotle was an asserter & Patron of connate Principles & Ideas—Aristotle, whose expressions in reprobation of such a doctrine are even violent. Quod igitur eas (scil. cognitiones) a naturâ habemus, absurdum est. Ἄτοπον![1] is the mildest phrase which he deigns to bestow on such an hypothesis. If Locke ever looked into the logical or metaphysical Works of Aristotle, I hazard a conjecture that this strange Blunder of his in matter of *fact* originated in a Blunder as to the meaning of a Word. Ἐγγίγ[ν]ομαι and ἐγγίνομαι are put together in some Lexicons as one word, and in all the Lexicons which I have consulted, they are given as synonimous with each other & with ἔνειμι, and all three are rendered by Insum, innascor. But in philosophical Greek γνώσεις ἐνοῦσαι, ἐγγιγνόμεναι, and ἐγγινόμεναι have each it's separate meaning—Γνώσεις ἐνοῦσαι (which is mentioned by Aristotle as a possible Hypothesis & disposed of with an 'absurdum est['])  is equivalent to connate or inherent Ideas, Mr Locke's Innate Ideas. γνώσεις ἐγγιγνόμεναι (which is used by Plato) = Ideas born *in* the Mind, or in Mr Locke's Language, Ideas derived from Reflection. But γνώσεις ἐγγινόμεναι, a *favorite* Phrase of Aristotle's, or ingenerated Ideas = Ideas acquired by Experience—cognitiones, quae a nobis *acquiruntur*, as Pacius rightly translates these passages. Hence Aristotle often has the sentence. Thus then these cognitions 'ἐγγίνονται τῇ ψυχῇ[']—are *ingenerated* in the Soul—i.e. by the action of external subjects on our senses. I guess therefore that Mr Locke carelessly & in a slovenly mood of mind, reading these passages, with a preconceived Opinion that the Peripatetic Philosophy was a congeries of false Hypotheses & verbal Subtleties, translated the words 'are *innate* (i.e. in *his* sense, *inherent*) in the mind,['] herein perhaps relying without scruple on the authority of his Lexicon, and the common use of the word in common Greek. I hope, that I am not treating Mr Locke with undue disrespect; for if I reject this, and all similar suppositions, I shall be reduced to the Belief that he charged upon a truly great man an opinion, which he himself deemed outrageously silly, without having ever read that great man's Works. Thus too in that express attack on Des Cartes in the 1st Chap. of his 2nd Book 'Men think not always' by translating the Cartesian 'Cogito' by the word

[1] Underlined once in MS.

'Think' he prepares his Reader to suppose that Des Cartes had taught that we are always *voluntarily* combining Ideas / for this, as Mr Locke himself observes, is the meaning of the English Word Think. Now Des Cartes expressly defines his cogitatio as a general *Term* for all our consciousnesses, whether of Impressions, Ideas, or mere Feelings.—Again in the words 'think not always' I need not point out to you the confusion in the word ('always') as combined with ('think not,') if we should admit Mr Locke's own account of Time as meaning nothing more than a *succession* of Thoughts, & that in this Proposition Mr Locke in order to rescue himself from absurdity must necessarily bewilder his Reader in obscure Notions of *Relative* Time as contradistinguished from Absolute.—The whole Reasoning (as far as Des Cartes' *Cogito* is not misconstrued) resolves itself into an equivocation in the word Consciousness, which is sometimes used for present Perception, & sometimes for the memory of a past Perception / for as to the wild & silly assertions, with which this Chapter is so amply stocked, it would be idle to include them under the term *reasoning*. These equivocations & these assertions are happily blended in the two following sentences. 'Those who do at any time sleep without dreaming can never be convinced that their Thoughts are sometimes for four hours together busy without their knowing it.'— And 'If the Soul doth think in a sleeping Man without being conscious of it, I ask whether during such thinking it has any pleasure or Pain or be capable of Happiness or Misery? I am sure, the *Man* is not, no more than the Bed or Earth he lies on. (!!!) For to be happy or miserable without being conscious of it seems to me utterly inconsistent & impossible.' This is a truly curious passage! First Des Cartes had expressly defined Thinking by Consciousness— thus then 'If the Soul is conscious without being conscious I ask whether during such consciousness it has any consciousness.[']—.
——Or what if a Cartesian should answer To be happy or miserable without being afterwards conscious of *having* been so seems to me neither inconsistent nor impossible——But if Mr Locke speaks of *present perception*, how came he to be so sure, that a sleeping man is devoid of Feeling?—'The man does not remember, that he had any.' Well (it may be answered) the natural Deduction from this is, that the Man had forgotten it. For to affirm that a man can breathe & turn himself & perform all the usual actions of sleep without any sensation is actually to affirm of men that same absurd Doctrine which Des Cartes is accused of having held concerning the Brutes, & which Mr Locke in his merry mood calls 'a step beyond the Rosecrucians.' This silly chapter with many others not much better originated in the little attention, which

## February 1801

Locke had given to the Law of association as explanatory of the Phaenomena both of Memory and of Reasoning— / for I find by his Preface what I first heard from Mr Mackintosh, that the trifling Chapter on Association was not introduced till the fourth Edition. It is true, that if we were to judge of Locke's merits by the first Book, & the first Chapter in the second Book of his Essay, we should sink him below his proper rank, even more than his present Reputation is above it. Yet if any one had read to me that chapter on 'Men think not always' without mentioning the Author, and afterwards read a passage in his fourth Book, in which it is asserted that Morals are equally susceptible of Demonstration as Mathematics, & then another passage in the conclusion of the eleventh [tenth] Chapter of Book the third, in which it [is] said 'all the figurative application of Words, Eloquence hath invented, are for nothing else but to insinuate wrong ideas, move the Passions, and thereby mislead the Judgement; and so indeed are perfect cheat'— I should have found myself incapable of believing the Author to be any thing but—what, I reverence even a great *name* too much to apply to Mr Locke.

It may not be amiss to remark, that the Opinion of Descartes respecting the Brutes has not been accurately stated. Malbranche indeed positively denies all feeling to Brutes, & considers them as purae putae Machines. But Des Cartes asserted only, that the Will and Reason of Man was a Something essentially distinct from the vital Principle of Brutes / and that we had no *proof* that Brutes are *not* mere automatons. Des Cartes, like Hartley & Darwin, held the possibility of a machine so perfect, & susceptible of Impulses, as to perform many actions of apparent Consciousness without consciousness / but the falsehood of a thing possible can never 'be *demonstrated*,['] tho' such demonstration may be superseded by intuitive Certainty. I am *certain* that I feel; and when I speak of men, I *imply* in the *word* 'Men' Beings like myself; but in the word 'Brutes' I imply Beings someway or other different from my own species, to them therefore I am not entitled to transfer my intuitive Self-knowlege / consequently, I cannot *prove* i.e. demonstrate, that any consciousness belongs to them. The strongest expression in all Des Cartes' Writings on this subject is 'etsi ratione careant, et *forte* omni cogitatione'.—This is, no doubt, egregious trifling, unworthy of Des Cartes, & hardly to be reconciled with other parts of his own Works, in which he shews that Nature acts upon us as Language, and that veracity is involved in the notion of Deity. However, to assert that a thing is so or so, and to assert that it *cannot* be demonstrated *not* to be so or so, form articles of Belief widely different from each other. Malbranche asserted that Brutes were machines devoid of all consciousness, Des Cartes only asserted, that no one could *demonstrate* the contrary.

I have abstained purposely from intermingling in these Letters any remarks of my own, not connected with matters of historical Fact / tho' I was greatly tempted to animadvert on the gross metaphor & at the same time bold assumption implied in the words 'inherent,' 'innate,' 'ingenerated,' 'object of the mind in thinking,' &c / I was likewise tempted to remark that I do not think the Doctrine of innate Ideas even in Mr Locke's sense of the Word so utterly absurd & ridiculous, as Aristotle, Des Cartes, & Mr Locke have concurred in representing it. What if instead of innate Ideas a philosopher had asserted the existence of *constituent* Ideas / the metaphor would not be a whit more gross, nor the hypothesis involved more daring or unintelligible, than in the former phrases / and I am sure, it would lead to more profitable Experiments & Analyses. In Mr Locke there is a complete Whirl-dance of Confusion with the words *we*, *Soul*, *Mind*, *Consciousness*, & Ideas. It is *we* as far as it is consciousness, and *Soul* & *Mind* are only other words for *we* / and yet nothing is more common in the Essay than such Sentences as these 'I do not say there is no *Soul* in *us* because *we* are *not sensible* of it in our sleep' &—'actions of our *mind unnoticed* by *us*[']—i.e. (according to Locke's own definitions of *mind* & *we*) 'actions of *our consciousness, of which our Consciousness is unconscious*.['] Sometimes again the Ideas are considered as objects of the mind in thinking, sometimes they stand for the mind itself, and sometimes we are the thinkers, & the mind is only the Thought-Box.—In short, the Mind in Mr Locke's Essay has three senses—the Ware-house, the Wares, and the Ware-house-man.— What is the *etymology* of the Word *Mind*? I think that I could make it as probable as could be expected in a conjecture on such a subject that the following is the history of the Word—In a Swabian Poet of the 13th Century I have found the word *Min* (pronounced mein); it is used by him for Geist, or Gemuth, the present German Words for Mind.—The same poet uses the word Minen, which is only the old Spelling for the present German *Meinen*—the old signification of Meinen (& which is still in many parts of Germany the *provincial* use of the word) *exactly corresponds* with the provincial use of the verb 'To mind' in England. Don't you *mind* that?—i.e. Do you not remember it.—Be sure, you *mind* him of that—i.e. remind him of that.—Hence it appears to be no other than provincial Differences of Pronunciation between the words Meinen, & Mahnen—which last word retains the old (*present provincial*) meaning of the word Meinen—i.e. to *mind* a person (of his Duty for instance). But the insertion of the *n* in the middle

( 696 )

*February 1801* [383

of a German verb is admitted on all hands to be *intensive* or *reduplicative* / as the Dictionary Phrase is. In reality it is no more than repeating the last syllable as people are apt to when speaking hastily or vehemently. Mahnen therefore is Mahenen, which is Mähen spoken hastily or vehemently. But the oldest meaning of the word mähen is to move forward & backward, yet still progressively—thence applied to the motion of the Scythe in mowing—from what particular motion the word was first abstracted, is of course in this as in all other instances, lost in antiquity. For words have many fates—they first mean particulars, become generals, then are confined to some one particular again, & so forth—as the word 'indorse' for instance.—To mow is the same as the Latin movere which was pronounced mow-ere—& monere in like manner is only the reduplicative of mow-ere—mow-en—mow-enen—mownen, or monen. This word in the time of Ennius was *menere*, & hence *mens*—the Swedish word for Mind is Mon—the Islandic Mene. The Greek μνάομαι, i.e. μενάομαι,[1] from whence μνήμη, the memory, is the same word—and all alike mean a repetition of similar motion, as in a scythe. It is even probable that the word meh, ma, & moe, the old German and English Words for *more* is of the same Birth & Parentage. All infinitives are in my opinion Imperatives with or without some auxiliar substantive / in our Language without, in Latin, German, etc *with*. What the Latin 're' and 'ri' are, I think I could make a bold guess at—and likewise at the meaning of the en, common to *all* the Gothic Dialects.—God bless you, my dear Sir! I would, I were with you to join in the Laugh against myself. S. T. Coleridge

### 384. To Josiah Wedgwood

MS. British Museum. Hitherto unpublished.

[February 1801]

Mr Locke's third Book is *on Words*; and under this head [he] should have arranged the greater number of the Chapters in his second Book. Des Cartes has said multum in parvo on the subject of words. He has said the same things as Mr Locke; but he has said them more perspicuously, more philosophically, & without any admixture of those errors or unintelligibilities into which Mr Locke suffered himself to be seduced by his Essences and Abstract Ideas.—Words (according to Des Cartes) are to be considered in three ways—they are themselves images and sounds; 2. they are connected with our Thoughts by associations with Images &

---

[1] μεν underlined once in MS.

Feelings; 3. with Feelings alone, and this too is the natural Tendency of Language. For as words are learnt by us in clusters, even those that most expressly refer to Images & other Impressions are not all learnt by us determinately; and tho' this should be wholly corrected by after experience, yet the Images & Impressions associated with the words become more & more dim, till at last as far as our consciousness extends they cease altogether; & Words act upon us immediately, exciting a mild current of Passion & Feeling without the regular intermediation of Images. Nam videmus, verba sive ore prolata sive tantum scripta, quaslibet in animis nostris cogitationes & commotiones excitare—& so forth. And if, says Des Cartes it be objected that these Words do not all excite *images* of the Battles, Tempests, Furies, &c, sed tantummodo *diversas intellectiones*[1]; this is true, but yet no wise different from the manner in which Impressions & Images act upon us. Gladius corpori nostro admovetur, et scindit illud; ex hoc sequitur Dolor, qui non minus diversus a gladii vel corporis locali motu, quam color vel sonus.[2] Words therefore become a sort of Nature to us, & Nature is a sort of Words. Both Words & Ideas derive their whole significancy from their coherence. The simple *Idea* Red dissevered from all, with which it had ever been conjoined would be as unintelligible as the word *Red*; the one would be a *sight*, the other a Sound, meaning only themselves, that is in common language, meaning nothing. But this is perhaps not in our power with regard to Ideas, but much more easily with regard to Words. Hence the greater Stability of the Language of Ideas. Yet both Ideas & Words whenever they are different from or contrary to our Habits either surprize or deceive us; and both in these instances deceive where they do not surprize. From inattention to this, it is conceivable, quantum in Catoptricis majores nostri aberrarent, quoties in speculis cavis et convexis locum Imaginum determinare conati fuerunt.[3]

With regard to Knowlege, & Truth, & Error & Falsehood I find no essential Difference whatsoever in the opinions of Locke & Des Cartes. Knowlege according to Des Cartes is clear & distinctive Perception, & Truth a clear & distinct Perception of the Relations which our Cognitions bear to each other. The causes of error & falsehood are such associations of Ideas with Ideas, of Words with Ideas, & of Words with Words, as are liable to be broken in upon. I associate the idea of a Red Coat with a Soldier, & herein I have not erred; but I have associated with the idea of a Red Coat nothing else but the Idea of a Soldier, & in consequence

---

[1] *Principia*, Pt. IV, Sect. cxcvii.      [2] Ibid.
[3] *Dioptrices*, Ch. VI, Sect. xix. For *aberrarent* read *aberrarint*.

a feeling of conviction that whenever I see a Red Coat coming, it must be a Soldier / but this is liable to be broken in upon—it is error.—The most common sources of error arise according[ly] from misunderstanding the nature of Abstract Ideas, and the confiding in certain propositions & verbal theses, as believing that we had formerly demonstrated them—quod multa putemus a nobis olim fuisse percepta, iisque memoriae mandatis, tanquam omnino perceptis, assentiamur, quae tamen revera nunquam percepimus.[1] To which he adds, as a motive for a wise and moderated scepticism, the action of early prejudices on our minds long after we have appeared to ourselves to have completely ridden our minds of them.——

If the facts, I have adduced, produce the same effect on you which they have produced on me, you will have been convinced that there is no Principle, no organic part, if I may so express myself, of Mr Locke's Essay which did not exist in the *metaphysical* System of Des Cartes—I say, the metaphysical / for with his Physics & in them with his notions of Plenum &c I have no concern. Yet it doth not follow that Des Cartes' System & Locke's were precisely the same. I think, if I were certain that I should not weary or disgust you by these long Letters, I could make it evident, that the Cartesian is bonâ fide identical with the Berkleian Scheme, with this Difference that Des Cartes has developed it more confusedly, and interruptedly than Berkley, and probably therefore did not perceive it in his own mind with the same steadiness & distinctness. Thus it is possible that in consequence of some brief Hints which your Brother gave me, & my after meditations on subjects connected with them, I may have formed in relation to visible & tangible Ideas opinions, which are not at present the same, but which would *coalesce* with his, instant[an]eously / but I am certain from the habits of my mind, that both my opinions & my modes of representing those opinions to my own mind, would be comparatively gross, *drossy* as it were, & unsteady too from the disturbing Forces of ordinary Language, with which I as a much & readily talking man have connected deeper Delights than he, & formed closer affinities. We may have the same point in view, but he is sailing thither, & I swimming. So Des Cartes's system is a *drossy* Berkleianism—and it is in consequence of it's dross & verbal Impurities, that the System of Locke is found so completely bodied out in it.—If I should not have been mistaken in this, it would follow that the famous Essay on the human Understanding is only a prolix Paraphrase on Des Cartes with foolish Interpolations of the Paraphrast's; the proper motto to which would be

[1] *Principia*, Pt. I, Sect. XLIV.

Nihil hîc Novi, plurimum vero superflui. A System may have no new Truths for it's component Parts, yet having nothing but Truths may be for that very reason a new System—which appears to me to be the case with the moral philosophy of Jesus Christ / but this, [which] is admitted on all hands, is not the case with Mr Locke's Essay. But if it's Truths are neither new nor unaccompanied by Errors and Obscurities, it may be fairly asked, wherein does Mr Locke's Essay['s] merit consist. Certainly not in his style, which has neither elegance, spirit, nor precision; as certainly not in his arrangement, which is so defective that I at least seem always in an *eddy*, when I read him / round & round, & never a step forward; but least of all can it be in his Illustrations, which are seldom accurate to the eye, & never interesting to the Affections.— I feel deeply, my dear Sir! what ungracious words I am writing; in how unamiable a Light I am placing myself. I hazard the danger of being considered one of those trifling men who whenever a System has gained the applause of mankind hunt out in obscure corners of obscure Books for paragraphs in which that System may seem to have been anticipated; or perhaps some sentence of half [a] dozen words, in the intellectual Loins of which the System had lain snug in *homuncular* perfection. This is indeed vile in any case, but when that System is the work of our Countryman; when the Name, from which we attempt to detract, has been venerable for a century in the Land of our Fathers & Forefathers, it is most vile. But I trust, that this can never be fairly applied to the present Instance—on the contrary I seem to myself as far as these facts have not been noticed, to have done a good work, in restoring a name, to which Englishmen have been especially unjust, to the honors which belong to it. It were well if we should rid ourselves of a fault that is common to us, in literary far more than in political Relations—the *hospitibus feros*,[1] attributed to us of old. No cautious man will affirm any thing of a People without Limitations that almost squeeze the poor Proposition to Death / With such exceptions however, as a prudent man must be understood to make, when he speaks of national character, I am inclined to say—that the French boast & flatter / the English neither boast nor flatter / but they assume and detract: that is, they take what they believe to be their absolute Bulk as a thing necessarily presupposed, & as it were, axiomatic, and they endeavor to increase their relative Size by levelling all around them.—Besides, Discoveries of these & similar Facts in literary History are by no means so unprofitable as might appear at the first view. They lessen that pernicious custom begun no doubt by the great Bacon, & in no small degree

[1] Horace, *Carm.* iii, 4, line 33.

fostered by Des Cartes, of neglecting to make ourselves accurately acquainted with the opinions of those who have gone before us, which doth only by rendering honest Fame insecure, greatly diminish a venial motive to worthy Efforts, but lays us open to many Delusions, & obnoxious to Sects & opinions of Sects which but for the charm of supposed novelty would have sunk at once, without gaining even the honors of Oblivion by having been once noticed. It is even better to err in admiration of our Forefathers, [than] to become all Ear, like Blind men, living upon the Alms and casual mercies of contemporary Intellect. Besides, Life is short, & Knowlege infinite; & it is well therefore that powerful & thinking minds should know exactly where to set out from, & so lose no time in superfluous Discoveries of Truths long before discovered. That periodical Forgetfulness, which would be a shocking Disease in the mind of an Individual relatively to it's own Discoveries, must be pernicious in the Species. For I would believe there is more than a metaphor in the affirmation, that the whole human Species from Adam to Bonaparte, from China to Peru, may be considered as one Individual Mind. But more than all, these little Detections are valuable as throwing [light] on the causes & growth of Reputation in Books as well as man. I hold the following circumstances to have [been] the main efficients of Mr Locke's Fame.[1] First & foremost, he was a persecuted Patriot, in the times of James the Second—closely connected with the Earl of Shaftesbury, the Earl of Peterborough, &c / and his works cried up by the successful Revolutionary Party with the usual Zeal & industry of political Faction. 2. The opinions of Gassendus, & Hobbes, had spread amazingly in the licentious & abominable Days of Charles the second & the controversial Reign of his Successor—All knowlege & rational Belief were derived from experience—we had no experience of a God, or a future state—therefore there could be no rational Belief. How fashionable these opinions & how popular the argument against Miracles of which Mr Hume seems to have conceited himself to have been the Discoverer, we need only read the Sermons of South[2] to be convinced of. When the fundamental Principles of the new Epicurean School were taught by Mr Locke, & all the Doctrines of Religion & Morality, forced into juxtaposition & apparent combination with them, the Clergy imagined that a disagreeable Task was fairly taken off their hands—they

---

[1] In Dec. 1810 Coleridge explained Locke's reputation with many of the same arguments he employs in this letter. See *Blake, Coleridge, Wordsworth, Lamb, etc. being Selections from the Remains of Henry Crabb Robinson*, ed. by Edith J. Morley, 1922, p. 36.

[2] Robert South (1634–1716) published his sermons in 6 volumes, 1679–1715.

could admit what they were few of them able to overthrow, & yet shelter themselves from the consequences of the admission by the authority of Mr Locke. The high Church Clergy were no friends to Mr Locke indeed; but they were popular chiefly among the Ignorant, and their popularity was transient. Besides, a small party violently & industriously praising a work will do much more in it's favor, than a much larger party abusing it can effect to it's disadvantage. But the low Clergy were no small party, & they had all the Dissenters to back. To this must be added the great spread of Arian notions among the Clergy / and it was no secret, that Mr Locke was an Arian. / Of this however the Clergy in the present Day take no notice; no Parson preaches, no Judge speechifies, no Counseller babbles against Deism, but the great Mr Locke's name is discharged against the Infidels, Mr Locke, that greatest of Philosophers & yet pious Believer. The effect, the Clergy have had in raising, extending & preserving Mr Locke's Reputation cannot be calculated—and in the meantime the Infidels were too politic to contradict them. The infidels attacked the Christians with Mr Locke's Principles, & the Christians fell foul on the Infidels with Mr Locke's authority.—3. Sir Isaac Newton had recently overthrown the whole system of Cartesian Physics, & Mr Locke was believed to have driven the plough of Ruin over the Cartesian Metaphysics.—This was a complete Triumph of the English over the French / the true origin of the union, now proverbial, of the two names—Newton & Locke.—5 [4]. After this came Leibnitz, & the Dispute concerning the Invention of the Infinitesimal &c and the bitterness & contempt with which this great man was treated not only by Newton's Understrappers, but by the whole English Literary Public, have not even yet wholly subsided.— Now Leibnitz not only opposed the Philosophy of Locke, but was believed & spoken of as a mere reviewer of the exploded Cartesian Metaphysics—a visionary & fantastic Fellow, who had only given Mr Locke occasion to 'fight his Battles o'er again & twice to slay the Slain.'—Leibnitz's notions of Plenum, pre-established Harmony &c were misrepresented with the most ludicrous blunders by Maclaurin[1] & other Lockists—& Voltaire in that jumble of Ignorance, Wickedness, & Folly, which with his usual Impudence he entitled a *Philosophical* Dictionary, made it epidemic with all the No-thinking Freethinkers throughout Europe, to consider Locke's Essay as a modest common sense System, which taught but little indeed—& yet taught all that *could* be known / & held it up in opposition to the dreams of the Philosophy of Leibnitz, whose mortal sin in the Mind of Voltaire & his Journeymen was, not his

---

[1] Colin Maclaurin (1698–1746), mathematician and natural philosopher.

monads, but that intolerable Doctrine of the Theodicee, that the system of the Universe demanded not only the full acquiescence of the Judgement in its perfection, but likewise the deepest devotion of Love & Gratitude. Berkley who owed much to Plato & Malebranch, but *nothing* to Locke,[1] is at this day believed to be no more than a refiner upon Locke—as Hume is complimented into a refiner on Berkley. Hence Mr Locke has been lately called the Founder of all the succeeding Systems of Metaphysics, as Newton of natural Philosophy——& in this sense his Name is revered tho' his Essay is almost neglected / —Those, who do read Mr Locke, as a part of Education or of Duty, very naturally think him a great Man / having been taught to suppose him the Discoverer of all the plain pre-adamitical Common sense that is to be found in his Book. But in general his Merit like that of a Luther, or a Roger Bacon, is not now an idea abstracted from his Books, but from History,—among the Overthrowers of Superstition, his Errors & Inaccuracies are sometimes admitted, now only to be weighed against the Bullion of his Truths, but more often as in other holy Books, are explained away—& the most manifest self-contradictions reconciled with each other / & on the plea, that so great a man has to be judged by the general Spirit of his Opinions, & not by the Dead Letter.—Lastly, we must take in as the main Pillar of Mr Locke's Reputation the general aversion from even the name of Metaphysics & the Discussions connected with it / arising 1. from the enormous commerce of the Nation, & the enormous increase of numbers in the Profession of the Law consequent hereon, and 2. from the small number of the Universities & the nature of the Tutorships & Professorships in them—& 3 & principally, from the circumstance that the preferment of the Clergy in general is wholly independent of their Learning or their Talents, but does depend very greatly on a certain passive obedience to the Impelling[?] articles of the Church. In the more than one or two Instances I have heard Clergymen confess that they did not read for fear that they might [be] rendered uneasy in their minds. How great a Loss this is to the Community will appear by the reflection, that of the three greatest, nay, only three *great* Metaphysicians which this Country *has* produced, B., B. & H.[2] / two were Clergymen of the Church of England. [MS. of this letter breaks off thus.][3]

---

[1] To say that Berkeley owed nothing to Locke is nonsense.

[2] 'I mean, Berkley & [Joseph] Butler / in whose company I place Hartley as a useful Writer.' [Cancelled sentence in MS.]

[3] The verso of the last page of this manuscript contains a rough draft of a small part of Letter 382.

## 385. To Josiah Wade

*Pub.* Early Rec. ii. 18.

March 6th, 1801

My very dear friend,

I have even now received your letter. My habits of thinking and feeling have not hitherto inclined me to personify commerce in any such shape as could tempt me to turn Pagan, and offer vows to the Goddess of our Isle. But when I read that sentence in your letter, 'The time will come I trust, when I shall be able to pitch my tent in your neighbourhood,' I was most potently tempted to a breach of the second commandment, and on my knees, to entreat the said Goddess, to touch your bank notes and guineas with her magical, multiplying wand. I could offer such a prayer for you, with a better conscience than for most men, because I know that you have never lost that healthy common sense, which regards money only as the means of independence, and that you would sooner than most men cry out, enough! enough! To see one's children secured against want, is doubtless a delightful thing; but to wish to see them begin the world as rich men, is unwise to ourselves, (for it permits no close of our labors) and is pernicious to them; for it leaves no motive to their exertions, none of those sympathies with the industrious and the poor, which form at once the true relish and proper antidote of wealth. . . .

Is not March rather a perilous month for the voyage from Yarmouth to Hamburg? danger there is very little, in the packets, but I know what inconvenience rough weather brings with it; not from my own feelings, for I am never sea sick, but always in exceeding high spirits on board ship, but from what I see in others. But you are now an old sailor. At Hamburg I have not a shadow of acquaintance. My letters of introduction produced for me (with one exception, viz. Klopstock the brother of the poet) no real service, but merely distant and ostentatious civility. And Klopstock will by this time have forgotten my name, (which indeed he never properly knew) for I could speak only English and Latin, and he only French and German. At Ratzeburgh (35 English miles N. E. from Hamburgh on the road to Lubec) I resided four months, and I should hope, was not unbeloved by more than one family, but this is out of your route. At Gottingen I stayed near five months, but here I knew only students, who will have left the place by this time, and the high learned professors, only one of whom could speak English, and they are so wholly engaged in their academical occupations, that they would be of no service to you. Other acquaintance in Germany I have none, and connection I never had any. For though I was much intreated by some of the Literati to correspond with them, yet my natural laziness, with the little value I attach to literary men, as literary men, and with my aversion from those letters, which are to be made up of studied sense, and unfelt compliments, combined to prevent me from availing myself of the offer. Herein and in similar instances, with English authors of repute, I have ill consulted the growth of my reputation and fame. But I have cheerful and confident hopes of myself. If I can hereafter do good to my fellow creatures, as a poet, and as a metaphysician, they will know it; and any other fame than this, I consider as a serious evil, that would only take me from out the number and sympathy of ordinary men, to make a coxcomb of me.

As to the Inns or Hotels at Hamburgh, I should recommend you to some German Inn. Wordsworth and I were at the 'Der Wilde Man,' and dirty as it was, I could not find any Inn in Germany very much cleaner, except at Lubec. But if you go to an English Inn, for heaven's sake, avoid the Shakspeare, at Altona, and the King of England, at Hamburgh. They are houses of plunder, rather than entertainment. The Duke of York's Hotel, kept by Seaman, has a better reputation, and thither I would advise you to repair; and I advise you to pay your bill every morning at breakfast time; it is the only way to escape imposition. What the Hamburgh merchants may be I know not, but the tradesmen are knaves. Scoundrels, with yellow-white phizzes, that bring disgrace on the complexion of a bad tallow candle. Now as to carriage, I know scarcely what to advise; only make up your mind to the very worst vehicles, with the very worst horses, drawn by the very worst postillions, over the very worst roads, (and halting two hours at each time they change horses) at the very worst inns; and you have a fair, unexaggerated picture of travelling in North Germany. The cheapest way is the best; go by the common post waggons, or stage coaches. What are called extraordinaries, or post chaises, are little wicker carts, uncovered, with moveable benches or forms in them, execrable in every respect. And if you buy a vehicle at Hamburgh, you can get none decent under thirty or forty guineas, and very probably it will break to pieces on the infernal roads. The canal boats are delightful, but the porters everywhere in the United Provinces, are an impudent, abominable, and dishonest race. You must carry as little luggage as you well can with you, in the canal boats, and when you land, get recommended to an inn beforehand, and bargain with the porters first of all, and never lose sight of them, or you may never see your portmanteau or baggage again.

My Sarah desires her love to you and yours. God bless your dear little ones! Make haste and get rich, dear friend! and bring up the little creatures to be playfellows and schoolfellows with my little ones!

Again and again, sea serve you, wind speed you, all things turn out good to you!

God bless you,<br>
S. T. Coleridge.

### 386. To William Godwin

*Address*: Mr Godwin | Polygon | Sommers Town | London—
*MS*. Lord Abinger. *Hitherto unpublished.*
*Postmark*: 10 March 1801. *Stamped*: Keswick.

Keswick, Cumberland   March 7, 1801

Dear Godwin

I have puzzled my brains to no purpose to find a plausible conjecture, *why* you have not written to me.—If I had in any way offended you, your simple & direct habits would have impelled you to write; and if you have been *employed*, I should have thought, it would have been some Cheering of Toil to have set a friend at a distance a sympathizing with you.—Do write—if it be only half a dozen Lines.—

Your's sincerely,<br>
S. T. Coleridge

### 387. To Thomas Poole

*Address*: Mr T. Poole | N. Stowey | Bridgewater | Somerset.
*MS. British Museum. Pub. with omis. Letters, i. 348.* About one-third of pages 3 and 4 has been torn from the holograph; the passages in brackets have been supplied from a transcript made by Thomas Ward.
*Stamped*: Keswick.

Monday Night. [16 March 1801]<br>
[Endorsed March 16, 1801]

My dear Friend

The interval since my last Letter has been filled up by me in the most intense Study. If I do not greatly delude myself, I have not only completely extricated the notions of Time, and Space; but have overthrown the doctrine of Association, as taught by Hartley, and with it all the irreligious metaphysics of modern Infidels— especially, the doctrine of Necessity.—This I have *done*; but I trust, that I am about to do more—namely, that I shall be able to evolve all the five senses, that is, to deduce them from *one sense*, & to state their growth, & the causes of their difference——& in this evolvement to solve the process of Life & Consciousness.——I write this to you only; & I pray you, mention what I have written to no one.—At Wordsworth's advice or rather fervent intreaty I have intermitted the pursuit—the intensity of thought, & the multitude of minute experiments with Light & Figure, have made me so nervous & feverish, that I cannot sleep as long as I ought & have been used to do; & the Sleep, which I have, is made up of Ideas so connected, & so little different from the operations of Reason, that it does not afford me the due Refreshment. I shall therefore take a Week's respite; & make Christabel ready for the Press—which I shall publish by itself—in order to get rid of all my engagements with Longman—My German Book I have suffered to remain suspended, chiefly because the thoughts which had employed my sleepless nights during my illness were *imperious* over me, & tho' Poverty was staring me in the face, yet I dared behold my Image miniatured in the pupil of her hollow eye, so steadily did I look her in the Face!——for it seemed to me a Suicide of my very soul to divert my attention from Truths so important, which came to me almost as a Revelation / Likewise, I cannot express to you, dear Friend of my heart!—the loathing, which I once or twice felt, when I attempted to write, merely for the Bookseller, without any sense of the moral utility of what I was writing.—I shall therefore, as I said, immediately publish my CHRISTABEL, with two Essays annexed to it, on the Praeternatural—and on Metre. This done I shall propose to Longman instead of my Travels (which tho' nearly done I am exceedingly anxious not to publish, because it brings me forward in a *personal* way, as a man who relates little adventures of himself to *amuse* people—& thereby exposes me to sarcasm & the malignity of anonymous Critics, & is besides *beneath me*—I say, *beneath me* / for to whom should a young man utter the pride of his Heart if not to the man whom he loves more than all others?) I shall propose to Longman to accept instead of these Travels a work on the originality & merits of Locke, Hobbes, & Hume / which work I mean as a *Pioneer* to my greater work, and as exhibiting a proof that I have not formed opinions without an attentive Perusal of the works of my Predecessors from Aristotle to Kant.—I am *confident*, that I can prove that the Reputation of these three men has been wholly unmerited, & I have in [what I have already written traced the whole history of the causes that effected this reputation entirely to Wordsworth's satisfaction.

You have seen, I hope, the lyrical Ballads—In the divine Poem called Michael, by an infamous Blunder of the Printer near 20 lines are omitted in page 210, which makes it nearly unintelligible—Wordsworth means to write to you & to send them together with a list of the numerous] Errata. The character of the Lyrical

Ballads is very great, & will increase daily. They have *extolled* them in the British Critic.[1]

Ask Chester (to whom I shall write in a week or so concerning his German Books) for Greenough's Address—& be so kind as to send it immediately. [Indeed, I hope for a *long* Letter from you—your opinion of the L. B, the preface &c—You know, I presume, that Davy is appointed Director of the Laboratory; and Professor at the Royal Institution?[2]—I received a very affectionate Letter from him on the Occasion. Love to all—We are all well, except perhaps myself—Write!—God love you

& S T Coleridge]

### 388. To Thomas Poole

*Address*: Mr T. Poole | N. Stowey | Bridgewater | Somerset.   *Single*
MS. British Museum. Pub. Letters, i. 350.
*Postmark*: 26 March 1801.   *Stamped*: Keswick.

My dear Friend                     Monday Night [23 March 1801]

I received your kind Letter of the 14th—I was agreeably disappointed in finding that you had been interested in the Letter respecting Locke—those which follow are abundantly more entertaining & important; but I have no one to transcribe them—nay, three Letters are written which have not been sent to Mr Wedgwood, because I have no one to transcribe them for me—& I do not wish to be without Copies— / of that Letter, which you have, I have no Copy.—It is somewhat unpleasant to me, that Mr Wedgwood has never answered my letter requesting his opinion of the utility of such a work,[3] nor acknowleged the receipt of the long Letter containing the evidence that the whole of Locke's system, as far as it was a system, & with the exclusion of those parts only which have been given up as absurdities by his warmest admirers, pre-existed in the writings of Des Cartes, in a far more pure, elegant, & delightful form.[4]——Be not afraid, that I shall join the party of the *Little-ists*[5]—I believe, that I shall delight you by the detection of their artifices—Now Mr Locke was the founder of this

---

[1] *British Critic*, Feb. 1801.

[2] Davy arrived in London on 11 Mar. 1801, and during the spring gave three courses of lectures at the Royal Institution. It was not until 15 July that he was officially appointed by the Managers.

[3] No such letter has come to light.

[4] See Letter 381, dated 18 Feb. 1801, and apparently sent at that time to both Josiah Wedgwood and Poole.

[5] In acknowledging Letter 381, Poole on 14 Mar. warned Coleridge not to become a Little-ist: 'Think before you join the herd of *Little-ists*, who, without knowing in what Locke is defective, wish to strip the *popular mind* of him, leaving in his place *nothing—darkness, total darkness*.' *Thomas Poole.* ii. 34.

## 23 March 1801

sect, himself a perfect Little-ist. My opinion is this—that deep Thinking is attainable only by a man of deep Feeling, and that all Truth is a species of Revelation. The more I understand of Sir Isaac Newton's works, the more boldly I dare utter to my own mind & therefore to *you*, that I believe the Souls of 500 Sir Isaac Newtons would go to the making up of a Shakspere or a Milton. But if it please the Almighty to grant me health, hope, and a steady mind, (always the 3 clauses of my hourly prayers) before my 30th year I will thoroughly understand the whole of Newton's Works—At present, I must content myself with endeavouring to make myself entire master of his easier work, that on Optics. I am exceedingly delighted with the beauty & neatness of his experiments, & with the accuracy of his *immediate* Deductions from them —but the opinions founded on these Deductions, and indeed his whole Theory is, I am persuaded, so exceedingly superficial as without impropriety to be deemed false. Newton was a mere materialist—*Mind* in his system is always passive—a lazy Looker-on on an external World. If the mind be not *passive*, if it be indeed made in God's Image, & that too in the sublimest sense—the Image of the *Creator*—there is ground for suspicion, that any system built on the passiveness of the mind must be false, as a system. / I need not observe, My dear Friend, how unutterably silly & contemptible these Opinions would be, if written to any but to another Self. I assure you, solemnly assure you, that you & Wordsworth are the only men on Earth to whom I would have uttered a word on this subject—. It is a rule, by which I hope to direct all my literary efforts, to let my Opinions & my Proofs go together. It is *insolent* to *differ* from the public *opinion* in *opinion*, if it be only *opinion*. It is sticking up little *i by itself i* against the whole alphabet. But one *word* with *meaning* in it is worth the whole alphabet together—such is a sound Argument, an incontrovertible Fact.—

*O for a lodge* in a Land, where human Life was an end, to which Labor was only a Means, instead of being, as it [is] here, a mere means of carrying on Labor.—I am oppressed at times with a true heart-gnawing melancholy when I contemplate the state of my poor oppressed Country.—God knows, it is as much as I can do to put meat & bread on my own table; & hourly some poor starving wretch comes to my door, to put in his claim for part of it.—It fills me with indignation to hear the *croaking* accounts, which the English Emigrants send home of America. The society is so bad— the manners so vulgar—the servants so insolent.—Why then do they not seek out one another, & make a society—? It is arrant ingratitude to talk so of a Land in which there is no Poverty but as a consequence of absolute Idleness—and to talk of it too with abuse comparatively with England, with a place where the laborious Poor are dying with Grass with[in] their Bellies!—It is idle to talk of the Seasons—as if that country must not needs be miserably misgoverned in which an unfavorable Season introduces a famine. No! No! dear Poole! it is our pestilent Commerce, our unnatural Crowding together of men in Cities, & our Government by Rich Men, that are bringing about the manifestations of offended Deity.——I am assured, that such is the depravity of the public mind, that no literary man can find bread in England except by misemploying & debasing his Talents—that nothing of real excellence would be either felt or understood. The annuity, which I hold, perhaps by a very precarious Tenure, will shortly from the decreasing value of money become less than one half of what it was when first allowed to me—If I were allowed to retain it, I would go & settle near Priestly, in America / I shall, no doubt, get a certain price for the two or three works, which I shall next publish—; but I foresee, they will not sell—the Booksellers finding this will treat me as an unsuccessful Author—i.e. they will employ me only as an anonymous Translator at a guinea a sheet—(I will write *across* my other writing in order to finish what I have to say.) I have no doubt, that I could make 500£ a year, if I liked. But then I must forego all desire of Truth and Excellence. I say, I would go to America, if Wordsworth would go with me, & we could persuade two or three Farmers of this Country who are exceedingly attached to us, to accompany us—I would go, if the difficulty of procuring sustenance in this Country remain in the state & degree, in which it is at present. Not on any romantic Scheme, but merely because Society has become a matter of great Indifference to me—I grow daily more & more attached to Solitude—but it is a matter of the utmost Importance to be removed from seeing and suffering *Want*.

God love you, my dear Friend!—

S. T. Coleridge.

### 389. *To Thomas Poole*

*Address*: Mr T. Poole | N. Stowey | Bridgewater | Somerset    Single Sheet.
*MS*. British Museum. *A few lines pub*. Thomas Poole, *ii*. 40.
*Postmark*: 27 March 1801. *Stamped*: Keswick.

My dearest Poole                Keswick, Tuesday, March 24. 1801

The latter half of my yesterday's Letter was written in 'a wildly-wailing strain.'[1] The truth is, I was horribly hypochondriacal. So

---

[1] Cf. a fragmentary poem concluding with the line, 'A wildly-wailing Note'. *Poems*, ii. 997.

many miserable Beings, that day, travelling with half-famished children, had levied contributions on us, that when I received the Newspaper, I could scarcely read the Debates; my heart swelled so within me at the brutal Ignorance & Hardheartedness of all Parties alike—Add to this, I was affected by a Rheumatism in the back part of my head—and Add to this too, that I was irritated by the necessity, I was under, of intermitting most important & hitherto successful Researches, in order to earn a trifle of ready money by scribbling for a Newspaper. Having given to my own conscience proof of the activity & industry of my nature I seemed to myself to be entitled to exert those powers & that industry in the way, I myself approved.—In that mood of mind nothing appeared to me so delightful as to live in a Land where Corn & Meat were in abundance—& my imagination pointed to no other place, than those inland parts of America where there is little communication with their foul Cities, & all the articles of *Life*, of course, to be had for a trifle.—But my Country is my Country; and I will never leave it, till I am starved out of it.—Do not mistake me, my dear Poole!—I am not alarmed for the present year. I know that what I shall have finished in two or three months will fetch a fair Price, & disembarrass me compleatly; but I foresee, that my works will not sell, & that the Booksellers finding this will have nothing to do with me, except as an anonymous Hack at starving Wages. The Country is divided into two Classes—one rioting & wallowing in the wantonness of wealth, the other struggling for the necessaries of Life.—The Booksellers feel this— Longman told me, that 'scarcely any, but Books of expence, sold well. Expensive Paper, & Ornaments &c were never layed out in vain. For the chief Buyers of Books were the Wealthy who bought them for Furniture.'—Now what can *I* write that could please the Taste of a Rich Man?—Dear Poole—a man may be so kindly tempered by nature, and so fortunately placed by unusual circumstances, as that for a while he shall, tho' rich, bear up against the anti-human Influences of Riches; but they will at last conquer him. It is necessary for the human Being in the present state of society to have felt the pressures of actual Hardships, in order to be a moral Being. Where these have been never & in no degree felt, our very deeds of Pity do to a certain point co-operate to deprave us. Consider for a moment the different Feelings with which a poor woman in a cottage gives a piece of Bread & a cup of warm Tea to another poor Woman travelling with a Babe at her Back, & the Feelings with which a Lady lets two pence drop from her Carriage Window, out of the envelope of perfumed Paper by which her Pocket is defended from the Pollution of Copper——

the difference is endless. But all this is better for our fire side Conversation, than for an eight-penny Letter.

I have sent you two more Letters,[1] & will send the Rest / all of which you must bring back with you when you come.—When you come, I shall beg you to bring me a *Present*—it is, three Prisms—they will cost you 8 shillings a piece.

Some time ago I mentioned to you a thought which had suggested itself to me, of making Acorns more serviceable. I am convinced that this is practicable simply by malting them.—There was a total failure of acorns in this country last year, or I would have tried it. But last week as I was turning up some ground in my garden, I found a few acorns just beginning to sprout—and I eat them—they were, as I had anticipated, perfectly *sweet* & fine-flavored, & wholly & absolutely without any of that particular & offensive Taste which Acorns, when crude, leave upon the Palate, & Throat.—I have no doubt that they would make both bread & beer, of an excellent taste & nutritious Quality.—It may be objected,—Suppose this—what gain?—They fatten pigs at present—. This is however inaccurately stated—Where there are large woods of Oak, a few Pigs may be fattened—but Acorns are so uncertain a Crop, that except in large woods Pigs can never be kept on that speculation—& in truth of the Acorns [drop]ped every year $\frac{9}{10}$ths are wasted. Secondly, Pigs fed with only acorns have a bad flavor / thirdly, *Pigs* are likewise & more regularly fatted with Potatoes & Barley-meal—& if the Objection, which I have stated, held good against the *humanization* of Acorns it would have held good against the introduction of Potatoes & Barley, as human Food—nay, it actually has been made in Germany & France against Potatoes.—What gain, said they?—they are already useful—we fatten our Pigs with them.——In this Country Oaks thrive uncommonly well, & in very bleak & rocky Places—and I have little doubt, that by extending & properly managing the Plantation of Oaks, there might be 20 Families maintained where now there is one——For Corn in this country is a most uncertain crop; but it so happens, that those very seasons which utterly destroy Corn produce an overflow of Acorns, & those Seasons, which are particularly favorable to Corn, prevent the Harvest of Acorns. Thus, the Summer before last all the Corn was spoilt, but there was a prodigious Crop of Acorns—last summer there was a fine Crop of excellent Corn in these Counties (which never want as much moisture as Corn needs) but no acorns.—If my hopes should be realized by my experiments, it would add another to the innumerable Instances of the Almighty's wisdom

---

[1] Letters 382 and 383.

& Love—making the Valleys & the Mountains supply, each the Failure of the other. When the Mountains are struck with drouth, the Valleys give Corn—when the Valleys are rotted with rain, the Mountains yield Acorns.——The great objection at present to the Planting of Oaks is their slow Growth (the young wood which is weeded out not paying sufficient for the *Board & Lodging* of the wood destined for Timber)—But very young Trees bear a certain proportion of acorns——Oaks, I apprehend, draw, even more than other T[rees], their nourishment from the moisture &c of the air, for they thrive in dry soils alone; yet are most fruitful in wet seasons. It is worth trying whether the Oak would be injured if the Leaves were taken off after the Acorns have fallen / they make a food for Horses, Cows, & Sheep.—Should it be true, that the Oak is fructified by superficial Irrigation, what a delightful Thing it would be if in every Plot adjacent to Mountain Cottages stood half a dozen noble Oaks, & the little red apple-cheeked children in drouthy seasons were turning a small Fire engine into the air so as to fall on them! Merciful God! what a contrast to the employment of these dear Beings by a wheel or a machine in a hellish Cotton Factory!—'See! see! what a pretty Rainbow *I* have made!'—&c &c *Write to me*—I cannot express to you what a consolation, I receive from your Letters! S. T. C.

My Wife has a violent Cold—Derwent is quite well—& Hartley has the worms. Do not forget to ask Chester for Greenough's address.—Love to your dear Mother.—

The Farmers in these Northern Counties are getting rich. Their Crops last year were excellent; but the County itself is starving. If it were found, that Potatoes would bear Carriage as well as Grain, there would be no Food left in the County. It would all go to Liverpool and Manchester, &c.

### 390. *To William Godwin*

*Address*: Mr Godwin | the Polygon | Sommers Town | London   Single
*MS. Lord Abinger. Pub. with omis.* William Godwin, ii. 77.
*Postmark*: 28 March 1801.   *Stamped*: Keswick.

Greta Hall, Keswick   Wednesday, March 25, 1801
Dear Godwin

I fear, your Tragedy[1] will find me in a very unfit state of mind to sit in Judgement on it. I have been, during the last 3 months, undergoing a process of intellectual *exsiccation*. In my long Illness I had compelled into hours of Delight many a sleepless, painful

[1] This was *Abbas, King of Persia*, which was not accepted for presentation at Drury Lane.

hour of Darkness by chasing down metaphysical Game—and since then I have continued the Hunt, till I found myself unaware at the Root of Pure Mathematics—and up that tall smooth Tree, whose few poor Branches are all at it's very summit, am I climbing by pure adhesive strength of arms and thighs—still slipping down, still renewing my ascent.—You would not know me—! all sounds of similitude keep at such a distance from each other in my mind, that I have *forgotten* how to make a rhyme—I look at the Mountains (that visible God Almighty that looks in at all my windows) I look at the Mountains only for the Curves of their outlines; the Stars, as I behold them, form themselves into Triangles—and my hands are scarred with scratches from a Cat, whose back I was rubbing in the Dark in order to see whether the sparks from it were refrangible by a Prism. The Poet is dead in me—my imagination (or rather the Somewhat that had been imaginative) lies, like a Cold Snuff on the circular Rim of a Brass Candle-stick, without even a stink of Tallow to remind you that it was once cloathed & mitred with Flame. That is past by!—I was once a Volume of Gold Leaf, rising & riding on every breath of Fancy—but I have beaten myself back into weight & density, & now I sink in quicksilver, yea, remain squat and square on the earth amid the hurricane, that makes Oaks and Straws join in one Dance, fifty yards high in the Element.

However, I will do what I can—Taste & Feeling have I none, but what I have, give I unto thee.———But I repeat, that I am unfit to decide on any but works of severe Logic.

I write now to beg, that, if you have not sent your Tragedy, you may remember to send Antonio with it, which I have not yet seen—& likewise my Campbell's Pleasures of Hope, which Wordsworth wishes to see.

Have you seen the second Volume of the Lyrical Ballads, & the Preface prefixed to the First?———I should judge of a man's Heart, and Intellect precisely according to the degree & intensity of the admiration, with which he read those poems———Perhaps, instead of Heart I should have said Taste, but when I think of The Brothers, of Ruth, and of Michael, I recur to the expression, & am enforced to say *Heart*. If I die, and the Booksellers will give you any thing for my Life, be sure to say—'Wordsworth descended on him, like the Γνῶθι σεαυτόν from Heaven; by shewing to him what true Poetry was, he made him know, that he himself was no Poet.'

In your next Letter you will perhaps give me some hints respecting your prose Plans.—.

God bless you<br>& S. T. Coleridge

I have inoculated my youngest child, Derwent, with the Cowpox—he passed thro' it without any sickness.—I myself am the Slave of Rheumatism—indeed, tho' in a certain sense I *am recovered* from my Sickness, yet I have by no means *recovered* it. I congratulate you on the settlement of Davy in London.—I hope, that his enchanting manners will not draw too many Idlers round him, to harrass & vex his mornings.—. . .[1]

P.S.—What is a fair Price—what might an Author of reputation fairly ask from a Bookseller for one Edition, of a 1000 Copies, of a five Shilling Book?—

### 391. To Thomas N. Longman

*Address*: Messrs. Longman and Rees | Paternoster Row | London
*MS. Professor C. B. Tinker. Hitherto unpublished.* This letter is written on a sheet the first page of which contains a letter from Wordsworth to Longman.
*Early Letters*, 265.
*Postmark*: 30 March 1801. *Stamped*: Keswick.

Friday Night, March 26 [27], 1801

Dear Sir

Mr Wordsworth was so good as to send me your Letter to him with his own unsealed, that I might write without putting you to the expence of two Letters.—

Had not my dear friend, Mr Wordsworth, taken my Debt to you on *his* Shoulders, & thereby liquidated it,[2] I should have been made seriously unhappy by the Delays of my long & tedious Illness—more unhappy, I may truly say, than ever before a pecuniary transaction had rendered me / and this because your behaviour to me has been marked by such uniform delicacy, & liberality.—My Sickness has left me in a state of mind, which it is scarcely possible for me to explain to you—one feature of it is an extreme Disgust which I feel at every perusal of my own Productions, & which makes it exceedingly painful to me not only to revise them, but I may truly add, even to look on the Paper, on which they are written.—This has been produced in part no doubt by Disease; but in part too by the very important Researches & Studies, in which I have been lately immersed, & which have made all subjects of ordinary Interest appear to me *trifling* beyond measure.—Conscious however, that this is truly Disease, I shall very soon remit you the manuscript of my 'Information collected during a

---

[1] Two lines heavily inked out in manuscript.

[2] 'I consider the 30£ which you advanced to Mr Coleridge as advanced on my account.' Wordsworth to Longman and Rees, 27 Mar. 1801. By 5 July Coleridge had repaid part of this indebtedness to Wordsworth. See Letter 403.

residence of 10 months in North Germany' / —considering however
my previous Agreement as in no wise binding on you. You will
look the work over, & then if you like to renew your former offer,
well and good!—If not, I shall be equally well-satisfied.—In the
mean time, I should rather wish to send forth a Poem first, which I
have reason to believe, from the concurring testimony of all the
Persons to whom I have submitted it, is more likely to be popular
than any thing which I have hitherto written—. It is in length
about the size of the Farmer's Boy, and I shall annex to it two
Discourses, Concerning Metre, & Concerning the Marvellous in
Poetry— / For this poem a friend of mine is now drawing for me
under my own direction some head-and tail-pieces, representing
the particular Scenes & Places, which are mentioned in the course
of the Tale, all of which he takes on the spot—and they are from
the wildest & most romantic parts of this County.—I wish to
know whether you are disposed to publish this poem in the manner
in which the FABLIAUX edited by Mr Ellis[1] are published / whether
you would venture on the expence of having the little Drawings
engraved or cut in wood /? The title of the Poem is CHRISTABEL,
a Legend, in five Books.—As to Terms, I wish them to be such as
would diminish the *Risk* as much as possible—that is to say, I
would leave the Terms to yourself, undetermined till the first
Edition was sold—and the trifle, I should request leave to draw
on you for, I would have put to my personal Account—to be
liquidated by my after labors, if the success of this Poem should
not answer my *wishes*: for *hopes* & *expectations* I do not waste on
things of such utter uncertainty.—Your's [ver]y truly,

S. T. Coleridge

## 392. To Robert Southey

*Pub.* Life and Corres. *ii. 146.* According to Cuthbert Southey, this letter was
waiting for Southey when he returned to England from Portugal in July 1801.

Greta Hall, Keswick; April 13. 1801

My dear Southey,

I received your kind letter on the evening before last, and I
trust that this will arrive at Bristol just in time to rejoice with
them that rejoice. Alas! you will have found the dear old place
sadly *minused* by the removal of Davy. It is one of the evils of long
silence, that when one recommences the correspondence, one has
so much to say that one can say nothing. I have enough, with what
I have seen, and with what I have done, and with what I have

---

[1] George Ellis edited G. L. Way's translations of select *Fabliaux* in 1796.
A second edition appeared in 1800.

*13 April 1801*

suffered, and with what I have heard, exclusive of all that I hope and all that I intend—I have enough to pass away a great deal of time with, were you on a desert isle, and I your *Friday*. But at present I purpose to speak only of myself relatively to Keswick and to you.

Our house stands on a low hill, the whole front of which is one field and an enormous garden, nine-tenths of which is a nursery garden. Behind the house is an orchard, and a small wood on a steep slope, at the foot of which flows the river Greta, which winds round and catches the evening lights in the front of the house. In front we have a giant's camp—an encamped army of tent-like mountains, which by an inverted arch gives a view of another vale. On our right the lovely vale and the wedge-shaped lake of Bassenthwaite; and on our left Derwentwater and Lodore full in view, and the fantastic mountains of Borrodale. Behind us the massy Skiddaw, smooth, green, high, with two chasms and a tent-like ridge in the larger. A fairer scene you have not seen in all your wandcrings. Without going from our own grounds we have all that can please a human being. As to books, my landlord, who dwells next door, has a very respectable library, which he has put with mine; histories, encyclopaedias, and all the modern gentry. But then I can have, when I choose, free access to the princely library of Sir Guilfred Lawson, which contains the noblest collection of travels and natural history of, perhaps, any private library in England; besides this, there is the Cathedral library of Carlisle, from whence I can have any books sent to me that I wish; in short, I may truly say that I command all the libraries in the county. . . .

Our neighbour is a truly good and affectionate man, a father to my children, and a friend to me. He was offered fifty guineas for the house in which we are to live, but he preferred me for a tenant at twenty-five; and yet the whole of his income does not exceed, I believe, 200*l.* a year. A more truly disinterested man I never met with; severely frugal, yet almost carelessly generous; and yet he got all his money as a common carrier, by hard labour, and by pennies and pennies. He is one instance among many in this country of the salutary effect of the love of knowledge—he was from a boy a lover of learning. . . . The house is full twice as large as we want; it hath more rooms in it than Allfoxen; you might have a bedroom, parlour, study, &c. &c., and there would always be rooms to spare for your or my visitors. In short, for situation and convenience,—and when I mention the name of Wordsworth, for society of men of intellect,—I know no place in which you and Edith would find yourselves so well suited. . . .[1]

[1] 'The remainder of this letter, as well as another of later date, was filled

## 393. *To George Bellas Greenough*

*Address*: — Greenough Esq. | No/21 Bedford Street | Covent Garden | London.
*Transcript* Professor Edith J. Morley. *Pub. with omis.* Wordsworth and Coleridge, ed. by E. L. Griggs, 1939, 235.
*Postmark*: 16 April 1801. *Stamped*: Keswick.

Greta Hall, Keswick, Cumberland.<br>Monday, April 13, 1801

Dear Greenough,

    I heard lately with a deep emotion, that you had visited Stowey & wrote immediately for your Address. This evening I received it. You have no doubt considered me as having behaved forgetfully towards you; & with justice, as far as the word 'behaved' implies an outward & visible Intercourse.—But, Greenough! I should calumniate myself most vilely, if I should admit that I had really been forgetful, or had felt one symptom of a cooling & alienated mind. Your name is familiar with all, whom I love / Yet where I have spoken of you once, I have thought of you a thousand times— aye, with the Heart's Thoughts.—My neglect was occasioned in the first Instance by perplexities domestic & pecuniary—since then I have been monthly more & more ignorant whither to direct to you / & my whole time I may say with severest Truth, has been parcelled out into wearisome occupation, changes of Residence, and long & tedious fits of Sickness, which have thrown me behind hand ever more & more in my literary engagements.—I was always a wretched Performer of epistolary Duties; but latterly I have almost wholly omitted them—I am situated here in a country that one may call *charming* & new-stamp the worn-out slang Phrase with definite meaning & sincere emotion. My House commands perhaps the noblest Prospects of any House in the Island / & my honored Friend, Wordsworth, has fixed his Cottage in the most *beautiful* Spot in Grasmere Vale—a few miles from me.—I would, that I could make out to my mind a distinct Hope of seeing you this Summer / possibly amid the dreary Goings on & burthensome Manners of daily Life it might be both pleasant & morally useful to you to dwell awhile with me & with Wordsworth & his Sister—for we are in some sort unusual Beings, inasmuch as we have seen a great deal of what is called the World, & acquired a great deal of what is called Knowlege, & yet have formed a deep conviction that all is contemptible that does not spring immediately out of an affectionate Heart. Possibly too it may be some

with a most gloomy account of his own health, to which my father refers in the commencement of his reply.' Note by Cuthbert Southey, *Life and Corres.* ii. 148–9.

inducement to you, that the probability of *having me to see* is yearly diminishing—I feel, that I 'to the Grave go down'—As a Husband, & a Father, as a young Man who had dar'd hope that he, even he, might sometime benefit his fellow creatures, I wish to live, but I have kept my *best* hope so unprofan'd by Ambition, so pure from the love of Praise, & I have so deep an intuition that *to cease to be* are sounds without meaning, that though I wish to live, yet the Thought of Death is never for a moment accompanied by Gloom, much less terror, in my feelings or imagination.—I write to you from a bed of Pain / with the fine weather I revive, like a Parlour Fly; but every change in this changeful Climate throws me on my back again, with inflamed eyes, rheumatic fever, & latterly a sort of irregular *Gout*——I am seldom in health three days together.—With the fall of the Leaf it is my present intention to pass over into a warmer climate / & I think of visiting the Azores, in order to ascertain the effect which a mere continuing summer may have.—I have written entirely concerning myself; for of you or of those whom we know in common, I am so ignorant where you are & what your pursuits & objects, that all I could write would be inquiries which possibly I might not be entitled to make.—But believe, dear Greenough, that as in Germany I loved & esteemed you more than any I met there, so neither since I have been in England, have I met any *new* acquaintance whom I love & esteem one tenth part so much. S. T. Coleridge.

I have opened the letter to beg you to forgive it's unseemly Form &c

### 394. To Thomas Poole

*Address*: Mr T. Poole | N. Stowey | Bridgewater | Somerset   *Single*
*MS. British Museum. A few lines pub.* Thomas Poole, *ii.* 44.
*Postmark*: 21 April 1801.   *Stamped*: Keswick.

Saturday, April 18. 1801

My dearest Poole

He must needs be an unthinking or a hard-hearted man who is not often oppressed in his spirits by the present state of the Country. There is a dearth of Wisdom still heavier than that of Corn / the mass of the inhabitants of the country are growing more & more acquainted with the blackness of the conspiracy, which the Wealthy have entered into, against their comforts & independence & intellect. But they perceive it only thro' the dimness of passions & personal indignation. The professed Democrats, who on an occasion of uproar would press forward to be the

Leaders, are without knowlege, talents, or morals. I have conversed with the most celebrated among them; more gross, ignorant, & perverted men I never wish to see again!—O it would have made you, my friend! 'a sadder & a wiser man', if you had been with me at one of Horne Tooke's public Dinners!—I could never discover by any train of Questions that any of these Lovers of Liberty had either [a] distinct *object* for their Wishes, or distinct views of the *means*.—All seemed a quarrel about names!—Taxes—national Debt—representation—overthrow of Tythes & Church Establishments—&c &c.——I believe, that it would be easy to enumerate the causes of the evils of the Country, & to *prove* that they & they alone were the great & calculable causes; but I doubt the *possibility* of pointing out a Remedy.—Our enormous Riches & accompanying Poverty have corrupted the *Morals* of the nation. All *Principle* is scouted—: by the Jacobins, because it is the death-blow of vainglorious Scepticism—by the Aristocrats, because it is visionary & theoretical—even our most popular Books of Morals, (as Paley's[1] for instance) are the corrupters & poisoners of all moral sense & dignity, without which neither individual or people can stand & be men.—O believe me, Poole! it is all past by with that country, in which it is generally believed that Virtue & Prudence are two words with the same signification—in which Vice is considered as evil only because it's distant consequences are more painful than it's immediate enjoyments are pleasurable—and in which the whole human mind is considered as made up of just four ingredients, Impression, Idea, Pleasure and Pain.—I said, that I doubted the possibility of pointing out a Remedy—my reason is this—The Happiness & Misery of a nation must ultimately be traced to the morals & understandings of the People. A nation where the Plough is always in the Hand of the owner, or (better still) where the Plough, the Horse, and the Ox have no existence, may be a great & a happy nation; and may be *called* so, relatively to others less happy, if it has only a manifest *direction* & *tendency* towards this 'best Hope of the World.' Now where there is no possibility of making the number of independent & virtuous men bear any efficient proportion to the number of the Tyrants & the Slaves—that country is fallen never to rise again! There is no instance in the World in which a Country has ever been regenerated which has had so large a proportion of it's Inhabitants crowded into it's metropolis, as we in G. Britain.—I confess, that I have but small Hopes of France; tho' the proportion there is not nearly so great.—So enormous a metropolis imposes on the Governors &

---

[1] William Paley (1743–1805), *Principles of Moral and Political Philosophy*, 1785.

People the necessity of Trade & Commerce—these become the Idols—and every thing that is lovely & honest fall[s] in sacrifice to these Demons.—It is however consoling to me in some small degree to find these opinions of the iniquity of Wealth & Commerce more & more common / especially, among the humbler Quakers in the North, & the more religious Part of the Day Labourers in this County. I assure you, they legislate respecting the Rights & Wrongs of Property with great Boldness & not without a due sense of the enormous Difficulties that would attend the Enthronement of Justice & Truth.—O merciful Heaven! if it were thy good Will to raise up among us *one* great good man, only *one* man of a commanding mind, enthusiastic in the *depth* of his Soul, calm on the *surface*—and devoted to the accomplishment of the *last End* of human Society by an Oath which no Ear of Flesh ever heard, but only the omnipresent God!—Even this unhappy nation might behold what few have the courage to dream of, and almost as few the goodness to wish.——

I trust, that your troubles & commotions are now over. What well grounded Objection can there be to the fixing the *Minimum* of Wages by some article of a *certain real value*? If at any time there should be so many Candidates for Labor, that, but for this Law, the Masters could get Labourers at a still cheaper Rate, then the Parishes might be obliged to employ a large number in the cultivation of Lands, &c. O there are ways enough, Poole! to *palliate* our miseries—but there is not honesty nor public spirit enough to adopt them.—Property is the bug bear—it stupifies the heads & hardens the hearts of our Counsellors & Chief Men!—They know nothing better than Soup-shops—or the boldest of them push forward for an abolition of Tythes!—*Honest Men!*—I trust, that these anti-tythe men will be the occasion of a miracle—they will make even our Priests utter aloud the *very Truth*. It will be a proud Day for me, when the Gentlemen of landed Property set in good earnest about plundering the Clergy——'When Rogues quarrel,' &c—the proverb is somewhat musty.—

I have written a long Letter & said nothing of myself. In simple verity, I am disgusted with that subject. For the last ten days I have kept my Bed, exceedingly ill. I feel and am certain, that 'I to the Grave go down.'—My complaint I can scarcely describe / it is a species of irregular Gout which I have not strength of constitution sufficient to ripen into a fair Paroxysm—it flies about me in unsightly swellings of my knees, & dismal affections of my stomach & head. What I suffer is mere *pain* is almost incredible; but that is a trifle compared with the gloom of my Circumstances.—I feel the transition of the Weather even in my bed—at present, the Disease has seized the whole Region of my Back, so that I scream mechanically on the least motion.—If the fine Weather continue, I shall revive—& look round me—& before the Fall of the Year make up my mind to the important Question—Is it better to die or to quit my native Country, & live among Strangers?—Another Winter in England would *do for me*.—Besides, I am rendered useless & wretched—not that my bodily pain afflicts me—God forbid! Were I a single man & independent, I should be ashamed to think myself wretched merely because I suffered Pain / that there is no Evil which may not ultimately be reduced into Pain, is no part of my Creed. I would rather be in Hell, deserving Heaven, than be in Heaven, deserving Hell. It is not my bodily Pain—but the gloom & distresses of those around me for whom I ought to be labouring & cannot.—

Enough of this——It is the last time, I shall ever write you in such a [. . .?]—you have perplexities enough of your own.—

God love you, & S. T. Coleridge—

### 395. *To John Thelwall*

*Address*: Mr Thelwall | Hereford    *Single*
MS. Pierpont Morgan Lib. *Hitherto unpublished.*
*Postmark*: 26 April 1801.    *Stamped*: Keswick.

April 23, 1801

Dear Thelwall

I wish you all joy & comfort on the Safety of your Wife—& congratulate you both for the Mother and the Child.—I should conjecture that you have written me some letter which must have miscarried, from the enigmatic style of some parts of that which I received yesterday; but that it is more probable that in the bustle & liveliness of your imagination you may have supposed that you had written what you had meant to write.—I allude to 'the secret expedition' which you talk of; the word 'secret' is a word, I detest—& I know of no expeditions but those to Holland, Ferrol, & Egypt.—And what connection your 'Lady of the Lake' has with this Expedition; in other words, the meaning of the phrase The Lady of the Lake, *therefore*, quite eludes my powers of decyphering, which are in truth sufficiently blunt.—I never likewise received a hint of your intention to translate the French Georgics—I suppose, you meant—his Country Gentleman, or Homme des Champs —or his Poems on Gardens—. / It is true, he has translated Virgil's Georgics—but you cannot have intended to translate a translation.[1]—

[1] Jacques Delille, the French translator of Virgil, published *L'Homme des Champs, ou Les Géorgiques Françaises*, in 1800.

## 23 April 1801

You say 'I should like to know your opinion on my mode of publication & my advertisement:'—and certes, if I believed, it was not too late, and I at all capable of influencing your conduct, I should think it my duty to give it freely. As it is, I see no use in it—especially in a letter, in which it is at all times difficult to make your full meaning understood, & very easy to occasion yourself to be misunderstood.—Besides, we are so utterly unlike each other in our habits of thinking, and we have adopted such irreconcileably different opinions in Politics, Religion, & Metaphysics, (& probably in Taste too) that, I fear—I fear—I do not know how to express myself——but such, I fear, is the chasm between us, that so far from being able to shake hands across it, we cannot even make our Words intelligible to each other.—Moral Esteem, frequent & kind wishes, & a lively Interest in your Welfare as a good Man & man of Talents make up in my mind for the too great want of similitude in our intellectual Habits & modes of Faith; (and, I presume, the same holds good in your feelings towards me) but this utter dissimilitude must needs render us fitter to do any other good service for each other, than to offer *advice*.—I shall briefly say therefore, that I am exceedingly glad, you have published by Subscription—first, because you have a *right* to do so, & secondly, I suspect, that in a very very short time the London Booksellers will be marvellously shy of Epic Poems.——The Lady of the Lake is rather an unlucky title; as since the time of Don Quixote the phrase has become a cant word in almost all European Languages for a Woman of Pleasure / A *dramatic Legend* is likewise not a happy combination. The Etyma of the words 'dramatic' & [']legend' directly contradict each other—tho' not so absurd as the phrase 'speaking Pantomime' it is too much of the same class.—Paternal Tears instead of Poems on that particular subject is a quaint &, at the same time, trite conceit. To call a poem *a Tear* is quite Italian—Milton was young enough to be your Son when he used the phrase 'melodious Tear.'—But these are trifles—I am more concerned at your publication of two Books of your Epic Poem. First of all, you mean to publish the whole—& then your Subscribers are to buy these two Books over again / but waiving this, it will appear a childish impatience if you have not finished the Poem; for then it is to be presumed that these books must be to a certain degree unfinished, at all events, not adjusted so as to be an harmonious part of the Whole.—At least no Poet has a right to be certain, that any Book of a Poem will remain what it is, until he has written the whole.[1]—But if you *have* written the whole,

---

[1] Thelwall's *Poems chiefly written in Retirement. The Fairy of the Lake, a Dramatic Romance; Effusions of Relative and Social Feeling: and Specimens of*

I should have advised you to have published *it alone* by Subscription.—The *Hope of Albion* is a very vague title—& would apply to a thousand Subjects.—You say no part of the contents of this Volume are to be political?—How is this possible if you give your Memoirs?——

My health is very, very bad—this day I have risen from my bed after another long confinement of fourteen Days / indeed, I feel & know, that (at all events, if I stay in this climate) I am going down to the Grave—an event which neither [alarms nor depresses] me.—[If I d]ie, and I do not expect to live many years, my Brothers will, I have reason to believe, protect my Wife & children—and from this Cause I am sure I need not request you not to mention my name in your memoirs[1]—.—I say this, not thinking it at all probable that you would do so; but because the thing may be of some importance to my poor Wife & children.

Your's &c S. T. Coleridge.

## 396. To William Godwin

*Address*: Mr Godwin | Polygon | Sommers' Town | London
*MS.* Lord Abinger. *Hitherto unpublished.*
*Postmark*: 1 May 1801.   *Stamped*: Keswick.

Keswick   Tuesday Evening, April 28, 1801

Dear Godwin

I have, this moment, received your manuscript: & this night, if I had not received it, I should have certainly written to you, to make the proper inquiries &c. Indeed, I should have written long ago; but that I feel the utmost aversion at writing an unnecessary Letter since the increase of the postage, that brutal Tax upon the affections & understanding—! You need not be half as poor as I am; & yet look *blank* & fretful on any *idle* Letter, that has taken a shilling from your pocket.———I do not know in what way you wish me to convey my remarks—whether by Letter to you, or en masse to be sent as a companion, when I send back the manuscript.—Spite of the strange Delay at Crosby & Letterman's, & afterwards, perhaps, at the Penrith Booksellers, no time has been lost— / since during the last three weeks I have kept my bed—to day I have crawled forth into the hot Sun, and, if this

---

the *Hope of Albion; or, Edwin of Northumbria: an Epic Poem,* 1801. The first edition is not available. In the second edition 'Fairy' rather than 'Lady' is used in all titles and sub-titles; 'dramatic romance' is used for 'dramatic legend'; and Thelwall apologizes for publishing an extract from his epic.

[1] No mention of Coleridge appears in the memoir prefixed to Thelwall's volume.

## 28 April 1801

weather continue, I have hopes of Health—at least, till next Autumn /. But this last Winter has truly been a hard one for me—one ugly Sickness has followed another, fast as phantoms before a vapourish Woman / in the mean time my expences increased, and I unable to write a line to defray them.—But enough of this—You, I doubt not, can find matter of gloom in London quite sufficient for all the stock of sympathy, which you may have, or wish to have.

I will give your manuscript my best attention, & what I think, I will communicate—but indeed, indeed, I am not dissembling when I express my exceeding scepticism respecting the sanity of my own Feelings & Tone of Intellect, relatively to a work of Sentiment & Imagination.—I have been compelled, (wakeful thro' the night, & seldom able, for my eyes, to read in the Day) to seek resources in austerest reasonings—& have thereby so denaturalized my mind, that I can scarcely convey to you the disgust with which I look over any of my own compositions—a disgust, which has rendered the few brief intervals of my Sicknesses profitless to me as to those engagements with my bookseller which I yet *must* fulfil or starve.—God be praised, I do not however owe my bookseller any thing—methinks, I would rather have my Butcher & Baker for Duns, than Printers & Booksellers.—

Have you seen Davy lately?—It has been an age since I heard *of* him or *from* him—.

It would have yielded me much satisfaction, in many an hour of Downheartedness, if I could have received from you some information respecting your literary Projects & Plans of Sustenance.—The Theatre—alas! alas! that is not to be *relied* on by you.—I have fears even concerning the managers / —and suspect, that your future warfare with theatrical Intrigue, & Duplicity will be worse, than any you have hitherto waged.—It is perhaps impertinent in me to offer advice to you concerning the choice of subjects &c—; but I cannot help wish[ing] that you would write a novel more on [the] plan of Tom Jones—taking up your Hero or Heroine at or before the Birth, & relating his story in the *third* Person or *first*—as your Judgement inclines.—

You will have seen the new Tragedy. When you write, devote half a dozen Lines to it.

My wife & children are well—I trust, that your little ones grow & flourish.—Your's sincerely

S. T. Coleridge

## 397. To Humphry Davy

*Address*: Mr Davy
MS. Royal Institution. Pub. with omis. Frag. Remains, *89*.

Monday, May 4, 1801

My dear Davy

I received a letter this evening from Dr Beddoes who immediately wants the Books in the inclosed Parcel. They should have been sent some 9 months ago—; but I have had enough to do &c—with my miseries & sicknesses——Be so good as to have the Parcel booked & forwarded immediately.—

I heard from Tobin the day before yesterday, nay, it was Friday—from him I learn that you are giving lectures on Galvanism. Would to God! I were one of your auditors.—My motive muscles tingled & contracted at the news, as if you had bared them & were *zincifying* the life-mocking Fibres.

When you have leisure & impulse, perfect leisure & a complete Impulse, write to me—but only then. For tho' there does not exist a man on earth who yields me greater pleasure by writing to me, yet I have neither Pain nor Disquietude from your Silence. I have a deep faith in the guardianship of Nature over you—of the Great Being whom you are manifesting.—Heaven bless you, my dear Davy!—I have been rendered uneasy by an account of a Lisbon Pacquet's non-arrival—lest Southey should have been on board it.—Have you heard from him lately?—

It would seem affectation to write to you & say nothing of my health / but in truth I am weary of giving useless pain. Yesterday I should have been incapable of writing you this scrawl; & tomorrow I may be as bad. '*Sinking, sinking, sinking!* I feel, that I am *sinking!*'—My medical attendant says that it is irregular Gout with nephritic Symptoms—. *Gout* in a young man of 29—!—! Swoln Knees, & knotty Fingers, a loathy Stomach, & a dizzy head—trust me, Friend! I am at times an object of moral Disgust to my own Mind.—But that this long long Illness has impoverished me, I should immediately go to St Miguel's, one of the Azores—the Baths & the delicious Climate might restore me—and if it were possible, I would afterwards send over for my Wife & children, & settle there for a few years—it being exceedingly cheap.—On this supposition Wordsworth & his Sister have with generous Friendship offered to settle there with me—& possibly our dear Southey would come too.—But of this I pray you, my dear fellow! do not say a syllable to any human Being—for the scheme from the present state of my circumstances is rather the Thing of a *Wish* than of a *Hope*.

## 4 May 1801

Tell Tobin I have received his letter, & expect the Books &c with impatience, & return him my best Thanks.—If you write to me, pray in a couple of sentences tell me whether Herschel's Thermometric *Spectrum* (in the Philos. Trans.) will lead to any Revolution in the chemical Philosophy.—As far as *words* go, I have become a formidable chemist—having got by heart a prodigious quantity of terms &c to which I attach *some* ideas—very scanty in number, I assure you, & right meagre in their individual persons. That which most discourages me in it is that I find all *power* & vital attributes to depend on modes of *arrangement*—and that Chemistry throws not even a distant rush-light glimmer upon this subject. The *reasoning* likewise is always unsatisfactory to me— I am perpetually saying—probably, there are many agents hitherto undiscovered. This cannot be *reasoning*; for in all conclusive reasoning we must have a deep conviction that all the *terms* have been exhausted. This is saying no more than that (with Dr Beddoes's leave) chemistry can never possess the same kind of certainty with mathematics—in truth, it is saying nothing. I grow however exceedingly interested in the subject.——

God love you, my dear Friend!—From Tobin's account I fear that I must give up a very sweet vision—that of seeing you this summer. The summer after my Ghost perhaps may be a *Gas*—Your's affectionately

S. T. Coleridge

### 398. To Robert Southey

*Address*: Mr C. Danvers | St James's Place | Kingsdown | Bristol    Single
(For Mr Southey)
*MS.* Lord Latymer. *Pub.* Letters, *i.* 354.
*Postmark*: 11 May 1801. *Stamped*: Keswick.

Greta Hall, Keswick.    May 6, 1801
My dear Southey

I wrote you a very very gloomy letter; & I have taken blame to myself for inflicting so much pain on you without any adequate motive. Not that I exaggerated anything as far as the immediate Present is concerned; but had I been in better health & a more genial State of Sensation, I should assuredly have looked out upon a more chearful Future.—*Since* I wrote you, I have had another & more severe fit of Illness—which has left me weak, very weak— but with so calm a mind, that I am determined to believe, that this Fit was bonâ fide the last.—Whether I shall be able to pass the next Winter in this Country, is doubtful; nor is it possible, I should know till the fall of the Leaf.—At all events, you will (I hope & trust, & if need were *intreat*) spend as much of the summer & autumn with us as will be in your power—& if our *Healths* should permit it, I am confident there will be no other solid objection to our living together in the same house, divided. We have ample Room—Room enough & more than enough—and I am willing to believe, that the blessed Dreams, we dreamt some 6 years ago may be auguries of something really noble which we may yet perform together.—

We wait impatiently, anxiously, for a letter announcing your arrival—indeed the article Falmouth has taken precedence of the *Leading Paragraph* with me for the last 3 weeks.—Our best Love to Edith.—Derwent is the Boast of the County—the little River-God is as beautiful as if he had been the Child of Venus Anaduomene previously to her Emersion.—Dear Hartley! we are at times alarmed by the state of his Health—but at present he is well—if I were to lose him, I am afraid, it would exceedingly deaden my affection for any other children I may have——[1]

> A little child, a limber Elf
> Singing, dancing to itself;
> A faery Thing with red round Cheeks,
> That always *finds*, and never *seeks*—
> Doth make a Vision to the Sight,
> Which fills a Father's Eyes with Light!
> And Pleasures flow in so thick & fast
> Upon his Heart, that he at last
> Must needs express his Love's Excess
> In Words of Wrong and Bitterness.
> Perhaps 'tis pretty to force together
> Thoughts so all unlike each other;
> To mutter and mock a broken charm;
> To dally with Wrong, that does no Harm—
> Perhaps, 'tis tender too & pretty
> At each wild Word to feel within
> A [s]weet Recoil of Love & Pity;
> And what if in a World of Sin
> (O sorrow & shame! should this be true)
> Such Giddiness of Heart & Brain
> Comes seldom, save from Rage & Pain,
> So talks, as it's most us'd to do.——

---

[1] These lines, of which no other manuscript version exists, were printed in 1816 as the conclusion to Part II of *Christabel*. Obviously they were inspired by Hartley Coleridge.

A very metaphysical account of Fathers calling their children rogues, rascals, & little varlets——&c——
God bless you, my dear Southey! I need not say, write!—
                                                    S. T. Coleridge

P.S. We shall have Pease, Beans, Turneps (with boiled Leg of mutton), cauliflowers, French Beans, &c &c—endless!—We have a noble Garden!

## 399. To Daniel Stuart

MS. *British Museum.* Pub. Letters from the Lake Poets, 17.

Keswick, Saturday, May 16, 1801
Dear Stuart

I should have been greatly affected by the contents of your letter at any time; and at present I felt them with a fellow-feeling added to brotherly sympathy.—You have had misery enough of your own & see enough immediately around you for any profitable purpose, to which Sufferance or compassion can conduce—were it not therefore necessary in some sort as a justification of my silence & inexertion, I should feel no impulse to tell you that since the first of January I have been, with the exception of 3 weeks and a few days, & this not continuous but interspersed, confined to my bed, with a succession of Disorders, i.e. Rheumatic Fever followed by an Hydrocele, & since then by what is called irregular or retrocedent Gout. My powers of mind never forsook me; but the act of writing (& in general, of conversation) was wholly out of my power.—Since the last 8 days I appear to myself to be really recovering; but I have had so many short Recoveries of one, two, and three days each, followed by such severe Relapses, that verily I am almost afraid to Hope. But chearful Thoughts come with genial sensations:—& Hope is itself no mean Medicine.

I thank you for your kindness in continuing to send the paper to us—it has been a great amusement to Mrs Coleridge during her long attendance on my sick bed—& latterly to me. It would give me more than a common pleasure if I could write any thing that would please you or do you an atom of service—as to any terms, they are out of the Question—my ill health & those habits of irresolution, which are perhaps the worst bad consequences of ill health, forbid me at present to rely on myself—but if you would write & point out to me any *subjects*, I would do any thing for you off hand with great pleasure—. I ask you for *subjects* & a little *information*—for I am wholly ignorant of the present state of the public Feeling.——

In the question respecting the Disfranchisement of the Clergy it appeared to me . . . [Remainder of manuscript missing.]

### 400. To Thomas Poole

*Address*: Mr T. Poole | N. Stowey | Bridgewater | Somerset    Single sheet
*MS*. British Museum. *A few lines pub.* Thomas Poole, *ii. 48*.
*Postmark*: 20 May 1801.    *Stamped*: Keswick.

May 17, 1801.—Sunday Evening
My dear Poole
I thank you with a full heart for your last Letter which was as wise as it was kind.—Ah dear friend! had you seen me a few days before the date of it, you would have needed no other evidence [to] have convinced you, that my gloom & forebodingness respecting pecuniary affairs were the effects, & in no degree the causes, of my personal indisposition.—I should take shame to myself indeed, if in an hour of health I had suffered 10 minutes unhappiness from the difficulty of living at 130£ a year—sadly minused as it is, & probably will continue to be, by Income Taxes & the other Gentry of that class.—No! Poole—I should be unworthy of your esteem as an ordinary man, & most deserving of your ridicule as a pretended Philosopher, if that gloom & the expressions, that conveyed it to you, had been other than perishing Maggots engendered in the weakly bowels of Disease. My pecuniary Embranglements indeed will cost me some trouble to cut through—if I regain my health, I shall arm my hands in a stout Pair of Hedger's & Ditcher's Gloves, & fall to with a light heart / if not, God's will be done!—I must do what I can / tho' it would be unusually painful to me to continue in Debt even to those who love me, desirous as I am that no one should with truth impute my disregard of wealth for myself to want of strict honesty & punctuality in my money-dealings with others.—I have written you many letters; and yet from all of them you will scarcely have been able to collect a connected story of my Health, & it's Downfalls.—I will give it now (as briefly as I can) that you may distinctly understand the plans which I shall after mention.—During the whole Fall of the year to Christmas I had been harrassed with all sorts of crazinesses, blood-shot eyes, swoln Eye lids, rheumatic pains in the back of my head & limbs, clusters of Boils in my neck, &c—from all which, but especially from a transient Puffiness of one of my hands, I learnt the doleful Tidings that the machine was crazed—& slight changes of weather affected me, & *Wet* cloathes, tho' pulled off immediately on my entering the house, never failed to throw me on my back.—The new year was ushered in with what I believed a Rheumatic Fever / tho' no

doubt part of the pains were nephritic.—This was followed by the Hydrocele & a tedious, tormenting, humiliating Visitant it was.— My general Health, after this was removed, was as you may suppose, but indifferent, sometimes better, sometimes worse, never good—& during this Interval I applied myself with great intensity of thought & application, far greater indeed than in all my former Life. Notwithstanding the Result, I still praise God that I did so.—In the course of these studies I tried a multitude of little experiments on my own sensations, & on my senses—and some of these (too often repeated) I have reason to believe did injury to my nervous system— / However this be, I relapsed—and a Devil of a Relapse it has been, to be sure!—. There is no Doubt, that it is irregular Gout combined with frequent nephritic attacks—I had not strength enough to ripen it into a fair Paroxysm—it made it's outward shews sometimes in one or other of my fingers, sometimes in one or more of my Toes, sometimes in my right Knee & Ancle; but in general it was in my left Knee and Ancle—here the Disorder has been evidently attempting to fix itself—my left knee was most uncouthly swoln & discolored, & gave me night after night pain enough, heaven knows, but yet it never came to a fair Paroxysm.— All this was mere nothing—but O dear Poole! the attacks on my stomach, & the nephritic pains in my back which almost alternated with the stomach fits—they were terrible!—The Disgust, the Loathing, that followed these Fits & no doubt in part too the use of the Brandy & Laudanum[1] which they rendered necessary—this

[1] This letter, with its passing reference to laudanum, gives a true account of the beginning of Coleridge's slavery to opium, and confirms his reiterated assertion, made in 1814, 1820, and 1826, that he unwittingly became a drug addict in an effort to alleviate pain. Thus in 1814 he tells Cottle how he was 'seduced into the ACCURSED Habit ignorantly. I had been almost bed-ridden for many months with swellings in my knees—in a medical Journal I unhappily met with an account of a cure performed in a similar case (or what to me appeared so) by rubbing in of Laudanum, at the same time taking a given dose internally—It acted like a charm, like a miracle! I recovered the use of my Limbs, of my appetite, of my Spirits—& this continued for near a fortnight. At length, the unusual stimulus subsided—the complaint returned—the supposed remedy was recurred to—but I can not go thro' the dreary history—' MS. New York Public Lib. (*Early Rec.* ii. 157). See T. Allsop, *Letters, Conversations and Recollections of S. T. Coleridge*, 1864, p. 41, and Gillman, *Life*, 246–8. See also Letter 516, p. 984 n. Although this letter to Poole does not contain any reference to medical reading, Letter 374 provides evidence of it.

Earlier letters show that Coleridge had previously taken opium both for medicinal purposes and to relieve the strain of agitated spirits and that he was well aware of the 'divine repose' it induced (see Letters 10, 108, 150, 151, 209, 238, and 309), but it seems evident that his habitual use of drugs did not begin until his illness of 1800–1. See also E. L. Griggs, 'Samuel Taylor Coleridge and Opium', *Huntington Lib. Quar.*, August 1954, pp. 357–78.

Disgust, Despondency, & utter Prostration of Strength, & the strange sensibility to every change in the atmosphere even while in my bed— / enough!—I pray God with a fervent heart, my beloved & honored Poole! that those words may for ever remain *Words* to you—unconstrued by your own experience.—On Monday, May 4th, I recovered, all at once as it were—my appetite returned, & my spirits too in some measure—On the Thursday following I took the opportunity of a return Post Chaise, & went to Grasmere— to do away doleful remembrances—& I grew better and better, till Tuesday last—indeed I was so stout that I had resolved on walking back to Keswick the next morning—but on Tuesday afternoon I took a walk of about six miles, & on my return was seized again with a shivering Fit followed by a feverish & sleepless night, & in the Morning my left Knee was swoln as much as ever.—I return'd to Keswick in a return post chaise on Friday Evening— my knee is still swoln, & my left [ancle?] in flames of fire, & last night these pretty companions kept me sleepless the whole night— hour after hour,

> I utter'd and suppress'd full many a groan,
> The Cur, Arthritis, gnawing my knee-bone—

but my stomach & head & back remain unaffected, & I am resolved to believe that I am really recovering, tho' I have had so many recoveries of two, & three days each, followed by such severe Relapses, that verily I am almost afraid to hope. But chearful Thoughts come with genial sensations; and Hope is itself no mean Medicine.—My plan is very short—when the swelling in my knee is gone, I shall take for a few weeks the Rust of Iron in pretty large Doses—& thro' the whole Summer I will observe every rule of the most scrupulous Prudence & Forecast with religious strictness, using *regulated* Diet & *regulated* Exercise—at the close of the summer if I should be so far re-established, that I no longer feel my health affected by the changes of the Weather, I shall have nothing to do, but to pass the Winter in quiet industry, with unremitted caution as to Wet & cold.—If the contrary should be the case, I am determined to go to St Miguel's (one of the Azores—see 'St Miguel' in your Encyc.)—I can go from Whitehaven, which is but sixteen miles from Keswick, for a mere trifle—perhaps, for nothing; & I can be lodged & boarded in a convent close by the Bath in the E. of the Island for the whole Winter for ten pound. Even in a pecuniary Light it will be a good plan / for my Letters will bring me at least a hundred Pound. Captn Wordsworth (W's Brother & worthy to be so) passed two months there, & warmly recommends a Wintering there, as almost a certain Cure of my

( 732 )

*17 May 1801* [400

Complaints.—When I am sick or in pain, I look forward to this scheme with a comforting satisfaction—but whenever I am quite at ease, I cannot bear even to think of it.—

I had hopes, when I began this Letter, that one Half of it would have sufficed for my story—& now I am at the end, & have no room to say aught about my disappointment in not seeing you—& now too the Country is in it's very lustre of beauty, & hitherto unpestered by the Tourists.—But if I can send a letter franked from London to you, by means of a parcel which I shall soon send to Longman, I will write again.—

God in heaven bless you & S. T. Coleridge

Love to your dear Mother—& to Ward—Mrs C. & the Children quite well—Derwent is a downright Beauty—. When you see your Sister & Mr K., remember us affectionately to them.

## 401. *To Humphry Davy*

*Address*: Mr Davy | Royal Institution | Albermarle Street | London    *Single*
MS. *Royal Institution. Pub. with omis.* Frag. Remains, *90.*
*Postmark*: 24 May 1801.    *Stamped*: Keswick.

Greta Hall, Keswick. May 20, 1801

My dear Davy

I rested my whole weight on my crutch, & laughed so that I could scarce hold myself on the crutch, at the question, you put to me, in Underwood's[1] name.—I suppose, that when I had begun to laugh, from my exceeding weakness I continued it nolens volens.—But wherein the laughable of the Question consists, it may be difficult to shew.—In the first place, I was excessively tickled by the sentence 'to love a woman called Hays *or* Taylor'. I did not (& do not) know how to understand these words—whether Underwood loves a woman whose name he had mentioned to you, but *you* had forgotten whether the name, he mentioned, was Hayes *or* Taylor—or whether the woman was really Hayes *alias* Taylor—i.e. had sometimes assumed one name, & sometimes another. On the first supposition, as no two Combinations of letters can well be more widely different from each other than Hayes & Taylor, it left me in no small scepticism as to the degree of attention, with which you had vitalized your auditory nerves at the moment that the little man had named his Amata to you; and of course, it became a possible case that neither Hayes nor Taylor

---

[1] T. R. Underwood, the artist. He was Tom Wedgwood's travelling companion to France and Switzerland in 1803. Coleridge sometimes referred to him as Subligno.

( 733 )

might be the Lady's name, but Saunderson, or Courtney, or any other. On the other supposition, it tickled me no little that a man should be in love before he had received a conviction even of the Woman's good character; but most of all at an inquiry into the character & honor of 'a woman named Hayes *alias* Taylor.'— Now Hayes *alias* Taylor may perhaps have had some other name, at the time I knew her— / for certes No Lady of either of these names do I recollect (except Miss Mary Hayes, of literary note, whom I once saw for half an hour.)—I went first thro' all the *virtuous* Women, I had ever known, as far as my Memory would assist—but it was all Blank. Then (& verily I, a Husband & a Father, & for the last seven years of my Life a very Christian Liver, felt oddly while I did it) then, I say, I went as far as memory served, thro' all the loose women I had known, from my 19th to my 22nd year, that being the period that comprizes my Unchastities; but as names are not the most recollectible of our Ideas, & the name of a loose Woman not that one of her adjuncts, to which you pay the most attention, I could here recollect no *name* at all—no, nor even a face nor feature. I remembered my vices, & the times thereof, but not their objects.——Bye the bye has not Underwood a wife & child?—And of what nature is this Love?—But I am not Underwood's confessor; & his creed & mine agree probably in very few articles. But it would give me great pleasure to save him from mischief, because there is much about the little man which I much like, tho' there is likewise more than a little which I could wish the Alchemist, Thought, to transmute. Therefore, when you see him, tell him from me that either from the confusion of *my* memory or of *yours* I am left ignorant, who it is, whom he means; but if he will bring back my former Self to me by a few Ubi Quando Circumstances—*where* I knew her, & *when*— &c &c, I will then communicate all I know with great pleasure. Ask him what he thinks of a Trip to the Azores with me—on a landskip scheme? It is a world of *great* & *peculiar* landskip-beauties; & I give it as my solemn advice, that the Oreads & the Dryads are the very best Ladies in the World for him to form a long *amatory* connection with:—*amatory*, I say, as contra-distinguished both from the *conjugal* and the *amicitial* connections.

Tho' we of the North must forego you, my dear Davy, yet I shall rejoice when I receive a letter from you from Cornwall. I must believe, that you have made some important discoveries in Galvanism, and connected the facts with other more interesting ones—or I should be puzzled to conceive how that subject could furnish matter for more than one Lecture. If I recollect aright, you have identified it with Electricity—& that indeed is a wide field.

## 20 May 1801

I shall dismiss my British Critic, & take in Nichol[son's] Journal—
& then I shall know something about you.[1] I am sometimes apprehensive, that my passion for science is scarcely true & genuine—it is but *Davyism*! that is, I fear that I am more delighted at *your* having discovered a Fact, than at the Fact's having been discovered.

My health is better—I am indeed eager to believe, that I am really *beginning to recover*—tho' I have had so many short recoveries followed by severe Relapses, that I am at times almost afraid to hope. But chearful thoughts come with genial sensations; & Hope is itself no mean Medicine.

I am anxious respecting Robert Southey! Why is he not in England?—Remember me kindly to Tobin. As soon as I have any thing to communicate, I will write to him. But alas! Sickness turns large districts of Time into dreary uniformity & sandy Desolation.——Alas for Egypt!—& Menou![2]—However, I trust the *English* will keep it if they take it—& something still will be gained to the cause of human Nature.—Heaven bless you!

S. T. Coleridge

### 402. To William Godwin

*Address*: Mr Godwin | the Polygon | Sommers' Town | London   *Single Sheet*
*MS.* Lord Abinger. *Pub. with omis.* Macmillan's Magazine, *April 1864, p. 528.*
*Postmark*: 26 June 1801.   *Stamped*: Keswick.

Grieta Hall, Keswick   Tuesday Evening, June 23, 1801

Dear Godwin

I have had, during the last three weeks, such numerous interruptions of my 'uninterrupted rural Retirement', such a succession of Visitors both indigenous & exotic, that verily I wanted both the time & the composure necessary to answer your Letter of the first of June. At present, I am writing to you from my bed. For in consequence of a very sudden change in the weather from intense Heat to a raw and scathing chillness my bodily Health has suffered a Relapse as severe as it was unexpected; but I find however, that I have gathered much strength in this last Interval. The Disease assumes an air of far greater Decision than it ever before manifested; and about 5 o/clock this morning I had a fair & full Paroxysm of the Gout in my left Knee & Foot, which, after a sojourn of some

---

[1] Coleridge refers to Nicholson's *Journal of Natural Philosophy, Chemistry, and the Arts*, 1797–1815, to which Davy contributed a number of articles.

[2] Jacques F. de Menou (1750–1810), the French general defeated at Alexandria, 21 Mar. 1801.

## To William Godwin

Hours, has left me in better spirits than it found me, tho' my knee remains swoln & exquisitely sore, and I am instructed too to expect a second Fit in the course of the Night. But I can bear even violent Pain with the meek patience of a Woman, if only it be unmingled with confusion in the Head, or sensations of Disgust in the stomach, for these, alas! insult and threaten the steadiness of our moral Being.

I have not yet received either Antonio or your Pamphlet in answer to Dr Parr & the Scotch Gentleman[1] (who is to be Professor of Morals to the young Nabobs at Calcutta with an Establishment of 3000£ a year!!)—Stuart was so kind as to send me Fenwick's Review of it in a paper called the Albion; & Mr Longman has informed me that by your orders the Pamphlet itself has been left for me at his House. The extracts, which I saw, pleased me much, with the exception of the introduction which is incorrectly & clumsily worded. But indeed I have before observed that whatever you write, the first Page is always the worst in the Book.—I wish, that instead of six days you had employed six months, and instead of a half a crown Pamphlet had given us a good half a guinea Octavo. But you may yet do this.—It strikes me that both in this work & in your second Edition of the Political Justice[2] your Retractations have been more injudicious than the assertions or dogmas retracted. But this is no fit subject for a mere Letter. If I had time, which I have not, I would write two or three sheets for your sole Inspection, entitled, History of the Errors & Blunders of the literary Life of William Godwin. To the World it would appear a Paradox to say, that you are all too persuadible a man; but you yourself know it to be the truth.—

I shall send back your manuscript on Friday, with my criticisms. You say, in your last, 'How I wish you were here!'—When I see how little I have *written* of what I could have *talked*, I feel with you that a Letter is but 'a mockery' to a full & ardent mind. In truth I feel this so forcibly, that if I could be certain that I should remain in this country, I should press you to come down, & finish the whole in my House; but if I can by any means raise the moneys, I shall go in the first Vessels that leave Liverpool for the Azores, (St Michael's to wit) & these sail at the latter end of July.—Unless I can escape one English Winter & Spring, I have not any rational prospect of Recovery. You 'cannot help regarding uninterrupted

---

[1] Cf. Godwin's *Thoughts occasioned by . . . Dr. Parr's Spital Sermon, . . . being a Reply to the Attacks of Dr. Parr, Mr. Mackintosh, the Author of an Essay on Population, and Others,* 1801. A copy of this work with Coleridge's annotations is in the British Museum.

[2] The second edition of *Political Justice* was published in 1796.

## 23 June 1801

rural retirement as a principal cause' of my ill-health. My ill-health commenced at Liverpool in the shape of blood-shot eyes & swoln Eyelids while I was in the daily habit of visiting the Liverpool Literati—these on my settling at Keswick were followed by large Boils in my neck & shoulders—these by a violent Rheumatic Fever—this by a distressing & tedious Hydrocele—& since then by irregular Gout, which promises at this moment to ripen into a legitimate Fit. What uninterrupted rural retirement can have had to do in the production of these outward & visible evils, I cannot guess! What share it has had in consoling me under them I know with a tranquil mind, & feel with a grateful Heart. O that you had now before your eyes the delicious picture of Lake, & River, & Bridge, & Cottage, & spacious Field with it's pathway, & woody Hill with it's spring verdure, & mountain with the snow yet lingering in fantastic patches upon it—this, even the same which I had from my sick bed, even without raising my head from the Pillow!— O God! all but dear & lovely Things seemed to be known to my Imagination only as Words—even the Forms which struck terror into me in my fever-dreams were still forms of Beauty—Before my last seizure I bent down to pick something from the Ground, & when I raised my head, I said to Miss Wordsworth—I am sure, Rotha! that I am going to be ill: for as I bent my head, there came a distinct & vivid spectrum upon my Eyes—it was one little picture —a Rock with Birches & Ferns on it, a Cottage backed by it, & a small stream.—Were I a Painter I would give an outward existence to this—but I think it will always live in my memory.——Bye the bye our rural Retirement has been honored by the company of Mr Sharp, and the poet Rogers—the latter, tho' not a man of very vigorous intellect, won a good deal both on myself & Wordsworth— for what he said evidently came from his own feelings, & was the result of his own observation. I doubt not that they both return to London with far other opinion respecting Wordsworth, than the Scotch Gentleman[1] has been solicitous to impress his Listeners with. But that Gemman's Lectures & Conversations are but the Steam of an Excrement, & truly animalcular must those Souls be, to whom *this* can form a cloud that hides from them the face of Sun or Star. He is a thing that must make itself known to all noses, sooner or later; but some men's olfactories are quicker than others'— / You for instance *smelt at* him & found him out—I & Wordsworth *winded* him at a distance.—

It gave me pain that you should so misunderstand a sentence in my former Letter respecting the Lyrical Ballads.[2] It was a mere Tirade, almost as compleatly so, as your apotheosis of

[1] James Mackintosh.       [2] See Letter 390.

*me* in your last Letter, &, as I supposed, it was sufficiently explained to be a Tirade by the spirit of the whole Epistle which I wrote while struggling with the most disquieting & depressing sensations, & which was indeed no more than the awkward Curvette of a heavy-loaded Beast of Burthen grown restive under his Load. The passage, which you quote, would have been grossly improper, addressed to a junior—addressed to you *seriously* it would have deserved no milder name than Coxcombry or Insolence. Yet *seriously* I should have small fellow-feeling with a man who could read 'the Brothers' & 'Michael' with indifference, or (as some have done) with merriment—& I must add too (in proof of a favorite opinion of my own, viz. that where the Temper permits a *sneer*, the Understanding most frequently makes a blunder) that there are few better reasons than the accidental circumstance of private Friend[ship] why, as a *touchstone* by which to come at a decision in my own mind concerning a Man's Taste & Judgment, the works of a contemporary writer hitherto without fame or rank ought 'to take the lead of Milton, Shakespear, & Burke.' I have myself met with persons who professed themselves idolatrous admirers of Milton, & yet declared it to be their opinion that Dr Darwin was as great a poet. Thousands *believe* that they have always admired Milton—who have never asked themselves, for what they admired him, or whether in naked matter of Fact they ever did admire him.—Likewise, dear Godwin! highly as I respect the powers of Edmund Burke, I feel a sort of confidence that I could *reason* any candid man into a conviction that he had acted lightly & without due *awe* when he placed Burke's name by the side of Milton's & Shakespear's.

My love to your dear little ones. Mrs Coleridge is well—& Hartley & Derwent. The latter is as fair & fat a creature, as ever had his naked Body circumnavigated by an old Nurse's kisses.—I feel my knee beginning to make ready for the reception of the Lady Arthritis.—God bless you and S. T. Coleridge

## 403. *To Thomas Poole*

*Address*: Mr T. Poole | Nether Stowey | Bridgewater | Somerset  *Single*
*MS. British Museum. Pub. E. L. G. i. 174.*
*Postmark*: 8 July 1801. *Stamped*: Keswick.

Sunday, July 7 [5], 1801.  Keswick
My dearest Poole

I had written you a letter some days ago, which by accident was not sent to the post—it's purport chiefly was to desire you to

*5 July 1801* [403

desire Mr King to pay Mrs Fricker 10£ in my name, which sum Mr Wedgewood will remit to you the first time he writes. I wrote to him on Wednesday night last, requesting him so to do. I adopt this mode of conveying the money to Mrs F. first to save her the expence of two double Letters, as I must *divide* the note in order to send it with certain safety, & four Shillings is a heavy Drawback from 10£—& secondly, from the great difficulty of procuring Bank of England Bills in this County. Nobody here will take them—they call them 'swindling notes'—the home business is carried on by the Bank Paper of the chief Towns in this & the adjoining Counties, & the London Business by means of Drafts.——

The remaining part of my Letter was written in so gloomy a spirit that I am glad it was delayed long enough for me to see & destroy it. On Wednesday Evening I received a friendly Letter from Jos. Wedgewood. He had seen a letter of mine to Tobin, written for the purpose of preventing him & a friend of his from paying me a visit this summer, (a *month's visit*) the reason I assigned was the uncertainty of my remaining in this country after this month, as I was determined to go to the Azores in the very first vessels, & winter there, if I could get the moneys necessary for *me to go* with, & for my *Wife & Babes* to be left behind with.— Mr Wedgewood says—'I shall be very glad to hear from you, when you have strength & spirits to write, as I suppose some plan must be settled as to your annuity. In the mean time I inclose a draft of 50£, as I think we are in your debt.'—This 50£ has, I doubt not, left me *their* debtor, as far as respects this year's annuity. It has enabled [me] to pay up to the present hour all our half yearly & quarterly Keswick Bills, rent, &c—& as much of the remainder of the Debt transferred from Longman to Wordsworth as is sufficient for W's present necessities.—Within a trifle, 4 or 5£ perhaps, *my Household* will go on very smoothly & easily till Christmas when I shall be able to draw again.—

I wrote to Tobin in the first gloomy moments of a sudden & severe Relapse: on the three following nights I had three sharp paroxysms of decided Gout which left me in apparent health & good spirits: & under these influences I wrote a very chearful answer to Mr Wedgewood, & informed him, that I had postponed, and I hoped relinquished the scheme of passing the Winter at St Michael's; but that I meant to try a course of Horse Exercise. Within two Hours, after I had dispatched this Letter I was again taken ill with fever & the most distressing stomach-attacks—on Friday Evening & night I was very ill—only a little better on Saturday—and I am still *very* sick & *somewhat* sad. I can bear pain, my dear Poole! I can bear even violent pain with the meek patience

( 739 )

of a Woman; but nausea & giddiness are far worse than pain—for they insult & threaten the steadiness of our moral Being—& there is one thing yet more deplorable than these—it is the direful Thought of being inactive & useless. Nine dreary months—and oh me! have I had even a fortnight's full & continuous health? I have hardly gained the Rock, ere a new Wave has overtaken & carried me back again. When I am well & employed as I ought to be, I cannot describe to you how independent a Being I seem to myself to be. My connection with the Wedgewoods I feel to be an honor to myself, & I hope, and *almost feel*, that it will hereafter be even something like an honor to them too—but—oh Poole! you know my heart & I need not reverse the picture. Now what am I to do? Mr Wedgewood says 'From all I have heard of the part of England where you are, I think it is very likely that you may have suffered from the wetness of the climate, & that you might probably derive great benefit from merely changing your place of Abode in England.' To this I make two remarks which I shall make into two paragraphs—a trick, I have learnt by writing for Booksellers at so much *per sheet*. Blank Spaces are a Relief to the Reader's eye & the Author's Brain—& the Printers too call them FAT.

First then, that beastly Bishop, that blustering Fool, Watson,[1] a native of this vicinity, a pretty constant Resident here, & who has for many years kept a Rain-gage, considers it as a vulgar Error that the climate of this County is particularly wet. He says, the opinion originates in this—that the Rain here falls more certainly in certain months, & these happen to be the months in which the Tourists visit us. William Coates said to me at Bristol—[']Keswick, Sir! is said to be the rainiest place in the Kingdom—it always rains there, Sir!—I was there myself three Days, & it rained the whole of the Time.'——Men's memories are not much to be relied on in cases of weather; but judging from what I remember of Stowey & Devon, Keswick has not been, since I have been here, wetter than the former, and not so wet as Devonshire.

Secondly, whither am I to go?—Nota bene, Poole! I have now no furniture: & no means whatever to buy any. Giving the requisite & merited attention to this circumstance, I say, I live cheaper here than I could do any where in England. I have delightful Prospects, heavenly Grounds for the children, a *solicitously kind* neighbour in my Landlord—& a mother to Hartley in his Housekeeper. But all this out of the question—I say, I *live cheaper* here than I could in any part of the Kingdom.—But then I find, alas! that I cannot endure the climate—but then I have not an

---

[1] Richard Watson, who was born in Westmorland, devoted much attention to chemistry and made discoveries concerning the thermometer.

atom of Belief, nor the most trifling Reason for believing, that the Climate in any other part of the Kingdom is one whit better for me—excepting *perhaps* some part of Cornwall. And how am I to get thither?—Every one has said to me—I hope, you may recover your health merely by living in Devonshire or Cornwall without going abroad. I have always answered thus—Going abroad—going out of the Kingdom, &c—are terrible *Words*—but what is the Thing itself?—I can go, by myself, to St Michael's for 5 guineas, & live there for 20£ a year—& if I send for my wife & children, the expence will be exactly in the same proportion—and the carriage of my Books will cost nothing additional. But if I go to the coasts of Devon, or Cornwall, by myself, the coasting-voyage is too dangerous for me to go by sea & it is intolerably tedious & uncertain: if I go by Land, I must often halt a day or two on the road, & it cannot cost me so little as 20 guineas—and as to *living*, Lord have mercy upon me!——if I go with my Wife & Children, the expence will be in the same proportion—& the Carriage of my Books will half ruin me!——. Add to this, that at St Michael's I have not only an exceedingly cheap country, a heavenly Country to look at, & Baths specific in the cure of my Disease, but I can gain twice as much as my voyage there & back, & my maintenance, by writing without half the effort which I am now using what I have seen & noticed.—I have therefore made up my mind to go & see the place at the end of this month, *if I can*.—And now all I have to do is to think *how* I can do it.—I could go if I had 30£ for myself, & 10£ to leave with Mrs Coleridge. This 40£ I think I could raise from the Booksellers without injuring my reputation by giving out unfinished works, merely in advance, provided I could get any one to be my Security for the repayment of the money in case that Death or Disease should occasion a non-performance of my Engagement.[1]—To the Wedgewoods I will not apply—it would look like borrowing money upon my annuity—and I am, and I ought to be, feverishly fearful & delicate with regard to my pecuniary connections with them, having yet done nothing in evidence that they did not do a hasty & imprudent thing in having done so much for me.—God bless them!——I am sure, I think often & often of them with a grateful & affectionate heart—. Neither do I apply to you—partly, because I am vexed that I have not yet

---

[1] Wordsworth opposed such a scheme in a letter to Poole: 'This plan, for my own part, though I did not like to say so abruptly to Coleridge, I greatly disapprove, as I am sure it would entangle him in an engagement which it is ten to one he would be unable to fulfil, and what is far worse, the engagement, while useless in itself, would prevent him from doing anything else.' *Early Letters*, 281.

been able to repay you the 37£, I already owe—& partly, because I know how manifold & vexatious your pecuniary responsibilities already are—and am somewhat too proud willingly to force you to think of *me* at the time you are thinking of poor —— or ——. I shall apply therefore elsewhere, if I can think of any body else— if not, I will try my rhetoric to persuade some Bookseller to advance the sum without security—and not till this have failed, shall I ask you.——Consider this Letter therefore only as one giving you occasion for writing to advise me, if you have any advice to offer, or any reason for believing that I am wrong in my present Determination. Something I must do, & that speedily—for Body & Soul are going—Soul is going into Body, and Body is going into Dung & Crepitus—with more of the latter than the former. Wordsworth mentioned to me that he meant to write you. I told him, I should certainly write myself, & was about to state what I meant to say— but he desired me not to do it, that he might write with his opinions unmodified by mine.[1]—*We* are all well but *I*.

Best Love to your mother.——

God for ever bless you, my | Dear Poole, | & |

S. T. Coleridge

## 404. To William Godwin

*Address*: Mr Godwin | Polygon | Sommers' Town | London  *Single*
MS. Lord Abinger. *Pub. with omis.* William Godwin, ii. 79.
*Postmark*: 11 July 1801. *Stamped*: Keswick.

Keswick. Wednesday.—[8 July 1801.]

Dear Godwin

I have this evening sent your Tragedy (directed to you) to Penrith to go from thence to London by the Mail. You will probably receive it on Saturday Morning.—It is the Carlisle Mail— you can easily enquire it out, if it should not arrive on Saturday— tho' perhaps it may be delayed one day in Penrith—if so, you will not receive it till Monday.—

It would be needless to recount the pains & evils that prevented me from sending it on the day, I meant to do. Your letter of this evening has given me some reason to be glad, that I was prevented. My Criticisms &c were written in a style & with a boyish freedom of censure & ridicule, that would have given pain & perhaps, offence. I will rewrite them, abridge them, or rather extract from them their absolute meaning, & send them in the way of [a] Letter.—In the Tragedy I have frequently used the following marks ※ ⊤. ⟊. #.—Of these the first, ※ calls your attention to

[1] See Letter 411.

## 8 July 1801

my suspicions, that your Language is false or intolerable English: the second ⊤. marks the passages, which struck me as *flat* or mean —the third ǂ. is a note of reprobation levelled at those sentences, in which you have adopted that worst sort of vulgar Language, common-place *book* Language—such as, [']Difficulties that mock narration'—[']met my view' [']bred in the lap of Luxury'——&c— ǂǂ implies bad metre.——I was much interested by the last three acts—indeed, I greatly admired your management of the story. The two first acts, I am convinced, you must entirely re-write / — I would indeed open the play with the Conspirators in Isfahan, confident of their success—& Bulac, who had fled from the army in some apparent Defeat (afterwards recovered by the Sefi) at the head of these Conspirators—In this way you might with great dramatic animation explain to the Audience all you wish, & give likewise palpable motives of Despair & Revenge to Bulac's after Conduct.—But this I will write to you—the papers, in which I have *detailed* what I think might be substituted, I really do not dare send—.

You must have been in an odd mood, when you could write to a poor fellow with a sick stomach, a giddy head, & swoln & limping Limbs, to a man on whom the Dews of Heaven cannot fall without diseasing him, 'You want, or at least you think you want neither accom[m]odation nor society as ministerial to your happiness[']— / and strangely credulous too, when you could gravely repeat that in the Island of St Michael's, the chief town of which contains 14000 Inhabitants, no other residence was procurable but 'an unwindowed Cavern scooped in the Rock'—!—I must have been an idle fool indeed to have resolved so deeply without having made due inquiries how I was to be housed & fed.—Accom[m]odations are necessary to my Life—& Society to my Happiness, tho' I can find that society very interesting & good, which you perhaps would find dull & uninstructive.—

One word more. You say—I do not tolerate you in the degree of partiality you feel for Mrs I.—will not allow your admiration of Hume, & the pleasure you derive from Virgil, from Dryden, even in a certain degree, from Rowe.——Hume & Rowe *I* for *myself* hold very cheap; & have never feared to say so—but never had any objection to any one's differing from me. I have received, & I hope, still shall, great delight from Virgil, whose versification I admire beyond measure, & very frequently his Language. Of Dryden I am & always have been a passionate admirer. I have always placed him among our greatest men.—You must have misunderstood me—& considered me as detracting when I considered myself only as discriminating.—But were my opinions otherwise I should rather fear that others would not tolerate *me* in holding opinions different from those of people in general, than feel any difficulty in tolerating others in their conformity with the general sentiment.—Of Mrs I. I once, I believe, wrote a very foolish sentence or two to you.[1]—And now for 'my late acquisitions of *friends*.[']—Aye—*friends*!—Stoddart indeed, if he were nearer to us and more among us, I should really number among such—he is a man of uncorrupted integrity & of a very, very kind heart—his talents are respectable—and his information such, that while he was with me I derived much instruction from his conversation.—Sharpe & Rogers had an introductory note from Mr Wedgewood—they are so much my friends, that my chief ground in etiquette to call on Sharpe would be his intimacy with Mr Wedgewood, & as to Mr Rogers—even if I wished it, and were in London the next week, I should never dream that any acquaintance, I have with him, would entitle me to call on him at his own house.—That Tobin thought of bringing Underwood & Dyson astonished both me & W.—they would neither have been in my house. The whole visit should have been from Tobin, whom I greatly venerate—tho' certainly a four weeks' visit from him with two unpleasant uninvited men in his train would have been somewhat too much.—Dyson I dislike—but little [Su]bligno—what has he done? Tobin & [Da]vy think well of him.—

God bless you & S. T. Coleridge.

## 405. To Robert Southey

*Address*: Mrs Danvers | Kings down Parade | Bristol | (For Mr Southey)
Single Sheet

MS. Lord Latymer. Pub. with omis. Letters, i. 356.
*Postmark*: 25 July 1801.

Wednesday, July 22, 1801

My dear Southey

Yesterday evening I met a boy on an ass, winding down *as picturish* a glen, as eye ever looked at—he & his Beast no mean part of the picture—I had taken a liking to the little Blackguard at a distance, & I could have downright hugged him when he gave me a letter with your hand-writing.—Well, God be praised! I shall surely see you once more, somewhere or other. If it be really impracticable for you to come to me, I will doubtless do any thing rather than not see you—tho' in simple truth travelling in chaises or coaches even for one day is sure to lay me up for a week.—But

[1] For Coleridge's opinion of Mrs. Inchbald see Letter 333.

## 22 July 1801

do, do, for heaven's sake, come—& go the shortest way, however dreary it be—for there is enough to be seen when you get to our house.—If you did but know what a flutter the Old Moveable at my left Breast has been in, since I read your letter—I have not had such a Fillip for a many months.—My dear Edith! how glad you were to see old Bristol again![1]——

I am again climbing up that rock of Convalescence, from which I have been so often so washed off, & hurried back—but I have been so unusually well these last two Days, that I should begin to look the damsel Hope full in the face, instead of sheep's eyeing her, were it not that the Weather has been so unusually hot—& that is my Joy!—Yes, Sir! we will go to Constantinople; but as it rains there, which my Gout loves as the Devil does Holy Water, the Grand Turk shall shew the exceeding attachment, he will no doubt form towards us, by appointing us his Vice-roys in Egypt— I will be Supreme Bey of that showerless District, & you shall be my Supervisor.—But for God's sake, make haste & come to me, and let us talk of the Sands of Arabia while we are floating in our lazy Boat on Keswick Lake, with our eyes on massy Skiddaw, so green & high. Perhaps, Davy might accompany you. Davy will remain unvitiated—his deepest & most recollectible Delights have been in Solitude, & the next to those with one or two whom he loved. He is placed no doubt in a perilous Desart of good things— but he is connected with the present Race of Men by a very awful Tie, that of being able to confer immediate benefit on them; and the cold-blooded venom-toothed Snake, that winds around him, shall be only his Coat of Arms, as God of Healing.—

I exceedingly long to see Thalaba—& perhaps still more to read Madoc over again.—I never heard of any third Edition of my Poems—I think, you must have confused it with the L. B.— Longman could not surely be so uncouthly ill-mannered, as not to write to me to know if I wished to make any corrections or additions.—If I am well enough, I mean to alter, with a devilish sweep of revolution, my Tragedy, & publish it in a little volume by itself with a new name, as a Poem. But I have no heart for Poetry— alas! alas! how should I? who have passed 9 dreary months with giddy head, sick stomach, & swoln knees.—My dear Southey!— it is said, that long sickness makes us all grow selfish by the necessity which it imposes of continual[l]y thinking about ourselves—but long & sleepless Nights are a fine Antidote—oh! how I have dreamt about you——Times, that *have been*, & never can return, have been with me on my bed of pain, and how I yearned

[1] After a little over a year in Portugal the Southeys arrived in Bristol on 10 July 1801: there they stayed with the Danvers for several weeks.

## To Robert Southey

toward you in those moments, I myself can know only by feeling it over again!—But come! 'strengthen the weak hands, & confirm the feeble knees. Then shall the lame man leap as a hart, and sorrow & sighing shall flee away.'——

I am here, in the vicinity of Durham, for the purpose of reading from the Dean & Chapter's Library an Ancient, of whom you may have heard—*Duns Scotus*![1] I mean to set the poor old Gemman on his feet again, & in order to wake him out of his present Lethargy, I am burning Locke, Hume, & Hobbes under his Nose—they stink worse than Feather or Assafetida.

Poor Joseph! he has scribbled away both head & heart. What an affecting Essay I could write on that Man's character.—Had he gone in his quiet way, on a little poney looking about him with a sheep's eye cast now & then at a short poem, I do verily think from many parts of the Malvern Hill, that he would at last have become a poet better than many who have had much fame—but he would be an Epic, & so

> Victorious o'er the Danes I Alfred preach,
> Of my own Forces Chaplain-general!—

I have a very large Boil in my neck a little to the right of my Wind-pipe, & it is poulticed—in consequence whereof I smell so exactly like a hot Loaf, that it would be perilous for me to meet a hungry blind man.—But it has broke, & is easy.—Write immediately, directing—Mr Coleridge, Mr George Hutchinson's, Bishop's Middleham, Rushiford, Durham[2]—& tell me, when you set off—& I will contrive to meet you at Liverpool—where, if you are jaded with the journey, we can stay a day or two at Dr Crompton's—& chat a bit with Roscoe & Curry, whom you will like as men far, far better than as writers—O Edith! how happy Sara will be—and little Hartley, who uses the air & the Breezes as skipping Ropes—& fat Derwent, so beautiful & so proud of his three Teeth, that there's no bearing of him. God bless you, dear Southey &

S. T. Coleridge

P.S. Remember me kindly to Danvers, & Mrs Danvers—

---

[1] The schoolman, Joannes Duns Scotus (1265?–1308?). In a marginal note Coleridge says he 'could find but one work of Duns Scotus's—that *De Sententiis*' in the Durham Library. See *Notes on English Divines*, ed. by Derwent Coleridge, 2 vols., 1853, ii. 21. See also Letter 528.

[2] At this time George Hutchinson was living at Bishop Middleham, near Durham, and apparently Sara kept house for him. Thomas Hutchinson was at Gallow Hill, near Scarborough, and Mary seems to have made her home there.

*25 July 1801* [406

406. *To Robert Southey*

*Address*: Mrs Danvers | Kingsdown | Bristol    for Mr Southey
*MS*. Lord Latymer. *Pub. with omis.* Letters, *i. 359.*
*Postmark*: 27 July 1801. *Stamped*: Durham.

Saturday, July 25, 1801. Durham

My dear Southey

I do loathe cities—that's certain. I am in Durham at an Inn—& that too I do not like—& have dined with a large parcel of Priests all belonging to the Cathedral—thoroughly ignorant & hard-hearted. I have had no small trouble in gaining permission to have a few books sent to me 8 miles from the place, which nobody has ever read in the memory of man.—Now you will think what follows a Lie—& it is not. I asked a stupid haughty fool, who is the Librarian of the Dean & Chapter's Library in this city, if he had Leibnitz. He answered—'We have no Museum in this Library for natural curiosities; but there is a mathematical Instrument-seller in the town, who shews such [an]imalcula thro' a glass of great magnifying powers.' Heaven & Earth!—he understood the word '*live Nits.*' Well, I return early tomorrow to Middleham, to a quiet good family, that love me dearly—a young farmer, & his Sister[1]—& he makes very droll verses in the northern dialect & in the metre of Burns, & is a great Humourist; & the woman is so very good a woman, that I have seldom indeed seen the like of her. —Death! that every where there should be one or two good & excellent People like these—& that they should not have the power given 'em to edit a crepitus strong enough to whirl away the rest to Hell—!

I do not approve the Palermo & Constantinople scheme—to be secretary to a fellow, that would poison you for being a poet while he is only a lame Verse-maker! But verily, dear Southey! it will not suit you to be under any man's controll—or biddances. What if you were a Consul—'twould fix you to one place, as bad as if you were a Parson. It won't do.—Now mark my scheme!— St Nevis is the most lovely as well as the most healthy Island in the W. Indies—Pinny's Estate is there—and he has a country House situated in a most heavenly way, a very large mansion. Now between you & me I have reason to believe that not only this House is at my service, but many advantages in a family way that would go one half to lessen the expences of living there—& perhaps, Pinny would appoint us sine-cure Negro-drivers at a hundred a

[1] Sara Hutchinson, who accompanied Coleridge to Gallow Hill a few days later. See Letter 407.

year each, or some other snug & reputable office—& perhaps, too we might get some office in which there is quite nothing to do, under the Governour. Now I & my family, & you & Edith, & Wordsworth & his Sister might all go there—& make the Island more illustrious than Cos or Lesbos. A heavenly climate—a heavenly country,—& a good House. The Sea shore so near us—dells & rocks, & streams— / Do now think of this! But say nothing about it—on account of old Pinny.—Wordsworth would certainly go, if I went. By the living God, it is my opinion, that we should not leave three such men behind us.

N.B. I have every reason to believe Keswick (& Cumberland & Westmoreland in general) full as dry a Climate as Bristol. Our rains fall more certainly in certain months; but we have fewer rainy days taking the year thro'.—As to cold, I do not believe the difference perceptible by the human Body.—But I feel, that there is no relief for me in *any part* of England.—Very hot weather brings me about in an instant—& I relapse as soon as it coldens.——

You say nothing of your voyage homeward or the circumstances that preceded it—this however I had far rather hear from your mouth than your Letter.——Come! and come quickly.

My love to Edith—& remember me kindly to Mary & Martha & Eliza, & Mrs Fricker.—My kind respects to Charles & Mrs Danvers. Is Davy with you?—If he is, I am sure, he speaks affectionately of me.—God bless you! Write. S. T. Coleridge

## 407. To Robert Southey

*Address*: Mrs Danvers | Kingsdown Parade | Bristol (For Mr Southey)
*MS*. Lord Latymer. *Pub. with omis.* Letters, *i. 361.*
*Postmark*: 3 August 1801.

Scarborough, Aug. 1. 1801

My dear Southey

On my return from Durham (I foolishly walked back) I was taken ill—& my left knee swelled, '*pregnant* with agony' as Mr Dodsley says in one of his poems. Dr Fenwick has earnestly persuaded me to try Horse-exercise & warm Sea-bathing—& I took the opportunity of riding with Sara Hutchinson to her Brother Tom, who lives near this place, where I can ride to & fro, & bathe with no other expence there than that of the Bath. The fit comes on me either at 9 at night, or 2 in the morning—in the former case it continues 9 hours, in the latter 5—I am often literally *sick* with pain.—In the day time however I am well—surprisingly so indeed considering how very little sleep I am able to snatch.—Your letter was sent after me, & arrived here this morning—and but that my

## 1 August 1801

letter *can* reach you on the 4th of this month, I would immediately set off again, tho' I arrived here only last night. But I am unwilling not to try the Baths for one week—. If therefore you have not made the immediate preparation, you may stay one week longer at Bristol—but if you have, you must look at the Lake, & play with my Babies 3 or four days—tho' this grieves me. I do not like it—I want to be with you, & to meet you even at the very verge of the Lake Country.—I would far rather that you would stay a week at Grasmere, (which is on the Road, 14 miles from Keswick) with Wordsworth than go on to Keswick, & I not be there. O how you will love Grasmere!

All I ever wish of you with regard to wintering at Keswick is to stay with me *till* you find the climate injurious.—When I read that chearful sentence 'we will climb Skiddaw this year, & scale Etna the next' with a right piteous & humorous Smile did I ogle my poor knee, which at this present moment is larger than the thickest part of my Thigh.——

A little quaker Girl (the daughter of the great quaker mathematician Slee, a friend of Anti-Negro-trade Clarkson who has a house at the foot of Ulswater, which Slee Wordsworth dined with— a pretty parenthesis!) this little Girl, 4 years old, happened after a very hearty meal to *eructate*, while Wordsworths were there. Her Mother *looked* at her—& the little creature immediately & *formally* observed—'Yan belks when yan's fu', & when yan's empty'—that is 'One belches when one's full, & when one's empty.'—Since that time this is a favorite piece of Slang at Grasmere & Greta Hall—whenever we talk of poor Joey, George Dyer, & other Perseverants in the noble Trade of Scriblerism.—

Wrangham, who lives near here, one of your Anthology Friends, has married again—a Lady of a neat 700£ a year—his Living by the Inclosure will be something better than 600—besides what little fortune he had with his last wife, who died in the first year. His present wife's *Cousin* observed—'Mr W. is a *lucky* man—his *present* Lady is very weakly & delicate.'——I like the idea of a man's *speculating in sickly Wives*. It would be no bad character for a farce.

That letter £ to which you allude was a kind-hearted honest well-spoken Citizen—the three Strokes, which *did* for him were, as I take it, First, the Ictus Cardiacus, which devitalized his moral *Heart*—2ndly, the Stroke of the Apoplexy in his *head*—& thirdly, a stroke of the Palsy in his Right hand—which produces a terrible shaking & impotence in the very attempt to reach his Breeches Pocket.—O dear Southey! what incalculable Blessings, worthy of Thanksgiving in Heaven, do we not owe to our being & *having been*,

407]  To Robert Southey

*Poor!* No man's Heart can wholly stand up against Property.——
My love to Edith. S. T. Coleridge

P.S. If you write again, before I see you, which I scarcely expect, direct your letter as before, to Mr George Hutchinson's, Bishops Middleham, Rushiford, Durham.—I shall be there in ten days, unless I should be worse, than I have the slightest reason to expect.—There I shall stay two days, merely for rest—& then proceed straight on to Keswick—at which place I trust that I shall arrive on the 15th of this month, or the 16th at farthest.——Kind Remembrances to Danvers!

### 408. To Francis Wrangham

*Transcript Coleridge family. Pub. E. L. G. i. 179.*

Dear Wrangham  Gallow Hill—Aug. 2—1801

I arrived here on Friday afternoon. Such is the state of my health that I could not venture to ride over to Hunmanby, uncertain whether or no you are at home—but I cannot satisfy myself unless in some way or other I convey to you my wish for the enduring happiness of yourself and those who are dear to you.[1] I shall remain here four or five days, or a week at the farthest: as Southey will at the conclusion of that time be (with Mrs Southey) on his road to Keswick. Have you any thoughts of visiting the Lakes this Autumn? I need not say, how happy we of Keswick & Grasmere shall be to give you the welcome in our own names & in that of Lady Nature—Wordsworth at least can introduce you to all her best things in all her mollissima tempora—for few men can boast, I believe, so intimate an acquaintance with her Ladyship.——

Believe me, dear Wrangham, Your's sincerely
S. T. Coleridge.

### 409. To Robert Southey

*Address*: Mrs Danvers | Kingsdown Parade | Bristol   *Single Sheet*   (for Mr Southey)
*MS. Lord Latymer. Pub. E. L. G. i. 179.*
*Postmark*: 15 August 1801. *Stamped*: Rushyford.

Bishop's Middleham, Wednesday, August 11. [12]
My dear Southey

I am glad that Longman played the Jew with you. Do not, whatever you do, do not send Madoc hastily out of your hands.—

[1] 'Alluding to my recent marriage with D. Cayley—July 14—1801.' [MS. note by Wrangham.]

## 12 August 1801

I have much (and as I believe some things of importance) to talk over with you respecting that poem. I cannot but believe that it will stand unrivalled in it's own kind—and that a very noble kind. I am *anxious* about that poem.—*Do not write for Stuart*—Hamilton is bad enough. 'Sdeath! is there nothing you can translate, to wit, anonymously?———I much wish, it were possible to bring your Mother with you. Change—& chearfulness—and Rest—they are the Physicians. I met two Lines in an old German Latin Book which pleased me—

> Si tibi deficiant Medici, Medici tibi fiant
> Haec tria, Mens hilaris, Requies, Moderata Diaeta.[1]

What you say of Davy, impressed me, melancholied me. After I had written what I wrote to you concerning him, & had sent off my letter, a reproof rose up in my heart—& I said to myself—O when wilt thou be cured of the idle trick of letting thy Wishes make Romances out of men's characters? I had one very affecting letter from Davy, soon after his arrival in London—& in this he complained in a deep tone of the ill effect which perpetual analysis had on his mind. I for my part never did think his sphere of utility extended by his removal to London; and I think those most likely to be *permanently* useful who most cherish their best feelings.

> Know thy own self & reverence the Muse!

What a thing, what a living thing, is not Shakespere & in point of real utility I look on Sir Isaac Newton as a very puny agent compared with Milton—and I have taken some pains with the comparison, & disputed with transient conviction for hours together in favor of the former.—However, you are right as an oracle when you add—we are all well in our way.—I have seen no new books except Godwin's which I met with by accident—& think of it precisely as you do. I was so much delighted with all the rest of the Pamphlet that I could have myself pulled his nose for that loathsome & damnable passage.

Dr Fenwick at Durham dissuaded me from bathing in *the open Sea*—he thought it would be fatal to me. I came out all at once on the Beach, and had Faith in the Ocean. I bathed regularly, frolicked in the Billows, and it did me a proper deal of good. When I received your letter this morning, I was packing up to go Keswickward—I returned from Scarborough last night—but now I shall

---

[1] See *De Conservanda Bona Valetudine.* Opusculum Scholae Salernitanae ... Cum Arnoldi Novicomensis ... brevissimis ac utilissimis ac Enarrationibus: Accuratius iam & emendatius edita per Ioannem Curionem, & Iacobum Crellium, Frankfurt, 1551, cap. i. Coleridge cites this Latin distich a number of times in his letters. See also Letters 443 and 550.

## To Robert Southey

stay a week at Dinsdale & bathe twice a day in the sulphur baths there. They work wonders. God bless you. I long to behold you. Love to Edith.—On my first emersion I composed a few lines which will please you as a symptom of convalescence—for alas! it is a long [time] since I have cropt a flowering weed on the sweet Hill of Poesy[1]—

### 1

God be with thee, gladsome Ocean!
How gladly greet I thee once more—
   Ships and Waves and endless Motion
And Life rejoicing on thy Shore.

### 2

Gravely said the sage Physician,
To bathe me on thy shores were Death;
   But my Soul fulfill'd her Mission,
And lo! I breathe untroubled Breath.

### 3

Fashion's pining Sons and Daughters
That love the city's gilded Sty,
   Trembling they approach thy Waters
And what cares Nature, if they die?

### 4

Me a thousand Loves and Pleasures
A thousand Recollections bland,
   Thoughts sublime and stately Measures
Revisit on thy sounding Strand—

### 5

Dreams, the soul herself forsaking,
Grief-like Transports, boyish Mirth,
   Silent Adorations, making
A blessed Shadow of this Earth!

### 6

O ye Hopes, that stir within me,
Health comes with you from above:
   God is with me, God is in me,
I cannot die, if Life be Love!

[1] *Poems*, i. 359.

## 410. To Miss Isabella Addison and Miss Joanna Hutchinson

*Address*: Miss Addison | Mr Hutchinson's | Gallow-Hill | Wykeham, | Malton | [Yorkshire]
*MS. Miss Joanna Hutchinson. Hitherto unpublished.* The holograph is torn; the bracketed passages were written on the manuscript by Emma Hutchinson.

Wednesday, Aug. 19. 1801
Respected Miss Is'bel,
    Joanna,[1] my Dear!
This comes to you hoping.—We're happy to hear
By a Pigeon, that early this morn did appear
At our window with two Billet-deux in it's Bill,
That safe, wind and limb, you had reach'd Gallow Hill
The Mare [all obedient to Isabel's will]
Two such beautiful Girls in so *knowing* a Pha'ton
(*Mem. A Board nail'd behind with a name and a date on*)
Two such *very* sweet Girls in a Taxer so green,
Miss Addison driving as bright as a Queen
And Joanna so gay—by the ghost of old Jehu,
It was well worth a shilling, my Lasses! to see you!
Why, even the Dust fell in love, I'll be bound,
With you both, and for Love could not rest on the ground
And Mary, for gladness & joy did not scant any
When she said Tom & you, with the Horse, Mare, and A[ntony.]
But this topic [I fear] I've ex[hausted 'twere better
With some news and advice to enliven my letter
But e]nough is as good as a feast—and for More,
Why, you know, it might surfeit—at least, make one snore.
But *one thing* indeed I am *forc'd* to declare,
You are both fair as Angels, and good as you're fair,
And I'll purchase a glazier's diamond, my Lasses,
To scribble your names on all windows & glasses.

Now for news.—There is none. My eyes I've not cock'd on
Brother George since last night: for he's gone into Stockton—
And on Saturday last, as that wit told you scoffing,
To Dinsdale I rode, & was boil'd in a coffin.
And then I *did* smell—aye, I smelt, by old Davy,
Like a Pole Cat serv'd up in an addle-egg gravy.
High in health I return'd; but on Sunday grew bad,
And on Monday was worse, & a fever I had,

[1] Isabella Addison later married John Monkhouse; Joanna Hutchinson was Sara's younger sister.

On Tuesday grew better, & on Wednesday, you see,
Am as gay as the Lark that sings high o'er the Lea.

And next for ADVICE.—Aye, of that I have plenty
If instead of but two you were 20 times 20.
There's a Lake by the fir-grove—don't bathe there, I say;
'Tis *tempting*, I own; but too much in the way
And it rouges, like Lamp-black—and then it were risible
To paint such fair Maids, as Joanna & Isabel.
A Brunette is a pretty complexion, *as such*—
But black & all black—why, 'tis somewhat too much.—
The sweet Lake hath a Die, that's too deep for a Lady—
So, pray, be content with what Nature has made 'e.

But, secondly—mind!—You'll be going to Scarborough—
I intreat and admonish you tho', not to harbour a
Thought of electing from Dukes or from Earls
A Husband to suit you—'twon't answer, my Girls.
A Baronet?—Why, if he's eager to wed you,
You may do as you like—*I* shall not forbid you.
But as plain Meat is all that the Healthy desire,
Were I you, I'd put up with a simple Esquire.
Such a one now *as me*. (*Nota bene. I'm married,
And Coals to Newcastle must never be carried!!*)

But thirdly & lastly, for Enough, as I tell you,
Is as good as a feast—and More would but swell you.—
At present, they are doctoring George's black Mare—
I intreat and admonish you, *do* have a care
(You, Miss Addison, YOU I now am addressing,)
As you love poor Joanna, & hope for my Blessing,
Do keep the Mare's Physic snug out of [her way]
For Enough is as good as a Feast, as I [say,]
She has taken three ounces of Salts with[out manna]
But she *may* take too much—& then farew[ell Joanna.]

My love to dear Mary—& tell Tom to bear in
Remembrance his promise to come after shearing.
He might visit all way from the Thames to the Tyne
And not meet a Welcome more glowing than mine.
And if Mary will come, a kind kiss I will gi' her,
And at Grasmere are Folks, will be happy to see her
At least, they will treat her with all due civility—
And Politeness is better than downright Hostility.

*19 August 1801* [410

Bless my soul! What, turn over!—Why, I've written a whole
Ridge—
Enough is a Feast—so adieu from

YOUR
COLERIDGE

P.S. Dear Girls! I had almost forgotten to say,
That I think, that you both possess charms in your way.

411. To Thomas Poole

*Address*: Mr. T. Poole | Nether Stowey | Bridgewater | Somerset   *Single*
*MS. British Museum. Pub. with omis.* Thomas Poole, *ii. 63*.

In July 1801 Wordsworth wrote to Poole 'solely on Coleridge's account', and suggested that £50 would make it possible for Coleridge to go to the Azores in search of health. 'My dear Poole,' Wordsworth concluded, 'you will do what you think proper on this statement of facts; if, in case of Coleridge's death, you could afford to lose 50£, or more if necessary, it may perhaps appear proper to you to lend him that sum, unshackled by any conditions, but that he should repay it when he shall be able; if he dies, if he should be unwilling that any debt of his should devolve on his Brothers, then let the debt be cancelled.' *Early Letters*, 279–81.

On 21 July 1801 Poole replied not to Wordsworth, but to Coleridge. After regretting Coleridge's ill health, Poole went on to say that he had proposed to the Wedgwoods that Coleridge accompany Tom to Sicily, but that he had received no answer. He suggested the advisability of Coleridge borrowing from his brothers. Then, after mentioning Wordsworth's letter and the request for £50, Poole said he had 'many claims', offered to lend £20, and added the comforting news that Coleridge's indebtedness was £52, not £37, as Coleridge had supposed. MS. British Museum.
*Postmark*: 10 September 1801.   *Stamped*: Keswick.

Keswick. Sept. 7. 1801

My dear Poole

It has been, you may be well assured, neither a Falling off of my affection to you, nor doubt of your's to me which has produced my long silence—; but simply confusion, & ignorance & indecision and want of means respecting the disposal of myself in order to the preservation of a Life, which heaven knows, but for a sense of duty I would resign as quietly & blessedly as a Baby fallen asleep lets the mother's nipple slip from it's innocent gums.—I have such an utter dislike to all indirect ways of going about any thing, that when Wordsworth mentioned his design of writing to you, but would not explain to me even by a hint *what* he meant to write, I felt a great repugnance to the idea, which was suppressed by my habitual deference to his excellent good sense. I wish, I had not suppressed it—he wrote without knowing you, or your circumstances, your habitual associations in the whole growth of your mind, or the accidental impressions of disgust made by your many Losses &

( 755 )

the squandering of your exertions on objects that had proved themselves unworthy of them. It is impossible that you should feel with regard to pecuniary affairs as Wordsworth or as I feel—or even as men greatly inferior to you in all other things that make man a noble Being. But this I always knew & calculated upon; & have applied to you in my little difficulties when I could have procured the sums with far less pain to myself from persons less dear to me, only that I might not estrange you wholly from the outward & visible Realities of my existence, my Wants & Sufferings. —In all my afflictions I never dreamt however for a moment of making such an application to you, as Wordsworth did—he acted *erroneously* but not wrongly—for you, I understand, had requested him to write to you freely on all that in his opinion concerned my Welfare.—However Error generates Error; his Letter untuned your mind—You wrote to me when you ought assuredly to have written to him—& you wrote to the Wedgewoods, & made a most precipitate & unwise request, which coming from you will, I am sorry to say, in all human probability connect in their minds a feeling of disgust with my character & my relations to them—a feeling of disgust, & a notion of *troublesomeness.*—Besides, the Request itself—! O God! how little you must have comprehended the state of my Body and mind not to have seen that to have accompanied Tom Wedgewood was the very last thing that I could have submitted to! Two Invalids—& two men so utterly unlike each other in opinions, habits, acquirements, & feeling! When I was well, I made the offer to him *as a duty*, provisionally that he could find no other person, that suited him; but in the state in which I now am, I should have felt it my duty to have declined it, had it been offered to me or even desired of me.—The other proposals I only sighed at—principally, that of applying to my family. What claims have I on my family? A name & nothing but a name. Had I followed the wishes of my family, Poole! think you, that ten times the paltry sum, that may be wanted by me, would have presented any difficulty to me.—My family—I have wholly neglected them—I do not love them—their ways are not my ways, nor their thoughts my thoughts—I have no recollections of childhood connected with them, none but painful thoughts in my after years—at present, I think of them habitually as commonplace rich men, bigots from ignorance, and ignorant from bigotry. —To me they have always behaved unexceptionably. I have a little to thank them for, & nothing to complain of—/ but what one claim can I have on their assistance or exertions? whence can it arise? Shall I say then—do it, because I am *called* your Brother? Or shall I say, do it because I *am* your Brother?—I who am not their Brother in any sense that gives to that title aught that is good or dear.—Or shall I say—Preserve my life, because if it is preserved, I shall most assuredly devote it with all it's powers & energies to the overthrow of all that you hold precious or sacred?— But enough of this—let us for the future abstain from all pecuniary matters—if I live, I shall soon pay all I at present owe—& if I die, the thought of being in *your* debt will never disquiet me on my sick bed. I love you too well to have one injurious thought respecting you.—You deem me, too often perhaps, an enthusiast—Enthusiast as I may be, Poole! I have not passed thro' Life without learning, that it is a heart-sickening Degradation to borrow of the Rich, & a heart-withering affliction to owe to the Poor.——

As to my health, I am *going*, as I suspect.—My knee & leg remains swoln & troublesome—but that is a trifle. Other symptoms of a more serious nature have lately appeared—a tendency to scrophulous Boils and Indurations in the Neck, a dry husky Cough, with profuse sweats at night confined to the Region of my Chest. Of course, it is my Duty not to stay in this climate—I have accordingly written to John Pinny of Somerton, requesting of him to let me have apartments in his Country House in the Isle of St Nevis, & even earnestly solicited him to contrive, that the expences of my food & necessary conveniences may by his means & letters be alleviated as much as possible. When I have heard from him, I will write again to you. My spirits are good—I am generally *cheerful*, & when I am not, it is only because I have exchanged it for a deeper & more pleasurable Tranquillity. The young Soldier rushes on the Bayonet & cries with his last breath—God save King George! I should have been strangely idle, an Hypocrite or a Dupe, if I have not learnt my Trade as well as he has learnt *his*. His Trade has been to follow a blind feeling—& thereby to *act*—mine has been to contemplate—& thereby to *endure*.

Southey is here with his Wife. Wordsworth is gone into Scotland to the Scotch Lakes with Sir William & Lady Rush & their six Daughters—to the eldest of whom Montague (who is with them) was to have been married on Thursday last at Edingburgh—& was so, I suppose. She is a fine girl, only 18.—

My Wife & children are both well.—How much Mrs C. was shocked at the death of poor Susan Chester, you may easily suppose. I felt a sort of pain—just enough to bring a tear upon my cheek, some five minutes after I heard the intelligence. Poor Mrs Chester!—

My best Love to your Mother—& kind Remembrances to Ward if he be with you.—Heaven bless you, my dear Poole, & your affectionate Friend,

S. T. Coleridge

## 412. To Thomas Poole

*Address*: Mr T. Poole | Nether Stowey | Bridgewater | Somerset
MS. British Museum. Pub. Letters, *i. 364.*
*Postmark*: 22 September 1801. *Stamped*: Keswick.

Greta Hall, Keswick. Sept. 19. 1801

By a letter from Davy I have learnt, Poole! that your Mother is with the Blessed.—I have given her the tears & the pang, which belong to her Departure; & now she will remain to me for ever what she has long been, a dear & venerable Image, often gazed at by me in imagination, and always with affection & filial piety. She was the only Being whom I ever *felt* in the relation of Mother: & She is with God! We are all with God!—What shall I say to *you*? I can only offer a prayer of Thanksgiving for you, that you are one who have habitually connected the act of Thought with that of Feeling; & that your Natural Sorrow is so mingled up with a sense of the Omnipresence of the Good Agent, that I cannot wish it to be other than what, I know, it is. The frail, & the too painful, will gradually pass away from you; & there will abide in your Spirit a great & sacred accession to those solemn Remembrances and faithful Hopes, in which and by which the Almighty lays deep the foundations of our continuous Life, and distinguishes us from the Brutes, that perish. As all things pass away, & those Habits are broken up which constituted our own & particular Self, our nature by a moral instinct cherishes the desire of an unchangeable Something, & thereby awakens or stirs up anew the passion to promote *permanent* Good, & facilitates that grand business of our Existence —still further, & further still, to generalize our affections, till *Existence* itself is swallowed up in *Being*, & we are in Christ even as he is in the Father.—It is among the advantages of these events that they learn us to associate a new & deep feeling with all the old good phrases, all the reverend sayings of comfort & sympathy, that belong, as it were, to the whole human Race—I felt this, dear Poole! as I was about to write my old—

God bless you & love you for ever and ever!

Your affectionate Friend,
S. T. Coleridge

Would it not be well, if you were to change the scene awhile!— Come to me, Poole!—No—No—no.—You have none that love you so well as I—I write with tears that prevent my seeing what I am writing.—

*19 September 1801*

### 413. To Daniel Stuart

*Address*: D. Stuart Esq. | No/ 335 | Strand | London
*MS*. British Museum. *Pub*. Letters from the Lake Poets, *19*.
*Postmark*: 22 September 1801.   *Stamped*: Keswick.

Saturday Evening, Sept. 19. 1801

Dear Stuart

I have received your *very* kind Letter (with the half of the 30£ note.) Meaning, what I do, by these words I need not expatiate on your liberality &c. Southey, I am certain, never thought otherwise than that you had behaved very handsomely with him; & will, I know, be more pleased with the 13 guineas, as an instance of generosity in the thing itself, than for the particular result to him. —I will assuredly make the attempt to write some good prose for you; but I must first give *the Poetics* a compleat *Jog*.[1] I shall certainly labor to make the poems in general suited to a daily morning Paper —every short poem, that has any merit at all, must be suitable in it's turn, whatever kind it may [be] of—but some kinds ought to recur more frequently than others—and these of course, temporary & political. What I have been doing, since I first wrote, has been this:—to get together a *fair stock in hand* of poems, serious & ludicrous, tales &c—& to send these off as things always to be had —& then, as the event, or occasion, or thought rises to send you from time to time something *of* the day & *for* the day.—Southey & I do well together in this Line; for I have always 50 subjects with all the ideas thereunto appertaining, but it is always a struggle with me to *execute*—and this Southey performs not only with rapidity, but takes great pleasure in doing it. Have you seen the Thalaba?—It is not altogether a poem exactly to my Taste; there are however three uncommonly fine passages in it. The first in Volume 1st beginning (p. 130) at the words 'It was the Wisdom & the Will of Heaven' continued to the end of the third Line, p. 134.— then omitting the intermediate pages, pass on to page 147. & recommence with the words *Their Father is their Priest*—to the last line of p. 166.—concluding with the words Of Thalaba went by.[2]— This would be a really good extract, & I am sure, none of the Reviews will have either feeling or Taste to select. You will see when you see the book, that the pages are almost entirely filled up with notes, so that the number of Lines is not great. Should it however be too great, you may begin it at p. 150, and entitle it THE LOVE OF ONEIZA FOR THALABA extracted &c.—

[1] Coleridge contributed five poems to the *Morning Post* in Sept. 1801.
[2] Cf. *Thalaba*, Book III, lines 229–370.

The next extract is in Volume the second, p. 126. beginning at the words All Waste! no sign of Life &c—to p. 131, ending with the words

She clapt her hands for Joy.[1]

The third passage is very short, & uncommonly lyrical—indeed, in versification & conception superior to any thing I have ever seen of Southey's—It must begin at the 3rd line of p. 142, Volume the second—and be entitled Khawla, or the enchantress's Incantation

'Go out, ye lights!' quoth Khawla &c

and go on to the last words of p. 143.[2]—There should be a little note saying, that Eblis is the Mahometan Name for the Evil Spirit.——

These three passages are excellently suited for a Paper, & would doubtless be of service to the Book.—Longman will, of course, gladly send you the Books.—

I feel myself much affected by the wish, you express, that I had applied to you in my pecuniary Distresses. Pinched we have been, no doubt; for Sickness increased my outgoings, while it cut off [a]ll the resources that depended on my own Industry. But the evil day is gone by & I have found that a little *wi[ll go]* a good way if there is an absolute necessity for it.—As to you, dear Stuart! I already consider myself independently of this our new engagement, as your Debtor; for I am not so blinded by Authorship, as to believe that what I have done is at all adequate to the money, I have received. But it is however something in a world like this to have a man really attached to your Interest for your sake as well as his own—& that man, believe me, Stuart! you have in me.

I have a favor to ask of you, which I am almost ashamed to ask too—it is this—Wordsworth & myself have one very dear Friend to whom the pleasure of seeing a paper during the time I wrote in it would be greater, than you can easily imagine. Would you send a paper for this next Quarter to her? Wordsworth will feel himself excited by his affections to do something—& whatever he does I shall conscientiously *add* & not substitute, as a sort of acknowlegement for this new Debt. The paper must be directed—

Miss S. Hutchinson, Bishops Middleham, Rushiford, Durham.

My children are both well, & their Mother. We expect Southey in a fortnight. Mrs Southey is with us.—I am so much better that I begin to hope, that I may be well enough to pass the winter near you—

Your's sincerely
S. T. Coleridge

[1] *Thalaba*, Book VIII, lines 287-390.   [2] Ibid., Book IX, lines 49 fol.

## 414. To William Godwin

*Address*: Mr Godwin | Polygon | Somers' Town | London
*MS*. Lord Abinger. *Pub. with omis.* William Godwin, *ii. 81.*
*Postmark*: 25 September 1801.

Greta Hall, Keswick, Cumberland   Tuesday, Sep. 22. 1801

Dear Godwin

When once a correspondence has intermitted from whatever cause, it scarcely ever recommences without some impulse ab extra. After my last Letter I went rambling after Health, or at least alleviation of Sickness—my Azores scheme I was obliged to give up, as well, I am afraid, as that of going abroad altogether, from want of money.—Latterly, I have had additional sources of Disquietude—so that altogether I have, I confess, felt little inclination to write to *you*, who have not known me long enough, nor associated enough of that esteem, which you entertain for the qualities, you attribute to me, with *me myself me*, to be much interested about the carcase, Coleridge.—So of Carcase Coleridge no more.——

At Middleham, near Durham, I accidentally met your Pamphlet, & read it—and only by accident was prevented from immediately writing to you. For I read it with unmingled delight & admiration, with the exception of that one hateful Paragraph, for the insertion of which I can account only on a superstitious hypothesis, that when all the Gods & Goddesses gave you each a good gift, Nemesis counterbalanced them all with the destiny, that in whatever you published, there should be some one outrageously *imprudent*, suicidal Passage. But you have heard enough of this. With the exception of this passage I never remember to have read a pamphlet with warmer feelings of sympathy & respect. Had I read it en masse when I wrote to you, I should certes have made none of the remarks, I once made, in the *first* Letter on the subject; but as certainly should have done so in my second. On the most deliberate reflection I *do* think the introduction clumsily worded—and (what is of more importance) I do think your retractations always imprudent, & not always just.—But it is painful to me to say this to you—I know not what effect it may have on your mind—for I have found, that I can not judge of other men by myself. I myself am *dead indifferent* as to *censures* of any kind—/ Praise even from Fools has sometimes given me a momentary pleasure, & what I could not but despise as *opinion* I have taken up with some satisfaction, as *sympathy*. But the censure or dislike of my dearest Friend, even of him, whom I think the wisest man, I know, does not give me the slightest pain

( 761 )

/ it is ten to one but I agree with him—& if I do, then I am glad. If I differ from him, the pleasure I receive in developing the SOURCES of our disagreement entirely swallows up all consideration of the disagreement itself. But then I confess, I have written nothing that I value myself *at all*—& that constitutes a prodigious difference between *us*—& still more this, that *no* man's opinion merely as opinion operates on me in any other way, than to make me review my own side of the Question. All this looks very much like self-panegyric—I cannot help it—it is the truth. And I find it to hold good of no other person, id est, to the extent of the *indifference*, which I feel—and therefore I am without any criterion, by which I can determine what I can say & how much without wounding or irritating.—I will never therefore willingly criticize any manuscript composition, unless the author and I are together / for then I know, that say what I will, he cannot be wounded—because my voice, my look, my whole manner, must convince any good man, that all I said was accompanied with sincere good-will & genuine kindness. Besides, I seldom fear to say any thing, when I can *develope* my reasons / but this is seldom possible in a Letter.

——It is not improbable, that is to say, not *very improbable*, that if I am absolutely unable to go abroad—(and I am now making the last effort by an application to Mr John Pinny respecting his House at St Nevis, & the means of living there) I may perhaps come up to London, & maintain myself, as before, by writing for the Morning Post.—If I come, I come *alone*.—Here it will be imprudent for me to stay, from the wet & the cold—even if every thing within doors were as well suited to my head & heart, as my head & heart would, I trust, be to every thing that was wise & amiable.[1]—My darling

---

[1] While Coleridge and his wife were an ill-assorted pair, the failure of their marriage is not evident until the winter of 1800–1 (see *Early Letters*, 273). Reluctant to go north, Mrs. Coleridge, who did not share in the intimacy with the Wordsworths, was sorely tried after her removal to Keswick by her husband's months of ill health and the resultant inability to provide for his family. It seems probable, too, that she was aware of his growing attachment to Sara Hutchinson, an attachment which ripened into love during Sara's protracted stay with the Wordsworths in the winter of 1800–1; and certainly, his month-long visit with the Hutchinsons in the summer of 1801 precipitated a crisis. Earlier Coleridge had been able to view the incompatibility between himself and Mrs. Coleridge with equanimity; indeed, he wrote to Southey on 12 Feb. 1800: 'My wife is a woman of absolutely pure mind and considerable intellect . . ., but her every-day self and her minor interests, alas, do not at all harmonize with my occupations, my temperament, or my weaknesses —we cannot be happy in all respects. In my early married life I was often almost miserable—now (as everything mellows) I am content, indeed, thankful!' Association with Sara Hutchinson, however, brought to Coleridge the heart-withering Conviction' that he could not but be miserable with his wife, an attitude bound to make married life intolerable alike for him and for her;

22 September 1801                    [414

Hartley has this evening had an attack of fever—but my medical friend thinks, it will pass off.—I think of your children not infrequently. God love them. Wordsworth is not at home. He has been in the Scotch [Lakes] with Montague & his new Father, S[ir] William Rush.—Your's, S. T. Coleridge.

### 415. To Daniel Stuart

*Address*: D. Stuart Esq. | No/ 335 | Strand | London
*MS. British Museum. Pub. with omis.* Letters from the Lake Poets, 23.
*Postmark*: 30 September 1801. *Stamped*: Keswick.

My dear Stuart                  [*Circa* 27 September 1801]

I have been afraid that my widow would have had to settle my 16 guineas with you—I have had a frightful seizure of the Cholera morbus, or bilious Colic—but the danger is past—& I am assured, that I shall be much improved in my general Health by the violent discharges. I write that you may not wonder at my silence—perhaps, you may not hear from me for 5 or 6 days, as I really find it more than merely expedient to lie in perfect calmness after so violent an agitation of the body & the spirits. It can be, I suppose, of no great importance when I begin with you / I think more & more seriously of coming to London.—I am in bed. I [cannot write] any further; but believe m[e,]
with great sincerity, | Your's
S. T. Coleridge

Of course, I received on Thursday the other half of the note.—

### 416. To Thomas Poole

*Address*: Mr T. Poole | Nether Stowey | Bridgewater | Somerset    Through London.
*MS. British Museum. Pub. with omis.* Thomas Poole, ii. 66.
*Postmark*: 8 October 1801. *Stamped*: Keswick.

Greta Hall, Keswick. Octob. 5. 1801
My dear Poole

I have this evening received your Letter. That I felt many & deep emotions of tenderness & sympathy, you will know without my telling you—and in truth minds, like mine & (in it's present mood) your's too, require to be *braced* rather than *suppled*. Your plan for your own life appears to me wise & judicious: and I cannot

and immediately after his return from the Hutchinsons he began to fill his letters with complaints about his domestic unhappiness and to talk of separation.

( 763 )

too earnestly impress upon you the solemn Duty, you owe to yourself, your fellow-men, & your maker, to exert your faculties, to give evidence of that which God has delivered to your keeping, first to your own mind, & next to that of your countrymen. Great Talents you undoubtedly possess—indeed, when I consider the vast disadvantages which you have laboured under as an *intellectual* Being, from the circumstances of having been born to a patrimony & of having had almost from your Birth hourly Doings with *money* —all dear Relationships, all hourly intercourses, in some measure modified, or interrupted, by influences of *money*— & compare with these disadvantages your opinions, powers, & habits of feeling, I feel an *indefiniteness* in my conception of your Talents—a faith, that they are greater than even to your own mind they have hitherto appeared to be. To some great work I exhort you to devote yourself, as soon as ever the Hurry of Grief & Mutation is over, as soon as the Darkness of Sorrow has thinned away into Gloom—to some great work, which shall combine a predominance of self-collected *fact & argument* with the necessity of wide & extensive Reading.—Poole! I have seen only two defects in your making up, that are of any importance—(let me premise before I write the next sentence that by family attachment I do not mean *domestic* attachment, but merely *family—cousinships*; not Brother, not Sister, not Son—for these are *real* relations; but family, as far as it [is] mere accident.) The two defects which I have seen in you, are, 1. Excess of *family* & of *local* attachment, which has fettered your moral free-agency, & bedimmed your intellectual vision. It has made you half a coward at times when (*I dream at least* that) *I* should [have] been more than brave.—2. A too great desire & impatience to produce *immediate* good—to *see* with your own eyes the plant, of which you have sown the seed. Mustard Cress may be raised this way; & we will raise Mustard Cress; but acorns, acorns—to plant these is the work, the calling, the labor of our moral Being.

This in this awful tone I have been powerfully impelled to say: tho' in general I *detest* any thing like the giving of Advice.—I was with an acquaintance lately, & we passed by a poor Ideot boy, who exactly answered my description—he

> Stood in the sun, rocking his sugar-loaf Head,
> And staring at a bough from Morn to Sunset
> *See-saw'd* his voice in inarticulate Noises.[1]

[1] For these lines in a somewhat different form see *Remorse*, Act II, Scene i, lines 189–91. Since the passage of which they are a part does not belong to *Osorio*, Coleridge must have been reworking that play as early as 1801. See Letter 405, in which he tells Southey of his intention to alter his tragedy 'with a devilish sweep of revolution', and to publish it 'as a Poem'.

I wonder, says my Companion, what that Ideot means to say.—
'To give advice,' I replied: 'I know not what else an Ideot can do,
& any Ideot can do that.' It is more accordant with my general
Habits of Thinking to resign every man to himself, & the quiet
influences of the great Being—& in that spirit, & with a *deep, a very
deep*, affection, I *now* say—God bless you, Poole!——

As to the plan, you propose for me, I see no *reasons* attached to
any part of it—& no *motives*, as well as no reasons, to the former
part of it, namely, that of my taking lodgings near London.—But
you do not know, you have never formed any conception, of the
real state of my health.—It is probable, that my plan will be this—
this Autumn & the winter I shall probably pass in Somersetshire &
Dorset with [the] Wedgewoods, Pinny, & you—& possibly, a week
or two at Ottery—& in the Spring, if I live so long which is more
than I myself expect, I shall go to St Nevis to Pinny's House—
where Pinny will by that time have prepared for me a comfortable
Home without expence—& there I shall pass a year. Farther on
than this I see no wisdom in attempting to look. Mrs Coleridge &
the children will, in all probability, stay where they are—in a more
delightful place or a more kind & respectful neighbourhood she
cannot be—& she is attached to the place & the people who live
next door to us.

I am sorry, that my letter affected you *so* painfully & I need
not say, what a pang I felt at the accident of the time, in which it
must have reached you. The letter itself I cannot, after the most
dispassionate Review, consider as objectionable. Why should you
feel pain at my affirming, that it is impossible for you & me to feel
alike in money concerns? From my childhood I have associated
nothing but *pain* with money—I have had no wish, no dream, no
one pleasure connected with wealth. The only pleasure which the
possession of a few pounds has ever given me has been simply this
—'Well—for a week or two I shall have no occasion to interrupt
my thoughts & feelings by any accursed Thoughts about money.'
—To[o] I have formed long & meditative habits of *aversion* to the
Rich, Lov[e for] the Poor or the *un*wealthy, & belief in the
excessive evils arising from Property. How is it *possible*, Poole! that
you *can* have all these feelings? You would not wish to have them.
—I still think that you erred in writing to Mr Wedgewood—and
still think of the idea of an application from me to my nominal
Brotherhood, as I then thought.—I WAS vexed that Wordsworth
should have applied to you—for I know enough of the human
heart to have felt, without any positive fact, that there is a great
difference between our fore-seeing that such or such an answer
*would be* the Result of such or such an application, & our knowing

that such & such an answer *has been* the Result. That *I* should not have refused the 50£, tho' it had been my only 50£, beyond the expences of the ensuing month, is saying nothing; because I should not have refused it on a less important necessity to many a man, for whom I have but a very *diluted* love & esteem, and to whom I should refuse many a sacrifice of much greater difficulty, which you would wittingly make for me. But different as our feelings are respecting money, I am assured that you would not have refused thrice the sum, if necessary, had you believed the state of my Health to be that which I know it to be. No—Poole! I love you, & know that you love me.—Even at this moment it almost irritates me, that Wordsworth should have applied to you—the money might have been raised from so many Quarters—indeed, I was prevented from going to the Azores not by this, but by intelligence received of the exceeding dampness of the Climate.—Southey has been with me for some time, but quits me on Wednesday morning for Ireland—he is appointed private secretary to Corry, the Irish Chancellor—half the year he spends in Dublin, & half in London. His salary is 200£ a year, & 200£ for travelling expences—this is nothing—but his society will be all the first & greatest people—and of course the *opening* is great.—Men of Talents are at present in great request by the Ministry—had I a spark of ambition, I have opportunities enough—but I will be either far greater than all this can end in, even if it should end in my being Minister of state myself, or I will be nothing.—Mrs Coleridge & both children are well—

God love you, my dear Poole! and restore you to that degree of cheerfulness which is necessary for virtue & energetic well-doing. May he vouchsafe the same blessing to your
      affectionate friend, S. T. [Coleri]dge.


### 417. To Robert Southey

MS. Lord Latymer. Pub. with omis. E. L. G. i. 182.

    Oct. 21. 1801.—The day after my Birth day—29 years of age!—Who on earth can say that without a sigh!

[De]ar Southey

You did not stay long enough with us to *love* these mountains & this wonderful vale. Yesterday the snow fell—and to day—O that you were here—Lodore full—[the] mountains snow-crested—& the dazzling silver of the Lake—this cloudy, sunny, misty, howling Weather!——After your arrival I move southward in the hopes that warm Rooms & deep tranquillity may build me up anew; & that I may be able to return in the Spring without the necessity of going abroad. I propose to go with you & Edith to London—& thence to Stowey or Wedgewood's, as circumstances direct.—My knee is no longer swoln, & this frosty weather agrees with me—but O Friend! I am sadly shattered. The least agitation brings on bowel complaints, & within the last week *twice* with an ugly symptom—namely—of sickness even to vomiting—& Sara—alas! we are not suited to each other. But the months of my absence I devote to *self*-discipline, & to the attempt to draw her nearer to me by a regular developement of all the sources of our unhappiness— then for another Trial, *fair* as I hold the love of good men dear to me—*patient*, as I myself love my own dear children. I will go believing that it will end happily—if not, if our mutual unsuitableness continues, and (as it assuredly will do, if it continue) increases & strengthens, why then, it is better for her & my children, that I should live apart, than that she should be a Widow & they Orphans. Carefully have I *thought thro'* the subject of marriage & deeply am I convinced of it's indissolubleness.—If I separate, I do it in the earnest desire to provide for her & [the]m; that while I live, she may enjoy the comforts of life; & that when I die, something may have been accumulated that may secure her from degrading Dependence. When I least love her, then m[ost] do I feel anxiety for her peace, comfort, & welfare. Is s[he] not the mother of my children? And am I the man not to know & feel this?—Enough of this. But, Southey! much as we differ in our habits, you do indeed possess my esteem & affection in a degree that makes it uncomfortable to me not to tell you what I have told you. I once said—that I *missed* no body—I only enjoyed the *present*. At that moment my heart misgave me, & had no one been present, I should have said to you —that you were the only exception— / for my mind is full of visions, & you had been so long connected with the fairest of all fair dreams, that I feel your absence more than I enjoy your society: tho' that I do not enjoy your society so much, as I anticipated that I should do, is wholly or almost wholly owing to the nature of my domestic feelings, & the fear, or the consciousness, that you did not & could not sympathize with him [them].—Now my heart is a little easy.—God bless you!——

Dear Davy!—If I have not overrated his intellectual Powers, I have little fear for his moral character. Metaphysicians! Do, Southey, keep to your own most excellent word (for the invention of which you deserve a pension far more than Johnson for his Dictionary) &

always say— *Metapothecaries*. There does not exist an instance of a *deep* metaphysician who was not led by his speculations to an austere system of morals—. What can be more austere than the Ethics of Aristotle—than the systems of Zeno, St Paul, Spinoza (in the Ethical Books of his Ethics), Hartley, Kant, and Fichte? —As to Hume, was he not—ubi non fur, ibi stultus—& often thief & blockhead at the same time? It is not *thinking* that will disturb a man's morals, or confound the distinctions, which *to think* makes. But it is *talking—talking—talking—that* is the curse & the poison. I defy Davy to *think* half of what he *talks*: if indeed he talk what has been attributed to him. But I must see with my own eyes, & hear with my own ears. Till then I will be to Davy, what Max was to Wallenstein. Yet I do agree with you that chemistry tends in it's present state to turn it's Priests into Sacrifices. One way, in which it does it—this however is an opinion, that would make Rickman laugh[1] at me if you told it him—is this—it prevents or tends to prevent a young man from falling in love. We all have obscure feelings that must be connected with some thing or other—the Miser with a guinea— Lord Nelson with a blue Ribbon—Wordsworth's old Molly with her washing Tub—Wordsworth with the Hills, Lakes, & Trees— / all men are poets in their way, tho' for the most part their ways are *damned bad ones*. Now Chemistry makes a young man associate these feelings with inanimate objects—& that without any moral revulsion, but on the contrary with complete self-approbation— and his distant views of Benevolence, or his sense of immediate beneficence, attach themselves either to Man as the whole human Race, or to Man, as a sick man, as a painter, as a manufacturer, &c—and in no way to man, as a Husband, Son, Brother, Daughter, Wife, Friend, &c &c—. That to be in love is simply to confine the feelings prospective of animal enjoyment to one woman is a gross mistake—it is to associate a large proportion of all our obscure feelings with a real form—A miser is *in love* with a guinea, & a virtuous young man with a woman, in the same sense, without figure or metaphor. A young poet may do without being in love with a woman—it is enough, if he loves—but to a young chemist it would be salvation to be downright romantically in Love—and unfortunately so far from the Poison & antidote growing together, they are like the Wheat & Barberry.—

You are not the first person who has sought in vain for Mole &

---

[1] John Rickman (1771–1840), statistician, was at this time secretary to Charles Abbot, Chief Secretary for Ireland. In 1802, when Abbot became Speaker in the House of Commons, Rickman remained his secretary. In 1814 he was appointed Second Clerk Assistant at the Table of the House of Commons.

# 21 October 1801

Mulla.[1]—I shall end this Letter with a prayer for your speedy arrival, & a couple of Sapphic Verses translated *in my way* from Stolberg—You may take your Oath for it, it was no admiration of the Thought, or the Poetry that made me translate them—

> To the Will o/ the Wisps[2]—
>
> But now I think of it—no—I will pursue my first thought——
>
> Lunatic Witch-fires! Ghosts of Light & Motion!
> Fearless I see you weave your wanton Dances
> Near me, far off me, You that tempt the Trav'ller
>                            Onward & onward,
>
> Wooing, retreating, till the Swamp beneath him
> Groans!—And 'tis dark!—This Woman's Wile—I know it!
> Learnt it from *thee*, from *thy* perfidious Glances,
>                            Black-ey'd Rebecca!—

It is more poetical than the original, of which this is a literal Translation—Still play, juggling Deceiver! still play thy wanton Dances, Fugitive child of Vapor, that fervently temptest onward the Wanderer's feet, then coyly fleest, at length beguilest into Ruin. These maiden Wiles—I know them—learnt them all out of thy blue eyes, fickle Nais.

                       Heaven bless you—.—S. T. Coleridge

## 418. To Thomas Poole

*Address*: Mr T. Poole | Nether Stowey | Bridgewater | Somerset    Through London.
*MS. British Museum. Pub. E. L. G. i. 186.*
*Postmark*: 24 October 1801. *Stamped*: Keswick.

                                          Oct. 21. 1801

My dear Poole

Was my society then *use*less to you during my Abode at Stowey? Yet I do not remember, that I ever once offered you *advice*! If indeed under this word you chuse to comprehend all that free communication of thought & feeling, which distinguished our inter-

---

[1] Cf. Spenser, *Colin Clouts Come Home Againe*, lines 56–59:
> One day (quoth he), I sat, (as was my trade)
> Under the foote of Mole, that mountaine hore,
> Keeping my sheepe amongst the cooly shade
> Of the greene alders by the Mullaes shore.

[2] *Poems*, ii. 979.

course, I have nothing to do but to subscribe to your *Meaning*, referring you to the Dictionary for the better wording thereof. By the 'quiet influences of the great Being' I wished to convey all that all things do from natural impulse, rather than direct and prospective Volition: not that I meant to interdict the latter—on the contrary, in that very letter I felt it my duty to give you *plump advice*—nay, I admit that man is an *advising* animal; even as he is a concupiscent one—Now as Religion has directed it's main attacks against concupiscence, because we are too much inclined to it, so does Prudence against *advice*-giving, & for the same reason. In short, I meant no more than that it is well to have a general *suspicion* of ourselves in the moment of an inclination to advise— this suspicion, not as a ham-stringer to cripple, but as a curb-rein to check. As to myself, advice from almost any body gives me pleasure, because it informs me of the mind & heart of the adviser —but from a very very dear Friend it has occasionally given me great pain—but, so help me Heaven, as I *believe* at least that I speak truly—on his account alone—or, *if* on my own, on my own only as a disruption of that sympathy, in which Friendship has it's Being. A thousand people might have advised all that you did, and I might have been pleased; but it [was] the *you you* part of the Business that afflicted me—tho' by what figure of speech any part of my Letter could be called outrageous, I can discover by the science of metaphysics, rather than by any hitherto published Art of Rhetoric.—And here ends, I trust, the Controversial—from which I have seldom seen much good come even in conversation— & never any thing but evil when Letters have been the Vehicle.—

I will come to you as soon as I can get the money necessary. There are a few bills here, which must be payed before I can leave Mrs Coleridge with comfort, to the amount of 10£ perhaps; I must leave her 5£; & my own Journey will cost me 10£. Any *part* of this money, that you can spare for the space of *four months*, I shall be glad to receive from you—& the rest, I will borrow from Pinny— as soon as I know of his arrival at Somerton. I have very particular Reasons for not anticipating any part of my next year's annuity by any draft on the Mr Wedgewoods.—

Mackintosh, (who is a large tall man) spent two days with me at Keswick, & was very entertaining & pleasant. He is every inch the Being, I had conceived him to be, from what I saw of him at Cote House. We talked of all & every thing—on some very affecting subjects, in which he represented himself by words as affected; on some subjects that called forth his verbal indignation—or exultation: but in no one moment did any particle of his face from the top of his forehead to the half of his neck, *move*. His face has no *lines* like that of a man—no softness, like that of a woman—it is smooth, *hard*, motionless—*a flesh-mask*!—As to his conversation, it was all uncommonly *well-worded:* but not a thought in it worthy of having been worded at all——He was however entertaining to me always; & to all around him then chiefly, when he talked of Parr, Fox, Addington,[1] &c &c. When I asked him concerning Davy—he answered *Oh!*—*little* Davy—Dr Beddoes' Eleve, you mean?—This was an exquisite trait of character.

The Irish Chancellor's Name is *Corry*, not Curry.

We, i.e. Wordsworth & myself, regard the Peace as necessary; but the Terms as most alarming.

My children are well—& I am better. My knee is quite gone down—& the frosty air has greatly improved my general health. But a fit of Rain, or a fit of Grief, undoes in three hours what 3 weeks had been doing. I am a crazy crazy machine!—God bless you

& S. T. Coleridge

What did you mean by my being 'the sport of the capricious advice of the most capricious'? It was quite an enigma to me.—

N.B. I never received a *double* letter from Mr Wedgewood that was not charged *single*, nor a *single* Letter from you that was not charged *double*.

Yesterday was my Birth day—29 years of age! O that I could write it without a sigh—or rather without occasion for one!—

### 419. To Thomas Poole

*Address*: Mr T. Poole | N. Stowey | Bridgewater | Somerset     *Single sheet*
MS. *British Museum. Hitherto unpublished.*
*Postmark*: 3 November 1801.     *Stamped*: Keswick.

Saturday Night, Nov. [October] 31. 1801

My dear Poole

I received both letters, inclosing the 25£ compleat—(N.B. Each letter charged only *single* —whereas all your *single* letters have been charged *double*)—If *I can*, I leave this place on Saturday next, go straight forward to London, in which place I shall settle all my literary concerns with advice for my future health, &c—My stay [t]here will certainly not exceed ten days—and from thence I proceed in the Bridgewater Mail for Bridgewater & you.—I purpose

---

[1] Henry Addington (1757–1844), later first Viscount Sidmouth, was at this time First Lord of the Treasury and Chancellor of the Exchequer. Under his government England made peace with France in 1802.

staying with you, & Mr Wedgewood, & Mr Pinny, & [at] Ottery till the last days of March / less than *two* months I shall assuredly not stay with *you*. Now for the words—*if I can*—. My health & personal appearance is much improved; but on Wednesday in stepping over a fence I had a Thorn run into my leg, some inch & a half from the Ancle close by the tendo Achilles—I have reason to fear that it has broke in—an incision has been made to no purpose—but the wound keeps open, & a suppuration is forming—& when formed, it may bring forth the *lurker*. I have suffered great agony—I am more than lame—for I cannot without torture move my leg from a super-horizontal position. Whether I exaggerate illness or no, remains to be proved; but this I will venture to say for myself, that there is scarcely a *Woman* in the Island that can endure Pain more quietly than I—tho' the Present is scarcely an Instance—for I have had such valuable Lights thrown upon me, with regard to the exceedingly interesting & obscure subject of *Pain*, in consequence of this accident, that I am quite in spirits about it. O! how I *watched* myself while the Lancet was at my Leg! —*Vivat Metaphysic*! And now, my dearest Poole! for a word or two respecting *your very interesting piece of News*. You will not suspect me, I know, of being warped by my dislike of old Symes, & my abhorrence of his moral dispositions—: I do not fear that you will suspect me of this—all I fear is, lest you should suspect that long, & solitary Broodings over the *elements* of Thought have diseased my notions of those *moral Relations* which result from the *great aggregates of Life*, the Father, the Husband, the Clergyman, the Brother, the Citizen.—Do not, I intreat you, think this of me. My opinions in Ethics are, if any thing, more austere than they ever were—but really, ignorant as I am of all the minor facts, & judging only from the facts which you have adduced, I can not see that Bradley has committed any error at all—or has done any thing which I would not have done in his place. A lewd Boy & a wanton Girl mutually seduce each other; but the Boy is willing to repair the evil, & to marry the Girl. If he do not, the Girl is hunted by Infamy, & perhaps hunted by it into the Toils of Guilt & habitual Depravity. This Girl is Bradley's Sister-in-law.—Old Symes who at first was 'a madman in fury,' & whose fury has now '*settled into a deep malignant rage*'—old Symes—i.e. a Man-shaped animal capable of 'a deep malignant Rage' & known to be so by every one that knew any thing of him—he surely was not a man to apply to, unless Bradley wished to do so as a substitute for necromancy to save himself the trouble of calling up a Devil from Hell to trumpet & blast abroad the infamy of his Sister—I should say, to make it infamy by his trumpetings.—You must know that Symes never

*31 October 1801*

would have consented to the marriage—& Bradley knew it—& if, Poole! you do not know that the young man did his duty in marrying the young woman, all I can say is that my moral system is more austere than your's—and I am sure that in this case your system is founded on Prudence of Men, & not on the Gospel of Christ.—Bradley saw that whatever Hubbub might at first be created, all would die away—Husband & Wife are Husband & Wife—and *warmth* of constitution is often connected with many excellent moral dispositions—the affair may have prevented her from being a Whore—& no doubt has prevented him from being, as the Stowey youths of his acquaintance all were, Whoremongers deep-died![1] ...As to the clandestineness, &c &c—they were only steps of prudence—if it were right to do the thing, it certainly could not be wrong to do it in the only way in which it could be done without uproar & desecration. I see no moral wrong in the clandestineness whatever—if I saw Bradley, & you had not convinced us [by] the adduction of new facts that I am in the wrong, I should give him my right hand, & say, *You* have acted, Sir! as a man, & a Christian —.—I will write again on the [day] I leave this place.
Most affect.—S.T.C.—

P.S. You will see, I take it for granted that the Girl is with child.—

### 420. To Humphry Davy

*Address*: Mr Davy | Royal Institution | Albermarle Street | London
MS. *Royal Institution*. Pub. Frag. Remains, *91*.
*Postmark*: 3 November 1801. *Stamped*: Keswick.

Greta Hall Keswick Cumberland. Oct. 31 1801.
My dear Davy

I do not know by what fatality it has happened; but so it is that I have thought more often of you, & I may say, *yearned* after your society more for the last 3 months than I ever before did—& yet I have not written to you. But you know that I honor you, & that I love whom I honor. Love & Esteem with me have no dividual Being; & where ever this is not the case, I suspect, there must be some lurking moral superstition which Nature gets the better of —& that the real meaning of the phrase—'I love him tho' I can not esteem him'—is— I esteem him but not according to my system of esteem—but *you*, my dear Fellow! *all* men love and esteem—which is the only *suspicious* part of your character—at least, according to the 5th Chapter of St Matthew.—God bless you—
And now for the Business of this Letter. *If I can*, I leave this

[1] Three or four words inked out in manuscript.

place so as to be in London on Wednesday the eleventh of next month—in London I shall stay a fortnight—but as I am in feeble health, & have a perfect phobia of Inns & Coffee-houses, I should rejoice if you or Southey should be able to offer me a bedroom for the fortnight aforesaid.— From London I move Southward.— Now for the Italicized words *if I can*—the cryptical & implicit import of which is—I have a damned Thorn in my leg, which the Surgeon has not been yet able to extract—& but that I have metaph[ys]icized most successfully on *Pain* in consequence of the accident, by the great Scatterer of Thoughts, I should have been half-mad.—But as it is I have borne it *like a Woman*—which I believe to be two or three degrees at least beyond *a Stoic*.—A suppuration is going on—and I endure in hope.—I have re-direct-[ed] one of Southey's Letters to you, taking it for granted that you will see him immediately on his arrival in Town—he left us yesterday afternoon.—Let me hear from you if it be only to say what I know already that you will be glad to see me.—O dear friend, thou one of the two human Beings of whom I dare hope with a hope, that elevates my own heart—O bless you!—

S. T. Coleridge

### 421. To Robert Southey

*Address*: R. Southey Esq.
*MS. Lord Latymer. Pub. E. L. G. i. 188.*

Novemb. 9 1801 Monday Night

Dear Southey

The thorn Mr Edmondson believes to be still in my leg—the wound does not heal,—or in the damn'd Scotch-English of the present day—*heals not*. But I leave this place to morrow morning for Eusemere, Mr Clarkson's Residence, whither Mrs Coleridge & my beloved children are already gone.—Whether I leave Eusemere Wednesday or Friday, I can not say—Friday is the latest day——I wish you immediately to write a penny post letter to Stuart (No / 335, Strand, London) informing [him] of this, & that I have received his letter, & that he will be the *second* person, I shall call on / *maning* you for the first.—Love to Edith.—Hartley was breeched last Sunday—& looks far better than in his petticoats. He ran to & fro in a sort of dance to the Jingle of the Load of Money, that had been put in his breeches pockets; but he did [not] roll & tumble over and over in his old joyous way—No! it was an *eager* & solemn gladness, as if he felt it to be an awful aera in his Life.— O bless him! bless him! bless him! If my wife loved me, and I my

9 November 1801

wife, half as well as we both love our children, I should be the happiest man alive—but this is not—will not be!—

Your's affectionately
S. T. Coleridge.

## 422. To William Godwin

*Address*: Mr Godwin | Polygon | Somers' Town
*MS*. Lord Abinger. *Pub. with omis.* William Godwin, *ii. 83.*
*Postmark*: 19 November 1801.

25, Bridge Street, Westminster[1]
Thursday Morning. [19 November 1801]

Dear Godwin

I arrived here late on Sunday Evening—& how long I shall stay, depends much upon my health. If I were to judge from my feelings of yesterday & to day, it will be a very short time indeed—for I am miserably uncomfortable. By your Letter to Southey I understand that you are particularly anxious to see me. To day I am engaged for 2 hours in the morning with a person in the city—after which I shall be at Lambe's—till past 7 at least——I had assuredly planned a walk to Somers' town; but I saw so many People on Monday and walked to & fro so much, that I have been ever since like a Fish in air, who, as you perhaps know, lies panting & dying from excess of Oxygen/ —A great change from the society of W. & his sister—for tho' we were three persons, it was but one God— —whereas here I have the amazed feelings of a new Polytheist, meeting Lords many, & Gods many—some of them very Egyptian Physiognomies, dog-faced Gentry, Crocodiles, Ibises, &c—tho' more odd fish, than rarae aves.—However as to the business of seeing you—it is possible that you may meet me this evening—if not, & if I am well enough, I will call on you—& if you breakfast at 10—breakfast with you to morrow morning/ it will be hard indeed if I cannot afford a half-a-crown Coach-fare to annihilate the sense at least of the Space.—I write like a Valetudinarian; but I assure you, that this morning I feel it still more—

Your's | &c | S. T. Coleridge
P.S. Southey's best Comp's—

[1] Southey's lodgings in London.

### 423. To Mrs. S. T. Coleridge

[Addressed and franked] London November twenty . . . | Mrs. Coleridge | Kesw[ick]    W. Williams Wynn
MS. Victoria University Lib. Hitherto unpublished.
Postmark: — November 18⟨01⟩.

[Circa 25 November 1801]

My dear Sara

I remain well—to day I remove to my Lodging, No/ 10, King Street, Covent Garden, London[1]—but how long I shall stay there, I know not—probably not more than 10 days: for the Letter, which you inclosed for me, was from T. Wedgewood, who asks me if it would be agreeable to me to pass 3 months with him in Cornwall—This of course I answered in the affirmative: it is of the first importance to me to make the connection with the Wedgewoods one of Love & *personal* attachment, as well as of moral calculation & intellectual Hope—which are subject to sad Caprices in this mortal Life.—O my dear Hartley—my Derwent! my [children]!—The night before last I dreamt [I saw] them so vividly, that I was quite ill in the morning—& wept my eyes red—which was good for me.—. . .[Remainder of manuscript missing.]

### 424. To Thomas Poole

Address: Mr T. Poole | Nether Stowey | Bridgewater | Somerset
MS. British Museum. Pub. E. L. G. i. 189.
Postmark: 14 ⟨December⟩ 18⟨01⟩.

Monday, Dec. 14. 1801

My dear Poole

That I *ought* to have written to you a month ago, I feel about as strongly as it is possible you can feel. But London has upset me—it is all buz buz buz with my poor Head—& like a creature robbed of his free agency I do what I *must* not what I *would*—I am writing for the Morning Post—& reading in the old Libraries[2] for my curious metaphysicial Work—; but I hate London & my intention is in a week's time to go to Gunville, & from thence in a few days to proceed to you with Tom Wedgewood—who spoke of you to me with an enthusiasm of Friendship that surprized me & brought such a gush of Tears into my eyes that I had well nigh made a fool

---

[1] 'I took a first floor for him in King Street, Covent Garden, at my tailor's, Howell's, whose wife was a cheerful good housewife, of middle age, who I knew would nurse Coleridge as kindly as if he were her son.' Daniel Stuart, *Gentleman's Magazine*, May 1838, p. 487.

[2] Among other books Coleridge was reading the *Parmenides* and the *Timaeus* of Plato. See Letter 459.

of myself in the Street.—I am better than I could expect—& would so much rather talk with you than write to you, that I am right glad that what I could write I shall soon be able to talk.—It would be no unpleasant subject for a day-dream—Davy, you, & I going into France together.—God bless you! My best remembrances to Ward.

S. T. Coleridge

### 425. To Thomas Poole

*Address*: Mr T. Poole | Nether Stowey | Bridgwater | Somerset
*MS. British Museum. Hitherto unpublished.*
*Postmark*: 24 December, 1801.

Thursday Evening [24 December 1801.]
My dear Poole

If it please God, I shall leave Town to morrow night in the Bridgewater Mail—& of course, shall be at Bridgewater, barring accidents, on Saturday. From thence I shall get to Stowey according as the Weather dictates.—I have had a fearful Bout of it this time —the Bell (for my Bedroom looks out into the great Church-yard) has tolled often & dolefully for those that died of the same Complaint—but my Hour was not come—nay, I seem to be on the whole of a lightened spirit since I have left my bed. I hope, T. W. is with you—. God bless you both—

&
S. T. C.

### 426. To Daniel Stuart

*Address*: D. Stuart Esq. | No/ 335 | Strand
*MS. British Museum. Pub.* Letters from the Lake Poets, 7.

Friday Night—[25 December 1801]
My dear Stuart

A Letter which I received this afternoon makes it proper for me to be off to Stowey as soon as I can—You will hear from me by Tuesday's Post, at the farthest—& this you may rely on—& I feel the inmost conviction that I shall do more for you the ten days of my absence than if I had been in London—I have borrowed 5 guineas of Mr Howel, which you will be so good as to pay him—and if you want money, I have written on the other side a draft for 25£, which you will use if you have any need—I am much your debtor at present; but please God! deliver me of this complaint. I will soon work it out.

Your's sincerely
S. T. Coleridge

( 777 )

## 427. To Robert Southey

*Address*: Mr Southey
MS. Lord Latymer. Pub. Letters, i. 365.

Dec. 31. 1801.—Nether Stowey, Bridgewater.

Dear Southey

On Xmas day I breakfasted with Davy, with the intention of dining with you; but I returned very unwell, & in very truth in so utter a dejection of spirits, as both made it improper for me to go any whither, & a most unfit man to be with you.—I left London on Saturday Morning 4 o/ clock—& for 3 hours was in such a storm, as I was never before out in: for I was a top of the Coach—Rain & Hail & violent wind with vivid flashes of Lightning, that seemed almost to alternate with the flash-like Re-emersions of the Waning Moon, from the ever shattered ever closing Clouds. However, I was armed cap-a-pie, in a compleat Panoply, namely, in a huge, most huge, Roquelaire, which had cost the Government 7 Guineas—& was provided for the Emigrants in the Quiberon Expedition, one of whom falling sick stayed behind & parted with his Cloak to Mr Howel who lent it me—. I dipped my head down, shoved it up, & it proved a compleat Tent to me. I was as dry as if I had been sitting by the fire—. I arrived at Bath at 11 o clock at Night—& spent the next day with Warren who has gotten a very sweet Woman to Wife, and a most beautiful House & situation at Whitcomb, on the Hill over the Bridge.—On Monday afternoon I arrived at Stowey—. I am a good deal better; but my Bowels are by no means derevolutionized.—So much for me.—

I do not know what I am to say to you of your dear Mother [1]/ Life passes away from us in all modes & ways—in our friends, in ourselves. We all 'die daily'.—Heaven knows that many & many & many a time I have regarded my Talents & Acquirements as a Porter's Burthen, imposing on me the Duty of going on to the end of the Journey, when I would gladly lie down by the side of the road, & become the Country for a mighty nation of Maggots—for what is Life, gangrened, as it is with me, in it's very vitals— domestic Tranquillity?——These things being so, I confess that I feel for *you* but not for the *event*; or for the *event* only by an act of Thought, & not by any immediate *shock* from the like Feeling within myself.——

When I return to Town, I can scarcely tell—I have not yet made up my mind whether or no I shall move Devonward. My Relations wish to see me, & I wish to avoid the uneasy feelings I shall have,

---

[1] Southey's mother died on 5 Jan. 1802.

*31 December 1801*

if I remain so near them without gratifying the wish / no very brotherly mood of mind, I must confess—but it is, $\frac{9}{10}$ths of it at least, a work of their own Doing.—

Poole desires to be remembered to you—Remember me to your wife, & to Mrs Lovell.

God bless you | &
S. T. Coleridge

### 428. To Mrs. S. T. Coleridge

*MS. Lord Latymer. Hitherto unpublished.*

Sunday Night. [17 January 1802][1]

[My] dear Sara

I must put you to the expence [of an]other Letter, to say, that I shall not go to [Otter]y; but shall return to London, on Tuesday —[prob]ably, with T. Poole.—I am ashamed to [sen]d such a Letter to you; but I am too much in a flurry to write more.—Davy begins his Lectures, much earlier than I expected—& I am determined to attend the whole course.—You will therefore write to me, directing as before—

No/ 10, King Street, Covent Garden, London.

If all things happen, as I from the very depth of my soul wish them to do, I expect to be with you by the middle of March—. I am at present improved in Health, spite of the intense Frost which at last has broken up/ I hope to God, you will make you[rself] flannel Drawers, &c, as I advised—[and] instantly, get the fluid Essence [of] Mustard—& that you have already [begun] to take the Mustard Pills, night & morning. Do it regularly & perseveran[tly,] or it will not signify a farthing.—

I will take care of the Letters, &c—My Love &c to Mr Jackson, & Mrs Wilson—

And O my dear Children!
S. T. Coleridge

### 429. To Sara Hutchinson

*Address:* Miss S. Hutchins[on] | Gallo[w Hill]   Single sheet.
*MS. Dove Cottage. Hitherto unpublished.* This fragment, consisting of the middle of one page, with part of the address on the opposite side, is the first letter from Coleridge to Sara Hutchinson to survive. There was evidently a large correspondence between them, later destroyed, and an entry in Coleridge's

---

[1] Since Coleridge arrived in London on Thursday, 21 Jan. 1802, this letter was probably written the previous Sunday. See Letter 431.

429]  *To Sara Hutchinson*

notebook gives some idea of the intimate nature of their letters: 'If I have not heard from you very recently, and if the last letter had not happened to be full of explicit love and feeling, then I conjure up shadows into substances—and am miserable.' T. M. Raysor, 'Coleridge and "Asra",' *Studies in Philology*, July 1929, p. 310. See also Letters 448 and 453.
*Postmark*: 18 January 1802.  *Stamped*: Bridgewater.

. . .—Peach[1] has left Greta Hall, & with him went his china men, & beasts, & unpetticoated Beauties—& of course, the Bull-dog, that so long had been Hartley's Bedfellow.—Mr Jackson saw that the poor Boy's eyes were *full*, & that he could scarce keep his heart down at the departure of the Bull-dog & the good creature could not stand it, but without saying a word walked into town & brought back four fourpenny Images, which now take it by turns to sleep in Hartley's arms. Mrs C. writes me, that she read the 10 commandments to him; but after the *second* he attended no longer; but was quite lost in thought.—'What is the matter, my Dear?[']——[']*I'se afraid, the Lord will be angry with me.*' [']And what for?' '*Because I've got four Images, & I take one to bed with me every night. But what* IS *worshipping Images?*[']—Poor Mrs C. has suffered a great deal from the Rheumatism lately.

This Evening the wind chopped round from South East to South...

### 430. To Daniel Stuart

*Address*: D. Stuart Esq. | No/ 335 | Strand | London
*MS*. British Museum. *Pub*. Letters from the Lake Poets, 24.
*Postmark*: 19 January 1802.  *Stamped*: Bridgewater.

Dear Stuart

I shall be with you without fail on Thursday morning at the latest—for the first 10 days after my arrival at Stowey, I had every evening a Bowel-attack—which layed my spirits prostrate—/ but by a severe adherence to a certain regular Diet & Regimen, I have, I hope, entirely got the better—I am certainly exceedingly improved in health, spirits, & activity—& as the Proof of the Pudding is in the eating, I hope, to bring some *proofs* of it with me.—

Be so good as to let Mr & Mrs Howel know of the Day of my Return—I left a Check for 25£ for you with them / as I did not like to leave Town so heavily in your Debt.—Mr T. Wedgewood, who has been with me at Poole's the whole time, informs me, that the Calcutta scheme is knocked on the head—& with it Mackintosh's Hopes in that Quarter—

---

[1] Mr. Peach was apparently a friend of Jackson's and a temporary resident of Jackson's part of Greta Hall. See Letter 476, and Dorothy Wordsworth's *Journals*, i. 73.

*19 January 1802*

What a pitiful Note that of Bonaparte's to the Legislature.—
Damn the fellow!—
> Your's sincerely,
> S. T. Coleridge

### 431. To William Godwin

*Address*: Mr Godwin | Polygon | Somers' Town
*MS*. Lord Abinger. *Hitherto unpublished.*
*Postmark*: 22 January 1802.

> King's Street, Covent Garden
> Thursday, 21.—[January 1802]

Dear Godwin

I left town on the 26 of December; & I returned this morning at 12 o/ clock—& found your letters on my mantle-piece. I was much affected by them / & can say with the strictest truth that I have been to you qualis ab incaepto. I thought indeed, that I had given you a sufficient proof of [it] by the confidence & openness, with which I spoke to you of my own most private concerns.—You perhaps took offence at my not calling on you; but ill-health has surely a privilege—if you had ever asked me & fixed a day, I should most certainly have come—not, that I wanted an invitation in any other light than as a mere determinant ab extra—for in London I never go any where, nor in any degree follow my free-inclination—I am *pushed* / & waste my time because of all words I find it most difficult to say, *No*.—I am sorry that you have suffered pain; tho' indeed there exists some consolation in the reflection, that you must be a far more privileged man, than I am, to be capable of suffering pain from such causes.—

I had never heard of your marriage[1]—in that & in all things I wish you from the depth & warmth of my spirit all happiness & moral progression. I will call on you as soon as I possibly can; & with your permission will introduce to you one of the very best, & among the most sensible men, in the Kingdom, my friend, T. Poole.—In the meantime if you have time let me see you—for I am very sincerely your's

> S. T. Coleridge

---

[1] Godwin married Mrs. Clairmont on 21 Dec. 1801.

432. *To William Godwin*

*Address*: Mr Godwin | Polygon | Somers' Town
*MS*. Lord Abinger. *Hitherto unpublished*.
*Postmark*: 22 January 1802.

Friday Morning, Jan. 22. 1802
King's Street, Covent Garden—

Dear Godwin

I wrote to you yesterday, immediately on my arrival, a few hasty Lines—went to the Lecture at the Royal Institution, & dined with Poole & Davy, in a large party—a sort of anniversary club Dinner, of a club with a long name of which Tobin is a member—Vapidarians,[1] I think, they call themselves. I returned at 9 o/ clock, went to bed, & this morning

I feel, that I have drunken deep
Of all the Blessedness of Sleep—[2]

No wonder—I have not slept two hours for the last three nights.—This morning I reperused your Letter—& I write again, because I fear, that in the fretfulness of fatigue & hurry I might not have answered it with the respect & affection due to you.—

I have no other wish, than that you should know 'the Truth, the whole Truth, & (if possible) nothing but the Truth' of me in the sum total of my character, much more in it's immediate relations to you. You date the supposed alteration of my feelings towards you, & consequent conduct, from Midsummer last; & my conduct since my arrival in town from the North you have regarded as an exacerbation of the Disease. My conduct since November I conceived that I have fully explained. You appear to me not to have understood the nature of my body & mind—. Partly from ill-health, & partly from an unhealthy & reverie-like vividness of *Thoughts*, & (pardon the pedantry of the phrase) a diminished Impressibility from *Things*, my ideas, wishes, & feelings are to a diseased degree disconnected from *motion & action*. In plain & natural English, I am a dreaming & therefore an indolent man—. I am a Starling self-incaged, & always in the Moult, & my whole Note is, Tomorrow, & tomorrow, & tomorrow. The same causes, that have robbed me to so great a degree of the self-impelling self-directing Principle, have deprived me too of the due powers of Resistances to Impulses from without. If I might so say, I am, as an *acting* man, a creature of mere Impact. 'I will' & 'I will not' are phrases, both of them

[1] In Apr. 1801 Davy was elected to the Tepidarian Society, so called because they drank nothing stronger than tea.
[2] Cf. *Christabel*, lines 375–6.

( 782 )

equally, of rare occurrence in my dictionary.—This is the Truth—I regret it, & in the consciousness of this Truth I lose a larger portion of Self-estimation than those, who know me imperfectly, would easily believe— / I evade the sentence of my own Conscience by no quibbles of self-adulation; I ask for Mercy indeed on the score of my ill-health; but I confess, that this very ill-health is as much an effect as a cause of this want of steadiness & self-command; and it is for mercy that I ask, not for justice.—To apply all this to the present case—

When you spent the Tuesday Evening with me at my Lodgings, I told you my scheme—i.e. that line of conduct, which I thought it my duty to pursue, & which I *wished* to realize.—If I deviated from it, it was (with the exception of two Saturdays, which I dined out, the one with Mackintosh & the other with Sharp, & which I did from *Principle*)—all the rest, (& I must add in favor of myself, that the whole scarcely amounted to more than half of half a dozen) was from the causes, I have stated. I was *taken* out to *dinner;* & if you had come & fixed a day, you too would have *taken* me.—But indeed, Godwin! you were offended, far too hastily. For a week & more I was exceedingly unwell; & in one instance, when I had fully intended to have met you, I had a hint given to me that it would be *unpleasant* to you, &c.—So much for my apparent or real Neglect of you since my arrival in town.—The altered Tone of my Letters previously, is a different affair. When I wrote to you, that I did not imagine you to be much interested about my personal existence, you think this may be fairly considered as a developement of the state of my feelings towards you.—No.——It developed nothing; but it hinted disappointment, & that my feelings of personal concern respecting you had been starved by the imagined want of correspondent feelings in your mind. I had been really & truly interested in you, & for you; & often in the heat of my spirit I have spoken of your literary Imprudences & Self-delusions with asperity, that if '*the good-natured* Friends' have conveyed it to you [they] would have conveyed a bare story of the constancy of my friendship—but the truth & the whole Truth, [is] that I have been angry because I have been *vexed*. My letters before Midsummer expressed what I felt——and nothing but what I felt. If I underwent any alteration of feelings, it was in consequence of my appearing to observe in your Letters a want of interest in me, my health, my goings on. This offended my *moral* nature, & (so help me God) not my personal Pride. I considered it as a great Defect in your character, & as I always write from my immedia[te] feelings (with more or less suppression) I suffered the Belief to appear in the tone of my language—I was struggling with sore calamities, with bodily pain, & languor—with pecuniary Difficulties—& worse than all, with domestic Discord, & the heart-withering Conviction—that I could not be happy without my children, & could not but be miserable with the mother of them.—Of all this you knew but a part, & that, no doubt, indistinctly / yet there did appear to me in your letters a sort of indifference—a total want of affectionate Enquiry—pardon me, if I dare express all my meaning in a harsh form—it did appear to me, as if without any attachment to me you were simply gratified by the notion of my attachment to you. But I must repeat (for if I know my own heart, it is the naked Truth) it offended my moral, & not my personal, feelings: for I have purchased Love by Love.—I am boisterous & talkative in general company; & there are those, who have believed that Vanity is my ruling Passion. They do not know me.—As an *Author*, at all events, I have neither Vanity nor ambition—I think meanly of all, that I have done; and if ever I hope proudly of my future Self, this Hot Fit is uniformly followed & punished by Languor, & Despondency—or rather, by lazy & unhoping Indifference.—In the 2nd Volume of Wordsworth's Lyrical Ballads you will find certain *parts*, & *superficies* of me *sketched* truly under the title—'A character in the antithetical manner.['][1]—I have written thus, and thus prolixly of myself, with far other feelings than those of Self-love, or of pleasure from the writing about myself—. You seemed to doubt my regard & esteem for you: to whom but to a man whom I regarded & esteemed, would I, or could I, have written this Letter?—Your's, S. T. Coleridge

### 433. To George Bellas Greenough

*Address*: G. B. Greenough Esq.—
*Transcript Professor Edith J. Morley. Hitherto unpublished.*

Monday morning, Jan. [25,] 1802

My dear Greenough

I found last night [a] letter (the first I have received from Germany) from the Pastor, with whom I lodged & boarded at Ratzeburg. It interested me, & I think will amuse you—'For we have all of us one human heart.' I send you likewise Godwin's Letter, of which you, of course, take care—& when you have read it, put it safely away till I see you.—Do be so kind (you humour me so, that I get impudent) as to mend for me the Pens, that are

[1] See E. L. Griggs, 'A Note on Wordsworth's *A Character*', *Rev. of Eng. Studies*, Jan. 1953, pp. 57–63.

25 January 1802

inclosed— / —I will mend my own head & heart as much as possible, that I may with better confidence subscribe myself, my dear
Greenough, | Your affectionate | Friend,
S. T. Coleridge

### 434. To Mrs. S. T. Coleridge

MS. *Victoria University Lib. Hitherto unpublished.* This fragment from the top of pages 1 and 2 of the manuscript is all that survives.

[February 1802][1]

My dear Sara

You did very wrong in not writing to me—and I did very wrong in writing to you so angrily. Anger on the strongest provocations is rather excusable, than justifiable; . . .
. . . beloved Children—my Hartley—that *apparition* of Love / & that Derwent, that creature, that Baby, the idea of whom lives almost as much in my Lips as in my Eyes; so intensely do I long to kiss him.—Sara's[2]. . .

### 435. To Mrs. S. T. Coleridge

*Address*: Mrs Coleridge | Greta Hall | Keswick | Cumberland
MS. Lord Latymer. *Pub. E. L. G. i. 191.*
*Postmark*: 19 February 1802.

No/ 10 King's St, Covent Garden—
Friday, Feb. 19, 1802

My dear Love

I dined with Southey yesterday, & incautiously [eat] some Greens, & after that some apple Pie; & on my return to my Lodgings to Tea I was taken very ill with colic Pains & Diarrhoea; & when that went off, one of my old shivery fits came / I went to bed—had a bad night, but about 4 o clock this morning I fell asleep, & awoke at 9 pretty well. With this exception my Health has continued upon the Mend, notwithstanding that the Weather, dank & chill & foggy, has been much against [me]. I attribute my amendment to the more tranquil State of my mind—& to the chearfulness inspired by the thought of speedily returning to you

---
[1] This fragment probably belongs to the early part of 1802. After the birth of his daughter Sara (23 Dec. 1802) Coleridge would no longer refer to Derwent as 'that Baby'.
[2] No doubt referring to Sara Hutchinson.

## To Mrs. S. T. Coleridge

in love & peace—I am sure, I drive away from me every thought but those of Hope & the tenderest yearnings after you—And it is my frequent prayer, & my almost perpetual aspiration, that we may meet to part no more—& live together as affectionate Husband & Wife ought to do.—I hope to leave Town this day fortnight, so as to be with you on the 7th of March / the intervening time I shall be very busy / and if I write twice more, it will be as much as I shall be well able to do.—On Sunday I shall dine with Sir William Rush, & on Monday Evening I am to have a Seat in their Box for Mrs Billington's Benefit—on Wednesday I dine with Mr Losh.—I shall exert all my influence to try to get George Fricker a place in the India House, or some other of the public Offices / Mary Lovell is to remain with the Southeys—in truth, Edith is so exceedingly valetudinarian, that some one or other seems almost necessary. The great Difference of expence will be in the Travelling / & that will be very heavy.

Little Subligno (alias, Underwood) fell in love lately with a fair Jewess—& went to Mr D'Israeli, requesting his interference, & offering immediately to become a convert, & be *circumcised*. This is *nakedly* the fact, without a word of Decoration—I like Subligno hugely.

What do you say to a two years' Residence at Montpellier—under blue skies & in a rainless air? In that case, we would go to Liverpool & spend a week or 10 days with the Cromptons—& from Liverpool to Bordeux by Sea—. But I must first work. Southey would go that way to Lisbon—& spend some months with us—.—

I wish, you would think of something that I may bring Hartley—I have puzzled my head, & cannot think of any thing that will at once delight him, & be durable.——And my sweet Derwent—! My thin child & my fat Child!

Remember me most kindly to Mr Jackson & Mrs Wilson— & to Mr & Mrs Wilkinson—

I hope, you receive the papers regularly. Are you not much affected by the highly sentimental Cast of Mr *Ross's* Advertisements—& his Wig-Statue of the lovely & much-lamented Queen of Scots?—

If you wish me to bring any thing from Town, write me what—& I will do it—

God bless you, | &
S. T. Coleridge

*19 February 1802*

### 436. To Thomas Poole

*Address*: Mr T. Poole | N. Stowey | Bridgewater | Somerset
*MS*. British Museum. Hitherto unpublished.
*Postmark*: 19 February 1802.

No /10 King's St Covent Garden
Friday, Feb. 19, 1802

My dear Poole

Of all colors Greens are the most refreshing to weak eyes; but of all vegetables Greens are not the most comforting to weak Bowels. I dined yesterday with Southey, & unfortunately eat some Cole/ went home soon after dinner to write something for Stuart, when I was taken most violently in my bowels, & after an hour's colic & diarrhoea seized with a shivering fit, & went to bed / I was in a high fever till four o/ clock, when I fell into a gentle sleep, & I woke this morning quite recovered. With this exception my health has been on the Mend, since you left town / nor have I had any occasion for opiates of any kind—neither did I take any last night. —Your Letter arrived *yesterday*, with the Bristol post mark, Feb. 17—tho' it was *dated* Monday night. I gave it to Davy, to execute the commissions therein.—I suppose that by this time you have reached Stowey—Remember me kindly to Ward. Mr Ridout[1] called on me, & spent half an hour with me. He is a truly amiable man. Indeed, that whole family are a spot of sunshine in the moral World. I scarcely remember having seen so interesting a young Woman, as Mary Ward.—You may be assured, that in a very short time the first sheet of my metaphysical work will go to the Press.—My plans are to leave London, in a fortnight/ which time I employ in consulting the Books &c / & in finishing the History of the opinions concerning Space & Time for Mackintosh[2]— When I am more at leisure, I will write you more at length. The anecdote of G. Burnet was very interesting—I suspected it in London & talked seriously with him; but he denied it. He is now however very happy—without one earthly Thing to do, but talk Jacobinism with Citizen Stanhope, that glorious Minority of one!— I have found it convenient to pay Howel for Cloathes &c with a

---

[1] J. G. Ridout, Thomas Ward's uncle. See Letter 499.
[2] 'A great metaphysical book is conceived and about to be born. Thomas Wedgewood the Jupiter whose brain is parturient—Mackintosh the man-midwife—a preface on the history of metaphysical opinions promised by Coleridge. This will perhaps prove an abortion. . . . It has, however, proceeded so far as to disturb the spiders, whose hereditary claim to Thomas Aquinas and Duns Scotus had not been disputed for many a year before. Time and Space are the main subjects of speculation.' Southey to William Taylor, 6 Feb. 1802. *Memoir of William Taylor*, i. 398–9.

draft—therefore you will be so good as to destroy your's, & I send you instead a check on Stuart, who will pay it at sight—I have deducted the 6£ 12/.

When next we meet, my dear Friend! may it be under bluer skies & a more genial Sun!—God bless you,

& your affectionate
S. T. Coleridge

P.S. We were in truth in much anxiety respecting your Draft on Cruckshank—& of course, rejoiced at your recovery of it—

### 437. To Mrs. S. T. Coleridge

Address: Mrs Coleridge | Greta Hall | Keswick | Cumberland
MS. Lord Latymer. Pub. Letters, i. 367.
Postmark: 24 February 1802.

Feb. 24th—[1802]

My dear Love

I am sure, it will make you happy to hear that both my Health & Spirits have greatly improved—& I have small doubt, that a residence of two years in a mild & even climate will, with God's Blessing, give me a new Lease in a better Constitution. You may be well assured, that I shall do nothing rashly / but our journey thither I shall defray by Letters to Poole & the Wedgewoods—or more probably addressed to Mawman, the Bookseller, who will honor my drafts in return.—Of course, I shall not go till I have earned all the money necessary for the Journey &c—The plan will be this —unless you can think of any better.—Wordsworth will marry soon after my return;[1] & he, Mary, & Dorothy will be our companions, & neighbours / Southey means, if it is in his power, to pass into Spain that way.——About July we shall all set sail from Liverpool to Bordeux &c—/ Wordsworth has not yet settled, whether he shall be married at Gallow Hill, or at Grasmere—only they will of course make a point that either Sara shall be with Mary, or Mary with Sara*h* / previous to so long a parting.—If it be decided, that Sarah is to come to Grasmere, I shall return by York, which will be but a few miles out of the way, & bring her /[2].—

---

[1] Wordsworth was not married until 4 Oct. 1802. Undoubtedly letters to and from 'poor Annette' Vallon (see *Journals*, i. 114–28) led him to delay his marriage until he had seen her and his daughter Caroline.

[2] Dorothy says she and Wordsworth were 'perplexed about Sara's coming'; as a matter of fact Sara did not go to Grasmere. Coleridge, nevertheless, arrived at Gallow Hill on Tuesday, 2 Mar., where he remained until 13 Mar. One passage in the original draft of *Dejection, an Ode* (see Letter 438, p. 792) describes an incident which probably occurred at Gallow Hill at this time.

## 24 February 1802

At all events I shall stay a few days at Derby—: for whom, think you, should I meet in Davy's Lecture Room but Joseph Strutt? He behaved most affectionately to me, & pressed me with great earnestness to pass thro' Derby (which is on the road to York) & stay a few days at his house among my old friends—I assure [you], I was much affected by his kind & affectionate [behavior] / tho' I felt a little awkward, not knowing *whom* I might venture to ask after / I could not bring out the word 'Mrs Evans'—& so I said— Your *Sister*, Sir! I HOPE—*she* is well!—/— On Sunday I dined at Sir William Rush's—and on Monday likewise—& went with them to Mrs Billington's Benefit—'Twas the Beggar's Opera—it was *perfection*!—I seem to have acquired a new sense by hearing her!— I wished you to have been there—/. I assure you, I am quite a man of *fashion*—so many titled acquaintances—& handsome Carriages stopping at my door—& fine *Cards*—and then I am such an exquisite Judge of Music, & Painting—& pass criticisms on furniture & chandeliers—& pay such very handsome Compliments to all Women of Fashion / that I do verily believe, that if I were to stay 3 months in town & have tolerable health & spirits, I should be a Thing in Vogue—the very *ton*ish Poet & Jemmy Jessamy fine Talker in Town / If you were only to see the tender Smiles that I occasionally receive from the Honorable Mrs Damer—you would scratch her eyes out, for Jealousy / And then there's the *sweet* (N.B. musky) Lady Charlotte—nay, but I won't tell you her name / you might perhaps take it into your head to write an Anonymous Letter to her, & disturb our little innocent amour.—

O that I were at Keswick with my Darlings! My Hartley / My fat Derwent!

God bless you, my dear Sara! I shall return in Love & chearfulness, & therefore in pleasurable Convalescence, if not in Health /— We shall try to get poor dear little Robert into Christ's Hospital / that Wretch of a Quaker will do nothing! The skulking Rogue,[1] just to lay hold of the time when Mrs Lovell was on a Visit to Southey—there was such low Cunning in the Thought—

Remember me most kindly to Mr & Mrs Wilkinson / & tell Mr Jackson, that I have not shaken a hand, since I quitted him, with more esteem & glad feeling, that I shall soon, I trust, shake his with—God bless you & your aff. & *faithful Hus.

S. T. Coleridge

---

[1] The grandfather of 'little Robert' Lovell. See Letter 124.
* notwithstanding the Honorable Mrs D. & Lady Charlotte—— [Note by S. T. C.]

### 438. To Sara Hutchinson

*MS. Dove Cottage. Pub. E. de Selincourt, 'Coleridge's Dejection: an Ode', Essays and Studies by Members of the English Association, 1937, vol. xxii, 7–25.*

This earliest draft of *Dejection* was addressed as a letter to Sara Hutchinson. When Coleridge first published the poem in the *Morning Post* on 4 October 1802 (the seventh anniversary of his own marriage and Wordsworth's wedding day) and later in *Sibylline Leaves*, he gave it a unity lacking in its epistolary form and omitted the most personal passages. Thus he turned a poetic letter full of self-revelation and self-pity into a work of art with a timeless and universal significance. See *Poems*, i. 362, and Letters 445, 449, 464 and 512.

A Letter to——

April 4, 1802.—Sunday Evening.

Well! if the Bard was weatherwise, who made
The grand old Ballad of Sir Patrick Spence,
This Night, so tranquil now, will not go hence
Unrous'd by winds, that ply a busier trade
Than that, which moulds yon clouds in lazy flakes,
Or the dull sobbing Draft, that drones & rakes
Upon the Strings of this Eolian Lute,
    Which better far were mute.
For, lo! the New Moon, winter-bright!
And overspread with phantom Light,
(With swimming phantom Light o'erspread
But rimm'd & circled with a silver Thread)
I see the Old Moon in her Lap, foretelling
The coming-on of Rain & squally Blast—
O! Sara! that the Gust ev'n now were swelling,
And the slant Night-shower driving loud & fast!

A Grief without a pang, void, dark, & drear,
A stifling, drowsy, unimpassion'd Grief
That finds no natural Outlet, no Relief
    In word, or sigh, or tear—
This, Sara! well thou know'st,
Is that sore Evil, which I dread the most,
And oft'nest suffer! In this heartless Mood,
To other thoughts by yonder Throstle woo'd,
That pipes within the Larch tree, not unseen,
(The Larch, which pushes out in tassels green
It's bundled Leafits) woo'd to mild Delights
By all the tender Sounds & gentle Sights
Of this sweet Primrose-month—& *vainly* woo'd

( 790 )

## 4 April 1802

O dearest Sara! in this heartless Mood
All this long Eve, so balmy & serene,
Have I been gazing on the western Sky
And it's peculiar Tint of Yellow Green—
And still I gaze—& with how blank an eye!
And those thin Clouds above, in flakes & bars,
That give away their Motion to the Stars;
Those Stars, that glide behind them, or between,
Now sparkling, now bedimm'd, but always seen;
Yon crescent Moon, as fix'd as if it grew
In it's own cloudless, starless Lake of Blue—
A boat becalm'd! dear William's Sky Canoe![1]
—I see them all, so excellently fair!
I see, not feel, how beautiful they are.

  My genial Spirits fail—
  And what can these avail
To lift the smoth'ring Weight from off my Breast?
  It were a vain Endeavor,
  Tho' I should gaze for ever
On that Green Light which lingers in the West!
I may not hope from outward Forms to win
The Passion & the Life whose Fountains are within!
These lifeless Shapes, around, below, Above,
  O what can they impart?
When even the gentle Thought, that thou, my Love!
  Art gazing now, like me,
  And see'st the Heaven, I see—
Sweet Thought it is—yet feebly stirs my Heart!

  Feebly! O feebly!—Yet
  (I well remember it)
In my first Dawn of Youth that Fancy stole
With many secret[2] Yearnings on my Soul.
At eve, sky-gazing in 'ecstatic fit'[3]
(Alas! for cloister'd in a city School
The Sky was all, I knew, of Beautiful)[4]
At the barr'd window often did I sit,
And oft upon the leaded School-roof lay,
  And to myself would say—

---

[1] Cf. Prologue to *Peter Bell*.
[2] gentle [Cancelled word in line above.]
[3] Milton, *The Passion*, line 42.
[4] Cf. *Frost at Midnight*, lines 51–53.

## To Sara Hutchinson

There does not live the Man so stripp'd of good affections
As not to love to see a Maiden's quiet Eyes
Uprais'd, and linking on sweet Dreams by dim Connections
To Moon, or Evening Star, or glorious western Skies—
While yet a Boy, this Thought would so pursue me
That often it became a kind of Vision to me!

    Sweet Thought! and dear of old
    To Hearts of finer Mould!
Ten thousand times by Friends & Lovers blest!
    I spake with rash Despair,
    And ere I was aware,
The Weight was somewhat lifted from my Breast!
O Sara! in the weather-fended Wood,
Thy lov'd haunt! where the Stock-doves coo at Noon,
    I guess, that thou hast stood
And watch'd yon Crescent, & it's ghost-like Moon.
And yet, far rather in my present Mood
I would, that thou'dst been sitting all this while
Upon the sod-built Seat of Camomile—[1]
And tho' thy Robin may have ceas'd to sing,
Yet needs for *my* sake must thou love to hear
The Bee-hive murmuring near,
That ever-busy & most quiet Thing
Which I have heard at Midnight murmuring.[2]

    I feel my spirit moved—
    And wheresoe'er thou be,
    O Sister! O Beloved!
    Those dear mild Eyes, that see
    Even now the Heaven, *I* see—
There is a Prayer in them! It is for *me*—
And I, dear Sara—*I* am blessing *thee*!

It was as calm as this, that happy night
When Mary, thou, & I together were,
The low decaying Fire our only Light,
And listen'd to the Stillness of the Air!
O that affectionate & blameless Maid,
Dear Mary! on her Lap my head she lay'd—
    Her Hand was on my Brow,
    Even as my own is now;

---

[1] Built by Coleridge and the Wordsworths, 10 Oct. 1801. See *Journals*, i. 77.
[2] Cf. *A Day-dream*, line 35.

And on my Cheek I felt thy eye-lash play.
Such Joy I had, that I may truly say,
My Spirit was awe-stricken with the Excess
And trance-like Depth of it's brief Happiness.[1]

Ah fair Remembrances, that so revive
The Heart, & fill it with a living Power,
Where were they, Sara?—or did I not strive
To win them to me?—on the fretting Hour
Then when I wrote thee that complaining Scroll
Which even to bodily Sickness bruis'd thy Soul!
And yet thou blam'st thyself alone! And yet
    Forbidd'st me all Regret!

And must I not regret, that I distress'd
Thee, best belov'd! who lovest me the best?
My better mind had fled, I know not whither,
For O! was this an absent Friend's Employ
To send from far both Pain & Sorrow thither
Where still his Blessings should have call'd down Joy!
I read thy guileless Letter o'er again—
I hear thee of thy blameless Self complain—
And only this I learn—& this, alas! I know—
That thou art weak & pale with Sickness, Grief, & Pain—
    And *I—I* made thee so!

O for my own sake I regret perforce
Whatever turns thee, Sara! from the Course
Of calm Well-being & a Heart at rest!
When thou, & with thee those, whom thou lov'st best,
Shall dwell together in one happy Home,
One House, the dear *abiding* Home of All,
I too will crown me with a Coronal—[2]
Nor shall this Heart in idle Wishes roam
    Morbidly soft!
No! let me trust, that I shall wear away
In no inglorious Toils the manly Day,
And only now & then, & not too oft,
Some dear & memorable Eve will bless
Dreaming of all your Loves & Quietness.

---

[1] The incident described in this stanza becomes the subject of *A Day-dream*. See *Poems*, i. 385.

[2] Cf. *Intimations Ode*, line 40, 'My head hath its coronal'. Coleridge's line, which appears in no other version of his poem, clearly links *Dejection* with Wordsworth's Ode, the first four stanzas of which were composed in Mar. 1802.

## To Sara Hutchinson

Be happy, & I need thee not in sight.
Peace in thy Heart, & Quiet in thy Dwelling,
Health in thy Limbs, & in thine Eyes the Light
Of Love, & Hope, & honorable Feeling—
Where e'er I am, I shall be well content!
Not near thee, haply shall be more content!
To all things I prefer the Permanent.
And better seems it for a heart, like mine,
Always to *know*, than sometimes to behold,
    *Their* Happiness & thine—
For Change doth trouble me with pangs untold!
To see thee, hear thee, feel thee—then to part
    Oh!—it weighs down the Heart!
To *visit* those, I love, as I love thee,
Mary, & William, & dear Dorothy,
It is but a temptation to repine—
The transientness is Poison in the Wine,
Eats out the pith of Joy, makes all Joy hollow,
All Pleasure a dim Dream of Pain to follow!
My own peculiar Lot, my house-hold Life
It is, & will remain, Indifference or Strife.
While *ye* are *well* & *happy*, 'twould but wrong you
If I should fondly[1] yearn to be among you—
Wherefore, O wherefore! should I wish to be
A wither'd branch upon on a blossoming Tree?

But (let me say it! for I vainly strive
To beat away the Thought) but if thou pin'd,
Whate'er the Cause, in body or in mind,
I were the miserablest Man alive
To know it & be absent! Thy Delights
Far off, or near, alike I may partake—
But O! to mourn for thee, & to forsake
All power, all hope of giving comfort to thee—
To know that thou art weak & worn with pain,
And not to hear thee, Sara! not to view thee—
    Not sit beside thy Bed,
    Not press thy aching Head,
    Not bring thee Health again—
    At least to hope, to try—
By this Voice, which thou lov'st, & by this earnest Eye—
Nay, wherefore did I let it haunt my Mind
    The dark distressful Dream!

[1] idly [Cancelled word in line above.]

## 4 April 1802

I turn from it, & listen to the Wind
Which long has rav'd[1] unnotic'd! What a Scream
Of agony by Torture lengthen'd out
That Lute sent forth! O thou wild Storm without!
Jagg'd Rock[2], or mountain Pond, or blasted Tree,
Or Pine-grove, whither Woodman never clomb,
Or lonely House, long held the Witches' Home,
Methinks were fitter Instruments for Thee,
Mad Lutanist! that in this month of Showers,
Of dark brown Gardens, & of peeping Flowers,
Mak'st Devil's Yule, with worse than wintry Song
The Blossoms, Buds, and timorous Leaves among!
Thou Actor, perfect in all tragic Sounds!
Thou mighty Poet, even to frenzy bold!
    What tell'st thou now about?
'Tis of the Rushing of an Host in Rout—
And many Groans from men with smarting Wounds—
At once they groan with smart, and shudder with the Cold!
'Tis hush'd! there is a Trance of deepest Silence,
Again! but all that Sound, as of a rushing Crowd,
And Groans & tremulous Shudderings, all are over—
And it has other Sounds, and all less deep, less loud!
    A Tale of less Affright,
    And temper'd with Delight,
As William's Self had made the tender Lay—[3]
    'Tis of a little Child
    Upon a heathy Wild,
Not far from home—but it has lost it's way—
And now moans low in utter grief & fear—
And now screams loud, & hopes to make it's Mother hear![4]

'Tis Midnight! and small Thoughts[5] have I of Sleep—
Full seldom may my Friend such Vigils keep—
O breathe She softly in her gentle Sleep!
Cover her, gentle Sleep! with wings of Healing.
And be this Tempest but a Mountain Birth!
May all the Stars hang bright above her Dwelling,
Silent, as tho' they *watch'd* the sleeping Earth![6]

---

[1] howl'd [Cancelled word in line above.]
[2] Steep Crag [Cancelled words in line above.]
[3] A reference to Wordsworth's *Lucy Gray*.
[4] See Letter 377 for the germ of this passage.
[5] Hope [Cancelled word in line above.]
[6] See Letter 567, at the end of which these two lines are quoted.

## To Sara Hutchinson

    Healthful & light, my Darling! may'st thou rise
        With clear & cheerful Eyes—
And of the same good Tidings to me send!
        For, oh! beloved Friend!
I am not the buoyant Thing, I was of yore—
When I like an own Child, I to Joy belong'd;
For others mourning oft, myself oft sorely wrong'd,
Yet bearing all things then, as if I nothing bore!

        Yes, dearest Sara! yes!
There *was* a time when tho' my path was rough,
The Joy within me dallied with Distress;
And all Misfortunes were but as the Stuff
Whence Fancy made me Dreams of Happiness:
For Hope grew round me, like the climbing Vine,
And Leaves & Fruitage, not my own, seem'd mine!
But now Ill Tidings[1] bow me down to earth /
Nor care I, that they rob me of my Mirth /
        But oh! each Visitation
Suspends what Nature gave me at my Birth,
        My shaping Spirit of Imagination!

I speak not now of those habitual Ills
That wear out Life, when two unequal Minds
Meet in one House, & two discordant Wills—
        This leaves me, where it finds,
Past cure, & past Complaint—a fate austere
Too fix'd & hopeless to partake of Fear!

But thou, dear Sara! (dear indeed thou art,
My Comforter! A Heart within my Heart!)
Thou, & the Few, we love, tho' few ye be,
Make up a world of Hopes & Fears for me.
And if[2] Affliction, or distemp'ring Pain,
Or wayward Chance befall you, I complain
Not that I mourn—O Friends, most dear! most true!
        Methinks to weep with you
Were better far than to rejoice alone—
But that my coarse domestic Life has known
No Habits of heart-nursing Sympathy,
No Griefs, but such as dull and deaden me,
No mutual mild Enjoyments of it's own,
No Hopes of it's own Vintage, None, O! none—

    [1] Misfortunes [Cancelled word in line above.]
    [2] when [Cancelled word in line above.]

## 4 April 1802

Whence when I mourn'd for you, my Heart might borrow
Fair forms & living Motions for it's Sorrow.
For not to think of what I needs must feel,
But to be still & patient all I can;
And[1] haply by abstruse Research to steal
From my own Nature all the Natural Man—
This was my sole Resource, my wisest plan!
And that, which suits a part, infects the whole,
And now is almost grown the Temper of my Soul.

   My little Children are a Joy, a Love,
     A good Gift from above!
But what is Bliss, that still calls up a Woe,
     And makes it doubly keen
Compelling me to *feel*, as well as KNOW,
What a most blessed Lot mine might have been.
Those little Angel Children (woe is me!)
There have been hours, when feeling how they bind
And pluck out the Wing-feathers of my Mind,
Turning my Error to Necessity,
I have half-wish'd, they never had been born!
*That* seldom! But sad Thoughts they always bring,
And like the Poet's Philomel, I sing
My Love-song, with my breast against a Thorn.

With no unthankful Spirit I confess,
This clinging Grief too, in it's turn, awakes
That Love, and Father's Joy; but O! it makes
The Love the greater, & the Joy far less.
These Mountains too, these Vales, these Woods, these Lakes,
Scenes full of Beauty & of Loftiness
Where all my Life I fondly hop'd to live—
I were sunk low indeed, did they *no* solace give;
But oft I seem to feel, & evermore I fear,
They are not to me the Things, which once they were.[2]

O Sara! we receive but what we give,
And in *our* Life alone does Nature live.
Our's is her Wedding Garment, our's her Shroud—
And would we aught behold of higher Worth
Than that inanimate cold World allow'd
To the poor loveless ever-anxious Crowd,

[1] Or [Cancelled word in line above.]
[2] Cf. *Intimations Ode*, line 9: 'The things which I have seen I now can see no more.' Coleridge's line appears only in this version of his poem.

## To Sara Hutchinson

Ah! from the Soul itself must issue forth
A Light, a Glory, and a luminous Cloud
    Enveloping the Earth!
And from the Soul itself must there be se[nt]
A sweet & potent Voice, of it's own Bir[th,]
Of all sweet Sounds the Life & Element.

O pure of Heart! thou need'st not ask of me
What this strong music in the Soul may be,
    What, & wherein it doth exist,
This Light, this Glory, this fair luminous Mist,
This beautiful & beauty-making Power!
Joy, innocent Sara! Joy, that ne'er was given
Save to the Pure, & in their purest Hour,
Joy, Sara! is the Spirit & the Power,
That wedding Nature to us gives in Dower
    A new Earth & new Heaven
Undreamt of by the Sensual & the Proud!
Joy is that strong Voice, Joy that luminous Cloud—
    We, we ourselves rejoice!
And thence flows all that charms or ear or sight,
All melodies the Echoes of that Voice,
All Colors a Suffusion of that Light.

Sister & Friend of my devoutest Choice!
Thou being innocent & full of love,
And nested with the Darlings of thy Love,
And feeling in thy Soul, Heart, Lips, & Arms
Even what the conjugal & mother Dove
That borrows genial Warmth from those, she warms,
Feels in her thrill'd wings, blessedly outspread—
Thou free'd awhile from Cares & human Dread
By the Immenseness of the Good & Fair
    Which thou see'st every where—
Thus, thus should'st thou rejoice!
To thee would all Things live from Pole to Pole,
Their Life the Eddying of thy living Soul—
O dear! O Innocent! O full of Love!
A very[1] Friend! A[2] Sister of my Choice—
O dear, as Light & Impulse from above,
Thus may'st thou ever, evermore rejoice!
                                    S. T. C.

[1] gentle [Cancelled word in line above.]
[2] O [Cancelled word in line above.]

## 439. To Thomas Poole

*Address*: Mr T. Poole | N. Stowey | Bridgewater | Somerset
*MS*. British Museum. *Pub. with omis.* E. L. G. i. 193.
*Postmark*: 10 May 1802. *Stamped*: Keswick.

My dear Poole
May 7, [1802.] Friday—Keswick

I were sunk low indeed, if I had neglected to write to you from any lack of affection / I have written to no human being—which I mention, not as an excuse, but as preventive of any aggravation of my fault. I have neither been very well, nor very happy; but I have been far from idle / and I can venture to promise you that by the end of the year I shall have disburthened myself of all my metaphysics, &c—& that the next year I shall, if I am alive & in possession of my present faculties, devote to a long poem.—All my small poems are about to be published, as a second Volume / & I mean to write few, if any, small poems, hereafter.—So much for myself—My children are well—Mrs Coleridge is indisposed, & I have too much reason to suspect that she is breeding again / an event, which was to have been deprecated.—Wordsworth is as well as he usually is; & has written a considerable number of small poems.—So much for us of the North.—

And you are going to France, Switzerland, Italy!—Good go with you, & with you return! I have, you well know, read nothing in French but metaphysical French / of French Books I know nothing —of French manners nothing—Wordsworth, to whom I shall send your Letter tomorrow, may perhaps have somewhat to communicate / he having been the same rout—but what can you want? I never saw you in any company in which you did not impress every one present as a superior man / and you will not be three days in France without having learnt the way of learning all you want—. I advise one thing only—that before you go you skim over Adam Smith, & that in France you look thro' some of their most approved writers on political Economy—& that you keep your mind *intent* on *this* / I am sure, that it is a Science in it's Infancy— indeed, Science it is none—& you, I would fain anticipate, will be a Benefactor to your Species by making it so.—Had I been you, I would have gone thro' France & Switzerland, & returned by Paris—& not gone to Paris first. Such a crowd of eager Englishmen will be there, at the same time with you, all pressing forward with their Letters of Recommendation / & you will find it difficult perhaps to remain disentangled by their society / To which as a more important Reason I may add the superior skill & fluency in French

439]                    *To Thomas Poole*

& french manners—the naturalization of Look & Tongue—which will enable you to converse with the Literati of Paris on a better footing, if you take Paris last.—I had offers made me by a London Bookseller of paying me the reasonable expences, of a tour thro' France & Switzerland, on the condition of a regular correspondence with him, which he was, of course, to publish / but tho' I had many strong domestic reasons impelling me to accept the offer, among others the benefit which my Health would have received from such a vacation from household Infelicity, yet I declined it—chiefly, but not altogether, from my ignorance of the French Language— / In Switzerland indeed they speak German; but there one uses one's Eyes more than one's Tongue or Ears— / It would be droll if we had met—you not knowing of my Scheme!—What an Æra in our Lives it would have been, to have passed thro' Switzerland together—

You will (tho' I have little claim upon you, I confess) give me the delight of hearing from you / especially, I am solicitous to know the price of provisions & house rent in the South of France—nearest Switzerland / I am glad, you have received the German Picture[1]—there is one (I see by the Newspaper) in the Exhibition of me / what it is, or whose, I do not know, but I guess, it must be the miniature, which Hazlitt promised to Mrs Coleridge; but did not give to her, because I never finished my sittings / Mine is not a *picturesque* Face / Southey's was made for a picture.—Poor old Cruckshank![2]—

Give my kind Love to Ward—I will not let this post go off without this Letter, dreary & vacant as it is—but I will write again, in a few days, when my heart is come back to me / but not to leave such a Blank I will transcribe 2 pleasing little poems of Wordsworth's—

To a Butterfly[3]

Stay near me! Do not take thy Flight!
A little longer stay in sight!
Much Reading do I find in thee,
    Historian of my Infancy!
Float near me! do not yet depart!
    Dead Times revive in thee—
Thou bring'st, gay creature as thou art,
A solemn Image to my Heart,
    My Father's Family.

---

[1] See p. 470.
[2] Poole had written Coleridge of the death of John Cruikshank, Lord Egmont's agent.          [3] *Wordsworth's Poet. Works*, i. 226.

( 800 )

O pleasant, pleasant were the Days
The time when in our childish plays
My Sister Emmeline & I
Together chac'd the Butterfly.
A very Hunter did I rush
Upon the Prey: with Leaps & Springs
I follow'd on from Brake to Bush—
But she, God love her! fear'd to brush
   The Dust from off it's wings.

      The Sparrow's Nest[1]
Look! five blue Eggs are gleaming there!
Few Visions have I seen more fair
Nor many Prospects of Delight
More pleasing than that simple sight!
I started, seeming to espy
The Home & little Bed,
The Sparrow's Dwelling which hard by
My Father's House, in wet or dry,
My Sister Emmeline & I
Together visited.

She look'd at it, as if she fear'd it,
Still wishing, dreading to be near it;
Such Heart was in her, being then
A little Prattler among men.
The Blessing of my later years
Was with me when a Boy,
She gave me eyes, she gave me ears,
And humble Cares & delicate Fears,
A heart the fountain of sweet Tears,
And love & thought & Joy!

I ought to say for my own sake that on the 4th of April last I wrote you a letter in verse; but I thought it dull & doleful—& did not send it——
          God bless you, dear Friend! & S. T. C.——

---

[1] *Wordsworth's Poet. Works*, i. 227.

### 440. To George Coleridge

*Address*: Revd G. Coleridge | Ottery St Mary | Devon   by favor of Revd Mr Froude
*MS.* Lady Cave. *Pub.* E. L. G. i. 196.

June 3, 1802. Keswick.

My dear Brother

I cannot let Mr Froude stay so long in this country without making him the Bearer of a Letter to you from me / especially, since he has given me so much cheerful Information respecting you, & your's, & the rest of my family. I pray God, that you may all continue as well and happy, as you are prosperous. I assure you I was much affected by the zeal & enthusiasm, with which Mr Froude spoke of you, & the Colonel. He seemed to feel as great a pride in your welfare, & high character, as if you had been *his* elder Brothers, instead of mine.—Froude is indeed a very amiable, liberal, & well-principled Man; & I sincerely hope, that he will take with him from among us an accession to his real comfort.——As to myself, I have little to communicate. My health is much better than it was; tho' I have still very frequent attacks in my Bowels. They are a seditious Crew; and I have need of the most scrupulous attention to my Diet to preserve them in any tolerable Order. The children are both well; and Derwent is, as Froude will no doubt inform you, a thorough Coleridge in his whole Cast. Hartley is more a thing sui Generis—but he is of a very sweet and docile Disposition, & possesses that, for which, I believe, *I* was somewhat remarkable when a child, namely, a memory both quick & retentive.—Mrs S. Coleridge is but poorly / however her Disorder menaces me with no other Event, I suspect, than that of *a New Life.*—

As to my Studies, they lie chiefly, I think, in Greek & German. (Hartley made me laugh the other day by saying, that Greek Letters were English Letters *dried up.*) Tho' I have a great prepossession in favour of all ancient usages, (τὰ ἀρχαῖα κρατείτω) yet I can not but conjecture, that it would be found both a feasible & profitable Scheme to teach Greek first. It seems wrong, that a language containing Books so much more numerous & valuable than the Latin, & in itself so much more easy & perspicuous, should be confined, as to the ready & fluent Reading of it, to a few Scholars. This is owing solely to the Teaching of the Greek thro' the medium of the Latin; whereas, according to my humble *Vote,* both Greek & Latin should be taught with direct reference to the English. What should we think of a Schoolmaster, who taught Italian thro' the medium of French?—But you are more likely to have formed correct opinions on this Subject than I.—I will only add, that at the time of the first Greek Dictionaries there were not Scholars enough in any one Country to take off so large an Edition, as it was necessary to print / they were therefore compelled to render the Greek into the universal Language / But the cause having so wholly ceased, it is pity but that the effect would likewise cease. Gilbert Wakefield was engaged, & had made good progress, in a Greek & English Lexicon / what is become of it, I have not heard. —I have read Vincent on the Greek Verb—in my opinion—— πάντα κόνις, καὶ πάντα τὸ μηδέν—It is too dull, to say—πάντα γέλως— πάντα ὕπνος, would be the aptest Supplement.

You have been, no doubt, interested in some measure by the French Concordat. I own, I was surprized to find it so much approved of by Clergymen of the Church / It appeared to me a wretched Business—& first occasioned me to think accurately & with consecutive Logic on the force & meaning of the word *Established* Church / and the result of my reflections was very greatly in favor of the Church of England maintained, as it at present is / and those scruples, which, if I mistake not, we had in common when I last saw you, as to the effects & scriptural propriety of this (supposed) alliance of Church & State were wholly removed.— Perhaps, you will in some measure perceive the general nature of my opinions, when I say—the Church of France at present ought to be called—*a standing* church—in the same sense as we say a *standing* army.—If the Subject interested you, I would willingly give you my opinions in full, with an historical account of the Objections of the Dissenters, & of the Warburtonian System of defence, which I rather dislike & *suspect*. Warburton's Faith was, I fear, of a very suspicious Cast.[1]—

You will give my love & Duty to my Mother, of whose health & good spirits I am delighted to hear—to my Brother James, his wife, & dear & lively family you will remember me with fraternal affection—& to Edward / —Above all, let me say how much I should be delighted to see your little ones, & Mrs G. Coleridge— and if I had written half as often as I have thought of you, (earnestly & seriously thought of you) you would have complained heavily of the Postage, & with good reason.—

God bless you, dear Brother, & your's affectionately & gratefully,
S. T. Coleridge

---

[1] See William Warburton, *The Alliance between Church and State*, 1736.

## 441. To Sara Hutchinson

*MS. Dove Cottage. Hitherto unpublished fragment.*

[Early Summer 1802][1]

... —Hartley told his Mother, that he was thinking all day—all the morning, all the day, all the evening—'what it would be, if there were *Nothing* / if all the men, & women, & Trees, & grass, and birds & beasts, & the Sky, & the Ground, were all gone / *Darkness & Coldness*—& nothing to be dark & cold.' His Mother ...

... [His] motto from infancy might have been *not me alone*! [']My *Thoughts* are my Darlings!'—Hartley's *attachments* are excessively strong—so strong, even to places, that he does not like to go into town—or on a visit / The field, garden, & river bank / his Kitchen & darling Friend—they are enough / & Play fellows are burthensome to him / excepting *me* / because I can understand & sympathize with, his wild Fancies—& suggest others of my own.— I am tolerably—My best Love ...


## 442. To Sara Hutchinson

*Address*: Miss S. Hutchins[on] | Gallow Hill | Wykeham | Malto[n] | Yorksh[ire]
*MS. Dove Cottage. Hitherto unpublished fragment.*

[Early Summer 1802]

... The [dear] Children are both well. Derwent, if I have re[mained] a long time without noticing him, comes to me, & says—*Tiss*!— He is such an angel!—Some time ago I watched Hartley under the Trees, down by the River—the Birds singing so sweetly above him / & he was evidently lost in thought. I went down, & asked him what his Thoughts were—so he hugged me, & said after a while 'I thought, how I love the sweet Birds, & the Flowers, & Derwent, and Thinking; & how I hate Reading, & being wise, & being Good.'—Does not this remind you of 'the pretty Boy' in my Foster Mother's Tale[2]—in the L.B.— ...

[1] This and the following fragment belong to 1802, before the birth of Sara.
[2] Cf. lines 28–35:

>And so the babe grew up a pretty boy,
>A pretty boy, but most unteachable—
>And never learnt a prayer, nor told a bead,
>But knew the names of birds, and mock'd their notes,
>And whistled, as he were a bird himself:
>And all the autumn 'twas his only play
>To get the seeds of wild flowers, and to plant them
>With earth and water, on the stumps of trees.

*1 July 1802*

### 443. To George Coleridge

*Address*: Revd G. Coleridge | Lymington | Hampshire
*MS*. Lady Cave. *Pub*. E. L. G. i. 199.
*Stamped*: Keswick.

Keswick, Thurs: July 1. 1802

My dear Brother

If you have had the same Tempest at Lymington, as has been playing it's freaks among our Lakes & mountains this whole Day, the sea must have 'shown off in a grand style', as the Tourists phrase it. May you have occasion to exclaim with the younger Pliny—'O Mare! O Littus! Verum secretumque Μουσεῖον, quàm multa invenitis, quàm multa dictatis!'[1] It gave me great pleasure to hear from yourself a confirmation of what Mr Froude had hin[ted] to me—namely, your intention of living hereafter for yourself—because I am well assured, that in so doing you will, in some way or other, be living still for the benefit of others. You have purchased for yourself a high earthly Reward, the Love & Honor of men, whom you yourself have been the main Instrument of rendering worthy to be themselves loved & honored.—It seems as if there were something originally amiss in the constitution of all our family—if that can be indeed without presumption called 'amiss' which may probably be connected intimately with our moral & [int]ellectual characters—but we all, I think, carry much passion, [& a] deep interest, into the business of Life—& when to this is supe[ra]dded, as in my Brother James's Case, great bodily fatigue, the organs of digestion will be soon injured—in weak men this in general produces affections of the Bowels, more or less painful, in strong men spasmodic hypochondria, that will appear to have it's head quarters in the Stomach, & the Secretories of Bile—and I suspect the latter to be my Brother's case, & that the only prescription is that of the old Latin Distich /

Si tibi deficiant Medici, Medici tibi fiant
Haec tria: Mens hilaris, Requies, moderata Diaeta.

The last is an old acquaintance of the Colonel's; & the two former depend but little on our own arbitrement: so that alas! like advice in general, it is very true, and yet but little worth.——I have been better of late—so much better, that I have hopes of soon becoming a tolerably healthy man / a stout man I never shall be.——From the latter part of your Letter I fear that I must have worded my Letter to you very inacc[ur]ately in what respected the change of sentiment—in saying that I had no longer my former scruples

---

[1] Pliny, *Epis*. I. ix, to Minicius Fundanus.

respecting the *establishment* of the Church of England, I did not mean in any way to refer to it's peculiar Doctrines—or to the Church of England in particular. The change in my opinions applies equally to the Gallic Church, antecedent to the Revolution, and to the regular & parochial Clergy of Spain & Portugal.—The Clergy are called in a statute of Queen Elizabeth 'the great, venerable, third *Estate* of the Realm'—that is to say, they & their property are an elementary part of our constitution, not created by any Legislature, but really & truly antecedent to any form of Government in England upon which any existing Laws can be built— They & their Property are *recognized* by the Statutes—even as the common Law frequently is—which was bona fide Law, & the most sacred Law, before the Statute / and recognized not for the purpose of having any additional authority conferred on it, but for the removing of any ambiguities & for the increasing of it's publicity. The Church is not depend[en]t on the Government, nor can the Legislature constit[ution]ally alter it's property without consent of the Proprietor—any [more] than it constitutionally could introduce an agrarian Law.—Now this is indeed an Establishment— res stabilita—it has it's own foundations / whereas the present church of France has no foundation of it's own—it is a House of Convenience built on the sands of a transient Legislature—& no wise differs from a *standing Army*. The colonial Soldiers under the Roman Emperors were an *established* Army, in a certain sense— & so were the Timariots under the Turks / —but the Church of France is a *standing* church, as it's army is a *standing* army. It *stands*; and so does a Child's House of Cards—but how long it shall stand depends on the caprice of a few Individuals.—This I hold to be indeed & in sad & sober Truth an antichristian union of the Kingdom of Christ with the Kingdom of this World—& in a less degree I look upon the manner, in which the Dissenting Clergy are maintained, as objectionable on the same grounds. Now herein, & only herein, lies the Change in my opinions.—When I was last with you, & we walked on a Sunday Evening with Mr Southey, toward the Head wier [Weir], you expressed your Dissent from Dr Priestley's opinions, & your disapprobation of the Spirit in which they had been made public; but you said, (& I had heard the same opinion from you before) that you did agree with him in thinking, that Church Establishments had been prejudicial to Christianity.— At that time I was wholl[y] of the same mind & so I remained till mor[e re]ading [and] Reflection removed that opinion, which I ha[d felt to be] common at that time to yourself & to me——. Wi[th regard] to the particular Doctrines of the Church, or to any [change] I had no motive to speak—for I have always [declared to] you the truth & the whole truth, when I have talk[ed with you] on this subject—& I could never discover any differen[ce in your] opinions and my own.—I understood that in common [with all] the best & greatest men of the Church, with Bishop Tay[lor, Archb]ishop Tillotson, Bishop Law—(not to mention W[illiam] Paley, & Jortin, because these are, rightly or wrongly believed to be semi-socinians) you regretted that so many scholastic Terms & nice Distinctions had been introduced into our Articles & Liturgy—I do no more. I have read carefully the original of the New Testament—& have convinced myself, that the Socinian & Arian Hypotheses are utterly untenable; but what to put in their place? I find [nothing so] distinctly revealed, that I should dare to impose my opinion as an article of Faith on others—on the contrary, I hold it probable that the Nature of the Being of Christ is left in obscurity —& that it behoves us to think with deep humility on the subject, & when we express ourselves, to be especially careful, on such a subject, to use the very words of Scripture.—Dearest Brother! is there a serious Clergyman of all your acquaintance who does not, when he puts the Question seriously to himself, wish that this could be—if it could be without too dear a purchase?—But we know by sad Experience, that Innovations are almost always dearly purchased—& I plead for no innovations—not even of the rash Anathemas of the Preface to the athanasian Creed—neither do I either with my Tongue or in my Heart censure those, who cling to the Church of England as they cling to their Wives—first, because there is great evil in change—& secondly, because all moral & all political attachment must be grounded, not on an immunity from defects & errors, but on the presence of Truths & Virtues practicable & suitable to us.——My Faith is simply this—that there is an original corruption in our nature, from which & from the consequences of which, we may be redeemed by Christ—not as the Socinians say, by his pure morals or excellent Example merely—but in a mysterious manner as an effect of his Crucifixion—and this I believe—not because I *understand* it; but because I *feel*, that it is not only suitable to, but needful for, my nature and because I find it clearly revealed.—Whatever the New Testament says, I believe—according to my best judgment of the meaning of the sacred writers.—Thus I have stated to you this whole of the Change which has taken place in me—which is however far from being 'the fi[rst] fruits' of my reverence for the τὰ ἀρχαῖα κρ[ατε]ίτω.—My kindest Love to Mrs G. Coleridge—in [whic]h & to you, & your dear little ones Mrs C. [joins]—

S. T. Coleridge

## 444. To William Sotheby[1]

*Address*: William Sotheby Esq. | Upper Seymour [St] | London    Single Sheet
*MS*. Colonel H. G. Sotheby. *Pub. with omis.* Letters, i. 369.
*Stamped*: Keswick.

Tuesday, July 13, 1802. Greta Hall, Keswick

My dear Sir

I had written you a letter, and was about to have walked to the Post with it, when I received your's from Longnor—it gave me such lively pleasure, that I threw my Letter into the Fire / for it related chiefly to the Erste Schiffer of Gesner[2] / and I could not endure that my first Letter to you should *begin* with a subject so little interesting to my Heart or Understanding.—I trust, that you are before this at the end of your Journey; and that Mrs and Miss Sotheby have so completely recovered themselves, as to have almost forgotten all the fatigue, except such instances of it as it may be pleasant to them to remember. Why need I say, how often I have thought of you since your departure, & with what Hope & pleasurable Emotion? I will acknowlege to you, that your very, very kind Letter was not only a Pleasure to me, but a Relief to my mind / for after I had left you on the Road between Ambleside & Grasmere, I was dejected by the apprehension, that I had been unpardonably loquacious, and had oppressed you, & still more Mrs Sotheby, with my many words so impetuously uttered. But in simple truth you were yourselves in part the innocent causes of it / for the meeting with you; the manner of the meeting; your kind attentions to me; the deep & healthful delight, which every impressive & beautiful object seemed to pour out upon you; kindred opinions, kindred pursuits, kindred feelings, in persons whose Habits & as it were *Walk* of Life, have been so different from my own—; these, and more than these which I would but cannot say, all flowed in upon me with unusually strong Impulses of Pleasure / and Pleasure, in a body & soul such as I happen to possess, 'intoxicates more than strong Wine.'—However, *I promise to be a much more subdued creature—when you next meet me* / for

---

[1] William Sotheby (1757–1833), poet, dramatist, and translator, became Coleridge's staunch friend from the time of their meeting in 1802.

[2] Coleridge's translation of Salomon Gessner's poem, *Der erste Schiffer*, was to be published with illustrations by the engraver, P. W. Tomkins. Although in subsequent letters Coleridge gives Sotheby the impression that he had completed the work, he wrote to Godwin in 1811 that he had composed only part of it: 'I once translated into blank verse about half of the poem, but gave it up under the influence of a double disgust, moral and poetical.' *William Godwin*, ii. 223. No trace of Coleridge's translation remains.

*13 July 1802* [444

I had but just recovered from a state of extreme dejection brought on in part by Ill-health, partly by other circumstances / and Solitude and solitary Musings do of themselves impregnate our Thoughts perhaps with more Life & Sensation, than will leave the Balance quite even.—But you, my dear Sir! looked [at a] Brother Poet with a Brother's Eyes—O that you were now in my study, & saw what is now before the window, at which I am writing, that rich mulberry-purple which a floating Cloud has thrown on the Lake—& that quiet Boat making it's way thro' it to the Shore!—We have had little else but Rain & squally weather since you left us, till within the last three Days—but showery weather is no evil to us—& even that most oppressive of all weathers, hot small *Drizzle*, exhibits the Mountains the best of any. It produced such new combinations of Ridges in the Lodore & Borrodale Mountains, on Saturday morning, that, I declare, had I been blindfolded & so brought to the Prospect, I should scarcely have known them again. It was a Dream, such as Lovers have—a wild & transfiguring, yet enchantingly lovely, Dream of an Object lying by the side of the Sleeper. Wordsworth, who has walked thro' Switzerland, declared that he never saw any thing superior—perhaps nothing equal—in the Alps.—The latter part of your Letter made me truly happy. Uriel himself should not be half as welcome / & indeed he, I must admit, was never any great Favorite of mine. I always thought him a Bantling of zoneless Italian Muses which Milton heard cry at the Door of his Imagination, & took in out of charity.—However, come horsed as you may, carus mihi expectatusque venies.[1] *De ceteris rebus, (si*[2] *quid agendum est, et quicquid*[2] *sit agendum) ut quam rectissime agantur, omni meâ curâ, operâ, diligentiâ, providebo.*[3]

On my return to Keswick I reperused the erste Schiffer with great attention; & the result was an increasing Disinclination to the business of translating it / tho' my fancy was not a little flattered by the idea of seeing my Rhymes in such a gay Livery—as poor Giordano Bruno says in his strange yet noble Poem De Immenso et Innumerabili

> Quam ganymedeo Cultu, graphiceque Venustus!
> Narcissis referam, peramârunt me quoque Nymphae.[4]

But the Poem was too silly. The first conception is noble—so very good, that I am spiteful enough to hope that I shall discover it not

---
[1] *Ciceronis Epis. ad Fam.* xvi. vii.
[2] Underlined twice in MS.  [3] Ibid. i. ii.
[4] 'The lines are taken, with some alterations, from a kind of *l'envoy* or epilogue which Bruno affixed to his long philosophical poem, *Jordani Bruni Nolani de Innumerabilibus Immenso et Infigurabili; seu de Universo et Mundis libri octo.* Francofurti, 1591, p. 654.' *Letters,* i. 371 n.

to have been original in Gesner—he has so abominably maltreated it.—First, the story is very inartificially constructed—we should have been let into the existence of the Girl & her Mother thro' the young Man, & after *his* appearance / this however is comparatively a trifle.—But the machinery is so superlatively contemptible & commonplace—as if a young man could not dream of a Tale which had deeply impressed him without Cupid, or have a fair wind all the way to an Island within sight of the Shore, he quitted, without Æolus. Æolus himself is a God devoted & dedicated, I should have thought, to the Muse of Travestie / his Speech in Gesner is not defici[ent] in Fancy—but it is a Girlish Fancy—& the God of the winds exceedingly disquieted with *animal* Love / ind[uces?] a very ridiculous Figure in my Imagination.—Besides, it was ill taste to introduce Cupid and Æolus at a time which we positive[ly] know to have been anterior to the invention & establishment of the Grecian Mythology—and the speech of Æolus reminds me perpetually of little Engravings from the Cut Stones of the Ancients, Seals, & whatever else they call them.—Again, the Girl's yearnings & conversations with [her] Mother are something between the Nursery and the Veneris Volgivagae Templa[1]—et libidinem spirat et subsusurrat, dum innocentiae loquelam, et virgineae cogitationis dulciter offensantis luctamina simulat.—It is not the Thoughts that a lonely Girl *could* have; but exactly such as a Boarding School Miss whose *Imagination,* to say no worse, had been somewhat stirred & heated by the perusal of French or German Pastorals, would suppose her to say. But this is indeed general in the German & French Poets. It is easy to cloathe Imaginary Beings with our own Thoughts & Feelings; but to send ourselves out of ourselves, to *think* ourselves in to the Thoughts and Feelings of Beings in circumstances wholly & strangely different from our own / hoc labor, hoc opus / and who has atchieved it? Perhaps only Shakespere. Metaphisics is a word, that you, my dear Sir! are no great Friend to / but yet you will agree, that a great Poet must be, implicitè if not explicitè, a profound Metaphysician. He may not have it in logical coherence, in his Brain & Tongue; but he must have it by *Tact* / for all sounds, & forms of human nature he must have the *ear* of a wild Arab listening in the silent Desart, the eye of a North American Indian tracing the footsteps of an Enemy upon the Leaves that strew the Forest—; the *Touch* of a Blind Man feeling the face of a darling Child— / and do not think me a Bigot, if I say, that I have read no French or German Writer, who appears to me to have had a *heart* sufficiently pure & simple to be capable of this or any thing like it. / I could say a great deal

[1] Cf. Lucretius iv. 1071.

more in abuse of poor Gesner's Poem; but I have said more than, I fear, will be creditable in your opinion to my good nature. I must tho' tell you the malicious Motto, which I have written on the first page of Klopstock's Messias—

> Tale tuum carmen nobis, divine Poeta,
> Quale *Sopor*![1]

Only I would have the words, *divine Poeta*, translated, *Verse-making* DIVINE. I read a great deal of German; but I do dearly dearly dearly love my own Countrymen of old times, and those of my contemporaries who write in their Spirit.

William Wordsworth & his Sister left me Yesterday on their way to Yorkshire / they walked yesterday to the foot of Ulswater, from whence they go to Penrith & take the Coach—I accompanied them as far as the 7th Mile Stone. Among the last things, which he said to me, was—'Do not forget to remember [me] to Mr [So]theby with whatever affectionate terms, so slight an Intercourse may permit—and how glad we shall all be to see him again.' —I was much pleased with your description of Wordsworth's character as it appeared to y[ou—] it is in few words, in half a dozen Strokes, like s[ome of] Mortimer's[2] Figures, a fine Portrait— The word '*homoge[neity*' gave] me great pleasure, as most accurate & happily expressi[ve. I must] set you right with regard to my perfect coinc[idence with] his poetic Creed. It is most certain, that that P[reface arose from] the heads of our mutual Conversations &c—& the f[irst pass]ages were indeed partly taken from notes of mine / for it was at first intended, that the Preface should be written by me—and it is likewise true, that I warmly accord with W. in his abhorrence of these poetic Licences, as they are called, which are indeed mere tricks of Convenience & Laziness. *Exemp. Grat.* Drayton has these Lines—

> Ouse having Ouleney past, as she were waxed mad,
> From her first stayder Course immediately doth gad,
> And in meandred Gyres doth whirl herself about,
> *That, this* way, here and there, back, forward, in and out,
> And like a wanton Girl oft doubling in her Gait
> In labyrinthine Turns & Twinings Intricate &c &c—[3]

the first poets observing such a stream as this, would say with truth & beauty—it *strays*—& now every stream shall *stray* wherever it prattles on it's pebbled *way*—instead of it's bed or channel / . (I

---

[1] Virgil, *Ecl.* v. 45–46.
[2] John Hamilton Mortimer (1741–1779), historical painter.
[3] Michael Drayton, *Poly-Olbion*, Song 22, lines 17–22.

have taken the instance from a Poet, from whom as few Instances of this vile commonplace trashy Style could be taken as from any writer—from Bowles's *execrable Translation* of that lovely Poem of Dean Ogle's,[1] vol. II. p. 27.— / I am confident, that Bowles good-naturedly translated it in a hurry, merely to give him an excuse for printing the admirable original.)—In my opinion every phrase, every metaphor, every personification, should have it's justifying cause in some *passion* either of the Poet's mind, or of the Characters described by the poet—But *metre itself* implies a *passion*, i.e. a state of excitement, both in the Poet's mind, & is expected in that of the Reader—and tho' I stated this to Wordsworth, & he has in some sort stated it in his preface, yet he has [not] done justice to it, nor has he in my opinion sufficiently answered it. In my opinion, Poetry justifies, as *Poetry* independent of any other Passion, some new combinations of Language, & *commands* the omission of many others allowable in other compositions / Now Wordsworth, me saltem judice, has in his system not sufficiently admitted the former, & in his practice has too frequently sinned against the latter.—Indeed, we have had lately some little controversy on this subject—& we begin to suspect, that there is, somewhere or other, a *radical* Difference [in our] opinions[2]—Dulce est inter amicos rarissimâ Dissensione condiri plurimas consensiones, saith St Augustine, who said more good things than any Saint or Sinner, that I ever read in Latin.—

Bless me! what a Letter!——And I have yet to make a request to you / I had read your Georgics[3] at a Friend's House in the Neighbourhood—and on sending for the book I find that it belonged to a Book Club, & has been returned. If you have a copy interleaved, or could procure one for me, and will send it to me per Coach with a copy of your original Poems I will return them to you with many thanks in the Autumn / & will endeavor to improve my own taste by writing in the blank Leaves my feelings both of the Original & your Translation / your poems I want for another purpose—of which hereafter.—Mrs Coleridge & my children are well—she desires to be respectfully remembered to Mrs & Miss Sotheby. Tell Miss Sotheby that I will endeavor to send her soon the completion of the Dark Ladié—as she was good-natured [enough] to be pleased with the first part——Let me hear

---

[1] *Poetical Works of Bowles*, ed. by G. Gilfillan, 2 vols., 1855, i. 100. Lines 1 and 2 of Bowles's translation read:

Oh thou, that prattling on thy pebbled way
Through my paternal vale dost stray.

[2] This is the first evidence of Coleridge's dissatisfaction with Wordsworth's Preface to *Lyrical Ballads*. See also Letter 449.

[3] Sotheby's translation of Virgil's *Georgics* was published in 1800.

from you soon, my dear Sir!—& believe me with heart-felt wishes for you & your's, in every day phrase, but indeed indeed not with every-day Feeling, your's most sincerely,

S. T. Coleridge.

I long to lead Mrs Sotheby to a Scene that has the grandeur without the Toil or Danger of Scale Force—it is called the White Water Dash.——

### 445. To William Sotheby

*Address*: W. Sotheby Esq. | Upper Seymour St | London     *Single* Sheet
*MS*. Colonel H. G. Sotheby. *Pub. with omis.* Letters, *i. 376*.
*Postmark*: 22 July 1802.    *Stamped*: Keswick.

July 19, [1802.] Keswick

My dear Sir

I trouble you with another Letter, to inform you that I have finished the first Book of the Erste Schiffer; it consists of about 530 Lines—the second Book will be a 100 lines less. I can transcribe both legibly in three single-sheet Letters—you will only be so good as to inform me, *whither* & *whether* I am to send them. If they are likely to be of any service to Tomkins, he is welcome to them / if not I shall send them to the Morning Post. I have given a *faithful* Translation in blank Verse / . To have *decorated* Gesner would have been indeed 'to spice the spices'—to have lopped & pruned *somewhat*, would have only produced incongruity / to have done it *sufficiently* would have been to have published a poem of my own, not Gesner's—I have aimed at nothing more than purity & elegance of English, a keeping & harmony in the color of the Style, & a smoothness without monotony in the Versification. If I have succeeded, as I trust, I have, in these respects, my Translation will be just so much better than the original, as metre is better than prose, in *their* judgments at least, who prefer blank Verse to Prose. —I was probably too severe on the *morals* of the Poem—uncharitable perhaps, but I am a homebrewed Englishman, and tolerate downright grossness more patiently than this coy and distant Dallying with the Appetites. 'Die Pflanzen entstehen aus dem Saamen, gewisse Thiere gehen aus den Eyern hervor, andre so, andre anders. *Ich hab' es alles bemerkt; was hab' ich auch sonst zu thun?*' *&c &c &c* Now I apprehend that it will occur to 19 readers out of 20, that a maiden so *very curious*, so exceedingly *inflamed & harrassed by a Difficulty*, & so *subtle* in the discovery of even comparatively *distant* analogies, would necessarily have seen the difference of sex in her Flocks & Herds, & the MARITAL as well as maternal character could not have escaped her /. Now I avow, that the grossness & vulgar plain Sense of Theocritus's Shepherd Lads, bad as it is, is in my opinion less objectionable than Gesner's Refinement—which necessarily leads the imagination to Ideas without *expressing them*—Shaped & cloathed—the mind of a pure Being would turn away from them, from natural delicacy of Taste / but in that shadowy half-being, that state of nascent Existence in the Twilight of Imagination, and just on the vestibule of Consciousness, they are far more incendiary, stir up a more lasting commotion, & leave a deeper stain. The Suppression & obscurity arrays the simple Truth in a veil of something like Guilt, that is altogether *meretricious*, as opposed to the *matronly majesty*—of our Scriptures, for instance— / —and the Conceptions, as they *recede* from distinctness of *Idea*, *approximate* to the nature of *Feeling*, & gain thereby a closer & more immediate affinity with the appetites.——But independently of this, the whole passage, consisting of precisely one fourth of the whole Poem, has not the least Influence on the *action* of the Poem / and it is scarcely too much to say, that it has nothing to do with the main Subject / except indeed it be pleaded that *Love* is induced by compassion for this maiden to make a young man *Dream* of her, which young man had been, without any influence of this said Cupid, deeply interested in the story—& therefore did not need the interference of Cupid at all ——any more than he did the assistance of Æolus, for a fair wind all the way to an Island, that was within sight of Shore.—

I translated the Poem, partly, because I could not endure to appear *irresolute & capricious* to you, in the first undertaking which I had connected in any way with your person—in an undertaking, which I connect with our journey from Keswick to Grasmere, the Carriage in which we were, your Son, your Brother, your daughter, & your wife—all of whom may God Almighty bless!—a Prayer not the less fervent, my dear Sir! for being a little out of place here—— & partly too, because I wished to force myself out of metaphysical trains of Thought—which, when I trusted myself to my own Ideas, came upon me uncalled—& when I wished to write a poem, beat up Game of far other kind—instead of a Covey of poetic Partridges with whirring wings of music, or wild Ducks *shaping* their rapid flight in forms always regular (a still better image of Verse) up came a metaphysical Bustard, urging it's slow, heavy, laborious, earth-skimming Flight, over dreary & level Wastes. To have done with poetical Prose (which is a very vile Olio) Sickness & some other & worse afflictions, first forced me into *downright metaphysics* / for I believe that by nature I have more of the Poet in me / In a poem written during that dejection to Wordsworth, &

the greater part of a private nature—I thus expressed the thought —in language more forcible than harmonious.[1]——

    Yes, dearest Poet, yes!
There was a time when tho' my Path was rough,
The Joy within me dallied with Distress,
And all Misfortunes were but as the Stuff
Whence Fancy made me Dreams of Happiness:
For Hope grew round me, like the climbing Vine,
And Fruit and Foliage, not my own, seem'd mine.
But now Afflictions bow me down to Earth—
Nor car'd[2] I, that they rob me of my Mirth;
But O! each Visitation
Suspends what Nature gave me at my Birth,
My shaping Spirit of Imagination!
— — — — — — — —
— — — — — — — — [sic]
For not to think of what I needs must feel,
But to be still & patient all I can;
And haply by abstruse research to steal
From my own Nature all the natural Man;
This was my sole Resource, my wisest Plan—
And that which suits a part infects the whole,
And now is almost grown the Temper of my Soul!

Thank Heaven! my better mind has returned to me—and I trust, I shall go on rejoicing.—As I have nothing better to fill the blank space of this Sheet with, I will transcribe the introduction of that Poem to you, that being of a sufficiently general nature to be interesting to you.—The first Lines allude to a stanza in the Ballad of Sir Patrick Spence—'Late, late yestreen, I saw the new Moon With the old Moon in her arms; and I fear, I fear, my master dear, There will be a deadly Storm.'—

   Letter written Sunday Evening, April 4.

### 1

Well! if the Bard was weatherwise who made
The dear old Ballad of Sir Patrick Spence,
This Night, so tranquil now, will not go hence
Unrous'd by Winds, that ply a busier Trade

---

[1] These selections from the 4 Apr. 1802 draft of *Dejection* indicate that Coleridge was already working over his poem some months before it was first published in the *Morning Post*.

[2] care [Cancelled word in line above.]

## To William Sotheby

Than that, which moulds yon Clouds in lazy Flakes,
Or the dull sobbing Draft, that drones and rakes
Upon the Strings of this Eolian Lute,
Which better far were mute.
For lo! the New-moon, winter-bright;
And overspread with phantom Light;
(With swimming phantom Light o'erspread,
But rimm'd and circled with a silver Thread;)
I see the old Moon in her Lap, foretelling
The coming on of Rain & squally Blast!
And O! that even now the Gust were swelling,
And the slant Night-shower driving loud & fast!

A Grief without a Pang, void, dark, & drear!
A stifling, drowsy, unimpassioned Grief,
That finds no natural Outlet, no Relief
In word, or Sigh, or Tear!
This, William! well thou know'st,
Is that sore Evil which I dread the most,
And oft'nest suffer. In this heartless Mood,
To other Thoughts by yonder Throstle woo'd
That pipes within the Larch-tree, not unseen—
(The Larch, that pushes out in Tassels green
It's bundled Leafits) woo'd to mild Delights
By all the tender Sounds & gentle Sights
Of this sweet Primrose-Month—& vainly woo'd!
O dearest Poet, in this heartless Mood
All this long Eve so balmy & serene
Have I been gazing on the western Sky
And it's peculiar Tint of yellow-green—
And still I gaze—& with how blank an eye!
And those thin Clouds above, in flakes & Bars,
That give away their Motion to the Stars;
Those Stars, that glide behind them or between,
Now sparkling, now bedimm'd, but always seen;
Yon Crescent Moon, as fix'd as if it grew
In it's own cloudless starless Lake of Blue—
A Boat becalm'd! thy own sweet Sky-Canoe!
I see them all, so excellently[1] fair!
I *see*, not *feel*, how beautiful they are!

  My genial Spirits fail,
  And what can these avail

[1] E. H. C. (*Letters*, i. 381) reads 'exquisitely'.

( 816 )

### 19 July 1802

To lift the smoth'ring Weight from off my Breast?
    It were a vain Endeavor,
    Though I should gaze for ever
On that green Light, that lingers in the West.
I may not hope from outward Forms to win
The Passion & the Life, whose Fountains are within.

O Wordsworth! we receive but what we give,
And in our Life alone does Nature live:
Our's is her Wedding-garment, our's her Shroud!
And would we aught behold of higher Worth
Than that inanimate cold World *allow'd*
To the poor loveless ever-anxious Crowd,
Ah! from the Soul itself must issue forth
A Light, a Glory, a fair luminous cloud
    Enveloping the Earth!
And from the Soul itself must there be sent
A sweet and pow'rful Voice, of it's own Birth,
Of all sweet Sounds the Life and Element!
O pure of Heart! thou need'st not ask of me
*What* this strong Music in the Soul may be—
What and wherein it doth exist,
This Light, this Glory, this fair luminous Mist,
This beautiful and beauty-making Power!
Joy, blameless Poet! Joy, that ne'er was given
Save to the Pure, and in their purest Hour,
Joy, William! is the Spirit & the Power
That wedding Nature to us gives in Dow[er]
    A new Earth and new Heaven
Undreamt of by the Sensual and the Proud![1]
Joy is that sweet Voice, Joy that luminous cloud—[2]
    We, we ourselves rejoice!
And thence comes all that charms or ear or sight,
All Melodies an Echo of that Voice,
All colors a suffusion from that Light!

Calm stedfast Spirit, guided from above,
O Wordsworth! friend of my devoutest choice,
Great Son of Genius! full of Light & Love!
    Thus, thus dost[3] thou rejoice.

---

[1] E. H. C. (*Letters*, i. 382) reads 'Undream'd of by the sensual and proud—'
[2] E. H. C. (ibid.) omits this line.
[3] may'st [Cancelled word in line above.]

## To William Sotheby

    To thee do all things live from pole to pole,
    Their Life the Eddying of thy living Soul!
    Brother & Friend of my devoutest choice,
    Thus may'st thou ever, ever more rejoice!

I have selected from the Poem which was a very long one, & truly written only for 'the solace of sweet Song', all that could be interesting or even pleasing to you—except indeed, perhaps, I may annex as a *fragment* a few Lines on the Eolian Lute, it having been introduced in it's Dronings in the 1st Stanza. I have used 'Yule' for Christmas.

    ——Nay, wherefore did I let it haunt my mind
      This dark distressful Dream?
I turn from it, & listen to the Wind
Which[1] long has rav'd unnotic'd! What a Scream
Of Agony by Torture lengthen'd out
That Lute sent forth![2] O thou wild Storm without,
Bare Crag, or mountain Tairn, or blasted Tree,
Or Pine-grove, whither Woodman never clomb
Or lonely House long held the Witches' Home,
Methinks, were fitter Instruments for Thee,
Mad Lutanist! that in this month of Showers,
Of dark-brown Gardens & of peeping Flowers
Mak'st Devil's Yule, with worse than wintry Song
The Blossoms, Buds, & timorous Leaves among!
Thou Actor, perfect in all tragic Sounds!
Thou mighty Poet, even to Frenzy bold!
    What tell'st thou now about?
'Tis of the rushing of an Host in Rout
With many Groans from men with smarting Wounds—
At once they groan with Pain, & shudder with the Cold!
But hush! there is a Pause of deepest[3] Silence!
Again!—but all that Noise, as of a rushing crowd,
With Groans, & tremulous Shudderings, all is over;
And it has other Sounds, less fearful & less loud.
    A Tale of less affright
    And temper'd with delight,
As thou thyself had'st fram'd the tender Lay—
    'Tis of a little Child
    Upon a heathy[4] Wild

    [1] That [Cancelled word in line above.]
    [2] E. H. C. (*Letters*, i. 383) reads 'out'.
    [3] E. H. C. (ibid.) reads 'deeper'.
    [4] E. H. C. (ibid. 384) reads 'heath'.

Not far from home—but she has lost her way;
And now moans low in utter Grief & Fear,
And now screams loud & hopes to make her Mother hear.—

My dear Sir! ought I to make an apology for troubling you with such a long verse-cramm'd Letter?—O that instead of it I could but send to you the Image now before my eyes—Over Bassenthwaite the Sun is setting, in a glorious rich *brassy* Light—on the top of Skiddaw, & one third adown it, is a huge enormous Mountain of Cloud, with the outlines of a mountain——this is of a starchy Grey—but floating fast along it, & upon it, are various Patches of sack-like Clouds, bags & woolsacks, of a shade lighter than the brassy Light of the clouds that hide the setting Sun—a fine yellow-red somewhat more than sandy Light—and these the highest on this mountain-shaped cloud, & these the farthest from the Sun, are suffused with the darkness of a stormy Color.—Marvellous creatures! how they pass along!——Remember me with most respectful kindness to Mrs & Miss Sotheby, & the Captains Sotheby——

truly, your's, S. T. Coleridge

### 446. To Messrs. Edwards, Templer, & Co.

*Address*: Messrs Edwards, Templer, and Co, | Bankers | Stratford Place | London    Post pay'd
*MS.* Maurice Inman, Inc. *Hitherto unpublished.*
*Postmark*: 23 July 1802.    *Stamped*: Keswick.

Greta Hall, Keswick, Cumberland
Tuesday, July 20, 1802

Sirs

I have this day drawn on your Bank for the sum of 50£, at six weeks' date, payable to Mr William Jackson or order—according to permission given me by Josiah Wedgewood Esq., this 50£ making up the whole of the 150£, which I was permitted to draw on you for, in the present year—

I remain, | Gentlemen, | with great respect | Your obedient humble | Servant

S. T. Coleridge.

### 447. To John Prior Estlin

*Address*: Revd Mr Estlin | Bristol    *Single sheet.*
MS. Bristol Central Lib. *Pub.* Letters to Estlin, 82.
*Postmark*: 29 July ⟨1802⟩.    *Stamped*: Keswick.

Greta Hall, Keswick, July 26, 1802
My dear Friend

Day after day, and week after week, have I been intending to write to you / to enumerate all the causes of the delay (superadded alas! to my inveterate habit of Procrastination) would make my present Letter a very different one from what I wish it to be / a doleful instead of a cheerful one. I am at present in better health than I have been—tho' by no means strong or well—*& at home all is Peace & Love.* I am about shortly to address a few Letters to the British Critic[1] on the use of the definitive article, & the inferences drawn from it by Grenville Sharp,[2] & since attempted to be proved in a very learned & industrious work by the Revd C. Wordsworth, a fellow of Trinity, our Wordsworth's Brother. Sharp's Principle is as follows—When καί connects two nouns (*not of the Plural number, and not Proper names*) if the article ὁ, or any of it's cases, precedes the first of the said Nouns or Participles, and is not repeated before the second Noun or Participle, the latter always relates to the same Person, that is expressed or described by the first Noun or Participle / ex. gr. Ὁ Θεὸς καὶ[3] Πατὴρ τοῦ Κυρίου ἡμῶν &c 2. Cor. 1.3.—Τυχικὸς ὁ ἀγαπητὸς Ἀδελφὸς καὶ[4] Διάκονος &c Eph. VI. 21.—from which rule he deduces absolute assertions of the Godhead of Christ from Acts XX. 28. Eph. V. 5. 2. Thessal. I. 12. 1. Timoth. V. 21. 2. Timoth. IV. 1. Titus II. 13. 2. Peter I. 1. Jude 4.—Kit Wordsworth's Book is occupied in proofs that *all* the *Greek* Fathers, & many & those the most learned of the Latin Fathers did so understand these Texts, when from the nature of the Arian Controversy it would have answered their purposes much better to have understood the words according to our present Versions.—The first thing, that stared me in the face & which I afterwards found true, is that all the instances, but two, are to all

---

[1] Chambers thinks the review of Christopher Wordsworth's *Six Letters to Granville Sharp*, 1802, in the *British Critic*, xx. 15, was probably written by Coleridge. *Life*, 159. In an unpublished passage from a letter to Poole, dated 28 Jan. 1810, however, Coleridge says: 'On the first appearance of Christopher Wordsworth's Book on the Subject I studied the matter seriously; [and] but for accidents should have published on it.'

[2] Granville Sharp, *Remarks on the Uses of the Definitive Article in the Greek Text of the New Testament*, 1798.

[3] Underlined twice in MS.

[4] Underlined once in MS.

intents & purposes *Proper Names* & consequently fall within Grenville Sharpe's own Exception—the two instances, which I have not found used as a Proper name, are Titus II. 13. & 2 Peter I. 1.— Now if you know any proof of Σωτήρ being used without an article, in any place where it stands by itself—in the same manner as Christ is, and God—and as Κύριος I can prove to be in a hundred instances in Greek—you would serve me—& what is a much greater inducement to you—throw Light on a very important subject / or if you know any instance in which Sharp's Rule is falsified. / In English now, *exem. causâ*, we might say, as I walked out to day, whom should I meet but the Carpenter & Shoemaker of our Village / ? it would certainly be more *accurate* to say *the* Carpenter & *the* Shoemaker / but the accuracy of Special Pleading is to be found in few Books—nor is it necessary—You would know that I had met TWO Persons, because you know that the trades of Carpenter & Shoemaker are not one in this country—whereas if I had said, the Carpenter & Joiner / tho' the form of Grammar would have been the same, you would have known instantly that I had met but *one* man. If you recollect in Aristophanes, &c or the Septuagint any instances to this purpose, you would oblige me by transmitting them to me. Unfortunately I have none of the Greek Fathers—neither have I the Septuagint—but I have found much that I want, in Suicerus's Thesaurus Patrum,[1] which I was lucky enough to buy for it's weight at a Druggist's——

In these Letters I purpose to review Horsley's & Priestley's controversy[2]—& in these you will see my *Confessio Fidei*, which as far as regards the Doctrine of the Trinity is *negative* Unitarianism— a non liquet concerning the nature & being of Christ—but a condemnation of the Trinitarians as being wise beyond what is written. / On the subjects of the original corruption of our Nature, the doctrines of Redemption, Regeneration, Grace, & Justification by Faith my convictions are altogether different from those of Drs Priestley, Lindsey, & Disney—neither do I conceive Christianity to be tenable on the Priestleyan Hypothesis. I read Lardner[3] often—not so much for the information, I gain from him—which is however very great—but for the admirable modesty & truly Christian Spirit which breathe thro' his works—& which I wish to imbibe as a man, & to imitate as a Writer—well aware of the natural Impetuosity & *Warburtonianism* of my own uncorrected

---

[1] J. C. Suicerus, *Thesaurus Ecclesiasticus e Patribus Graecis* . . . , 2 vols., 1682.
[2] Joseph Priestley, *Defences of Unitarianism for the Years 1788 and 1789. Containing Letters to Dr. Horsley* . . . , 1790.
[3] Nathaniel Lardner, *Works*, 11 vols., 1788, the edition to which Coleridge refers.

Disposition. My dear Friend—believe no idle Reports concerning me / *if* I differ from you, & *wherein* I differ from you, it will be that I believe *on the whole more* than you, not less—of which I give, I trust, the best proof in my power, by breeding up my Child in *habits* of awe for Deity, & undoubted Faith in the truth in Christ. ——I thank you from the Bottom of my Heart for the pleasure & instruction which I have received from your sermon on the Sabbath—which I have read *repeatedly*—& shall take occasion to speak of, as in my humble opinion incomparably the best work that has been written on the Subject—as far as I have seen / & a sufficient answer to (what I had before believed unanswerable) Paley's objections.—It grieved me that you should have [applied] the word *Genius* so emphatically (p. 26) to Evanson[1] / for surely you wrote it unthinkingly—Is not Evanson egregiously a *weak & vain* man? God forgive me, if I *speak* uncharitably—I am sure I do not feel so—but his Book on the Dissonance of the Evangelists struck me as the silliest & most vapid Book, I ever perused / . Σφόδρα τοι σμικρὸς ὢν τὸν νοῦν, ὡς ἂν ἐκ τῶν αὐτοῦ λόγων τεκμηράμενον εἰπεῖν, φαίνεται[2]—the Papias among the Unitarians. (La[r]dn. Vol. II. p. 108.)—I wish, you would give us in some form or other, in Magazine or separate Publication, a real History in the spirit of Lardner of all that can be collected of the opinions of the Jews, & Jewish Doctors, concerning the Messiah / antecedent to the time of Christ, & since that time.——I have been rather dissatisfied with Lardner's answer to the IVth & last objection to the philosophical explication of the Daemoniacs—Do be so good as to look to the passage—Vol. I. p. 483.[3]—Dr Lardner intimates that it was not Christ's business to instruct men in Physics—that it was foreign to his Mission—that he was engaged in teaching the principles of *true* Religion—& that any debate on this error might have diverted him from his main work. The Jews were not in danger of Idolatry—there was therefore no urgent necessity [—and he a]dds two insta[nces] in which our Lord studiously declined to concern himself with things foreign to the office of a Prophet—. Now the first of these Instances seems to me to weigh against Lardner / Christ might have confuted a dangerous error without involving any question of natural or metaphysical philosophy—he did not decide for or against the doctrine of Pre-existence; but he most effectually quashed the pernicious *moral* error of attributing all afflictions to direct Judgments of God upon the Individual so

---

[1] Edward Evanson, *Arguments against the Sabbatical Observance of the Sunday*, 1792.
[2] Eusebius' comment on Papias, *Historia Ecclesiastica*, iii. 39, par. 13.
[3] Coleridge refers to Lardner's *The Credibility of the Gospel History*.

*26 July 1802*

afflicted. If the Evangelists had in any one passage merely called the Daemoniacs Diseased men, or insane men, 'whose diseases are believed by the people to proceed from Daemons'—or—diseases, the true causes of which are not revealed to us, but which are believed to proceed from Daemons / there would have been, I conceive[, no] physical hypothesis implied, & yet the Gospel saved fro[m the] apparent Ignominy of having confirm[ed by] it's author[ity a beli]ef so wild & inhuman. In Dr Lardner's sec[ond] Instance I [do not] agree with him that 'it could not but [be a good] work to decide' that cause, as the Brother required—On th[e contrary it] appears to me, that if Christ had done so, he would have [recognized?] institutions of individual Property / & the alliance of spiritu[al] authority with concerns of a purely secular Nature. But to [be more] orderly—. 1. It was not his business to instruct men in natural [phil]osophy—*Answer*. True! But it was a grievous *moral* Error—as well as physical absurdity—& might have been removed without any decision in physics, at least so far as that his Religion could not have been chargeable with aiding & *confirming* it. 2. It was foreign to his Mission, which was to instruct men in the Principles of true Religion. *Answer*. True Principles cannot be taught but by the subversion of false ones. This is eminently the practice in the Gospel of Christ—more than half of Christ's Discourse on the Mount is consumed in exploding errors—elsewhere he is open & urgent in the same—even so with St Paul / . Do, my dear Friend! read what Lardner says p. 462. 463. & 464.—& then decide in your own mind on the baseness & pernicious effects of such a superstition / You know human Nature too well not to know that a mind in terror of Spirits & attributing diseases to their malice may not be strictly *idolatrous*—but it is impossible that such a mind can be a *worshipper of the true* God— in the proper, Christian, & spiritual meaning of worshippers in Spirit & in Truth. But not only did it imply frightful corruption, in the great article of all Religion, the moral attributes of God; but it must needs have had a bad effect & an anti-social Influence, on the intercourse between man & man.—It is not fair, my dear Sir! to state it as a mere popular *opinion* / it was a reigning & inveterate superstition accompanied by the most wicked practices —all the impostures & delusions of Exorcism / vide p. 486. 487. Yet so far are these Exorcists from being condemned by Christ, that their Innocence is cited by him to prove his own. Matth. XII. 27. 28.—Dr Lardner's Exposition of these two Verses, p. 489. appears to me exceedingly arbitrary, & utterly destitute of probability or plausibility—. Indeed, I confess, it shocked me, in so dear & every way excellent a man / . If you see this matter in a different

Light, & approve of Lardner's Exposition, I will state my objections to it at length / at present I have no room on the paper. 3. It was not immediately connected with his Mission—& there was no urgent Necessity. *Answer.* It *was* (ὥς μοι δοκεῖ) immediately connected with his Mission / For how could those be deemed sane or proper judges of true miracles, who gave evidence in favor of false ones? St Paul (as Dr Lardner himself shews, p. 453) directly asserts the existence of wicked Spirits swarming in the air, [&] in a state of enmity to man. Eph. VI. 11. 12. Without pressing at all too hardly on the nature of evidence I think we may be permitted to say, that men who believed that six thousand Spirits dwelt in the Body of one man, & after they were forced to leave it, went into two thousand Pigs, three Devils to one Pig, must have been credulous or unreasoning men / & might, as far as this remained without a counterbalance / have been fairly challenged as unfit to be upon a Jury in a question of miracles. But God be praised! we can shew that an ample counterbalance did exist—yet still Christianity is chargeable with having confirmed & *taught* a pernicious error— / The infidelical argument from Christian Wars, Crusades, &c is childish / Christianity was the pretext, not the cause—but of the horrible Burnings & Drownings of thousands of Men & Women, as Witches, and all the irreverent & inhuman feelings towards aged & hypochondriacal People Christianity might seem to have been directly & properly the cause—For when the Physicians & natural Philosophers earnestly laboured to inculcate humane & true opinions on this subject, they were silenced by the authority of the Gospel, and their efforts for a long time frustrated, as you may easily convince yourself by reading the controversies concerning Witches / I have stated the argument, as I wish to state every argument, with as much force as if I were a compleat convert to it—. I hope to hear from you on the subject / and then I will give you all I can say in solution of the Difficulty—which I confess appears to me a very serious one. I meant to have said much to Mrs Estlin—& I am at the end of the Paper. May God preserve & bless her, & you, & your little ones,

    your affect. & grateful Friend, S. T. Coleridge

## 448. *To Sara Hutchinson*

*Address*: Miss S. Hutchinson | Gallow Hill | Wykeham | Malton | Yorkshire
Single Sheet
*MS. Dove Cottage. Pub. with omis. Chambers, Life, 336.*
*Stamped*: Keswick.

Tuesday, July 27, 1802

My dearest Sara

If the weather with you be what it is here, our dear Friends[1] must have had a miserable Day yesterday. It rained almost incessantly at Keswick; till the late Evening, when it fell a deep Calm, & even the Leaves, the very topmost Leaves, of the Poplars & Aspens had Holiday, & like an overworked Boy, consumed it in sound Sleep. The whole Vale presented a curious Spectacle / the Clouds were scattered by the wind & rain in all shapes & heights, above the mountains, on their sides, & low down to their Bases—some masses in the middle of the valley—when the wind & rain dropt down, & died—and for two hours all the Clouds, white & fleecy all of them, remained without motion, forming an appearance not very unlike the Moon as seen thro' a telescope. On the Mountains directly opposite to our House (in Stoddart's Tobaccojuice Picture) the Clouds lay in two ridges ‗ ‗ ‗ ‗ ‗ ‗ with a broad, strait *road* between them, they being the *walls* of the Road. Blessings on the mountains! to the Eye & Ear they are always faithful. I have often thought of writing a set of *Play-bills* for the vale of Keswick—for every day in the Year—announcing each Day the Performances, by his Supreme Majesty's Servants, Clouds, Waters, Sun, Moon, Stars, &c.—To day the weather is mild—tho' (as Mrs Bancroft informed my wife in a note last week) '*the humid Aspect of the general Atmosphere is eminently hostile to my fondly-cherished Hopes.*' For I wait only for a truly fine Day to walk off to St Bees. Best compliments to the River Bee, & if he have any commands to the Saint, his Relation, I shall be happy to communicate the same.—I write now in order to send dear Tom word of an advertisement in the Whitehaven Paper of to day—concerning Lord Lowther's Farms—'To be let by private Contract, & entered upon at Candlemas, 1803—I Woodhouse Demesne, in the Parish of Barton, 274 acres. 2. Sockbridge Demesne, in the said Parish, with Sockbridge High Field, & High Field Closes, containing together about 323 acres, with ten Cattle Gaits on Tirrill High Moor. 3. The Lands in Sockbridge called Louth. But, with the House & Croft in Sockbridge (late Stockdale's) containing together about 48 acres,

[1] On 26 July William and Dorothy Wordsworth left Gallow Hill for London, on their way to France.

448]  *To Sara Hutchinson*

with 5 Cattle Gaits on Tirrill High Moor. 4. A Farm in Clifton called Town-end Tenement, with Long Lands containing together about 112 acres. 5. A Farm, called Abbots' Farm, near Melkinthorpe, about 95 acres, with FOSTER PASTURE, about 30 acres. 6. Lands near Lowther, called WALKER'S GRASSING about 30 acres. 6. KNIPE SCARS, with the Land called WARTHEY'S & SHAP BECK TENEMENT, about 587 acres. 7. WHALE ING near WHALE (expressively so called) about 48 acres. N.B. Grows capital Train Oil, & Bones for Old Maids' Stays. I recommend this Farm to Tom's particular attention.—8. Lands, part of Meaburn Demesne, with the Park, about 268 acres. 9. Hartson Demesne with it's extensive Sheep Heaths. 10. Wet Sleddale Demesne. 11. Wastdale Head & Foot with Demings & it's extensive Sheep Heaths. (The Farm of the three last Farms may be accommodated at a fair Price with what number they choose of the same Heath-going Sheep &c) 12. Frenchfield Estate, near Penrith, 170 acres, recommended to adventurers in Manufactures—All persons desirous of taking any of these to transmit their Proposals in Writing under Seal to John Richardson, Esquire, at Lowther Hall, Westmoreland, before the 29th of September next.[']—O would that Lot 11 were as good for FARMER Tom, as it would be for FRIEND TOM. I know it well—the situation is fine beyond description, eleven miles from Keswick, thro' Borrodale!! Ravenglass is it's market Town. I have no doubt the Farm would answer capitally, but for one Thing—The People of England, 'od rabbit 'em! are not Stone-eaters—if they were, I don't know a Place in which there is a greater Plenty & variety of that solid & substantial Food. What soft washy pap-like Stuff is a piece of Beef compared with a stout Flint! But there is no persuading People to their own good! So we will have done with it.—As I have been transcribing, I must give you a touch out of WARNER's [']Tour thro' the northern Counties'[1]—. P. 14. Vol. 1. 'In the walks of Literature &c &c Bristol has made & still makes a figure, &c &c. The gigantic Intellect & sublime Genius of COLERIDGE, which were here first publicly developed, &c &c. CHATTERTON, second only to his MONODIST (see COLERIDGE's monody on the Death of Chatterton) &c. Southey's Muse also poured forth those beautiful &c & the two COTTLES have given from *their own Press* works which would add to the fame of any Poets *of the Day*.'—Ha! Ha! Ha!—even to the fame of GIANT COLERIDGE, I suppose!—Now isn't this a Proof, that it does not depend altogether on a man's own Prudence whether or no he is to become ridiculous. Vol. 2. p. 100. 'The animated, enthusiastic, & accom-

---

[1] Richard Warner, *A Tour through the Northern Counties of England, and the Borders of Scotland*, 2 vols., 1802.

*27 July 1802*

plished COLERIDGE, whose residence at Keswick gives additional charm to it's impressive Scenery, inspired us with Terror (A LYING SCOUNDREL!) while he described the universal Uproar (O Lord! what a lie!) that was awakened thro' the mountains by a sudden Burst of involuntary Laughter in the Heart of their Precipices; an incident, which a kindred Intellect, his Friend & Neighbour at Grasmere, WORDSWORTH (whose L.B. exclusively almost of all modern Compositions, breathe the true nervous & simple Spirit of Poetry) has worked up into the following admirable effusion / ['] here follows *Joanna*.—Could you believe now, that the Rogue made up all this out of my telling him, that Wordsworth's Echo, tho' purposely beyond Nature, was yet only an *exaggeration* of what really would happen—for that I myself with John Wordsworth & William had laughed aloud at Stickle Tarn in Langdale, & that the effect was quite enough to justify the Poem from being more extravagant, than it was it's purpose to be.—Whatever I told him, the Fellow has murdered in this way—a book fuller of Lies & Inaccuracies & Blunders was, I believe, on my conscience, never published. From foolish men, that write Books, Lord deliver me!— It has been my Lot to be made a Fool of by Madmen, & represented as a Madman by Fools!

Mrs Coleridge is but poorly—the Children are tolerable—I am but so so / this Weather has been my Enemy. O that I may be well & look bonny when you all come to us!——Dear Hartley—!— I picked up a parcel of old Books at Wilkinson's which he gave me / among them is an old System of Philosophy by some FANTASTIC or other, with a large Print of Sun, Moon, & Stars, Birds, Beasts, & Fishes——with Adam & Eve, rising out of a Chaos!— Derwent immediately recognized the Horse & Cow—Hos! CU!—& then putting his finger to Eve's Bosom, said—*Ma!*—*Ma!* PAP!— Ma—pap!—i.e. his Mother's or Mary's bosom / into which he puts his little Hand when he is petting. But I asked Hartley what he thought of it—& he said—[']it is *very* curious! A Sea not in a World, but a World rising out of a Sea! (these were his own umprompted words, & entirely his own idea)—There they all are— Adam & all!—Well! I dare say, they stared at one another finely!' —This strikes me as a most happy image of the Creation—Yesterday, *crazy* Peter Crosthwaite (not the Museum Peter) came in to Mr Jackson—(and Mrs Wilson & Hartley only were at home)— Hartley soon found out that he was crazy, turned pale & trembled —& Mrs W. snatched him up & brought him in to us / as soon as he came in, he cried aloud in an agony, nor could we appease him for near a quarter of an hour—When I talked to him how foolish it was, Well! says he, you know, I am always frightened at things that are not like other things. But, Hartley! said I—you would not be frightened if you were to see a number of new Beasts or Birds or Fishes in a Shew—Yes—said he! when I was a little Boy, I was frightened at the Monkey & the Dromedary in London (*so he was, poor fellow! God knows*)—but now I am not frightened at them, *because they are like themselves*. What do you mean, Hartley? —'Don't ask me so many questions, Papa! I can't bear it. I mean, that I am frightened at men that are not like men / a Monkey is a monkey—& God made the Dromedary—but Peter is a crazy man—he has had a chain upon him!'—Poor fellow! when he recovered, he spent the whole afternoon in whirling about the Kitchen, & telling Mrs Wilson wild Stories of his own extempore composition about mad men & mad animals—all frightful: for tho' he cannot endure the least approximation to a sorrowful Story from another Person, all his own are most fantastically tragical. ——O dear Sara!—how dearly I love you! Dear Mary! Heaven bless you & send back our dear Friends to you! S. T. Coleridge.

### 449. To Robert Southey

*Address*: R. Southey Esq. | St James's Place | King's Down | Bristol     *Single Sheet*
MS. Lord Latymer, *Pub. with omis.* Letters, *i. 384.*
*Postmark*: 31 July 1802.    *Stamped*: Keswick.

July 29, 1802. Greta Hall, Keswick
My dear Southey

Nothing has given me half the pleasure these many many Months as last week did Edith's Heralding to us of a minor Robert: for that it will be a boy, one always takes for granted. From the bottom of my heart, I say it, I never knew a man that better deserved to be a Father by right of virtues that eminently belonged to him, than yourself /; but besides this, I have cheering hopes that Edith will be born again—& be a healthy woman.—When I said, nothing had given me half the pleasure, I spoke truly, and yet said more than you are perhaps aware of—for by Lord Lonsdale's Death there are excellent Reasons for believing, that the Wordsworths will gain 5000£ / the share of which (and no doubt Dorothy will have more than a mere share) will render William Wordsworth & his Sister quite independent. They are now in Yorkshire—& he returns in about a month, *one of us*.—A part of your today's Letter shocked me exceedingly—it is the first Breath that I have heard respecting it—I mean, Wade's Failure / for so, I suppose, I am to understand it—and it is heavy to me in a double way, for William Read's Loss. Wade ever behaved to me with steady & uniform affection / his Distresses or Misfortunes would afflict me severely—& what are these compared with immoral conduct? I trust & have full faith, that he is more sinned against than sinning. Estlin's Sermons, I fear, are mere moral Discourses. If so, there is but small chance of their Sale. But if he had published a *volume* of sermons, of the same kind with those which he has published singly—i.e. apologetical & ecclesiastico-historical, *I am almost* confident, they would have a respectable circulation. Single Sermons to *publish* is almost always a foolish thing—like single sheet quarto poems— / Estlin's sermon on the Sabbath really surprized me / it was well-written, in style I mean / and the reasoning throughout is not only sound, but has a cast of novelty in it—a superior Sermon altogether it appeared to me——I am myself a little theological—and if any Bookseller will take the risque, I shall in a few weeks, possibly, send to the Press a small Volume under the Title of 'Letters to the British Critic concerning Grenville Sharp's Remarks on the uses of the Definitive article in the Greek Text of the new Testament, & the Revd C. Wordsworth's Six Letters to G. Sharp Esq. in confirmation of the same / together with a Review of the Controversy between Horsley & Priestly respecting the faith of the Primitive Christians.'—This is no mere Dream, like my Hymns to the Elements / for I have written more than half the work / —I purpose afterwards to publish a Book—Concerning Tythes & Church Establishment—for I conceit, that I can throw great Light on the Subject / You are not apt to be much surprized at any change in my mind, active as it is—but it will perhaps please you to know, that I am become very fond of History—and that I have read much with very great attention. / — I exceedingly like the Job of Amadis de Gaul[1]—I wish, you may half as well like the Job, in which I shall very shortly appear. Of it's sale I have no doubt; but of it's prudence?—There's the Rub. —Concerning Poetry, & the characteristic Merits of the Poets, our Contemporaries—one Volume Essays, the second Selections / the Essays are on Bloomfield, Burns, Bowles, Cowper, Campbell, Darwin, Hayley,[2] Rogers, C. Smith, Southey, Woolcot,[3] Wordsworth—the Selections from every one, who has written at all, any way above the rank of mere Scribblers—Pye & his Dative Case Plural, Pybus,[4] Cottle &c &c[5]—The object is not to examine what is good

[1] Southey's *Amadis of Gaul*, 1803.
[2] William Hayley (1745–1820), author of *The Triumph of Temper*, 1781.
[3] John Wolcot (Peter Pindar) (1738–1819), poet and satirist.
[4] H. J. Pye (1745–1813), poet laureate, and C. S. Pybus, author of *The Sovereign. Addressed to Paul, Emperor of All the Russias*, 1800.
[5] Concerning these projected works, Southey wrote in reply: 'You spawn

in each writer, but what has ipso facto pleased, & to what faculties or passions or habits of the mind they may be supposed to have given pleasure / Of course, Darwin & Wordsworth having given each a defence of *their* mode of Poetry, & a disquisition on the nature & essence of Poetry in general, I shall necessarily be led rather deeper—and these I shall treat of either first or last / But I will apprize you of one thing, that altho' Wordsworth's Preface is half a child of my own Brain / & so arose out of Conversations, so frequent, that with few exceptions we could scarcely either of us perhaps positively say, which first started any particular Thought—I am speaking of the Preface as it stood in the second Volume [edition?]—yet I am far from going all lengths with Wordsworth / He has written lately a number of Poems (32 in all) some of them of considerable Length / (the longest 160 Lines) the greater number of these to my feelings very excellent Compositions / but here & there a daring Humbleness of Language & Versification, and a strict adherence to matter of fact, even to prolixity, that startled me / his alterations likewise in Ruth perplexed me / and I have thought & thought again / & have not had my doubts solved by Wordsworth / On the contrary, I rather suspect that some where or other there is a radical Difference in our theoretical opinions respecting Poetry— / this I shall endeavor to go to the Bottom of—and acting the arbitrator between the old School & the New School hope to lay down some plain, & perspicuous, tho' not superficial, Canons of Criticism respecting Poetry.—What an admirable Definition Milton gives quite in an obiter way—when he says of Poetry—that it is '*simple, sensuous, passionate.*'!—It truly comprizes the whole, that can be said on the subject. In the new Edition of the L. Ballads there is a valuable appendix, which I am sure you must like / & in the Preface itself considerable additions, one on the Dignity & nature of the office & character of a Poet, that is very grand, & of a sort of Verulamian Power & Majesty—but it is, in parts, (and this is the fault, me judice, of all the latter half of that Preface) obscure beyond any necessity—& the extreme elaboration & almost constrainedness of the Diction contrasted (to my feelings) somewhat harshly with the general style of the Poems, to which the Preface is an Introduction. Sara (why, dear Southey! will you write it always, Sara*h*?—Sar*a*, methinks, is associated with times that you & I cannot & do not wish ever to forget) Sara said with some acuteness, that she wished all that Part of the Preface to have been in Blank Verse—& vice versa &c—However, I need not say, that any diversity of opinion

plans like a herring; I only wish as many of the seed were to vivify in proportion.' *Life and Corres.* ii. 190.

### 29 July 1802

on the subject between you & myself, or Wordsworth and myself, can only be small, taken in a *practical* point of view. /

I rejoice that your History marches on so victoriously.[1] It is a noble Subject, and I have the fullest confidence of your success in it—The influence of the Catholic Religion—the influence of national Glory on the individual morals of a people—especial[l]y in the Downfall of the Nobility of Portugal—the strange fact (which seems to be admitted as with one voice by all Travellers) of the vileness of the Portuguese Nobles compared with the Spanish —and of the superiority of the Portuguese Commonalty to the same Class in Spain / the effects of Colonization on a small & not very fruitful Country / the effects, important & too often forgotten effects, of absolute *accidents*, such as the particular Character of a race of Princes, on a nation—O what aweful subjects these are!— I long to hear you read a few Chapters to me——But I conjure you, do not let Madoc go to Sleep. O that without words I could cause you to *know* all that I think, all that I feel, all that I hope, respecting that Poem! As to myself, all my poetic Genius, if ever I really possessed any *Genius*, & it was not rather a mere general *aptitude* of Talent, & quickness in Imitation / is gone—and I have been fool enough to suffer deeply in my mind, regretting the loss— which I attribute to my long & exceedingly severe Metaphysical Investigations—& these partly to Ill-health, and partly to private afflictions which rendered any subject, immediately connected with Feeling, a source of pain & disquiet to me /

> There was a Time when, tho' my Path was rough,
> I had a heart that dallied with distress;
> And all Misfortunes were but as the Stuff,
> Whence Fancy made me dreams of Happiness:
> For Hope grew round me, like the climbing Vine,
> And Fruits and Foliage, not my own, seem'd mine!
> But now Afflictions bow me down to Earth—
> Nor car'd I, that they robb'd me of my Mirth /
> But oh! each Visitation
> Suspends what Nature gave me at my Birth,
> My shaping Spirit of Imagination!

(Here follow a dozen Lines that would give you no pleasure & then what follows—)

> For not to *think* of what I needs must *feel*;
> But to be still and patient all, I can—
> And haply by abstruse Research to steal

---

[1] Southey did not complete his projected history of Portugal.

From my own Nature all the natural Man /
This was my sole Resource, my wisest Plan!
And that which suits a part, infects the Whole,
And now is almost grown the Temper of my Soul.——

Having written these Lines, I rejoice for you as well as for myself, that I am able to inform you, that now for a long time there has been more Love & Concord in my House, than I have known for years before. I had made up my mind to a very aweful Step—tho' the struggles of my mind were so violent, that my sleep became the valley of the Shadows of Death / & my health was in a state truly alarming. It did alarm Mrs Coleridge—the thought of separation wounded her Pride—she was fully persuaded, that deprived of the Society of my children & living abroad without any friends, I should pine away—& the fears of widowhood came upon her—And tho' these feelings were wholly selfish, yet they made her *serious*—and that was a great point gained—for Mrs Coleridge's mind has very little that is *bad* in it—it is an innocent mind—; but it is light, and *unimpressible*, warm in anger, cold in sympathy—and in all disputes uniformly *projects* itself *forth* to recriminate, instead of turning itself inward with a silent Self-questioning. Our virtues & our vices are exact antitheses—I so attentively watch my own Nature, that my worst Self-delusion is, a compleat Self-knowlege, so mixed with intellectual complacency, that my q[uick]ness to see & readiness to acknowlege my faults is too often frustrated by the small pain, which the sight of them give[s] me, & the consequent slowness to amend them. Mrs C. is so stung by the very first thought of being in the wrong that she never amends because she never endures to look at her own mind at all, in it's faulty parts—but shelters herself from painful Self-enquiry by angry Recrimination. Never, I suppose, did the stern Match-maker bring together two minds so utterly contrariant in their primary and organical constitution. Alas! I have suffered more, I think, from the amiable propensities of my nature than from my worst faults & most erroneous Habits—and I have suffered much from both—But as I said—Mrs Coleridge was made *serious*—and for the first time since our marriage she felt and acted, as beseemed a Wife & a Mother to a Husband, & the Father of her children—She promised to set about an alteration in her external manners & looks & language, & to fight against her inveterate habits of puny Thwarting & unintermitting Dyspathy—this immediately—and to do her best endeavors to cherish other *feelings*. I on my part promised to be more attentive to all her feelings of Pride, &c &c and to try to correct my habits of impetuous & bitter censure—. We have both kept our Promises—& she has found herself so much more happy, than she had been for years before, that I have the most confident Hopes, that this happy Revolution in our domestic affairs will be permanent, & that this external Conformity will gradually generate a greater inward Likeness of thoughts, & attachments, than has hitherto existed between us. Believe me, if you were here, it would give you a deep delight to observe the difference of our *minutely* conduct towards each other, from that which, I fear, could not but have disturbed your comforts, when you were here last. Enough. But I am sure, you have not felt it tedious—

So Corry & you are off? I suspected it; but Edith never mentioned an iota of the Business to her Sister.—It is well. It was not your Destiny. Where ever you are, God bless you!—My health is weak enough; but it is so far amended that it is far less dependent on the influences of weather. The mountains are better friends in this respect.—Would that I could flatter myself, that the same would be the case with you. The only objecti[on] on my part is now, God be praised! done away—the services, & benefits, I should receive from your society & the spur of your example, would be incalculable. The house consists, the first Floor, or rather ground Floor, of a Kitchen, & a Back Kitchen, a large Parlour, & two nice small Parlours—the second Floor, of three Bed rooms, one a large one, & one large Drawing Room / the third Floor or Floors, of three Bed rooms—in all of 12 Rooms—besides these, Mr Jackson offers to make that nice Out-house, a Workshop, either two Rooms, or one noble Large one, for a Study—if I wish it.—If it suited you, you might have one Kitchen or (if Edith & Sara thought it would answer) we might have the two Kitchens in common / —You might have, I say, the whole Ground Floor, consisting of two sweet Wing-rooms, commanding that loveliest view of Borrodale, & the great Parlour / and supposing we each were forc'd to have two servants, a nurse-maid & a housemaid—the two house-maids would sleep together in one of the upper Rooms and the Nursemaids have each a room to herself—One of the Wing Rooms on the Ground Floor must be your & Edith's Room / and if Mary be with you, the other hers— / We should have the whole second Floor—consisting of the Drawing Room, which would be Mrs Coleridge's Parlour, two Bedrooms, which (as I am so often ill, & when ill cannot rest at all, unless I have a bed to myself) is absolutely necessary for me / & one room, for you, if occasion should be / or any friend of your's or mine.—The highest Room in the house is a very large one, intended for two; but suffered to remain one by my Desire. It would be [a] capital, healthy Nursery.—The outhouse would become my Study—and I *have* a Couch-Bed, on which I am now sitting (*in bed*) & writing to you—it is now in the Study—of course, would be removed to the Outhouse, when that became my Study—and would be a second Spare-bed.—I have no doubt, but that Mr Jackson would willingly let us retain my present Study—which might be your Library & Study Room.—My dear Southey—I merely state these Things to you. All our Lot on earth is Compromise—Blessings obtained by Blessings foregone, or by Evils undergone. I should be glad, no doubt, if you thought that your Health & Happiness would find a home under the same Roof with me; and I am sure, you will not accuse me as indelicate or obtrusive in mentioning things as they are / but if you decline it altogether, I shall know that you have good reasons for so doing—& be perfectly satisfied—for if it detracted from your comfort, it could of course be nothing but the contrary of all advantage to me. You would have access to 4 or 5 Libraries—Sir W. Lawson's, a most magnificent one but chiefly in Natural History, Travels—&c—Carlton House (I am a PRODIGIOUS Favorite of Mrs Wallis, the Owner & Resident, mother of the Privy Counsellor Wallis), Carlisle Dean & Chapter, the Library at Hawkshead School, & another (of what value, I know not) at St Bees—whither I mean to walk tomorrow, & spend 5 or 6 days, for Bathing—it is four miles from Whitehaven by the Sea side.——

Mrs Coleridge is but poorly—children well. Love to Edith & Mary—& to all, in whom I am at all interested. God love you—. If you let me hear from you, it is among my FIRMEST RESOLVES, god ha' mercy on 'em! to be a regular Correspondent of your's—

S. T. Coleridge

P.S. Mrs C. must have one room on the ground floor—but this is only putting one of your rooms on the second Floor——

### 450. To Sara Hutchinson

*Transcript Sara Hutchinson, in Mr. A. H. B. Coleridge's possession. Pub. Wordsworth and Coleridge, ed. by E. L. Griggs, 1939, pp. 150–7.* The original of this letter, along with those of Letters 451 and 456, has disappeared, but the text has survived in the form of a journal made from them by Sara Hutchinson. This letter and the one following describe the first six days of a solitary tour, begun 1 August and completed 9 August, which carried Coleridge to the top of Scafell.

[1–5 August 1802]

On Sunday Augt. 1st—½ after 12 I had a Shirt, cravat, 2 pair of Stockings, a little paper & half a dozen Pens, a German Book (Voss's Poems) & a little Tea & Sugar, with my Night Cap, packed up in my natty green oil-skin, neatly squared, and put into my *net* Knapsack / and the Knap-sack on my back & the Besom stick in my hand, which for want of a better, and in spite of Mrs C. & Mary, who both raised their voices against it, especially as I left the Besom scattered on the Kitchen Floor, off I sallied—over the Bridge, thro' the Hop-Field, thro' the Prospect Bridge at Portinscale, so on by the tall Birch that grows out of the center of the huge Oak, along into Newlands——Newlands is indeed a lovely Place—the houses, each in it's little Shelter of Ashes & Sycamores, just under the Road, so that in some places you might leap down on the Roof, seemingly at least—the exceeding greenness & pastoral beauty of the Vale itself, with the savage wildness of the Mountains, their Coves, and long arm-shaped & elbow-shaped Ridges—yet this wildness softened down into a congruity with the Vale by the semicircular Lines of the Crags, & of the bason-like Concavities. The Cataract between Newlands & Kescadale had but little water in it / of course, was of no particular Interest— / I passed on thro' the green steep smooth bare Kescadale / a sort of unfurnished Passage or antechamber between Newlands & Buttermere, came out on Buttermere & drank Tea at the little Inn, & read the greater part of the Revelations—the only part of the new Testament, which the Scotch Cobler read—because why? *Because it was the only part that he understood.* O 'twas a wise Cobler! . . .[1] Conceive an enormous round Bason mountain-high of solid Stone / cracked in half & one half gone / exactly in the remaining half of this enormous Bason, does Buttermere lie, in this [2] beautiful & stern Embracement of Rock / I left it, passed by Scale Force, the white downfal[l] of which glimmered thro' the Trees, that hang before it like bushy Hair over a madman's Eyes, and climbed 'till I gained the first Level / here it was 'every man his own pathmaker,' & I went directly cross it—upon soft mossy Ground, with many a hop, skip, & jump, & many an occasion for observing the Truth of the old Saying: where Rushes grow, A Man may go. Red Pike, a dolphin-shaped Peak of a deep red, looked in upon me from over the Fell on my Left, on my right I had, first Melbreak (the Mountain on the right of Crummock, as you ascend the Lake) then a Vale running down with a pretty Stream in it, to Loweswater / then Heck [Hen] Comb, a Fell of the same height & running in the same direction with Melbreak, a Vale on the other side too,—and at the bottom of both these Vales the Loweswater Fells running abreast. Again I reached an ascent, climbed up, & came to a ruined Sheepfold—a wild green view all around me, bleating of Sheep & noise

[1] Three-quarters of line inked out in MS.
[2] Small diagram at this point which is not reproduced here.

( 835 )

of waters—I sate there near 20 minutes, the Sun setting on the Hill behind with a soft watery gleam; & in front of me the upper Halves of huge deep-furrowed Grasmire [Grassmoor] (the mountain on the other side of Crummock) & the huge Newland & Buttermere Mountains, & peeping in from behind the Top of Saddleback. Two Fields were visible, the highest cultivated Ground on the Newland side of Buttermere, and the Trees in those Fields were the only Trees visible in the whole Prospect.—I left the Sheepfold with regret—for of all things a ruined Sheepfold in a desolate place is the dearest to me, and fills me most with Dreams & Visions & tender thoughts of those I love best—Well! I passed a bulging roundish-headed green Hill to my Left, (and to the left of it was a frightful Crag) with a very high round-head right before me; this latter is called Ennerdale-Dodd, and bisects the ridge between Ennerdale & Buttermere & Crummock—I took it on my right hand, & came to the top of the bulging green Hill, on which I found a small Tarn, called Flatern [Floutern] Tarn, about 100 yds. in length, & not more than 7 or 8 in breadth, but O! what a grand Precipice it lay at the foot of! The half of this Precipice (called Herd house) nearest to Ennerdale was black, with green moss-cushions on the Ledges; the half nearest to Buttermere a pale pink, & divided from the black part by a great streamy Torrent of crimson Shiver, & Screes, or Shilly (as they call it). I never saw a more heart-raising Scene. I turned & looked on the Scene which I had left behind, a marvellous group of mountains, wonderfully & admirably arranged—not a single minute object to interrupt the oneness of the view, excepting those two green Fields in Buttermere—but before me the glorious Sea with the high Coast & Mountains of the Isle of Mann, perfectly distinct—& three Ships in view. A little further on, the Lake of Ennerdale (the lower part of it) came in view, shaped like a clumsy battle-dore—but it is, in reality, exactly *fiddle-shaped*. The further Bank & the higher part, steep, lofty, bare bulging Crags; the nether Bank green & pastoral, with Houses in the shelter of their own dear Trees.—On the opposite Shore in the middle & narrow part of the Lake there bulges out a huge Crag, called angling Stone / being a famous Station for anglers—and the reflection of this Crag in the Water is admirable —pillars or rather it looks like the pipes of some enormous Organ in a rich golden Color.—I travelled on to Long Moor, two miles below the foot of the Lake, & met a very hearty welcome from John Ponsonby, a Friend of Mr. Jackson's—here I stayed the night, [1 August] & the greater part of Monday—the old man went to the head of the Lake with me / the mountains at the head of this Lake & Wast-dale are the Monsters of the Country, bare bleak

*1–5 August 1802*

Heads, evermore doing deeds of Darkness, weather-plots, & storm-conspiracies in the Clouds—their names are Herd house, Bowness, Wha Head, Great Gavel, the Steeple, the Pillar, & Seat Allian [Seatallan].—I left Long Moor after Tea, & proceeded to Egremont, 5 miles—thro' a very pleasant Country, part of the way by the River Enna [Ehen], with well wooded Banks, & nice green Fields, & pretty houses with Trees, and two huge Sail-cloth Manufactories—went to Girtskill, a mercer, for whom I had a Letter, but he was at Workington, so I walked on to St. Bees, 3 miles from Egremont—when I came there could not get a Bed—at last got an apology for one, at a miserable Pot-house; slept [2 August] or rather dozed, in my Clothes—breakfasted there—and went to the School & Church ruins—had read in the history of Cumbd. that there was an 'excellent Library presented to the School by Sr. James Lowther,' which proved to be some 30 odd Volumes of commentaries on the Scripture utterly worthless—& which with all my passion for ragged old Folios I should certainly make serviceable . . .[1] for fire-lighting. Men who write Tours and County histories I have by woeful experience found out to be *damned Liars*, harsh words, but true!—It was a wet woeful oppressive morning—I was sore with my bad night—walked down to the Beach, which is a very nice hard Sand for more than a mile / but the St. Bees Head which I had read much of as a noble Cliff, might be made a song of on the Flats of the Dutch Coast—but in England 'twill scarcely bear a looking-at.—Returned to Egremont, [3 August] a miserable walk—dined there, visited the Castle, the Views from which are uncommonly interesting—I looked thro' an old wild Arch—slovenly black Houses, & gardens, as wild as a Dream, over the hills beyond them, which slip down in one place making a noticeable Gap—had a good Bed, slept well—& left Egremont this morning [4 August] after Breakfast, had a pleasant walk to Calder Abbey—an elegant but not very interesting Ruin, joining to a very han[d]some Gentleman's House built of red freestone, which has the comfortable warm look of Brick without it's meanness & multitude of puny squares. This place lies just within the Line of circumference of *a Circle* of woody Hills—the area, a pretty Plain half a mile perhaps in diameter—and completely cloathed & hid with wood, except one red hollow in these low steep hills, & except behind the Abbey, where the Hills are far higher, & consist of green Fields almost (but not quite) to the Top. Just opposite to Calder Abbey, & on the Line of the Circumference, rises Ponsonby Hill, the Village of Calder Bridge, & it's interesting Mill, all in Wood, some hidden, some roofs just on a line with the

[1] Two or three words inked out in MS.

Trees, some higher, but Ponsonby Hall far higher than the rest.—
I regained the Road, and came to Bonewood, a single Alehouse on
the top of the hill above the Village Gosforth—drank a pint of
Beer (I forgot to tell you that the whole of my expences at St. Bees,
a glass of Gin & Water, my Bed, & Breakfast amounted to 11d.)—
from this Bonewood is a noble view of the Isle of Man on the one
side, & on the other side all the bold dread tops of the Ennerdale
& Wastdale Mountains / . Indeed the whole way from Egremont
I had beautiful Sea Views, the low hills to my right dipping down
into inverted Arches, or Angles, & the Sea, often with a Ship seen
thro'—while on my left the Steeple, & Sca' Fell facing each other,
far above the other Fells, formed in their interspace a great Gap
in the Heaven.—So I went on, turned eastward, up the Irt, the
Sea behind & Wastdale Mountains before—& here I am—

Wed. Afternoon[1] ½ past 3, Augt. 4th. 1802—
Wastdale, a mile & half below the Foot of the Lake, at an Alehouse
without a Sign, 20 strides from the Door, under the Shade of a
huge Sycamore Tree, without my coat—but that I will now put
on, in prudence—yes here I am / and have been for something
more than an hour, & have *enjoyed* a good Dish of Tea (I carried
my Tea & sugar with me) under this delightful Tree. In the House
there are only an old feeble Woman, and a '*Tallyeur*' Lad upon
the Table—all the rest of the Wastdale World is a haymaking,
rejoicing and thanking God for this first downright summer Day
that we have had since the beginning of May.—And now I must
go & see the Lake / for immediately at the Foot of the Lake runs
a low Ridge so that you can see nothing of the Water till you are
at it's very Edge.

Between the Lake and the Mountains on the left, a low ridge of
hill runs parallel with the Lake, for more than half it's length; &
just at the foot of the Lake there is a Bank even & smooth & low
like a grassy Bank in a Gentleman's Park. Along the hilly Ridge
I walked thro' a Lane of green Hazels, with hay-fields & Hay-
makers on my Right, beyond the River Irt, & on the other side
of the River, Irton Fell with a deep perpendicular Ravine, & a
curious fretted Pillar of Clay crosier-shaped, standing up in it—
next to Ireton Fells & in the same line are the Screes, & you can
look at nothing but the Screes tho' there were 20 quaint Pillars
close by you. The Lake is wholly hidden 'till your very Feet touch
it, as one may say / and to a Stranger the Burst would be almost
overwhelming. The Lake itself seen from it's Foot appears indeed

---

[1] This passage on the alehouse appears at the beginning of the Sara Hutchin-
son journal but is placed here to preserve the chronology of Coleridge's tour.

*1–5 August 1802*

of too regular shape; exactly like the sheet of Paper on which I am writing, except it is still narrower in respect of it's length. (In reality however the Lake widens as it ascends, and at the head is very considerably broader than at the foot.) But yet, in spite of this it is a marvellous sight / a sheet of water between 3 & 4 miles in length, the whole (or very nearly the whole) of it's right Bank formed by the Screes, or facing of bare Rock of enormous Height, two thirds of it's height downwards absolutely perpendicular; & then slanting off in *Screes*, or Shiver, consisting of fine red Streaks running in broad Stripes thro' a stone colour—slanting off from the Perpendicular, as steep as the meal newly ground from the Miller's spout.—So it is at the foot of the Lake; but higher up this streaky Shiver occupies two thirds of the whole height, like a pointed Decanter in shape, or an outspread Fan, or a long-waisted old maid with a fine prim Apron, or—no, other things that would only fill up the Paper.—When I first came the Lake was a perfect Mirror; & what must have been the Glory of the reflections in it! This huge facing of Rock *said* to be half a mile in perpendicular height, with deep Ravin[e]s the whole *winded* [wrinkled?] & torrent-worn, except where the pink-striped Screes come in, as smooth as silk / all this reflected, turned into Pillars, dells, and a whole new-world of Images in the water! The head of the Lake is crowned by three huge pyramidal mountains, Yewbarrow, Sca' Fell, & the great Gavel; Yewbarrow & Sca' Fell nearly opposite to each other, yet so that the *Ness* (or Ridge-line, like the line of a fine Nose,) of Sca' Fell runs in behind that of Yewbarrow, while the Ness of great Gavel is still farther back, between the two others, & of course, instead of running athwart the Vale it directly faces you. ⟨ ⟩ The Lake & Vale run nearly from East to west and this figure below will give you some idea of it.—[1]

Melfell [Middle Fell] (lying South [north] of the Lake) consists of great mountain steps decreasing in size as they approach the Lake.

My Road led along under Melfell & by Yewbarrow—& now I came in sight of it's other side called Keppel Crag & then a huge enormous bason-like Cove called Green Crag [Red Pike?] / as I suppose, from there being no single Patch of Green to be seen on any one of it's perpendicular sides—so on to Kirk Fell, at the foot of which is Thomas Tyson's House where W[ordsworth] & I slept Novr. will be 3 years—& there I was welcomed kindly, had a good Bed, and left it after Breakfast.

[1] But the Transcriber has not ingenuity enough to copy it, nor the full length Portrait of the Author—so they must be dispensed with—[Note by Sara Hutchinson.]

## To Sara Hutchinson

Thursday Morning, Augt. 5th—went down the Vale almost to the water head, & ascended the low Reach between Sca' Fell and the Screes, and soon after I had gained it's height came in sight Burnmoor Water, a large Tairn \\/ nearly of that shape, it's Tail towards Sca' Fell, at its head a gap forming an inverted arch with Black Coomb & a peep of the Sea seen thro' it.—It lies directly at the Back of the Screes, & the stream that flows from it down thro' the gap, is called the Mite—and runs thro' a Vale of it's own called Miterdale, parallel with the lower part of Wastdale, and divided from it by the high Ridge called Ireton Fells. I ascended Sca' Fell by the side of a torrent, and climbed & rested, rested & climbed, 'till I gained the very summit of Sca' Fell—believed by the Shepherds here to be higher than either Helvellyn or Skiddaw—Even to Black Coomb—before me all the Mountains die away, running down westward to the Sea, apparently in eleven Ridges & three parallel Vales with their three Rivers, seen from their very Sources to their falling into the Sea, where they form (excepting their Screw-like flexures) the *Trident* of the Irish Channel at Ravenglass——O my God! what enormous Mountains these are close by me, & yet below the Hill I stand on / Great Gavel, Kirk Fell, Green Crag, & behind the Pillar, then the Steeple, then the Hay Cock—on the other side & behind me, Great End, Esk Carse [Hause], Bow-fell & close to my back two huge Pyramids, nearly as high as Sca' Fell itself, & indeed parts & parts of Sca' Fell known far & near by these names, the hither one of Broad Crag, and the next to it but divided from it by a low Ridge Doe Crag, which is indeed of itself a great Mountain of stones from a pound to 20 Ton weight embedded in wooly Moss. And here I am *lounded*—so fully lounded—that tho' the wind is strong, & the Clouds are hast'ning hither from the Sea—and the whole air seaward has a lurid Look—and we shall certainly have Thunder—yet here (but that I am hunger'd & provisionless) *here* I could lie warm, and wait methinks for tomorrow's Sun / and on a nice Stone Table am I now at this moment writing to you—between 2 and 3 o'Clock as I guess / surely the first Letter ever written from the Top of Sca' Fell! But O! what a look down just under my Feet! The frightfullest Cove that might ever be seen / huge perpendicular Precipices, and one Sheep upon it's only Ledge, that surely must be crag! Tyson told me of this place, & called it Hollow Stones. Just by it & joining together, rise two huge Pillars of bare lead-colored stone— / I am no measurer / but their height & depth is terrible. I know how unfair it is to judge of these Things by a comparison of past Impressions with present—but I have no shadow of hesitation in saying that the Coves & Precipices of Helvellin are nothing to these! But [from] this sweet lounding Place I see directly thro' Borrowdale, the Castle Crag, the whole of Derwent Water, & but for the haziness of the Air I could see my own House —I see clear enough where it stands——

Here I will fold up this Letter—I have Wafers in my Inkhorn / & you shall call this Letter when it passes before you the Sca' Fell Letter[1] / —I must now drop down, how I may into Eskdale—that lies under to my right—the upper part of it the wildest & savagest surely of all the Vales that were ever seen from the Top of an English Mountain / and the lower part the loveliest.——

## 451. To Sara Hutchinson

*Transcript Sara Hutchinson, in Mr. A. H. B. Coleridge's possession. Pub. Wordsworth and Coleridge, ed. by E. L. Griggs, 1939, pp. 158–63.*

Eskdale, Friday, Augt. 6th. [1802] at an Estate House called Toes

There is one sort of Gambling, to which I am much addicted; and that not of the least criminal kind for a man who has children & a Concern.—It is this. When I find it convenient to descend from a mountain, I am too confident & too indolent to look round about & wind about 'till I find a track or other symptom of safety; but I wander on, & where it is first *possible* to descend, there I go—relying upon fortune for how far down this possibility will continue. So it was yesterday afternoon. I passed down from Broad-crag, skirted the Precipices, and found myself cut off from a most sublime Crag-summit, that seemed to rival Sca' Fell Man in height, & to outdo it in fierceness. A Ridge of Hill lay low down, & divided this Crag (called Doe-crag) & Broad-crag—even as the Hyphen divides the words broad & crag. I determined to go thither; the first place I came to, that was not direct Rock, I slipped down, & went on for a while with tolerable ease—but now I came (it was midway down) to a smooth perpendicular Rock about 7 feet high—this was nothing—I put my hands on the Ledge, & dropped down / in a few yards came just such another / I *dropped* that too / and yet another, seemed not higher—I would not stand for a trifle / so I dropped that too / but the stretching of the muscle[s] of my hands & arms, & the jolt of the Fall on my Feet, put my whole Limbs in a *Tremble*, and I paused, & looking down, saw that I had little else to encounter but a succession of these little Precipices—

[1] 'The Sca' Fell Letter' was posted to Sara Hutchinson at Gallow Hill, Yorkshire, from Ambleside on Sunday evening, 8 Aug. Cf. Letter 453. The transcript contains no conclusion or signature.

it was in truth a Path that in a very hard Rain is, no doubt, the
channel of a most splendid Waterfall.—So I began to suspect that
I ought not to go on / but then unfortunately tho' I could with
ease drop down a smooth Rock 7 feet high, I could not *climb* it / so
go on I must / and on I went / the next 3 drops were not half
a Foot, at least not a foot more than my own height / but every
Drop increased the Palsy of my Limbs—I shook all over, Heaven
knows without the least influence of Fear / and now I had only
two more to drop down / to return was impossible—but of these
two the first was tremendous / it was twice my own height, & the
Ledge at the bottom was [so] exceedingly narrow, that if I dropt
down upon it I must of necessity have fallen backwards & of course
killed myself. My Limbs were all in a tremble—I lay upon my
Back to rest myself, & was beginning according to my Custom to
laugh at myself for a Madman, when the sight of the Crags above
me on each side, & the impetuous Clouds just over them, posting
so luridly & so rapidly northward, overawed me / I lay in a state
of almost prophetic Trance & Delight—& blessed God aloud, for
the powers of Reason & the Will, which remaining no Danger can
overpower us! O God, I exclaimed aloud—how calm, how blessed
am I now / I know not how to proceed, how to return / but I am
calm & fearless & confident / if this Reality were a Dream, if I were
asleep, what agonies had I suffered! what screams!—When the
Reason & the Will are away, what remain to us but Darkness &
Dimness & a bewildering Shame, and Pain that is utterly Lord
over us, or fantastic Pleasure, that draws the Soul along swimming
through the air in many shapes, even as a Flight of Starlings in
a Wind.—I arose, & looking down saw at the bottom a heap of
Stones—which had fallen abroad—and rendered the narrow Ledge
on which they had been piled, doubly dangerous / at the bottom
of the third Rock that I dropt from, I met a dead Sheep quite
rotten—This heap of Stones, I guessed, & have since found that
I guessed aright, had been piled up by the Shepherd to enable him
to climb up & free the poor creature whom he had observed to be
crag-fast—but seeing nothing but rock over rock, he had desisted
& gone for help—& in the mean time the poor creature had fallen
down & killed itself.—As I was looking at these I glanced my eye
to my left, & observed that the Rock was rent from top to bottom
—I measured the breadth of the Rent, and found that there was
no danger of my being *wedged* in / so I put my Knap-sack round
to my side, & slipped down as between two walls, without any
danger or difficulty——the next Drop brought me down on the
Ridge called the How / I hunted out my Besom Stick, which I had
flung before me when I first came to the Rocks—and wisely gave

*6 August 1802*

over all thoughts of ascending Doe-Crag—for now the Clouds were again coming in most tumultuously—so I began to descend / when I felt an odd sensation across my whole Breast—not pain nor itching—& putting my hand on it I found it all bumpy—and on looking saw the whole of my Breast from my Neck [to my Navel][1] —& exactly all that my Kamell-hair Breast-shield covers, filled with great red heat-bumps, so thick that no hair could lie between them. They still remain / but are evidently less—& I have no doubt will wholly disappear in a few Days. It was however a startling proof to me of the violent exertions which I had made.—I descended this low Hill which was all hollow beneath me—and was like the rough green Quilt of a Bed of waters—at length two streams burst out & took their way down, one on [one] side a high Ground upon this Ridge, the other on the other—I took that to my right (having on my left this high Ground, & the other Stream, & beyond that Doe-crag, on the other side of which is Esk Halse, where the head-spring of the Esk rises, & running down the Hill & in upon the Vale looks and actually deceived me, as a great Turnpike Road—in which, as in many other respects the Head of Eskdale much resembles Langdale) & soon the channel sank all at once, at least 40 yards, & formed a magnificent Waterfall—and close under this a succession of Waterfalls 7 in number, the third of which is nearly as high as the first. When I had almost reached the bottom of the Hill, I stood so as to command the whole 8 Waterfalls, with the great triangle-Crag looking in above them, & on the one side of them the enormous & more than perpendicular Precipices & *Bull's-Brows*, of Sca' Fell! And now the Thunder-Storm was coming on, again & again!—Just at the bottom of the Hill I saw on before me in the Vale, lying just above the River on the side of a Hill, one, two, three, four Objects, I could not distinguish whether Peat-hovels, or hovel-shaped Stones—I thought in my mind, that 3 of them would turn out to be stones—but that the fourth was certainly a Hovel. I went on toward them, crossing & recrossing the Becks & the River & found that they were all huge Stones—the one nearest the Beck which I had determined to be really a Hovel, retained it's likeness when I was close beside / in size it is nearly equal to the famous Bowder stone, but in every other respect greatly superior to it—it has a complete Roof, & that perfectly *thatched* with weeds, & Heath, & Mountain-Ash Bushes—I now was obliged to ascend again, as the River ran greatly to the Left, & the Vale was nothing more than the Channel of the River, all the rest of the interspace between the mountains was a tossing up & down of Hills of all sizes—and the place at which I am now

[1] Words in brackets inked out in MS.

writing is called—*Te-as*, & spelt, *Toes*—as the Toes of Sca' Fell—.
It is not possible that any name can be more descriptive of the
Head of Eskdale—I ascended close under Sca' Fell, & came to a
little Village of Sheep-folds / there were 5 together / & the redding
Stuff, & the Shears, & an old Pot, was in the Passage of the first
of them. Here I found an imperfect Shelter from a Thunder-shower
—accompanied with such Echoes! O God! what thoughts were
mine! O how I wished for Health & Strength that I might wander
about for a Month together, in the stormiest month of the year,
among these Places, so lonely & savage & full of sounds!

After[1] the Thunder-storm I shouted out all your names in the
Sheep-fold—when Echo came upon Echo / and then Hartley &
Derwent & then I laughed & shouted Joanna[2] / It leaves all the
Echoes I ever heard far far behind, in number, distinctness &
*humanness* of Voice—& then not to forget an old Friend I made
them all say Dr. Dodd[3] &c.—

After the Storm I passed on & came to a great Peat-road, that
wound down a hill, called Maddock How, & now came out upon
the first cultivated Land which begins with a Bridge that goes
over a Stream, a Waterfall of considerable height & beautifully
wooded above you, & a great water-slope under you / the Gill down
which it falls, is called Scale Gill—& the Fall Scale Gill Force.
(The word Scale & Scales is common in this Country—& is said
by . . .[4] to be derived from the Saxon Sceala; the wattling of
Sheep—but judging from the places themselves, *Scale Force* & this
Scale Gill Force—I think it as probable that it is derived from
Scalle—which signifies a deafening Noise.) Well, I passed thro'
some sweet pretty Fields, & came to a large Farm-house where
I am now writing / The place is called Toes or *Te* as—the master's
name John Vicars Towers—they received me hospitably / I drank
Tea here & they begged me to pass the Night—which I did &
supped of some excellent Salmonlings, which Towers had brought
from Ravenglass whither he had been, as holding under the Earl
of Egremont, & obliged 'to ride the Fair'—a custom introduced
during the times of Insecurity & piratical Incursion for the Protection of Ravenglass Fair. They were a fine Family—and a Girl
who did not look more than 12 years old, but was nearly 15, was
very beautiful—with hair like vine-tendrils—. She had been long

---

[1] This paragraph, which forms the conclusion of this letter in the Sara Hutchinson journal, has been transferred to keep the events of the tour in chronological order.
[2] Cf. Wordsworth's poem, *To Joanna*.
[3] A reference to Dr. William Dodd, the forger.
[4] Name omitted in MS.

*6 August 1802* [451

ill—& was a sickly child—[']Ah poor Bairn! (said the Mother) worse luck for her / she looks like a Quality Bairn, as you may say.' This man's Ancestors have been time out of mind in the Vale / and here I found that the common Names, Towers, & Tozers are the same— / *er* signifies 'upon'—as Mite-er-dale the Dale upon the River Mite / Donnerdale—a contraction of Duddon-er-dale the Dale upon the River Duddon—So Towers, pronounced in the Vale *Te*-ars—& Tozers is [are] those who live on *the Toes*—i.e. upon the *Knobby* feet of the Mountain / Mr. *T*ears has mended my pen.— This morning after breakfast I went out with him, & passed up the Vale again due East, along a higher Road, over a heathy upland, crossed the upper part of Scale Gill, came out upon Maddock How, & then ascending turned directly Northward, into the Heart of the mountains; on my left the wild Crags under which flows the Scale Gill Beck, the most remarkable of them called Cat Crag (a wild Cat being killed there) & on my right hand six great Crags, which appeared in the mist all in a file—and they were all, tho' of different sizes, yet the same shape all triangles—. Other Crags far above them, higher up the Vale, appeared & disappeared as the mists passed & came / one with a waterfall, called Spout Crag— and another most tremendous one, called Earn [Heron] Crag—I passed on, a little way, till I came close under a huge Crag, called Buck Crag—& immediately under this is Four-foot Stone—having on it the clear marks of four foot-steps. The Stone is in it's whole breadth just 36 inches, (I measured it exactly) but the part that contains the marks is raised above the other part, & is just $20\frac{1}{2}$ Inches. The length of the Stone is $32\frac{1}{2}$ Inches. The first foot-mark is an Ox's foot—nothing can be conceived more exact—this is $5\frac{3}{4}$ Inches wide—the second is a Boy's shoe in the Snow, $9\frac{1}{2}$ Inches in length / this too is the very Thing itself, the Heel, the bend of the Foot, &c.—the third is the Foot-step to the very Life of a Mastiff Dog—and the fourth *is Derwent's very own first little Shoe*, 4 Inches in length & O! it is the sweetest Baby shoe that ever was seen.—The wie-foot in Borrowdale is contemptible; but this really does work upon my imagination very powerfully / & I will try to construct a Tale upon it / the place too is so very, very wild. I delighted the Shepherd by my admiration / & the four foot Stone is my own Christening, & Towers undertakes it shall hereafter go by that name for hitherto it has been nameless.—And so I returned & have found a Pedlar here of an interesting Physiognomy—& here I must leave off—for Dinner is ready[1]——

[1] Sara Hutchinson's transcript breaks off with Friday, 6 Aug. On 10 Aug. (Letter 453), after his return to Keswick, Coleridge wrote to Sara that he had not yet finished this 'Great-sheet' letter. Probably he never did so, for shortly

## 452. To Robert Southey

*Address*: Robert Southey Esq. | St James's Place | King's Down | Bristol
*Single Sheet*
MS. Lord Latymer. Pub. with omis. Letters, *i*. 393.
*Postmark*: 12 August 1802. *Stamped*: Keswick.

Monday Night, August 9, 1802

My dear Southey

Derwent can say his Letters—and if you could but see his darling Mouth, when he shouts out Q!—This is a Digression.—On Sunday August I. after morning church I left Greta Hall, crossed the fields to Portinscale, went thro' Newlands, where 'Great Robinson looks down upon Maiden's Bower,' and drank Tea at Buttermere—crossed the mountains to Ennerdale, & slept at a farm House a little below the foot of the Lake / Spent the greater part of the next Day mountaineering, & went in the evening thro' Egrement to St Bees & slept there—returned next day to Egremont & slept there—went by the Sea Coast as far as Gosforth, then turned off, & went up Wasdale, & slept at T. Tyson's at the head of the vale / Thursday morning crossed the mountains, & ascended Sca' fell, which is more than a 100 yards higher than either Helvellin or Skiddaw / spent the whole day among clouds, & one of them a frightening thunder-cloud—slipt down into Eskdale, & there slept—& spent good part of the next day—proceeded that evening to Devock Lake, & slept at Ulpha Kirk / on Saturday passed thro' the Donnerdale Mountains to Broughton Vale, Torvor Vale, & in upon Coniston / Sunday surveyed the Lake &c of Coniston, & proceeded to Bratha, and slept at Lloyd's House / this Morning walked from Bratha to Grasmere, & from Grasmere to Greta Hall—where I now am, quite sweet and ablute / & have but even now read thro' your Letter—which I will answer by the night's post, & therefore must defer all account of my very Interesting Tour—saying only that of all earthly things which I have beheld, the view *of* Sca' fell & *from* Sca' Fell, (*both* views from it's own summit) is the most heart-exciting. And now for business— The rent of the whole House, including Taxes, & the Furniture we have, will be not under 40£, & not above 42£ a year / You will have half the house, & half the furniture, and of course, your share will be either 20£ or 20 guineas. As to furniture, the house certainly will not be wholly, i.e. compleatly, furnished by Jackson / two rooms we must somehow or other furnish between us—but not *immediately*—you may pass the winter without it—& it is hard, if

afterwards Charles and Mary Lamb arrived at Greta Hall for a visit lasting three weeks.

we cannot raise 30£ in the course of the winter between us / and whatever we buy, may be disposed of any Saturday, to a moral certainty at it's full value / or Mr Jackson, who is uncommonly desirous that you should come, will take it—but we can put on for the winter well enough / .—Your Books may come all the way from Bristol either to Whitehaven, Maryport, or Workington / sometimes directly, always by means of Liverpool. In the latter case they must be sent to Whitehaven / from whence waggons come to Keswick twice a week.—You will have 20 or 30 shillings to lay out in Tin & Crockery—& you must bring with you, or buy here, which you may do at 8 months' credit, knives & forks, &c, and all your Linen from the diaper subvestments of the young Jacobin to diaper Table Cloths, Sheet[s], Napkins, &c. But these, I suppose, you already have.—What else I have to say, I can not tell / & indeed shall be too late for the Post. But I will write soon again /

I was exceedingly amused with the Cottelism / but I have not time to speak of this or of other parts of your Letter. I believe that I can execute the Criticisms with no Offence to Hayley, & in a manner highly satisfactory to the admirers of the Poet Bloomfield, & to the Friends of the Man Bloomfield. But there are certainly other objections of great weight.—Sara is well—and the children pretty well. Hartley is almost ill with transport at my Sca' Fell expedition / That child is a Poet, spite of the Forehead '*villainous low*,'[1] which his Mother smuggled into his Face. Derwent is more beautiful than ever—but very backward with his Tongue—altho' he can say all his Letters—N.B. Not out of Books. God bless you! & your's—

&

S. T. Coleridge

If you are able to determine, you will of course let me know it, without waiting for a second Letter from me / as if you determine in the affirmative of the Scheme, it will be a great motive with Jackson, indeed a most infallible one, to get immediately to work—so as to have the whole perfectly finished six weeks at least before your arrival.——

Another reason for your writing immediately is that we may lay you in a Stock of Coals during the summer, which is a saving of some Pounds.——When I say *determine*, of course, I mean—such determination, as the thousand Contingencies, black & white, permit a wise man to make / & which would be enough for me to act on.——

[1] *The Tempest*, IV. i. 250.

Sara will write to Edith soon—

*Sara* did not catch the ᵃ itch,[1] before her concubition with Abram / .—

I have just received a Letter from Poole—but I have found so many Letters, that I have opened your's only.——

### 453. To Sara Hutchinson

*Address*: Miss S. Hutchinson | Gallow Hill | Wykeham | Malton | Yorkshire
*MS. Dove Cottage. Pub. with omis. Chambers*, Life, *339*.
*Stamped*: Keswick.

August 10, 1802. Tuesday Evening

My dearest Sara

You will this morning, I trust, have received the Letter which I left at the Ambleside Post (the first, I came to) on Sunday Evening. I have half such another, the continuation of my tour, written; but on my arrival yesterday at my home, about 8 o'clock in the evening, I found 7 Letters for me / I opened none for an hour, I was so overglad to see the children again / and the first, I opened, I was forced to answer directly—which was as much as I could do, to save the Post—& to day I have been so busy letter-writing, that I have not time to finish the Great-sheet Letter—so must send a short one, briefly to say that I have received your two Letters, one of Monday, Aug. 2. inclosing the 5£—which I read last night, & had better left it alone, as I did 5 others—for it kept me awake longer than I ought to have been—and one this evening. I am well, & have had a very delightful & feeding Excursion, or rather Circumcursion.—When you did not hear from me, & in answer too to a letter containing a note, you should surely have concluded, my Darling! that I was not at home: for when do I neglect these things to those, I love? Other things, & weighty ones, God help me! I neglect in abundance / for instance / two little Boxes, which Dorothy fears, (& with abundant Reason) are lost— & which contain, besides my cloathes & several very valuable Books, all my written collections made in Germany—which taken merely in a pecuniary point of view are not worth less than 150£ to me.——More Rain coming! I broke off writing to look at the Sky / it was exactly 35 minutes after 7, which [was] 4 minutes after the real Sunset, and long long after the apparent sun-set behind our Vales—& I saw such a sight as I never before saw. Beyond Bassenthwaite at the end of the view was a Sky of bright yellow-green; but over that & extending all over Bassenthwaite,

[1] Coleridge again refers to Southey's spelling of Mrs. Coleridge's name— Sara*h*. Cf. Letter 449.

*10 August 1802*

& almost up to Keswick church a Cloud-Sky of the deepest most fiery Orange—Bassenthwaite Lake look'd like a Lake of 'blood-red Wine'—and the River Greta, in all it's winding, before our house, & the upper part of the Keswick Lake, were fiery red—even as I once saw the Thames when the huge Albion Mills were burning, amid the Shouts of an exulting Mob—but with one foot upon Walla Crag, and the other foot exactly upon Calvert's House at Windy Brow was one great Rainbow, *red* and *all* red, entirely formed by the Clouds——I have now seen all the Rain-bows, that, I suppose, are possible—the Solar Rainbow, with it's many colors, the grey lunar Rainbow, & a fiery red Rainbow, wholly from the Clouds after sunset!—

I seem, I know not why, to be beating off all Reference to Dorothy & William, & their Letters—I heard from Sotheby of their meeting—(tho' I did not read his Letter till after I had read your's—) I wish, I wish, they were back!——When I think of them in Lodgings at Calais, Goslar comes back upon me; & of Goslar I never think but with dejection.—[Dear little Caroline!—Will she be a ward of Annette?—Was the subject too delicate for a Letter? —][1] I suppose so.——To morrow morning they will leave Calais, if they indeed leave it 10 days after the Date of Dorothy's Letter / so that they will probably be with you, I would fain hope, by Monday next.—I saw old Molly yesterday / She was weakly, but '*mended*' from what she had been / the Rheumatic Pain & weakness had left her Back, & gone into her arms—I slept at Bratha on Sunday Night—& did not go on to Grasmere, tho' I had time enough, and was not over-fatigued; but tho' I have no objection to sleep in a lonely House, I did not like to sleep in *their* lonely House. I called the next day—went into the garden—pulled some Peas, & shelled & drest them, & eat them for my dinner with one rasher of Bacon boiled—but I did not go up stairs, nor indeed any where but the Kitchen. Partly I was very wet & my boots very dirty—& Molly had set the Pride of her Heart upon it's niceness— & still more—I had small desire to go up!

It was very kind in you, my Darlings! to send the 5£; (which I have now sent back) but it was not very wise. I could have easily procured 3 or 4£ from Mr Jackson / but I gave up the Residence at St Bees, because I began to reflect that in the present state of my finances I ought not to *spend* so much money. Thomas Ashburner's call was the *occasion* of my resolve not to go to St Bees; but my own after reflections were the *cause*.—In the course of my

---

[1] The words enclosed in brackets are heavily inked out in the manuscript. This is the only surviving reference to Annette and Caroline Vallon in Coleridge's letters.

Tour (& I was absent 9 days) I gave away to Bairns, & foot-sore Wayfarers four shillings, & some odd pence; & I *spent* nine shillings—sum total, £0″ 13s 0d—but to this must be added the wear & tear of my Boots, which are gone to be mended; & sixpence for a great knee-patch for my Pantaloons, which will not however be worn an hour the shorter time for the said large knee-patch. I have now *no clothes but what are patched at the elbows, & knees, & in the seat*—& I am determined to wear them *out & out*—& to have none till after Christmas.——Hartley is in good spirits; but he does not look well. Derwent too looks less rosy than usual—for we cannot keep him from the Gooseberries—Hartley says—[']He is far over wicked; but it's all owing to Adam, who did the same thing in Paradise.'—Derwent can *repeat* all the Letters; & can point out six or seven / O! that you could see his Darling mouth, when he shouts out Q.—But notwithstanding his *erudition*, he is very backward in his Tongue.—Lloyd's children are nice fair Babies; but there is nothing *lovely* in their countenances or manners.—I have seldom seen children, I was so little inclined to caress—fair & clean, as they were. O how many a cottage Bairn have I kissed or long'd to kiss, whose Cheeks I could scarce see for the healthy dirt—but these I had no wish to kiss!—There is a something in children that makes Love flow out upon them, distinct from beauty, & still more distinct from good-behaviour / I cannot say, God knows! that our children are even decently well-behaved—& Hartley is no beauty—& yet it has been the Lot of the two children to be beloved. They are the general Darlings of the whole Town: & wherever they go, Love is their natural Heritage.

Mrs Coleridge is now pretty well.—

God bless my darling Sara!—& thee, dear Mary! I will finish my long Letter, as soon as possible / but for the next 3 or 4 days I shall be exceedingly busy. Write immediately. Kind Remembrances to Tom & Joanna.—Bless you, my Darling!

                                     &

                                  S. T. Coleridge

I have received a large Wedgewood Jug, & a large Cup, finely embossed with figures, & thick-rimmed with silver, as a present, from—*Lady Rush*! with a *kind Note*.—I had a shrewd suspicion, that I was a favorite.——

Inclosed is the £5, 5s note.—

### 454. To Sara Hutchinson

*Address*: Miss S. [Hutchinson]   [*Sin*]*gle sheet*.
*MS. Dove Cottage. Hitherto unpublished.* These few lines, with a fragment of the address on the opposite side, are all that remain of Coleridge's letter.

[August 1802?][1]

... —the black thick Cloud indeed is still over my head, and all the Landscape around me is dark & gloomy with it's shadow—but the wind has risen, Darling! it blows this way a strong & steady gale, & I see already with the eye of confident anticipation the laughing blue sky, & no black thick Cloud!— ...

... write next to
... [Wor]dsworth, Gr ...
... [s]hall assuredly be ...
... [begin]ning of next wee[k] ...
... [ne]ver cease to do ...
... lovely!—S. T. C[oleridge]
... consumptive, is gone ...
... of gloomy Thoughts.—


### 455. To Robert Southey

[Addressed by Mrs. S. T. Coleridge] Mrs Southey | St James's-place | Kingsdown | Bristol.
*MS. Lord Latymer. Hitherto unpublished.* Coleridge's letter was written on the address sheet of a letter from Mrs. Coleridge to her sister, Mrs. Southey.
*Postmark*: ⟨1⟩4 August ⟨1802⟩. *Stamped*: Keswick.

[*Circa* 12 August 1802][2]

My dear Southey

Do let me hear from you / what of the Cow Pox & Loyola?— Marius, an Ecclesiastic of noble birth, a Swiss, who died Anno Domini 601—wrote a Latin Chronicle of his own Time, to be met with in Du Cheyne[3]—in *the year 570* he speaks of the Small Pox,

---

[1] This letter must have been written shortly after 10 Aug. 1802, because of the reference to Grasmere and to Wordsworth. In Letter 453 Coleridge speaks of the probable arrival of the Wordsworths at Gallow Hill by 'Monday next'.

[2] In the summer of 1802 the Southeys took a furnished house in the same row as the Danvers's home, where they had had lodgings the year before. The fact that Mrs. Coleridge did not use the name Danvers in the address, as well as references in her letter, indicates a date in Aug. 1802.

[3] *Marii Aventicensis Episcopi Chronicon* appeared in the first volume of André Du Chesne's *Historiae Francorum Scriptores* ... , 5 vols., 1636–49.

which was first introduced by the Abyssinians into Arabia when they conquered the Province of Hamyen [Yemen?]; & they called it the Locust-plague, believing it to have originated in the huge heaps of putrefying Locusts in the Desert.—From Arabia it was carried by Greek merchants to Constantinople—& from thence by the armies of Justinian in his Gothic War to Italy, Switzerland, & France. Marius expressly says of it; ['animalia bubula maxime interierunt—the Oxen & Cows *chiefly* died of it /' tho' he had before stated it's devastations among men as quite frightful. The Cattle plague in 1769 was pronounced by the Physicians in Denmark to be the genuine Small Pox—it was eradicated in England, Flanders, & the South of France by burying all the diseased Cattle with the Carcases entire, & with their Litter; but in Denmark it became *naturalized*—& they prevented it's ill effects by *inoculating* the Calves, which answered in all cases exactly as inoculation in the human species.—These facts seem to place the identity of the Small & cow pox out of all doubt—be so good as to mention them to Mr King & Dr Beddoes—& learn from them, whether the Facts have been adduced in any of the pamphlets of Jenner, Woodville,[1] & the rest of the Cow po[x men]. God bless you, dear Friend! &

S. T. Coleridge.

## 456. To Sara Hutchinson

*Transcript Sara Hutchinson, in Mr. A. H. B. Coleridge's possession. Pub. Inquiring Spirit, ed. by Kathleen Coburn, 1951, pp. 240–2.* This fragment is all that remains of what was probably a journal letter begun on 25 Aug., the same day Coleridge visited 'Buttermere Halse Fall' (Moss Force). The concluding paragraph of this fragment mentions an excursion of Sunday, 29 Aug., to Lodore, which Coleridge compares with Moss Force and Scale Force.

Charles and Mary Lamb were with Coleridge at this time, and it is quite likely that Lamb was his companion on both the short excursions mentioned in this letter. Lamb wrote afterwards that Coleridge 'received us with all the hospitality in the world, and gave up his time to show us all the wonders of the country. . . . We have clambered up to the top of Skiddaw, and I have waded up the bed of Lodore.' *Lamb Letters*, i. 315.

Keswick, Augt. 25th, 1802

All night it rained incessantly—& in a hard storm of Rain this morning, at ½ past 10, I set off, & drove away toward Newlands—there is a Waterfall, that divides Great Robinson from Buttermere Halse Fell, which when Mary & Tom [Hutchinson], & I passed, we stopped & said—what a wonderful Creature it would be in a hard Rain—dear Mary was especially struck with it's latent Great-

[1] Edward Jenner (1749–1823), discoverer of vaccination; and William Woodville (1752–1805).

ness—& since that time I have never passed it without a haunting wish to see it in it's fury—it is just 8 miles from Keswick. I had a glorious Walk—the rain sailing along those black Crags & green Steeps, white as the wooly Down on the under side of a Willow Leaf, & soft as Floss Silk / & silver Fillets of Water down every mountain from top to bottom that were as fine as Bridegrooms. I soon arrived at the Halse—& climbed up by the waterfall as near as I could, to the very top of the Fell—but it was so craggy—the Crags covered with spongy soaky Moss, and when bare so jagged as to wound one's hands fearfully—and the Gusts came so very sudden & strong, that the going up was slow, & difficult & earnest —& the coming down, not only all that, but likewise extremely dangerous. However, I have always found this *stretched & anxious* state of mind favorable to depth of pleasurable Impression, in the resting Places & *lownding* Coves. The Thing repaid me amply / it is a great Torrent from the Top of the Mountain to the Bottom / the lower part of it is not the least Interesting, where it is beginning to slope to a level—the mad water rushes thro' it's *sinuous* Bed, or rather prison of Rock, with such rapid Curves, as if it turned the Corners not from the mechanic force, but with foreknowledge, like a fierce & skilful Driver / great Masses of Water, one after the other, that in twilight one might have feelingly compared them to a vast crowd of huge white Bears, rushing, one over the other, against the wind—their long white hair shattering abroad in the wind / The remainder of the Torrent is marked out by three great Waterfalls—the lowermost apron-shaped, & though the Rock down which it rushes is an inclined Plane, it shoots off in such an independence of the Rock as shews that it's direction was given it by the force of the Water from above. The middle, which in peaceable times would be two tinkling Falls, formed in this furious Rain one great *Water-wheel* endlessly revolving / & double the size & height of the lowest—the third & highest is a mighty one indeed / it is twice the height of both the others added together / nearly as high as Scale Force / but it rushes down an inclined Plane—and does not *fall*, like Scale Force / however, if the Plane had been smooth, it is so near a Perpendicular that it would have *appeared* to fall—but it is indeed so fearfully savage, & black, & jagged, that it tears the flood to pieces—and one great black Outjutment divides the water, & overbrows & keeps uncovered a long slip of jagged black Rock beneath, which gives a marked *character* to the whole force. What a sight it is to look down on such a Cataract!— the wheels, that circumvolve in it—the leaping up & plunging forward of that infinity of Pearls & Glass Bulbs—the continual *change* of the *Matter*, the perpetual *Sameness* of the *Form*—it is an awful Image & Shadow of God & the World.[1]—When I reached the very top, where the Stream flows level, there were feeding three darling Sheep, with their red ochre Letters on their sides, as quiet as if they were by a Rill in a flat meadow, flowing clear over smooth tressy water-weeds, & thro' by long Grass—Bless their dear hearts what darlings mountain Sheep are!—A little above the summit of the Waterfall I had a very striking view—the Lake & part of Keswick in a remarkably interesting point of view seen at the end of the Vista formed by the vale of Newlands—this was on my right—and as I turned to my left, the Sun burst out—& I saw close by me part of the Lake of Buttermere, but not an inch of any one of it's Shores or of the Vale—but over away beside Crummock a white shining dazzling view of the Vale of Lorton & the Sea beyond it.—

I went to Lodore on Sunday [29 August]—it was finer than I had ever seen it before—never were there three Waterfalls so different from each other, as Lodore, Buttermere Halse Fall, & Scale Force.—Scale Force is a proper Fall between two very high & narrow Walls of Rock, well tree'd—yet so that the Trees rather add to, than lessen the precipice Walls.—Buttermere Halse Fall is a narrow, open, naked Torrent with three great Water-slopes individualized in it one above another, large, larger, largest—. Lodore has it's Walls, but they are scarcely Walls, they are wide apart, & not upright, & their beauty & exceeding Majesty take away the Terror—and the Torrent is broad & wide, & from top to bottom it is small Waterfalls, abreast, & abreast. Buttermere Halse Fall is the War-song of a Scandinavian Bard—Lodore is the Precipitation of the fallen Angels from Heaven, Flight & Confusion, & Distraction, but all harmonized into one majestic Thing by the genius of Milton, who describes it. Lodore is beyond all rivalry the first & best Thing of the whole Lake Country. Indeed

---

[1] In two letters contributed to *The Times Literary Supplement* on 28 Sept. and 26 Oct. 1951, Mr. A. P. Rossiter examines the sources of Coleridge's *Hymn before Sun-rise, in the Vale of Chamouni*, and he convincingly demonstrates that the passage above found lyrical expression in the following lines of the poem. 'Who', asks the poet, called forth the 'five wild torrents'

> Down those precipitous, black, jaggéd rocks,
> For ever shattered and the same for ever?
> Who gave you your invulnerable life,
> Your strength, your speed, your fury, and your joy,
> Unceasing thunder and eternal foam? (*Poems*, i. 379.)

One can only agree with Mr. Rossiter that the account of Buttermere Halse Fall is reflected in Coleridge's poem and that the Falls of Lodore, described later in this letter, also may have stimulated the poet's imagination. For further comment on Coleridge's sources see Letter 459.

26 August 1802 [457

(but we cannot judge at all from Prints) I have seen nothing equal to it in the Prints & Sketches of the Scotch & Swiss Cataracts.

### 457. To William Sotheby

*Address*: [W.] Sotheby Esq. | Lodge | Loughton | Essex
*MS. Colonel H. G. Sotheby. Pub. with omis. Letters, i. 396.*
*Postmark*: 30 August 1802. *Stamped*: Keswick.

Thursday, August 26, 1802

My dear Sir

I was absent on a little Excursion, when your Letter arrived—& since my return I have been waiting & making every enquiry in the hopes of announcing the receipt of your Orestes[1] & it's companions, with my sincere thanks for your kindness. But I can hear nothing of them. Mr Lamb however goes to Penrith next week, & will make strict scrutiny. I am not to find the Welch Tour[2] among them; & yet I think I am correct in referring the Ode, NETLEY ABBEY, to that collection / a poem which I believe I can very nearly repeat by heart—tho' it must have been four or five years since I last read it. I well remember, that after reading your Welch Tour, Southey observed to me, that you, I, & himself had all done ourselves harm by suffering our admiration of Bowles to bubble up too often on the surface of our Poems. In perusing the second Volume of Bowles, which I owe to your kindness, I met a line of my own which gave me great pleasure / from the thought, what a pride & joy I should have had at the time of writing it, if I had supposed it possible that Bowles would have adopted it—The line is

>   Had MELANCHOLY mus'd herself to Sleep[3] /

I wrote the lines at 19—& published them many years ago in the Morning Post as a fragment—and as they are but 12 lines I will transcribe them[4] /

>   Upon a moulder'd Abbey's broadest Wall,
>   Where ruining Ivies prop the Ruins steep,
>   Her folded Arms wrapping her tatter'd Pall
>   Had MELANCHOLY mus'd herself to sleep.
>   The FERN was press'd beneath her Hair;

---

[1] Sotheby's *Orestes*, 1802.
[2] Sotheby's *A Tour through Parts of Wales, Sonnets, Odes, and Other Poems*, 1794.
[3] See Bowles's *Coombe-Ellen*, lines 36–37:
>   Here Melancholy on the pale crags laid,
>   Might muse herself to sleep.
[4] First published *Morning Post*, 12 Dec. 1797. *Poems*, i. 73.

> The dark-green* ADDER's tongue was there;
> And still, as came the flagging Sea-gales weak,
> The long lank Leaf bow'd fluttering o'er her cheek.
>
> Her pallid Cheek was flush'd: her eager Look
> Beam'd, eloquent in slumber. Inly wrought
> Imperfect Sounds her moving Lips forsook,
> And her bent Forehead work'd with troubled Thought.——

\* Asplenium Scolopendrium, more commonly called the Hart's Tongue. [S. T. C.]

I met these Lines yesterday by accident—& ill as they are written, there seem'd to me a force & distinctness of Image in them, that were buds of Promise in a school-boy performance / tho' I am giving them perhaps more than their Deserts in thus ensuring them a Reading from you.——I have finished the First Navigator; and Mr Tomkins may have it, whenever he wishes. It would be gratifying to me if you would look it over, & alter any thing, you like / my whole wish & purpose is to serve Mr Tomkyns—& you are not only much more in the habit of writing verse than I am, but must needs have a better Tact of what will offend that class of Readers, into whose hands a shewy Publication is likely to fall. I do not mean, my dear Sir! to impose on you 10 minutes' thought / but often, currente oculo, a better phrase or position of words will suggest itself. As to the 10£, it is more than the Thing is worth, either in German or English / & Mr Tomkins will better give the true value of it by kindly accepting what is given with kindness. Two or three copies presented in my name, one to each of the two or three Friends of mine, who are likely to be pleased with a fine Book—this is the utmost, I desire, or will receive.—I shall for the ensuing quarter send occasionally verses, &c to the Morning Post, under the signature "Εστησε[1]—& I mention this to you, because I have some intention of translating Voss's Idills[2] in English Hexa-

---

[1] Underlined twice in MS.

[2] J. H. Voss, *Luise, ein ländliches Gedicht in drei Idyllen*, 1795. In the Mitchell Library of New South Wales, Sydney, Australia, there is an autograph manuscript of Coleridge containing eight lines from this poem. The lines are headed: 'The prefatory Verses to Voss's Louise translated almost verbally, & in the original metre.'

### Before Gleim's Cottage

Up, up! noble old Man! *Who knocks there?* Friend & Acquaintance
  *Friends should more quietly knock.* True! but you would not have heard.
*Hush! ye'll awaken the Maidens.* They love us. *Hush! it is Midnight.*
  *And could ye wish them to rise?* Rise & receive the Belov'd.
*Whom, prithee?* Know you the Vicar of Greeno? *What? & Luisa?*
  She and her Husband. *But where's Mother?* And Mother, to boot.

## 26 August 1802

meters, with a little prefatory Essay on modern Hexameters.—I have discovered, that the poetical Parts of the Bible, & the best parts of Ossian, are little more than slovenly Hexameters—and the rhythmical Prose of Gesner is still more so— / & reads exactly like that metre in Boetius' & Seneca's Tragedies which consists of the latter half of the Hexameter—.——The Thing is worth an Experiment; & I wish it to be considered merely as an Experiment. I need not say, that the greater number of the verses signed "Εστησε will be such as were never meant for any thing else but the peritura charta of the M. Post.[1]—

I had written thus far when your Letter of the 16th arrived, franked on the 23rd from Weymouth with a polite apology from Mr Bedingfeld (if I have rightly decyphered the Name) for it's detention.—I am vexed, that I did not write immediately on my return home / but I waited, day after day, in hopes of the Orestes, &c. It is an old proverb that Extremes meet, & I have often regretted that I had not noted down as they incurred the interesting Instances, in which the Proverb is verified. The newest subject —tho' brought from the Planets (or *Asteroids*) Ceres & Pallas, could not excite my curiosity more than Orestes.—I will write immediately to Mr Clarkson, who resides at the foot of Ulswater, & beg him to walk in to Penrith, & ask at all the Inns, if any Parcel have arrived—if not, I will myself write to Mr Faulder, & inform him of the Failure.—There is a subject of great merit in the ancient mythology hitherto untouched—I believe so at least— but for the *mode* of the Death which mingled the ludicrous & horrible, but which might be easily altered, it is one of the finest subjects for Tragedy that I am acquainted with—Medea after the murder of her children fled to the Court of the old King, Pelias, was regarded with superstitious Horror, & shunned or insulted by the Daughters of Pelias—till hearing of her miraculous Restoration of Æson they conceived the idea of recalling by her means the youth of their own Father. She avails herself of their credulity— & so works them up by pretended magical Rites, that they consent to kill their Father in his sleep, & throw him into the magic Cauldron—which done, Medea leaves them with bitter Taunts & triumph.—The daughters are called, Asteropaea, Antonoe, & Alcestis—Ovid alludes briefly to this story in the couplet

*Up up, Girls! make ready the Best!* Nay, nothing but Shelter—
    Shelter and welcoming Smiles. *Dear Souls! come in—it is cold!*
This translation is on the verso of Coleridge's rough draft of an outline for a poem on Mahomet. See Letter 292.

[1] In addition to a number of epigrams, Coleridge contributed such poems as *Dejection, The Day Dream, Chamouny,* and *Ode to the Rain* to the *Morning Post* over this signature.

## To William Sotheby

Quid referam Peliae natas pietate nocentes
Caesaque virgineâ membra paterna manu?[1]

What a thing to have seen a Tragedy raised on this Fable by Milton in rivalry of the Macbeth of Shakespere!—The character of Medea, wand'ring & fierce, and invested with impunity by the strangeness & excess of her Guilt—& truly an injured woman, on the other hand / & possessed of supernatural Powers—The same story is told in a very different way by some authors—and out of their narrations matter might be culled that would very well coincide with, & fill up, the main incidents / Her Imposing the sacred Image of Diana on the Priesthood at Iolcus, & persuading them to join with her in inducing the daughters of Pelias to kill their Father / the Daughters under the Persuasion that their Father's youth would be restored, the Priests under the Faith, that the Goddess required the Death of the old King—& that the safety of the Country depended on it—In this way Medea might be suffered to escape, under the direct Protection of the Priesthood—who may afterward discover the Delusion. The moral of the Piece would be a very fine one.——

Wordsworth wrote me a very animated account of his Difficulties & his joyous meeting with you which he calls the happy Rencontre or Fortunate Rain-storm.—O that you had been with me during a thunder-storm, on Thursday August the 5th / I was sheltered (in the phrase of this country, *lownded*) in a sort of natural Porch on the summit of Sca' Fell, the central mountain of our Giants, said to be higher than Skiddaw or Helvellin / & in chasm, naked Crag, bursting Springs, & Waterfall the most interesting, without a rival / When the Clouds pass'd away, to my right & left & behind me stood a great national Convention of Mountains which our ancestors most descriptively called Copland, i.e. the Land of Heads —before me the mountains died away down to the Sea in eleven parallel Ridges—Close under my feet as it were, were three Vales, Wastdale with it's Lake, Miterdale, & Eskdale, with the three Rivers, Irt, Mite, and Esk seen from their very fountains to their Fall into the Sea at Ravenglass Bay, which with these Rivers form to the Eye a perfect Trident—🔱—Turning round I looked thro' Borrodale out upon the Derwentwater & the vale of Keswick even to my own House where my own children were.—Indeed, I had altogether the most interesting walk—thro' Newlands to Butter-

---

[1] Ovid, *Heroides*, xii, lines 129–30. See also Pausanias, VIII. xi. 3.

mere, over the Fells to Ennerdale, to St Bees, Egremont, Gosforth, up Wasdale, to Sca' Fell, down Eskdale, to Devock Lake, Ulpha Kirk, Broughton Mills, Torver, Coniston, Wyndermere, Grasmere, Keswick / If it would entertain, I would transcribe my notes—& send them you by the first opportunity. I have scarce left Room for my best respects to Mrs & Miss Sotheby—& affectionate wishes for your happiness & all who constitute it. With unfeigned Esteem, dear Sir! your's &c, S. T. Coleridge.

P.S. I am ashamed to send you a scrawl so like in form to a servant wench's first letter / You will see that the first half was written before I received your last Letter——

## 458. To Robert Southey

*Address*: Robert Southey Esq. | St James's Place | Kings Down | Bristol
*Single Sheet*
MS. Lord Latymer. Pub. with omis. E.L.G. i. 203.
*Postmark*: 6 September 1802. *Stamped*: Keswick.

Thursday, Sept. 2, 1802

Dear Southey

I have received your's of 29th ult. & Sara has received Mary's—both this evening—and we are sadly perplexed. Edith & Mary cannot have counted the rooms accurately. Exclusive of the Kitchen & Back Kitchen, there are ten rooms in the House—two very large, two tolerably large, & six small ones. The two very large ones would of course be your parlour & mine, the two next in size your Bedroom & mine / there remain six—the two largest & pleasantest of which must be our two Studies / of the remaining four, two will be the Maids' rooms. Supposing, we have but three Servants—a Cook, and two Nursery-maids who must make the beds—& I hope & believe, that these will be enough—& suppose too, that the Infants sleep with their mothers—yet still three maids must have two Rooms—first, because their rooms will be small—& secondly because Derwent will sleep with that one, who has a bed to herself—there now are but two—of these Mary has one, and Tom the other——What follows? I have not a single bed to offer to a Friend / & it will be impossible for Mr & Mrs Wordsworth, & Miss Wordsworth ever to pay us a visit—& not only that, but when Mrs Coleridge lies in, there must be a little bed in her room for the Nurse— / & of course for 5 or 6 weeks I must have a bed room for myself / indeed, I could not at any time do without one / for if I am in the least unwell, I am utterly sleepless unless I have a bed

( 859 )

to myself—and a bed room too.—There is an outhouse which I hoped to have had turned into a study for myself—& it would have been so large, that I might [have] occasionally slept in it wholesomely—which I could not do in the little wing room, which will otherwise be my Study / but I find that it is impossible to have it fitted up till next year / & I *thought*, that when I mentioned it, Jackson enumerated the *costs* of flooring &c, as if it would be more money than he could conveniently hazard / as it would be of no use to him, if I were to go away. At present, it is merely the brick walls, & the blue Slates above.—I fear too, that the new House will not be finished till the middle of November / tho' Jackson has promised me to bestir himself—This however is a trifle / the days are so short at the close of October, that it will make but little difference your not coming till a month later / Besides, you might come / & have furnished Lodgings at Keswick, for a month / at least, either for you & Edith, & child—or for Mary & Tom / for half of you we could certainly either find or make room for. / The former objections are more weighty.—Mrs Coleridge will write in a day or two an exact account of the furniture, that we have—and of what will be wanted / supposing, these objections can be done away.—It is absolutely necessary, that I should have one spare Room always ready for Wordsworth & his Wife / and tho' Dorothy would, of course, always accompany them, yet I suppose, Mrs Lovell would give her half her Bed. It would be *convenient* to have a second Bedroom for myself—but this I can easily waive / when Wordsworth was not expected, of course, I should use *his* Room, as I have been accustom[ed] to call it—and when there, I shall either be well, & Mrs C. likewise, & we sleep in one room / or I can put the little lazy bed, that the Nurse will sleep in, into my Study, for the few nights, that he may be at Keswick.—I told you that you might have half the house—i.e. 5 rooms, besides the Kitchen / & unless we retained 5, we should be as straightened, as if we were in Lodgings—& in case of sickness, we should [be] so thronged as to be quite miserable.—So much for Business. Sara will write to Mary or Edith / & when you have the whole before you, you must then settle it.—Now for the remainder.

The Letter to Estlin is not the existing half, nor the 20th part, of the existing half of my *Letters* to the B.C.—W. Taylor's notion that Christ was the author of the Wisdom of Solomon seems to me a silly one / unless he can shew the Gospel & Epistles of John to be not only forgeries, but forgeries without any foundation in the real doctrines & tenets of Jesus. He says, that [']the Apostles often quote the Book.' God bless him!!—why not—'the Book often quotes the Apostles.'?—The Wisdom of Solomon is supposed by

Eichhorn[1] to have been written in the second Century by an Alexandrian Christian.—As to the latter part, I was never more astonished in my Life, than when I read that sentence in your Letter—'the latter Solution is so strikingly probable that I know not how it should now first be made.'—I should suppose, that nothing was ever older. Before I went to Germany, I spoke to Estlin of the great importance of the Miracle of the Ascension, without which the Resurrection could never be proved to be a miracle at all—or any thing more than resuscitation / as the body was not putrefied, & as Xst was so manifestly *favored* both by Pilate & the Soldiers. Estlin admitted it—but spoke of the objection as a very old one.—Either, he said, the Ascension is true or a lie / if true, it confirms the miraculous nature of the Resurrection / if a lie, what need of any ingenious hypothesis about the Resurrection / why not *both* Lies ?—My mind misgave me at that time, that thousands who would die rather than tell a Lie for a Lie, will tell 20 to *help out* what they believe to be a certain Truth / and the idea made great impression on my mind, tho' without the least suspicion that it was any thing but an old objection. In Germany, I found it the *universal* Solution / & at Göttingen I understood that it was publickly stated, as the probable truth, by Eichhorn / & passages from Plutarch, as well as the Passage, you refer to, in Josephus—cited by him—on my return home, Dr Beddoes in Biggs' Shop detailed this as a general opinion——and lo & behold, in Herder's Von der Auferstehung, als Glauben, Geschichte & Lehre,[2] i.e. Of the Resurrection, as an Article of Faith, of History, & of Doctrine, I found the whole developed in a delightful manner —with the curious passages in Plutarch / & a bold Laugh at those who lay'd any stress on the Ascension.—I detailed this to you at Keswick, if I am not greatly mistaken / & I am positive, that both Davy & myself entered fully into it at your Rooms, when Northmore was there. Indeed, it would be strange, if I had never mentioned it to you—for I believe, you would be the only one of my acquaintance to whom I have not mentioned & dwelt upon it.— I cannot believe, that W. Taylor considers this as any discovery of his own / Before the time of Grotius's de Veritate Christianâ no *stress* was lay'd on the judicial, law-cant kind of evidence for Christianity which has been since so much in Fashion / & Lessing very sensibly considers Grotius as the greatest Enemy that Xtianity ever had. Since his Time I cannot but think, that this hypothesis would be found in very many Authors long before

[1] J. G. Eichhorn (1752–1827), *Einleitung in die apokryphischen Bücher des Alten Testaments*, 1795.
[2] A copy of this work, 1794, annotated by Coleridge is in the British Museum.

Herder or Eichhorn / neither does Herder in the book now before me lay any claim to originality—& this Book, if I am not mistaken, W. Taylor *reviewed*. He certainly did, two other little tracts that usually accompany it /. I need not say that Herder (who is a sort of German Bishop) writes very slyly—& admits the possibility of this resuscitation, as a mere natural occurrence, & the probability of it, as if nothing were lost to Xtianity by the admission. I will quote one sentence, p. 120. They held that to be a miracle which probably was no miracle; they believed that this Resurrection was effected by the omnipotence of God, when perhaps it was merely a natural resuscitation in consequence of the powerful Perfume of Nicodemus.—Plank has written a very large & most fact-full History of the Reformation.[1]—God bless you & S. T. C.

As soon as the new House is finished, the whole front of the old one will be pulled down, if it does not fall before: so we *cannot* have any rooms in that.

An excellent Story that Eagle of Brass!


### 459. *To William Sotheby*

*Address*: W. Sotheby Esq. | Lodge | Loughton | Essex   *Single Sheet*
MS. Colonel H. G. Sotheby, Pub. with omis. Letters, *i. 401*.
*Postmark*: 13 September 1802.   *Stamped*: Keswick.

Friday, Sept. 10, 1802. Greta Hall, Keswick
My dear Sir

The Books have not yet arrived, and I am wholly unable to account for the Delay. I suspect, that the cause of it may be Mr Faulder's mistake in sending them by the Carlisle Waggon—they should have been sent by the Kendal & Whitehaven Waggon. A person is going to Carlisle on Monday from this place—& will make diligent enquiry—& if he succeed, still I cannot have them in less than a week—as they must return to Penrith, & there wait for the next Tuesday's Carrier. I ought perhaps to be ashamed of my weakness / but I must confess, I have been downright *vexed* by the Business—every Cart, every return-Chaise from Penrith, has renewed my Hopes, till I begin to play tricks with my own Impatience—& say—Well—I take it for granted, that I sha' n't get [them] for these 7 days, &c &c—with other of those Half-lies, that Fear begets upon Hope.—You have imposed a pleasing task on

---

[1] G. J. Planck, *Geschichte der Entstehung der Veränderungen und der Bildung unsers protestantischen Lehrbegriffs vom Anfang der Reformation bis zu der Einführung der Concordienformel*, 6 vols., 1791–1800.

me in requesting the minutiae of my opinions concerning your Orestes—whatever these opinions may be, the disclosure of them will be a sort of *map* of my mind, as a Poet & Reasoner—& my curiosity is strongly excited. I feel you a man of Genius in the choice of the subject. It is my Faith, that the 'Genus irritabile' is a phrase applicable only to *bad* poets[1]—Men of great Genius have indeed, as an essential of their composition, great sensibility, but they have likewise great confidence in their own powers—and Fear must always precede anger, in the human mind. I can with truth say, that from those, I love, mere general praise of any thing, I have written, is as far from giving me pleasure, as mere general censure—in any thing, I mean, to which I have devoted much time or effort. 'Be minute, & assign your Reasons often, & your first impressions always—& then blame or praise—I care not which —I shall be gratified'—These are *my* sentiments, & I assuredly believe, that they are the sentiments of all, who have indeed felt *a true Call* to the Ministry of *Song*. Of course, I too 'will act on the golden rule of doing to others, what I wish others to do unto me.'—But while I think of it, let me say that I should be much concerned, if you applied this to the First Navigator—It would absolutely mortify me, if you did more than look over it—& when a correction suggested itself to you, take your pen, & make it—& then let the copy go to Tomkyns—What they have been, I shall know when I see the Thing in Print—for it must please the present times, if it please any—and you have been far more in the fashionable World, than I, & must needs have a finer & surer Tact of that which will offend or disgust in the higher circles of Life.——Yet it is not what I should have advised Tomkyns to do—& that is one reason why I *can not* & *will not* except more than a brace of copies, from him. I do not like to be associated in a man's mind with his Losses—if he have the Translation gratis, he must take it on his own judgment—but when a man pays for a thing, & he loses by it, the Idea will creep in, spite of himself, that the Failure was, in part, owing to the badness of the Translation. While I was translating the Wallenstein, I told Longman, it would never answer—when I had finished it, I wrote to him / & foretold that it would be waste paper on his Shelves, & the dullness charitably layed upon my Shoulders. It happened, as I said—Longman lost 250£ by the work / 50£ of which had been payed to me—poor pay, Heaven knows! for a thick Octavo volume of blank Verse— & yet I am sure, that Longman never thinks of me but Wallenstein & the Ghosts of his departed Guineas dance an ugly Waltz round my Idea.—This would not disturb me a tittle, if I thought well of

[1] Cf. *Biographia Literaria*, ch. ii.

the work myself—I should feel a confidence, that it would win it's way at last / but this is not the case with Gesner's Der erste Schiffer. —It may as well lie here, till Tomkins wants it—let him only give me a week's notice, and I will transmit it to you with a large margin.—Bowles's Stanzas on Navigation are among the best in that second Volume / but the whole volume is woefully inferior to it's Predecessor. There reigns thro' all the blank verse poems such a perpetual trick of *moralizing* every thing—which is very well, occasionally—but never to see or describe any interesting appearance in nature, without connecting it by dim analogies with the moral world, proves faintness of Impression. Nature has her proper interest; & he will know what it is, who believes & feels, that every Thing has a Life of it's own, & that we are all *one Life*. A Poet's *Heart & Intellect* should be *combined, intimately* combined & *unified*, with the great appearances in Nature—& not merely held in solution & loose mixture with them, in the shape of formal Similies. I do not mean to *exclude* these formal Similies—there are moods of mind, in which they are natural—pleasing moods of mind, & such as a Poet will often have, & sometimes express; but they are not his highest, & most appropriate moods. They are 'Sermoni propiora' which I once translated—'*Properer for a Sermon*.' The truth is—Bowles has indeed the *sensibility* of a poet; but he has not the *Passion* of a great Poet. His latter Writings all want *native* Passion—Milton here & there supplies him with an appearance of it—but he has no native Passion, because he is not a Thinker—& has probably weakened his Intellect by the haunting Fear of becoming extravagant / Young somewhere in one of his prose works remarks that there is as profound a Logic in the most daring & dithyrambic parts of Pindar, as in the "Οργανον of Aristotle—the remark is a valuable one /

> Poetic Feelings, like the flexuous Boughs
> Of mighty Oaks, yield homage to the Gale,
> Toss in the strong winds, drive before the Gust,[1]
> Themselves one giddy storm of fluttering Leaves;
> Yet all the while, self-limited, remain
> Equally near the fix'd and parent Trunk
> Of Truth & Nature, in the howling Blast[2]
> As in the Calm that stills the Aspen Grove.[3]—

That this is deep in our Nature, I felt when I was on Sca' fell—. I involuntarily poured forth a Hymn in the manner of the *Psalms*,

---

[1] Blast [Cancelled word in line above.]
[2] Storm [Cancelled word in line above.]
[3] Lines 34–41 of *To Matilda Betham from a Stranger, Poems*, i. 374.

## 10 September 1802

tho' afterwards I thought the Ideas &c disproportionate to our humble mountains[1]—& accidentally lighting on a short Note in some swiss Poems, concerning the Vale of Chamouny, & it's Mountain, I transferred myself thither, in the Spirit, & adapted my former feelings to these grander external objects. You will soon see it in the Morning Post—& I should be glad to know whether & how far it pleased you.—It has struck [me] with great force lately, that the Psalms afford a most compleat answer to those, who state the Jehovah of the Jews, as a personal & national God—& the Jews, as differing from the Greeks, only in calling the minor Gods, Cherubim & Seraphim—& confining the word God to their Jupiter. It must occur to every Reader that the Greeks in their religious poems address always the Numina Loci, the Genii, the Dryads, the Naiads, &c &c—All natural Objects were *dead*—mere hollow Statues—but there was a Godkin or Goddessling *included* in each—In the Hebrew Poetry you find nothing of this poor Stuff —as poor in genuine Imagination, as it is mean in Intellect— / At best, it is but Fancy, or the aggregating Faculty of the mind—not

---

[1] The remainder of this sentence is omitted in *Letters*, i. 405. Mr. A. P. Rossiter, whose two letters to *The Times Literary Supplement* of 28 Sept. and 26 Oct. 1951 examine the sources of *Chamouny*, has kindly supplied the following note: 'Presumably these lines were cut out by E. H. C. as a result of De Quincey's exposure of the "unacknowledged obligation" to "Frederica Brun, a female poet of Germany" (*Tait's Magazine*, 1834), and the subsequent charges of "plagiarism". S. T. C. never admitted using the *poem* (given in *Poems*, ii. 1131), and I believed that his detailed use of her *notes* was unknown before 1951 and my two letters in *T.L.S.* (Letter 456.) Since then M. Adrien Bonjour has sent me his Lausanne dissertation of 1942, which anticipated some of my points on these notes, without tracing S. T. C.'s sources beyond Frau Brun. I believe that these include echoes from Stolberg's poem on a cataract (*Poems*, ii. 1126, and i. 308), possibly others from Brun's alpine verses, and that both form and substance are strongly influenced by Bowles's *Coombe Ellen*—a rhapsodic blank verse nature-poem, in which (lines 16 f.) will be found the *point d'appui* of the inconsequent disquisition in this letter on the Greeks, Numina Loci, etc. S. T. C. leaves this poem unmentioned, in a way most suspiciously like his silence on the Brun poem. The inference is, that the involuntary hymn story was an estecian myth, an imposition on the guileless Sotheby. Letter 450 records what he did do on Scafell, and is well backed by a scribbled page near the end of Notebook 2 (p. 32), where he has jotted down the mountain-panorama; and neither gives any more hint of a poem than will be found in the letter to Sotheby of August 26th (Letter 457)—written three weeks after his ascent. This silence, with the pregnant imaginative image from Buttermere Halse Fall (Letter 456), suggests that the *Chamouny* verses were not written till after Aug. 26th *at earliest*; and that S. T. C. was well aware of his "obligations" both to the somewhat *un*-fairy godmother Friederike and to that insidious *God*father, Bowles: from whose verses his apposite comments appositely rebound on his own *Hymn* (as it was to be entitled after the original publication in the *Morning Post*, September 11th 1802).'

*Imagination*, or the *modifying*, and *co-adunating* Faculty.[1] This the Hebrew Poets appear to me to have possessed beyond all others—& next to them the English. In the Hebrew Poets each Thing has a Life of it's own, & yet they are all one Life. In God they move & live, & *have* their Being—not *had*, as the cold System of Newtonian Theology represents / but *have*. Great pleasure indeed, my dear Sir! did I receive from the latter part of your Letter. If there be any two subjects which have in the very depth of my Nature interested me, it has been the Hebrew & Christian Theology, & the Theology of Plato. Last winter I read the Parmenides & the Timaeus with great care—and O! that you were here, even in this howling Rain-Storm that dashes itself against my windows, on the other side of my blazing Fire, in that great Arm Chair there—I guess, we should encroach on the morning before we parted. How little the Commentators of Milton have availed themselves of the writings of Plato / Milton's Darling! But alas! commentators only hunt out verbal Parallelisms—*numen abest*. I was much impressed with this in all the many Notes on that beautiful Passage in Comus from l. 629 to 641[2]—all the puzzle is to find out what Plant Haemony is—which they discover to be the English Spleenwort—& decked out, as a mere play & licence of poetic Fancy, with all the strange properties suited to the purpose of the Drama—They thought little of Milton's platonizing Spirit—who wrote nothing without an interior meaning. 'Where more is meant, than meets the ear' is true of himself beyond all writers. He was so great a Man, that he seems to have considered Fiction as profane, unless where it is consecrated by being emblematic of some Truth / What an unthinking & ignorant man we must have supposed Milton to be, if without any hidden meaning, he had described [it] as growing in such abundance that the dull Swain treads on it daily—& yet as never *flowering*—Such blunders Milton, of all others, was least likely to commit—Do look at the passage—apply it as an Allegory

---

[1] Cf. also Letter 535.

[2] Amongst the rest a small unsightly root,
But of divine effect, he cull'd me out;
The leaf was darkish, and had prickles on it,
But in another country, as he said,
Bore a bright golden flow'r, but not in this soil:
Unknown, and like esteem'd, and the dull swain
Treads on it daily with his clouted shoon:
And yet more med'cinal is it than that moly
That Hermes once to wise Ulysses gave;
He call'd it haemony, and gave it me,
And bad me keep it as of sovereign use
'Gainst all inchantments, mildew, blast, or damp,
Or ghastly furies' apparition.

of Christianity, or to speak more precisely of the Redemption by the Cross—every syllable is full of Light!—[']a *small unsightly Root*[']—to the Greeks Folly, to the Jews a stumbling Block—[']The leaf was darkish & had prickles on it[']—If in this Life only we have hope, we are of all men the most miserable / & [a] score of other Texts—[']But in another country, as he said, Bore a bright golden Flower'—the exceeding weight of Glory prepared for us hereafter / —[']but [not] in this soil, unknown, & like esteem'd & the dull Swain treads on it daily with his clouted shoon['] / The Promises of Redemption offered daily & hourly & to all, but accepted scarcely by any—[']He called it Haemony[']—Now what is Haemony? Αἷμα-οἶνος—Blood-wine.—And he took the wine & blessed it, & said—This is my Blood— / the great Symbol of the Death on the Cross.—There is a general Ridicule cast on all allegorizers of Poets—read Milton's prose works, & observe whether he was one of those who joined in this Ridicule.—There is a very curious Passage in Josephus—De Bello Jud. L. 7. cap. 25 (al. vi. §§ 3) which is, in it's literal meaning, more wild, & fantastically absurd than the passage in Milton—so much so that Lardner quotes it in exultation, & asks triumphantly—Can any man who reads it think it any disparagement to the Christian Religion, that it was not embraced 'by a man who could believe such stuff as this?—God forbid! that it should affect Christianity, that it is not believed by the learned of this world.'—But the passage in Josephus I have no doubt, [is] wholly allegorical.—῎Εστησε signifies— *He hath stood*[1]—which in these times of apostacy from the principles of Freedom, or of Religion in this country, & from both by the same persons in France, is no unmeaning Signature, if subscribed with humility, & in the remembrance of, Let him that stands take heed lest he fall—. However, it is in truth no more than S. T. C. written in Greek. *Es tee see*—

Pocklington will not sell his House—but he is ill—& perhaps, it may be to be sold—but it is sunless all winter. God bless you, & [your's,] & S. T. Coleridge

Mrs Coleridge joins me in most respectful remembrances to Mrs & Miss Sotheby.—

---

[1] ῎Εστησε signifies 'He hath placed' not 'He hath stood'. The word should have been ῎Εστηκε, but then the play on Coleridge's initials would have been lost. Elsewhere he called it 'Punic Greek'. Subsequently Coleridge wrote in a copy of his *Conciones ad Populum*: 'Qualis ab initio, εστησε ΕΣΤΗΣΕ = S.T.C. July, 1820.' The echo from *Ars Poetica*, 127 ('Qualis ab incepto processerit, et sibi constet'), suggests that he found in Horace's 'sibi constet' a confirmation of his forced interpretation. Cf. C. C. Seronsy, 'Marginalia by Coleridge in Three Copies of His Published Works', *Studies in Philology*, July 1954, p. 471, and *Poems*, i. 453.

### 460. To William Sotheby

*Address*: William Sotheby Esq. | Lodge | Loughton | Essex.
*MS.* Colonel H. G. Sotheby. *Pub.* E. L. G. i. 207.
*Postmark*: 22 September 1802. *Stamped*: Keswick.

Sunday Evening, Sept. 19th. 1802. Greta Hall, Keswick

My dear Sir

Late yesterday evening, on my return from Braighton,[1] I had the pleasure of finding the long expected Parcel. It arrived at Keswick on Friday night. It is so splendid a present, that my first Feeling was not wholly unmixed—I did not know what I had asked.—Immediately on my return I had a slight attack of Fever —and am but just risen from bed—of course, I write now merely to acknowlege the receipt of the Parcel.

You asked me in your last concerning Barrow. Mr Pocklington is very ill, & in case of his Decease it is on the whole rather probable than otherwise, that it will be put up for sale—tho' he is so strange, & so intensely selfish, a character, that no one would be surprized, if knowing how many People are anxious to have it, he should prevent it's sale by a direct clause in his Will.—Should this not be the case, yet still I cannot advise you to think of it. Depend on it, it will go at an extravagant Fancy Price—I know myself three people agape for it—Sir Wilfrid Lawson, who has a noble, I might well say, a kingly Mansion at Braighton, is enamoured of Barrow— Sir W. is a man, who never lets money stand in the way of any of his inclinations / & he told me himself on Saturday morning, that tho' he would not make a fool of himself by giving an extravagant price for it, yet he would bid hard.—However, there could be no objection to your bidding your own Sum / but the House itself is in many respects objectionable. During the whole of the winter Months it is utterly sunless; & tho' the Rooms themselves may not be damp, yet the situation is exceedingly so. How often do I see the spot, where the House lies, involved in mist, when all the vale beside, is free! Add to this, that like the rest of Mr Pocklington's Houses, it is built compleatly in the Spirit of a Batchelor—all the other rooms are sacrificed to the Dining Room—That is a noble Room, made for a whole Neighbourhood—but it is the only room / the Bedrooms are mere Pigeon Holes.—If it were possible to find a truly fine situation, with ground enough about it for a couple of Cows, & a few Horses, it would certainly be better economy to build a House—: for if the situation were well chosen, & the House built with *good* sense in it's inside, & *fine* sense in it's outside, it is

---

[1] Brayton Hall, the seat of Sir Wilfrid Lawson.

( 868 )

what in the common language of men would be called a *Certainty*, that whenever you were tired of it, it might be either let or sold without any Loss—& most probably, to a great Advantage. But I cannot say, that I *know* any such situations. The one at Applethwaite is indeed in point of the exquisitely picturesque confined view on the one side, & the glorious view of the whole vale & lakes on the other / in point of the dryness of the Roads immediately around, & the number of lovely Walks close by—the place, to which I have long & uniformly given the preference over any other spot in the whole Vale, from the Gorge of Borrodale to the outlet of Bassenthwaite / But there is no Land around it—at least, not more than an acre.——If however your partiality to this Country should continue, & you should wish to pass any number of months here, this Greta Hall will be finished in less than two months—& you might have 5 rooms (two very large ones) & a kitchen, Cellar & Stable—with as much garden ground as you wished—& you might have it for any length of time, from three months to three years—the House would be perfectly distinct from our's—it would be just half-furnished—& the *annual* rent including Taxes would not exceed 25£. Any furniture sells here by auction 9 times out of 10 at *more* than it's original value—at the worst, no one loses more than a very moderate per centage for it's use.—I have stated this—because it exists—& because I wish you to know all that there is, & all that there is not, in the vale—leaving the Things to persuade or dissuade, according as their nature &c may be.—It would make me truly happy, if [you] should feel an impulse to come & look out for yourself—We can make up three beds for you at an hour's warning.

We have had dismal weather lately—the last three days have been hot summer weather—& it is interesting to see under Skiddaw the Hay, the *first fruits* of the Soil, in the same fields with the Corn-sheaves.—Did you see a very fine Sonnet on Buonaparte in the Morning Post of Wednesday or Thursday last—? It was written by Wordsworth—& comes upon my Feelings, as in the spirit of the best of Milton's Sonnets.

Present my kindest & most respectful remembrances to Mrs and Miss Sotheby, & believe me, my dear Sir,
      with unfeign'd & affectionate Esteem your's
          truly, S. T. Coleridge

Sir Wilfrid Lawson has a most splendid Library at Braighton / in Voyages, Travels, & Books of Natural History it is no doubt the first in the Island—next to Sir Joseph Banks's. He is an extremely liberal & good-natured Creature—. We have had Sir Charles &

Lady Boughton here, with Miss Boughton—& with them Miles Peter Andrews, & Captn Topham. Sir Charles perfectly *astounded* me by the diversity of his attainment—Musician, both as composer, & Player—Draftsman—Poet—& a Linguist, both of the western, & oriental Languages, almost to a prodigy.

### 461. To Basil Montagu

*Address*: Basil Montague Esq. | Christ's College | (or at his Lodgings, opposite Jesus College) | Cambridge   *Single Sheet*
MS. *Huntington Library. Pub. E. L. G. i. 210.*
*Stamped*: Keswick.

Greta Hall, Keswick    Tuesday, Sept. 21. 1802.
My dear Montague

I received your Letter last night, inclosing two pound—& another two pound in a Letter from Dorothy—which is amply sufficient for me. I am at ease.—I am puzzled how to read the Direction, you have sent—I suppose, it is Christ College—and yet I know not how it can be that, as you lodge opposite Jesus—You would have heard from me some days ago had I known your address—& by the close of this week you will hear from me to some purpose. Be under no alarm concerning any other Selections—were there twenty, it would increase not diminish the probable Sale of our's—it may possibly be prudent to give the work a more extensive name—ex. gr. 'Examination of the Style of our English Prose Writers under Charles I. & the Commonwealth, chiefly in reference to Jeremy Taylor, & Milton, with illustrative Selections.'[1] —I do not see that the Book Mackintosh mentions will be of any use to me, sufficient to repay the expence of Carriage. I have Milton's Works, Hall's Works, & all Taylor's, together with Harrington's.

We have been plagued to death with a swarm of Visitors—I thought of having a Board nailed up at my Door with the following Words painted on it—Visited *out*, & removed to the Strand, opposite to St Clement's Church, for the Benefit of Retirement.

You tell me—you are very very happy. How can you be otherwise? You have no overburthening cares—you have an active mind—a kind & gentle Heart—and a wife devoted to you, a beautiful Woman, pure & innocent as her own dear Babe—affectionate, as yourself, & her affections moving in the same Directions. Beside which, she has a Voice & a Harp that would make me as

[1] In 1805 Montagu published *Selections from the Works of Taylor, Hooker, Hall, and Lord Bacon. With an Analysis of the Advancement of Learning.*

*21 September 1802* [461

great a Poet as Milton (I sometimes think) if I lived near you.—May the Almighty bless you both, & continue you to be the sources of each other's Goodness as well as Comfort.—

What are your motives for a residence at Cambridge?

I went last week to Braighton to Sir Wilfrid Lawson's who unites a kingly House with a most kingly Library. On my return I called at a Friend's or Acquaintance's rather who lay ill in a nervous Fever—on my Return I experienced an attack of the same—a sudden loss of Strength & Spirits, with a very quick & very feeble pulse. My pulse was 120 in the course of the night. I had been myself a witness of the vast efficacy of the muriatic Acid in low Fever—& took a large Dose—& it assuredly stopped the Progress of the Fever. I am very weak—& my bowels deranged by the violence of the Acid—but my Spirits have recovered from the utter Prostration, into which they fell on the commencement of the attack / & my pulse is fuller, & less frequent.

Hartley was six years old lately—& Derwent 2 years last Tuesday—on which day he could tell all his Letters—& tell the names of upwards of 60 animals, on the picture Cards. He is as quick a Learner for his age as any child I know of—& there is not a child of his age in Christendom that I love so well. I am grieved that Dorothy has been stopped in London by a violent Cold.—My best prayers for your Infant—& to Laura a Brother's affectionate kind wishes.—Your's, dear Montague, most sincerely,

S. T. Coleridge

P.S. I shall write again on Saturday, if I am alive.—

### 462. To William Sotheby

*MS. Lord Latymer. Pub. Letters, i. 408.* This seems to be the 'half of a letter' referred to in Letter 463. It is unfinished and has no address sheet; and since it is not among the Coleridge letters in the possession of Colonel H. G. Sotheby, it was probably not posted.

Tuesday, Sept. 27 [28]. 1802. Greta Hall, Keswick

My dear Sir

The River is full, and Lodore is full, and silver Fillets come out of Clouds, & glitter in every Ravine of all the mountains; and the Hail lies, like Snow, upon their Tops; & the impetuous Gusts from Borrodale snatch the water up high & continually at the bottom of the Lake; it is not distinguishable from Snow slanting before the wind—and under this seeming Snow-drift the Sunshine *gleams*, & over all the hither Half of the Lake it is *bright*, and *dazzles*—a cauldron of melted Silver boiling! It is in very truth a sunny,

( 871 )

misty, cloudy, dazzling, howling, omniform, Day / & I have been
looking at as pretty a sight as a Father's eyes could well see—
Hartley & little Derwent running in the Green, where the Gusts
blow most madly—both with their Hair floating & tossing, a
miniature of the agitated Trees below which they were playing /
inebriate both with the pleasure—Hartley whirling round for joy—
Derwent eddying half willingly, half by the force of the Gust—
driven backward, struggling forward, & shouting his little hymn
of Joy. I can write thus to you, my dear Sir! with a confident
spirit / for when I received your Letter of the 22nd, & had read
'the family History', I layed down the sheet upon my Desk, &
sate for half an hour thinking of you—dreaming of you—till the
Tear grown cold upon my cheek awoke me from my Reverie. May
you live long, long, thus blest in your family—& often, often may
you all sit around one fire-side. O happy should I be, *now & then*,
to sit among you / your Pilot & Guide in some of your summer
walks /

> Frigidus at sylvis Aquilo si increverit, aut si
> Hyberni pluviis dependent nubibus Imbres,
> Nos habeat domus, et multo Lar luceat igne.
> Ante focum mihi parvus erit, qui ludat, Iulus,
> Blanditias ferat, et nondum constantia verba:
> Ipse legam magni tecum monumenta Platonis!

Or what would be still better, I could *talk* to you (& if you were
here now, to an accompaniment of Winds that would well suit
the subject) instead of *writing* to you concerning your Orestes.
When we talk, we are our own living Commentary / & there are
so many *running Notes* of Look, Tone, and Gesture, that there
is small danger of being misunderstood, & less danger of being
imperfectly understood—in *writing*—but no! it is foolish to abuse
a good substitute, because it is not all that the original is.—So
I will do my best—& believe me, I consider this Letter which I am
about to write, as merely an exercise of my own judgment—a
something that may make you better acquainted perhaps with
the architecture & furniture of *my* mind, tho' it will probably
convey to you little or nothing that had not occurred to you before,
respecting your own Tragedy. One thing I beg solicitously of you /
that, if any where I appear to speak positively, you will acquit
me of any correspondent Feeling / I hope, that it is not a frequent
Feeling with me in any case, & that if it appear so, I am belied by
my own warmth of manner / in the present instance it is impossible
—I have been too deeply impressed by the work—& I am now
about to give you not criticisms nor decisions, but a History of my

Impressions—& for the greater part, of my first Impressions / & if any where there seem any thing like a tone of Warmth or Dogmatism, do, my dear Sir! be kind enough to regard it as no more than a way of conveying to you the *whole* of my meaning— or (for I am writing too seriously) as the dexterous *Toss*, necessary to turn an Idea out of it's Pudding-bag round & unbroken.—

### 463. To William Sotheby

*Address*: W. Sotheby Esq. | Lodge | Loughton | Essex    *Single Sheet*
*MS. Colonel H. G. Sotheby. Pub. E. L. G. i. 212.* This letter is written on the fourth page of a foolscap sheet containing Coleridge's critical notes on Sotheby's *Orestes*, 1802. These notes are too detailed for inclusion here, but two examples may be cited. Concerning the lines, 'Be but Orestes safe, and life new-born / Will glow in every vein', Coleridge has this to say: '—*glow.?*—Pope played the devil with that word, wearing it to rags & tatters; & I never will use it except in it's original sense—the visible vibratory motion in red hot Iron.' Having carried his comments through the first three acts of *Orestes*, Coleridge gave up further criticism with the following comment: 'Men almost always write most correctly when they write most passionately. It is a common opinion, but I will ever *assert*, that [it] is a compleat vulgar error that cold writers are the correct writers. Passion is the common Parent both of Harmony [and of correctness] / —Now whether it be that the latter part of the Tragedy (rolling shoreward in larger billows of Passion) is indeed faultless in language, or that tho' I have read it over three times, I am still incapable of reading it with sufficient calmness to detect any minute faults—I know not. The effect is certain—I cannot find the dot of an I amiss in it.—'
*Postmark*: 6 October 1802. *Stamped*: Keswick.

Friday, Oct. [1, 18]02. Keswick

My dear Sir

I had written about half of a letter to you on the Orestes, as *a Poem, & a Tragedy*—on it's excellencies & Beauties, and on it's defects—when some necessary business, joined with ill-health, came & stopped me. Eam reverentiam cum Literis ipsis, tum scriptis tuis, debeo, ut sumere in manus illa, nisi vacuo animo, irreligiosum putem.—But I shall have a day's Leisure in the beginning of next week / & believe me, I have no pleasanter employment to anticipate. In the mean time, I find lying before me a sheet of *minutiae minutissimae*, which I send you, *half-ashamed*. After I had looked at the building with something of the eye of an architect, to turn myself into a *fly*, & creep over it with *animalcular* feet, & peer microscopically at the sand-grit of it's component Stones / this may give you no great idea of my Taste, but I am persuaded, it will please you as proof of the zeal, with which I read, while I read.——I have prefixed to the Sheet a significant *?* I mean to imply, that all below are mere Queries—&

that if any word or sentence have a dogmatic tone, this was merely a mode of conveying the whole idea in my mind fully & broadly; & was absolutely unaccompanied by any *feeling* of dogmatism. How deeply I admire the Tragedy, & how sincerely / —I flatter myself, I shall prove to you by proving that I *understand* it. It is matter of regret with me, that my Greek Tragedies are not yet come from London / but some future time I will write you yet another Letter (unconscionable Scribe that I am) giving a comparative analysis &c.—

Wordsworth will be married, Deo volente, on next Monday, Oct. 4.—& purposes to be at his own Cottage at Grasmere on Wednesday, Oct. 6.—He has every reason for a confident Hope, that Lord Lowther will pay the Debt.—

I am so extremely busy in the Morning Post at present, & shall continue so, for the ensuing fortnight, that I shall scarcely have time to look over & transcribe the First Navigator, till the 14th of this month / I would therefore fix the 20th (which is my 30th Birthday) for the time of sending it off to you / but yet if Mr Tomkyns really *want* it before, I will *make* time. My next letter will be dated two days earlier than this / for it will not be worth while to transcribe it—

I have had a very serious attack of low Fever—& stopped it compleatly by the use of the muriatic acid—which has however deranged my bowels, & both the Disease & the Remedy have left me very weak—

S. T. Coleridge

My most respectful remembrances to Mrs & Miss & Captn Sotheby.—

### 464. To Thomas Wedgwood

*Address*: Thomas Wedgewood Esq. | Eastbury | Blandford | Dorset
*MS.* Wedgwood Museum. *Pub.* E. L. G. i. 214.
*Postmark*: 23 October 1802.  *Stamped*: Keswick.

Oct. 20, 1802. Greta Hall, Keswick

My dear Sir

This is my Birth-day, my thirtieth. It will not appear wonderful to you therefore, when I tell you that before the arrival of your Letter I had been thinking with a great weight of different feelings concerning you & your dear Brother. For I have good reason to believe, that I should not now have been alive, if in addition to other miseries I had had immediate poverty pressing upon me. I will never again remain silent so long. It has not been altogether

## 20 October 1802

Indolence or my habits of Procrastination which have kept me from writing, but an eager wish, I may truly say, a Thirst of Spirit to have something honorable to tell you of myself——at present, I must be content to tell you something cheerful. My Health is very much better. I am stronger in every respect: & am not injured by study or the act of sitting at my writing Desk. But my eyes suffer, if at any time I have been intemperate in the use of Candle-light.—This account supposes another, namely, that my mind is calmer & more at ease.—My dear Sir! when I was last with you at Stowey, my heart was often full, & I could scarcely keep from communicating to you the tale of my domestic distresses. But how could I add to your depression, when you were low? or how interrupt or cast a shade on your good spirits, that were so rare & so precious to you?—After my return to Keswick I was, if possible, more miserable than before. Scarce a day passed without such a scene of discord between me & Mrs Coleridge, as quite incapacitated me for any worthy exertion of my faculties by degrading me in my own estimation. I found my temper injured, & daily more so; the good & pleasurable Thoughts, which had been the support of my moral character, departed from my solitude—I determined to go abroad—but alas! the less I loved my wife, the more dear & necessary did my children seem to me. I found no comfort except in the driest speculations—in the ode to dejection, which you were pleased with, these Lines in the original followed the line—My shaping Spirit of Imagination.

> For not to think of what I needs must feel,
> But to be still and patient, all I can,
> And haply by abstruse Research to steal
> From my own Nature all the natural Man—
> This was my sole resource, my only plan,
> And that which suits a part infects the whole
> And now is almost grown the Temper of my Soul.—[1]

I give you these Lines for the Truth & not for the Poetry—.—However about two months ago after a violent quarrel I was taken suddenly ill with spasms in my stomach—I expected to die—Mrs C. was, of course, shocked & frightened beyond measure—& two days after, I being still very weak & pale as death, she threw herself upon me, & made a solemn promise of amendment—& she

---

[1] These lines were not included in the version of *Dejection* appearing in the *Morning Post* and were first published in 1817, nor do they follow, as Coleridge says, the line on imagination in the original draft of the poem; instead, they follow a passage referring to his domestic woes and need for sympathy. See Letters 438, 445, and 449.

has kept her promise beyond any hope, I could have flattered myself with: and I have reason to believe, that two months of tranquillity, & the sight of my now not colourless & cheerful countenance, have really made her feel as a Wife ought to feel. If any woman wanted an exact & copious Recipe, 'How to make a Husband compleatly miserable', I could furnish her with one—with a Probatum est, tacked to it.—Ill tempered Speeches sent after me when I went out of the House, ill-tempered Speeches on my return, my friends received with freezing looks, the least opposition or contradiction occasioning screams of passion, & the sentiments, which I held most base, ostentatiously avowed—all this added to the utter negation of all, which a Husband expects from a Wife—especially, living in retirement—& the consciousness, that I was myself growing a worse man / O dear Sir! no one can tell what I have suffered. I can say with strict truth, that the happiest half-hours, I have had, were when all of a sudden, as I have been sitting alone in my Study, I have burst into Tears.—— But better days have arrived, & are still to come. I have had visitations of Hope, that I may yet be something of which those, who love me, may be proud.—I cannot write that without recalling dear Poole—I have heard twice—& written twice—& I fear, that by a strange fatality one of the Letters will have missed him.— Leslie[1] was here sometime ago. I was very much pleased with him.—And now I will tell you what I am doing. I dedicate three days in the week to the Morning Post / and shall hereafter write for the far greater part such things as will be of as permanent Interest, as any thing I can hope to write——& you will shortly see a little Essay of mine justifying the writing in a Newspaper. My Comparison of the French with the Roman Empire was very favorably received.[2]—The Poetry, which I have sent, has been merely the emptying out of my Desk. The Epigrams are wretched indeed; but they answered Stuart's purpose better than better things—/. I ought not to have given any signature to them whatsoever / I never dreamt of acknowleging either them or the Ode to the Rain. As to feeble expressions & unpolished Lines—there is the Rub! Indeed, my dear Sir! I do value your opinion very highly—I should think your judgment on the sentiment, the imagery, the flow of a Poem decisive / at least, if it differed from

---

[1] Sir John Leslie (1766–1832), mathematician and natural philosopher, to whom Tom Wedgwood granted an annuity in 1797.

[2] In addition to a number of epigrams and poems which appeared in the *Morning Post* in September and October, Coleridge published a series of twelve articles between 21 Sept. and 9 Nov. 1802. See *Essays on His Own Times*, ii. 478–592.

my own, & after frequent consideration mine remained different—it would leave me at least perplexed. For you are a perfect electrometer in these things— / but in point of poetic Diction I am not so well s[atisf]ied that you do not require a certain *Aloofness* from [the la]nguage of real Life, which I think deadly to Poetry. Very shortly however, I shall present you from the Press with my opinions in full on the subject of Style both in prose & verse—& I am confident of one thing, that I shall convince you that I have thought much & patiently on the subject, & that I understand the whole strength of my Antagonists' Cause.—For I am now busy on the subject—& shall in a very few weeks go to the Press with a Volume on the Prose writings of Hall, Milton, & Taylor—& shall immediately follow it up with an Essay on the writings of Dr Johnson, & Gibbon—. And in these two Volumes I flatter myself, that I shall present a fair History of English Prose.—If my life & health remain, & I do but write half as much and as regularly, as I have done during the last six weeks, these will be finished by January next—& I shall then put together my memorandum Book on the subject of poetry. In both I have sedulously endeavoured to state the Facts, & the Differences, clearly & acutely—& my reasons for the Preference of one style to another are secondary to this.—Of this be assured, that I will never give any thing to the world in propriâ personâ, in my own name, which I have not tormented with the File. I sometimes suspect, that my foul Copy would often appear to general Readers more polished, than my fair Copy—many of the feeble & colloquial Expressions have been industriously substituted for others, which struck me as artificial, & not standing the test—as being neither the language of passion nor distinct Conceptions.—Dear Sir! indulge me with looking still further on to my literary Life. I have since my twentieth year meditated an heroic poem on the Siege of Jerusalem by Titus—this is the Pride, & the Stronghold of my Hope. But I never think of it except in my best moods.—The work, to which I dedicate the ensuing years of my Life, is one which highly pleased Leslie in prospective / & my paper will not let me prattle to you about it.——I have written what you most wished me to write—all about myself—.—Our climate is inclement, & our Houses not as compact as they might be / but it is a stirring climate / & the worse the weather, the more unceasingly entertaining are my Study Windows—& the month, that is to come, is the Glory of the year with us. A very warm Bedroom I can promise you, & one that at the same time commands our finest Lake—& mountain-view. If Leslie could not go abroad with you, & I could in any way mould my manners & habits to suit you, I should of all things like to be your companion. Good nature, an affectionate Disposition, & so thorough a sympathy with the nature of your complaint that I should feel no pain, not the most momentary, in being told by you what your feelings required, at the time in which they required it—this I should bring with me. But I need not say, that you may say to me—'you don't suit me', without inflicting the least mortification.—Of course, this Letter is for your Brother, as for you—but I shall write to him soon. God bless you, & S. T. Coleridge

## 465. To Thomas Wedgwood

*Address*: Thomas Wedgewood Esq. | Gunville | Eastbury | Blandford | Dorset
*MS. Wedgwood Museum. Pub.* Tom Wedgwood, *118*.
*Postmark*: 6 November 1802. *Stamped*: Brough.

Wednesday, Nov. 3. 1802. Keswick

Dear Wedgewood

It is now two hours since I received your Letter; and after the necessary consultation, Mrs Coleridge herself is fully of opinion that to lose Time is merely to lose Spirits. Accordingly, I have resolved not to look the children in the Face (the parting from whom is the only downright Bitter in the Thing) but to take a chaise tomorrow morning, ½ past Four, for Penrith, & go to London by tomorrow's Mail. Of course, I shall be in London (God permitting) on Saturday Morning—I shall rest that day and the next, and proceed to Bristol by the Monday Night's Mail. At Bristol I will go to Cote, and there wait your coming.——If the Family be not at home, I shall beg a Bed at Dr Beddoes's, or at least leave word where I am.—At all events, barring serious Illness, serious Fractures, and the et cetera of serious *Unforeseens*, I shall be at Bristol, Tuesday Noon, Nov. 9th. You are aware, that my whole knowlege of French does not extend beyond the power of limping slowly, not without a Dictionary Crutch, thro' an easy French Book: & that as to Pronunciation, all my Organs of Speech, from the bottom of the Larynx to the Edge of my Lips, are utterly and naturally Anti-gallican.—If only I shall have been any Comfort, any Alleviation, to you—I shall feel myself at ease—& whether you go abroad or no, while I remain with you, it will greatly contribute to my comfort, if I know that you will have no hesitation, nor pain, in telling me what you wish me to do or not to do. I regard it among the Blessings of my Life that I have never lived among men whom I regarded as my artificial Superiors; that all the respect, I have at any time payed, has been wholly to supposed Goodness or Talent. The consequence has been, that I have no alarms of Pride, no cheval de frise of Independence. I have always lived among Equals. It never occurs to me, even for a moment, that I am otherwise. If I have quarreled with men, it has been, as Brothers, or School-fellows quarrel. How little any man can give me, or take from me, save in matters of Kindness and esteem, is not so much a Thought, or Conviction, with me, or even a distinct Feeling, as it is my very Nature.—Much as I dislike all formal Declarations of this kind, I have deemed it well to say this. I have as strong feelings of Gratitude as any man. Shame upon me, if in the Sickness & the Sorrow which I have had, and which have been kept unaggravated & supportable by your kindness & your Brother's, shame upon me if I did not feel a kindness, not unmixed with reverence, towards you both / but yet I never should have had my present Impulses to be with you, and this confidence that I may be an occasional comfort to you, if independently of all gratitude I did not thoroughly esteem you; and if I did not appear to myself to *understand* the nature of your sufferings, & within the last year in some slight degree to have *felt*, myself, something of the same. Forgive me, my dear Sir! if I have said too much—it is better to *write* it than to *say* it—& I am anxious that in the event of our travelling together you should feel yourself at ease with me, even as you would with a younger Brother, to whom from his childhood you had been in the Habit of saying, Do this, Col.—or—don't do that—.———

I have been writing fast lest I should be too late for the Post—forgetting that I am myself going with the Mail, & of course had better send the Letter from London with the intelligence of my safe arrival there——Till then, all Good be with us.—

S. T. Coleridge

Penrith | Thursday Morn—

If this Letter reaches you without any further writing, you will understand by it, that all the Places in the Mail are engaged—& that I must wait a day—but this will make no difference in my arrival at Bristol——

## 466. *To Mrs. S. T. Coleridge*

*Address* [Mr]s Coleridge | Greta Hall | Keswick | Cumberla[nd]
*MS. Victoria University Lib. Hitherto unpublished.* This fragment comprises parts of the first, second, third, and fourth pages of the manuscript.

Undoubtedly the missing passages in this letter included an account of the time Coleridge spent in the company of Sara Hutchinson at Penrith on his way to London. The letters immediately following show that Mrs. Coleridge, cognizant of her husband's intimacy with Sara Hutchinson and thoroughly angered by it, wrote in high dudgeon of this visit. Thus Coleridge was led to berate his wife for her jealousy and to offer analyses of her and of himself; and while he was solicitous about her coming confinement, it is evident that her failure either to look with favour on his affection for Sara Hutchinson and the Wordsworths or 'to give them any Share of *your* Heart', was an important source of friction between them.

*Postmark*: 8 ⟨November⟩ 18⟨02⟩.

[8 November 1802][1]

. . . his wife a nasty hard-hearted, hatchet-fac'd, droop-nos'd, eye-sunken, rappee-complexioned, [old Bitch.—][2] The first night we stopp'd at 10 o clock—& slept at [Leeming Lane][2]—the next night at 12, & slept at Newark—Sunday afternoon 2 o clock brought us to Stamford—where I took the Mail for London / a horrible stinking Jew crucified my Nose the whole way—It is fact, that I never knew what a true *foul* stench was, before—O it was a STINKING JEW! We arrived at the Bull & Mouth Inn at ½ past 5 this morning—I sate by the fire in the dark Coffee-house till ½ past 7, when I got my Breakfast / & took a hackney Coach for King's Street, where the Howells received me with great Joy—, & seemingly true affection.—My Cloathes are just gone off, & Books[3]— so that I have been under the necessity of ordering a new suit, immediately—& I shall stay in Town till Wednesday or perhaps Thursday—but shall see no body but Stuart & John Wordsworth— of this you may depend——. If any Letter come from the Colonel i.e. my Brother—or from Mr Dennys, . . .

. . . you had better direct the Letter to Mr Estlin's, where I will leave my Address—if I shall have quitted Bristol.—It must be a Joy to you to hear, that I have borne the Journey so well—it cost me two pound, perhaps, more than it would have done, if I could have taken my place in the Mail—but it was money well-spent—for both the first & second night my Limbs were quite crazed & feverous, & my inside hot as fire—so that in all probability had I not had sound sleep each night, I should have been layed up. My Journey has cost me, all in all, £8₁₁ 11s₁₁ 6D. I will send you down some money in a post or two—

My dear Love—write as chearfully as possible. I am tenderer, & more fluttery, & bowel-weak, than most—I can not bear any thing gloomy, unless when it is quite necessary.—Be assured, I

---

[1] Coleridge left Keswick on 4 Nov. as he had planned (see Letter 465), stayed in Penrith overnight, and arrived in London on 8 Nov.

[2] The words in brackets are inked out in the manuscript.

[3] On 4 Nov. 1802 Lamb wrote to Coleridge that his books, &c., which had been left in London, were to leave by the Kendal wagon the following day. *Lamb Letters*, i. 328.

*8 November 1802* [466

will bring back (come home when I will) a pure, affectionate, & husbandly Heart to ...
 Again & again & for ever more
God bless & preserve you, my Love! & me for your sake, & the sake of our dear Children / —& try to *love* & be *kind* to, those whom I love.——I am, & will remain,
 Your faithful & affectionate Husband
 S. T. Coleridge

### 467. *To Mrs. S. T. Coleridge*

*MS. Victoria University Lib. Pub. E.L.G. i. 190.*

[Saturday Morning, 13 November 1802][1]

... when they ... the trains of my ideas, they fall in, & form part of ... as to what is thought or said of me by persons, whom I do not particularly esteem or love, & by whom I am not esteemed or loved. 4. An independence of, & contempt for, all advantages of external fortune, that are not immediately connected with bodily comforts, or moral pleasures. I love warm Rooms, comfortable fires, & food, books, natural scenery, music &c; but I do not care what *binding* the Books have, whether they are dusty or clean— & I *dislike* fine furniture, handsome cloathes, & all the ordinary symbols & appendages of artificial superiority—or what is called, *Gentility*. In the same Spirit, I dislike, at least I seldom like, Gentlemen, gentlemanly manners, &c. I have no Pride, as far as Pride means a desire to be *thought* highly of by others—if I have any sort of Pride, it consists in an indolent ...

So much for myself—& now I will endeavor to give a short sketch of what appears to be the nature of your character.—As I seem to exist, as it were, almost wholly within myself, in *thoughts* rather than in *things*, in a particular warmth felt all over me, but chiefly felt about my heart & breast; & am connected with *things without* me by the pleasurable sense of their immediate Beauty or Loveliness, and not at all by my knowlege of their average value in the minds of people in general; & with *persons without* me by

[1] This fragment is from the letter to which Coleridge refers in the first sentence of Letter 468: 'I wrote to you from the New Passage, Saturday Morning, Nov. 13.—' While this scrap is all that remains of Coleridge's impetuous letter, we may judge of its tenor from a second reference to it in Letter 470: 'I did not write to you that Letter from the Passage without much pain, & many Struggles of mind.... Had there been nothing but your Feelings concerning Penrith I should have passed it over—... but there was one whole sentence of a very, very different cast. It immediately disordered my Heart, and Bowels.'

467]      *To Mrs. S. T. Coleridge*

no ambition of their esteem, or of having rank & consequence in their minds, but with people in general by general kindliness of feeling, & with my especial friends, by an intense delight in fellow-feeling, by an intense perception of the Necessity of LIKE to LIKE; so you on the contrary exist almost wholly in the world *without you* / the Eye & the Ear are your great organs, and you depend upon the eyes & ears of others for a great part of your pleasures. . . .

### 468. *To Mrs. S. T. Coleridge*

*Address*: Mrs Coleridge | Keswick | Cumberland
*MS. Lord Latymer. Pub. with omis.* Letters, *i. 410.*
*Postmark*: 18 November 1802.

St Clear, Carmarthen. Tues. Nov. 16. 1802
My dear Love

I wrote to you from the New Passage, Saturday Morning, Nov. 13.—We had a favorable Passage—dined on the other side, & proceeded in a Post-chaise to Usk, and from thence to Abergavenny, where we supped, slept, & breakfasted—a vile supper, vile beds, & vile breakfast.—From Abergavenny to Brecon, thro' the vale of Usk, I believe—19 miles of most delightful Country—it is not indeed comparable with the meanest part of our Lake Country—but Hills, Vale, & River, Cottages & Woods, are nobly blended, & thank Heaven! I seldom permit my past greater pleasures to lessen my enjoyment of present Charms—Of the things, which this 19 miles has in common with our whole vale of Keswick, (which is about 19 miles,) I may say that the two vales, & the two Rivers are equal to each other / that Keswick Vale beats the Welch one, all hollow, in Cottages—; but is as much surpassed by it in Woods, and Timber Trees. I am persuaded, that every Tree in the South of England has three times the number of *Leaves*, that a Tree of the same sort & size has in Cumberland or Westmoreland—and there is an incomparably larger number of very large Trees. Even the Scotch Firs luxuriate into beauty, & pluminess, & the Larches are magnificent Creatures indeed—in S. Wales.—I must not deceive you however / with all these advantages, S. Wales—if you came into it with the very pictures of Keswick, Ulswater, Grasmere, &c in your fancy, & were determined to hold them & S. Wales together—with all it's richer fields, woods, & ancient Trees, S. Wales would needs appear flat & tame, as ditch-water. I have no firmer persuasion than this—that there is no place in our Island—(& saving Switzerland—none in Europe, perhaps) which really equals the vale of Keswick, including Borrodale, Newlands, & Bassenthwaite—. O Heaven! that it had but a more genial Climate!—It is now going on for the 18th week, since they have had any Rain here, more than a few casual refreshing Showers—& we have monopolized the Rain of the whole Kingdom! From Brecon to Trecastle / a Church Yard two or three miles from Brecon is belted by a circle of the largest & noblest Yews, I ever saw—in a belt, to wit—they are not as large as the Yew in Borrodale, or that in Lorton / but so many, so large & noble, I never saw before—and quite *glowing* with those heavenly coloured silky-pink-scarlet Berries.—From Trecastle to Llandovery, where we found a nice Inn, an excellent Supper, & good Beds—. From Llandovery to Llandilo—from Llandilo to Carmarthen, a large Town, all white-washed—the Roofs of the Houses all white-washed! a great Town in a Confectioner's shop, on Twelfth cake Day / or a huge Show piece at a distance / . It is nobly situated along a Hill, among Hills, at the Head of a very extensive Vale.—From Carmarthen after Dinner to St Clear— a little Hamlet nine miles from Carmarthen, three miles from the Sea (the nearest Sea-port being Langarn, pronounced *Larn*, on Carmarthen Bay—look in the Map) and not quite 100 miles from Bristol.—The Country immediately round is exceedingly bleak & dreary—just the sort of Country, that there is around Shurton, &c—But the Inn, the BLUE BOAR, is the most comfortable little Public House, I was ever in—. Miss S. Wedgewood[1] left us this morning (we arrived here, at ½ past 4 Yesterday Evening) for Crescella, Mr ALLEN's Seat (the Mrs Wedgewoods' Father)[2] 15 miles from this place—and T. Wedgewood is gone out, Cock shooting, in high glee & spirits. He is very much better than I expected to have found him / he says, the Thought of my coming, & my really coming so immediately, has sent a new Life into him.— He will be out all the mornings—the evenings we chat, discuss, or I read to him. To me he is a delightful & instructive Companion. He possesses the *finest*, the *subtlest* mind & taste, I have ever yet met with.—His mind resembles that miniature Sun seen, as you look thro' a Holly Bush, as I have described it in my Three Graves—[3]

> ' A small blue Sun! and it has got
> A perfect Glory too!
> Ten thousand *Hairs* of color'd Light
> Make up a Glory gay & bright
> Round that small orb so blue![']——

[1] Sarah Wedgwood was the sister of Tom and Josiah.
[2] John Bartlett Allen of Cresselly was the father of Mrs. John and Mrs. Josiah Wedgwood.          [3] *Poems*, i. 284, lines 509–13.

### To Mrs. S. T. Coleridge

I continue in excellent Health, compared with my state at Keswick—my bowels give me but small Disquiet—all, I am troubled with, is a frequent oppression, a suffocating Weight, of Wind—Sunday Night I was obliged to *sit up* in my bed, an hour & a half—& at last, was forced to make myself sick by a feather, in order to throw off the Wind from my Stomach—. But I have now left off Beer too, & will persevere in it—I take no Tea—in the morning Coffee, with a tea spoonful of Ginger in the last cup—in the afternoon a large Cup of Ginger Tea— / & I take Ginger at 12 o clock at noon, & a glass after supper. I find not the least inconvenience from any Quantity, however large—I dare say, I take a large Table spoonful in the course of the 24 hours—& once in the 24 hours (but not always at the same hour) I take half a grain of purified opium, equal to 12 drops of Laudanum—which is not more than [an] 8th part of what I took at Keswick, exclusively of B[eer,] Brandy, & Tea, which last is undoubtedly a pernicious S[timulant—] all which I have left off—& will give this Regimen a *fair, compleat* Trial of one month—with no other deviation, than that I shall sometimes lessen the opiate, & sometimes miss a day. But I am fully convinced, & so is T. Wedgewood, that to a person, with such a Stomach & Bowels as mine, if any stimulus is needful, Opium in the small quantities, I now take it, is incomparably better in every respect than Beer, Wine, Spirits, or any *fermented* Liquor—nay, far less pernicious than even Tea.—*It is my particular Wish, that Hartley & Derwent should have as little Tea as possible—& always very*[1] *weak, with more than half milk.* Read this sentence to Mary, and to Mrs Wilson.—I should think, that Ginger Tea with a good deal of Milk in it would be an excellent Thing for Hartley. A Tea spoonful piled up of Ginger would make a pot full of Tea, that would serve him for two days—And let him drink it half milk—I dare say, that he would like it very well—for it is pleasant, with sugar—& tell him that his dear Father takes it instead of Tea, & believes, that it will make his dear Hartley grow, & cure the Worms. The whole Kingdom is getting *Ginger*-mad.

My dear Love! I have said nothing of Italy: for I am as much in the Dark as when I left Keswick—indeed, much more. For I now doubt very much whether we shall go or no. Against our going you must place T. W's improved state of Health, & his exceeding dislike to continental Travelling, & horror of the Sea, & his exceeding attachment to his Family / for our going you must place his past experience—the transiency of his enjoyments, the craving after change, & the effect of a cold winter, especially if it should come on *wet*, or *sleety*. His determinations are made so rapidly,

---
[1] Underlined twice in MS.

that two or three days of wet weather with a raw cold air might have such an effect on his Spirits, that he might go off immediately for Naples, or perhaps for Teneriff—which latter place he is always talking about. Look out for it in the Encyclopaedia.—Again, these latter causes make it not impossible or improbable, that the pleasure, he has in me, as a companion, may languish—. I must subscribe myself in haste

Your dear Husband<br>S. T. Coleridge

The Mail is waiting

### 469. To Mrs. S. T. Coleridge

*MS. Lord Latymer. Hitherto unpublished.*

St. Clear's, Carmarthen. Sunday, Nov. 21. 1802

My dear Sara

It is a bleak Country this, & the Rain has come on / tho' to day is a sunshiny Day. I have nothing to tell you therefore, except that I am this instant going to Crescelly, 17 miles from hence, to the Seat of Mr Allen, the Mrs Wedgewoods' Father / that we purpose to return hither to morrow to dinner / but for fear any accident should keep us longer, I now write these few Lines in a hurry—which yet, I trust, will be worth postage, because they will inform you that my Health continues to improve / & if I remain tranquil, I may return to you, a new Creation. I think it not improbable that we may go from hence to Bodmin, in Cornwall / but I know nothing —& T.W. knows as little.

I shall write to Stuart immediately to send you some money—I can not ask Wedgewood—& he has not said any thing to me / but merely borrowed from me the money, I had, saying—that it was impossible, we could have any but joint expences. I hope to find a Letter from you on my return / all about yourself, i.e. your Health, & the dear children. Remember me most affectionately to Mr Jackson—& Mrs Wilson—& give my Love to Mary—& be sure to tell her & Mrs Wilson not to let Derwent & Hartley have any Tea. Milk & water equally hot—& they won't know the difference. A weak Ginger Tea would certainly be useful to Hartley's Bowels.

God bless you, my dear Love, | &<br>S. T. Coleridge

### 470. To Mrs. S. T. Coleridge

*Address*: Mrs Coleridge | Greta Hall | Keswick | Cumberland
*MS. Lord Latymer. Pub. with omis. E.L.G. i. 218.*
*Postmark*: 25 November 1802.

St Clear's, Carmarthen.
Tuesday MORNING, ½ past 5!! Nov. 22 [23]. 1802

My dear Love

We left this place some two hours before your Letter arrived; & returned hither yesterday Afternoon, ¼ past I—half an hour too late for me to answer your Letter by yesterday's Post. I know, that this will be a Morning of Bustle: & the desire of writing you lay so heavy on my mind, that I awoke at 4 o/clock this morning. The fires here in every room keep in all day & all night; & yet they do not use as much coal on the whole, as we do. It burns like a Brick-kiln Fire—is never touched—& never goes out, till the last cinder falls out of the Grate. Would to Heaven! you had only a few Waggon loads of them for the next 3 or 4 months!—A little after the Clock struck 5, I rose & lit my Candle, found the untended Fire in the parlour bright & clear; & am sitting by it, writing to you—to tell you, how very much I was & am affected by the tidings of your Fainting—& to beg you, INSTANTLY to get a Nurse. If Mary's Aunt cannot come, do write immediately to Mrs Clarkson, & try to get Mrs Railton. To be sure, there is a mawkish '*so-vāry-good*'-ness about her character, & her Face & Dress have far too much of the SMUG-DOLEFUL in them, for *my* Taste; but I believe, she is really a well-intentioned honest woman, & she is certainly an excellent Nurse.—At all events, get somebody immediately—have a fire in your Bedroom—& have nothing to do with Derwent, either to mind or to dress him. If you are seriously ill, or unhappy at my absence, I will return at all Hazards: for I know, you would not *will* it, tho' you might *wish* it, except for a serious cause.

I shall write to Mr Estlin for my Letter. You speak too of a Letter from Mr Dennis. Where is it? I have received none. If I want the Old Man of the Alps, I will write for it.—

Indeed, my dear Love! I did not write to you that Letter from the Passage[1] without much pain, & many Struggles of mind, Resolves, & Counter-resolves. Had there been nothing but your Feelings concerning Penrith I should have passed it over—as merely a little tiny Fretfulness—but there was one whole sentence of a very, very different cast. It immediately disordered my Heart,

[1] See Letter 467.

and Bowels. If it had not, I should not have written you; but it is necessary, absolutely necessary for you to know, how such things do affect me. My bodily Feelings are linked in so peculiar a way with my Ideas, that you cannot *enter into* a state of Health so utterly different from your own natural Constitution—you can only see & know, that so it is. Now, what we know only by the outward fact, & not by sympathy & inward experience of the same, we are ALL of us too apt to forget; & incur the necessity of being *reminded* of it by others. And this is one among the many causes, which render the marriage of unequal & unlike Understandings & Dispositions so exceedingly miserable. Heaven bear me witness, [I often say inly—in the words of Christ—Father forgive her! she knows not what she does][1]—Be assured, my dear Love! that I shall never write otherwise than *most* kindly to you, except after great *Aggressions* on your part: & not then, unless my reason convinces me, that some good end will be answered by my Reprehensions.— My dear Love! let me in the spirit of love say two things / 1. I owe duties, & solemn ones, to you, as my wife; but I owe equally solemn ones to Myself, to my Children, to my Friends, and to Society. Where Duties are at variance, dreadful as the case may be, there must be a Choice. I can neither retain my Happiness nor my Faculties, unless I move, live, & love, in perfect Freedom, limited only by my own purity & self-respect, & by my incapability of loving any person, man or woman, unless I at the same time honor & esteem them. My Love is made up $\frac{9}{10}$ths of fervent wishes for the permanent *Peace* of mind of those, whom I love, be it man or woman; & for their Progression in purity, goodness, & true Knowlege. Such being the nature of my Love, no human Being can have a right to be jealous. My nature is quick to love, & retentive. Of those, who are within the immediate sphere of my daily agency, & bound to me by bonds of Nature or Neighbourhood, I shall love each, as they appear to me to deserve my Love, & to be capable of returning it. More is not in my power. If I would do it, I could not. That we can love but one person, is a miserable mistake, & the cause of abundant unhappiness. I can & do love many people, dearly—so dearly, that I really scarcely know, which I love the best. Is it not so with every good mother who has a large number of Children—& with many, many Brothers & Sisters in large & affectionate Families?—Why should it be otherwise with Friends? Would any good & wise man, any warm & wide hearted man marry at all, if it were part of the Contract—Henceforth this Woman is your only friend, your sole beloved! all the rest of mankind, however amiable & akin to you, must be only

---

[1] The passage in brackets is carefully inked out in the manuscript.

your *acquaintance*!—? It were well, if every woman wrote down before her marriage all, she thought, she had a *right* to, from her Husband—& to examine each in this form—By what *Law* of God, of Man, or of general reason, do I claim *this* Right?—I suspect, that this Process would make a ludicrous Quantity of Blots and Erasures in most of the first rude Draughts of these Rights of Wives—infinitely however to their own Advantage, & to the security of their true & genuine Rights. 2.—Permit me, my dear Sara! without offence to you, as Heaven knows! it is without any feeling of Pride in myself, to say—that in sex, acquirements, and in the quantity and quality of natural endowments whether of Feeling, or of Intellect, you are the Inferior. Therefore it would be preposterous to expect that I should see with your eyes, & dismiss my Friends from *my* heart, only because you have not chosen to give them any Share of *your* Heart; but it is not preposterous, in me, on the contrary I have a *right* to expect & demand, that you should to a certain degree love, & act kindly to, those whom I deem worthy of my Love.—If you read this Letter with half the Tenderness, with which it is written, it will do you & both of us, GOOD; [& contribute it's share to the turning of a mere Cat-hole into a Dove's nest!][1] You know, Sally Pally! I must have a Joke— or it would not be me!—

Over frightful Roads we at last arrived at Crescelly, about 3 o/clock—found a Captain & Mrs Tyler there (a stupid Brace) Jessica, Emma, & Frances Allen—all simple, good, kind-hearted Lasses—& Jesse, the eldest, uncommonly so. We dined at $\frac{1}{2}$ past 4—just after dinner down came Old Allen—O Christ! Old Nightmair! An ancient Incubus! Every face was saddened, every mouth pursed up!—Most solemnly civil, like the Lord of a stately Castle 500 years ago! Doleful & plaintive eke: for I believe, that the Devil *is* twitching him home. After Tea he left us, & went again to Bed—& the whole party recovered their Spirits. I drank nothing; but I eat sweet meats, & cream, & some fruit, & talked a great deal, and sate up till 12, & did not go to sleep till near 2. In consequence of which I arose sickish, at $\frac{1}{2}$ past 7—my breakfast brought me about—& all the way from Crescelly I was in a very pleasurable state of feeling; but my feelings too tender, my thoughts too vivid—I was *deliciously* unwell. On my arrival at St Clear's I received your Letter, & had scarcely read it, before a fluttering of the Heart came on, which ended (as usual) in a sudden & violent Diarrhoea / I could scarcely touch my Dinner, & was obliged at last to take 20 drops of Laudanum—which now that I have for 10 days left off all stimulus of all kinds, excepting $\frac{1}{3}$rd of a grain of

[1] The passage in brackets is carefully inked out in the manuscript.

opium, at night, acted upon me more [pow]erfully than 80 or 100 drops would have done at Keswick.—I slept sound what I did sleep; but I am not *quite* well this morning; but I shall get round again in the course of the Day.—You must see by this, what absolute necessity I am under of *dieting* myself—& if possible, the still greater Importance of *Tranquillity* to me.—All the Woodcocks seem to have left the Country; T. Wedgewood's hopes & schemes are again all afloat; to day we leave this place for Narbarth, 12 miles from hence—shall probably return to Crescelly—& then— God knows, where! Cornwall perhaps—Ireland perhaps—perhaps, Cumberland—possibly, Naples, or Madeira, or Teneriffe. I don't see any likelihood of our going to the Moon, or to either of the Planets, or fixed Stars—& that is all, I can say. Write immediately, my dear Love! & direct to me—where?—That's the Puzzle—to be left at the Post Office, Carmarthen.—God bless you, my dear Love! & speed me back to you & our dear H. & D, *& etc.* Mr T. Wedgewood desires his best respects to you—he is just come down.—God bless you again & S. T. Coleridge

Best respects to Colonel Moore—& his Lady & Miss D'arcy— & always remember me affectionately to Mr Jackson, & Hartley's other Mother.——

### 471. To Mrs. S. T. Coleridge

*Address*: Mrs Coleridge | Greta Hall | Keswick | Cumberland
*MS*. Lord Latymer. *Pub*. *E.L.G. i. 222.*
*Postmark*: 7 December 1802. *Stamped*: Narberth.

Saturday Night, Dec. 4 1802.   Crescelly, near Narbarth

My dearest Love

I will not disappoint you of a Letter, tho' by a joint Blunder of mine & the Post Boy's I cannot send the Draft, till tomorrow: & for fear of accident do not expect it till this day week—tho' I hope, it will arrive on Friday: supposing this Letter to arrive on Thursday.—I have vexed & fretted myself that I did not send it a fortnight ago—there was no earthly reason, why I should not. You know, how hateful all Money-thoughts are to me!—& how idly & habitually I keep them at arm's length.—

I received to night your's+Lady Rush—with a Letter from Col. Moore—& one from Clarkson. I was affected by your Letter with such Joy & anxious Love—so overpowered by it, that I could not endure to read Lady Rush's—nor have I yet done it.— God love you & have you in his keeping, my blessed Sara!—& speedily restore me to you.—I have a faith, a heavenly Faith, that our future Days will be Days of Peace, & affectionate Happiness.—

## To Mrs. S. T. Coleridge

O that I were now with you! I feel it very, very hard to be from you at this trying Time—I dare not think a moment concerning you in this Relation, or I should be immediately ill. But I shall soon return—& bring you back a confident & affectionate Husband. Again, and again, my dearest dearest Sara!—my Wife & my Love, & indeed my very Hope / May God preserve you!—And do you above all things take care of yourself—if you have no other serious objection but the expence, to Mrs Railton—I desire, I *command* you, to have her instantly. Heaven forbid we should save a few pounds at this time.——

If you want the money immediately, & cannot without discomfort wait another Day——but this is idle—one or two Days can make no Difference—. I have some thoughts of sending 50£, which you may change by paying Miss Crosthwaite's Bill.——I shall write to Colonel Moore to morrow—.

To morrow morning T. Wedgewood goes to Treharn, about 13 miles from hence—to see a Cottage which he means to take / on Wednesday or Thursday he will receive an answer from Gunville—& before this I trust, he will receive an Answer from Luff[1]—In all probability we shall leave this place for Gunville on Friday or Saturday—& from thence, after a short Stay, proceed together to Keswick. I cannot doubt that I at least, shall be with you by New-Year's Day / —tho' *possibly* I may be obliged to leave you again for two or three months—. But the Future is a Cloud.

Josiah Wedgewood has been ill in the rheumatism / he has written, in a Letter to Tom W. (received this evening) a most affectionate Paragraph to me, assuring me of his Love & perfect Regard. It affected me greatly.

It is one o clock—& I must finish this Letter for it is to go off tomorrow morning at 8.

I am very comfortable here. Sally Wedgewood is really the most perfectly good woman, I ever knew / & the three Allens are sweet, cheerful, & most innocent Girls. I cannot help being idle among them. What sweeter & more tranquillizing pleasure is there, than to feel one's self completely innocent among compleatly innocent young Women—! Save when I think of home, my mind is calm & soundless.—Sally Wedgewood plays on the Piano Forte *divinely*—Warm Rooms, warm Bedrooms, Music, pleasant Talking, & extreme Temperance—all this agrees with me—& the best Blessing, that results from all, is a *placid Sleep*—no *difficulties* in my Dreams, no Pains, [no Desires][2]—.

[1] Captain Charles Luff, a young friend of the Wordsworths and Clarksons, lived at Glenridding in Patterdale.
[2] Words in brackets inked out in manuscript.

There is an old Aunt in the House, a large fat old Lady, (her name Mrs Jones) foolishly good-tempered, & of frisky Spirits.— She is old Allen's own Sister—& has another Brother, Joshua Allen, a great oddity, & enthusiastic Methodist. It is notorious to every one but himself that he neither does care, or ever has cared, a farthing for his Wife or Children—This man descanted on Religion in the following words—'All our sinful affections give way to the blessed Graces of Religion. *I am so compleatly a new Creature by means of Religion, tho' it is well known what Love I bear my Wife & children, yet if a man were to murder them before my face, I am positive, that I should not feel the least spark of resentment.'*—[']Nay, nay, Brother Josh (exclaimed the old Lady who looks up to him as to an Angel) *there* you *do* go somewhat too far. *I* SHOULD be a *little offended* at it.'——Jessica Allen was present—& told me the Story with infinite Humour.——

Give my best Love to Mr Jackson, & Mrs Wilson— And O! My sweet Hartley! & my Derwent!——

God bless you & S. T. Coleridge

Josiah Wedgewood's Esqre Gunville, near Blandford, Dorset— will be my next address.

### 472. To Mrs. S. T. Coleridge

MS. Lord Latymer. Pub. E.L.G. i. 225.

Crescelly, Dec. 5. 1802

My dearest Love

I inclose a Draft for 50£; dated Monday, Decemb. 13th & payable two months after date. I would have you pay Miss Crosthwaite's Bill—ordering in all you will want for the next month—& so paying up for the whole year at once. Mr Jackson will be so good as to pay the Bill for you—& indorse the Draft which I have drawn in his name. Whether you can likewise send 10£ to your Mother, you will see, after you have paid all that is needful or well to pay. J'Anson & the Carriers must be payed off hand.—Be sure not to leave yourself with less than 10£, if possible —& therefore as I would have you pay the Butcher & Flour Woman, you had better not think of your Mother.

T. Wedgewood did not go to day to Treharn—; but I go with him tomorrow.—As I must get up early, I must not write longer to keep myself awake. I have been listening to sweet Music till I am much effeminated, & if I were to indulge in any Thoughts respecting Keswick I should not close my eyes for hours. God bless

( 891 )

472] *To Mrs. S. T. Coleridge*

you, my dear Love!—Don't you think, Crescelly Coleridge, would be a pretty name for a Boy?—If a Girl, let it be Gretha Coleridge—not *Greta*—but—Gretha—unless you prefer Rotha—or Laura. What do you think of Bridget?—Only it ought to end with a vowel. You may take your choice of Sara, Gretha, or rather Algretha, Rotha, Laura, Emily, or Lovenna.—. The Boy must be either Bracey, or Crescelly.—Algretha Coleridge will needs be a beautiful Girl.——

God bless you, my dear Life [sic]—& our sweet children—& your affectionate Husband

S. T. Coleridge

For God's sake don't let the expence weigh with you about a Nurse. You ought to think of a Servant. I hope, Sara Hutchinson will be well enough to come in, while you are lying in / both she & Mary Wordsworth are good Nurses.——

### 473. *To John Prior Estlin*

*Address*: Revd J. P. Estlin | St Michael's Hill | Bristol
MS. *Bristol Central Lib. Pub. with omis.* Letters, i. 414.
*Stamped*: Narberth.

Dec. 7. 1802.—Crescelly, near Narbarth, Pembrokeshire

My dear Friend

I took the Liberty of desiring Mrs Coleridge to direct a Letter for me, to you—fully expecting to have seen you—but I passed rapidly thro' Bristol, & left it with Mr Wedgewood immediately—& literally had *no time* to see any one. I hope however to see you on my return / for I wish very much to have some hours' conversation with you on a subject, that will not cease to interest either of us, while we *live* at least—and I trust, that this is a Synonime of—'for ever!'—As Mr T. Wedgewood however is rapid in his movements, & sudden in his resolves, it is possible, that we may strike up directly thro' Wales into the North, without taking Bristol in our way—I must therefore request that you will be so good as to re-direct any Letter or Letters, which there may be for me, to J. B. Allen's, Esqre, Crescelly, near Narbarth, Pembrokeshire—by the return of Post.

Have you seen my different Essays in the Morning Post?—The Comparison of Imperial Rome, & France—the 'Once a Jacobin, always a Jacobin[']—& the two Letters to Mr Fox?—Are my Politics your's?—

Have you heard lately from America? A Gentleman informed

me, that the Progress of religious Deism in the middle Provinces is exceedingly rapid—that there are numerous Congregations of Deists—&c &c. Would to heaven, this were the case in France!— Surely, religious Deism is infinitely nearer the religion of our Saviour, than the *gross* Idolatry of Popery, or the more decorous, but not less genuine, Idolatry of a vast majority of Protestants.— If there be meaning in words, it appears to me that the Quakers & Unitarians are the only Christians, altogether pure from Idolatry— and even of these, I am sometimes jealous, that some of the Unitarians make too much an *Idol* of their *one* God. Even the worship of one God becomes Idolatry, in my convictions, when instead of the Eternal & Omnipresent, in whom we live, & move, & *have* our Being, we set up a distinct Jehovah tricked out in the *anthropomorphic* Attributes of Time & *Successive* Thoughts—& think of him, as a PERSON, *from* whom we had our Being. The tendency to *Idolatry* seems to me to lie at the root of all our human Vices—it is our Original Sin.—When we dismiss *three Persons* in the Deity, only by subtracting *two*, we talk more intelligibly, but I fear, do not feel more religiously—for God is a Spirit, & must be worshipped in Spirit.

O my dear Sir! it is long since we have seen each other—believe me, my esteem & grateful Affection for you & Mrs Estlin has suffered no abatement, or intermission—nor can I persuade myself, that my opinions fully stated & fully understood would appear to you to differ *essentially* from your own. My creed is very simple— my confession of Faith very brief. I approve altogether & embrace entirely the *Religion* of the Quakers, but exceedingly dislike the *sect*, & their own notions of their own Religion.—By Quakerism I understand the opinions of George Fox rather than those of Barclay—who was the St Paul of Quakerism.—

I pray for you, & your's!—

S. T. Coleridge—

## 474. To Mrs. S. T. Coleridge

*Address*: Mrs Coleridge | Greta Hall | Keswick | Cumberland   Single Sheet
*MS.* Lord Latymer. *Pub. E.L.G. i. 226.*
*Postmark*: 15 December 1802.   *Stamped*: Narberth.

Crescelly
Monday, Dec. 13. 1802—Morning, 8 o/clock

My dear Love

A few minutes remain, before the Post, for me to tell you, that here I still am—& that nothing has happened—& that my Health seems stationary, saving that my half boot with a hard Fold has

## To Mrs. S. T. Coleridge

bruised the cross of my foot, which swells and inflames at evenings & gives me much pain & some concern. We waited for a Letter from Luff—& one from Gunville—my Letter to Luff has been blown about by Cross winds. When that from Gunville arrives, which surely will come tomorrow, we shall, I suppose, leave this place—but probably not for Gunville—but for Keswick. Supposing this to be the case, & supposing we set off on Wednesday or Thursday Morning, we shall be eight Days at least in the Journey—so that we cannot be there before Christmas Day—it is my intention, as you will then be confined, to leave T. Wedgewood at Clarkson's. But all this may all happen differently—! I sent you, a week ago, a draft, dated from this day, for 50£.—I will give you notice, as soon as I know myself, where a Letter from you will meet me.—I hope, that Sara Hutchinson is well enough to have come in—it would be a great comfort, that one or the other of the three Women at Grasmere should be with you—& Sara rather than the other two because you will hardly have another opportunity of having her by yourself & to yourself, & of learning to know her, such as she really is. How much this lies at my Heart with respect to the Wordsworths, & Sara, and how much of our common Love & Happiness depends on your loving those whom I love,—why should I repeat?—I am confident, my dear Love! that I have no occasion to repeat it.

Considering how long I have been here, & how without a single Interruption I have continued for three weeks to think of you with love & tenderness, & that this, I regard, as an omen of the Future—I should like the child to be called *Crescelly*—purely on the account, I have stated——

I will write again to morrow—

My dearest Love! with 10 thousand wishes & fervent prayers for you, I am

Your faith. & aff. Husband<br>S. T. Coleridge

### 475. To James Coleridge

*Address*: Col/l Coleridge | Ottery St Mary | Honiton | Devon
*MS. British Museum. Hitherto unpublished.*

Crescelly, Pembroke. Dec. 14. 1802

My dear Brother

I left Keswick, Nov. 5 [4], & proceeded immediately to my friend, Mr T. Wedgewood, the state of whose Health & Feelings made me feel it my duty to answer a Letter of his, only by going to him. Since that time we have been moving from one place to

## 14 December 1802 [475

another; & your Letter has been so tossed about by cross-winds, that I did not receive it till late, yester evening.—Indeed, my dear Brother! the account of your health was most deeply interesting to me. I will run the risk of being smiled at by you, by adding my opinions to those you have already received. When George tells you, you are bilious, Ned that you have an acid in your stomach, and Mother, that you have the rheumatic Gout, they all unconsciously equivocate—in one sense it is false, in another sense true, but trifling. Who does not know, that there exists a close sympathy between the Lungs & the Stomach, & between the Stomach & the Liver? Where the stomach & Lungs are confessedly diseased, the Liver will always secrete the Bile, at times, diseasedly—in quality or quantity. But what does this tell you more, than if a man should tell you, that you looked yellow, or coughed much? Your own Looking-glass, and your own ears will have informed you whether this is true or no.—So no doubt a Stomach that turns even Fat acid, will often have an acid in it—& a Stomach, that generates wind in such quantities, must needs afflict the body with these flying pains, which my Mother calls the rheumatic Gout—.—All this is true, but it is likewise trifling. But if they mean more, & say—that such is the *cause* of your disorder, they speak without proof—& I suspect, against probability—they confound the *Symptoms* with the primary Disease. Your own account is exceedingly rational— I have no doubt, that you see the Truth / but I suspect, that you do not see it in all it's Bearings. There is only one sentence in your account that I object to—but that sentence is the most important & has made me very anxious. 'In short, I am not in a Decline because I lose no flesh, and look very healthy.'—I was with a very shrewd & *common sense* physician lately, who had much experience in pulmonary consumption, and was enumerating the sources of delusion, which led pulmonary Patients to disbelieve the fact till it became of no use to know it. Among others he particularly stated this one—almost in your very words. Indeed, indeed, my dear Brother, in the *early* stage of pulmonary Consumption many Patients even *gain* flesh, & look more than usually healthy. My little Berkley grew fat and looked healthy to the Hour of his Death—he was opened, & found to have died of ulcers in his Lungs, & the Lungs exceedingly inflamed.—Whatever may be the *cause* of your disorder, whether the circumstances, you have stated, or any thing more latent in your original constitution—or more probably, both in combination—the effect however is admitted & certain. You have a weak Stomach, that generates acids & gasses; & you have weak Lungs—that is, Lungs in an inflamed State, & that inflammation easily exasperated.—Now do ask any experienced Apothecary, whether slight causes would not *convert* such a State of Body into pulmonary Consumption? Stomach Weakness, when not relieved by natural Paroxysms of Gout, have [has] a *frequent* termination in consumption; but surely there is no possible description of pulmonary consumption, which would not include heated & inflammable Lungs, with something like a permanent Cold in the Head, as pulmonary consumption in it's *first approaches* at least, if not in it's earliest Stage. Probably, there may be 20 different Diseases confounded under one name of pulmonary Consumption / . The Disease, when the same, will probably be greatly modified by the circumstance of it's arising from constitutional predisposing weakness, or from direct personal exposure & overaction. The latter is pretty clearly your case—& I have not the least doubt, that you would be completely renovated by a year passed in a warm & even climate, without those *Drafts* of air, & those irritating particles of Sea-coal, which make an English Fire-side (that Father & Mother of all genuine English Virtues) a very stepmother to pulmonary Patients. As to myself, I am determined to pass the next year or two of my Life either at Madeira, or Teneriffe, or Lisbon—with my Family.—All this I have written on my own score of information / but let it all go for mere Prattle—only do let me *intreat* you, my dear Brother! to write a detailed account of your Health to Dr Beddoes. You & I, I dare say, think much alike of Beddoes's general mind. He is a very ingenious man, of great Learning & very extensive practice— but precipitant, & bold, even to daring—a passionate Innovator. But there is no man in Europe who has had under his inspection so many cases of Scrofula, Hypochondriasis (or Complaints of the Stomach & other digestive organs) and of consumption, whether purely organical & pulmonary, or scrofulous, or hypochondriac, or all conjoined—& these in all possible stages of the Disorders, & modified by all possible Differences of Age, Habits, Sex, & Constitution—. Many sensible Physicians, who hold Beddoes very cheap in general, admit that in the detection of Diseases, & in his deductions from Symptoms, he is perhaps unrivalled.—It will cost you but a guinea, & it is probable, that from some respect & kindness, he bears to me, he may give more *thought* to it, than to an ordinary Letter. I wish you only to learn from him what your disorder *is*—how far you will adopt his mode of curing it, is quite an after question—Yet while I write thus, I seem to feel, that no two enlightened Physicians, who had been tolerably conversant with pulmonary cases, could have two different opinions on your case. You are evidently not in a *Decline*; but as evidently [you have] the *Basis*, the *precurrent* & *predisposing* Causes, of pul-

## 14 December 1802

monary Consumption / tho' I have no doubt that if only you will see it, & be *somewhat afraid*, you will not have the least reason to be *alarmed*. A warm climate would certainly & immediately effect a cure in your case—without any danger of relapse on your return to this country—& I should hope, that even in England care, with a very cautious use of the Tincture of Digitalis, would produce the same effect. But believe me, I am not quite so mad as to wish that you should place any Reliance on *my* prescriptions.—May God Almighty preserve you for your family & for your Country!——

I expect to return to Keswick in a day or two, & that Mr T. Wedgewood will accompany me—As soon as I arrive, I shall certainly write either to you or to George, & give you all I know of my own plans—& state to you the principles & the feelings, that prevent me from forming others. At present, my main plan must be to recover my health. My stomach is weak—& disposed to flatulence with all it's pains & heavinesses—& I have no [doubt that] there is a taint of Scrofula in my constitution. [By Scroful]a I mean no more than an inirritable State [of] the muscles, with deficient venous action, & a languor of the absorbents—accompanied with an undue sensibility of the nervous system, or of whatever unknown parts of our body are the more immediate Instruments of Feeling & Idea. Where you find a man indolent in body & indisposed to definite action, but with lively Feelings, vivid ideal Images, & a power & habit of continuous Thinking, you may always, I believe, suspect a somewhat of Scrofula—With me it is something more than a suspicion—I had several glandular Swellings at School—& within the last four years a Lump has formed on my left cheek, just on the edge of my whisker—. The swellings in my knees were from the same cause.—For my Stomach I have found great relief in taking Ginger Tea with milk & sugar—& just at the moment of dinner, two or three pills, containing in the whole—four or five Grains of Rhubarb mixed up in gum water with an equal or greater quantity of Ginger. This no doubt must have been often recommended to you—[& no doubt] you have tried it. In my diet I prefer simple to seasoned, solids to fluids, and animal food to vegetable—I sacredly abstain from Tea, which turns acid on my stomach, & is assuredly a poison to weak stomachs—likewise as sacredly from all wine, spirits, & fermented liquors. If I am at any time very languid, & a faint head-ach & troubled bowels give me the warning, I prefer ether in small quantities with camphorated Julep, or half a grain of opium, to wine or spirit—& my Health has improved, astonishingly, since I adopted this regimen. But warmth, warm cloathing, & tranquillity of mind, are things of absolute necessity with me.—

475]    *To James Coleridge*

I doubt whether I shall reach Keswick before I have to announce another Coleridge to you—I long very much—indeed, my whole inside *yearns*—to see you all—& your dear little ones.—My best duty to my Mother—my Love to Mrs James, love to the big Children, & kisses to the little ones—love to George, Mrs George, to Edward & his Wife. May Heaven bless you all!

I am, dear Brother, your's with unfeigned Affection, & a deep Esteem

S. T. Coleridge—

I write from Mr Allen's Seat—one of whose Daughters is married to Mr Drew:——& 2 others to John & Josiah Wedgewood.

### 476. *To Mrs. S. T. Coleridge*

*Address*: Mrs Coleridge, or Mr Jackson, | Greta Hall, | Keswick | Cumberland
*MS. Lord Latymer. Pub. E. L. G. i. 227.*
*Postmark*: 18 December 1802. *Stamped*: Narberth.

Thursday Morning, 7 o/clock. Thursday, Dec. 16. 1802
Crescelly

My dear Love

I write with trembling—at what time or in what state my Letter may find you, how can I tell? Small need is there for saying, how anxious I am, how full of terrors & prayers!—I trust in God, that this Letter, which I write with a palpitating heart, you will read with a chearful one—the new Baby at your breast. O may God Almighty preserve you!

We leave this place in less than an hour—our rout lies thro' St Clear's, Carmarthen, Llandilo, Llandovery, Trecastle, Brecon, Hay, Hereford, Worcester, Birmingham, Litchfield, Abbot's Bromley, Uttoxeter, Ashborn, New Inn, Buxton, Stockport, Manchester, Bolton, Preston, Garstang, Lancaster, Burton, Kendal, Ambleside, Keswick—346 miles. From Keswick I must go with T. Wedgewood to Mr Clarkson's—& so on to Luff's. I calculate that we shall not much exceed forty miles a day: & that we shall be at Ambleside, Thursday Evening, Dec. 23rd.——
Mrs Wilson will be so good, as to have a Fire kept in Peach's Parlour, & likewise in Peach's Bedroom / & great care taken, that the Bed & Bedding shall be thoroughly and thoroughly warmed, & air[ed]. I should think it would be advisable to order immediately a pair of best Blankets from Miss Crosthwaite's.——My dearest Love! T. W. will not stay above a day or two in Keswick—& for God's sake, do not let [him] be any weight or bustle on your mind—let him be entirely Mr Jackson's Visitor—& let a Girl from

the town come up for the time, he stays—& Mrs J'Anson will probably accomodate you with a Fowl or two.—But above all, Mr Jackson will be so good as immediately to write a Line, to be left for me at the Post Office, Kendal—informing me, how you are—*and of all, I am to know*. Any Letters, you may have written to Gunville, will be sent back again to Keswick.— Mrs Wilson will be so good as to procure a pound or so of the best salt potted Butter—which Mr T. Wedgewood likes.——

Again & again, my dear Love! God bless you<br>S. T. Coleridge

If Mr Jackson open this, he will, I am sure, excuse the Liberty I take with him—& accept of my best & kindest remembrances. And the same to dear Mrs Wilson.——
I sent 50£, Monday before last.

### 477. To Thomas Poole

*Address*: T. Poole Esqre | Nether Stowey | Bridgewater | Somerset
*MS*. British Museum. *Pub*. E.L.G. i. 228.
*Stamped*: Brecknock.

Trecastle, Friday Night, Dec. 17. 1802

My dear Poole

Both T. Wedgwood & myself are sorry that we cannot congratulate you on your return to England, with unmingled pleasure —but this damned Dutch Ague—I pray God, you may have Stoweyized it to the Devil—or back again to the low Countries, which I should suppose a worse punishment for an Ague—unless indeed, like Milton's Devils, it should move alternately from the fiery to the icy end of hell.—And now let me defend myself against the charge of neglecting you—. When your Letter arrived at Keswick I was absent—out among the mountains on a fortnight's Tour—your Letter came the very day, I left home—. Mrs Coleridge will bear witness for me, how vexed & wounded I was that a Letter from you should have been a fortnight unanswered—& how immediately & exclusively I set about answering it. I wrote you a *long*, & (for my head & heart were both full) not an ineloquent, or valueless Letter—& if it were at all in my character to set any price on my own compositions, I should be vexed that I had not taken a copy. I wished to do it—but did not, for eagerness to forward it to you. This Letter *must* have arrived at your Lodgings in Paris, the day you left it—. Did you not pass thro' Paris on your return?— You yourself, my dear friend! are not wholly blameless in having stayed so long at Paris without writing to me. On receiving your second Letter, I wrote to you at the Poste restante, Geneva—not indeed immediately, but time enough in all conscience for it to have reached the place—before your arrival. This was a mere Letter of affection, with a little effusion of old English Gall contra Gallos. It grieves me that you have not received these Letters—because it does a friendship no good for a man to have felt resentfully or *woundedly* towards his friend for 3 or 4 months—even tho' he finds afterwards that he has wronged his Friend.—Now of all earthly Things I detest explanations—after the Day of Judgment there will be an end to them / veniat regnum tuum!—And now for information respecting myself & our friend.—I received on the 3rd of November a Letter from T. Wedgwood, which, I felt, could be properly answered only by immediately going to him. I left Keswick the next morning—passed thro' London to Bristol—met T. W. at Cote—proceeded with him & Sally Wedgwood into Wales—spent a week or so at St Clear's—& then to Crescelly, the Seat of the Mrs Wedgwoods' Father, old Allen—where we have passed the last 3 weeks in much comfort. Miss S. Wedgewood is a truly excellent woman / her whole Soul is clear, pure, & deep, as an Italian Sky—Jessy, Fanny, & Emma Allen are all sweet Girls —& Jessy & Fanny very interesting. We had plenty of music & *plenty of Cream*: for at Crescelly (I mention it as a remarkable circumstance it being the only place, I was ever at, in which it was not otherwise) *tho'* they have a Dairy, & *tho'* they have plenty of milk, yet nevertheless they are not at all stingy of it. In all other Houses, where Cows are kept, you may drink six shillings' worth of wine a day, & welcome / but use threepenny worth of Cream & O Lord! the Feelings of the Household & their Looks would curdle the Cream Dish. I have never been able to understand or analyse this strange Folly——it is a perfect mystery, that threepenny worth of Cream should be more costly than a shilling's worth of Butter.[1]——

Our friend's Health is as nearly as possible what it was last Christmas—& I conceive, that he must go to a warmer Climate sooner or later. He would not hesitate an hour, but that he feels that he is not likely to be happy, at a distance from, & out of reach of, Josiah.—He is determined to give England a fair Trial—& a scheme has started, which he thinks himself bound to act upon tho' the success of it, in it's first approaches, is extremely problematical. The Detail of it he will acquaint you with, as soon as he can ascertain any thing respecting it—and on this scheme he is now going strait onwards to Cumberland—and will return into

[1] C— used to be very fond of the *clouted cream*—eating more than my Dairy-maid thought sufficient—The reproof within is meant for her—or *me*. [Note written in the manuscript by Thomas Poole.]

South Wales, about the middle or perhaps end of January. It is a sense of Duty—no movement of pleasure—that impels him to the North, instead of to Stowey—according to our former plan. He has taken a Shooting Cottage at Trewern, 5 miles from Narbarth, 13 from Crescelly, in Pembrokeshire—. This afternoon as we were on our way from Llandovery to this place, he had a very serious fit indeed, brought on by long detention of indurated faeces—he is now relieved—but God Almighty shield him from a second. I should extremely dread an inflammation in the Bowels, as the consequence.——

My own Health is certainly better than it was when you last saw me—much better. But it is far, very far from what it ought to be. My Stomach is exceedingly weak—and all sort of food produces flatulence—& my Bowels are weak. I find every month an increased necessity of austere Diet—I have left off all wine, Spirit, & fermented liquor—& I *try* to prefer solids to fluids, & animal food to vegetable—: simple food to seasoned I prefer naturally. But deep & pleasurable Tranquillity of Mind—& an even warmth of Body—are absolutely necessary for me, as far at least as Health is necessary. The latter I can gain only by settling in Sicily, or Teneriffe, or the W. Indies—& this I should not hesitate concerning, if I could ensure the former, which you well know does not depend on myself.—However, Mrs C. & I go on with less

——of those habitual Ills
That wear out Life when two unequal minds
Meet in one house, & two discordant wills—[1]

We have been at peace.—I return home with a palpitating heart—for I expect to hear at Kendal, that I have a new Child.—From Keswick I shall write again; but T. Wedgwood joins with me in begging & entreating that you will immediately write to him, or me, at Keswick—informing us, how you are—for in very truth we are both anxious.—Give my love to Ward—to whom Mr Wedgewood desires his friendly remembrance. And if Miss Ward is at Stowey, I send her my best good wishes—for she is of the better clay—there is a susceptibility of the good & the beautiful in her heart & mind.——

God bless you, my dear friend! I still believe, that I shall see you in a few months.

S. T. Coleridge

We shall arrive at Keswick Dec. 24 or 25th God willing.—

[1] Cf. Letter 438, p. 796.

## 478. To Robert Southey

*Address*: Robert Southey Esqre | St James's Place | Kingsdown | Bristol
*MS*. Lord Latymer. *Pub*. Letters, *i. 415*.
*Postmark*: 29 December 1802. *Stamped*: Keswick.

Christmas Day, 1802

My dear Southey

I arrived at Keswick, with T. Wedgewood, on Friday Afternoon—that is to say, yesterday—& had the comfort to find that Sara was safely brought to bed, the morning before—i.e. Thursday ½ past six, of a healthy—GIRL! I had never thought of a Girl as a possible event—the word[s] child & man child were perfect Synonimes in my feelings—however I bore the sex with great Fortitude—& she shall be called Sa*ra*. Both Mrs Coleridge & the Coleridgiella are as well as can be—I left the little one sucking at a great rate. Derwent & Hartley are both well.—

I was at Cote in the beginning of November—and of course had calculated on seeing you & above all on seeing little Edith's physiognomy, among the certain things of my expedition—but I had no sooner arrived at Cote, than I was forced to quit it— T. Wedgewood having engaged to go into Wales with his Sister—I arrived at Cote in the afternoon, & till late evening did not know or conjecture that we were to go *off* early on the next morning.—I do not say this for you—you must know, how earnestly I yearn to see you—but for Mr Estlin, who expressed himself wounded by the circumstance. When you see him therefore, be so good as to mention this to him.—

I was much affected by Mrs Coleridge's account of your health & eyes. God have mercy on us!—We are all sick, all mad, all slaves!—It is a theory of mine that Virtue & Genius are Diseases of the Hypochondriacal & Scrofulous Genus—& exist in a peculiar state of the Nerves, & diseased Digestion—analogous to the beautiful Diseases, that colour & variegate certain Trees.—However, I add by way of comfort, that it is my Faith that the Virtue & Genius produce the Disease, not the Disease the Virtue &c—tho' when present, it fosters them. Heaven knows! there are fellows who have more vices than scabs, & scabs countless—with fewer Ideas than Plaisters.——

As to my own Health, it is very indifferent. I am exceedingly temperate in every thing—abstain wholly from wine, spirits, or fermented Liquors—almost wholly from Tea—abjure all fermentable & vegetable food—bread excepted—& use *that* sparingly— live almost entirely on Eggs, Fish, Flesh, & Fowl—& thus contrive not to be *ill*—but well I am not—& in this climate never shall be.

( 902 )

## Christmas Day 1802 [478

A deeply ingrained, tho' mild Scrofula, is diffused thro' me: & is a very Proteus. I am fully determined to *try* Teneriffe or Gran Canaria, influenced to prefer them to Madeira solely by the superior cheapness of living. The Climate & Country are heavenly—the Inhabitants Papishes, all of whom I would burn with fire & faggot—for what didn't they do to us Christians under bloody Queen Mary? O the Devil sulphur-roast them—! I would have no mercy on them, unless they drowned all their Priests—& then spite of the Itch (which they have in an inveterate degree, Rich & Poor, Gentle & simple, old & young, Male & female) would shake hands with them unglov'd.——By way of *one* impudent Half-Line in this meek & mild Letter—will you go with me?—'*I*' & 'you' mean mine & your's—of course.——

Remember, you are to give me Thomas Aquinas & Scotus Erigena.[1]—

God bless you | &
S. T. Coleridge

I can have the best Letters of recommendation.——

My Love & their Sister's to Edith & Mary—& if you see Mrs Fricker, be so good as to tell her that she will hear from me or Sara in the course of ten days.——

### 479. To Mary Robinson

*Address*: Miss Robinson | Englefield Cottage | Windsor | London
*MS. Dove Cottage. Pub. E.L.G. i. 232.*

Greta Hall, Keswick. Dec. 27. 1802

My dear Miss Robinson

I was in Wales when your Letter arrived; and am even now returned to my Home. The cause of the Delay in answering your Letter will be my apology.—If I were writing to a mere Stranger, or to one with whose name I had connected nothing serious or interesting, it would be sufficient for me to say (& I could say it with strict Truth) that I have almost wholly weaned myself from the habit of making Verses, and for the last three years uninterruptedly devoted myself to studies only not *quite* incompatible with poetic composition. Poetic composition has become laborious & painful to me.—The Gentlemen, with whose names you would wish to associate mine, are of such widely diffused literary celebrity, that no one will accuse me of mock humility, or an affectation of

---

[1] A copy of Johannes Scotus Erigena's *De Divisione Naturae*, 1681, with marginal notes by Coleridge is in the British Museum. Coleridge was reading the volume in 1803. See Letters 504 and 506.

( 903 )

modesty, when I say (confining my meaning exclusively to *literary* celebrity) that my name would place their's in company below their rank. But I, you know, am not a man of the World: and there are other qualities which I value infinitely higher than Talents or the fame arising from them—among other things the use, to which those Talents have been applied.—Much solitude, & absence from cities & from the manners of cities, naturally make a man somewhat serious——& in this mood I cannot help writing to *you*. Your dear Mother is more present to my eyes, than the paper on which I am writing—which indeed swims before my sight—for I can not think of your Mother without Tears. Let not what I say offend you—I conjure you, in the name of your dear Mother! let it not do so. Others flattered her—I admired her indeed, as deeply as others—but I likewise esteemed her *much*, and yearned from my inmost soul to esteem her *altogether*. Flowers, they say, smell sweetest at eve; it was my Hope, my heart-felt wish, my Prayer, my Faith, that the latter age of your Mother would be illustrious & redemptory—that to the Genius & generous Virtues of her youth she would add Judgement, & Thought—whatever was correct & dignified as a Poetess, & all that was matronly as Woman. Such, you best know, were her own aspirations—One of her poems written in sickness breathes them so well & so affectingly, that I never read it without a strange mixture of anguish & consolation.—In this Feeling I cultivated your Mother's acquaintance, thrice happy if I could have soothed her sorrows, or if the feeble Lamp of my Friendship could have yielded her one ray of Hope & Guidance. Your Mother had indeed a good, a very good, heart—and in *my* eyes, & in *my* belief, was in her latter life a blameless Woman.—Her memoirs I have not seen—I understood that an excessively silly copy of Verses, which I had absolutely forgotten the very writing of, disgraced me & the volumes[1]—this publication of a private Letter (an act so wholly unjustifiable, & in it's nature subversive of all social confidence) I attributed altogether to the Man, at whose Shop the Volumes were published—. I was sorry, no doubt, that so very silly a Poem had been published—for your mother's sake still more than for my own— yet I was not displeased to see my Name joined to your Mother's— I have said every where & aloud, that I thought highly both of her Talents & of her Heart, & that I *hoped* still more highly of both. I was not grieved at an occasion, which compelled me often to

---

[1] Coleridge's poem, *A Stranger Minstrel*, was published in Mrs. Robinson's posthumous *Memoirs*, 4 vols., 1801, iv. 141. The work also contained poetical contributions by Peter Pindar and others. Miss Robinson included Coleridge's *The Mad Monk* in her *Wild Wreath*, 1804.

## 27 December 1802

stand forth, as her Defender, Apologist, & Encomiast. But, my dear Miss Robinson! (I pray you, do not be wounded—rather consider what I am about to say as a pledge of my esteem, & confidence in your honor & prudence, a confidence beyond the dictates of worldly caution)—but I have a wife, I have sons, I have an infant Daughter—what excuse could I offer to my own conscience if by suffering my name to be connected with those of Mr Lewis, or Mr Moore, I was the *occasion* of their reading the Monk, or the wanton poems of Thomas Little Esqre? Should I not be an infamous Pander to the Devil in the seduction of my own offspring?—My head turns giddy, my heart sickens, at the very thought of seeing such books in the hands of a child of mine. I neither have or profess an excess of religious Faith or Feeling—I write altogether from the common feelings of common Honesty. The mischief of these misery-making Writings *laughs* at all calculation. On my own account therefore I must in the most emphatical manner decline all such connection. But I cannot stop here—! Indeed, indeed, I write with Tears on my cheek. What, dear Miss Robinson! ought *you* to feel for yourself—& for the memory of a MOTHER—of all names the most awful, the most venerable, next to that of God! On *your* conduct, on *your* prudence, much of her reputation, much of her justification will ultimately depend. Often & proudly have I spoken of you, as being in your manners, feelings, & conduct a proof of the inherent purity of your Mother's mind—Such, I am sure, you will always remain—. But is it not an *oversight*—a *precipitancy*—is it not to revive all which Calumny & the low Pride of Women (who have no other chastity than that of their mere animal frames) love to babble of your dear Mother, when you connect her posthumous writings with the poems of men, whose names are highly offensive to all good men & women for their licentious exercise of their Talents? It is usual in certain countries to plant the Night violet on Graves—because it sends forth it's odours most powerfully during the Darkness, & absence of the Sun. O dear Miss Robinson! exert your own Talents—do you plant the night violets of your own Genius & Goodness on the Grave of your dear Parent—not Hensbane, not Hemlock! Do not mistake me! I do not suspect, that the Poems, you mean to publish, have themselves aught in the least degree morally objectionable—; but the *names* are those of men, who have sold provocatives to vulgar Debauchees, & vicious School boys——in no other Light can many of their writings be regarded by a Husband & a Father.— As to Peter Pindar—!—By all the Love & Honor, I bear to your dear Parent's memory, by the anguish & the indignation at my inmost heart, I swear to you that my flesh creeps at his name!!—

479]  *To Mary Robinson*

You have forgotten, dear Miss Robinson!—yes, you had altogether forgotten, that in a published Poem he called an infamous & mercenary Strumpet *'the Mrs Robinson of Greece'*—. Will you permit the world to say—her own Daughter does not resent it—her own Daughter connects the fame of her Mother with that of the man, who thus assassinated her reputation?—No! No!—I am sure, you had forgotten it—. I feel that I should insult you if I supposed the possibility of this Letter's being read by any but yourself. It has long been my intention to write a poem of some length expressly in honor of your mother, which I meant to have addressed to you—having previously requested your permission. I mention this merely to prove to you, how much I am interested in, how gladly I should assent to, any plan that I could think truly honorable to your Mother or yourself.

I remain most sincerely your Friend & Well wisher,

S. T. Coleridge

### 480. *To Thomas Poole*

*Address*: T. Poole Esqre | N. Stowey | Bridgewater | Somerset
*MS.* British Museum, *Pub. E.L.G. i. 235.*
*Postmark*: ⟨1⟩ January 180⟨3⟩. *Stamped*: Keswick.

Wednesday, Dec. 29. [1802]

My dear Friend

I have such a mass of Letters to answer, that I can write you but a few Lines. We arrived safely on Friday afternoon—and on the morning before, at ½ past six, Mrs Coleridge was brought to bed of a healthy Girl, who is to be called Sarah. Both Mother & Babe are well.—I am middling—. My plans are these—it is probable, that I shall return with our Friend, either to Gunville or Trewern, & there employ myself for six weeks or 2 months—at the end of which time it is my firm resolution to go myself to the Canary Islands & see them—& know whether a comfortable House & the common Comforts of Life are to be had in Gran Canaria or Teneriffe—if so, I shall return, & by the next vessel transport my family, myself, & my books. If not, I shall attempt to see Sicily and the South of Italy—for the same purposes.— T. Wedgewood is much as usual—his Spirits indifferent, his appetite tolerable. He leaves Keswick with me tomorrow morning, & goes to Ulswater—whether he returns to Keswick, or goes on to Newcastle upon Tyne, is uncertain. At all events, he means to have come back to the South before the last week of January.— After I had last written you, & sent off the Letter, my heart misgave me that I had written triflingly, & in a tone unworthy of you & of myself—in a first Letter on your return to your native Country after your first absence—& that too on so unpleasant a necessity, & in ill health to boot. But I was not writing for myself only—& this writing ½ for myself, & ½ as a kind of Amanuensis untuned my feelings.—I found your Letter here: both T. W. & myself mourn, that your ill-health clings about you.—I doubt not, I shall see you soon.—As you know, I often joke with a Tear in my eye—so I could not help saying, that as your digestive organs were disordered, it was no wonder, that the Cream turned sour on your Stomach.—I received a Letter from Sharp a few days ago with this Post script—'I like your friend, Poole, most EXCEEDINGLY.' Sharp is a clever ready-cut-&-dried-speech-retailer, and a friendly man who, tho' he has no heart, has a neat thing enough of a cardioeidĕs Automaton, that answers all the purposes of a heart to all the demands & interests of simple acquaintanceship. As your Greek is not French or Latin or English, I must lexiconize *my* 'Cardioeidous[']—which signifies something in the likeness of a Heart— / a puppet Heart——

What a misery that the Canarians are Catholics! O the Devil sulphur-roast all Papishes! I would burn every Mother's child of them with Fire & Faggot in remembrance of what they did to us Christians in the time of bloody Queen Mary.—

T. W.'s Love.——

To Ward, & to his Sister remember me kindly—

And when you write to Bristol, do be so good as to remember [me] in more than common terms to your Sister & Mr King.—

God bless you, my dear Poole! | & | Your affectionate & | faithful—
S. T. Coleridge

T. Wedgewood sent you a dozen Pound of Honey—at least, left word to have sent to you—before he left Gunville.—

## 481. *To Mrs. S. T. Coleridge*

*Address*: Mrs Coleridge | Greta Hall | Keswick | Cumberland    by favor of Agatha Fleming.
*MS. Lord Latymer. Pub. E.L.G. i. 237.* The bottom of pages 1 and 2 and the top and bottom of pages 3 and 4 of the manuscript have been cut off.

Glenridden, Jan. 5. 1802.—[1803] Wednesday night

My dear Wife & dear Love

I considered it as more than usually unlucky that the both times, that Letters went from Grasmere to Keswick, I should have been in Bed & *unfit* to write to you. I say *unfit*; because I was so low & so unwell, that if I had written, I must either have deceived or depressed you. And yet still I was vexed afterwards that I had not added one Line or so—lest you should think me neglectful, or unaffectionate. And heaven knows! I build up my best hopes on my attempts to conciliate your Love, & to call it forth into hourly exercise, & gentle compliances, by setting you the example of respectful & attentive manners. We cannot get rid of our faulty Habits all at once; but I am fully sensible, that I have been faulty in many things; tho' justice to myself compels me to add, not without provocation. But I wish to confine my whole attention to my own faults—& it is my hourly & serious Resolve to endeavor to correct all little overflows of Temper, & offensive vehemence of manner, look, & language—& above all things never, never either to blame you, or banter you in the presence of a third person. On the other hand, you must make up your mind to receive with love & a ready & docile mind any thing that I say seriously & lovingly to you, when we are alone: because, my dear Love! I must needs grow desperate, if I should find, that it is not only the *manner* of being found fault with that i[rritated you, but I canno]t & will not endure to . . .

. . . encourage every Thought & Feeling that may tend to make me love you more—& make a merit to myself of bearing with your little corrosions, & apparent unimpressibilities. You are a good woman with a pleasing person, & a healthy understanding superior certainly to nine women in ten, of our own rank, or the rank above us—& I will be not only contented but grateful, if you will let me be quite tranquil—& above all, my dear dear Sara! have confidence in my honor & virtue—& suffer me to love & to be beloved without jealousy or pain. Depend on it, my dear Wife! that the more you sympathize with me in my kind manners & kind feelings to those of Grasmere, the more I shall be likely to sympathize with you in your opinions respecting their faults & imperfections. I am no Idolater at present; & I solemnly assure you, that if I prefer many parts of *their* characters, opinions, feelings, & habits to the same parts of your's, I do likewise prefer much, very much of your character to their's—Of course, I speak *chiefly* of Dorothy & William—because Mrs Wordsworth & her Sister are far less remote from you than they—& unless I am grievously deceived, will in some things become less so still.—God send us Peace & Love—My dear Love! what a new year's Blessing it would be—O & surely it shall be. My heart is full of Hope & full of Love!—

I walked on Sunday with William, Mary & Sara to John Stanley's

## 5 January 1803

to meet Dorothy—got wet in my feet, & half forgetful, half stupid, suffered them to *smoke* & *steam* away, while on my feet, holding them close by the Fire. I was not well when I came home as Dorothy informed you—indeed, I was . . .

. . . which is 3 miles of the road—the whole Distance being 13 miles. But these 3 miles are almost as much as the other ten. I arrived safe & well. How I found T. Wedgewood, & what his Plans are, I would rather tell you by word of mouth—I fear, that I shall leave you in a week perhaps—& go to Gunville.— / At all events, I must consult with Wordsworth on a very important subject—& then finally consult with you, & with you arrange it—I go therefore from hence to Grasmere tomorrow morning—& shall *strive* to be at Keswick tomorrow night— / & *possibly* may come in on a double horse, with Sara Hutchinson—whom I have *some few reasons* for wishing to be with you immediately, which I will inform you of—but one of the least, & yet the most ostensible, is the necessity of one or more of her Teeth being drawn without Delay—for I never saw a human Being's Health so much affected *generally* by the Tooth ache as her's appears to be— / yet this Tooth ache I suspect to be in part nervous—& the cause, which, I more than suspect, has called this nervousness into action, I will tell you when I am alone with you.[1] In one thing, my dear Love! I do prefer you to any woman, I ever knew—I have the most unbounded Confidence in your Discretion, & know it to be well grounded. Mr Wedgewood will certainly not come back to Keswick.

O my dear Love! I have very much to say respecting our children—indeed, indeed, some very vigorous & persevering measures *must* be taken. Sitting up till 11 o clock at night—coffee in the morning—&c &c &c—and this for a child whose nerves are as wakeful as the Strings of an Eolian Harp, & as easily put out of Tune! What . . .

. . . Trash & general irregularity of Diet!—I know, you will say that you were dieted, & yet had worms. But this is no argument at all—for first it remains to be proved that you were *properly* dieted—secondly, it is as notorious as the Sun in heaven, that bad Diet will & does bring worms—& lastly, Derwent has been manifestly tea-poisoned—as well as Hartley—& both of them are eat up by worms. Mary would not say, that Derwent had no Tea given him—she only said, that *he had but little.* Good God! what in-

---

[1] 'What was Coleridge going to tell his wife?' asks Chambers; and suggests that Coleridge probably believed and intended to tell her that 'Sara Hutchinson was likely to become the wife of John Wordsworth'. *Life*, 164. In 1808 Coleridge wrote to Stuart: 'Had Captn Wordsworth lived, I had hopes of seeing her blessedly married, as well as prosperously.'

fatuation!—as if a little child could know the difference between Tea, & warm milk & water—& out of mere laziness, because the Tea is in the cup, to give or . . . & their mother—if I have twenty children, Tea . . .

### 482. To Robert Southey

*Address*: Robert Southey Esqre | St James's Parade | Kingsdown | Bristol
MS. Lord Latymer. *Pub. with omis. E.L.G. i. 240.*
*Postmark*: 11 January 1803. *Stamped*: Keswick.

Keswick, Saturday Evening, Jan. [8,] 1803
My dear Southey

Your whole conduct to George Burnet has been that of a kind & truly good man. For myself, I have no heart to spare for a Coxcomb mad with vanity & stupified with opium. He may not have a bad heart; but he wants a good one. With much sorrow from without, much pain, & disease, & not a little self-dissatisfaction, & with some real distresses of valuable men in my immediate view, I verily can scarcely afford even to pity a fool. Yet better stars be with him!—I grieve sincerely that there should be such helpless self-tormenting Tormentors; tho' I cannot say, that it adds much to my grief, that one of them is called George Burnet.—At least, if it does, it is for his friends & not for his own sake.—

Believe me, dear Southey! your account of your improved health & eyesight was a real comfort to me. I love my Milton / & will not endure any other Poet's addresses to his Blindness—Yet of the two fearful evils I would rather, you were blind, than stomach-deranged to any high degree—. You know enough, dear friend! of this latter to guess what it must be, when in the excess in which T. Wedgewood has it. Your diet is, I am persuaded by my own experience, a wise one. I take the chalybeated Aquafortis, with benefit—& find considerable benefit from eating nothing at breakfast, & taking only a single cup of strong Coffee— then at eleven o'clock I take a couple of eggs, kept in boiling water one minute, folded up in a napkin for a minute & a half, & then put into the boiling water, which is now to be removed from the fire, & kept there with the saucepan covered from 4 to 6 minutes, according to the size of the eggs, & quantity of water in the saucepan.—The superiority of eggs thus boiled to those boiled in the common way proves to me the old proverb—there is reason in roasting of Eggs.—I empty the eggs out into a glass or tea cup, & eat them with a little salt & cayenne peper—but no bread.—What a pretty Book one might write, entitled 'Le petite Soulagement, or

## 8 January 1803

Little Comforts, by a Valetudinarian[']—comprizing cookery, sleeping, travelling, conversation, self-discipline—poetry, morals, metaphysics—all the alleviations, that reason & well-regulated self-indulgence, can give to a good sick man.—Sara sends her best Love to you & Edith & Margaret—& she will write as soon as she has strength. She is in a middling way—nothing to lament, nothing to boast of. The Sariola is well—save the Thrush in her mouth—of which I have noted nothing but that it does not sing, from whence I conclude it is a different kind of Thrush from the Turdus Communis or Throstle of the South Counties— / On the 30th of Dec. I accompanied Wedgewood to Patterdale, at the head of Ullswater, to Mr Luff's—whom he has some thoughts, I believe, of getting as a companion. On New year's Day I walked over Kirkstone, an awful Road over a sublime mountain by Tairn & waterfall, to Ambleside & Grasmere—the next day, I walked more than halfway to Keswick to meet Miss Wordsworth, & back again / but unfortunately got wet in my feet—& on the day after, Monday, Jan. 3. in the evening I had an attack of Dysentery, in kind the same, & in degree nearly equal, to that which I had at Keswick when Stoddart & Edith were there. Dear Edith will remember it well. The same deadly sweats—the same frightful Profluvium of burning Dregs, like melted Lead—with quantities of bloody mucus from the Coats of the Intestines.—I was better after—& had a good night—& was so well the next day, that I determined to perform the promise, I had made—& accordingly walked back again to Mr Luff's over Kirkstone, just 15 miles from Grasmere—I stayed Wednesday at Luff's—& on Thursday Wedgewood seemed to have made up his plans, & I found I could go to my home, for a week or so—but having something of importance to talk to Wordsworth about concerning Luff I was forced to go by Grasmere—but took a little Poney & a woman to bring it back again, to take me to the top of the mountain; but before I got half way up, the storm was so horrid & pitiless that the woman seemed frightened—& I thought it unmanly to let her go on. So I dismounted, & sent her home with the Storm to her Back. I am no novice in Storms; but such as this I never before witnessed, combining the violence of the wind & rain with the intensity of the cold. My hands were shrivelled like a Washer-woman's: & the rain was pelted, or rather *slung*, by the wind against my face, like splinters of Flint; and seemed to *cut* my flesh.—A violent pain attacked my right eye— which, I own, greatly alarmed me—. On turning the mountain, at the first step of descent, all was calm, breathless—it seemed as if there was a great Fountain of wind & Tempest at the summit that rolled down a Niagara of Air towards Patterdale—I arrived at

Grasmere, soaked thro'—& the next day walked to Keswick—but in consequence of all this, I have had another attack of disentery, & am very poorly.—I have been thus prolix—because it will give you a good idea of the nature of my health—& what a degree & scrupulousness of care it requires to ward off fits of Distemper from my Bowels.—

My plans are these—or rather Wedgewood's—to go to Gunville, to his Brother's, in about ten days—stay there a month or so—& then to go together to Paris, thro' Switzerland, to Rome, Naples, & perhaps Sicily.—I am indifferent—this is well—& to stay at home would perhaps be better. God knows my heart! it is for my wife's & children's sakes that I go far more than for my own. Yet I could be well-content to try what great care, scrupulous Diet, & a perfect system of cloathing would do, at Keswick. For I love the place with a perfect Love.—Next to Keswick I would live at Bristol beyond any other place in the Island & of course am glad that you are to live there.—I have a great deal more to say; but I am getting weak.—The Ode on Switzerland?—O!—you must mean the old Ode, entitled France—which Stuart has reprinted.[1] As to my politics, given in the Letters to Fox, & in the Essays on France, they are quite my own—& Stuart's *chiefly* in consequence of my conversations with him. So far from writing those Letters under Stuart's influence, he kept them 3 weeks—afraid to publish them—& at last did it, roused to indignation by an account given him by one of Fox's warmest Friends of Fox's conduct in Paris.— As to Switzerland I know nothing—if you can procure me any information from King, I would thank you. You well know, that all valuable information may [be] compressed into a very moderate Letter. As to my Letters to Fox, I wish, you had *read* them—You would have seen, that only a few conciliatory Passages were Stuartian, but all the reprehensory parts *I myself I*—. If I have erred, how gladly should I have it pointed out to me! But men of all parties have read the Letters with a compleat Sympathy of Faith—& what am I to understand by your remark, my dear Southey?—Have you heard any thing from France, which inclines you to think favorably of Bonaparte, of the French Government, or of Fox's apparent Adulation?—But I shall write two or three more Essays—& then collect them into a Pamphlet—& so I shall have your opinion cool[l]y.—I heard of the Edingburgh review,[2] & heard the name of your Reviewer—but forgot it—. Reviews may sell 50 or 100 copies in the first three months—& there their Influence ends. Depend on it, no living Poet possesses the *general*

---

[1] *Morning Post*, 16 Apr. 1798; reprinted 14 Oct. 1802.
[2] See *Edinburgh Review*, Oct. 1802, p. 63, for a review of *Thalaba*.

reputation, which you possess. Blomfield is the Farmer's Boy, not a Poet—in the mind of the Public—and Rogers is never thought of, tho' every School Girl has his pleasures of memory. W. Wordsworth's reputation is hitherto *sectarian*—my *name* is perhaps nearly as well known & as much talked of as your's—but I am talked of, as the man of Talents, the splendid Talker, & as a Poet too—but not, as you are, as a Poet, κατ' ἔμφασιν—I rejoice that Madoc is to be published speedily.—God bless you!—write to me here—& if I go, your Letter will be sent after me—& I will endeavor to write more livelily.—I am become a gentle & tranquillized Being, but, O Southey! I am not the Coleridge, which you knew me. S. T. C.—

My AFFECTIONATE ESTEEM to C. Danvers. God bless him!!

### 483. *To Thomas Wedgwood*

*Address*: T. Wedgewood Esqre | C. Luff's Esqre | Glenridden | Ulswater.
*MS. Wedgwood Museum. Pub. with omis.* Letters, *i. 417.*
*Stamped*: Keswick.

Greta Hall, Keswick. Sunday, Jan. 9th. 1803

My dear Wedgewood

I send you two Letters, one from your dear Sister, the latter half of which relates to business of your's—& the second from Sharp— by which you will see, at what short notice I must be off, if I go to the Canaries. If your last plan continue in full force in your mind, of course, I have not even the phantom of a Wish thitherward struggling; but if aught have happened to you, in the things without, or in the world within, to induce you to change the plan in itself or the plan relatively to me, I think, I should raise the money at all events, & go & see. But I would a thousandfold rather go with you, whithersoever you go.—I shall be anxious to hear how you have gone on since I left you—. I have been in much dread respecting your long detention of the faeces—that alone seems to me to decide in favor of a hotter climate, somewhere or other. The best scheme, I can think of, is that in some part of Italy or Sicily, which we both liked, I would look about for two houses—Wordsworth & his family would take the one, & I the other—& then you might have a home, either with me, or if you thought of Mr & Mrs Luff, under this modification, one of your own—& in either case you would have neighbors—& so return to England when the homesickness pressed heavy on you, & back to Italy, when it was abated, & the climate of England began to poison your comforts. So you would have abroad in a genial climate a certain comfort of society among simple & enlightened men & women, your country folks; & I should be an alleviation of the pang, which you will necessarily feel always, as often as you quit your own family. I know no better plan: for travelling in search of objects is at best a dreary business, and whatever excitement it might have had, you must have exhausted it.—God bless you, my dear friend! I write with dim eyes: for indeed, indeed, my heart is very full of affectionate sorrowful thoughts towards you.

I found Mrs Coleridge not so well, as I expected; but she is better to day. And I myself write with difficulty, with all the fingers, but one, of my right hand very much swoln. Before I was half up Kirkstone, the storm had wetted me thro' & thro'—& before I reached the Top, it was so wild & outrageous, that it would have been unmanly to have suffered the poor woman to continue pushing on her Face & Breasts up against such a torrent of wind & rain. So I dismounted, & sent her home with the storm to her Back. I am no novice in mountain-mischiefs; but such a storm as this was I never witnessed, combining the intensity of the Cold with the violence of the wind & rain. The rain-drops were pelted, or rather *slung*, against my face, by the Gusts, just like splinters of Flint; & felt, as if every drop *cut* my flesh. My hands were all shrivelled up, like a washerwoman's; & so benumbed, that I was obliged to carry my stick under my arm. O it was a wild business! Such hurry-skurry of Clouds, such volleys of sound! In spite of the wet & the cold I should have had some pleasure in it, but for two vexations—first, an almost intolerable pain came into my right eye, a *smarting & burning* pain / & secondly, in consequence of riding with such cold water under my *fork* extremely uneasy & burthensome Feelings attacked my Groin & right Testicle—so that what with the pain from the one, & the alarm from both, I had no enjoyment at all. Just on the brow of the Hill I met a man, dismounted who could not keep on horse-back—he seemed quite scared by the uproar—& said to me with much feeling—O Sir! it is a perilous Buffeting, but it is worse for you than for me—for I have it at my Back.——However I got safely over—and immediately on the Descent all was calm & breathless, as if it was some mighty Fountain just on the summit of Kirkstone, that shot forth it's volcano of Air, & precipitated a huge stream of invisible Lava down the Road to Patterdale.—I called at Wilcock's, delivered your orders respecting the Trout—& on to Grasmere—I was not at all unwell when I arrived there, tho' wet of course to the Skin, & my right eye had nothing the matter with it, either to the sight of others, or to my own Feeling— / but I had a bad night, with distressful Dreams, chiefly about my eye, & awaking often in the dark I thought, it was the effect of mere recollection / but it appeared in the morning, that my right eye was blood-shot, & the Lid swoln—. That morning however I walked home—& before I reached Keswick, my eye was quite well—but I felt unwell all over—& yesterday afternoon I had another sad bowel-attack—& continued unusually unwell all over me till about 8 o/clock in the evening. I took no opium or laudanum /; but at 8 o/clock, unable to bear the stomach uneasiness & the bowel threatenings, & the achings of my Limbs, I took two large Tea spoonfuls of Ether in a wine glass of Camphorated Gum water / and a third Tea spoonful at 10 o/clock—I received compleat relief, my body calmed, my sleep placid; but when I awoke in the morning, my right hand, with three of the Fingers was swoln & inflamed. The swelling of the Hand is gone down; & of two of the fingers somewhat abated—but the middle finger is still twice it's natural size—so that I write with some difficulty. This has been a very rough attack; but tho' I am much weakened by it, & look sickly & hagged, yet I am not out of heart: for such a Bout, such a *'perilous Buffeting'* was enough to have hurt the health of a strong man—Few Constitutions can bear to be long wet thro' in intense Cold.—I fear, it will tire you to death to read this prolix scrawled Story—but my health, I know, interests you.—Do contrive to send me a few lines by the market people on Tuesday—I shall receive it on Tuesday Evening.

Affectionately, dear friend! | your's ever
S. T. Coleridge.

It is most unlucky that Aggy did not go—it is as far to Penrith or farther, as to Keswick—so if you have any thing to communicate, you had better send a lad at once to Keswick.—

[I] send this by the Post, lest Aggy should be detained tomorrow too.—I am sic sic, i.e. so so.

### 484. To Thomas Wedgwood

*Address*: T. Wedgewood Esqre | C. Luff's Esqre | Glenridden | Ulswater—
*MS. Wedgwood Museum. Pub. with omis.* Tom Wedgwood, *132.*

Friday Night, Jan. 14. 1803
Dear Friend

I was glad at heart to receive your Letter (which came to me on Thursday morning, I do not know how) and still more gladdened by the reading of it. The exceeding kindness, which it breathed, was literally medicinal to me; & I firmly believe, cured me of a nervous rheumatism in my head & teeth.—I daresay, that you mixed up the scolding & the affection, the acid & the oil, very compleatly at Patterdale; but by the time, it came to Keswick, the oil was all atop.—You ask, in God's name, why I did not return when I saw the state of the weather? The true reason is simple, tho' it may be somewhat strange—the thought never once entered my head. The *cause* of this I suppose to be, that (I do not remember it at least) I never once in my whole life turned back in fear of the weather. Prudence is a plant, of which I, no doubt, possess some valuable specimens—but they are always in my hot-house, never out of the glasses—& least of all things would endure the climate of the mountains. In simple earnest, I never find myself alone within the embracement of rocks & hills, a traveller up an alpine road, but my spirit courses, drives, and eddies, like a Leaf in Autumn: a wild activity, of thoughts, imaginations, feelings, and impulses of motion, rises up from within me—a sort of *bottom-wind*, that blows to no point of the compass, & comes from I know not whence, but agitates the whole of me; my whole Being is filled with waves, as it were, that roll & stumble, one this way, & one that way, like things that have no common master. I think, that my soul must have pre-existed in the body of a Chamois-chaser; the simple image of the old object has been obliterated—but the feelings, & impulsive habits, & incipient actions, are in me, & the old scenery awakens them. The farther I ascend from animated Nature, from men, and cattle, & the common birds of the woods, & fields, the greater becomes in me the Intensity of the feeling of Life; Life seems to me then a universal spirit, that neither has, nor can have, an opposite. God is every where, I have exclaimed, & works every where; & where is there *room* for Death? In these moments it has been my creed, that Death exists only because Ideas exist / that Life is limitless Sensation; that Death is a child of the organic senses, chiefly of the Sight; that Feelings die by flowing into the mould of the Intellect, & becoming Ideas; & that Ideas passing forth into action re-instate themselves again in the world of Life. And I do believe, that Truth lies inveloped in these loose generalizations.—I do not think it possible, that any bodily pains could eat out the love & joy, that is so substantially part of me, towards hills, & rocks, & steep waters! And I have had some Trial. On Monday Night I had an attack in my stomach, & right side, which in pain & the length of it's continuance appeared to me by the far the severest, I ever had—I was under the necessity of having a person set up with me till 3 in the morning / tho' about one o/clock the pain passed out of my stomach, like Lightning from a cloud, into the extremities of my right foot—my Toe swelled & throbbed —& I was in a state of delicious ease, which the pain in my Toe did not seem at all to interfere with. On Tuesday I was uncommonly well all the morning, & eat an excellent dinner; but playing too long & too rompingly with Hartley & Derwent I was very unwell that evening—on Wednesday I was well—& after dinner wrapt myself up warm, & walked with Sara Hutchinson to Lodore—I never beheld any thing more impressive than the ⁓⋏⋏‾ wild outline of the *black* masses of mountain, over Lodore & so on to the Gorge of Borrodale seen thro' the bare Twigs of a grove of Birch Trees, thro' which the road passes—and on emerging from the Grove, a red planet, (so very red that I never saw a star so red, being clear & bright at the same time) stood on the edge of the point where I have put an Asterisk / it seemed to have sky behind it—it *started*, as it were, from the Heaven, like an eye-ball of Fire. I wished aloud for you to have been with me at that moment. The walk appeared to have done me good; but I had a wretched Night —had shocking pains in my head, occiput, & teeth—& found in the morning that I had two blood-shot eyes. But almost immediately after the receipt & perusal of your Letter the pain left me, & I have bettered to this hour—& am now indeed as well as usual, saving that my left eye is still very much blood-shot. It is a sort of duty with me to be particular respecting facts that relate to my health / I am myself not at all dispirited. I have retained a good sound appetite thro' the whole of it—without any craving after exhilarants or narcotics—& I have got well, as in a moment. Rapid recovery is constitutional with me; but the two former circumstances I can with certainty refer to the system of Diet, abstinence from vegetables, wine, spirits, & beer, which I have adopted by your advice. I have no dread or anxiety respecting any fatigue which either of us are at all likely to undergo even in continental Travelling. Many a healthy man would have been layed up with such a Bout of thorough Wet & intense Cold at the same time, as I had on Kirkstone. Would to God that also for your sake I were a stronger man; but I have strong wishes to be with you, & love your society; & receiving much comfort from you, & believing that I receive likewise much improvement, I find a delight (very great, my dear friend! indeed it is) when I have reason to imagine that I am in return an alleviation of your destinies, & a comfort to you. *I* have no fears: & am ready to leave home at a two days' warning— / for myself I should say 2 hours; but bustle & hurry might disorder Mrs Coleridge. She & the three children are quite well.—

I grieve, that there is a lowring in politics—. The Moniteur contains almost daily some bitter abuse on our ministers &

parliament—& in London there is great anxiety & omening. I have dreaded war from the time, that the disastrous fortunes of the Expedition to St Domingo under Le Clerc was known in France.[1]—

I have sent some Ginger—& have tried to cater some thing for you at Keswick—but could not succeed—I could get neither Fish nor Hare. My kind remembrances to Mr & Mrs Luff. I have sent my three Razors, which I beg, Luff will regenerate for me upon the Golding—& I will give him a Draft to any amount on the first Banking House, he will point out to me, on any part of Parnassus.——The newspapers have been sent, while I was in bed, to Grasmere—I will send a whole parcel of them to Penrith on Monday Night—& if I can send any thing else, you will write me word by the man / at all events, write me one or two lines—as few, as you like—only just how you are.—Pray, is the Lake opposite to Glenridden frozen over?—I am afraid, that in a few days there will be a great Fall of Snow.—At the end of 5 days we shall have two beds vacant, for you—& for Mr & Mrs Luff—if it would be any change to you to come over to Keswick—.—

Heaven bless us all!—

I remain, | my dear Wedgewood | with most affectionate esteem & | grateful attachment | your sincere Friend
S. T. Coleridge

### 485. To Samuel Purkis

*Address*: Samuel Purkis Esqre | Brentford | Middlesex
*MS. Huntington Lib. Pub. E. L. G. i. 244.*
*Postmark*: 2 February 1803.

Southey's, St James's Parade, Kingsdown, Bristol. Feb. 1. 1803
My dear Purkis

For the last 5 months of my Life I seem to have annihilated the present Tense with regard to place—you can never say, where *is* he?—but only—where *was he*? where *will* he be?—From Keswick —to London—Bristol—Pembroke—Birmingham—Manchester / Keswick—Etruria—Bristol—& in a few days to Blandford— probably, Stowey, Exeter—possibly, the Land's End. I am with

---

[1] In Dec. 1801 General Leclerc, Napoleon's brother-in-law, left France for Hispaniola at the head of a large expedition to conquer the island. Leclerc died of yellow fever in Nov. 1802 and was succeeded by General Rochambeau. His troops decimated by sickness and the ferocious resistance of the Negroes, Rochambeau capitulated to Dessalines in Nov. 1803. Thus France lost for ever the rich colony of Saint-Domingue. See *Henry Christophe and Thomas Clarkson*, ed. by E. L. Griggs and C. H. Prator, 1952, pp. 21–32.

*1 February 1803*

Mr T. Wedgewood—and expect after six weeks' stay with him in England to go thro' France, & Italy—& to winter in Sicily—but I am a Comet tied to a Comet's Tail, & our combined Path must needs be damnably eccentric, & a defying Puzzle to all Astronomers from La Lande & Herschell to YZ, who with 20 more Alphabetonymists *likewise* gave a solution to an astronomical problem in the last Lady's Diary.—If I had not gone with Wedgewood, or if I should not go, I shall probably go to Gran Canaria or Teneriffe— for my health is miserable. While in warm rooms, all goes well; but any exposure inevitably diseases, almost disorganizes me. Cold & Wet are my He and She Devil. I am however *better* tho' not stronger / for I abstain, & have for the last 4 months, from all wine, spirits, beer—& from all narcotics & exhilarants, whether from the Vintner's Shop or the Apothecary's—My appetite is very keen in consequence—but I am not stronger / nor at all more hardy.——I shall shortly publish a second Volume of Poems[1]—

My Poverty, & not my Will consenting—

I have likewise written a Tragedy & a Farce / & have planned out a long comic Poem / of regular & epic construction / as long as Hudibras; but tho' with infinitely less Wit, yet I trust with more humour, more variety of character, & a far, far more entertaining, & interesting Tale. Each book will be in a different metre / but all in rhyme—& each book a regular metre. It seems to me, that a comic Epic Poem lies quite new & untouched to me—Hudibras is rather a series of Satires than a comic Poem.—My plan does not exclude the utmost beauty of Imagery & poetic Diction / and some parts will be serious & pathetic.—So much of myself—only let me add as interesting to dear Mrs Purkis—that a day or two before last Christmas Day Mrs Coleridge was safely delivered of a fine Girl, whom we have baptized Sara.—My wife & all my children are well.—

I write now to ask a little favor of you. There is a preparation of the Indian Hemp, called Bhang, or Bang, or Banghee—the same Drug, which the Malays take, & under it's influence become most pot-valiant Drawcansirs, run a muck, &c. My friend, T. Wedgewood, is exceedingly desirous to obtain a small specimen of it: from what he has heard of it, he conceives it possible that it may afford some alleviation to his most hopeless malady—which is a dreadful inirritability of the intestinal Canal. Now I know that Sir Joseph Banks has a quantity of it—and if you should see him shortly, & could procure a small quantity of it—(you may mention, if you choose, for whom you want it—& Sir Joseph was an intimate

[1] Cf. Letter 505.

Friend of old Mr Wedgewood's, & no stranger to T. Wedgewood) you would oblige me greatly—For my poor Friend's Spirits are so very low, that he has no heart even to write half a dozen Lines himself. O Purkis! Purkis!—what an awful Sight is this! A man of Genius (I know not his superior) of exquisite & various Taste, of extensive Information & subtle & inventive faculties—active beyond example from nature—add to these most affectionate Dispositions, a man loving many, & beloved by many—deeply attached to a prosperous Family, who deserve & return his attachment / & deriving honors & cheering recollections from his noble Father, and crown all these things with a large Fortune, a fine person, a most benevolent Heart, which a calm & comprehensive & acute understanding organizes into genuine Beneficence /—and what more can you think, as constituent of compleat Happiness!—All these Things unite in T. Wedgewood: & all these things are blasted by—a thickening of the Gut!—O God! Such a Tree, in full blossom—it's fruits all medicinal & foodful—& a grub—a grub at the root!—

I am sad to hear of T. Poole's Health! O I yearn to be with him.—Remember me kindly to Mrs Purkis—& my best wishes attend your little ones.—If you could succeed in your request, be so good as to send it by Coach to me, Josiah Wedgewood's Esqre, Gunville, Blandford, Dorset. God bless you & S. T. Coleridge

### 486. To Thomas Poole

*Address*: Thos Poole Esqre | Nether Stowey | Bridgewater
*MS. British Museum. Hitherto unpublished.*
*Postmark*: 3 February 1803. *Stamped*: Bristol.

St James's Parade Bristol. Wednesday Evening [2 February 1803]
My dear Poole

We arrived at Cote, on the afternoon of the Tuesday of last week—I did not stay there, but went immediately to Southey's—where I now am. Mrs Wedgewood is very unwell—& John Wedgewood is no favorite of mine / & T. Wedgewood is in very low Spirits—too low to move out—I have therefore determined to come by myself to Stowey—& Wedgewood will write to me where & when I am to join him. I have been, & still am, miserably afflicted by the Cold—incapable of stirring out of the House without immediate ill effects—I must beg of you therefore to let me have a fire in a tolerably roomy bedroom. I shall leave this place on Friday morning—& be at Bridgewater on Friday Noon / if you send in for me, well & good—if not, I must take a post-chaise.—More when we meet.—God bless you & S. T. Coleridge

*10 February 1803*

487. *To Thomas Wedgwood*

MS. *Wedgwood Museum. Pub. E. L. G. i. 247.*

Nether Stowey, Bridgewater. Feb. 10th. 1803. Thursday

Dear Wedgewood

Last night Poole & I fully expected a few lines from you—& when the newspaper came in without it, we felt as if a dull Bore of a Neighbour had been ushered in after a knock of the Door, which had made us all rise up, & start forward to welcome some long-absent Friend. Indeed in Poole's case this Simile is less overswoln than in mine: for in contempt of my convictions & assurances to the contrary Poole (passing off the Brommagem Coin of his Wishes for sterling Reasons) had persuaded himself fully, that he should really see *you* in propriâ personâ.—The truth is, we had no *right* to expect a letter from you / & I should have attributed your not writing to your having nothing to write, to your bodily dislike to writing—or (tho' with reluctance) to low Spirits—but that I have been haunted with the fear, that your Sister is worse—& that you are at Cote in the mournful office of comforter to your Brother.— God keep us from idle Dreams! Life has enough of real pains.—

I wrote to Captn Wordsworth about the Chinese or India Drawings, from 50£ to 100£—as you desired me—& desired him likewise to get me some Bang—. Wordsworth, in an affectionate Letter, answers me—'Mr Wedgewood shall have the pictures if we return to bring them home. Indeed, I should find the greatest pleasure in serving or pleasing him in any thing. *But I hope, I shall be able to get some for him before we sail.* The Bang if possible shall also be sent: if any country Ship arrives, I shall certainly get it. We have not got any thing of the Kind in our China Ships.'—Now the words *Italicized* may perhaps not be what you wish. If so—if you would much rather that they should be brought by Wordsworth himself from China—give me a line, that I may write & tell him not to get any before he sails.—

We shall hope for a letter from you to night—. I need not say, dear Wedgewood, how anxious I am to hear the particulars of your Health & Spirits.—On Saturday I had a $\Delta\iota\alpha\rho\rho$'hoea diarrhoeissima, et con furore, which continued on me for about 18 hours; & left me, weak indeed, but free from rheumatic pains & the accompanying feverishness. I am now pretty well—if I continue as well, all will do!—

Poole's account of his Conversations &c in France are very interesting & instructive——If your inclinations led you hither, you would be very comfortable here—but I am ready at an hour's warning, ready in heart & mind, as well as body & moveables.—

487]  *To Thomas Wedgwood*

With respectful remembrances & affectionate good wishes to your Brother & Sister

I am, | dear Wedgewood, | Your's most truly ever,
S. T. Coleridge

### 488. *To Thomas Wedgwood*

*Address*: Thos Wedgewood Esqre | Cote House | Bristol
*MS. Wedgwood Museum. Pub. with omis.* Tom Wedgwood, *135.*
*Stamped*: Bridgewater.

Feb. 10th, 1803. Thursday Night. Stowey

My dear Wedgewood

The Boy, who will take this Letter to Bridgewater time enough for the morning's mail, will carry a letter to Captn J. Wordsworth, & prevent him from thinking further of the Drawings.—I will likewise, as on my own account, ask, what you desire, of Seeds &c.——You bid Poole not reply to your letter. Dear Friend! I *could* not—if I had wished it. Only with regard to myself & my accompanying you, let me say thus much. My health is not worse, than it was in the North / indeed, it is much better. I have no fears. But if you feel that my health being what you know it to be, the inconveniences of my being with you will be greater than the advantages, feel no reluctance in telling me so. It is so entirely an affair of Spirits, that the conclusion must be made by you, not in your reason, but purely in your Spirits, & Feelings. Sorry indeed should I be to know, that you had gone abroad with one, to whom you were comparatively indifferent—Sorry, if there should be no one with you, who could by fellow-feeling & general like mindedness yield you sympathy in your sunshiny moments. Dear Wedgewood! my heart swells within me, as it were——I have no other wish to accompany you, than what arises immediately from my personal attachment to you, and a deep sense in my own heart that let us be as dejected as we will, a week together cannot pass in which a mind, like your's, would not feel the want of affection, or be wholly torpid to it's pleasurable influences.——I can not bear to think of your going abroad with a mere travelling companion—with one, at all influenced by Salary or personal conveniences. You will not suspect me of flattering you—but indeed, dear Wedgewood! you are too good & too valuable a man to deserve to receive tendance from a Hireling, even for a month together, in your present state.——If I do not go with you, I shall stay in England only such time, as may be necessary for me to raise the travelling money—& go immediately to the South of France.—I should probably cross the Pyrenees to Bilboa, [*sic*] see the Country of Biscay, & cross the North of Spain to Perpignan, & so on to the North of

Italy—& pass my next winter at Nice. I have every reason to believe, that I can live, even as a Traveller, as cheap as I do in England.—

Poole & Ward are Maltsters, & will send Mr Wedgewood 50 bushels of as good malt as can be had any where; but Poole wishes to know whether it is to be for Ale or Beer, that is, high-coloured, or *pale*—as in this Neighbourhood Beer is made with *pale* malt—likewise whether he wishes it ground or unground—& whether he wishes Hops to be sent with it, & what quantity.—There is fine Flour to be had here, of which Poole will send any quantity, your Brother wishes.—

I will write to Gunville tomorrow.—

God bless you!——I will repeat no professions even in the subscription of a Letter.—You know me—& that it is my serious simple wish, that in every thing respecting me you would think altogether of yourself, & nothing of me—& be assured, that no Resolve of your's, however suddenly adopted, or however nakedly communicated, will give me any pain—any at least arising from my own Bearings—

Your's ever,
S. T. Coleridge

P.S. I have been so overwhelmed that I have said nothing of Poole—what indeed can or ought I to say?—You know what his feelings are, even to men whom he loves & esteems far less than you.—He is deeply affected.——

Perhaps, Leslie would accompany you.

### 489. To Robert Southey

*Address*: Robert Southey Esqre | St James's Parade | Kingsdown | Bristol
*Single Sheet*
MS. Lord Latymer. Pub. with omis. E. L. G. i. 248.
*Stamped*: Bridgewater.

Nether Stowey, Tuesday, Feb. 15. 1803

My dear Southey

I arrived in safety—and after many days of anxious suspense have at length received a Letter from T. Wedgwood, written in dreadful gloom of spirit, desiring me to go by myself to Gunville—and adding that he thinks, my Health incapacitates me for accompanying him to the Continent—whither he intends going in May.—For myself, I should wish that he may continue to think so; but as my Health is rather better than what he knew it to be, when he last took me from the North, expressly under the idea of going with him to Italy in the *middle of March*, I conclude that this last

Thought is the mere child of unusually low spirits, & that when I meet him at Gunville, he will recur to his former plan. Poor fellow! my whole Heart aches for him.—If I went by myself, I should go to Bordeaux—Bayonne—over the Pyrenees to Bilboa—to Pampelona—& so on, keeping as close under the Pyrenees as possible to Perpignan, & so on into Italy—from Italy, if the year permitted, into Switzerland—& pass my next winter at Nice. I go to Gunville on Friday next—but probably shall not reach it till Saturday. My address, 'Josiah Wedgewood, Esqre, Gunville, near Blandford, Dorset, for Mr Coleridge.'—I understood you to say, that the Southerliest part of France was equally southerly as, or more so, than, the South of Spain. If I did not grossly misunderstand you, do, my dear fellow! turn to a map of Europe, & stare a bit at the State of your geographical knowlege. I stared & doubted, as you must remember; but gave up at last to you & Tom, being indeed on all occasions the humblest Creature on earth. Spain in all it's Latitudes runs parallel with Italy & Sicily. Surely I must have misunderstood you—yet so. I cannot imagine what the Dispute could have been.—I shall stay at Gunville from six [weeks] to two months, as I at present suppose. T. Poole is nearly well: his account[s] of his Travels & Conversations in France & Switzerland are exceedingly interesting & instructive: he became acquainted with Reding, Zelviger,[1] & the other Swiss Chieftains. He desires to be kindly remembered to you; & to Mrs Southey. We will take care that some Laver shall be procured as soon as possible. You promised Poole the 2nd Volume of the Anthology, which he has not received.—My health is at it's average. The Saturday before last I had a Διάρροια diarrhoeissima, con furore /

Νῶτα δ' ὑπεχθείνων πέτρας ἀπὸ σκληροκιρυγδοῦς
Σ'λισσλόσιται Ἀχιλεὺς φλοίσβας[2] ἐπὶ ῥωαρίμοιο.
                                                    Ὅμηρ

What a poor syllable the Greek σκυτ is to our $Squ[i]t$—and the Greek Σ'λισσλος—to our Shlishshlosh!!—It held upon me nearly 18 hours, & left me, weak indeed, but freed from rheumatic pains & feverishness. Since then I have been *pretty middling*, as the phrase goes; I do not stir out of the House; & as I have a delicious Wood fire in my bedroom, I am very comfortable here. A little boy, about 9 years old, a sharp Child, waits on me. I dearly love to be waited on by children. A penny, & cheerful Praise, *mills* them like chocolate.—Besides, it is right & *isocratic!*——

I promised to write to Mrs Lovell from this place. But on re-

[1] Coleridge refers to Aloys, baron de Reding (1765–1818), and Jakob Zellweger (1770–1821).
[2] S. T. C. *wrote* phlosh bosh *immediately below*.

flection I find that I can write nothing from hence which I did not say to her at Bristol / & that I had better, of course, go first to Gunville—& see what can be done. Mrs Coleridge suggests to me her apprehensions, that the circumstance of her having been on a stage may be an objection. I fear, that it may. Yet would to Heaven, there were no greater. If only I could say with Truth, that Mrs Lovell is of a cheerful unrepining Disposition & fond of children, I should not fear of success. But indeed, indeed, Southey! it is necessary to impress on Mrs Lovell's mind the conviction, that all must ultimately depend on herself. If she could derive from the thought, that by her own exertions she was about to make herself truly independent, [and exhibit] pleasure & a lightness & joyousness of Heart, there can be little doubt, that situations of some kind or other, & respectable ones, might be found. But if she goes into the affair with a predetermination to be offended—to meet with *Pride, proud* condescensions, &c &c &c—what can be done? Pride in a person, on whom I was really dependent, receiving without returning, would be indeed intolerable to me; but Pride in those, for whose guinea I still gave a Guinea's worth, I should think little of—except to laugh at it. Those who feel very differently from me, must have a great deal of Pride of their own; & then the Quere is, whether they are not as likely to *fancy* it, as to meet with it. Mrs Lovell not understanding French or Drawing or any of the ordinary [Gover]ness-accomplishments, it becomes more needful tha[t I sh]ould speak warmly of her good sense & prudent & irreproachable conduct (& this I can do with pleasure & satisfaction to myself) & of her sweetness of Disposition, & Temper; which how can I do?—If I do not succeed—if Mr W. is provided, or Mrs L. will not suit the place—& I can hear of no other, I assuredly, were I she, would advertise for a situation, either as a Governess, or as a Companion. But again & again she ought to be sensible, that unless she *accord* in her feelings, all must needs be baffled.

Now for Keswick. I still think, that it will answer most admirably, that is to say, if there be only Edith, & you, & the Passionate Pearl. Not that there will not be room for any Visitors, you may have at any time, but inter nos, I know from Mrs Coleridge that it would make her unhappy to live as House-mate with Mary: & loved & honoured, as you will be, by some very good & pleasant people at Keswick, I should be sorry that such impressions should be blended with the Feelings, which your Brother will inspire—/ not when he is by himself, but from his disrespectful & unbrotherly spirit of thwarting & contradicting you. Indeed, I cannot help saying that I have not for a very long time met with a young man who has made so unpleasant an impression on my mind.——But if you are only your own happy Selves, I do warmly recommend you to go to Keswick / I shall certainly be absent—even if I live—two years. There will be a good Nursery-room—& I should think that, if the Infants are healthy, the two Mothers may very well contrive to do with one Nurse maid, & one House-maid. When the children are both awake at the same time, the Mothers can take it by turns to take one child.—You will have no furniture to buy—& all your Books, & if you chose, yourselves too might go by water.—And you might go to Lisbon from Liverpool. You would save at least a 100£ in the two years—& all the interest of the furniture money—& Mrs Southey & Mrs Coleridge will, I doubt not, be great Comforts to each other. Of course you being but 3 in family, you would live in common, as Mrs Southey could come to you, in your Study, whenever she wished to be alone with you—. The annual expences of the whole family, Servants & every thing, will be short of 200£—so that you will live, House rent & all, for a little more than 100£ a year—you are paying half at least of your whole Keswick Expences at your present House. N.B.—I would by no means thwart Bella's wish to stay in Bristol: but on the contrary encourage her. She will not be happy at Keswick.— Before I leave England, I shall—if my phiz. will pass muster—make myself a member of the Equitable [Assuran]ce Society, & by an annual payment of 27£ during my Life ensure [100]0£ to Mrs C. at my Death. I fear, I must *rouge* a little. God b[less you] & S. T. Coleridge. Kisses to the Pearl—& remembrances to the Mother of Pearl.—

P.S. If the Equitables won't pass me, I shall ask the Wedgewoods to allow me 120£ instead of 150£ during Mrs Fricker's Life, & after her death 100£, & to allow Mrs Coleridge 50 or 60£ a year after my Death. I do not like this, simply because I could ask it only for Mrs C's *widowhood*; whereas nothing would give me greater pleasure on my Death bed, than the probability of her marrying a second time, happily.——

490. *To Samuel Purkis*

*Pub.* The Life of Sir Humphry Davy, *by John A. Paris, 2 vols., 1831, i. 173.* This letter is not included in a one-volume edition of the same work also issued in 1831.

Nether Stowey, Feb. 17, 1803

My dear Purkis,

I received your parcel last night, by post, from Gunville, whither (crossly enough) I am going with our friend Poole to-morrow morning. I do from my very heart thank you for your prompt and friendly exertion, and for your truly interesting letter. I shall write to Wedgwood by this post; he is still at Cote, near Bristol; but I shall take the *Bang* back with me to Gunville, as Wedgwood will assuredly be there in the course of ten days. Jos. Wedgwood is named the Sheriff of the County. When I have heard from Wedgwood, or when he has tried this *Nepenthe*, I will write to you. I have been here nearly a fortnight; and in better health than usual. Tranquillity, warm rooms, and a dear old friend, are specifics for my complaints. Poole is indeed a very, very good man. I like even his incorrigibility in small faults and deficiencies: it looks like a wise determination of Nature to let well alone; and is a consequence, a necessary one perhaps, of his immutability in his important good qualities. His journal, with his own comments, has proved not only entertaining but highly instructive to me.

I rejoice in Davy's progress. There are three Suns recorded in Scripture:—Joshua's, that stood still; Hezekiah's, that went backward; and David's, that went forth and hastened on his course, like a bridegroom from his chamber. May our friend's prove the latter! It is a melancholy thing to see a man, like the Sun in the close of the Lapland summer, meridional in his horizon; or like wheat in a rainy season, that shoots up well in the stalk, but does not *kern*. As I have hoped, and do hope, more proudly of Davy than of any other man; and as he has been endeared to me more than any other man, by the being a Thing of Hope to me (more, far more than myself to my own self in my most genial moments,)—so of course my disappointment would be proportionally severe. It were falsehood, if I said that I think his present situation most calculated, of all others, to foster either his genius, or the clearness and incorruptness of his opinions and moral feelings. I see two Serpents at the cradle of his genius, Dissipation with a perpetual increase of acquaintances, and the constant presence of Inferiors and Devotees, with that too great facility of attaining admiration, which degrades Ambition into Vanity—but the Hercules will strangle both the reptile monsters. I have thought it possible to exert talents with perseverance, and to attain true greatness wholly pure, even from the impulses of ambition; but on this subject Davy and I always differed.

When you used the word 'gigantic', you meant, no doubt, to give me a specimen of the irony I must expect from my Philo-Lockian critics. I trust, that I shall steer clear of almost all offence. My book is not, strictly speaking, metaphysical, but historical. It perhaps will merit the title of a History of Metaphysics in England from Lord Bacon to Mr. Hume, inclusive. I confine myself to facts in every part of the work, excepting that which treats of Mr. Hume:—*him* I have assuredly besprinkled copiously from the fountains of Bitterness and Contempt. As to this, and the other works which you have mentioned, 'have patience, Lord! and I will pay thee all!'

Mr. T. Wedgwood goes to Italy in the first days of May. Whether I accompany him is uncertain. He is apprehensive that my health may incapacitate me. If I do not go with him, (and I shall be certain, one way or the other, in a few weeks,) I shall go by myself, in the first week of April, if possible.

Poole's kindest remembrances I send you on my own hazard; for he is busy below, and I must fold up my letter. Whether I remain in England or am abroad, I will occasionally write you; and am ever, my dear Purkis, with affectionate esteem,

Your's sincerely,
S. T. Coleridge.

Remember me kindly to Mrs. Purkis and your children. T. Wedgwood's disease is not painful: it is a complete *taedium vitae*; nothing pleases long, and novelty itself begins to cease to act like novelty. Life and all its forms move, in his diseased moments, like shadows before him, cold, colourless, and unsubstantial.

### 491. *To Robert Southey*

*Address*: Robert Southey Esqre | St James's Parade | Kingsdown | Bristol
*Single Sheet*
*MS. Lord Latymer. Pub. E. L. G. i. 253.*
*Stamped*: Bridgewater.

Nether Stowey, Thursday Morning, Feb. 17. 1803

My dear Southey

I received your Letter at ten o'clock last night: it occasioned me a restless night. Partly, I was greatly oppressed to think, that there should hang such weights from your wings—& partly, I harrassed myself by the apprehension that I had expressed myself abruptly in my last Letter, & not with sufficient delicacy, as to your living at Keswick—making previous *conditions*, as in a Bargain. But I was heavy with thought & with *want* of Sleep, tho' not with the desire of it: and one is apt to say bluntly what must be said & cannot be said without pain. I feel myself awkwardly situated; I shall either be guilty of a Breach of Confidence to Mrs Coleridge or I must request of you not to mention what I say to Mrs Southey —& I am not certain, that this Latter is not in the teeth of part of your marriage Code. But Mrs Coleridge, who would be too happy,

## 17 February 1803

as the phrase [goes], if you & Mrs Southey & the Pearl were with her, has most expressly in a Letter to me declared that she will not live with Mrs Lovell; nor with Tom. This last article is not altogether in consequence of the opinion & feelings, I expressed to her, respecting him, & his unbrotherly manners to you; but from the necessity of an additional Servant, & the consequent crowding of the House, to which Mr Jackson has objected, for his own Quiet's sake, & to which Mrs C. objects for her own. Assuredly, I have no right to do any thing that will in the least degree diminish Mrs Coleridge's Comforts & Tranquillity. In an evil Day for me did I first pay attentions to Mrs Coleridge; in an evil day for me did I marry her; but it shall be my care & my passion, that it shall not be an evil day for her; & that whatever I may be, or may be represented, as a Husband, I may yet be unexceptionable, as her Protector & Friend.—

O dear Southey! I am no Elm!—I am a crumbling wall, undermined at the foundation! Why should the Vine with all it's clusters be buried in my rubbish?—As to my returning to Keswick, it is not to be calculated on.—

I advise you at all events to emancipate yourself. Allow Mrs Lovell 20£ a year, till she can get a situation; & let her live in some family, where she will make herself in some way useful, so as to make up for the small Allowance. If nothing better can be done (& I will try my very utmost) do this—but I conjure you, at all events, & whatever it cost you, emancipate yourself.—Good heaven! what a shocking Thing that there should be such unnecessary canker worms in your Happiness!—You only need a little courage to give a little pain. You are happy in your marriage Life; & greatly to the honor of your moral self-government, Qualities & manners are pleasant to, & sufficient for, you, to which my Nature is utterly unsuited: for I am so weak, that warmth of manner in a female House mate is as necessary to me, as warmth of internal attachment. This is weakness; / but on the other hand I ought to say, in justice to myself, that I am happy & contented in solitude, or only with the common Inhabitants of a Batchelor's House: / —an old woman, and a sharp Child.—But you, who want nothing to be happy—who are prevented from happiness, & consequent Greatness, only by unnecessary Appendages—I cannot endure to think of it——Go to Keswick—or to the South of France—first, compleatly clear yourself—& then live within your income, & do nothing but great works.——

My Disease is probably anomalous. If it can be called any thing, by a lucky Guess, it may be called irregular scrophulous Gout. But as to King's notion, that if it be irregular Gout, change of climate is no remedy—this is in the teeth of every medical writer of Note on the gout, who have all prescribed hot Climates for gouty people—& what weighs more with me, in the teeth of particular facts in my own knowlege.—Besides, what gouty Medicines are there that I have not used? What gouty regimen? Have I not wholly abandoned wine, spirits, & all fermented Liquors? And taken Ginger in superabundance? 'Tis true, I have not taken Dr Beddoes's North American Fruit—nor do I intend to do it.—What can I want more decisive than my own experience—in hot rooms I am well—in hot weather I am well—Cold, wet, & change of weather uniformly disease me.—It is astonishing how well I was three *hot* weeks in last summer—a cold rain came on, & I was ill as instantly as if it had poisoned me. I should be an ideot, if I wished any thing more decisive than this. My Disease, whatever it may be called, consists in an undue sensibility with a deficient irritability—muscular motion is languid with me, & venous action languid—my nerves are unduly vivid—the consequence is, a natural tendency to obstructions in the glands, &c; because glandular secretion requires the greatest vigor of any of the secretories. My only medicine is an universal & regular Stimulus—Brandy, Laudanum, &c &c make me well, during their first operation; but the secondary Effects increase the cause of the Disease. Heat in a hot climate is the only regular & universal Stimulus of the external world; to which if I can add Tranquillity, the equivalent, & Italian climate, of the world within, I do not despair to be a healthy man.

When I shall see you, I cannot tell—certainly not for 5 weeks. I go to Taunton on Friday; and leave it on Saturday morning 5 o'clock—& shall be at Gunville, on Saturday evening. Josiah Wedgewood is high Sheriff of the County.—You will see by my Letter that T. Wedgewood wrote to me what Tobin told you. Selfishly speaking, I should wish he might continue of that mind; but I love & honor him so much, that on the whole I do not wish it. For I am desirous above all things, that he should make a fair Trial of a good climate; which he cannot do, unless he has both a field companion with him, and a man who in the sum of his faculties is his Equal—& one who is with him purely from affectionate Esteem.—

Do not mind the Cid. I do not think, I shall be able to do any thing in the poetry Line.—

God bless you | &
S. T. Coleridge.

Poole's kind remembrances—& will send you Laver quam citissime.—I have opened the Letter to beg that you will procure me from King a Bottle of the red Sulfat, and one of the Compound Acid—& to send them well secured to Mr T. Wedgewood, Cote—for me: & this must be within a week.—

### 492. To Thomas Wedgwood

*Address*: [T. Wedge]wood Esqre | Cote House | Bristol
*MS. Wedgwood Museum. Pub. with omis*, Tom Wedgwood, *137*.
*Stamped*: Bridgewater.

Poole's, Thursday, Feb. 17. 1803

My dear Wedgewood

I do not know that I have any thing to say that justifies me in troubling you with the Postage & Perusal of this Scrawl.—I received a short & kind Letter from Josiah last night—he is named the Sheriff—Poole, who has received a very kind Invitation from your Brother in a Letter of last Monday, and which was repeated in the last night's Letter, goes with me, I hope, in the full persuasion, that you will be there before he is under the necessity of returning home. He has settled both his Might-have-been-lawsuits in a perfectly pleasant way, exactly to his own wish. He bids me say, what there is no occasion of saying, with what anxious affection his Thoughts follow you.—Poole is a very, very good man. I like even his incorrigibility in little faults, & deficiencies—it looks like a wise determination of Nature 'to let well alone.'—

Are you not laying out a scheme that will throw your Travelling in Italy into an unpleasant & unwholesome part of the year? From all, I can gather, you ought to leave this country in the first days of April, at the latest. But no doubt, you know these things better than I.—If I do not go with you, it is very probable that we shall meet somewhere or other / at all events, you will know where I am / & I can come to you if you wish it. And if I do go with you, there will be this advantage, that you may drop me where you like, if you should meet any Frenchman, Italian, or Swiss, whom you liked—& who would be pleasant & profitable to you—.—But this we can discuss at Gunville.

As to Mackintosh, I never doubted that he *means* to fulfil his engagements with you; but he is one of those weak-moraled men, with whom the meaning to do a thing means nothing. He promises with $\frac{99}{100}$ of his whole Heart; but there is always a little speck of cold felt at the core, that transubstantiates the whole Resolve into a Lie, even in his own consciousness.—But what I most fear is that he will in some way or other embroider himself upon your Thoughts; but you, no doubt, will see the Proof Sheets, & will prevent this from extending to the injury of your meaning. Would to Heaven, it were done!¹ I may with strictest truth say, that I have *thirsted* for it's appearance.—

I have written to Captn Wordsworth, by the yesterday's Post. His address is 'Mr Wordsworth, Staples Inn, Holborn, London. For Captn J. Wordsworth.' His own Lodgings were, & probably are, No 9 Southampton Buildings; but the former Address is sure to find him.—

I remain in comfortable Health. Warm Rooms, an old Friend, & Tranquillity, are specifics for my Complaint.—With all my ups & downs I have a deal of Joyous feeling, that I would with gladness give a good part of to you, my dear Friend!—God grant, that Spring may come to you with healing on her wings!—

My respectful remembrances to your Brother, and Mrs J. Wedgewood—& desire Mrs J. Wedgewood, when she writes to Crescelly, to remember me with affection to Miss Allen, & Fanny, & Emma—& to say, how often I think with pleasure on them & the weeks, I passed in their society. When you come to Gunville, please not to forget my Pens. Poole & I quarrel once a day about Pens. /

God bless you, my dear Wedgewood!

I remain with most affectionate esteem & regular attachment & good wishes

Your's ever,
S. T. Coleridge

If Southey should send a couple of Bottles, one of the red Sulfat, & one of the Compound Acid, to Cote for me, will you be so good as to bring them with you to Gunville.—

If Poole goes with [me to Gunville, we will hire a one]² horse chair— ——

### 493. To Thomas Wedgwood

*Address*: T. Wedgewood Esqre | Cote | Bristol
*MS. Wedgwood Museum, Pub. with omis. E. L. G. i. 252.*
*Stamped*: Bridgewater.

Nether Stowey—    Thursday, Feb. 17. 1803

My dear Wedgewood

Last night I received a four ounce parcel-Letter by the Post,

---

¹ Coleridge again refers to an abortive plan whereby Mackintosh was to prepare an essay incorporating Tom Wedgwood's philosophical opinions. It was this work for which Coleridge had earlier agreed to write a preface. See Letter 436. When Mackintosh sailed for India in Feb. 1804, he took with him Tom Wedgwood's manuscripts. 'The first moment after my books are placed on their shelves', he promised, 'shall be devoted to Time and Space.' *Tom Wedgwood*, 157–9.

² MS. torn. See letter 494 for Coleridge's mode of travel.

*17 February 1803* [493

which, Poole & I concluded, was the mistake or carelessness of the Servant, who had put the parcel, your Sister gave him, into the *Post* Office instead of the *Coach* Office. I *should* have been indignant, if dear Poole's *Squirt* of Indignation had not set me a laughing.—On opening it it contained my Letter from Gunville, & a parcel, a small one, of *Bang* from Purkis. I will transcribe the parts of his Letter which relate to it—but I have been harrassed by the apprehension that you may be vexed at Purkis's having mentioned your name.[1]—

Feb. 7. 1803. Brentford.

'My dear C. I thank you for your Letter, & am happy to be the means of obliging you. Immediately on the Receipt of your's I wrote to Sir Joseph Banks (who, I verily believe, is one of the most excellent and most useful men of this Country) requesting a small Quantity of Bang, & saying that it was for the use of Mr Wedgewood. I yesterday received the parcel which I now send—accompanied with a very kind Letter, & as part of it will be interesting to you & your Friend, I will transcribe it. "The Bang, you ask for, is the powder of the Leaves of a kind of Hemp that grows in the Hot Climates. It is prepared, and used, I believe, in all parts of the East, from Morocco to China. In Europe, it is found to act very differently on different Constitutions. Some it elevates in the extreme: others it renders torpid & scarcely observant of any evil that may befall them. In Barbary it is always taken, if it can be procured, by Criminals condemned to suffer amputations, & it is said to enable these *Miserables* to bear the rough operations of an unfeeling Executioner more than we Europeans can the keen knife of our most skilful Chirurgeons. This it may be necessary to have said to my friend, Mr Wedgewood, whom I respect as much as his Virtues deserve, & I know them well. I send a small quantity only, because I possess but little: if however it is found to agree, I will instantly forward the whole of my Stock, & write without delay to Barbary, from whence it came, for more."

[']Sir Joseph adds in a postscript—"It seems almost beyond a doubt, that the Nepenthe was a preparation of the Bang known to the Ancients."

[']Sir J. B. has not given me any directions or hints as to the quantity of *Bang* to be taken at a time; but it will occur to Mr W. that it is to be taken in very small Doses, & with the utmost caution &c &c &c—[']

Now I had better take the small parcel with me to Gunville. If I send it by the Post, besides the heavy expence, I can not rely

---

[1] Coleridge had authorized Purkis to use Wedgwood's name. See Letter 485.

493]  *To Thomas Wedgwood*

on the Stowey Carriers of Letters, who are a brace of as careless & dishonest Rogues, as had ever claims on that article of the Hemp & Timber Trade, called the Gallows.—Indeed, I verily believe that if all Stowey (Ward excepted) does not go to Hell, it will be by the supererogation of Poole's Sense & Honesty.—*Charitable*!

We go off early to morrow morning. I shall hear from you of course.—Respectful Remembrances to the Family at Cote.—We will have a fair Trial of *Bang*—Do bring down some of the Hyoscyamine Pills—& I will give a fair Trial of opium, Hensbane, & Nepenthe. Bye by the bye, I always considered Homer's account of the *Nepenthe* as a *Banging* lie.——

God bless you, | my dear Friend, | &
S. T. Coleridge


494. *To Robert Southey*

*Address*: Robert Southey Esqre | St James's Parade | Kingsdown | Bristol
Single Sheet.
*MS*. Lord Latymer. *Pub. E. L. G. i. 257.*
*Stamped*: Blandford.

Thursday, Feb. 24. 1803. 'Josiah Wedgwood's Esqre,
Gunville, Blandford, Dorset.'
Dear Southey

I have delayed writing in expectation of a Letter from you: & I still hope, that I shall receive one this evening—& shall therefore send this Letter by tomorrow's Post. I left Stowey with Poole on Friday Morning: instead of taking a Post-chaise & arriving at Gunville the same evening Poole *would* hire a one horse Chair (that Pandora Box of Accidents) & all happened as I most minutely foretold—breakings down, delays, wettings, & arrival at Gunville late on Sunday Afternoon. Here I shall remain a month at least. I need not say, that I am up to my chin in comforts.—

And now for Mrs Lovell.—It is as I feared. Mr Wedgwood had already opened a negociation for a Governess.—I have felt the less—at least the less immediate regret—from this circumstance / because I seem to have perceived, that Mrs L. & the Wedgwoods would not have suited each other. Indeed, Mr W. layed such *stress*, & so repeatedly, on good & even temper, & good and even spirits, that I could not have had the courage to have said any thing about it / And I think it possible to meet with situations, where the Governess lives on more familiar Terms with the Master & Mistress of the Family. I have it in my mind to write to Dr Crompton.—

My health is, as the weather is: & my spirits low indeed.

( 934 )

I do not feel convinced that the block-stamping of Cards had any connection whatever with the Discovery of Printing.—If this could have led to it, Sealing Letters, with engraved Seals, would have done it some 10 centuries before—& Common Coinage of money would have done it.—There is no strength in the affair in my mind, unless the whole process can be traced historically—nay more, with legal evidence such as is used & held valid, in quashing a Patent.—

In the early parts of your History be careful to collect with care all that can be known, & all that can even be guessed, about the Dresses, Manufactures, commerce, domestic Habits, & modifications of the feudal Government &c—or else your History will have the air & the character of a Story-Book. You do not need the Advice, I almost *know*; but *needless* Advice is no very unpleasant thing in a world, where there is such plenty of *useless* Advice.

The Letters are come in. I had no other particular wish to hear from you at present, than what arose from the Apprehension that what I had written concerning Keswick, might have wounded you. Yet as to the *matter* at least, it is impossible that I could with propriety write otherwise.

But I am in no spirits to talk of these Things.—Hartley has had both the Scarlet Fever & the Croup. He is tolerably well at present; but my mind misgives me, that I shall never see him more.

God bless you | &
S. T. Coleridge.

### 495. To Robert Southey

*Address*: Robert Southey Esqre | St James's Parade | Kingsdown | Bristol
*Single Sheet*
MS. Lord Latymer. Pub. E. L. G. i. 258.
*Stamped*: Blandford.

Saturday Night, 12 o clock. March 12. [1803]
My dear Southey

I received your Letter this evening, & was very glad to receive it.—Before I speak of it's contents, let me refer to a former Letter. You surely misunderstood my argument respecting the Cards—I layed no Stress on the Figures; but I contended that if stamping Cards *with Texts* was printing, Stamping Metal Medals with Figures & *Inscriptions* (many of them *long Inscriptions*) was Printing—every Seal with *words* in it was a species of Printing. You say, that the Figures led to the Texts—so be it! But still you have to prove that this led to *our Printing* or had any thing to do with it. Between these Stereotypes & moveable Types there is as great a distance as between—I will not say, picture-writing and Alphabetical Language; for that would be too much—but *precisely* as great as between the Chinese character Language & Alphabetical Language. —That Coins & Seals did not lead the Greeks & Romans to printing, first their Laws, & then their great Authors (Homer &c) by Stereotypes, does appear strange. Luck & Accident must be taken into the account, tho' it is impossible to ascertain the degree & weight of their action—but I think, that the multitude of Slaves, & the circumstance that the manuscript Trade was in the Hands of the wealthiest Nobles will of itself account for the phaenomenon / What Instrument for shortening field-labor was ever invented in the W. Indies ? There were none in Europe, till the commercial Feeling extended itself to Agriculture.—

Your prophecy concerning the Edingburgh Review did credit to your penetration. The second number is altogether despicable—the hum-drum of pert attorneys' Clerks, very pert & yet prolix & dull as a superannuated Judge. The passage you quote has been a slang Quotation at Gunville for the last week. The whole Pamphlet on the Balance of Power is below all Criticism—& the first article on Kant you may believe on my authority to be impudent & senseless Babble.

I rejoice at your account of Ritson's Book.[1]—Do you read Italian ? Whether or no (for there exists a good old English Translation) I conjure you to read thro' the historical & political Works of Machiavel. I prefer him greatly to Tacitus.—Now for myself—

T. Wedgwood arrived here the Tuesday before last, hopeless, heartless, planless. There seemed to be no thought at all of my accompanying him / & I accordingly settled every thing for going without him. On Sunday last I wrote to London, to make inquiries for him respecting a young man, who has been lately on the continent, for his companion / for his objections to me were, my health, & my ignorance of French & Italian, & the absolute necessity of his having some one to take the whole business of the road off his hands. Yet still he could not bear to come to the point—& Jos. was anxious, I believe, that Tom should not go without me—however, on Wednesday Jos. came to me & said—that T. W. could not bear the idea of losing me—that he would dismiss his present Servant, & at any price procure a capapee accomplished Travelling Gentleman Servant, &c—& that we would go together to London on Monday, March 14—& to France as soon as the Servant was procured—/—Of course, I assented / for I had promised that till the second week of April I would be at his Service, & that I would

---

[1] Joseph Ritson (1752–1803), *Ancient Engleish Metrical Romanceës*, 3 vols., 1802.

accomodate myself to his resolutions however rapidly changed or nakedly communicated—/ All being thus settled, *pounce*! comes this damned War-business!—However, we still go on Monday. Josiah Wedgwood goes with us—he has a [Dorset?] Address to present, as High Sheriff—. Where I shall be, I do not know—for there is no bed for me at York St. However a letter will find me there—'Messrs Wedgwood & Byerley, York Street, St James's Place, London'—& I *intreat* you, mention to no soul alive that I am in London / & communicate no part of this Letter to Tobin.——

You would greatly oblige me, if you would immediately gain from Mr King or Dr Beddoes information, where in London I can procure a Bottle of the Gout medicine. I admire Dr Beddoes's part of the Pamphlet very much. It is far superior to the Hygeia[1] in Style, & Reasoning. And yet with the exception of the Essay on Mania the Hygeia is a valuable & useful work. Indeed when I think how Beddoes bestirs himself, I take shame to myself for having suffered tittle-tattle Stories respecting him to warp my personal feelings—especially as to me he has always behaved with uncommon kindness. I do think, that Tobin's maxim of conduct is wise & good—always keep on the best terms, you can, with an acquaintance, as long as, & in proportion as, he is an active & useful Man—& this not only in your outward demeanour, but in your inner feelings.—

I wish from my heart's heart, that you were at Keswick—& that Mary were pensioned off. My heart bleeds for her often / in my deepest conviction, her real misfortune is her heart & temper. Could I have dared answer Wedgwood's Question in the affirmative—'Is she kind, gentle, of a sweet & affectionate Temper?' I will not disguise from you, that I could have procured the Situation for her—& she would never, never have been abandoned by them. But in proportion as Mr & Mrs Wedgwood are delightful in their own domestic character—the children delightful—& their intentions to a Governess, who should prove another mother & guardian to the children, in the highest degree liberal & grateful—in the same proportion, you feel, that I could not dare recommend any one without my warmest & sanest Convictions. Indeed, it would have been as silly as wicked. For their penetration is fully equal to their goodness of Heart.—

Would to Heaven, you were at Keswick. Wordsworth means to reside $\frac{1}{2}$ a mile from it—& you & he would agree far better now, than you might perhaps have done 4 or 5 years ago—& he is now

[1] Thomas Beddoes, *Hygëia: or Essays Moral and Medical, on the Causes affecting the Personal State of our Middling and Affluent Classes*, 3 vols., 1802–3.

495]    *To Robert Southey*

fonder of conversation & more open.—Kiss the Pearl, the dispassionate Pearl for me—Little Darling! I have a Father's Heart for all of her age—how much more for a child of your's, linked together as we have been, by good & evil, ple[asure] & pain. Would to God, to God, that in *one* thing, in which I am most unlik[e you,] that I were like you altogether! But the Time is past.—S. T. Coleridge.

### 496. To Thomas Poole

*Address*: Single Sheet. | T. Poole Esqre | Nether Stowey | Bridgwater | Somerset
*MS. British Museum. Hitherto unpublished.*
*Stamped*: Blandford.

Sunday March 13 1803. Gunville

My dear Poole

I have not written to you—excepting Mrs C. I have written to no one—because I have been in bad health & worse Spirits.—T. W. arrived the Tuesday after you quitted us, worse than I ever saw him both in health & spirits—hopeless, heartless, planless! He recovered however in a few days—on Sunday last I wrote to town for him, on the beat up for a companion—& on Wednesday wrote home positively that I was not to accompany T. W. but should immediately go off myself for Bilboa—but that Evening Tom sent Jos. to me to say, that he would dismiss his present Servant, and at any price however high procure a perfect Travelling Servant, who could take the whole business of the road upon him—that he could not think of giving me up, &c, & claimed my former promise —&c. Tom had had thoughts of [T. R.][1] Underwood—& I wrote to Davy about it, by his desire (& Davy has never thought fit to answer the Letter, which for his sake I trust in God has miscarried)— BUT THIS MUST BE A SECRET.—Jos. was uneasy manifestly—and communicated Tom's last message to me in a manner that sufficiently shewed how much it had been at his heart that his Brother should not go without me.—As to myself, it was a matter made wholly indifferent to me only by my affection for T. W.—Otherwise I would rather have gone on my own Bottom. However of course I assented—& it was settled that we should leave this place on Monday (i.e tomorrow) for London—. T. W. fitted me out with clothes &c / when lo! pounce comes down the King's Message, & a *War*!— However, we still go to London tomorrow—Jos. goes with us, to carry up the Dorset Address as High Sheriff—& stays as long as we stay. There are but two Beds at York St—& where I shall lodge, I cannot say—I have some thoughts of stopping at Purkis's—I have a mortal Dread of London Society.—When any thing is concluded,

[1] Initials heavily inked out in manuscript.

I will write to you of course. T. W. has been much better since he settled his plan—he talks of taking a covered Gig or something of that kind with one strong Horse—& to have a good Saddle-horse—& so to walk & ride & be carried, as one's feelings direct. In this way we should be 3 months perhaps in reaching Naples—I should like the plan extremely—but I am prepared for all & every thing to burst like a Bubble.[1]

There is nothing to be done at present with Mr W.'s Life.—There are no materials at present—& whether any can be collected, seems doubtful. A most valuable work *might* be made, I have no doubt.—But this, if ever, is for a future time.—

Remember me to Ward.—Whenever I feel my heart thawing, & my state of feeling pleasurable, I will not fail to write to you—at present I am a bottle of Brandy in Lapland.—God bless you /
My dear Friend! &<br>S. T. Coleridge

I have torn open my Letter—Jos. & Mrs W. & T. W. would be outrageous if I should say, I had written to you, & not remembered them [most] kindly to you.

I conjure you mention to no Soul alive, not t[o] Purkis, not to Davy, not to any one, that I am in London, for if it be possible, I shall try to see no one. I am quite menschenscheu, as the Germans say—i.e. man-shy——

Oblitusque meorum, obliviscendus et illis![2]

## 497. To Mrs. S. T. Coleridge

*Address*: Mrs . . .
*MS. Dove Cottage. Hitherto unpublished.* The holograph of this letter contains only a portion of pages 3 and 4. The original hangs on the wall in Dove Cottage.
*Postmark*: 24 March 1803.

. . . If there should be War, I shall immediately come to Keswick —& if there be any little things, you wish me to bring, write, & I will do it. Tell Wordsworth, that I have seen John 3 or 4 times—tho' he is so busy, that it has been only for an hour or less at a time. I had some notion that I should hear from them to day.

Remember me affectionately to Mr Jackson and Mrs Wilson—and my love to Mary—and make my best respects to Mr and Mrs Wilkinson, & Mr and Mrs Calvert—and I remain
with affectionate anxiety<br>your's &c S. T. Coleridge

---

[1] T. Wedgwood finally left for France on 25 Mar. 1803, taking with him as a companion not Coleridge but T. R. Underwood. He returned to England on 16 May, just at the outbreak of war. *Tom Wedgwood*, 141.

[2] Horace, *Epis.* I. xi. 9.

## To Mrs. S. T. Coleridge

[P.S.] ... & drink beer. If you do not, leave off your Beer at Supper, and take instead, a glass of warm brandy and water—not with your supper, nor immediately after, but just, as you are going to bed.—Of what kind are the Dreams? I mean, are they accompanied with distinct bodily feelings—*whizzings up* into the Head, fear of strangulation—&c—or simply great Fear from fearful Forms and Combinations—or both at once?—

### 498. To Mrs. S. T. Coleridge

*Address*: Mrs Coleridge | Greta Hall | Keswick | Cumberland
*MS. Lord Latymer, Pub. with omis.* Letters, i. 420.
*Postmark*: 4 April 1803.

Monday, April 4 1803

My dear Sara

I have taken my place for Wednesday Night; & barring accidents, shall arrive at Penrith on Friday Noon. If Friday be a fine morning, i.e. if it do not rain / you will get Mr Jackson to send a lad with a horse or poney to Penruddock / and my Trunk must come by the Carrier. I will walk to Penruddock.—The boy ought to be at Penruddock by 12 o clock, that his Horse may bait & have a feed of Corn.—But if it be rain, there is no choice but that I must take a chaise—at all events, if it please God, I shall be with you by Friday, 5 o'clock, at the latest—. You had better dine early—I shall take an egg or two at Penrith / & drink Tea at home.—For more than a fortnight we have had burning July Weather / the effect on my Health was manifest—but Lamb objected very sensibly —how do you know, what part may not be owing to the excitement of bustle & company?—On Friday Night I was unwell & restless —& uneasy in limbs & stomach / tho' I had been extremely regular —I told Lamb on Saturday morning, that I guessed that the weather had changed. But there was no mark of it—it was hotter than ever— on Saturday evening my right knee, & both my ancles swelled, & were very painful—& within an hour after there came on a storm of wind & rain / it continued raining the whole night— Yesterday it was a fine day, but cold—to day the same / but I am a great deal better / & the swelling in my ancles is gone down, & that in my right knee much decreased.—Lamb observed, that he was glad he had seen all this with his own eyes—he now *knew*, that my illness was truly linked with the weather / & no whim or restlessness of disposition in me.—It is curious; but I have found that the Weather glass changed on Friday Night, the very hour that I found myself unwell.—I will try to bring down something for Hartley; tho' Toys are so outrageously dear—& I so short of money—that I shall be puzzled.—

To day I dine again with Sotheby. He ha[s] informed me, that ten gentlemen, who have met me at his House, desired him to solicit me to finish the Christabel, & to permit them to publish it for me / & they engaged that it should be in paper, printing, & decorations the most magnificent Thing that had hitherto appeared.—Of course, I declined it. The lovely Lady shan't come to that pass!—Many times rather would I have it printed at Soulby's on the true Ballad Paper /——However, it was civil—and Sotheby is very civil to me.

I had purposed not to speak of Mary Lamb—but I had better write it than tell it. The Thursday before last she met at Rickman's a Mr Babb, an old old Friend & Admirer of her Mother / the next day she *smiled* in an ominous way—on Sunday she told her Brother that she was getting bad, with great agony—on Tuesday morning she layed hold of me with violent agitation, & talked wildly about George Dyer / I told Charles, there was not a moment to lose / and I did not lose a moment—but went for a Hackney Coach, & took her to the private Madhouse at Hogsden / She was quite calm, & said—it was the best to do so—but she wept bitterly two or three times, yet all in a calm way. Charles is cut to the Heart.—

You will send this note to Grasmere—or the contents of it / tho' if I have time I shall probably write myself to them to d[ay or] tomorrow.

Your's affectionately<br>S. T. Coleridge

## 499. *To William Godwin*

MS. Lord Abinger. Hitherto unpublished.

Tuesday Morning—[5 April 1803]¹

Dear Godwin

I am going to day to the equitable Assurance Society with Mr Ridout, one of the Managers, to ensure my Life for 1000£—Mr Ridout, who is a medical man, is my chief Affidavit / but as I must give reference to two persons, I shall refer them to you / it is simply a matter of form, to state that I have no distemper that tends to the shortening of Life—taken in the popular sense of the words.—

---

¹ Coleridge's Equitable Assurance Policy, T20743, is dated '7th April 1803', and this letter, therefore, was probably written on the Tuesday preceding. Furthermore, Godwin's son was born on 28 Mar. 1803, and Mary Lamb was taken to an asylum on 29 Mar. (See Letter 498.) She was much improved by 13 Apr. (*Lamb Letters*, i. 344.)

If I find that persons living in chambers may be Referees, I shall not trouble you; but shall refer to Mr White, or Mr Wordsworth. With all kind wishes for Mrs Godwin, & the least of your little ones, I am, dear Godwin, yours with much esteem & much affection

S. T. Coleridge

P.S. I *hope*, that Mary Lamb is rather better / her indisposition will prevent Charles from calling to know how Mrs Godwin is—for some days.—

### 499 A. *To J. G. Ridout*

MS. Mr. F. H. Harrop (*transcribed by Miss Helen Darbishire*). *Hitherto unpublished.* Although the address sheet of this manuscript is missing, it seems certain that the letter was intended for J. G. Ridout, one of the managers of the Equitable Assurance Society. See Letter 499.

Greta Hall, Keswick, Friday Night
April 15, 1802 [1803]

My dear Sir

I have been rather anxious from the not having heard from you, or received the Assurance Policy. I begin to suspect, that your Letter must have miscarried.—Do, be so good as to give me a couple of Lines—

I arrived here safe on Good Friday Evening,[1] but caught the Influenza in the coach / I cured myself immediately by a grain of opium taken with Camphor & Rhubarb.—

I heard briefly from James Tobin / Remember me most affectionately to John Tobin, whom I like & esteem more & more / the more I know him.—

The Influenza spares no one at Keswick & in the circumjacency—
Farewell! I am, | my dear Sir, | with no every day feeling of esteem | your obliged & | sincere Friend

S. T. Coleridge

### 500. *To Robert Southey*

[Addressed by Mrs. S. T. Coleridge.] To | R. Southey Esqre | Saint-James's place. | Kingsdown | *Bristol*
MS. *Lord Latymer. Hitherto unpublished.*
*Postmark*: 20 May 1803.  *Stamped*: Keswick.

17th May. [1803]

My dear Southey

What mouldering Temples we seem to be! I arrived at Keswick on Good Friday, with the Influenza which I caught of an old man

[1] 8 Apr.

in the Mail. It affected my eyes & stupified my Head, in a perfectly new way to me—However, I had nearly got rid of it, tho' my faculties were in a state of confusion & unexampled weakness, when I caught cold by some accident; & the Influenza returned in the shape of a rheumatic fever, severer for it's continuance (3 fits in the 24 hours) than any attack since my first terrific one at Xt Hospital—it was sufficiently distinguished however from simple Rheumatic Fever by the immediate & total Prostration of Strength, confusion of senses & faculties, long tearing fits of coughing with great expectoration, & clammy treacle-sweats on awaking.—At the same time we were all layed up, but Hartley / Maid, Mistress, Baby, & Derwent: so that we had a [h]ouse of Squawling as well as of Mourning. Again I a[m] raising myself up—and again I have a relapse—a[nd] that I write you this Letter is literally, my dear Friend! the extent & stretched Tether of my Powers.—Poor Mrs Danvers!—dear old Mrs Poole!—Old People, good dear old Ladies, are like Infants, that die at 9 months old / they gain by Death an unchangeable sort of Being in the minds of the Survivors. I did not love Mrs Danvers, as I loved Mrs Poole—but I loved her so well, that I understood compleatly how you loved her / & thinking of old Mrs Poole, I not only understood—but I *had*—your identical Feeling.—If I had such a mother, infirm, but her infirmity threatening nothing, methinks, I could go on with a full & an unyearning Heart——I will write as soon as I am able / I will do all I can respecting Robert Lovell.

You were mistaken as to the Essay on the men who had risen from the Dead not existing in Plutarch / Lamb had *your* Plutarch from Rickman / old Philemon [1] / & I found it immediately / So little ought we to rely on a *negation* of our memory against another's *Positive*.—My Plans remain the same / if Spain can continue neuter, I shall go in the late Autumn to Valencia / otherwise I must go to Madeira / which will be *our's* in some shape or other.—No one who lived a month with me *could* have the least doubt as to the *barometrical* nature of my Health. / I am weary & ashamed of talking about my intended works / I am still in hopes that this summer will not pass away without something worthy of me.—If you are in London, by all means insure your Life for 1000£ at the equitable Insurance Society. It will cost you 31£, for the first year, & 27£ for every succeeding one / and at your Death your widow &c have a 1000£, & besides an equal proportionate Share of the Profits of the Society for the whole time of your Membership.——I have

---

[1] Philemon Holland, *The Philosophie, commonly called the Morals, written by the learned Philosopher Plutarch of Chaeronea, translated out of Greek into English, and conferred with Latin and French*, 1603.

done it—& I cannot express what a comfort it has been to me / what a weight off my mind. Rickman objects to the value, it makes you set upon your Life, in case of going out on a water-party, or a Sea voyage / for this sort of Death, Hanging, & Suicide deprive you of the Benefits—I answer, the care you have in every other circumstance / mail coaches overturn & break necks, as well as Boats overset & drown / Every body (attorneys & men of the world) agrees, that it is the best *possible* way of saving money.—Bless you

& S. T. Coleridge.

## 501. To Mrs. Thomas Clarkson

MS. Mr. Basil Cottle. Hitherto unpublished fragment.

[May 1803][1]

... exceedingly precious—in a prudential as well as moral view.—I have not alluded to your dear Mother. On these occasions the impression on me is so nakedly an idealess feeling, that I have nothing to say save only that I *feel*.—For you, and Mr Clarkson, and for all whose Happiness ...

... interruptions have thrown me so dreadfully behind hand.—Again & again may God bless & restore you!—Your sincere Friend,

S. T. Coleridge

Mrs Coleridge joins in my anxious wishes for you.—
P.S. I should greatly wish Mr C. to write to Kendal immediately to know, if any of the Schoolmen were in that Library—speci ...[2]

## 502. To Thomas Poole

Address: Thomas Poole, Esqre | Nether Stowey | Bridgewater | Somerset—
MS. British Museum. Pub. E. L. G. i. 262.
Postmark: 23 May 1803. Stamped: Keswick.

May 20, 1803. Keswick

My dear Poole

Since Good Friday, the time of my arrival at Keswick, I have been not only very ill—& for a large part of the time actually bedridden—but the Disorder seized in my head in such a way, that the

---

[1] Having been ill for some time, Mrs. Clarkson left the Lake Country for Bury St. Edmunds in July 1803. Her mother died a year later, after a protracted illness, when Coleridge was in Malta. This letter was probably written in May, before Mrs. Clarkson's departure. The first sentence seems to refer to Coleridge's insurance policy, which, he wrote to both Southey and Poole, had been so great a comfort to him during his illness. See Letters 500 and 502.

[2] Possibly the result of this inquiry led Coleridge to request Thelwall to bring Duns Scotus's *De Sententiis* on the way from Kendal to Keswick. See Letter 528.

very idea of writing became terrible to me.—It was the Influenza, which shewed itself in the form of rheumatic Fever—crippling my loins—but distinguished from it by immediate prostration of Strength, confusion of Intellect on any attempt to exert it, a tearing Cough with constant expectoration, & clammy honey-dew sweats on awaking from my short Sleeps.—I am now only somewhat better / & feel the infinite Importance of the deepest Tranquillity. —It has been an inconceivable Comfort to me during my illness that when in London I had made myself a member of the Eq. Ass. Society for 1000£, which cost me 31£—but henceforward it will only be 27£. I made my will too, bequeathing the Interest of the Sum to Mrs C.—and after her Death the Sum itself to my Daughter if she be alive / if not, to my two boys or the one who is alive—. I ventured without writing to you to take the liberty of leaving the money to you in trust—& in case of your Death, to Wordsworth. But I shall employ the first months of my returning Health in arranging my MSS, to be published in case I should be taken off— & I will send you instructions with respect to my Letters &c— which should be collected—& I shall leave it entirely to you & Wordsworth to choose out of them such as with necessary omissions, & little corrections of grammatical inaccuracies may be published ——; but if God grant me only tolerable Health this summer, I pledge myself to all who love me, that by next Christmas the last three years of my Life shall no longer appear a Blank.—I wish exceedingly that you could come to me this Summer, or Autumn / and God knows my heart, I *wish* very few things.—

Dear Poole! in the present Instance I have been incapable of writing to you / but at no time judge of my affection & esteem by the frequency or infrequency of my Letters. While I live, I shall always hold you dear in the first degree.—Farewell!

S. T. Coleridge

At one time every Soul in my house was confined to bed, & we were tended on by strange faces. Many have died of the complaint in & about Keswick / & no one has been quite as well since as before.—Love to Ward. Mrs Coleridge's Love to you.——

### 503. To Francis Freeling[1]

*MS. Mr. Walter T. Spencer. Hitherto unpublished.*

Greta Hall, Keswick   Friday Night, May 20, 1803

Sir

In consequence of a request, expressed to me by Mr Stuart of the Morning Post Office, I take the Liberty of informing you, that my

[1] Francis Freeling (1764–1836), of the London Post Office.

## To Francis Freeling

paper, the Morning Post, did not arrive yesterday Afternoon—the paper for Tuesday, May 17th I waited till this evening, in case two papers should come together, as they often do; but the paper for Wednesday, 18th, arrived by itself. It is very seldom, that for so many Days together my paper should have come so regularly as it has done for the last fortnight—on an average of some months it has missed once a week.

I am, / Sir, / with great respect, / Your ob. humb. Servant,
S. T. Coleridge

### 504. To William Godwin

*Address*: Mr Godwin | Polygon | Sommers' Town | London
*MS. Lord Abinger. Pub. with omis.* William Godwin, ii. 92.

As the preceding letters show, Coleridge had been planning a philosophical work since early 1801, and in this letter he proposes an '*Instrument* of practical Reasoning'. No such work was published during his lifetime, but there is evidence that he had begun his task at this time. 'In the possession of the Coleridge family at Leatherhead', Miss Alice Snyder notes in her *Coleridge on Logic and Learning*, 1929, pp. 52–53, 'is a partly filled notebook that contains a section of the "familiar introduction to the common system of Logic", the first four chapters of the History, and a part of the fifth chapter. Moreover, the text offers clear evidence that the continuation of the manuscript was to follow in general the outline for the remaining chapters sketched in the letter to Godwin. . . . The fragment must . . . be tentatively assigned to 1803.' Miss Snyder prints the notebook in full. Ibid. 54–66 and 139–52. In Letter 505 Coleridge says 'the work is half-written *out*, & the *materials* of the other Half are all on paper—or rather, on papers'.
*Postmark*: 7 June 1803.

Saturday Night, June 4, 1803. Greta Hall, Keswick

My dear Godwin

I trust, that my dear Friend, C. Lamb, will have informed [you] how seriously ill I have been. I arrived at Keswick on Good Friday —caught the Influenza, have struggled on in a series of convalescence & relapse, the disease still assuming new shapes & symptoms —and tho' I am certainly better than at any former period of the Disease, and more steadily convalescent; yet it is not mere Low Spirits that makes me doubt, whether I shall ever wholly surmount the effects of it.—I owe this explanation to you: for I quitted Town with strong feelings of affectionate Esteem toward you, & a firm resolution to write to you within a short time after my arrival at my home. During my illness I was exceedingly affected by the Thought, that month had glided away after month, & year after year, & still had found & left me only *preparing* for the experiments, which are to ascertain whether the Hopes of those, who have hoped proudly of me, have been auspicious Omens, or mere Delusions—

and the anxiety to realize something, & finish something has, no doubt, in some measure retarded my Recovery.—I am now however ready to go to the Press, with a work which I consider as introductory to a *System*, tho' to the public it will appear altogether a Thing by itself. I write now to ask your advice respecting the Time & manner of it's Publication, & the choice of a Publisher.—I entitle it Organum verè Organum, or an *Instrument* of practical Reasoning in the business of real Life: to which will be prefixed 1. a familiar INTRODUCTION to the common System of Logic, namely, that of Aristotle & the Schools. 2. a concise and simple, yet full, Statement of the Aristotelean Logic, with references annexed to the Authors, & the name & page of the work, to which each part may be tra[ced,] so that it may be at once seen, what is Aristotle's, what Porphyry, wh[at] the addition of the Greek Commentators, & what of the Schoolmen.—3. Outline of the History of Logic in general. 1. Chapt.—The origin of Philosophy in general, and of Logic speciatim. 2 Chapt. Of the Eleatic & Megaric Logic. 3. of the Platonic Logic. 4. of Aristotle, containing a fair account [of] the Ὄργανον of which Dr Reid in Kaimes' Sketches of man[1] has given a most false, & not only erroneous, but calumnious Statement—as far as this account had not been anticipated in the second Part of my work—namely, the concise & simple, yet full, &c &c.—5. a philosophical Examination of the Truth, and of the Value, of the Aristotelean System of Logic, including all the after additions to it. 6. on the characteristic Merits & Demerits of Aristotle & Plato, as Philosophers in general, & an attempt to explain the fact of the vast influence of the former during so many ages; and of the influence of Plato's works on the restoration of the Belles Lettres, and on the reformation.—7. Raymund Lully. 8. Peter Ramus[2]. 9. Lord Bacon—or the Verulamian Logic. 10. Examination of the same, & comparison of it with the Logic of Plato (in wch I attempt to make it probable, that tho' considered by Bacon himself as the antithesis & Antidote of Plato, it is bonâ fide the same, & that Plato has been grossly misunderstood.)[3] 10 [*sic*].—Des Cartes / 11. Condillac —& a philosophical examination of *his* Logic, i.e. the Logic, which he basely purloined from Hartley.—Then follows my own Organum verè Organum—which consists of a Σύστημα of all *possible* modes of true, probable, & false reasoning, arranged philosophically, i.e. on a strict analysis of those operations & passions of the mind, in which they originate, & by which they act, with one or more

---

[1] Coleridge refers to Thomas Reid's 'A Brief Account of Aristotle's Logic', which was published in Lord Kames's *Sketches of the History of Man*, 1774.

[2] Raymond Lully (1235?–1315) and Petrus Ramus (1515–72).

[3] Cf. *The Friend*, 1818, iii. 193–216.

striking instances annexed to each from authors of high Estimation —and to each instance of false reasoning, the manner in which the Sophistry is to be detected, & the words, in which it may be exposed.—The whole will conclude with considerations of the value of the work, & it's practical utility—in scientific Investigations; especially, the first part, which contains the strictly demonstrative reasonings, and the analysis of all the acts & passions of the mind, which may be employed to the discovery of Truth—in the arts of healing, especially, in those parts that contain a catalogue &c of *probable* reasoning—: lastly, to the Senate, the Pulpit, & our Law courts, to whom the whole, but especially in the latter ¾ths of the work—viz. the probable & the false, will be useful—and finally, instructions, how to form a commonplace Book by the aid of this Instrument, so as to read with practical advantage—& (supposing average Talents) to *ensure* a facility & rapidity in proving & in confuting. /—I have thus amply detailed the contents of my work, which has not been the labour of one year or of two / but the result of many years' meditations, & of very various Reading.—The size of the work will, printed at 30 lines a page, form one Volume Octavo / 500 pages to the Volume—& I shall be ready with the first half of the work for the Printer, at a fortnight's notice.—Now, my dear Friend! give me your Thoughts on the subject—would you have me offer it to the Booksellers, or by the assistance of my Friends print & publish on my own account—? if the former, would you advise me to sell the copyright at once, or only one or more Editions? Can you give me a general notion, what terms I have a right to insist on / in either case? And lastly, to whom would you advise me to apply?—Longman & Rees are very civil; but they are not liberal / and they have no notion of me, except as of a Poet—nor any *sprinklings* of philosophical knowlege that could in the least enable them to judge of the value, or probable success, of such a Work.—Phillips is a pushing man, & a book is sure to have fair play, if it be his *Property*—& it could not be other than pleasant to me to have the same Publisher with yourself—*but.*— Now if there be any thing of importance, that with truth & justice ought to follow that '*but,*' you will inform me.—It is not my *habit* to go to work so seriously about matters of pecuniary business; but my ill-health makes my Life more than ordinarily uncertain / & I have a wife, & 3 little ones. If your judgment led you to advise me to offer it to Phillips, would you take the trouble of talking with him on the subject? & give him your real opinion, whatever it may be, of the work, and of the powers of the Author.——

When this Book is fairly off my hands, I shall, if I live & have sufficient health, set seriously to work—in arranging what I have already written, and in pushing forward my Studies, & my Investigations relative to the omne scibile of human Nature—*what we are, & how we become* what we are; so as to solve the two grand Problems, how, being acted upon, we shall act; how, acting, we shall be acted upon. But between me & this work there may be Death.

I hope, that your wife & little ones are well.—I have had a sick family—at one time, every Individual, Master, Mistress, children, & servants were all layed up in bed; & we were waited on by persons hired from the Town for the week. But now all are well, I only excepted.—If you find my paper smell, or my Style savour, of scholastic quiddity, you must attribute it to the infectious quality of the Folio, on which I am writing—namely, Jo. Scotus Erigena de divisione Naturae, the fore runner, by some centuries, of the Schoolmen.—I cherish all kind & honorable feelings toward you, & am, dear Godwin, your's most sincerely, S. T. Coleridge.

You know the high character, & present scarcity of Search's Light of Nature.[1] 'I have found in this writer (says PALEY in his Preface to his Mor. & Pol. Phil.) more original thinking & observation upon the several subjects, he has taken in hand, than in any other, not to say, in all others put together. His Talent also for illustration is unrivalled. But his Thoughts are diffused thro' a long, various, & irregular work,' &c. A friend of mine, every way calculated by his Taste, & prior Studies for such a work is willing to abridge & systematize that work from 8 to 2 Vol.—in the words of Paley 'to dispose into method, to collect into heads, & articles, and to exhibit in more compact & tangible masses, what, in that otherwise excellent performance, is spread over too much surface.' —I would prefix to it an Essay containing the whole substance of the first Volume of Hartley, entirely defecated from all the corpuscular hypotheses—with new illustrations—& give my name to the Essay.[2] Likewise, I will revise every sheet of the Abridgement. I should think, the character of the work, & the above quotation from so high an Authority (with the present Public, I mean) as Paley, would ensure it's success.—If you will read (or transcribe & send) this to Mr Phillips, or to Mr Mawman, or to any other Publisher (Longman & Rees excepted) you would greatly oblige me— that is to say, my dear Godwin, you would essentially serve a

---

[1] Abraham Tucker published *The Light of Nature Pursued*, in four volumes, under the name Edward Search in 1768. Three posthumous volumes appeared in 1778.

[2] Coleridge refers to William Hazlitt, who was apparently in the north at this time. Hazlitt's one-volume *Abridgement of The Light of Nature Pursued* was published in 1807, but without Coleridge's proposed essay.

young man of profound Genius and original mind, who wishes to get his *Sabine* Subsistence by some Employment from the Booksellers, while he is employing the remainder of his Time in nursing up his Genius for the destiny, which he believes appurtenant to it. Qui cito facit, bis facit. Impose any Task on me in return.

### 505. To William Godwin

*Address*: Mr Godwin | Polygon | Sommers' Town | London
*MS.* Lord Abinger. *Pub.* Macmillan's Magazine, *April 1864, p. 532.*
*Postmark*: 13 June 1803. *Stamped*: Keswick.

Friday, June 10, 1803. Greta Hall

My dear Godwin

Your Letter has this moment reached me, & found me writing for Stuart, to whom I am under a positive engagement to produce three Essays by the beginning of next week.[1] To promise therefore to do, what I could not do, would be somewhat worse than idle: & to attempt to do, what I could not do well, from distraction of mind, would be trifling with my Time, & your patience.—If I could convey to you any tolerably distinct notion of the state of my Spirits of late, & the train & the sort of my ideas consequent on that state, you would feel instantly, that my non-performance of the promise is matter of *Regret* with me indeed, but not of *Compunction*. It was my full intention to have prepared immediately a second volume of poems for the Press;[2] but tho' the poems are all either written, or composed, excepting only the conclusion of one Poem (= to 4 days' common work) & a few corrections, & tho' I had the most pressing motives for sending them off; yet after many attempts I was obliged to give up the very Hope—the attempts acted so perniciously on my disorder.—Wordsworth too wished, & in a very particular manner expressed the wish, that I should write to him at large on a poetic subject, which he has at present sub malleo ardentem et ignitum—I made the attempt —but I could not command my recollections. It seemed a Dream, that I had ever *thought* on Poetry—or had ever written it—so remote were my Trains of Ideas from Composition, or Criticism on Composition.—These two instances will in some measure explain my non-performance; but indeed I have been VERY ILL—& that I have done any thing in any way is a subject of wonder to

---

[1] No such contributions to the *Morning Post* have been identified.

[2] Although Coleridge did not issue a 'second volume', the third edition of his *Poems* was published by Longman and Rees in 1803. It was seen through the press by Charles Lamb. (*Lamb Letters*, i. 346–50.)

( 950 )

myself, and of no causeless Self-complacency.—Yet I am anxious to do something, which may convince you of my sincerity & Zeal; and if you think that it will be of any service to you, & will send down the Work, I will instantly give it a perusal con amore—& partly by my reverential Love of Chaucer, & partly from my affectionate Esteem for his Biographer, the summer too bringing increase of Health with it, I doubt not, that my old mind will recur to me; and I will FORTHWITH write a series of Letters containing a critique on Chaucer, & on the Life of Chaucer by W. Godwin,[1] and publish them with my name either at once in a small volume—or in the Morning Post in the first instance—& republish them afterwards—. The great Thing to be done is to present Chaucer stripped of all his adventitious matter—his Translations &c—to analyse his own real productions—to deduce his Province, & his Rank / then to compare him with his Contemporaries, or immediate both Prede-and Successors, first as an Englishman, & secondly as a Europaean—then with Spencer, & with Shakespere, between whom he seems to stand mid way, with however a manner of his own which belongs to neither—both a manner & an excellence—lastly, to compare Dante, & Chaucer, (& inclusively Spencer, & Shakespere) with the Ancients, to abstract the characteristic Differences, & to develope the causes of such Differences.—(For instance, in all the writings of the ancients I recollect nothing that strictly examined can be called Humour—yet Chaucer abounds with it —and Dante too, tho' in a very different way—Thus too, the passion for Personifications—& me judice, strong sharp practical good Sense, which I feel to constitute a strikingly characteristic Difference in favor of the *feudal* Poets.)

As to information, I could give you a critical sketch of Poems, written by contemporaries of Chaucer, in Germany—[an] Epic, to compare with his Palamon & Arcite—Tales with his Tales——descriptive & fanciful with those of the same kind in our own Poet—. In short, a Life of Chaucer ought in the work itself, & in the appendices of the work, to make the Poet explain his Age, & to make the Age both explain the Poet, & evince the superiority of the Poet over his Age.——I think that the publication of such a work would do *your* work some little service in more ways than one / it would occasion *necessarily* a double Review of it in all the Reviews—& there is a large Class of fashionable men, who have been pleased of late to take me into high favor, & among whom even my name might have some influence, & my praises of you some Weight.—But let me hear from you on the Subject.—

Now for my own business.—As soon as you possibly can do

[1] Godwin's *Life of Chaucer* was published in Oct. 1803.

## To William Godwin

something respecting the Abridgement of Search, do so: you will, on my honor, be doing *good*, in the best sense of the word.—Of course, I cannot wish you to do any thing till after the 24th—unless it should lie *pat* in your way to read that part of [my] Letter to Phillips.

As to my own work, let me correct one or two imperfect conceptions of your's respecting it.—I could, no doubt, induce my friends to publish the work for me: but I am possessed of facts, that deter me—I know, that the Booksellers not only do not encourage, but that they use unjustifiable artifices to injure works published on the Author's own account—It never answered, as far as I can find, in any instance. And even the sale of a first Edition is not without Objections, on this Score—to this however I should certainly adhere —& it is my resolution.—But I must do something *immediately/* Now if I *knew* that any Bookseller would purchase the first Edition of this work, as numerous as he pleases, I should *put the work out of hand at once, totus in illo*—but it was never my intention to send one single sheet to the Press, till the *whole* was bonâ fide *ready* for the Printer, that is, both written, & fairly written.—The work is half-written *out*; & the *materials* of the other Half are all on paper —or rather, on papers—&c in my Hand. I should not expect one farthing, till the work was delivered entire—and I would deliver it all at once, if it were wished. But if I cannot engage with a Bookseller for this, I must do something else *first*—which I should be sorry for.——

Your Division of the sorts of works acceptable to Booksellers is just—& what has been always my own notion—or rather knowlege —but tho' I detailed the whole of the contents of my work so fully to you, I did not mean to lay any Stress with the Bookseller on the first Half, but simply state it as preceded by a familiar Introduction, & critical History of Logic—on the Work itself I meant to lay all the Stress, as a work really in request—& non-existent, either well or ill-done—& to put the work in the *same class* with Guthrie, & Books of practical Instruction—for the Universities, first Classes of Schools, Lawyers, &c &c—— It's profitable Sale will greatly depend on the Pushing of the Bookseller, and on it's being considered as a *practical* Book—*Organum verè organum*—a book, by which the Reader is to acquire not only Knowlege, but likewise *Power*.—I fear, that it may extend to 700 pages—& would it be better to publi[sh] the Introduction & History separately, either after or before?—God bless you—& all Hon[or] to you & your Chaucer—all Happiness [to] you, your Wife,

& your—S. T. C.

P.S. If you read to Phillips any part of my Letter respecting my own work, or rather detailed it to him, you would lay all the Stress on the *Practical*.

### 506. To Robert Southey

*Address*: Mr Southey | St James's Place | Kingsdown | Bristol
*MS*. Lord Latymer. *Pub*. Letters, *i. 422*.
*Postmark*: 2 July 1803. *Stamped*: Keswick.

Wednesday—Keswick. [29 June 1803]

My dear Southey

You have had much illness as well as I, but I thank God for you, you have never been equally diseased in voluntary power with me. I knew a Lady, who was seized with a sort of asthma, which she knew would be instantly relieved by a dose of Ether—she had the full use of her Limbs—& was not an arm's length from the Bell— yet could not command voluntary power sufficient to pull it—& might have died but for the accidental Coming-in of her Daughter. —From facts such as these the doctrines of Materialism, & mechanical necessity have been deduced; & it is some small argument against the Truth of these Doctrines, that I have perhaps had a more various experience, a more intuitive knowlege, of such facts than most men——yet do not believe these Doctrines.—My health is *middling*. If this hot weather continue, I hope to go on endurably —and O! for peace!—for I forebode a miserable Winter in this country. Indeed, I am rather inclined to determine on wintering in Madeira, rather than staying at home.—I have inclosed 10£ for Mrs Fricker. Tell her, that I wish it were in my power to increase this poor half-year's Mite; but ill-health keeps me poor.——Bella is with us: & seems likely to recover.—I have not seen the Edingburgh Review—the truth is, that Edingburgh is a place of literary Gossip—& even *I* have had my portion of Puff there—& of course, my portion of Hatred & Envy.—One man puffs me up—he has seen & talked with me—another hears him, goes & reads my poems, written when almost a boy—& candidly & logically hates me, because he does not admire my poems in the proportion in which one of his acquaintances had admired me.—It is difficult to say whether these Reviewers do you harm or good.—

You read me at Bristol a very interesting piece of Casuistry from Father Somebody, the Author, I believe, of the Theatro Critico, respecting a double Infant—If you do not immediately want it, or if my using it in a book of Logic, with proper acknowlegement, will not interfere with your use of it—I should be extremely obliged to you, if you would send it me without delay.—I rejoice to hear of the Progress of your History. The only Thing, I dread, is the division of the Europaean & Colonial History—. In style, you have only to beware of short, biblical, & pointed Periods. Your general Style is delightfully natural & yet striking.

You may expect certain Explosions in the Morning Post, Coleridge versus Fox—in about a week. It grieved me to hear (for I have a sort of affection for the man) from Sharp, that Fox had not read my two Letters;[1] but had heard of them, & that they were mine—& had expressed himself more wounded by the circumstance than any thing that had happened since Burke's Business. Sharp told this to Wordsworth—& told Wordsworth, that he had been so affected by Fox's manner, that he himself had declined reading the two Letters—Yet Sharp himself thinks my opinions right & true: but Fox is not to be attacked—& why? Because he is an amiable man—& not by me—because he had thought highly of me—&c &c—O Christ! this is a pretty age in the article, *Morality*! —When I cease to love Truth best of all things; & Liberty, the next best; may I cease to live—nay, it is my creed, that I should thereby cease to live / for as far as any thing can be called probable in a subject so dark, it seems most probable to me, that our Immortality is to be a work of our own Hands.—All the children are well—& I love to hear Bella talk of Margaret.

Love to Edith—& to Mary.

God bless you, | &
S. T. Coleridge

I have received great delight & instruction from Scotus Erigena. He is clearly the modern founder of the School of Pantheism—indeed he expressly defines the divine Nature, as quae fit et facit, et creat et creatur—& repeatedly declares Creation to be *manifestation*—the Epiphany of Philosophers.——The eloquence with which he writes, astonished me, but he had read more Greek than Latin—and was a Platonist rather than an Aristotelean.—There is a good deal of omne meus oculus in the notion of the *dark* Ages,[2] &c, taken intensively—in extension it might be true—. They had *Wells;* we are flooded, ancle-high—& what comes of it but grass rank or rotten? Our age eats from that Poison-tree of Knowlege, yclept, Too much and too little.—Have you read Paley's last Book?[3] Have you it to review?—I could make a dashing Review of it.—

[1] Except for Coleridge's two Letters to Charles James Fox of 4 and 9 Nov. 1802, no further contributions concerning Fox have been identified.

[2] 'Coleridge says there has never been a single line of common-sense written about the dark ages. He was speaking of the knowledge and philosophy of that period; and I believe his assertion is true in a more extensive sense.' Southey to Rickman, *Southey Letters,* i. 228.

[3] William Paley, *Natural Theology; or Evidence of the Existence and Attributes of the Deity collected from the Appearances of Nature,* 1802.

507. *To Robert Southey*

Pub. Life and Corres. *ii. 217.*

Keswick, July, 1803

My dear Southey,

... I write now to propose a scheme, or rather a rude outline of a scheme, of your grand work. What harm can a proposal do? If it be no pain to you to reject it, it will be none to me to have it rejected. I would have the work entitled Bibliotheca Britannica, or an History of British Literature, bibliographical, biographical, and critical.[1] The two *last* volumes I would have to be a chronological catalogue of all noticeable or extant books; the others, be the number six or eight, to consist entirely of separate treatises, each giving a critical biblio-biographical history of some one subject. I will, with great pleasure, join you in learning Welsh and Erse: and you, I, Turner, and Owen,[2] might dedicate ourselves for the first half year to a complete history of all Welsh, Saxon, and Erse books that are not translations, that are the native growth of Britain. If the Spanish neutrality continues, I will go in October or November to Biscay, and throw light on the Basque.

Let the next volume contain the history of *English* poetry and poets, in which I would include all prose truly poetical. The first half of the second volume should be dedicated to great single names, Chaucer and Spenser, Shakespeare, Milton and Taylor, Dryden and Pope; the poetry of witty logic,—Swift, Fielding, Richardson, Sterne: I write *par hazard*, but I mean to say all great names as have either formed epochs in our taste, or such, at least, as are representative; and the great object to be in each instance to determine, first, the true merits and demerits of the *books;* secondly, what of these belong to the age—what to the author *quasi peculium*. The second half of the second volume should be a history of poetry and romances, everywhere interspersed with biography, but more flowing, more consecutive, more biblio-

---

[1] The idea for Southey's 'Bibliotheca Britannica' arose from conversations between Coleridge and Southey. Coleridge and I have often talked of making a great work upon English literature', Southey wrote to Taylor on 23 June 1803. (*Memoir of William Taylor*, i. 461.) Late in June, Southey set forth for London to make business arrangements for his venture, and he probably communicated his plans to Coleridge while there. Soon after his return to Bristol on 12 July he must have received this extraordinary letter from Coleridge. In Aug. 1803 Longman decided not to publish the work for the present, and it fell through, to be realized, perhaps, a century later in the *Cambridge History of English Literature.*

[2] Sharon Turner (1768–1847), author of the *History of England from the earliest period to the Norman Conquest*, 4 vols., 1799–1805; and William Owen, later Pughe (1759–1835), Welsh antiquary and lexicographer.

graphical, chronological, and complete. The third volume I would have dedicated to English prose, considered as to style, as to eloquence, as to general impressiveness; a history of styles and manners, their causes, their birth-places and parentage, their analysis. . . .

These three volumes would be so generally interesting, so exceedingly entertaining, that you might bid fair for a sale of the work at large. Then let the fourth volume take up the history of metaphysics, theology, medicine, alchemy, common, canon, and Roman law, from Alfred to Henry VII.; in other words, a history of the dark ages in Great Britain. The fifth volume—carry on metaphysics and ethics to the present day in the first half; the second half, comprise the theology of all the reformers. In the fourth volume there would be a grand article on the philosophy of the theology of the Roman Catholic religion. In this (fifth volume), under different names,—Hooker, Baxter, Biddle, and Fox,—the spirit of the theology of all the other parts of Christianity. The sixth and seventh volumes must comprise all the articles you can get, on all the separate arts and sciences that have been treated of in books since the Reformation; and, by this time, the book, if it answered at all, would have gained so high a reputation, that you need not fear having whom you liked to write the different articles —medicine, surgery, chemistry, &c. &c., navigation, travellers, voyagers, &c. &c. If I go into Scotland, shall I engage Walter Scott to write the history of Scottish poets? Tell me, however, what you think of the plan. It would have one prodigious advantage: whatever accident stopped the work, would only prevent the future good, not mar the past; each volume would be a great and valuable work *per se*. Then each volume would awaken a new interest, a new set of readers, who would buy the past volumes of course; then it would allow you ample time and opportunities for the slavery of the catalogue volumes, which should be at the same time an index to the work, which would be, in very truth, a pandect of knowledge, alive and swarming with human life, feeling, incident. By the by, what a strange abuse has been made of the word encyclopaedia! It signifies, properly, grammar, logic, rhetoric, and ethics and metaphysics, which last, explaining the ultimate principles of grammar—log., rhet., and eth.—formed a circle of knowledge. . . . To call a huge unconnected miscellany of the *omne scibile*, in an arrangement determined by the accident of initial letters, an encyclopaedia, is the impudent ignorance of your Presbyterian bookmakers. Good night!

God bless you!<br>S. T. C.

## 508. To William Wordsworth

MS. Dove Cottage. Pub. E. L. G. i. 266.

Saturday—[23 July 1803][1]

My dearest William

You would be as much astonished at Hazlitt's coming, as I at his going.—Sir G. & Lady B.[2] who are half-mad to see you—(Lady B. told me, that the night before last as she was reading your Poem on Cape RASH JUDGEMENT, had you entered the room, she believes she should have fallen at your feet) Sir G. & his wife both say, that the Picture[3] gives them an idea of you as a profound strong-minded Philosopher, not as a Poet—I answered (& I believe, truly—) that so it must needs do, if it were a good Portrait—for that you were a great Poet by inspirations, & in the Moments of revelation, but that you were a thinking feeling Philosopher habitually— that your Poetry was your Philosophy under the action of strong winds of Feeling—a sea rolling high.—

What the Devil to do about a Horse!—I cannot hear of one/ Keswick is not the Place/ & Mr Moore has sent me a Letter which makes it scarcely possible for me to buy the Jaunting Car under 15£. He expresses the utmost sorrow, that his finances relatively even to mine would make it unjust & pusillanimous in him to give way to his habitual Feelings, which would impel him to insist on my accepting it—that he had repeatedly refused 15£—but that I might deduct from that what I chose—. Dearest dearest dearest Friends—I will have 3 dearests, that there may be one for each— (and Godson John[4] shall have one for himself) I begin to find that a Horse & Jaunting Car is *an anxiety*—& almost to wish that we

---

[1] This letter must have been written on 23 July 1803, for on 17 July Nathaniel M. Moore, whose letter Coleridge mentions, wrote from Devonshire as follows: 'I had the Pleasure of receiving your Letter this Morning and now rejoice very sincerely in what I once felt as a great Disappointment, my not being able to sell the Jaunting Car. It is much at your Service. I wish I was able to do as my Heart would dictate. Is it worth £15—that I often refused— deduct from it what you please— . . . A Sale between you and me is very repugnant to my Feelings.' The jaunting car was purchased for the Scotch tour, which began on 15 Aug.

[2] Sir George Beaumont (1753–1827), artist and art patron, and his wife lodged with Jackson at Greta Hall in the summer of 1803 and soon became Coleridge's friends. Through Coleridge they came to know Wordsworth.

[3] Hazlitt, who was in the Lake Country at this time, executed portraits of Wordsworth, Coleridge, and Hartley Coleridge. P. P. Howe notes that the Wordsworth portrait was destroyed and that the whereabouts of the other two is unknown. *The Life of William Hazlitt*, 1947, p. 395.

[4] 'Godson John' Wordsworth was born 18 June 1803, and baptized 15 July 1803. Coleridge and Richard and Dorothy Wordsworth were the god-parents.

had adopted our first thought, & *walked*: with one pony & side saddle for our Sister Gift-of-God.—I was on horse just now with Sir G. & Lady B.—when Lord Lowther came riding up to us—so of course all dismounted—& he is now with his Jockey Phiz in with Sir G.—But I looked at him—& gave him a downright & heart-deep kind feeling for behaving honestly to all you——

Lady Beamont—I can describe her to you in few words—She is a miniature of Madame Guion /

> A deep Enthusiast, sensitive,
> Trembles & cannot keep the Tears in her eye—
> Such ones do love the marvellous too well
> Not to believe it. You may wind her up
> With *any* Music!—[1]

but *music* it must be, of some sort or other.—I have not as yet received any thing from Fletcher but the Side Portrait, which I shall prize deeply.—I am quoad health in excellent Trim for our Journey —foot or horse—. The children are all well—& Sara is an engaging meek Baby.—Yesterday evening we had a *Cram*—Mrs Wilkinson, General & Mrs Peché,[2] and two Andersons, Mrs Dauber & Miss Hodgins—Mrs Wilkinson *swears*, that your Portrait is 20 years too old for you—& mine equally too old, & too lank[3] /—Every single person without one exception cries out!—What a likeness!— but the face is too long! you have a round face!—Hazlitt knows this; but he will not alter it. Why?—because the Likeness with him is a secondary Consideration—he wants it to be a fine Picture —Hartley knew your's instantly—& Derwent too / but Hartley said—it is very like; but Wordsworth is far handsomer.—Our Mary says—it is very *leek;* but it is not canny enough—tho' Mr Wordsworth is not a *canny* man, to be sure.—She thinks Mr Cook's face, I believe, the ideal of Beauty—but you & I, dear William, pass for an ugly Pair with the lower order / which I foretel, Dorothy will not admit.—The two defects of it as a likeness are that the eyes are TOO OPEN & FULL—& there is a heaviness given to the forehead, from parting the Hair so greasily & pomatumish—there should have been a few straggling hairs left.—Hazlitt's paints are come from London /—God love you all W. D. M + dearest John. —[No signature on MS.]

[1] *Osorio*, II. i. 32–36. *Poems*, ii. 536.

[2] Coleridge refers to General John Peché, an East Indian officer. See Southey, *Life and Corres.* ii. 245.

[3] In 1805 Wordsworth wrote to Beaumont: 'We think, as far as mere likeness goes, Hazlitt's is better [than Northcote's portrait of Coleridge]; but the expression in Hazlitt's is quite dolorous and funereal.' *Early Letters*, 497. Southey said that Hazlitt 'made a very fine picture of Coleridge for Sir George Beaumont, which is said to be in Titian's manner'. *Life and Corres.* ii. 238.

## 1 August 1803

### 509. To Robert Southey

*Address*: Mr Southey | St James's Parade | Kingsdown | Bristol
*MS.* Lord Latymer. *Pub.* E. L. G. i. 263.
*Postmark*: 5 August 1803. *Stamped*: Keswick.

Monday Evening, August 1. 1803

My dear old friend

On whatever plan you determine, I will be your faithful Servant and Fellow-Servant. If you were with me, and Health were not far away, I could now rely on myself; but my Health is a very weighty, perhaps insuperable, Objection. Else the sense of responsibility to my own mind is growing deeper & deeper with me from many causes—chiefly, from the knowlege that I am not of no signifiance, relatively to, comparatively with, other men, my contemporaries. —I was thought *vain* / if there be no better word, to express what I was, so let it be / but if Cottle be *vain*, Dyer be vain, J. Jennings be *vain*, the word is a vague one / — it was in me the heat, bustle, and overflowing of a mind, too vehemently pushed on from within to be regardful of the object, upon which it was moving—an instinct to have my power proved to me by transient evidences, arising from an inward feeling of weakness, both the one & other working in me unconsciously—above all, a faulty delight in the being beloved, without having examined my heart, whether, if beloved, I had any thing to give in return beyond general kindness & general Sympathy—both indeed unusually warm, but which, being still *general*, were not a return in kind, for that which I was unconsciously desiring to inspire / —All this added together might possibly have been a somewhat far worse than *Vanity*—but it would still have been different from it—far worse if it had not existed in a nature where better Things were indigenous.—A sense of weakness—a haunting sense, that I was an herbaceous Plant, as large as a large Tree, with a Trunk of the same Girth, & Branches as large & shadowing—but with *pith within* the Trunk, not heart of Wood /—that I had *power* not *strength*—an involuntary Imposter— that I had no real Genius, no real Depth / — / This on my honor is as fair a statement of my habitual Haunting, as I could give before the Tribunal of Heaven / How it arose in me, I have but lately discovered / —Still it works within me / but only as a Disease, the cause & meaning of which I know / the whole History of this Feeling would form a curious page in a Nosologia Spiritualis—/——Your other objection is not equally well-founded—My plan would take in all & every body. I undertake for this—that every page which your plan would admit, mine should / neither is it accurate, that the greater part could only be done by me / —However, I give it up as contentedly as I offered it quietly / if any part I should desire you to retain, it would be the first Volume—to make that exhaust all Welch, Saxon, & Erse Literature. However, let me know as soon as is convenient your plan, whatever it be / —Good heavens! if you & I, Rickman & Lamb, were to put our Shoulders to one volume / a compleat History of the Dark Ages—if Rickman would but take the physics, you the Romances & Legendary Theology, I the Metaphysics, and Lamb be left to say what he liked in his own way— what might not be done / as to the Canon & Roman Law, it is done admirably for all Countries by Hugo of Göttingen, & I would abridge his Book—/ This alone would immortalize us—in Physics I comprehend Alchemy & Medicine / —Enough of all this.—I write only to say, that my zealous & continued Services are your's, on *any* plan—tho' as to Longman, I have assuredly a right to demand more than four guineas a sheet for the *Copy right* of so compleat a work as my Chaucer, Spenser, Shakespear, Milton, Taylor, &c &c will be—without boasting, a great Book of Criticism respecting Poetry & Prose—He ought to consider, that every Syllable which I shall write in the work is not for that work merely, but might every page be published in a work per se——&c &c.—

If no strange Accident intervene, I leave Home on Monday Next for my Scotch Tour / —We shall be 5 or 6 days in getting to Glasgow—and after that I know no place of Direction but Edingburgh. If therefore you wish to write within a day or two, direct to the Post Office, Glasgow / if not, I shall expect a Letter in a month or 5 weeks at Edingburgh.—

We are all pretty well. Sara is a quiet Creature—Derwent a great Beauty—both sadly nettle-rashy; but I am afraid to do any thing with it, it seems to keep them both in high health. Hartley is his own Self—piscis rarissima [*sic*]. Young Hazlitt has taken masterly Portraits of me & Wordsworth, very much in the manner of Titian's Portraits—he wishes to take Lamb—& you.—S. T. Coleridge—


### 510. To Robert Southey

*Address*: Mr Southey | St James's Parade | Kingsdown | Bristol—
*MS.* Lord Latymer. *Pub. with omis.* Letters, *i. 427.*
*Postmark*: 1⟨0⟩ August ⟨1803.⟩  *Stamped*: Keswick.

Sunday, Keswick—/ [7 August 1803]

Read the last Lines first.—I send this Letter merely to shew you, how anxious I have been about your Work.—

My dear Southey

The last 3 days I have been fighting up against a restless wish to write to you. I am afraid, lest I should infect you with my fears rather than furnish you with any new arguments—give you impulses rather than motives—and prick you with *spurs*, that had been dipt in the vaccine matter of my own cowardliness—. While I wrote that last sentence, I had a vivid recollection—indeed an ocular Spectrum—of our room in College Street—/ a curious instance of association / you remember how incessantly in that room I used to be compounding these half-verbal, half-visual metaphors. It argues, I am persuaded, a particular state of general feeling—& I hold, that association depends in a much greater degree on the recurrence of resembling states of Feeling, than on Trains of Idea / that the recollection of early childhood in latest old age depends on, & is explicable by this—& if this be true, Hartley's System totters.—If I were asked, how it is that very old People remember *visually* only the events of early childhood—& remember the intervening Spaces either not at all, or only verbally—I should think it a perfectly philosophical answer / that old age remembers childhood by becoming 'a second childhood.' This explanation will derive some additional value if you would look into Hartley's solution of the phaenomena / how flat, how wretched!—Believe me, Southey! a metaphysical Solution, that does not instantly *tell* for something in the Heart, is grievously to be suspected as apocry[p]hal. I almost think, that Ideas *never* recall Ideas, as far as they are Ideas—any more than Leaves in a forest create each other's motion—The Breeze it is that runs thro' them / it is the Soul, the state of Feeling—. If I had said, no *one* Idea ever recalls another, I am confident that I could support the assertion.——And this is a Digression.—My dear Southey, again & again I say, that whatever your Plan be, I will continue to work for you with equal zeal if not with equal pleasure / —But the arguments against your plan weigh upon me the more heavily, the more I reflect—& it could not be otherwise than that I should feel a confirmation of them from Wordsworth's compleat coincidence—I having requested his deliberate opinion without having communicated an Iota of my own.—You seem to me, dear friend! to hold the dearness of a scarce work for a proof, that the work would have a general Sale—if not scarce.—Nothing can be more fallacious than this. Burton's anatomy used to sell for a guinea to two guineas—it was republished / has it payed the expence of reprinting? Scarcely.—Literary History informs us, that most of those great continental Bibliographies &c were published by the munificence of princes, or nobles, or great monasteries.—A Book from having had little or no sale, except among great Libraries, may become so scarce, that the number of competitors for it, tho' few, may be proportionally very great. I have observed, that great works are now a days bought—not for curiosity, or the amor proprius—but under the notion that they contain all the *knowlege*, a man may ever want / and if he has it on his *Shelf*, why there it is, as snug as if it were in his *Brain*. This has carried off the Encyclopaedia,—& will continue to do so /. I have weighed most patiently what you have said respecting the persons, & classes likely to purchase a Catalogue of all British Books—I have endeavored to make some rude calculation of their numbers according to your own numeration table—& it falls very short of an adequate number—. Your scheme appears to be, in short, faulty—1. because every where the generally uninteresting—the catalogue part, will overlay the interesting parts / —2. because the first Volume will have nothing in it tempting or deeply valuable—for there is not time or room for it.—3. because it is impossible, that any one of the volumes can be executed as well as they would otherwise be, from the to & fro, now here now there, motion of the mind & employment of the Industry—O how I wish to be talking, not writing—for my mind is so full, that my thoughts stifle & jam each other / & I have presented them as shapeless Jellies / so that I am ashamed of what I have written, it so imperfectly expresses what I meant to have said.—My advice certainly would be— that at all events / you should make *some Classification* / Let all the Law Books form a catalogue per se / & so forth / otherwise it is not a book of reference / without an Index half as large as the work itself.—I see no well-founded Objection to the plan, which I first sent / the two main advantages are, that stop where you will, you are in Harbour—you sail in an Archipelago so thickly clustered—at each Island you take in a compleatly new Cargo / & the former cargo is in safe Housage: & 2ndly, that each Labourer working by the *Piece*, & not by the *Day*, can give an undivided attention, in some instances for 3 or four years—& bring to the work the whole weight of his Interest & Reputation. / One half, or at least one third, of every volume would be exactly what you have so well described / a delightful miscellany of noticeable Books, briefly characterized, & when they are worthy of it, & have not been anticipated in the former part of the volume, *analyzed*—striking the Line wherever you chuse—& going on to another with no other bond of connection than that of time /—& differing from your plan only in this—that it will be all interesting—all readable—/ & the two last Volumes will be bought of necessity—& be truly valuable / all the books treated of in the preceding eight Volumes being here printed in small Capitals, the vol. & page mentioned in which they are treated of—. An encyclopaedia appears to me a worthless monster. What Surgeon, or Physician, professed Student of pure or mixed Mathematics, what Chemist, or Architect, would go to an Encyclopaedia for *his* Books?—If valuable Treatises exist on these subjects in an Encycl., they are out of their place—an equal hardship on the general Reader, who pays for whole volumes which he *cannot* read, and on the professed Student of that particular Subject, who must buy a great work which he does not want in order to possess a valuable Treatise, which he might otherwise have had for six or seven Shillings. You omit those things only from your Encyclop. which are excrescences—each volume will *set up* the reader, give him at once connected trains of thought & facts, & a delightful miscellany for lownge-reading—. Your Treatises will be long in exact proportion to their general Interest.—Think what a strange confusion it will make, if you speak of each book, according to it's Date, passing from an Epic Poem to a Treatise on the Treatment of Sore Legs? No body can become an enthusiast in favor of the work /. I feel myself—but that is nothing—I have heard from more, than I remember ever to have heard any one observation / what wearisome & unrememberable Reading Reviews are. Considering how much Talent has been employed in Reviews, it is astonishing —till you perceive the cause of it—how little of one's knowlege one can distinctly trace back to these books—whereas Hayley's Notes on his Epic Poems & Historical Works almost every literary man speaks of with pleasure & gratitude.—In short, do what you will—only put together all the books, palpably of the same Class—& let the absolutely uninstructive (—tho' curious & useful as a Catalogue to be referred to) come all together, at the bottom of the *Pottle*.—When I know your final & total Plan, I will within a few weeks inform you in detail what articles I will attempt to furnish you with—& at what time.—

A great change of weather has come on / heavy rains & wind / & I have been *very* ill—& still I am in uncomfortable restless Health / I am not even certain whether I shall not be forced to put off my Scotch Tour /—but if I go, I go on Tuesday—I shall not send off this Letter, till this is decided.—God bless you & S. T. C.—

Sunday Night. I have this moment received your Letter. I have nothing to say. God grant that it may not put both you & Longman into ill-humour with each other—all I have to observe for myself is —that if all the Schoolmen, nay, if all the Centuries from Alfred to Edward 6th are to be crowded into *one* volume, it is not in my nature to do any thing in that volume /. However I will write to you, stating what I will do—& what space I must have. I can rely with the most heartfelt confidence, that you will not suffer me to hurt the work, or the work to hurt me / both which would take place, if my Quota were heterogeneous, & out of the Plan of the

Work at large.—Your Letter has answered some of my objections —yet I cannot for my Life see the advantage of having something of each in each volume—instead of putting down the whole of each subject at once.—My Health is an insuperable Objection to my plan, I admit—& one insuper. Ob. is enough. Else the Plan [is] feasible—& equally adapted to you, as to me.—God bless you & your affect. S. T. [C.]

### 511. *To Sir George and Lady Beaumont*

*Address*: Sir George Beaumont, Baronet, | at the | Right Honorable Lord Lowther's, | Lowther Hall | Penrith—
*MS.* Pierpont Morgan Lib. Pub. with omis. Memorials of Coleorton, ed. by William Knight, 2 vols., 1887, i. 1.

Greta Hall, Keswick. Friday, Aug. 12. 1803

Dear Sir George and Lady Beaumont

I returned, an hour and a half after your departure, with Hartley and Derwent, & with Wordsworth, his Wife, Sister, and the Baby. On Wednesday Afternoon, just when the Weather had cleared up, & we were preparing to set off, Miss Wordsworth was taken ill—one of her bilious Attacks brought on by the hurry & bustle of packing &c: and I myself was too unwell to walk home. There is a something in all the good & deep emotions of our nature, that would ever prevent me from purposely *getting out of the way* of them—it was painful to me to anticipate that you would be gone, painful to find that you were gone; and I only *endeavored* to satisfy myself with the thought, that it would have been more painful to have taken leave of you—. It will give a lasting Interest to the Drawing of the Waterfall, that I first saw it through tears. I was indeed unwell and sadly nervous; and I must not be ashamed to confess to you, my honoured Friends! that I found a bodily relief in weeping, and yielded to it.—On Tuesday Evening Mr Rogers, the author of the Pleasures of Memory, drank Tea & spent the evening, with us at Grasmere—& this had produced a very unpleasant effect on my Spirits. Wordsworth's mind & body are both of a stronger texture than mine; & he was amused with the envy, the jealousy, & the other miserable Passions, that have made their Pandaemonium in the crazy Hovel of that poor Man's Heart—but I was downright melancholy at the sight. If to be a Poet or a Man of Genius entailed on us the necessity of housing such company in our bosoms, I would pray the very flesh off my knees to have a head as dark and unfurnished, as Wordsworth's old Molly has, if only I might have a heart as careless & as loving.—But God be praised!

## 12 August 1803

these unhappy Beings are neither Poets, nor men of Sense—Enough of them!—Forgive me, dear Sir George! but I could not help being pleased, that the Man disliked you & your Lady—& he lost no time in letting us know it. If I believed it possible that the man liked me, upon my soul I should feel exactly as if I were tarred & feathered. —I have a *cowardly* Dread of being hated even by bad men; but in this instance Disgust comes in to my assistance, & the greater Dread of being called Friend.—I do seriously believe, that the chief cause of Wordsworth's & Southey's having been classed with me, as a *School*, originates entirely in our not hating or envying each other / it is so unusual, that three professed Poets, in every respect unlike each other, should nevertheless take pleasure in each other's welfare—& reputation. What a refreshment of heart did I not find last night in Cowper's Letters. Their very defects suited me. Had they been of a higher class, as exhibitions of Intellect, they would have less satisfied the then craving of my mind. I had taken up the Book merely as connected with you; & had I hunted thro' all the Libraries of Oxford & Cambridge I should have found no one that would have been so delightful on it's own account.—The Wordsworths are gone to Applethwait with Mrs Coleridge/ it would be no easy matter to say, how much they were delighted with the two Drawings, as two poems, how much affected by them, as marks of your kindness & attention.—O dear Sir George! indeed, indeed my heart is very full toward you, & Lady Beaumont—it is a very mixed feeling—& Gratitude expresses but a small part of it.—

Poor little Derwent has been in such a Crowd, that he did not seem to know that you were gone, till this afternoon; when we two had the House to ourselves. Then he went to your Room, & he has been crying piteously—'Lady Beaumont's gone away, & I WILL be a naughty boy—Lady Beaumont's gone away!' He is a very affectionate little fellow—.

If my health permit, we are to commence our [to]ur on Monday/ but this is very uncertain. I have now no doubt, that my Complaint is *atonic Gout*—& tho' the excitement & exercise, which the Journey will afford, would be of service to me, yet the chance of Rainy Weather & damp Beds is a very serious Business. I am rather better this evening; but I incline still to go to Malta with Stoddart, or to Madeira—which I can do at the same expense as I can make the Scotch Tour. I shall settle this in the course of to morrow—& by tomorrow's night post shall send you a large coarse Sheet, containing the Leech Gatherer which Miss Wordsworth has copied out—& such of my own verses as appeared to please you—. I have written a strange rambling Letter—for in truth I have written under a sort of perplexity of moral feeling—my head prompting respect, my heart confident affectionateness—the one tells me, it is my first Letter to you, the other lets me know that unless I write to you as old friends I can not write to you at all.—Be so good therefore as with your wonted kindness to think of this Letter as of a sort of awkward *Bow* on entering a room/ I shall find myself more at my ease when I have sate down.—Believe me, I write every day words with no every day feeling when I subscribe myself, dear Sir George, and dear Lady Beaumont, with affectionate Esteem your obliged and grateful S. T. Coleridge

## 512. To Sir George and Lady Beaumont

*Address*: *Single Sheet.* | Sir George Beaumont, Baronet, | at the | Right Honorable Lord Lowther's | Lowther Hall | Penrith.
*MS. Pierpont Morgan Lib.* Pub. B. Ifor Evans, '*Coleorton Manuscripts of "Resolution and Independence" and "Ode to Dejection"*', Modern Language Review, *July–October 1951, p. 355.*

Coleridge's letter is preceded by a copy of *Resolution and Independence* transcribed by Dorothy Wordsworth and an incomplete version of *Dejection* in Coleridge's handwriting. Mr. Evans points to 'the confirmation of the close relationship of Wordsworth's poem with that of Coleridge by their presentation in this joint form to the Beaumonts'; while Professor Meyer, in a careful study of the first draft of *Dejection*, composed on 4 April 1802, and of *Resolution and Independence*, begun on 3 May 1802, suggests that Wordsworth's poem 'is an answer to Coleridge's'. (Cf. B. Ifor Evans, op. cit. 355, and George W. Meyer, '*Resolution and Independence*: Wordsworth's Answer to Coleridge's *Dejection: An Ode*', *Tulane Studies in English*, ii, 1950, p. 66.)
*Stamped*: Keswick.

Saturday Night. [13 August 1803]

There was a roaring in the wind all night;[1]
The rain came heavily, & fell in floods;
But now the sun is rising calm and bright,
The birds are singing in the distant woods;
Over his own sweet voice the stock dove broods,
The jay makes answer as the magpie chatters;
And all the air is fill'd with pleasant noise of waters.

All things that love the sun are out of doors;
The sky rejoices in the morning's birth,
The grass is bright with rain-drops, on the moors
The hare is running races in her mirth,
And with her feet she from the plashy earth
Raises a mist, which, glittering in the sun,
Runs with her all the way wherever she doth run.

---

[1] *Poet. Works*, ii. 235. This version of *Resolution and Independence* differs considerably from that of the published text.

## 13 August 1803

I was a Traveller then upon the Moor,
I saw the hare that rac'd about with joy,
I heard the woods and distant waters roar,
Or heard them not, as happy as a Boy;
The pleasant season did my heart employ,
My old remembrances went from me wholly,
And all the ways of men so vain and melancholy.

But, as it sometimes chanceth from the might
Of joy in minds that can no farther go,
As high as we have mounted in delight
In our dejection do we sink as low
To me that morning did it happen so;
And fears and fancies thick upon me came,
Dim sadness & blind thoughts I knew not, nor could name.

I heard the sky-lark singing in the sky
And I bethought me of the playful hare;
Even such a happy Child of earth am I,
Even as these happy creatures do I fare;
Far from the world I walk & from all care
But there may come another day to me;
Solitude, pain of heart, distress and poverty.

My whole life I have liv'd in pleasant thought
As if life's business were a summer mood,
And they who liv'd in genial faith found nought
That grew more willingly than genial good
But how can he expect that others should
Build for him, sow for him, and at his call
Love him who for himself will take no heed at all.

I thought of Chatterton, the marvellous Boy,
The sleepless soul who perish'd in his pride:
Of him who walk'd in glory and in joy
Behind his plough upon the mountain side;
By our own spirits are we deified:
We Poets in our youth begin in gladness;
But thereof comes in the end despondency & madness.

Now whether it was by peculiar grace,
A leading from above, a something given,
Yet it befel that in that lonely place,
When up and down my fancy thus was driven,

## To Sir George and Lady Beaumont

And I with these untoward thoughts had striven,
I spied a Man before me unawares;
The oldest Man he seem'd that ever wore grey hairs.

My course I stopp'd as soon as I espied
The Old Man in that naked wilderness;
Close by a Pond upon the hither side
He stood alone: a minute's space, [I gue]ss,
I watch'd him, he continuing motionless.
To the Pool's further margin then I drew,
He all the while before me being full in view.

As a huge stone is sometimes seen to lie
Couch'd on the bald top of an eminence,
Wonder to all that do the same espy,
By what means it could thither come & whence;
So that it seems a thing endued with sense,
Like a Sea-beast crawl'd forth, which on a Shelf
Of rock or sand reposeth, there to sun itself.

Such seem'd this Man, not all alive nor dead,
Nor all asleep; in his extreme old age
His body was bent double, feet and head
Coming together in their pilgrimage;
As if some dire constraint of pain, or rage
Of sickness felt by him in times long past
A more than human weight upon his age had cast.

Himself he propp'd, both body, [limb, and face,][1]
Upon a long grey staff of shaven woo[d],
And still as I drew near with gentle pace
Beside the little Pond or moorish flood
Motionless as a cloud the Old Man stood,
That heareth not the loud winds when they call,
And moveth altogether if it moves at all.

He wore a Cloak the same as women wear
As one whose blood did needful comfort lack;
His face look'd pale as if it had grown fair,
And furthermore he had upon his back
Beneath his Cloak a round & bulky Pack,
A load of wool or raiment as might seem
That on his shoulders lay as if it clave to him.

[1] MS. torn.

## 13 August 1803

At length, himself unsettling, he the Pond
Stirr'd with his staff, & fixedly did look
Upon the muddy water which he conn'd
As if he had been reading in a book;
And now such freedom as I could I took
And, drawing to his side, to him did say,
'This morning gives us promise of a glorious day.'

A gentle answer did the Old Man make
In courteous speech which forth he slowly drew;
And him with further words I thus bespake,
'What kind of work is that which you pursue?
'This is a lonesome place for one like you.'
He answer'd me with pleasure & surprize,
And there was while he spake a fire about his eyes.

His words came feebly from a feeble chest,
Yet each in solemn order follow'd each
With something of a pompous utterance drest,
Choice word & measur'd phrase, beyond the reach
Of ordinary men, a stately speech,
Such as grave livers do in Scotland use,
Religious Men who give to God & Man their dues.

He told me that he to the Pond had come
To gather Leeches, being old and poor,
That 'twas his calling, better far than some,
Though he had many hardships to endure:
From Pond to Pond he roam'd, from Moor to Moor,
Housing with God's good help by choice or chance,
And in this way he gain'd an honest maintenance.

The Old Man still stood talking by my side,
But soon his voice to me was like a stream
Scarce heard, nor word from word could I divide,
And the whole body of the Man did seem
Like [one w]hom I had met with in a dream;
Or like a Man from some far region sent
To give me human strength, & strong admonishment.

My former thoughts return'd, the fear that kills,
The hope that is unwilling to be fed,
Cold, pain, and labour, & all fleshly ills,
And mighty Poets in their misery dead;

And now, not knowing what the Old Man had said,
My question eagerly did I renew,
'How is it that you live? & what is it you do?'

He with a smile did then his words repeat
And said, that wheresoe'er they might be spied
He gather'd Leeches, stirring at his feet
The waters in the Ponds where they abide.
Once he could meet with them on every side;
But fewer they became from day to day,
And so his means of life before him died away.

While he was talking thus the lonely place,
The Old Man's shape & speech all troubl'd me;
In my mind's eye I seem'd to see him pace
About the weary Moors continually,
Wandering about alone and silently.
While I these thoughts within myself pursu'd,
He, having made a pause, the same discourse renew'd.

And now with this he other matter blended
Which he deliver'd with demeanor kind,
Yet stately in the main; & when he ended
I could have laugh'd myself to scorn to find
In that decrepit Man so firm a mind;
'God,' said I, 'be my help & stay secure!
'I'll think of the Leech-gatherer on the lonely Moor.[']

Dejection, an Ode.[1]— (Imperfect) *April 4th, 1802*

'Late, late yestreen I saw the new Moon
'With the old Moon in her Arm,
'And I fear, I fear, my dear Mastér,
'We shall have a deadly Storm.[']

THE BALLAD OF SIR PAT. SPENCE.

Well! if the Bard was weatherwise, who made
The grand old Ballad of Sir Patrick Spence,
This Night, so tranquil now, will not go hence
Unrous'd by Winds that ply a busier Trade
Than that which moulds yon Clouds in lazy Flakes,
Or the dull sobbing Draft, that drones and rakes
Amid the Strings of this Eolian Lute,
   Which better far were mute!

[1] *Poems*, i. 362.

## 13 August 1803

For lo! the New moon, winter-bright!
And overspread with phantom Light,
With swimming phantom Light o'erspread
But rimm'd and circled with a silver Thread,
I see the Old Moon in her Lap, foretelling
The coming on of Rain and squally Blast!
And O! that even now the Gust were swelling,
And the slant Night-shower driving loud & fast!
Those Sounds which oft have rais'd me while they aw'd
    And sent my Soul abroad,
Might now perhaps their wonted Influence give,
Might startle this dull Pain, and make it move and live.

A Grief without a Pang, void, dark, and drear,
A stifled, drowsy, unimpassion'd Grief,
That finds no natural Outlet, no Relief
In Word, or Sigh, or Tear—
O dearest William! in this heartless Mood
To other Thoughts by yonder Throstle woo'd,
All this long Eve, so balmy and serene,
Have I been gazing on the western sky
And it's celestial Tint of yellow green—
And still I gaze! and with how blank an eye!
And those thin Clouds, above, in flakes and bars,
That give away their motions to the Stars;
Those Stars, that glide behind them or between,
Now sparkling, now bedimm'd, but always seen;
Yon crescent moon, as fix'd as if it grew
In it's own starless cloudless Lake of Blue;
I see them all so excellently fair—
I *see*, not *feel*, how beautiful they are!

    My genial Spirits fail,
    And what can these avail
To lift the smoth'ring Weight from off my Breast?
    It were a vain Endeavor
    Tho' I should gaze for ever
On that green Light, which lingers in the West:
I may not hope from outward forms to win
The Passion and the Life, whose Fountains are within!

O William! we *receive* but what we *give*:
And in our Life alone does Nature live.
Our's is her Wedding-garment, our's her Shroud!

## To Sir George and Lady Beaumont

And would we aught behold of higher Worth
Than that inanimate cold World *allow'd*
To the poor loveless ever-anxious Crowd—
Ah! from the Soul itself must issue forth
A Light, a Glory, a fair luminous Cloud
    Enveloping the Earth!
And from the Soul itself must there be sent
A sweet and potent Voice, of it's own Birth,
Of all sweet Sounds the Life and Element!

O pure of Heart! thou need'st not ask of *me*,
What this strong Music in the Soul may be—
What, and wherein doth it exist,
This Light, this Glory, this fair luminous Mist,
This beautiful, and beauty-making Power?
Joy, dearest Bard! but such as ne'er was given
Save to the Pure, and in their purest Hour,
Joy, effluent, & mysterious, is the Power[1]
Which wedding Nature to us gives in Dower
A new Earth and new Heaven
Undreamt of by the Sensual and the Proud!
This[2] is the sweet Voice, This[2] the luminous Cloud,
    Our hidden Selves rejoice![3]
And thence flows all that charms or Ear or Sight,
All Melodies the echoes of that Voice,
All Colours a Suffusion from that Light!

    Yes, dearest William! Yes!
There was a Time, when tho' my Path was rough,
This Joy within me dallied with Distress;
And all Misfortunes were but as the Stuff
Whence Fancy made me Dreams of Happiness:
For Hope grew round me, like the climbing Vine,
And Fruits and Foliage, not my own, seem'd mine.
But now Afflictions bow me down to Ear[th:]
Nor care I, that they rob me of my Mirth—
    But O! each Visitation
Suspends what Nature gave me at my Birth,
    My Shaping Spirit of Imagination!

    \*   \*   \*   \*   \*   \*   \*

---

[1] Joy, is the Spirit and mysterious Power [Cancelled version of line above.]
[2] Joy [Cancelled word in line above.]
[3] We, we ourselves, rejoice! [Cancelled version of line above.]

( 972 )

I am so weary of this doleful Poem that I must leave off / & the other Poems I will transcribe in a Sheet by themselves.[1]—I have been very ill—& it is well for those about me, that in these visitations of the Stomach my Disgusts combine with myself & my own Compositions—not with others or the works of others.——I received the Applethwaite Writings from the Lawyer, made over to W. Wordsworth in due form, with much parchment Parade.[2]—I have consulted Mr Edmondson as to the safety & propriety of my going into Scotland in an open Carriage. He is confident, that he can relieve me by the use of Carminative Bitters—& that the Exercise &c will be highly beneficial. I shall probably try it therefore / but shall stay two days to enable myself to guess at the effect of the Bitters—& the Steel Medicine.——All are well: & Wordsworth['s] most respectful & affectionate Remembrances I am to convey to you, in terms as warm as respect & propriety will permit me. But Heaven bless me! I am a wretched Hand at apportioning these Things!—

I trust, that you are both pretty well—My wishes, my prayers, are your's—and I remain,

    dear Sir George, and | dear Lady, Beaumont, | with affectionate & grateful respect & esteem | Your's most sincerely,

                                  S. T. Coleridge

John Fisher, Wordsworth's Neighbour, on reading Lord Lowther's circulatory Paper exclaimed to me—[']Well, Mr Coleridge! they shall do me na Injury, till they have kill't me! I'll *feet* (fight) till I dee (die)—& I'll dēē with Honor.' He is a Shoemaker—a fine enthusiastic noble minded Creature—who has got a Son, his only one, in the Army.—Peggy Ashburner, another Neighbour, on reading the little Pamphlet sent to the Minister of the Parish—cries out —Lord bless a' (pronounce it as *au*)—Lord bless a', and pray God! why, it is eneugh to freeten yan to Deeth!—And truly that Pamphlet is an over-dose of Stimulus.—

---

[1] See Letter 521.

[2] Beaumont had 'purchased a small property at Applethwaite, about three miles to the west [north] of Greta Hall, . . . and presented it to Wordsworth, whom as yet he had not seen'. Writing to Wordsworth in Oct. 1803, Beaumont says: 'I had a most ardent desire to bring you and Coleridge together. I thought with pleasure on the increase of enjoyment you would receive from the beauties of Nature, by being able to communicate more frequently your sensations to each other.' *Memorials of Coleorton,* i, pp. xii–xiii.

## 513. To Robert Southey

*Address*: Mr Southey | St James's Parade | Kingsdown | Bristol
MS. Lord Latymer. *Pub. with omis.* E. L. G. i. 268.
*Stamped*: Penrith.

Sunday, Aug. 14. 1803

My dear Southey

Your Letter affected me very deeply: I did not feel it so much the two first Days, as I have since done. I have been very ill, & in serious dread of a paralytic Stroke in my whole left Side. Of my disease there now remains no Shade of Doubt: it is a compleat & almost heartless Case of Atonic Gout. If you would look into the Article Medicine, in the Encyc. Britt. Vol. XI. Part 1.—No 213.— p. 181.—& the first 5 paragraphs of the second Column / you will read almost the very words, in which, before I had seen this Article, I had described my case to Wordsworth.—The only non-agreement is—'an imaginary aggravation of the slightest Feelings, & an apprehension of danger from them.'—The first sentence is unphilosophically expressed / there is a state of mind, wholly unnoticed, as far as I know, by any Physical or Metaphysical Writer hitherto, & which yet is necessary to the explanation of some of the most important phaenomena of Sleep & Disease / it is a transmutation of the *succession* of *Time* into the *juxtaposition* of *Space*, by which the smallest Impulses, if quickly & regularly recurrent, *aggregate* themselves—& attain a kind of visual magnitude with a correspondent Intensity of general Feeling.—The simplest Illustration would be the *circle* of Fire made by whirling round a live Coal—only here the mind is passive. Suppose the same effect produced ab intra—& you have a clue to the whole mystery of frightful Dreams, & Hypochondriacal Delusions.—I merely *hint* this; but I could detail the whole process, complex as it is.— Instead of 'an imaginary aggravation &c' it would be better to say —'an *aggregation* of slight Feelings by the force of a diseasedly retentive Imagination.'—*As to the apprehension of Danger*—it would belong to my Disease, if it could belong to me. But Sloth, Carelessness, Resignation—in all things that have reference to mortal Life—is not merely *in* me; it is *me*. (Spite of Grammar— i.e. Lowth's[1]—for I affirm, that in such instances 'it is *me*,' is genuine English & philosophical Grammar.)—Mr Edmondson, whom I have consulted on the possibility or propriety of my tour into Scotland, recommends it. He is confident—O that I were— that by the use of Carminative Bitters I may get rid of this truly poisonous, & body-&-soul-benumming Flatulence and Inflation:

---
[1] Robert Lowth, *A Short Introduction to English Grammar*, 1762.

& that if I can only get on, the Exercise & the Excitement will be of so much service as to outweigh the chances of Injury from Wet or Cold. I will therefore go: tho' I never yet commenced a Journey with such inauspicious Heaviness of Heart before. We—Wordsworth, Dorothy, and myself—leave Keswick tomorrow morning.[1] We have bought a stout Horse—aged but stout & spirited—& an open vehicle, called a Jaunting Car—there is room in it for 3 on each side, on hanging seats—a Dicky Box for the Driver / & a space or hollow in the middle, for luggage—or two or three Bairns.—It is like half a long Coach, only those in the one seat sit with their *back* to those in the other / instead of face to face.—Your feet are not above a foot—scarcely so much—from the ground / so that you may get off & on while the Horse is moving without the least Danger / there are all sorts of Conveniences in it /. We came from Grasmere last Thursday in it—Wordsworth in the Dicky—Dorothy, Mrs Wordsworth, our Mary, I, Hartley, Derwent, & Johnney Wordsworth / & this morning the same party—only instead of me Mrs Coleridge & Sara / are gone to set Mrs Wordsworth 7 miles of the way on to Grasmere.—What a nice Thing for us, if you & Edith were to take the other half of this House—& my Health gave any probability of my stay in England. But I swear by my Maker, that I will no longer trifle. I will try this Tour / if I cannot bear it—I shall return from Glasgow /—I will try the new Gout Medicine / & you would be doing me an essential Service, if you would call on Dr Beddoes—say, that I had long meditated a very long Letter to him on subjects, which have interested us both, in the shape of friendly remarks on his Hygeia / but I was hurried off from Gunville, where the Book was—& partly the not having the Book to refer to, tho' I have the most *thing-like* Recollections of it's contents—& far far more, the miserable State of my Health—& the quantity, I wished to say—have prevented me /—& now I am ashamed to write on a mere selfish Concern.—I read his Pamphlet on the new Medicine with sincere *admiration*/. With the single exception of the last Page, it seemed to me to have all the character-

---

[1] In a letter postmarked 25 Aug. 1803 Mrs. Coleridge has this to say to Southey: 'Last Monday [15 Aug.] my husband, W. Wordsworth, and D. W. set off for Scotland in an Irish-Car and one horse—W. is to drive all the way, for poor Samuel is too weak to undertake the fatigue of driving—he was very unwell when he went off, and was to return in the *Mail* if he grew worse. . . . I hope he will be able to go for if the weather be tolerable it will do him much good, so Mr. Edmondson thinks. . . . My husband is a good man—his prejudices—and his prepossessions sometimes give me pain, but we have all a somewhat to encounter in this life—I should be a very, very happy Woman if it were not for a few things—and my husband's ill health stands at the head of these evils!' MS. Lord Latymer.

istic excellencies of his manner *clarified* from his characteristic Defects—I have been made to understand, that this new medicine is not to be procured without great Difficulty from the Empiric, nor without very heavy Expence / however whatever the expence be, I will give it one Trial—& should be very greatly obliged to Dr Beddoes if *he* would desire Mr Wells to send down a sufficient Quantity of the Medicine, if he think it likely to be serviceable in a clear Case of atonic Gout / a case of capricious Appetite—indigestion / costiveness that makes my evacuations at times approach in all the symptoms to the pains of Labor—viz—distortion of Body from agony, profuse & streaming Sweats, & fainting—at other times, looseness with griping—frightful Dreams with screaming —*breezes* of Terror blowing from the Stomach up thro' the Brain / always when I am awakened, I find myself stifled with wind / & the wind the manifest cause of the Dream / frequent paralytic Feelings—sometimes approaches to Convulsion fit—three times I have wakened out of these frightful Dreams, & found my legs so *locked* into each other as to have *left* a bruise—/ Sometimes I am a little giddy; but very seldom have the Headach / And on the whole my Head is wonderfully *clear*, considering—tho' less so than in an earlier Stage of the Disease / & this being the strongest part of my Constitution, when that goes, all goes—/ My hands & fingers occasionally swell—my feet are often inflamed / with pulsations in the Toes—& twice last week I was lame in my left Leg, & the ancle was swoln / but these inflammatory Symptoms soon go off. My Mouth is endlessly full of water—itself no small Persecution—but above all, the *asthmatic Stuffing*—which forms a true suspension of the Habeas Corpus Act.—I live very temperately—drinking only one tumbler of Brandy & Water in the 24 hours / —but when I awake screaming, I take Tea or Coffee, with an egg & a good deal of Cayenne Pepper / which seems to procure me ease & sometimes Sleep—tho' no doubt it injures me in the long run. But what can I do?—I am sure, if Dr Beddoes lived near me, or in the same house with me, he would soften down his opinions respecting the inefficiency of Climate in Gout Cases. The effects of weather are to the full as palpable upon me, as upon the little Old Lady & Gentleman in the weather Box—or on the Sea Weed in the Barber's Shop. However, my dear Southey! do call on Dr Beddoes—& read such parts of this Letter to him, as you think fit—Say, that I would have written to him *formally* as to a Physician; but that never having done so, if I should send a fee, it would seem as if I were willing to forget all his prior kindness to me, & all my Obligations to him for the many Letters of medical advice which he has heretofore sent me, as the richer Man to the Poorer. It is neither my

Theory nor my Practice to do any thing *from* Gratitude; but if I live & regain my powers of manifesting my Powers, I will act *with* Gratitude: for indeed Dr Beddoes has been very kind to me / & I am often uncomfortable in my inner feelings at having permitted myself to be affected by little calumnious tittle-tattle respecting him—instead of daring to tell him with equal simplicity & honest zeal, wherein he is truly great & useful, & wherein he manifestly injures his own powers of benefiting his Fellow-Creatures.——What I want is to have a quantity of the Gout Medicine sent to Greta Hall, Keswick, Cumberland—by the waggon either from London or Bristol—so that on my return from Scotland I may find it here. Whatever the expence may be, do you defray it for me / & I will remit you the money within a week of the receipt of your Letter which shall inform me of the Amount.—If this fail, I then, *by God!* go off to Malta or Madeira / Madeira is the better place; but Stoddart is gone to Malta with a wife, with a place of 1500£ a year—& has given me a very kind Invitation/—You had better write to me, the Post Office, Edingburgh.—I shall write to you from Glasgow.—Mrs C. is but middling: the children are quite well—Derwent & Sara are as beautiful as Angels. I never saw a child so improved, as Sara is—& she is quietness itself—very lively, & joyous; but all in a quiet way of her own / She feeds on her Quietness, & 'has the most truly celestial expression of countenance, I ever beheld in a human Face.' —Now I have set you the example, & you may give loose to the Father, & write about dear little Margaret.—Only let me say, the words 'quoted' are Wordsworth's, not mine—& Wordsworth's words always *mean* the whole of their possible Meaning. She h[as larg]e blue eyes.— S. T. C.

### 514. To Mrs. S. T. Coleridge

*Address*: Mrs Coleridge | Greta Hall | Keswick | Cumberland | S. Britain
*MS. Lord Latymer. Pub. with omis.* Letters, *i. 431.*
*Stamped*: Fort William.

Friday Afternoon, 4 o clock. Sept. [2 1803]

My dear Sara

I write from the Ferry of Ball[achulish;] here a Letter may be *lucky* enough to go, & arrive at it's destination. This is the first Post, since the Day I left Glasgow——we went thence to Dumbarton (look at Stoddart's Tour, where there is a very good view of Dumbarton Rock & Tower) thence to Loch Lomond, and a single House, called Luss—horrible Inhospitality & a fiend of a Landlady!—thence 8 miles up the Lake to E. Tarbet—where the Lake is so like Ulswater, that I could scarcely see a difference /

crossed over the Lake, & by a desolate Moorland walked to another Lake, Loch Ketterin, up to a place called Trossachs, the Borrodale of Scotland & the only thing which really beats us—You must conceive the Lake of Keswick pushing itself up, a mile or two, into Borrodale, winding round Castle Crag, & in & out among all the nooks & promontories—& you must imagine all the mountains more *detachedly* built up, a general Dislocation—every rock it's own precipice, with Trees young & old—& this will give you some faint Idea of the Place—of which the character is extreme intricacy of effect produced by very simple means—one rocky high Island, four or 5 promontories, & a Castle Crag, just like that in the Gorge of Borrodale but not so large— / ——. It rained all the way—all the long long day—we slept in a hay loft, that is, Wordsworth, I, and a young man who came in at the Trossachs & joined us— Dorothy had a bed in the Hovel which was varnished *so rich* with peat smoke, an apartment of highly polished [oak] would have been poor to it: it would have wanted the *metallic* Lustre of the smoke-varnished Rafters.—This was [the pleasantest] Evening, I had spent, since my Tour: for [Wordsworth's] Hypochondriacal Feelings keep him silent, & [self]-centered—. The next day it still was rain & rain / the ferry boat was out for the Preaching—& we stayed all day in the Ferry [house] to dry, wet to the skin / O such a wretched Hovel!—but two highland Lasses who kept house in the absence of the Ferry man & his Wife, were very kind—& one of them was beautiful as a Vision / & put both me & Dorothy in mind of the Highland Girl in William's Peter Bell.—We returned to E. Tarbet, I with the rheumatism in my head / and now William proposed to me to leave them, & make my way on foot, to Loch Ketterin, the Trossachs, whence it is only 20 miles to Stirling, where the Coach runs thro' for Edingburgh—He & Dorothy resolved to fight it out—I eagerly caught at the Proposal: for the *sitting* in an open Carriage in the Rain is Death to me, and somehow or other I had not been quite comfortable. So on Monday I accompanied them to Arrochar, on purpose to see THE COB[B]LER, which had impressed me so much in Mr Wilkinson's Drawings—& there I parted with them, having previously sent on all *my* Things to Edinburgh by a Glasgow Carrier who happened to be at E. Tarbet. The worst thing was the money—they took 29 Guineas, and I six—all our remaining Cash! I returned to E. Tarbet, slept there that night— the next day walked to the very head of Loch Lomond to Glen Falloch—where I slept at a Cottage Inn, two degrees below John Stanley's but the good people were very kind—meaning from hence to go over the mountain to the Head of Loch Ketterin again—but hearing from the gude man of the House that it was

[40] miles to Glen Coe, of which I had formed an Idea from Wilkinson's Drawings—& having found myself so happy alone—such blessing is there in perfect Liberty!—that I walked off—and have walked 45 miles since then—and except the last mile, I am sure, I may say, I have not met with ten houses. For 18 miles there are but 2 Habitations!—and all that way I met no Sheep, no Cattle— only one Goat!—all thro' Moorlands with huge mountains, some craggy & bare, but the most green with deep pinky channels worn by Torrents—. Glen Coe interested me; but rather disappointed me—there was no *superincumbency* of Crag, the Crags not so bare or precipitous, as I had expected / — / I am now going to cross the Ferry for Fort William—for I have resolved to eke out my Cash by all sorts of self-denial, & to walk along the *whole line of the Forts*. I am unfortunately shoeless—there is no Town where I can get a pair, & I have no money to spare to buy them—so I expect to enter Perth Barefooted—I burnt my shoes in drying them at the Boatman's Hovel on Loch Ketterin / and I have by this mean hurt my heel— likewise my left Leg is a little inflamed / & the Rheumatism in the right of my head afflicts me sorely when I begin to grow warm in my bed, chiefly, my right eye, ear, cheek, & the three Teeth / but nevertheless, I am enjoying myself, having Nature with solitude & liberty; the liberty natural & solitary, the solitude natural & free!

——But you must contrive somehow or other to borrow 10£—or if that cannot be—5£, for me—& send it without delay, directed to me at [the Pos]t office, Perth. I guess, I shall be there [in 7] days, or 8 at the furthest—& your Letter will be two days getting thither (counting the day you put it in to the Office at Keswick as nothing) —so you must calculate / and if this Letter does not reach you in time—i.e. within 5 days from the Date hereof—you must then direct the Letter to Edingburgh / (I will *make* 5£ do. You must borrow it of Mr Jackson.—) & I must *beg* my way for the last 3 or 4 days!—It is useless repining; but if I had set off myself, in the Mail for Glasgow or Stirling, & so gone by foot as I am now doing, I should have saved 25£; but then Wordsworth would have lost it.——.

I have said nothing of you or my dear Children—God bless us all!— I have but one untried misery to go thro'—the Loss of Hartley or Derwent—aye, or dear little Sara!——In my health I am middling —While I can walk 24 miles a day, with the excitement of new objects, I can *support* myself—but still my Sleep & Dreams are distressful—& I am hopeless; I take no opiates but when the Looseness with colic comes on; nor have [I] any Temptation: for since my Disorder has taken this asthm[atic turn,] opiates produce none but positively unplea[sant effects.   S. T. C.]

### 515. *To Mrs. S. T. Coleridge*

*Address*: Mrs Coleridge | Greta Hall | Keswick | Cumberland | S. Britain. Single
MS. Lord Latymer. *Pub. E. L. G. i. 272. The bottom of each page of the holograph has been cut off.*
*Stamped*: Fort William.

Saturday, Sept. 3.—Fort William. 1803

My dear Sara

I learnt at the Ferry that it would be safer to take my Letter with me to this place, as the same Post took it, & did not go off till early on Sunday Morning.—I walked on very briskly, when now Night came on / my road lay all the way by a great Sea Lake, Rocks or Woods, or Rocks among woods close by my right hand, great mountains across the Sea on my left /—and now I had walked 28 miles in the course of the Day, when being thirsty I drank repeatedly in the palm of my hand, & thinking of writing to Sir G. Beaumont I was saying to myself—this using one hand instead of a Cup has one disadvantage that one literally does not know when one has had enough—and we leave off not because the Thirst is quench'd but because we are tired of Stooping.—Soon after (in less than a furlong) —a pain & intense sense of fatigue fell upon me, especially within my Thighs—& great Torture in my bad Toe—However I dragged myself along; but when I reached the Town, I was forced to lean on the man that shewed me my Inn (to which I had been recommended by a Dr Hay Drummond who met me at Kingshouse, & *created* an acquaintance in the most farcical manner imaginable—) Mrs Munro, the Landlady, had no room at all—and I could not stand—however she sent a boy with me to another little Inn, which I entered—& sitting down. . .
an affair altogether of the Body, not of the mind—that I had, it was true, a torturing pain in all my limbs, but that this had nothing to do with my Tears which were hysterical & proceeded from the Stomach— / Just as I had said this, a kind old man came in to me, who had crossed the Ferry with me, & being on horseback had been here half an hour before me / and I had had some chat with him in the Boat, told him of the Gout in my Stomach, & that this Tour was an experiment for Exercise—&c—/['] I never saw a man, ['] says he, ['] walk so well or so briskly as this young Gentleman did—and indeed he must have done so, for I rode as hard as I could, & yet have not been in much more than $\frac{1}{2}$ an hour—or three quarters.'— I told him with faltering voice that I should have been in half an hour sooner, but that the last mile & a half I could scarcely drag my Limbs along: & that the Fatigue had come upon me all at once. —'Whoo! Whoo! Whoo!' says the old man— ['] you drank water

by the road-side then ?[']—I said, yes!——'And you have Gout in the Stomach—/ indeed, but you are in *peril*.'—By this time they had gotten me a dish of Tea; but before I could touch it, my Bowels were seized violently, & there . . .
Gallon of nasty water——and so went to bed. Had a Bason of hot Tea brought up to me—slept very soon, and more soundly than I have done since I have been in Scotland. I find myself a little stiffish, this morning / 30 miles was perhaps too much for one day —yet I am positive, I should not have felt it, but for that unfortunate Drench of Water!— I might have gone on; but I wished to have a Shirt & Stockings washed / I have but *one* pair of Stockings—& they were so clotted & full of holes that it was a misery to *sit* with them on/. So I have sent them, & sit with none. —I had determined to buy a pair of Shoes whatever befell me, in the way of money distresses; but there are none in the Town ready made—so I shall be obliged to go as far as Inverness with these—perhaps to Perth / & I speak in the simplest earnest when I say, that I expect I shall be forced to throw them away before I get to Inverness, & to walk barefoot—My bad great Toe, on my left Foot, is a sore Annoyance to me.—

I am bepuzzled about this money. This Letter will not reach you, I fear, till Wednesday Night—However, you must at all events send me the money (I can & will make 5£ do) Mr Coleridge, to be left at the Post Office, Perth, N. Britain.—

I have been so particular in my account of that hysterical Attack, because this is now the third seizure / & the first from mere physical causes. The two former were the effect of agitated Feelings. —I am sure, that neither Mr Edmondson nor you have any adequate notion, how seriously ill I am. If the Complaint does not settle—& very soon too—in my extremities, I do not see how it will be possible for me to avoid a paralytic or apoplectic Stroke. . . .moment. . .[1]

I have no heart to speak of the Children!—God have mercy on them; & raise them up friends when I am in the Grave.—

Remember me affectionately to Mr Jackson and to Mrs Wilson. —Remember me too to Mr Wilkinson & Mrs W.—& tell Mr W. that if I return in tolerable Health, I anticipate a high Feast in looking over his [Drawings.]. . . him for flattering. . .

[1] Five and a half lines heavily inked out at the top of page 4 of the manuscript.

## 516. To Robert Southey

*Address*: Single Sheet | Mrs Coleridge | Greta Hall | Keswick | Cumberland | S. Britain   For Mr Southey.
*MS.* Lord Latymer. *Pub. with omis.* Letters, i. 434. This letter and the one following were written on the same sheet. Coleridge wrote to both Southey and Mrs. Coleridge from Perth; then on his arrival in Edinburgh the next day, he added a postscript to his letter to Mrs. Coleridge and posted the sheet containing both letters.
*Postmark*: 12 September 1803.

[Perth,] Sunday Night, 9 o clock—Sept. 10 [11]. 1803

My dearest Southey

I arrived here half an hour ago—& have only read your Letters—scarce read them.—O dear friend! it is idle to talk of what I feel—I am stunned at present—& this beginning to write makes a beginning of living feeling within me. Whatever Comfort I can be to you, I will.—I have no Aversions, no dislikes, that interfere with you—whatever is necessary or proper for you, becomes ipso facto agreeable to me. I will not stay a day in Edinburgh—or only one to hunt out my clothes. I can[not] chit chat with Scotchmen, while you are at Keswick, childless.—Bless you, my dear Southey! I will knit myself far closer to you than I have hitherto done—& my children shall be your's till it please God to send you another.——

I have been a wild Journey—taken up for a spy & clapped into Fort Augustus—& I am afraid, they may [have] frightened poor Sara, by sending her off a scrap of a Letter, I was writing to her.—I have walked 263 miles in eight Days—so I must have strength somewhere / but my spirits are dreadful, owing entirely to the Horrors of every night—I truly dread to sleep / it is no shadow with me, but substantial Misery foot-thick, that makes me sit by my bedside of a morning, & *cry*—. I have abandoned all opiates except Ether be one; & that only in *fits*—& that is a blessed medicine! —& when you see me drink a glass of Spirit & Water, except by prescription of a physician, you shall despise me—but still I can not get quiet rest—

> When on my bed my limbs I lay,[1]
> It hath not been my use to pray
> With moving Lips or bended Knees;
> But silently, by slow degrees,
> My spirit I to Love compose,
> In humble trust my eyelids close,

---

[1] *Poems*, i. 389. These lines, in revised form, were first published in the *Christabel* volume of 1816 as *The Pains of Sleep*.

## 11 September 1803

With reverential Resignation,
No Wish conceiv'd, no Thought exprest,
Only a *Sense* of Supplication,
A *Sense* o'er all my soul imprest
That I am weak, yet not unblest:
Since *round* me, *in* me, every where,
Eternal Strength & Goodness are!—

But yesternight I pray'd aloud
In Anguish & in Agony,
Awaking from the fiendish Crowd
Of Shapes & Thoughts that tortur'd me!
Desire with Loathing strangely mixt,
On wild or hateful Objects fixt:
Pangs of Revenge, the powerless Will,
Still baffled, & consuming still,
Sense of intolerable Wrong,
And men whom I despis'd made strong
Vain-glorious Threats, unmanly Vaunting,
Bad men my boasts & fury taunting[1]
Rage, sensual Passion, mad'ning Brawl,
And Shame, and Terror over all!
Deeds to be hid that were not hid,
Which, all confus'd I might not know,
Whether I suffer'd or I did:
For all was Horror, Guilt & Woe,
My own or others, still the same,
Life-stifling Fear, Soul-stifling Shame!

Thus two nights pass'd: the Night's Dismay
Sadden'd and stunn'd the boding Day.
I fear'd to sleep: Sleep seem'd to be
Disease's worst malignity.
The third night when my own loud Scream
Had freed[2] me from the fiendish Dream,
O'ercome by Sufferings dark & wild,
I wept as I had been a Child—
And having thus by Tears subdued
My Trouble to a milder mood—

---

[1] Sense of intolerable Wrong,
    Vain-glorious Threats, unmanly Vaunting,
    Revenge still baffled by a Throng
    Of insults then my fury taunting;
[Cancelled version of the four lines above.]
[2] wak'd [Cancelled word in line above.]

Such Punishment[s], I thought, were due
To Natures, deepliest stain'd with Sin,
Still to be stirring up anew
The self-created Hell within;
The Horror of their Crimes to view,
To know & loathe, yet wish & do!
With such let Fiends make mockery—
But I—O wherefore this on *me*?
Frail is my Soul, yea, strengthless wholly,
Unequal, restless, melancholy;
But free from Hate, & sensual Folly!
To live belov'd is all I need,
And whom I love, I love indeed[1]—& &c &c &c &c &c—

I do not know how I came to scribble down these verses to you —my heart was aching, my head all confused—but they are, doggrels as they may be, a true portrait of my nights.—What to do, I am at a loss:—for it is hard thus to be withered, having the faculties & attainments, which I have.—

We will soon meet—& I will do all I can to console poor dear Edith.—O dear dear Southey! my head is sadly confused. After a rapid walk of 33 miles your Letters have had the effect of perfect intoxication on my head & eyes—Change! change! change!—O God of Eternity! when shall we all be at rest in thee?—S. T. Coleridge.

## 517. *To Mrs. S. T. Coleridge*

*MS. Lord Latymer. Pub. E. L. G. i. 274.*
*Postmark*: 12 September 1803.

[Perth, 11 September 1803]

For Mrs Coleridge.[2]

My dearest Sara

I was writing to you from Fort Augustus when the Governor & his wise Police Constable seized me & my Letter—Since then I have

[1] In an unpublished letter of 1814 Coleridge quotes a fragment of this poem in greatly amended form. He says the lines are from a poem entitled *Diseased Sleep* and composed in 1803, and adds that they were 'part of a long letter in verse written to a friend, while I yet remained ignorant that the direful sufferings, I so complained of, were the mere effects of Opium, which I even to that hour imagined a sort of Guardian Genius to me!' In the 1814 letter Coleridge says the lines are 'an exact and most faithful portraiture of the state of my mind under influences of incipient bodily derangement from the use of Opium, at the time that I yet remained ignorant of the cause, & still *mighty proud* of my supposed grand discovery of Laudanum, as the Remedy or Palliative of Evils, which itself had mainly produced'.

[2] See headnote to preceding letter.

written to nobody. On my return, if God grant! we will take the Map of Scotland, & by help of my pocket Book I will travel my rout over again, from place to place. It has been an instructive tho' melancholy Tour.—At Fort Augustus I got a pair of Shoes—the day before I had walked 36 miles, 20 the WORST in conception, & up a Mountain—so that in point of effort it could not be less than 46 miles / the shoes were all to pieces / and three of my Toes were skinless, & I had a very promising Hole in my Heel.—Since the new Shoes I have walked on briskly—from 30 to 35 miles a day, day after day—& three days I lived wholly on Oat cake, Barley Bannock, Butter, & the poorest of all poor Skim-milk Cheeses—& still I had horrors at night!—I mention all this to shew you, that I have strength somewhere—and at the same time, how deeply this Disease must have rooted itself.—I wrote you my last Letter, overclouded by Despondency—say rather, in a total eclipse of all Hope & Joy—and as all things propagate their Like, you must not wonder, that Misery is a Misery-maker. But do you try, & I will try; & Peace may come at last, & Love with it.—I have not heard of Wordsworth; nor he of me. He will be wondering what can have become of me—. —I have only read the first Letter—& that part of Southey's, containing the 10£ note, which relates to himself— for they have stunned me—and I am afraid of Hysterics, unless a fit of vomiting which I feel coming on, should as I hope it will, turn it off—I must write no more / it is now 10 o clock / & I go off in the Mail at 4 in the Morning—. It went against the Grain to pay 18 shillings for what I could have made an easy Day's walk of: & but for my eagerness to be with dear Southey, I should certainly have walked from Edinburgh home / —O Sara! dear Sara!—*try* for all good Things in the spirit of unsuspecting Love / for miseries gather upon us. I shall take this Letter with me to Edinburgh —& leave a space to announce my safe arrival, if so it please God.—Good night, my sweet Children!

S. T. Coleridge

Monday Morning, 12 o clock.

I am safe in Edinburgh—& now going to seek out news about the Wordsworths & my Cloathes—I do not expect to stay here above this Day—Dear Southey's Letter had the precise effect of intoxication by an overdose of some narcotic Drug—weeping— vomiting—wakefulness the whole night, in a sort of stupid sensuality of Itching from my Head to my Toes, all night.—I had drunken only one pint of weak Porter the whole Day.—This morning I have felt the soberness of grief. God bless you all, & S. T. Coleridge—

## 518. To A. Welles

MS. New York Public Lib. Pub. E. L. G. i. 276. The condition of the manuscript indicates that it is a rough draft of the letter sent to Welles. Obviously Coleridge was pleased with his letter, for he told Southey: 'I was very much amused by Welles's Letter—& have written him a droll one enough in return—of which, if I am not too lazy, I will take a Copy.' Letter 519.

Welles's letter, which drew forth Coleridge's reply, reads in part: 'It is seldom that I feel more satisfaction in any action than I do in the one I am now ingaged in. A letter from Dr. Beddoes yesterday informed me you were gouty—he need not have added that you wished to be cured——for I should have supposed it. I have in my possession a kind of Nectar / for it removes pain, & of course promotes pleasure—& may in the end immortalize—me / which I freely offer to you. I will further add the prediction, founded on experience, that you may be relieved from the gout, & your general health improved into the bargain. For confirmation of this you may consult Sir Wilfred Lawson Bart. Brayton Hall Cockermouth, who is near you.'

Tuesday: Feb. [September] 13. 1803. Edinburgh

Dear Sir

I have, but even now, received your very obliging Letter, which comforted as well as amused me. I will give the medicine the fullest, and fairest Trial, yield the most implicit obedience to your Instructions, and add to both every possible attention to Diet and Exercise. My Disorder I believe to be atonic Gout: my Sufferings are often sufficiently great by day; but by patience, effort of mind, and hard walking I can contrive to keep the Fiend at arm's length, as long as I am in possession of Reason & Will. But with Sleep my Horrors commence; & they are such, three nights out of four, as literally to *stun* the intervening Day, so that more often than otherwise I fall asleep, struggling to remain awake. Believe me, Sir! Dreams are no Shadows with me; but the real, substantial miseries of Life. If in consequence of your Medicine I should be at length delivered from these sore Visitations, my greatest uneasiness will then [be], how best & most fully I can evince my gratitude:—should I commence Preacher, raise a new Sect to your honor, & make, in short, a greater clamour in your favor, as the Antipodagra, 'that was to come, and is already in the world', than ever the Puritans did against the poor Pope, as the Antichrist—Ho! all ye, who are heavy laden—come, and draw waters of Healing from the *Wells* of Salvation. This in my own opinion I might say without impiety, for if to clear men's body [bodies] from Torture, Lassitude & Captivity, their understandings from mists & broodings, & their very hearts & souls from despair, if to enable them to go about their Duty steadily & quietly, to love God, & be chearful—if all this be not a work of Salvation, I would fain be informed, what is.—

## 13 September 1803

Or I have thought of becoming theorizing Physician of demonstrations, (for that is the fashionable word) that all Diseases are to be arranged under Gout, as the Genus generalissimum / that all our faulty Laws, Regulations, national mismanagements, Rebellions, Invasions, Heresies, Seditions, not to mention public Squabbles & commissions of Bankruptcies have originated in the false Trains of Ideas introduced by diseased Sensations from the Stomach into the Brains of our Senators, Priests, & Merchants—of our great & little men / hence to deduce, that all Diseases being Gout & your M. curing the G. your medicine must cure *all* Diseases—then, joining party with Thomas Taylor, the Pagan (for whom I have already a sneaking affection on account of his devout Love of Greek) to re-introduce the Heathen Mythology, to detect in your per[son] another descent & metamorphosis of the God of the Sun, to erect a Temple to you, as Phoebo Sanatori; & if you have a Wife, to have her deified, by act of Parliament, under the name of the Nymph, Panacea. But probably it would not be agreeable to you to be taken up, like the Tibetan Delha Llama [Dalai Lama], and to be imprisoned during life * for a God. You would rather, I doubt not, find your deserved reward in an ample independent fortune, & your sublunary Immortalization in the praises, & thanks of good and sensible men: of all who have suffered *in* themselves or *for* others.—And in sober earnest, my dear Sir! (dropping All Joke, to which your lively & enlivening Letter has led me) to this last reward I shall be most happy to become instrumental, by being first a proof, & ever after an evidence & zealous Witnesser, of the powers & virtues of your discovery.—I leave Edinburgh tomorrow morning, having walked 263 miles in eight days in the hope of forcing the Disease into the extremities: & if the Coachman does not put an end to all my earthly Ills by breaking my neck, I shall be at Greta Hall, Keswick, Thursday Afternoon—at which place I shall wait, with respectful Impatience, for a Letter & Parcel from you. In the mean time, dear Sir! accept the best Thanks & warmest wishes

of your obliged & grateful | humble Servant<br>S. T. Coleridge

* P.S. Great & well-founded however as your objection may be to my proposed national apotheosis of your Person, yet as whatever, Verse or Prose, I write hereafter, would be chiefly owing to the cure by you performed, at all events 'eris *mihi* magnus Apollo.[']—[Note by S. T. C.]

## 519. To Robert Southey

*Address*: Robert Southey Esqre | Greta Hall | Keswick | Cumberland | S. Britain.
*MS*. Lord Latymer. *Pub. with omis.* Letters, i. 437.
*Postmark*: 13 September 1803.

Edinburgh   Tuesday Morning [13 September 1803]
My dear Southey

I wrote you a strange Letter, I fear: but in truth your's affected my wretched Stomach, & that my head in such a way, that I wrote mechanically in the *wake* of the first vivid Idea. No Conveyance left or leaves this place for Carlisle earlier than to morrow morning —for which I have taken my place. If the Coachman do not turn Panaceist, and cure all my Ills by breaking my neck, I shall be at Carlisle on Wednesday Midnight—& whether I shall go on in the Coach to Penrith, & walk from thence, or walk off from Carlisle at once, depends on 2 circumstances—whether the Coach goes on with no other than a common Bait to Penrith, & whether—if it should not do so—I can trust my cloathes &c to the Coachman safely, to be left at Penrith—There is but 8 miles difference in the walk—& eight or nine Shillings difference in the expence. At all events, I trust, that I shall be with you on Thursday by dinner time, if you dine at ½ past 2 or 3 o clock.— God bless you! I will go call on Elmsley.[1]—What a wonderful City Edinburgh is!—What alternation of Height & Depth!—a city looked at in the polish'd back of a Brobdignag Spoon, held lengthways—so enormously *stretched-up* are the Houses!— When I first looked down on it, as the Coach drove in on the higher Street, I cannot express what I felt—such a section of a wasp's nest, striking you with a sort of bastard Sublimity from the enormity & infinity of it's littleness— the infinity swelling out the mind, the enormity striking it with wonder. I think I have seen an old Plate of Montserrat, that struck me with the same feeling—and I am sure, I have seen huge Quarries of Lime or Free-Stone, in which the Shafts or Strata have stood perpendicularly instead of horizontally, with the same high Thin Slices, & corresponding Interstices!—I climbed last night to the Crags just below Arthur's Seat, itself a rude triangle-shaped bare Cliff, & looked down on the whole City & Firth, the Sun then setting behind the magnificent rock, crested by the Castle /—the Firth was full of Ships, & I counted 54 heads of mountains, of which at last 44 were cones or pyramids—the smokes rising up from ten thousand houses, each smoke from some one family—it

[1] Peter Elmsley (1773–1825), classical scholar and college friend of Southey's.

was an affecting sight to me!—I stood gazing at the setting Sun, so tranquil to a passing Look, & so restless & vibrating to one who looks stedfast; & then all at once turning my eyes down upon the City, it & all it's smokes & figures became all at once dipped in the brightest blue-purple—such a sight that I almost grieved when my eyes recovered their natural Tone!—Meantime Arthur's Crag, close behind me, was in dark blood-like Crimson—and the Sharp-shooters were below, exercising minutely, & had chosen that place on account of the fine Thunder-Echo, which indeed it would be scarcely possible for the Ear to distinguish from Thunder. The passing a day or two, quite unknown, in a strange City, does a man's heart good—He rises 'a sadder and a wiser man.'—I had not read that part in your second Letter requesting me to call on Elmsley—else perhaps I should have been talking away instead of learning & feeling. Walter Scott is at Laswade, 5 or 6 miles from Edinburgh—his House in Edinburgh is divinely situated—it looks up a street, a new magnificent Street, full upon the Rock & the Castle, with it's zig-zag Walls like Painters' Lightning—the other way down upon cultivated Fields, a fine expanse of water, either a Lake or not to be distinguished from one, & low pleasing Hills beyond—the Country well-wooded & chearful. I' faith, I exclaimed, the Monks formerly, but the Poets now, know where to fix their Habitations.—There are about four Things worth going into Scotland for, to one who has been in Cumberland & Westmoreland / —the view of all the Islands at the Foot of Loch Lomond from the Top of the highest Island, called Inch devannoc [Inchtavannach]: 2. the Trossachs at the foot of Loch Ketterin 3. The Chamber & anti-chamber of the Falls of Foyers—(the Fall itself is very fine—& so after Rain is White water Dash—7 miles below Keswick & very like it—& how little difference in the feeling a great real difference in height makes, you know as well as I—no Fall, of itself, perhaps can be worth go[ing] a long Journey to see, to him who has seen any Fall of Water, but the Pool, & whole Rent of the Mountain is truly magnificent—) 4th & lastly, the City of Edinburgh.—Perhaps, I might add Glen Coe: it is at all events a good Make-weight—& very well worth going to see, if a Man be a Tory & hate the memory of William the Third—which I am very willing to do—for the more of these fellows, dead & living, one hates, the less Spleen & Gall there remains for those, with whom one is likely to have any thing to do, in real Life.

I was very much amused by Welles's Letter—& have written him a droll one enough in return—of which, if I am not too lazy, I will take a Copy.—I am tolerably well, meaning, the Day Time, for my last night was just such a noisy night of horrors, as 3 nights out of 4 are, with me. O God! when a man blesses the loud Scream of Agony that awakes him, night after night; night after night!—& when a man's repeated Night-screams have made him a nuisance in his own House, it is better to die than to live. I have a Joy in Life, that passeth all Understanding; but it is not in it's present Epiphany & Incarnation. Bodily Torture! all who have been with me can bear witness that I bear it, like an Indian / it is constitutional with me to sit still & look earnestly upon it, & ask it, what it is?—Yea often & often, the seeds of Rabelaism germinating in me, I have laughed aloud at my own poor metaphysical Soul.—But these Burrs, by Day, of the Will & the Reason, these total Eclipses by night—O it is hard to bear them. I am complaining bitterly when I should be administering Comfort; but even this is one way of comfort. There are States of mind, in which even a Distraction is still a Diversion. We must none of us *brood*: we were not made to be *Brooders.*—God bless you, dear Friend,

&

S. T. Coleridge

Mrs C. will get clean Flannels ready for me.

### 520. *To Thomas Wedgwood*

*Address*: T. Wedgwood Esqre | Mr Allen's Chambers | 12. Paper Buildings | Temple | London
*MS. Wedgwood Museum. Pub. E. L. G. i. 278.*
*Postmark*: 19 September 1803. *Stamped*: Keswick.

Greta Hall, Keswick. Sept. 16. [1803.] Friday

My dear Wedgwood

I reached home on yesterday noon; & it was not a Post Day.—William Hazlitt is a thinking, observant, original man, of great power as a Painter of Character Portraits, & far more in the manner of the old Painters, than any living Artist, but the Object must be *before* him / he has no imaginative memory. So much for his Intellectuals.—His manners are to 99 in 100 singularly repulsive—: brow-hanging, shoe-contemplative, *strange* / Sharp seemed to like him / but Sharp saw him only for half an hour, & that walking—he is, I verily believe, kindly-natured—is very fond of, attentive to, & patient with, children / but he is jealous, gloomy, & of an irritable Pride—& addicted to women, as objects of sexual Indulgence.[1] With all this, there is much good in him—he is dis-

---

[1] Coleridge's judgement was soon confirmed, for Hazlitt involved himself in an amatory escapade during his 1803 visit to the Lakes. See Letter 531. Both Coleridge and Wordsworth have left accounts of the sequel, in which

## 16 September 1803

interested, an enthusiastic Lover of the great men, who have been before us—he says things that are his own in a way of his own—& tho' from habitual Shyness & the Outside & bearskin at least of misanthropy, he is strangely confused & dark in his conversation & delivers himself of almost all his conceptions with a Forceps, yet he says more than any man, I ever knew, yourself only excepted, that is his own in a way of his own—& oftentimes when he has warmed his mind, & the synovial juice has come out & spread over his joints, he will gallop for half an hour together with real Eloquence. He sends well-headed & well-feathered Thoughts straight forwards to the mark with a Twang of the Bow-string.—If you could recommend him, as a Portrait-painter, I should be glad. To be your Companion he is, in my opinion, utterly unfit. His own Health is fitful.—I have written, as I ought to do, to you most freely imo ex corde / you know me, both head & heart, & will make what deductions, your reason will dictate to you. I can think of no other person. What wonder? For the last years I have been shy of all mere acquaintances—

> To live belov'd is all, I need,
> And whom I love, I love indeed.[1]

I never had any ambition; & now, I trust, I have almost as little Vanity.—

For 5 months past my mind has been strangely shut up. I have taken the paper with an intention to write to you many times / but it has been all one blank Feeling, one blank idealess Feeling. I had nothing to say, I could say nothing. How deeply I love you, my very Dreams make known to me.—I will not trouble you with the gloomy Tale of my Health. While I am awake, by patience, employment, effort of mind, & walking I can keep the fiend at Arm's length; but the Night is my Hell, Sleep my tormenting Angel. Three Nights out of four I fall asleeep, struggling to lie awake—& my frequent Night-screams have almost made me a nuisance in my own House. Dreams with me are no Shadows, but the very Substances & foot-thick Calamities of my Life. Beddoes, who has been to me ever a very kind man, suspects that my Stomach 'brews Vinegar'—it may be so —but I have no other symptom but that of Flatulence / shewing itself by an asthmatic Puffing, & transient paralytic Affections / this Flatulence has never any acid Taste in my mouth / I have now

---

they were instrumental in helping Hazlitt to escape the vengeance of the local residents. See E. L. G. ii. 178–9, 196–7; *Henry Crabb Robinson on Books and their Writers*, ed. by Edith J. Morley, 3 vols., 1938, i. 169–70; and Chambers, *Life*, 176.

[1] These are the concluding lines of *The Pains of Sleep*.

no bowel-rumblings. I am too careful of my Diet—the supercarbonated Kals. does me no service, nor magnesia—neither have I any headach. But I am grown hysterical.—Meantime my Looks & Strength have improved. I myself fully believe it to be either atonic, hypochondriacal Gout, or a scrophulous affection of the mesenteric Glands. In the hope of driving the Gout, if Gout it should be, into the feet, I walked, previously to my getting into the Coach at Perth, 263 miles in eight Days, with no unpleasant fatigue: & if I could do you any service by coming to town, & there were no Coaches, I would undertake to be with you, on foot, in 7 days.—I must have strength somewhere / My head is indefatigably strong, my limbs too are strong—but acid or not acid, Gout or Scrofula, Something there is [in] my stomach or Guts that transubstantiates my Bread & Wine into the Body & Blood of the Devil— Meat & Drink I should say—for I eat but little bread, & take nothing, in any form, spirituous or narcotic, stronger than Table Beer.—I am about to try the new Gout Medicine / & if it cures me, I will turn Preacher, form a new Sect in honor of the Discoverer, & make a greater clamour *in his Favor*, as the Antipodagra, 'that was to come & is already in the world', than ever the Puritans did *against* the poor Pope, as Anti-christ.—All my Family are well. Southey, his Wife & Mrs Lovell are with us. He has lost his little Girl, the unexpected Gift of a long marriage, & stricken to the very Heart is come hither for such poor comforts as my society can afford him.——To diversify this dusky Letter I will write in a Post-script an Epitaph, which I composed in my Sleep for myself, while dreaming that I was dying. To the best of my recollection I have not altered a word—Your's, dear Wedgwood, and of all, that are dear to you at Gunville, gratefully & most affectionately, S. T. Coleridge

Epitaph[1]

Here sleeps at length poor Col, & without Screaming,
Who died, as he had always liv'd, a dreaming:
Shot dead, while sleeping, by the Gout within,
Alone, and all unknown, at E'nbro' in an Inn.

It was on Tuesday Night last at the Black Bull, Edinburgh—

[1] *Poems*, ii, 970.

### 521. *To Sir George and Lady Beaumont*

*Address*: Sir G. Beaumont, Bart | Dunmow | Essex
*MS*. Pierpont Morgan Lib. *Pub. with omis*. Memorials of Coleorton, *i*. 6 and 26.
*Postmark*: 26 September ⟨1803⟩.  *Stamped*: Keswick.

Greta Hall, Keswick. Sept. 22. 1803

My dear Sir George | and | Dear Lady Beaumont

I reached my home this day week. Need I say that I have been ill or that I should have written immediately? The attacks of the Gout, now no longer doubtful, have become formidable in the Stomach, & my nature is making continual tho' hitherto alas! fruitless efforts to throw the Disease into the Extremities / and as it never rains but it pours I have an intermittent Fever with severe Hemicrania, which returns every evening at ½ past 5, & has hitherto baffled the use of Bark. Yet I am strong, & have far better appetite than usual, & never in my Life *looked* so well, which is owing in part to the *Tan* from Sun, wind, & Rain. At Perth I received two Letters from Southey, the first informing me of his approaching Loss, the second of his arrival at Keswick / I altered my plans immediately—took my place in the Mail, & hastened home to yield him what small comfort, my society might afford. Previously to my taking the Coach, I had walked 263 miles in 8 days, in the hope of forcing the Disease into the extremities—and so strong am I, that I would undertake at this present time to walk 50 miles a day for a week together. In short, while I am in possession of my will & my Reason, I can keep the Fiend at arm's Length; but with the Night my Horrors commence—during the whole of my Journey three nights out of four I have fallen asleep struggling & resolving to lie awake, & awaking have blest the Scream which delivered me from the reluctant Sleep. Nine years ago I had three months' Visitation of this kind, and I was cured by a sudden throwing-off of a burning corrosive acid—these Dreams with all their mockery of Guilt, Rage, unworthy Desires, Remorse, Shame, & Terror formed at that time the subject of some Verses, which I had forgotten till the return of the Complaint, & which I will send you in my next as a curiosity.[1]—But God be praised! tho' it be hard to bear up, I do bear up, in the deep faith that all things work together for Good to him who in the simplicity of his Heart desires Good.—To morrow I expect to receive the new Gout medicine from Welles, who in consequence of a Request

---

[1] There is no corroboration of a 'three months' Visitation' in 1794, nor is there any evidence, beyond the statement here, that Coleridge composed *The Pains of Sleep* at that time. See Letter 516.

## To Sir George and Lady Beaumont

from my friend, Dr Beddoes, has written me a very obliging Letter. If he cure me, I will raise up a new Sect in his honor, & make a greater clamour *in his favor* as the Anti-podagra, 'that was to come & is already in the World' than ever the Puritans did *against* the poor Pope, as the Anti-christ.—I left Wordsworth & his Sister at Loch Lomond / I was so ill that I felt myself a Burthen on them / & the Exercise was too much for me, & yet not enough.—I sent my cloathes &c forward to Edinburgh / & walked myself to Glen Coe, & so on as far as Cullen, then back again to Inverness, & thence over that most desolate & houseless Country by Aviemore, Dalnacardoch, Dalwhinny, Tummel Bridge, Kenmore, to Perth, with various Digressions & mountain climbings.—At the Bridge of the Sark, which divides England from Scotland I determined to write to you—at the foot of Loch Ketterin, under the agitation of Delight produced by the Trossachs, I began a Letter to you / but my fits became so violent & alarming, that I was truly incapable of doing more, than taking a few notes in my pocket-book. At Fort William on entering the public House I fell down in an hysterical Fit with long & loud weeping to my own great metaphysical amusement, & the unutterable consternation & *bebustlement* of the Landlord, his Wife, children, & Servants, who all gabbled Gaelic to each other, & sputtered out short-winded English to me in a strange Style.—So much 'all about myself'. I will send you my whole Tour in the course of the ensuing fortnight, in two or three successive Letters.—Wordsworths will be home, Deo volente, on Saturday.—Poor Mrs Southey droops, but not so much as I expected: & I suspect & hope, that the best consolation is about to be given them /. Southey who is a very amiable man & very much improved in every respect, bears it well—it is a Loss which will never leave his memory, nor master his fortitude & resignation.

My dear & honored Friends! my spirit has been with you day after day. Yesterday Afternoon I found among Southey's Books a Tetraglott Edition of Paschal's Provincial Letters / I seized it, O how eagerly! It seemed to me as if I saw Lady Beaumont with my very eyes; and heard over again the very sounds of those words, in which she had expressed her enthusiastic Admiration of him. Tho' but a wretched French Scholar, I did not go to bed before I had read the Preface & the two first Letters. They are not only excellent; but the excellence is altogether of a new kind to me. Wit, Irony, Humour, Sarcasm, Scholastic Subtilty, & profound Metaphysics all combined—& this strange combination still more strangely co-existing with child-like Simplicity, Innocence, unaffected Charity, & the very soul of Christian Humility.—And the Style is a robe of pure Light.—

## 22 September 1803

We have Mr Clarkson here / so that we have a houseful—& my wife is chin-deep in occupation with the children & the meals—for we have but one Servant, & can procure no other till November. She will however write to Lady B. in answer to her kind Letter of to day as speedily as possible.—I send with this a Sheet full of Verses, that I had promised / your kindness, my dear Sir G., will make you think them almost worth the Postage.—In a few weeks I shall, if I live & am tolerably well, send you three Specimens of my *Translations* from your Drawings. If you should really like them, I will go on & make a Volume / I cannot help saying, & it seems as if I had more Love toward you than toward myself in my heart while I am saying it, that I myself have been unusually pleased with what I have done—My honored Friends! [with un-] affected esteem, gratitude & affectionate Admirati[on,]

[Y]our's, S. T. C.—

Mont Blanc, the summit of the Vale of Chámouny, an Hour before Sunrise—An Hymn.[1]

>Hast thou a charm to stay the Morning Star
>In his steep Course? So long he seems to pause
>On thy bald awful Top, O Chamouny!
>The Arve and Arveiron at thy Base
>Rave ceaselessly; but thou, dread Mountain Form!
>Risest from out thy silent Sea of Pines,
>How silently! Around thee, and above,
>Deep is the Sky and black! transpicuous, black,
>An ebon Mass! Methinks, thou piercest it,
>As with a Wedge!——
>              But when I look again,
>It is thy own calm Home, thy chrystal Shrine,
>Thy Habitation from Eternity!
>O dread and silent Form! I gaz'd upon thee,
>Till thou, still present to my bodily sense,
>Didst vanish from my Thought—entranc'd in prayer,
>I worshipp'd the Invisible alone.
>Yet thou meantime wast working on my Soul,
>Even like some deep enchanting Melody,
>So sweet, we know not, we are list'ning to it:
>Now I awake! and with a busier mind
>And active Will self-conscious, offer now
>Not, as before, involuntary Prayer
>And passive Adoration!

---

[1] *Poems*, i. 376. See Letters 456 and 459.

## To Sir George and Lady Beaumont

       Hand and Voice,
Awake, awake! And thou, my Heart, awake!
Green Fields and icy Cliffs! all join my Hymn!

And thou, thou silent Mountain, lone and bare!
O* struggling with the Darkness all the Night
And visited all night by Troops of Stars,
Or when they climb the Sky, or when they sink;
Companion of the Morning Star at Dawn,
Thyself Earth's rosy Star, and of the Dawn
Co-herald—wake, O wake, and utter praise!
Who sank thy sunless Pillars deep in Earth?
Who fill'd thy Countenance with rosy Light?
Who made thee Father of perpetual Streams?

And You, ye five wild Torrents, fiercely glad!
Who call'd you forth from Night and utter Death,
From Darkness let you loose and icy Dens,
Down those precipitous, black, jagged Rocks
For ever shatter'd, and the same for ever!
Who gave you your invulnerable Life,
Your Strength, your Speed, your Fury, and your Joy,
Eternal Thunder, and unceasing Foam?
And who commanded (and the Silence came)
Here shall your Billows stiffen and have rest?

Ye Ice-falls! Ye that from the Mountain's brow
*Adown†  enormous* RAVINES *steeply slope,*
Torrents, methinks, that heard a mighty Voice
And stopp'd at once amid their maddest Plunge,
Motionless Torrents! silent Cataracts!
Who made you glorious, as the Gates of Heaven,
Beneath the keen full Moon? Who bade the Sun
Cloathe you with Rainbows? who with ‡ lovely Flowers
Of living Blue spread garlands at your Feet?

---

 * I had written a much finer Line when Sca' Fell was in my Thoughts— viz—

   O blacker than the Darkness all the Night,
   And visited &c— [Note by S. T. C.]

 † *a bad line*; & I hope to be able to alter it. [S. T. C.]

 ‡ The Gentiana major grows in large companies a stride's distance from the foot of several of the Glaciers—It's *blue* Flower, the Colour of Hope—is it not a pretty Emblem of Hope creeping onward even to the edge of the Grave— to the very Verge of utter Desolation? [Note by S. T. C.]

## 22 September 1803

God! let the Torrents, like a Shout of Nations,
Utter! Thou Ice-plain, burst, and answer, God!
God, sing, ye Meadow-streams with gladsome Voice,
Ye Pine-groves, with your soft and soul-like Sound!
And ye too have a Voice, ye Towers of Snow!
Ye perilous Snow-towers, fall and thunder, God!
Ye azure Flowers, that skirt the eternal Frost!
Ye wild-goats bounding by the eagle's Nest!
Ye Eagles, play-mates of the Mountain Storm!
Ye Lightnings, the dread Arrows of the Clouds!
Ye Signs and Wonders of the Element—
Utter forth, God! and fill the Hills with Praise!

And thou, thou silent Mountain, lone and bare!
Whom as I lift again my Head, bow'd low
In Adoration, I again behold!
And from thy Summit upward to thy Base
Sweep slowly with dim Eyes suffus'd with Tears!
Rise, mighty Form! even as thou *seem'st* to rise!
Rise, like a Cloud of Incense, from the Earth!
Thou kingly Spirit thron'd among the Hills,
Thou dread Ambassador from Earth to Heaven,
Great Hierarch! tell thou the silent Stars,
Tell the blue Sky, and tell the rising Sun,
Earth with her thousand Voices calls on God!

    4 last Stanzas of an Ode to Tranquillity.[1]

Tranquillity! thou better Name
Than all the Family of Fame!
Thou ne'er wilt leave my riper Age
To low Intrigue and factious Rage:
For O! dear child of thoughtful Truth!
To Thee I gave my early Youth,
And left the Bark, and blest the stedfast Shore,
Ere yet the Tempest rose and scar'd me with it's roar!

Who late and lingering seeks thy Shrine,
On him but seldom, Power divine!
Thy Spirit rests!—Satiety
And Sloth, poor Counterfeits of Thee,
Mock the tir'd Worldling: idle Hope
And dire Remembrance interlope,
And scare the fev'rish Slumbers of his Mind—
The Bubble floats before, the Spectre stalks behind!

[1] *Poems*, i. 360.

But me the Power divine will lead
At Morning thro' th' accustom'd Mead;
And in the sultry summer Heat
Will build me up a mossy Seat;
And when the Gust of Autumn crowds
And breaks the busy moonlight Clouds—
Thee best the thought will lift, the heart attune,
Light as the busy Clouds, calm as the gliding Moon.

The feeling Heart, the searching Soul,
To HER I dedicate the Whole!
And while within myself I trace
The greatness of some future Race,
Aloof with hermit eye I scan
The present Works of present Man—
A wild and dream-like Trade of Blood & Guile,
Too foolish for a Tear, too wicked for a Smile!
S. T. Coleridge

Extempore—to a Child of six years old—[1]
Do you ask what the Birds say? The Linnet, the Dove,
The Blackbird, the Thrush, say, I love and I love!
In the Winter they're silent, the Wind is so strong—
What *It* says, I don't know, but it sings a loud Song.
But green Leaves, and blossoms, and sunny warm weather,
And singing and loving all come back together.
I love and I love almost all the Birds say
From Sunrise to Star-rise, so gladsome are they;
But the Lark is so brimful of Gladness and Love,
The green fields below him, the blue Sky above,
That he sings and he sings and for ever sings he—
I love my Love, and my Love loves me!     S. T. Coleridge—

## 522. *To Sir George and Lady Beaumont*

*Address*: Single Sheet | Sir George Beaumont, Bart | Dunmow | Essex
[Readdressed in another hand] Coleorton | hall | Ashby De la Zouch | Lastershire
*MS. Pierpont Morgan Lib. Pub. with omis.* Memorials of Coleorton, *i. 12.*
*Postmark*: 4 October 1803.

Grieta Hall, Keswick. Oct. 1. 1803.—11 o/clock

My dear & honored Friends

I received your kind Letter this afternoon; and yet have but this moment read it—I have been fighting up against so severe a tooth

[1] *Poems*, i. 386.

& face ache / Every morning, since my last, I have risen calculating on the pleasure—& indeed & indeed it is a very great one—of writing a long Letter to you; but what with the Disease & what with the medicine, I have been unable to do any thing but read in silence, or listen to my friend's recitations. Mr Edmondson has no doubt, that I have Gout; but very serious doubts whether my worst sufferings do not originate in an affection of the mesenteric Glands. However, I shall give a fair Trial to this new Gout medicine;[1] tho' it is a very rough Handler of my inner man, dies me thro' & thro'—makes a stir & push & bustle in my Legs & Feet, so that I nightly expect a full fit; but hitherto it has gone off in a profuse perspiration. These Lines I have written with the new medicine—a good Ink for an Author, if it stands—(at least, according to a Printer's patter) his pages would continue to be thoroughly medicinal!—I have thought of writing an Ode on Punning, of which the first words were to be, SPELLING ... state.

O dear Sir George! you bid me 'above all things abstain from reading by night.' Believe me, nine times out of ten I have transgressed in this way, only from the *dread* of falling asleep; & I contracted the Habit from awaking in terrors about an hour after I had fallen asleep, & from the being literally afraid to trust myself again out of the leading-strings of my Will & Reason. So I have lit my Candle, stirred up my fire, & studied till day light. I fear, I fear, that a hot climate is my only medicine; & it seems better to die than to live out of England. I have been extremely affected by the death of young Emmett[2]—just 24!—at that age, dear Sir George! I was retiring from Politics, disgusted beyond measure by the manners & morals of the Democrats, & fully awake to the inconsistency of my practice with my speculative Principles. My speculative Principles were wild as Dreams—they were 'Dreams linked to purposes of Reason'; but they were perfectly harmless— a compound of Philosophy & Christianity. They were Christian, for they demanded the direct reformation & voluntary act of each Individual prior to any change in his outward circumstances, & my whole Plan of Revolution was confined to an experiment with a dozen families in the wilds of America: they were philosophical, because I contemplated a possible consequent amelioration of the Human Race in it's present state & in this world; yet christian still, because I regarded this earthly amelioration as important chiefly for it's effects on the future State of the Race of man so

---

[1] The remainder of this paragraph, which Coleridge wrote with his gout medicine instead of ink, has faded and is all but illegible.

[2] Robert Emmet (1778–1803), the Irish patriot, was executed on 20 Sept. 1803 for leading an uprising in which Lord Kilwarden was murdered.

ameliorated. Dear good Mrs Carter thought wisely and accurately as well as charitably. For what is the nature & the beauty of Youth? Is it not this—to know what is right in the abstract, by a living feeling, by an intuition of the uncorrupted Heart? To body forth this abstract right in beautiful Forms? And lastly to project this phantom-world into the world of Reality, like a catoptrical mirror? Say rather, to make ideas & realities stand side by side, the one as vivid as the other, even as I have often seen in a natural well of translucent water the *reflections* of the lank weeds, that hung down from it's sides, standing upright, and like Substances, among the substantial water-plants, that were growing on the bottom.— And thus far all was well—the mists of the Dawn of Reason coloured by the rich clouds, that precede the rising Sun. But my relations, & the Churchmen & 'Aristocrats,' to use the phrase of the Day—these too conceited my phantoms to be substances / only what I beheld as Angels they saw as Devils, & tho' they never ceased to talk of my Youth as a proof of the falsehood of my opinions they never introduced it as an extenuation of the error. My *opinions* were the Drivel of a Babe, but the Guilt attached to them, this was the Grey Hair & rigid Muscle of inveterate Depravity. To such Bigotry what was an enthusiastic young man likely to oppose? They abhorred my person, I abhorred their actions: they set up the long howl of Hydrophoby at my principles, & I repayed their Hatred & Terror by the bitterness of Contempt. Who then remained to listen to me? to be kind to me? to be my friends —to look at me with kindness, to shake my hand with kindness, to open the door, & spread the hospitable board, & to let me feel that I was a man well-loved—me, who from my childhood have had no avarice, no ambition—whose very vanity in my vainest moments was $\frac{9}{10}$ths of it the desire, & delight, & necessity of loving & of being beloved?—These offices of Love the Democrats only performed to me; my own family, bigots from Ignorance, remained wilfully ignorant from Bigotry. What wonder then, if in the heat of grateful affection & the unguarded Desire of sympathizing with these who so kindly sympathized with me, I too often deviated from my own Principles? And tho' I detested Revolutions in my calmer moments, as attempts, that were necessarily baffled & made blood-horrible by the very causes, which could alone justify Revolutions (I mean, the ignorance, superstition, profligacy, & vindictive passions, which are the natural effects of Despotism & false Religion)—and tho' even to extravagance I always supported the Doctrine of absolute unequivocal non-resistance—yet with an ebullient Fancy, a flowing Utterance, a light & dancing Heart, & a disposition to catch fire by the very rapidity of my own motion, & to speak vehemently from mere verbal associations, choosing sentences & sentiments for the very reason, that would have made me recoil with a dying away of the Heart & an unutterable Horror from the actions expressed in such sentences & sentiments—namely, because they were wild, & original, & vehement & fantastic!—I aided the Jacobins, by witty sarcasms & subtle reasonings & declamations full of genuine feeling against all Rulers & against all established Forms!—Speaking in public at Bristol I adverted to a public Supper which had been given by Lord —— I forget his name, in honor of a victory gained by the Austrians, & after a turbid Stream of wild Eloquence I said—'This is a true Lord's Supper in the communion of Darkness! This is a Eucharist of Hell! A sacrament of Misery!—Over each morsel & each Drop of which the Spirit of some murdered Innocent cries aloud to God, This is *my* Body! & this is my Blood!—'—These words form alas! a faithful specimen of too many of my Declamations at that Time / fortunately for me, the Government, I suppose, knew that both Southey & I were utterly unconnected with any party or club or society—(& this praise I must take to myself, that I disclaimed all these Societies, these Imperia in Imperio, these Ascarides in the Bowels of the State, subsisting on the weakness & diseasedness, & having for their final Object the Death of that State, whose Life had been their Birth & growth, & continued to be their sole nourishment—. All such Societies, under whatever name, I abhorred as wicked Conspiracies—and to this principle I adhered immoveably, simply because it was a principle, & this at a time when the Danger attached to the opposite mode of conduct would have been the most seducing Temptation to it—at a time when in rejecting these secret associations, often as I was urged to become a member now of this & now of that, I felt just as a religious young officer may be supposed to feel, who full of courage dares refuse a challenge—& considered as a Coward by those around him often shuts his eyes, & anticipates the moment when he might leap on the wall & stand in the Breach, the first & the only one.—) This insulation of myself & Southey, I suppose, the Ministers knew / knew that we were Boys: or rather, perhaps, Southey was at Lisbon, & I at Stowey, sick of Politics, & sick of Democrats & Democracy, before the Ministers had ever heard of us: for our career of Sedition, our obedience to Sympathy & pride of Talent in opposition to our own—certainly, to *my* own—uniform principles, lasted but 10 months. Yet if in that time I had been imprisoned, as in the rigor of the Law, I doubt not, I might have been 50 times —for the very clank of the Chains, that were to be put about my Limbs, would not at that time have deterred me from a strong

Phrase or striking Metaphor, altho' I had had no other inducement to the use of the same except the wantonness of luxuriant Imagination, & my aversion to abstain from any thing simply because it was dangerous—yet if in that time I had been imprisoned, my health & constitution were such as that it would have been almost as certain Death to me, as the Executioner has been to poor young Emmett. Like him, I was very young, very enthusiastic, distinguished by Talents & acquirements & a sort of turbid Eloquence; like him, I was a zealous Partisan of Christianity, a Despiser & Abhorrer of French Philosophy & French Morals; like him, I would have given my body to be burnt inch by inch, rather than that a French Army should have insulted my native Shores / & alas! alas! like him, I was unconsciously yet actively aiding & abetting the Plans, that I abhorred, & the men, who were more, far more unlike me, in every respect, in education, habits, principles & feelings, than the most anathematized Aristocrat among my opponents. Alas! alas! unlike *me*, he did not awake! the country, in which he lived, furnished far more plausible arguments for his active Zeal than England could do; the vices of the party, with whom he acted, were so palpably the effect of darkest Ignorance & foulest oppression, that they could not disgust him / the worse the vices, & the more he abhorred them, the more he loved the men themselves, abstracting the men from their vices, the vices from the men, & transferring them, with tenfold Guilt, to the state of Society & to the Orange Faction holding together that State of Society, which he believed to be the cause of these Vices! Ah woe is me! & in this mood the poor young Enthusiast sent forth that unjustifiable Proclamation, one sentence of which clearly permitted unlimited assassination—the only sentence, beyond all doubt, which Emmett would gladly have blotted out with his Heart's Blood, & of which at the time he wrote it he could not have seen the Import—& the only sentence, which was fully realized in action—! This moment it was a few unweighed words of an empassioned Visionary, in the next moment it became the foul Murder of Lord Kilwarden!—O my heart give praise, give praise!—not that I was preserved from Bonds, or Ignominy or Death! But that I was preserved from Crimes that it is almost impossible not to call Guilt!—And poor young Emmet[t!] O if our Ministers had saved him, had taken his Oath & word of honor, to have remained in America or some of our Colonies for the next 10 years of his Life, we *might* have had in him a sublimely great man, we assuredly sh[ould] have had in him a good man, & heart & soul an *Englishman*!—Think of Lord Mansfield![1]—About the Age of poor Emmett he drank the Pre-

[1] William Murray (1705–93), later Earl of Mansfield, was accused of 'toast-

tender's Health on his Knees, & was obnoxious to all the pains & penalties of high Treason. And where lies the Difference between the two? Murray's Plot had for it's object a foul Slave[ry] under the name of Loyalty; Emmett's as foul a Slavery under the nam[e of] Liberty & Independence.—But whatever the Ministers may have done, Heaven h[as] dealt kindly with the young man. He has died, firm, & in the height & heat of his Spirit, beholding in his Partizans only the wickedly oppressed, in his enemies the wicked oppressors.—O if his mad mad Enterprize had succeeded /!—Thou most mistaken & bewildered young Man, if other Punishment than the Death thou hast suffered, be needful for thy deadly Error, what better Punishment, what fitter Purgatory can be imagined, than a Vision presented to thee & conceived as real, a Vision of all the Massacres, the furious Passions, the Blasphemies, Sensualities, Superstitions, the bloody Persecutions, and mutual Cannibalism of Atheist & Papist, that would have rushed in, like a Torrent of Sulphur & burning Chaos, at the Breach which thou thyself hadst made—till thou, yea, even thou thyself hadst called out in agony to the merciless Gaul, & invoked an army of Slave-fiends to crush the more enormous evil of a mob of Fiends in Anarchy.—My honored Friends! as I live, I scarcely know what I have been writing; but the very circumstance of writing to *you*, added to the recollection of the unwise & unchristian feelings, with which at poor Emmett's Age *I* contemplated all persons of *your* rank in Society, & *that* recollection confronted with my present Feelings towards you—it has agitated me, dear Friends! and I have written, my Heart at a full Gallop adown Hill.—And now, good night—I will finish this Letter tomorrow morning. The moon is in the very height & 'keystone' of the Sky, & all the mountains thro' the whole vale are, in consequence, things of the Earth: a few Hours ago when the Moon was rising from behind Latterig, & when the clouds on Causa & Grisedale Pikes, opposite my study window, caught it's Light; then all the mountains belonged to the Sky.—No one who has not suffered what I suffer in my sleep can conceive the depth & fervor, with which I wish that you may be asleep, dreamless or with such Dreams as leave no other trace behind them but the dim recollection that you had been dreaming!—Sunday Morning—I o clock.

Sunday Noon.—I was much affected by the beautiful passage, which Lady Beaumont was so good as to extract from her Sister's Letter. I would, that she & you two, were all here, even now, & looking out from my Study window. Great indeed is the charm,

ing the Pretender in old days at the house of a Jacobite mercer in Ludgate', but in 1752–3 his denial was accepted by the Cabinet.

which yearning memory gives to the Forms of Things; yet the *Present* would plead it's cause most eloquently from Skiddaw & Swinside, rich with all the hues of decaying Fern, the colour of the unripe Lime, of the ripe Lemon, of the bright orange, even to the depth of dried orange Peel / & when the whole shall have become of this last colour, then [the] decaying Birches will have put on the very same lovely Lemon-colour, which the Ferns have in their middle Stage of Decay. How kind Nature is to us—! where Decay is pernicious, she renders it offensive, as in all animal substances / but where it is innocuous, she makes it rival the Spring-tide *Growth* in Beauty. I use the word 'Nature' partly to avoid the too frequent use of a more awful name, & partly to indulge the sense of the *motherliness* of general Providence—when the Heart is not strong enough to lift itself up to a distinct contemplation of the Father of all things.—

It gives me sincere pleasure, that my Ode has pleased you—sometime or other I hope to finish it. I have sent Lady Beaumont the poems entitled Chamouny, the Inscription for the Fountain,[1] & Tranquillity.—Of the poems on your Sketches, dear Sir George! I hope thus much / that they will give evidence that the Drawings acted upon my mind as Nature does, in it's after workings—they have mingled with my Thoughts, & furnished Forms to my Feelings.—

Southey seems very happy, at present. His eyes plague him; but he is a hard Task-master to them. He is the most industrious man, I know or have ever known. His present occupations are, the re-composition of his Madoc, an epic Poem / & his great History of Portugal—of which he has written considerably more than a Quarto Volume.——We have not heard of or from Hazlitt. He is at Manchester, we suppose: & has both Portraits with him.[2]—The children are all well / & Derwent is a cube of Fat. Little Sara must be on the brink of Teething—she is 9 months old, & has no signs of a Tooth / the next 2 months will probably be a hard Time for her.—The pain & dangerous Diseases incident to Teething I have ever regarded as the most anomalous of the Dispensations of Nature, & their final cause the most obscure.—Bless me, what a Letter!——I am almost ashamed to send it—unless I might dare to say with St Augustine, Ep. 72. A *tedious* Length! sed non

---

[1] Actually Coleridge had sent *Extempore* instead.

[2] Hazlitt returned to Keswick in October. Notebook entries show that he was there by 24 Oct. and that Coleridge again sat for his portrait on 27 Oct. (Information kindly supplied from Coleridge's notebook by Miss Kathleen Coburn.) Apparently Hazlitt had returned to put some finishing touches on Coleridge's portrait. See P. P. Howe, *The Life of William Hazlitt*, 1947, p. 71.

apud te, cui nulla est pagina gratior quam quae me loquaciorem apportat tibi.——I remain, my honored Friends, with grateful & affectionate Esteem

your's ever & truly, S. T. Coleridge.

P.S. How does your Health bear up under the bustle of military Preparation? Are you much engaged in it?—

### 523. *To George Coleridge*

*Address*: Reverend G. Coleridge | Ottery St Mary | Honiton | Devon.
*MS. Lady Cave and Victoria University Lib. Pub. E. L. G. i. 281.* After filling four pages of a letter to his brother and not having exhausted himself, Coleridge wrote the conclusion on a sheet containing a letter from his wife to Mrs. George Coleridge.
*Postmark*: 5 ⟨October⟩ ⟨1803.⟩   *Stamped*: Keswick.

Greta Hall, Keswick. Oct. 2. 1803. Sunday Evening

My dear Brother

I have this moment received your's of Sept. 28th /. It is indeed very long since I have written to you—the sole reason has been, that I had nothing to communicate that was not of a depressing nature: & I am sick to the very soul of speaking or writing concerning my bodily miseries. My Disorder is supposed to be atonic Gout; in addition to which my medical friends suspect a scrofulous affection of the mesenteric Glands. While I am awake, & retain possession of my Will & Reason, I can contrive to keep the Fiend at Arm's length; but Sleep throws wide open all the Gates of the beleaguered City—& such an Host of Horrors rush in—that three nights out of four I fall asleep struggling to lie awake, and start up & bless my own loud Screams, that have awakened me. In the Hope that change of Scene might relieve me, & that hard Exercise might throw the Disease into the *Extremities*, I left my Home on August 15th & made the Tour of Scotland /—and I am certainly better since my return, tho' I have a troublesome intermittent fever, that recurs with very severe Hemicrania, about 5 o clock every afternoon—& which has hitherto baffled the use of Bark.—Meantime I am neither weakened nor emaciated. The last 8 days of my walk I walked 263 miles—about 34 miles a day on an average. Since my return I have been trying the celebrated new Gout medicine, & have had less affrightful Nights, & some symptoms of a disease ripening in the feet. No Bridegroom ever longed for rapture with more impatience than I do for Torture. So much of myself—which I have written not without reluctance.—Just before my arrival at Perth my heart had been visited with many tender Yearnings

## To George Coleridge

toward you & your family—and indeed to all my Kin. I resolved if my Health should be endurable, & if I could arrange my money-matters so as to make such a journey right & convenient—to leave this place in the latter end of October with my family, & having passed a week or so with Sir G. Beaumont at Dunmow to push forward for Ottery—& there to stay till Spring. But at Perth I found Letters from Southey—his little Girl, an unexpected Gift after a 7 years' marriage, died of water on the Brain from teething —and Southey & his Wife, almost heart-broken, immediately left Bristol, & came to Keswick, Southey for the comforts, he expected from my society, & Mrs Southey to be with her Sister.—Still it is not improbable, that I may spend my Christmas among you—only I shall come alone.——

These, dear Brother! are awful Times; but I really see no reason for any feelings of Despondency. If it be God's will, that the commercial Gourd should be canker-killed—if our horrible Iniquities in the W. India Islands & on the coasts of Guinea call for judgment on us—God's will be done!—Yet Providence seldom destroys a nation without first degrading it—the Romans were effeminate, cowardly, basely oblivious of all public virtues, & below all comparison inferior to their barbarian Overwhelmers in domestic virtues, when Rome fell before the Huns—Now bad as we may be, we assuredly are the best among the nations—in strength & *individual* Valour superior to our enemies, & not so much their inferior in military Skill as to counterbalance our vast advantage in point of numbers. The times are awful—I keep my spirit still & in a kind of devotional Calm; & I trust, would meet 'the sweet & Graceful Death pro patriâ' with as high an enthusiasm, as ever Spartan did. But I seriously think, that this Invasion, if attempted in vehement good earnest by the Corsican Tippoo Saib,[1] will be a Blessing to this Country & to Europe. Let us be humble before our Maker, but not spirit-palsied before our blood-thirsty Enemies. We will tremble at the possible punishment, which our national crimes may have made us worthy of, from retributive Providence; we will tremble at what God may do; but not at what our enemies can do, of themselves. When were we a more united People? When so well prepared? The very nature of the Invasion will cut off from the French army most of the opportunities of military Tactics—& bring the affair, man to man, bayonet against bayonet.—

That this day was coming, I foresaw at the conclusion of the Peace—& have not ceased in various ways & in various publications to warn & alarm the country—& it is a comfort to me, far

---

[1] Tippoo Sahib, Sultan of Mysore, long a foe of the British, was finally killed at the storming of Seringapatam, 4 May 1799.

beyond all the little vanities of Authorship, that my Essays & Alarum-trumpets in the Morning Post had an immediate & very extensive effect. Heaven knows! what a sacrifice I made in thus forcing myself away from the abstruse Researches, in which I am engaged, to embark on this stormy Sea of Politics—but I felt it my Duty, the more especially as my former Essays during the Peace were those that had so extravagantly irritated the First Consul. In March, 1800, I published in the Morning Post a long & very severe 'Character of Mr Pitt,' promising at the same time a Character of Bonaparte. Since the Time of Junius no single Essay ever made more noise in a newspaper than this—& day after day my character of Bonaparte was promised. I did not do it for reasons that appeared very forcible to me / in somewhat more than a month after the appearance of 'PITT,' Otto[1] sent privately to Stuart, & inquired when the character of Bonaparte would appear—Stuart returned some evasive answer—& Otto then sent a confidential friend to Stuart to beg a particular answer, & this Friend communicated to Stuart, that the question was asked at the instance of Bonaparte himself, who had been extremely impressed with the character of Pitt, & very anxious to see his own—which, no doubt he expected, would be a pure eulogy.—Stuart immediately came to me, & was in very high spirits on the occasion—I turned sad, & answered him—['] Stuart, that man will prove a Tyrant, & the deadliest enemy of the Liberty of the Press.'—'Indeed?'—['] Yes! a man, the Dictator of a vast Empire, to be so childishly solicitous for the *panegyric* of a Newspaper Scribbler—! will he not be equally irritable at the *Abuse* of newspaper Scribblers!—I am sick & sad, to feel how important little men become, when madmen are in power.'—Stuart has often talked of publishing this conversation of mine as an instance of political prophecy.—This will remind you of the Memoirs of P. P. Clerk of this Parish![2]—alas! that were no Burlesque in the present Day: & poor Dennis's request to the D. of Ma[r]lborough would now have nothing ridiculous in it.[3] The mad Vanity, & low *Detail* of vindictive Plans, of the first Consul are almost incredible. I will finish in my Wife's Letter.—

Continuation of my Letter.

Enough of Politics—at least, in *words*! I should have wholly ab-

[1] Louis-Guillaume Otto, French diplomat, who was sent to London in 1800 to arrange for the exchange of prisoners of war.

[2] For Pope's burlesque of Bishop Burnet, 'Memoirs of P. P. Clerk of This Parish', see *Works of Pope*, ed. by W. Elwin and W. J. Courthope, 10 vols., 1871–89, x. 435.

[3] John Dennis is said to have told the Duke of Marlborough of his fear that the French would make a stipulation for his extradition at the Peace of Utrecht.

stained from a subject that is truly wearisome to my Spirit, if your Letter, dear Friend of my Childhood, had not appeared to me to breathe despondency beyond the occasion.—I am sincerely & not slightly grieved that I have been silent so long. It is but a wretched Excuse to say, that all my friends have the same complaint to make: & in very truth my heart has been strangely shut up within itself.

> 'For not to *think* of what I needs must *feel*,
> But to be still and patient all, I can—
> And haply by abstruse Research to steal
> From my own Nature all the natural Man—
> This was my sole Resource, my wisest Plan!
> And that, which suits a Part, infects the Whole,
> And now is almost grown the Habit of my Soul!——'

I have sometimes derived a comfort from the notion, that possibly these horrid Dreams with all their mockery of Crimes, & Remorse, & Shame, & Terror, might have been sent upon me to arouse me out of that proud & stoical Apathy, into which I had fallen—it was Resignation indeed, for I was not an Atheist; but it was Resignat[ion]—witho[ut] religion because it was without struggle, without d[iff]iculty—because it originated in the Understanding & a stealing Sp[irit of] Contempt, not in the affections.——But amid all my [struggles I] have been a severe, perhaps, too severe a Student—[I have written] much & prepared materials for more—& yet I trus[t that I do not] deceive myself when I say, that I could leave al[l I have done] without a pang—. I have not read on an average less than 8 hours a day for the last three years—but all is vanity—I feel it more & more—all is vanity that does not lead to Quietness & Unity of Heart, and to the silent aweful idealess Watching of that living Spirit, & of that Life within us, which is the motion of that Spirit—that Life, which passeth all understanding.——Before I finish, let me say that there is yet one other cause of my silence —Your last Letter on Faith & Reason had affected me very deeply —I was sure, that we agreed in the depth & bottoms of our meaning —yet I thought that you had expressed yourself inaccurately—& began to reflect & make notes on the true Boundaries of Faith & Reason—till I found that I should have written a Treatise instead of a Letter.—However, it is my firm Intention, that in future no such unbrotherly Silence shall take place, on my part. You I have always loved & honored as more than mere Brother: & it was not my fault, that the mere names of Brother & of Kindred were of necessity less powerful in my feelings, than in those of other men who with perhaps vastly less Sensibility have had the good fortune to have been more domestically reared. But what I am is in consequence of what I have been; & there is enough in that, which I am, to be honorable & useful to my fellow-men, if the great Giver of all things give me the grace & the perseverance to call it forth wisely, & to apply it prudently.—I shall hope to hear soon again from you—in the mean time present my best Duty to our venerable Mother—my kindest Love to your Wife & fatherly wishes for your Children—to the Colonel, & all of his Family, & to Edward & those of his Household, a Brother's Love——& the same to Mrs Luke. My Derwent appears to me very like what William was when of the same age—

With affectionate Esteem & grateful & rememb'ring Love I am, my dearest Brother, ever your's, S. T. C.——

### 524. To Thomas Poole

*Address*: T. Poole, Esqre | Nether Stowey | Bridgewater | Somerset   *Single Sheet*
*MS. British Museum. Pub. E. L. G. i. 286.*
*Postmark*: 6 October 1803.

Oct. 3. 1803. Keswick

My dearest Friend

Tho' I should write but half a dozen Lines, I will write; for my long Silence affects [me] almost with a sense of Guilt. Continual Ill-health, & Discomforts almost worse than that, have shut me up strangely—I have written to no one—God forbid that my worst Enemy should ever have the Nights & the Sleeps that I have had, night after night—surprized by Sleep, while I struggled to remain awake, starting up to bless my own loud Screams that had awakened me—yea, dear friend! till my repeated Night-yells had made me a Nuisance in my own House. As I live & am a man, this is an unexaggerated Tale—my Dreams became the Substances of my Life—

> A lurid Light, a ghastly Throng—[1]
> Sense of insufferable wrong—
> And whom I scorn'd, they only strong!—
> Thirst of Revenge, the powerless will
> Still baffled, & yet burning still—
> Tempestuous pride, vain-glorious Vaunting,
> Base Men my vices justly taunting——
> Desire with Loathing strangely mixt,
> On wild or hateful Objects fix'd—
> Fantastic Passions, mad'ning Brawl,
> And Shame & Terror over all!—

[1] An amended version of *The Pains of Sleep*, lines 18–32. See *Poems*, i. 389.

> Deeds to be hid, that were not hid,
> Which, all confus'd I might not know,
> Whether I suffer'd or I did:
> For all was Guilt, & Shame, & Woe—
> My own or others', still the same,
> Life-stifling Fear, soul-stifling Shame!——

All symptoms conspired to prove that I had *Gout*, atonic stomach Gout, for one Disease—& my medical attendant suspected Mesenteric Scrofula, in addition.—I went into Scotland with Wordsworth & his Sister; but I soon found that I was a burthen on them / & Wordsworth, himself a brooder over his painful hypochondriacal Sensations, was not my fittest companion / so I left him & the Jaunting Car, & walked by myself far away into the Highlands—in the hopes of forcing the Disease into my extremities—at what a rate, you may guess, when I tell you, that the last eight Days I had walked 263 miles. At Perth I received two Letters from Southey, the first informing me of the certain Death of his Infant Child, & of the deplorable heart-stricken State in which he & his Wife were—& of their wish to be at Keswick, he expecting comfort from me, Edith from her Sister / the second informed me of their arrival at Keswick —I accordingly took a place in the Mail & hastened home / —Soon after I received a large *Cag* of the new Gout medicine / & assuredly, it has been of manifest service to me—& I write with my left hand swoln, & with strong symptoms of a fair full fit of the Gout in my Feet. No Bridegroom ever longed for Rapture more impatiently than I for Torture—It is wonderful, how this has relieved me! how balsam-sweet & profound my Sleep has been—how freely I breathe —how freely my Spirits seem to move within me!——So much of myself.

Southey seems very happy in my society—& tho' overpowered at moments, acts like a man.—

How are you employed? what part have you taken in this Alarm? —As to me, I think, the Invasion must be a Blessing. For if we do not repel it, & cut them to pieces, we are a vile sunken race / & it is good, that our Betters should *crack* us—And if we do act as Men, Christians, Englishmen—down goes the Corsican Miscreant, & Europe may have peace. At all events, dulce & decorum est pro patriâ mori—& I trust, I shall be found rather seeking than shunning it, if the French army should maintain it's footing, even for a fortnight.—Let me hear from you. It is not possible that you can feel any resentment now you know how calamitously I have been environed / Tell me all about yourself—what you are doing, what meditating—whether you can infuse any simple plain sense into

3 October 1803

the cerebellum of that foolish, well meaning Driveller, the Minister. —Southey tells me, that Rickman meant to apply to you[1]—Love to Ward—

S. T. Coleridge

## 525. To Thomas Poole

Address: T. Poole Esqre | N. Stowey | Bridgewater | Somerset  Single Sheet
MS. British Museum. Pub. with omis. E. L. G. i. 288.

Friday, Oct. 14. 1803. Greta Hall, Keswick

My dearest Poole

I received your letter this evening, thank you for your kindness in answering it immediately, and will prove my thankfulness by doing the same. In answer to your Question respecting Leslie & T. Wedgwood,[2] I say—to the best of my Knowlege, *Not a word, at any time*. I have examined & cross-examined my recollective Faculty with no common earnestness; and I cannot produce in myself even the dimmest *Feeling* of any such conversation. Yet I talk so much & so variously, that doubtless I say a thousand Things that exist in the minds of others, when to my own consciousness they are as if they had never been. I lay too many Eggs in the hot Sands with Ostrich Carelessness & Ostrich oblivion—And tho' many are luckily trod on & smashed; as many crawl forth into Life, some to furnish Feathers for the Caps of others, and more alas! to plume the Shafts in the Quivers of my Enemies and of them 'that lie in wait against my Soul.' But in the present instance, if I had mentioned any thing of the Kind, T. Wedgwood has so great a Love for you, as well as respect & affectionate Regard for Leslie, that he would have both suffered & expressed great Pain / I should have instantly felt that I had done wrong—& events of this sort I *never forget*. Likewise, I admire Leslie, & cherish high Hopes of him; & thought at the time, that part of your Dislike had been ill-founded, & that you had disliked him for a cause which had made you more than once treat me very harshly—namely, a supposed disposition in me to detract from the merits of two or three, whom you from childhood had been taught to contemplate with religious awe; but whom I thought very second rate Men / not sufficiently considering, that for one man whom Leslie or myself might *lower* in the Symposium of Genius, there are 10 faces unknown at present to you, whom we

[1] In Dec. 1803 Poole came to London on Rickman's invitation to prepare an abstract of returns concerning the poor ordered by the House of Commons from the parish overseers.
[2] Poole had asked Coleridge in a letter dated 9 Oct. 1803: 'Did you ever mention to T.W. that I disliked Leslie? tell me and what you said.'

should place at the head of the Table & in the places of Honor—in other words, that there is perhaps a larger mass (& a more frequent calling of it into activity) of awe & love of the great departed in my mind than in your's—This was in my Heart—for I suffered a great deal from your Expressions between Blandford & Gunville—& would of itself, have restrained me from making your Dislike a subject of Conversation / & as *to the other* cause of your Dislike, it is so very serious a Thing, that I should have thought myself downright a Rogue if I had mentioned it.—I think therefore, that without the least rashness I may *assert* at once, that I never did speak to T. W. on the subject. If any thing of this nature have come to his ears from me, it must have been thro' some third or fourth Person—Tobin for instance, who is an exceeding mischiefmaker, his Blindness, poor Fellow! making this sort of Gossip a high Treat to him / but I do not recollect having mentioned it to him—or to any one, but, I believe, to Wordsworth / and I hope therefore, that it will not have originated in me at all. It would be very, very painful to me. But I cannot be as confident of this, as of the former.[1] Since I finished the Letter, I seem to have some *dim*, very *dim*, Feeling of having mentioned it once to *Davy*. I seem to feel, as if I had not mentioned it to Wordsworth—but that *it was Davy*. But this is very likely to be all the mere straining of the memory—colours in the eyes from staring in the Dusk & rubbing them. Whoever mentioned [it] to T. W. acted a very unwise part—to use the mildest phrase. If I mentioned your Dislike of Leslie to T. W., it would have been assuredly mentioned as common to myself & to Leslie [you?]—and as arising from the same Cause—tho' the Dislike in my instance was only for the moment, a bubble broken by the agitation that gave it Birth.—O deeply, deeply do I detest this rage for Personality: & it is among the clamours of my Conscience, that I have so long delayed the Essay, which for so many years I have planned & promised!——

Wordsworth is in good health, & all his family. He has one LARGE Boy, christened John. He has made a Beginning to his Recluse. He was here on Sunday last: his Wife's Sister,[2] who is on a visit at Grasmere, was in a bad hysterical way, & he rode in to consult our excellent medical men. I now see very little of Wordsworth: my own Health makes it inconvenient & unfit for me to go thither one third as often, as I used to do—and Wordsworth's Indolence, &c keeps him at home. Indeed, were I an irritable man, and an unthinking one, I should probably have considered myself as having

---

[1] The three following sentences are interlined here in the MS.

[2] This refers to Joanna Hutchinson. See *Early Letters*, 336, for an account of her illness.

been very unkindly used by him in this respect—for I was at one time confined for two months, & he never came in to see me / me, who had ever payed such unremitting attentions to him. But we must take the good & the ill together; & by seriously & habitually reflecting on our own faults & endeavouring to amend them we shall then find little difficulty in confining our attention as far as it acts on our Friends' characters, to their good Qualities.—Indeed, I owe it to Truth & Justice as well as to myself to say, that the concern, which I have felt in this instance, and one or two other more *crying* instances, of Self-involution in Wordsworth, has been almost wholly a Feeling of friendly Regret, & disinterested Apprehension—I saw him more & more benetted in hypochondriacal Fancies, living wholly among *Devotees*—having every the minutest Thing, almost his very Eating & Drinking, done for him by his Sister, or Wife—& I trembled, lest a Film should rise, and thicken on his moral Eye.—The habit too of writing such a multitude of small Poems was in this instance hurtful to him—such Things as that Sonnet of his in Monday's Morning Post, about Simonides & the Ghost[1]— / I rejoice therefore with a deep & true Joy, that he has at length yielded to my urgent & repeated—almost unremitting—requests & remonstrances—& will go on with the Recluse exclusively.—A Great Work, in which he will sail; on an open Ocean, & a steady wind; unfretted by short tacks, reefing, & hawling & disentangling the ropes——great work necessarily comprehending his attention & Feelings within the circle of great objects & elevated Conceptions—this is his natural Element—the having been out of it has been his Disease—to return into it is the specific Remedy, both Remedy & Health. It is what Food is to Famine. I have seen enough, positively to give me feelings of hostility towards the plan of several of the Poems in the L. Ballads: & I really consider it as a misfortune, that Wordsworth ever deserted his former mountain Track to wander in Lanes & allies; tho'in the event it may prove to have been a great Benefit to him. He will steer, I trust, the middle course.—But he found himself to be, or rather to be called, the Head & founder of a *Sect* in Poetry: & assuredly he has written—& published in the M. Post, as W. L. D.[2] & sometimes with no signature —poems written with a *sectarian* spirit, & in a sort of Bravado.— I know, my dear Poole, that you are in the habit of keeping my Letters; but I must request of you, & do *rely* on it, that you will be so good as to destroy this Letter—& likewise, if it be not already

---

[1] *Poet. Works*, iii. 408. Wordsworth never reprinted the sonnet.

[2] In 1803 Wordsworth printed seven sonnets in the *Morning Post* with the signature W.L.D. The initials, Thomas Hutchinson suggests, stand for Wordsworthius Libertati dedicavit. *Poet. Works*, iii. 452.

done, that Letter which in the ebulliency of indistinct Conceptions I wrote to you respecting Sir Isaac Newton's Optics—& which to my *Horror* & Shame I saw that Ward had transcribed—a Letter which if I were to die & it should ever see the *Light* would damn me forever, as a man mad with Presumption.—[1]

Hartley is what he always was—a strange strange Boy—'*exquisitely wild*'![2] An utter Visionary! like the Moon among thin Clouds, he moves in a circle of Light of his own making—he alone, in a Light of his own. Of all human Beings I never yet saw one so utterly naked of *Self*—he has no Vanity, no Pride, no Resentment / and tho' *very passionate*, I never yet saw him *angry with* any body. He is, tho' now 7 years old, the merest Child, you can conceive—and yet Southey says, that the Boy keeps him in perpetual Wonderment—his Thoughts are so truly his own. [He is] not generally speaking an *affectionate* Child / but his Dispositions are very sweet. A great Lover of Truth, and of the finest moral nicety of Feeling —apprehension all over—& yet always Dreaming. He said very prettily about half a year ago—on my reproving him for some inattention, & asking him if he did not see something—[']My Father!['] quoth he with flute-like Voice—'I see it—I saw it—I see it now—& tomorrow I shall see it when I shut my eyes, and when my eyes are open & I am looking at other Things; but Father! it's a sad pity—but it can't be helped, you know—but I am always being a bad Boy, because I am always *thinking of my Thoughts*.'— He is troubled with Worms—& to night has had a clyster of oil & Lime water, which never fails to set him to rights for a month or two—. If God preserve his Life for me, it will be interesting to know what he will be—for it is not my opinion, or the opinion of two or of three—but all who have been with him, talk of him as of a thing that cannot be forgotten / Derwent, & my meek little Sara, the former is just recovering of a very bad epidemic Intermittent Fever, with tearing cough—& the other sweet Baby is even now suffering

---

[1] Coleridge was so disturbed over his letter of 23 Mar. 1801 (Letter 388) that he wrote again about it on 30 Jan. 1804 (Letter 544). Despite his wishes, both the original letter and Ward's copy still exist.

[2] Cf. *To H.C. Six Years Old*:

> O blessèd vision! happy child!
> Thou art so exquisitely wild,
> I think of thee with many fears
> For what may be thy lot in future years.
>
> . . . . . .
>
> Nature will either end thee quite;
> Or, lengthening out thy season of delight,
> Preserve for thee, by individual right,
> A young lamb's heart among the full-grown flocks.
>
> Wordsworth's *Poet. Works*, i. 247.

under it—. He is a fat large lovely Boy—in all things but his Voice very unlike Hartley—very vain, & much more fond & affectionate —none of his Feelings so profound—in short, he is just what a sensible Father ought to wish for—a fine, healthy, strong, beautiful child, with all his senses & faculties as they ought to be—with no chance, as to his person, of being more than a good-looking man, & as to his mind, no prospect of being more or less than a man of good sense & tolerably *quick parts.*—Sara is a remarkably interesting Baby, with the finest possible Skin & large blue eyes—& she smiles, as if she were basking in a sunshine, as mild as moonlight, of her own quiet Happiness.[1] She has had the Cow-pock. Mrs Coleridge enjoys her old state of excellent Health. We go on, as usual—except that tho' I do not love her a bit better, I quarrel with her much less. We cannot be said to live at all as Husband & Wife / but we are peaceable Housemates.—Mrs Lovell & Mrs Southey have miserable Health; but Mrs Southey, I hope, is breeding—& Mrs Lovell never can be well, while there exist in the world such Things as Tea, and Lavender & Hartshorn Slops, & the absence of religious, & the presence of depressing, Passions.—Southey I like more & more / he is a good man / & his Industry stupendous! Take him all in all, his regularity & domestic virtues, Genius, Talents, Acquirements, & Knowlege—& he stands by himself.— But Mrs S. & Mrs Lovell are a large, a very large Bolus!—but it is astonishing, how one's Swallow is enlarged by the sense of doing one's Duty—at least where the Pill is to pass off some time or other —& the Medicine to be discontinued.—But scarcely can even the sense of Duty reconcile one to taking Jalap regularly instead of Breakfast, Ipecacuanha for one's Dinner, Glauber's salt in hot water for one's Tea, & the whole of the foregoing in their different Metempsychoses after having passed back again thro' the mouth, or onwards thro' the Bowels, in a grand Maw-wallop for one's Supper.—My own Health is certainly improved by this new Gout medicine / I cannot however get delivered in a full natural way of this child of Darkness & Discomfort—always threatening & bullying—but the swelling never inflames sufficiently & all is commonly carried off in a violent Sweat—a long sudden soaking Sweat. But God be praised! my Nights since I last wrote have been astonishingly improved & I am confident now that my Complaint is nothing but flying Gout with a little Gravel.—This Letter I meant to be

[1] These descriptions of Hartley, Derwent, and Sara in some measure prognosticate the future of each child. Hartley was to become a poet and one of fortune's ne'er-do-wells, Derwent a successful clergyman and schoolmaster, and Sara a children's poet and editor, who with her husband strove to put her father's house in order. See E. L. Griggs, *Hartley Coleridge*, 1929, and *Coleridge Fille*, 1940.

## To Thomas Poole

about myself—O that I could but be in London with you. It seems to me that you are entering on the porch of a Temple, for which Nature has made & destined you to be the Priest. But more of this hereafter.——

I have been, to use a mild word, agitated by two INFAMOUS atrocious Paragraphs in the Morning Post of Thursday & Friday last—I believe them to be Mackintosh's—*O that they were*! I would hunt him into Infamy.—I am now exerting myself to the utmost on this Subject. Do write me *instantly what* you think of them / or rather, what you thought, what you felt, what you said!—

S. T. Coleridge

Many articles in the M. P. not mine are attributed to me. Very probably, those infamous articles may—Stuart has sold the paper for 15000£—he netted 8000£ a year—it was scarcely 2 years' purchase.—Do write instantly on the subject of this *No Quarter!*—
——I have written twice to Stuart who still, I believe, superintends the paper in part—& can get no answer from him.—Ever & for ever, dearest Friend, gratefully & with affectionate Esteem your's—

### 526. To Sir George Beaumont

*Address*: Sir G. Beaumont, Bart. | Dunmow | Essex [Readdressed in another hand] Sir Geo. Beaumont, Bart. | North Aston | Near Woodstock | Oxfordshire.
*MS. Cornell University Lib. Pub.* Some Letters of the Wordsworth Family, ed. by L. N. Broughton, 1942, p. 101.
*Postmark*: 22 October 1803. *Stamped*: Penrith.

Dear Sir George     Keswick, Monday, Oct. 16 [17]. 1803

I have had a large Sheet of Verses lying on my Desk for the last ten days, intended for Lady Beaumont: and I have wanted the heart to correct & send them off. They seemed so flat in themselves—and so unseasonable in the present awful crisis. I have been haunted with anxieties concerning you—my eyes ever & anon on the Map, now on Essex, & now on the Coast of France.—Dear Sir George, you are not a military man, nor possessed of military Science—night after night, I have been framing wishes that you were in Leicestershire, doing there what no one but yourself can do so well, namely, raising and organizing your Tenantry & Colliers—instead of remaining in the very heart of the Danger & the Anxiety, and where, I presume, all the Good has been done which your Presence was calculated to do. The form of Lady Beaumont & the imagined Form of your venerable Mother, are present to me / and I cannot help wishing & wishing that they were farther inland.

Do forgive me, dear Sir George! if I have presumed too far, in giving words to my feelings; but I am convinced, that there is no real Danger that threatens G. Britain as an Empire; but that the Plan of the Miscreant is that of a man mad with Hatred of Englishmen as Englishmen, & that he anticipates a relief to this infernal Passion by spreading Bloodshed & pitiless Devastation over particular Tracts—whatever part he may be able to disgorge his Troops on / tho' at the certainty of their final Destruction. If contrary to my deepest conviction, I find the Country in real Danger, I will stand or fall with it—and I trust, that I should not be found in my Study if the French remained even 10 days on British Ground. But merely to place one's self close by the Sluice-gate of the Stream, with no chance of doing any good that ten thousand cannot do better than you, 10,000 men, who can do nothing else, on whom their Country have no other Call, and Posterity no Claims——but I write in pain—my nature turns away with Terror from the Idea of appearing obtrusive or presumptuous to you.—
——I received last night two Volumes of Dr Barrow[1]—the admirable Passage on Wit, in which Lady Beaumont had put a paper, is an old friend & favorite of mine. Beyond any other passage in any Language it carries along a regular Admiration with a still increasing Surprize, till the mind rests at length in pure *Wonder*.—I pray, that I may read these excellent Sermons to such an effect, as will be considered by her Ladyship as the best possible Thanks.— We have quite a sick House—Southey's Eyes are very bad, Mrs Southey & her Sister are very poorly—Derwent is just recovering of a bad epidemic Cough & Fever, & poor little Sara is at this moment very ill indeed with it—tho' Mr Edmondson hopes & believes, that there is no danger. Mrs Coleridge is well: & I am better than usual.—I am very anxious to hear from you, and am with respectful affection your obliged & grateful, S. T. Coleridge.

### 527. To Mrs. John Thelwall

*Address*: Mrs Thelwall | Kendal
*MS. Pierpont Morgan Lib. Pub. E.L.G. i. 295.*
*Stamped*: Keswick.

Tuesday Night. [22 November 1803.][2]    Greta Hall, Keswick

Dear Mrs Thelwall

I did not receive your Husband's Letter, &c till the day before yesterday, when Mr Clarkson delivered it to me / I was vexed at

[1] Isaac Barrow's theological works were published posthumously under the editorship of Tillotson in four volumes, 1683–9.
[2] Clarkson was at Greta Hall on 19 Nov. 1803, for Southey, writing to John

the delay—as Thelwall would naturally think my silence a proof of neglect & forgetfulness of past kindness.—To all other purposes the Delay did no harm / for I have been so VERY, VERY ill, with such a complication of bodily miseries, for the last 3 weeks that I could not possibly have come over to Kendal—. As Thelwall is a Land-Nautilus & drives on in his own Shell, there can be no reason why he should not go from Kendal to Ambleside, to Grasmere (where he will see Wordsworth) & thence to Keswick / from Keswick to Carlisle by Newmarket Hesket, which is 25 miles—the whole journey from Kendal to Carlisle thro' Keswick is 55 miles—[a]bout 12 miles or so round about, as I guess. The road from Keswick to Carlisle I myself travelled this year in an Irish Car.—If your Husband adopt this plan, & immediately on his arrival at Kendal will give me a few Lines, stating the day, on which he intends to leave it, &c, I will—if my miserable Carcase be in any tolerable state of subservience to my wishes—walk to Kendal, & so return with him, in order to see you & your family—& to have the more of his Conversation.

Believe me, I have never ceased to think with tenderness—& have often thought with an *anxious* tenderness—of him, & his—& sincerely do I rejoice in his Well-doing & Well-being—sincerely rejoice that (to use the words of Milton a little altered) he has disembarked from a troubled Sea of Noises and hoarse disputes, to behold the bright countenance of Truth in the quiet and still Air of delightful Disquisition.—I could not guess at his System from his Syllabus[1] / and my curiosity therefore has still it's first *edge* on it.—I dread at Edingburgh the effects of the inordinate Self-sufficiency & Disputatiousness that deform the character of the literary part of it's Inhabitants / if report is not a Liar. Unanswerable Truth is a Torment to a mind, that has formed it's whole Taste & habit of pleasure in *answering*—to men, who have dubbed the monosyllable 'But', gentleman-usher to all their Sentences.—I have seen hitherto little Truth struck out by the so much boast[ed] *Collision* of Sentiment, in *Conversation*.——

I have 3 children, 2 boys & a girl—& they & my Wife are well. I sincerely wish, we were near Kendal—or rather that Kendal were very near to this Heaven upon Earth / that the two families might be comforts to each other. I shall be too late for the Post, if

King of Bristol on that day, says his letter 'will be delivered to you by Mr., once the Reverend Thomas Clarkson.' *Southey Letters*, i. 245. The next day, so Dorothy reports, Clarkson arrived at Grasmere and stayed a few hours, before leaving to join his wife in Bristol. *Later Years*, iii. 1344. This letter, then, must have been written on 22 Nov.

[1] Presumably a syllabus for the lectures on elocution Thelwall was delivering at this time. See *Southey Letters*, i. 255.

I write more / & my Health is so precarious, that what I do not write this Hour I may be unable to write the next——
With my kindest Remembrances to your Husband & yourself, & ardent well-wishing for you,
I remain, | dear Mrs Thelwall, | with simple & sincere Esteem & Affection | Your faithful Friend
S. T. Coleridge


528. *To John Thelwall*

*Address*: Mr John Thelwall | Kendal
*MS*. Pierpont Morgan Lib. *Pub.* E.L.G. i. 296.

Nov. 26th [25], 1803. Friday Night

My dear Thelwall

I received your Wife's kind & very interesting Letter; but was too ill to answer it by return of Post. I cannot without the most culpable Imprudence attempt to reach Kendal; especially, as I could not possibly arrive there time enough to spend any time at all with your Family—but I will go to Grasmere, & meet you there, if you come that way—as by Mrs Thelwall's Letter I promise myself, that you will.—I shall very soon—certainly in a week or ten days—leave this Country, to seek a vessel either for Malta or Madeira—for I dare stay no longer in this climate. But I will assuredly see Mrs Thelwall—& her friend—whose attachment to one unknown or at least unseen, affected & pleased me—not for myself—Heaven knows! she might easily have found a less unworthy object of her favorable opinion—but because such feelings of Esteem & Affection for persons, who are known to us only in spirit, are the exclusive property of minds at once fervent & pure & formative:—minds untamed by 'the dreary Intercourse' of common Life, & inspired by their own natures to believe, & have a Joy in the goodness of others.—

My Health is in a most distressful State; my Bowel & Stomach attacks frequent & alarming. But I bear Pain with a woman's Fortitude/ it is constitutional with me to look quietly and steadily in it's face, as it were, & to ask it—What & whence it is?——

If this Letter reach you in time, you will oblige me by going to the best Druggist in Kendal for me, & purchasing an Ounce of crude opium, & 9 ounces of Laudanum, the Latter put in a stout bottle & so packed up as that it may travel a few hundred miles with safety.—The whole will cost, I believe, half a guinea—& you will bring them with you in your gig.—Robert Southey is with me at present. He is a good man, a faithful Lover of all that good men once hoped for & must for ever desire / & he has a great respect & kindness for you——Wordsworth is likewise here / he came in last night to see me, I being very ill—but to day I am a good deal better / & hope to derive from you a stimulus strong enough to make your all too short Sojourn with us pleasant to you & representative of old Times. With best good wishes for you & your's

I am as ever, dear Thelwall, | your's
S. T. Coleridge

P.S. Do you know G. Braithwaite, Junr—a Quaker of our friend, Clarkson's, Acquaintance?—If you do, I wish you would call on him, present my regards, & in my name request him to procure for me Scotus in Sententias from the Sandys' Library,[1] which you can bring with you /—You will laugh heartily at travelling in a Gig with old Duns Scotus for your Companion /—God bless the old Schoolmen! they have been my best comforts, & most instructive Companions for the last 2 years.——Could you have believed, that I could have come *to this?*—

529. To Matthew Coates

*Address*: M. M. Cotes, Esqre | Mall | Clifton | Bristol     *Single Sheet*
MS. Mr. Merl F. Renz. Pub. with omis. Letters, *i*. 441.
*Postmark*: 8 December 1803.   *Stamped*: Keswick.

Greta Hall, Keswick. Dec. 5, 1803

Dear Sir

After a time of Sufferings great, as mere bodily Afflictions can well be conceived to be, and which the Horrors of my Sleep, and Night-screams (so loud & so frequent as to make me almost a

---

[1] Mr. Robert H. Pilling of the Kendal Grammar School has given me the following information concerning the Sandes Library in Kendal: 'Thomas Sandes founded in 1659 the Sandes Hospital "for the use of eight poor widows—and for the use of a schoolmaster to read prayers to the said widows twice a day and to teach poor children—". He left to the care of the schoolmaster the library which he had accumulated with instructions to allow "men of quality and learning" to be admitted thereto. The books were chained and so remained until at least 1722. In 1886 the endowments of the Sandes School (commonly called "the Blue Coat School") were amalgamated with those of the Grammar School. The Sandes School was then closed and the library transferred to the Grammar School, where it still remains. The library consists for the most part of the writings of the Early Fathers, Biblical commentators, religious controversialists, and ecclesiastical historians. In addition there are a number of secular histories and cosmographies.' Among the books in the Sandes Library is Scotus, *Super tertio Sententiarum*, 1505.

Nuisance in my own house [)] seemed to carry beyond mere Body —counterfeiting, as it were, the Tortures of Guilt, and what we are told of the Punishments of a spiritual World—I am at length a Convalescent—but dreading such another Bout as much as I dare dread a Thing which has no immediate connection with my Conscience. My left Hand is swoln, & inflamed; and the least attempt to bend the Fingers very painful, tho' not half so much as I could wish: for if I could but fix this Jack o'Lanthorn of a Disease in my Hand or Foot, I should expect a year or two's Furlow. But tho' I have no hope of this, yet I have a Persuasion, strong as Fate, that from 12 to 18 months' Residence & perfect Tranquillity in a genial Climate would send me back to dear old England, a sample of the first Resurrection. W. Wordsworth, who has seen me in all my Illnesses for nearly four years, and noticed their strange dependence on the state of my moral Feelings and the State of the Atmosphere conjointly, is decisively of the same opinion.—Accordingly, after many sore Struggles of mind from reluctance to quit my children, for so long a Time, I have arranged my affairs fully and finally, and hope to set sail for Madeira in the first Vessel that clears out from Liverpool for that Place: tomorrow or next day I expect a Letter from Dr Crompton, with particular Information. Robert Southey, who lives with us at present, informed me, that Mrs M. Cotes had a near Relation—a Brother, I believe, on the Island— the Dr Adams, who wrote a very nice little Pamphlet on Madeira relatively to the different sorts of Consumptions, & which I have now on my Desk.[1] I need not say, that it would be a great Comfort to me to be introduced to him by a Letter from you or Mrs C., intreating him to put me in the way of living as cheaply as possible. I have no Appetites, Passions, or Vanities that lead to expense: it is now absolute Habit with me indeed to consider my Eating & Drinking, as a course of Medicine: in Books only am I intemperate. They have been both Bane & Blessing to me. For the last 3 years, I have not read less than 8 hours a day, whenever I have been well enough to be out of Bed, or even to sit up in it—Quiet, therefore, a comfortable Bed and Bed room; and that [still] bett[er] Comfort of kind Faces—English Tongues & English Hearts—now and then —this is the Sum Total of my *Wants*. The last article indeed is not so much a *Want*, as it is a Thing, which I *need*. I am far too contented with Solitude. The same Fullness of Mind, the same

---

[1] Dr. Joseph Adams (1756–1818) obtained his M.D. degree at Aberdeen and settled in Madeira as a physician. In 1801 he published *A Guide to the Island of Madeira*. In 1805, after his return to England, he was elected physician to the Small-pox Hospital. It was Dr. Adams 'who in 1816 recommended Coleridge to the care of Mr. James Gillman'. *Letters*, i. 442 n.

## To Matthew Coates

Crowding of Thoughts, & Constitutional Vivacity of Feeling, w[hich] makes me sometimes the First Fiddle, & too often [a] Watchman's Rattle, in Society, renders me likewise [independent] of it.—However, I am wondrously calmed down, si[nce] you knew m[e—c]hiefly perhaps by unremitting Disease, [and] somewhat, I would fain hope, [by] Reflection and Self-discipline.

Mrs Coleridge desires me to remember her with respectfu[l regards] to Mrs Cotes, and to enquire into the History of your little [family. I] have three Children living, Hartley Coleridge, 7 years ol[d, Derwent,] 3 years old, and Sara a year old, on the 23rd of this Month. Hartley is considered as a Genius by Wordsworth, & Southey —indeed, by every one who has seen much of him—/ but (what is of much more consequence, & much less doubtful) he has the sweetest Temper & the most awakened moral Feelings of any Child, I ever saw. He is very backward in his Book-learning—cannot write at all, and a very lame Reader. We have never been anxious about it, taking it for granted that loving me & seeing how I love books, he would come to it of his own accord. And so it has proved. For in the last month he has made more progress than in all his former life. Having learnt every thing almost from the mouths of People, whom he loves, he has connected with his Words & notions a Passion & a Feeling which would appear strange to those who had seen no Children but such as had been taught almost every thing in Books.—Derwent is a large, fat, beautiful Child, quite the *Pride* of the Village, as Hartley is the *Darling*—Southey says, that all Hartley's Guts are in his Brains, and all Derwent's Brains in his Guts.—Verily, the constitutional Differences in Children are great indeed. From earliest Infancy Hartley was absent, a mere Dreamer, at his meals; put the food into his mouth by one effort, and made a second effort to remember that it was there & to swallow it—With little Derwent [it] is a time of Rapture & Jubilee —and any Story, that has no Pie or Cake in it, comes very flat to him.—Our Girl is a Darling little Thing with large blue eyes, a quiet Creature that as I have often said, seems to bask in a Sunshine, as mild as Moonlight, of her own Happiness.—O bless them! next to the Bible, Shakespere, & Milton, they are the three Books from which I have learnt the most—and the most important— & with the greatest Delight. I have been thus prolix about me & mine, purposely, to induce you to tell me something of yourself & your's. Believe me, I have never ceased to think of you with respect & a sort of yearning—you were the first man, from whom I heard that article of my Faith distinctly enunciated, which is the nearest to my Heart, the pure Fountain of all [my] moral & religious Feelings & [C]omforts—I mean, the absolute Impersonality of the

[D]eity. The Many would deem me an Atheist; alas! I know them to be Idolaters.—
    I remain, my dear Sir, with unfeigned Esteem & kind Wishes,
Your's, &c, S. T. Coleridge.—

P.S.—Be so good as to direct me as above: if I should be at Liverpool, the Letter (and, if I have not idly flattered myself, the Letters) will be forwarded to me. Do you know, whether there is any Trade from any Devonshire Port, any Vessels that go to, or touch at, Madeira?—I have not been without some Fears, while writing this Letter, lest you should have received some gloomy Intelligence from Madeira—but Dr Adams is so well known, that if there had been, it would assuredly have been mentioned—have escaped in the very first Boiling-up of the News.—There have been in the memory of middle-aged Persons two 'Borsten Clouds' in the mountains round Keswick; & have left the History of their Doings —one of them, in naked Rock adown the whole side of a high Mountain, in aforetime covered with vegetations:—but now written over with Vees, Ys and Ws, of no easy erasure—in winter time & after hard Rains they become Literae *vocales* with a vengeance— each one the bed of a Torrent.—S.T.C.

### 530. *To Sara Hutchinson*

*MS. Dove Cottage. Hitherto unpublished fragment.*

[*Circa* 19 December 1803][1]

... Sum, to be repayed by Wordsworth at the end of the Year in case I should not be able to do it[2] / & the plan which I had lit on, of taking up the money by a Draft on my own Annuity, W. to let Mrs C. have it by Installments quarterly, did not suit William /—& to confess the Truth to you, I am heart-sick and stomach-sick of talking, writing, and thinking about myself.—Besides all this, I found that I had been wandering in a mist; that there are so many Bills to pay, & heavy ones too, in addition to the 28 or 29£. . . & Mrs C's Mother's annual Pittance, that 150£ will not. . .

[1] In this letter Coleridge speaks 'of going to Grasmere tomorrow'. Since he went on 20 Dec. 1803, this letter was probably written the day before. See Letter 539.

[2] Writing to Coleridge about this time Dorothy Wordsworth says: 'As to the money William bids me say that whatever best accommodates you he should best like, only that it would be more pleasant to us (other things being nearly equal) to have nothing to pay till the end of next summer as John will then be at home, and our affairs settled.' *Early Letters*, 352. In Mar. 1804 William Sotheby gave Coleridge £100 for which Wordsworth stood security. See Letter 569.

## To Sara Hutchinson

. . . Dear little Derwent! he is a sad naughty Boy, but very beautiful. I forgot to tell a sweet anecdote of him, that happened some months before we went into Scotland / He was whirling round & round in the Kitchen, till (and no doubt for the first time in his conscious Life) he made himself compleatly giddy—he turned pale with fear, his pretty Lips began to quiver, and pawing with his two arms as if he was pulling something back, he cries out repeatedly with trembling Voice, The Kisshen is running away from Derwent! The Kishen (Kitchen) is running away from Derwent!—you never saw so pretty a sight.— To this Hour Derwent believes that there are two Derwents, & believes that the Reflection in the Looking-Glass is a real Being / & when I endeavored to convince him of his mistake by shewing him that he could not feel it / [']Well![ '] says little Cumbria—['] but you know, the Glass an't broke, & that's the reason, I can't get at *him.*'—Dear Hartley is just what he was—if possible, more thoughtful, joyous, and loveworthy than ever. He has afforded me a striking instance of the effect of local association / Since we have moved Houses, Hartley has been 9 times with us where he came once before, & has shewn most manifestly a great increase of affection to me—& to his Mother.—I think of going to Grasmere tomorrow—to stay there a couple of Days, & if possible to take Derwent & leave him there— & thence to London. . . .or Wednesday—. . .thence. . .Bath, & Exeter—. . .

[S.T.] C.

### 531. To Mrs. S. T. Coleridge

*Address*: Mrs Coleridge | Greta Hall | Keswick
*MS.* Lord Latymer. *Hitherto unpublished.* This fragment and the one following must have been written during Coleridge's stay at Grasmere, a visit prolonged by ill health and bad weather from 20 December 1803 to 14 January 1804. The references to the sending of ink relate the two letters, the ink, as a cancelled passage in the following letter suggests, being for the Wordsworths.

[Early January 1804]

. . . are as much to him & in his feelings, almost as Southey's Madoc to Southey & far more & with more reason than my Xstabel to me. I beseech you, endeavor to have the word of his Letter exactly obeyed/ & perhaps dear Southey will be so kind as to overlook the man, & to satisfy himself that the Pictures will receive no Harm, as far as the Packing goes.[1]—You must not send the rude Sketches of

[1] Presumably Hazlitt had written to Coleridge to send him his pictures, which had been left behind at the time of his precipitous departure from the Lakes. See Letter 520. Obviously Hazlitt also inquired of Wordsworth

my Face, nor Hartley[1] / the Latter belongs to the Wordsworths, partly as an Equivalent for my Portrait, & partly, as a something [for] the money he & I—(he 3 guineas) have payed—. Both William & Dorothy had been planning to get this picture, & it certainly almost belongs to them, & must be their's—yet in many respects it would have been highly gratifying to my Feelings to have presented it to Mr Jackson & to Mrs Wilson / or to speak more accurately—it is positively painful to me not to do so—but the Right both in blunt & in delicate feeling is clearly theirs.[2]—As to that rude Sketch of my Face, up in the upper Book room Garret, if you have no wish for it, & if on her coming into the Country Sara Hutchinson should be at all pleased with it, as a rude Sketch of me, it would gratify me that she should have it.—If Southey can spare it, be so good as not to forget to send the very first time a small Phial of Southey's Ink to Grasmere, & with them [it] the *Quills* on my Mantle piece in the Study, & those on the Table &c.—

I slept well—& am middling—this is sad rainy weather / —My Love to Southey—& with kindest well-wishing for all I am, as ever,

most anxiously yours &c
S. T. Coleridge

### 532. To Mrs. S. T. Coleridge

MS. Victoria University Lib. Hitherto unpublished fragment.

[Early January 1804]

... put in by accident in a cracked Bottle—out came a bit of the side, & the Ink was all spilled on the Carpet.—You must therefore send another very small Phial, wrapped up in brown paper, *by itself*, in the Parcel—& with the word, I N K, on it. Of myself I can not bear to say more than this / the Weather has been very bad, & I have been very ill / 4 days out of 5 prevented from going by Rain, & the 5th day by [G]outy Stomach-affections. At this present, all things, man, [w]oman & child, float be[fore me in] a sick Mist.— On...

... [I] mean to go off on Sunday, if possible—nay, to morrow, if possible—for London / & there to try to arrange the means of going abroad—& thence to Ottery, with the same Views.——

---

concerning his personal effects left at Keswick, for on 5 Mar. Wordsworth wrote to him: 'No body durst venture to seize your clothes or box.' *Later Years*, iii. 1349.

[1] Coleridge apparently refers to Hazlitt's portraits of himself and Hartley.

[2] On 4 Feb. Coleridge again mentions the portrait of Hartley (see Letter 552); it was in the possession of the Wordsworths by March. See *Later Years*, iii. 1349.

Derwent is a VERY, VERY good boy—I do not think, that he has cried 5 times since he has been here / tho' the Rooms are so small & the Rain so incessant. He has slept with me till last night when I was in too high a fever to endure a bedfellow. W. M. & D. all think [him] the best-tempered Child, they ever knew / &. . .

### 533. To Robert Southey

*Address*: Mr Southey.
*MS. Lord Latymer. Hitherto unpublished.*

Wednesday Night.—[11 January 1804]

My dear Southey

I have been vexed more than I ought to have been by poor old Molly's Silliness, to which your non-receival of Malthus is owing— I leave him to you / he is too stupid for any thing—.—I have stated the true pit of the argument over & over / but I beseech you to scourge him for that accursed Sophism / I mean, the ridiculing Godwin &c for even hinting the *possibility* of Exposure & Abortion, and disguising from his Readers, that he (as far as he pleads against the hopes of the progressive Improvement of mankind) is pleading for the real existence not only of these Crimes, but of a thousand others, and of the *misery & brutal Ignorance*, the production of which does alone render those Actions crimes!— And if he does not plead against the possibility of progressive Improvement, he is clearly a convert to the Godwinian Doctrine / —for where in God's name do they differ? If man can restrain his passions, in a conceivable state of knowlege & good Nurture, what is to stop this Improvement? or to prevent this Happiness?— Is he by growing a little better become a *Reprobate*; i.e. hopeless of being ever better?——You possess a real excellence, that of saying what you have to say, *fully, strikingly,* & yet in a nut-shell.—Do take some pains, and exhibit this Talent / —'from p. 17 to p. 355. Mr Malthus retails & details, from others' Travels & from his own, facts of all nations & all ages in all states of Society to prove, that Man has been[']—here enumerate the different curses stated, bad government, bad farmers, priesthood, &c &c / & that all these have made men wicked & poor & miserable / & that men in wickedness, & misery, & dearth of subsistence do not rear, even if they beget, as large families, as happy & good people would do.—Now, I put it seriously to Mr M's good sense, whether or no, if he had simply stated this in one sentence of half a dozen or half a score Lines, any one individual in Europe would have felt the least inclination to contradict the statement.—In short, the whole of these pages would make a sensible first sentence of an Essay in a Newspaper on the subject of population / for it is right to begin with a statement, which no one can or can wish to controvert / but 355 pages to say it out in![1]—The Minerva Press is not more merciless to Paper & Printer's Ink, nor Scotch Doctors when they write Quarto Volumes on Metaphysics more remorseless to the Pockets of their Purchasers. /

I thank you, my dear Friend! for your very entertaining Letter / your's are the only Letters which I open at once & with avidity—. —O dear Southey! my Health is pitiable—so mere a Slave to the Weather. In bad weather I can not possess Life without opiates— & with what aversion I take them, tho' I can not hitherto detect any pernicious Effect of it—nothing certainly compared with the effect of Spirits /—in fine weather I have not a Feeling about me that ever reminds me that I have been ill—and I can take my small Beer, & talk over it like a Burkite, or read or write or make verses—I want nothing—& wish nothing.—I must go into a hot climate / I can not but think my Disease—& windy Gout or Rheumatic Gout in general—no genuine gout, but primarily a Disease of the Skin, & affecting the Digestive organs by the diseased Action of the Skin / Physicians are as utterly ignorant of the Skin, as the Metaphysicians / & if I am not a mere Dreamer, it is of the last Importance in both / —I have no doubt, that a violent Eruption which perhaps a hot Climate might bring on, would cure me—/ for that the Stomach is not primarily affected, my non-emaciation, my non-head aches, & the instant effect of *dry Air*, be it hot or cold, seem to me to make more than probable.—Besides, my Skin is often deformed with bumps &c &c—& my childhood was vexed perpetually by sore heads, & swellings—

If it be fair, I go without fail tomorrow; but alas! it is now dark & rainy. I have a strong wish to go thro' Keswick /. O my sweet Children / By the time, I return, may I have to shake your hand for Edith's Safety & a dear one.—

My Love to all.—All here are very kind to me. Derwent is not quite well—there is something amiss within him / the extr'ordinary fetor of his Stools & preliminary tho' a posteriori Gasses seem to prove it.—But he is not ill at all—& is very sweet & good.—I write from Kendal to Mrs Coleridge—& to you from my next Stage.—

God love us all & S. T. C.—

P.S. I find by old Molly, that I had blamed her falsly—& that

---

[1] A copy of the 1803 edition of Malthus's *Essay on Population*, with marginal notes by Coleridge, is now in the British Museum. Southey's review appeared in the *Annual Review* for 1803.

Fletcher's People did not go on Tuesday on account of the Snow / —and all seems in confusion. However, I will not delay it any longer—I have therefore unpacked the Book & taken out my former Note, which was a shade too deep in the gloomy Line, & send it off to Fletcher's, pitch dark as it is.—

### 534. To Robert Southey

*Address*: Mr Southey | Greta Hall | Keswick
*MS. Lord Latymer. Hitherto unpublished.*

Friday, Jan. 13. 1804. Grasmere

Rain, soaking Rain: and my two last Nights have been poisoned by it. Yesterday morning after a bad breakfast, having been almost wholly sleepless during the Night, I fell sound asleep—the weather, as I thought, promising to clear up. I hoped that I should awake in Sun shine. But in less than 10 minutes after I had fallen asleep, the Rain came down in a storm; & whether any way connected with this, I cannot say—but I dreamt among other wild melancholy Things, all steeped in a deep dejection but not wholly unmingled with pleasure, that I came up into one of our Xt Hospital Wards, & sitting by a bed was told that it was Davy in it, who in attempts to enlighten mankind had inflicted ghastly wounds on himself, & must henceforward live bed-ridden. The image before my Eyes instead of Davy was a wretched Dwarf with only three fingers; which however produced, as always in Dreams, no Surprize. I however burst at once into loud & vehement Weeping, which at length, but after a considerable continuance, awakened me / My cheeks were drowned in Tears, my pillow & shirt collar quite wet / & the hysterical Sob was lingering in my breast.—Yester afternoon & evening I slept a profound death-like Sleep—I awoke at Ten— walked about, &c; but soon sunk down on the Floor-bed, and dozing in a strange way felt, as often as I opened my Eyes, as if I could not live. I could find no other words to express the strange Sensation— My Night's Sleep was distressful—loud Screams, that disturbed the Household—& yet this morning I am pretty well—& if the Rain were to clear up, & a frosty air to succeed, I should have nothing, but Pleasure and elastic Health, from the crown of my Head to the Soles of my Feet.—I will assuredly try a Wash-Leather Procutis. I do not suspect my skin of diseased Irritability; but of inirritability—if of either: for possibly neither word touches the specific nature of the Case. It is hardly possible to give even a plausible conjecture, while we remain ignorant of the secret means & subtle passages of that sympathy that exists in so remarkable a degree between the Skin & Stomach. The most sense-like-*sounding* account perhaps may be this: that on the slightest action of an uncongenial Air, from without, on the Skin, or of distressing disquieting Thoughts on the Digestive Organs from within, the *Secretories* of the Skin commence a diseased Action / if the *Absorbents* become languid, I have swellings, with moveable Fluid, in my knees or ancles, & am bed-ridden / if by means of opiates I revivify the action of the Absorbents, I have no swellings nor eruptions— no bad knees, no Boils in my neck, & Thighs, no little agony-giving ulcers in my mouth, et super Scrotum / but *then* the diseased Action of the Secretories of the Skin seems to be propagated into the Stomach, unless I so far increase the Dose, as to enable the Stomach to repel it—in which case the whole System obtains a *Temporary* Peace by the Equipoise of hostile Forces.—How dim & dusky all this is, I feel as strongly as you can / briefly therefore I will say, that I shall find words & a theory to explain my own Disease by, when any medical Philosopher shall have summed up in intelligible Language the state of the System at the Time of the Absence of the Nettle Rash on the Skin, & the presence of distressful Sensations in the Stomach / & vice versâ the Reappearance of this tormenting Rash upon the Skin, & the immediately consequent Ease of the Stomach. Mrs Wilson was for many years according to her own account in a state of bad Health almost to identity like mine / miserable Dependence on the weather, continual craving for stimulants, spices, hot liquors, &c—affrightful Dreams, & epileptic Breezes from the Stomach & still lower up to the Brain &c &c—after many years burst out a burning Eruption on her Skin, which still remains tho' somewhat pacified, & since that time she has been well.—I fully believe, that I have that which common people mean, when they say / that an Eruption has been driven *in*, or driven back into the Blood.—And with regard to weather, I do not conceive that damp air injures me altogether as damp air; but that, probably, there is a defect of electrical, or other imponderable fluid instrumental to vital action, in the air at such times. Else how could the Weather affect me in a warm bed, under four thick blankets, in a close room with a good Fire in it?—yet that it does, I know; & every one, who suffers under complaints similar to mine, affirms the same.—Finally, if I can pass a year, a whole year, in a hot climate, I feel a deep confidence, that I shall (in some way or other) recover my Health / & gladly should I purchase it at the price of an Eruption, that would kill all Love not purely spiritual.——Hereafter I trust, that a single Sentence will comprize the whole, I shall have to say on my Health viz: 'As usual'—or 'better than usual'—or 'worse than usual.'——

I was grieved to hear, that another Batch of Books had arrived. I cannot express to you, how anxious I am, at times, that you should devote yourself exclusively to Madoc. Your History you cannot finish; but Madoc you can. And most passionately do I desire that you should have one great work out of the power of Accidents—of those that might prevent, & (to think less gloomily) of those, that might suspend & interrupt. I do intreat you therefore do, do lay aside your History—& all reviewing after this Batch / & if you want money, borrow it, rather than earn it—& devote every hour to Madoc, that is capable of being devoted to composition.— When I see you, I shall talk to you concerning one thing which I have always been eager that you should remove—which indeed you have *altered*—but not removed. I *know, that I am right*—an arrogant phrase, but unaccompanied by any even the slightest Feeling of Arrogance.—. I may state it thus.—Suppose a reader of Madoc well & intimately acquainted with the Voyages, Travels, & Chronicles, & by means of them & the like with all the Exploits & Fortunes of the heroic Discoverers & Conquerors of South America / I conjecture, that *at first* he would feel his moral Taste a little offended by seeing any of their Adventures & Stratagems crowning in so divine a poem an obscure Welch Prince, whose ever approaching America is little more than a blind Guess—but on observing the moderation, with which you had availed yourself of these assistances, the great differences, varieties, &c &c, his Feeling of Offence would lessen & lessen, & at last be converted into positive pleasure & admiration / if only he came to those parts of your poem in good Humour. Now in order to this I assuredly could have wished that the Voyage of Madoc should have had altogether no *Resemblance* to that of Columbus / you once told me, that the same Events *must* have happened to both. But I cannot help believing, that your Heart & Imagination had been so pre-occupied by Wales, & by S. America, so *filled* with Thoughts & Images relating to these, that *at that time* you had not *room* for a true poetic Conception of the Voyage.—How admirably you have described the Mutiny, Madoc's feelings, &c—& how much excellent writing would be lost—I feel perhaps more strongly than you, who write with such facility, would permit yourself to feel—but spite of this I do seem to perceive within myself, that far more exquisite Lines & a far more interesting situation might be produced by making the men remain faithful—at least, such a majority—& those of course, the best, bravest, & wisest—as to overawe & overshame the rest—& those to *console* Madoc—'they are taken away from Guilt & Slavery—if they die, they die innocent, in an heroic Cause—Madoc is overpowered by seeing so many brave men *together* dying thus—had as many been known to die separately scattered over a kingdom, it would have raised a far less stormy feeling / &c' / —& for you to make *Madoc* the person, who had resolved to return, unable to think of sacrificing men of such tried Heroism, then to blame himself for leaving his dear native Land / his beloved Brother, & young Nephew so wronged, so beset with perils—&c &c &c—and then comes in the Tempest—and all afterwards as before.——I do not say it as any thing decisive; every man's opinion is something —but Wordsworth feels the weight of this resemblance to Columbus as strongly as I, tho' of course, I am the more haunted by it.——

God bless you.—I am most eager to be off—to be doing something—for this is mere Misery—not that I have been altogether idle tho'—my mind has been very active, & I have filled (since I have been at Grasmere) a full Third of that *large* Metallic Pencil Pocket-book with Hints, Thoughts, Facts, Illustrations, &c &c— the greater number relating to my Comforts & Consolations.[1] My kind remembrances to your Wife & to Mrs Lovell—. Tell Sara, that I would come thro' Keswick but for my Boxes—the heavy Expence & Delay of getting them back from Kendal &c—. My very Bowels yearn after my little Sara / to see her tottling alongside the Sopha —. Soon after I have taken my departure, Dorothy & Mary will come in with Derwent / he is by no means ill—is very happy, &c— but yet he is not in sound Health. Indeed, I think—& Sara, I believe, thinks so too / that he is never quite well when his Skin is quite clear of Nettle Bumps / Tell Sara, that nothing would give me greater pleasure than that Hartley should *immediately* be taught at least to *read* Hand Writing—& that if she will immediately set about it—(You can give her a little distinct Writing for him to read) in about a fortnight I will write him a Letter by the Post in very plain writing—but she must not give him a Hint of this.—— Again & again God bless you. S. T. Coleridge.

How goes on Edward?—The new Burnettianum amused me hugely.—

## 535. To Richard Sharp

*Transcript Coleridge family. Pub. with omis. Letters, ii. 447.*

King's Arms, Kendal. Jan. 15, 1804—Sunday Morning
My dear Sir

I give you thanks—and, that I may make the best of so poor & unsubstantial a Return, permit me to say, that they are such Thanks, as can only come from a Nature unworldly by Constitution

---

[1] For a fuller description of this unrealized project, see Letter 536.

and by Habit, and now rendered more than ever impressible by sudden Restoration—Resurrection I might say—from a long long sick bed. I had gone to Grasmere to take my Farewell of William Wordsworth, his Wife, and his sister—and thither your Letters followed me—O dear Sir! I am heart-sick and stomach-sick of speaking and writing concerning myself—nay, let me be proud, not my self—but concerning my miserable carcase—the Caterpillar Skin which, I believe, the Butterfly Elect is wriggling off, tho' with no small Labor and Agony.—I was at Grasmere a whole month—so ill, as that till the last week I was unable to read your letters—not that my inner Being was disturbed—on the contrary, it seemed more than usually serene and self-sufficing—but the exceeding Pain, of which I suffered every now and then, and the fearful Distresses of my sleep, had taken away from me the connecting Link of voluntary power, which continually combines that Part of us by which we know ourselves to be, with that outward Picture or Hieroglyphic, by which we hold communion with our Like—between the Vital and the Organic—or what Berkley, I suppose, would call—Mind and it's sensuous Language. I had only just strength enough to smile gratefully on my kind Nurses, who tended me with Sister's and Mother's Love, and often, I well know, wept for me in their sleep, and watched for me even in their Dreams. O dear Sir! it does a man's heart good, I will not say, to know such a Family, but even—to know, that there *is* such a Family. In spite of Wordsworth's occasional Fits of Hypochondriacal Uncomfortableness—from which more or less, and at longer or shorter Intervals, he has never been wholly free from his very Childhood—in spite of this hypochondriacal *Graft* in his Nature, as dear Wedgwood calls it, his is the happiest Family, I ever saw—and *were* it not in too great Sympathy with my Ill health—*were* I in good Health and their Neighbour—I verily believe, that the Cottage in Grasmere Vale would be a proud sight for Philosophy. It is with no idle feeling of Vanity that I speak of my Importance to them—that it is *I* rather than another, is almost an Accident; but being so very happy within themselves they are too good, not the more for that very reason to want a Friend and common Object of Love out of their Household.—I have met with several genuine Philologists, Philonoists, Phisiophilists, keen hunters after knowledge and Science; but Truth and Wisdom are higher names than these—and *revering* Davy, I am half angry with him for doing that which would make me laugh in another man—I mean, for prostituting and profaning the name of Philosopher, great Philosopher, eminent Philosopher &c &c &c to every Fellow, who has made a lucky experiment, tho' the man should be frenchified to the

Heart, and tho' the whole Seine with all it's filth & poison flows in his Veins and Arteries—Of our common Friends, my dear Sir! I flatter myself that you and I should agree in fixing on T. Wedgwood, and on Wordsworth, as genuine Philosophers—for I have often said (and no wonder, since not a day passes but the conviction of the truth of it is renewed in me and with the conviction the accompanying Esteem and Love) often have I said that T. Wedgwood's Faults impress me with Veneration for his moral and intellectual character more than almost any other Man's Virtues: for under circumstances like his, to have a Fault only in that Degree is I doubt not in the eye of God to possess a high Virtue. Who does not prize the Retreat of Moreau[1] more than all the Straw-blaze of Bonaparte's Victories?—and then to make it (as Wedgwood really does) a sort of crime even to think of his Faults by so many Virtues retained, cultivated and preserved in growth & blossom, in a climate—where now the Gusts so rise and eddy, that deeply-rooted must *that* be which is not snatched up & made a play thing of by them;—and now 'the parching Air Burns frore.'[2]—Mr. Wordsworth does not excite that almost painfully profound moral admiration, which the sense of the exceeding Difficulty of a given Virtue can alone call forth, & which therefore I feel exclusively toward T. Wedgwood; but on the other hand, he is an object to be contemplated with greater complacency—because he both deserves to be, and *is*, a happy man—and a happy man, not from natural Temperament—for therein lies his main obstacle—not by enjoyment of the good things of this world—for even to this Day from the first Dawn of his Manhood he has purchased Independence and Leisure for great & good pursuits by austere frugality and daily Self-denial—nor yet by an accidental confluence of amiable and happy-making Friends and Relatives, for every one near to his heart has been placed there by Choice and after Knowlege and Deliberation—but he is a happy man, because he is a Philosopher —because he knows the intrinsic value of the Different objects of human Pursuit, and regulates his Wishes in Subordination to that Knowlege—because he feels, and with a *practical* Faith, the Truth of that which you, more than once, my dear Sir, have with equal good sense & Kindness pressed upon me, that we can do but one thing well, & that therefore we must make a choice—he has made that choice from his early youth, has pursued & is pursuing it— and certainly no small part of his happiness is owing to this Unity of Interest, & that Homogeneity of character which is the natural consequence of it—& which that excellent man, the Poet Sotheby,

---

[1] The famous retreat of Jean-Victor Moreau took place in 1796.
[2] *Paradise Lost*, ii. 594–5.

noticed to me as the characteristic of Wordsworth. Wordsworth is a Poet, a most original Poet—he no more resembles Milton than Milton resembles Shakespere— no more resembles Shakespere than Shakespere resembles Milton—he is himself: and I dare affirm that he will hereafter be admitted as the first & greatest philosophical Poet—the only man who has effected a compleat and constant synthesis of Thought & Feeling and combined them with Poetic Forms, with the music of pleasurable passion and with Imagination or the *modifying* Power in that highest sense of the word in which I have ventured to oppose it to Fancy, or the *aggregating* power—in that sense in which it is a dim Analogue of Creation, not all that we can *believe* but all that we can *conceive* of creation. Wordsworth is a Poet, and I feel myself a better Poet, in knowing how to honour *him*, than in all my own poetic Compositions, all I have done or hope to do—and I prophesy immortality to his *Recluse*, as the first & finest philosophical Poem, if only it be (as it undoubtedly will be) a Faithful Transcript of his own most august & innocent Life, of his own habitual Feelings & Modes of seeing and hearing.[1]
—My dear Sir! I began a Letter with a heart, heaven knows! how full of gratitude toward you—and I have flown off into a whole-Letter-full respecting Wedgwood & Wordsworth. Was it that my Heart demanded an outlet for grateful Feelings—for a long *stream* of them—and that I felt it would be oppressive to you if I wrote to you of yourself half of what I wished to write? or was it that I knew I should be in Sympathy with you—& that few subjects are more pleasing to you than the Details of the merits of two men, whom, I am sure, you *esteem* equally with myself—tho' accidents have thrown me or rather Providence has placed me in a closer connection with them, both as confidential Friends, & the one as my Benefactor, & to whom I owe that my Bed of Sickness has not been in a House of Want, unless I had *bought* the contrary at the Price of my Conscience by becoming a Priest.—

I leave this place this afternoon having walked from Grasmere yesterday. I walked the 19 miles thro' mud & Drizzle, fog & stifling air, in four hours and 35 minutes—& was not in the least fatigued so that you may see that my sickness has not much weakened me—Indeed the Suddenness & seeming Perfectness of my Recovery is [are] really astonishing. In a single hour I have changed from a state that seemed next to Death, swoln Limbs, racking Teeth, & sick & convulsed stomach to a state of elastic Health—so that I have said—If I have been dreaming yet you, Wordsworth, have been awake. And Wordsworth has answered—I could not

[1] Cf. *Biographia Literaria* for Coleridge's elaboration of these ideas more than a decade later.

*15 January 1804* [535

expect any one to believe it who had not seen it—These changes have always been produced by sudden changes of the weather—dry hot weather or dry frosty weather seem alike friendly to me, and my persuasion is strong as the Life within me that a year's residence in Madeira would renovate me. I shall spend two days in Liverpool —& hope to be in London, Coach & Coachmen permitting, on Friday Afternoon or Saturday at the furthest—And on this day week I look forward to the pleasure of thanking you personally— for I still hope to avail myself of your kind Introductions—I mean to wait in London till a good Vessel sails for Madeira, but of this when I see you—believe me my dear Sir,

With grateful & affectionate thanks | Your sincere Friend
S. T. Coleridge

### 536. *To Thomas Poole*

*Address*: T. Poole, Esqre | 16 | Abingdon Street | Westminster
*MS. British Museum. Pub. with omis. Letters, ii. 452.*
*Postmark*: 19 January 1804.   *Stamped*: Kendal.

Sunday, Jan. 15. 1804. Kendal

My dear Poole

My Health is as the weather / that for the last month has been unusually bad—& so has my Health. I left my home, Jan. [December] 20th / meaning to stay one day at Grasmere—then for Kendal—& so for London—where I hoped to talk with you—& if I could realize the plan, to go immediately to Madeira—if not to go into Devonshire—. The next day after my arrival the Weather altered from a fine dry Frost to Thaw & Rain / & since then we have had little else than Rain, or Snow, or Thaw—or Drizzle—or Thaw-Winds—all deadly Poisons to me /—and I have indeed been very, very ill—for days together so weak, as scarcely to be able to smile with tenderness & thanks on Mrs Wordsworth & Dorothy, who have nursed me with more than Mother's Love.—However, I am somewhat better—and so far from weak now that I walked yesterday, tho' suffering grievously from asthma in consequence of the Drizzle, Fog, & Stifling Air, the 19 miles from Grasmere to Kendal in four hours & 35 minutes, & was not in the least fatigued—. My state of Health is a Riddle; but I think, I have solved it: as far as it is possible to solve any Skin or Stomach Complaint, while the marvellous Sympathy between the Skin & Stomach is known as a fact, but the means & passages of it are hidden & unguessed. I believe, that the *primary* Seat of the Disease is the Skin / & that any great Eruption would restore me to my inner Health—but of this when we meet—

I go by the heavy Coach this afternoon—shall be at Liverpool tomorrow Night—Tuesday & Wednesday I shall stay there—not more *certainly*, for I have taken my place all the way to London, & this Stay of two Days is an Indulgence & entered in the Road Bill—/—so I expect to be in London, on Friday Evening, about 6 o clock, at the Saracen's Head, Snow Hill. Now, my dearest Friend! will you send a twopenny post Letter directed, Mr Coleridge (Passenger in the Heavy Coach from Kendal & Liverpool) to be left at the Bar, | Saracen's Head, | Snow Hill—informing me, whether I can have a Bed at your Lodgings—or whether Mr Rickman could let me have a Bed for one or two Nights—for I have such a Dread of sleeping at an Inn or Coffee House in London, that it quite unmans me to think of it—. To love & to be beloved makes hot-house Plants of us, dear Poole.—Tho' wretchedly ill, I have yet not been deserted by Hope—less dejected than in any former Illness—& my Mind has been active, & not vaguely but to that determinate purpose which has employed me the last three months—& I want only one fortnight's steady Reading to have got *all* my materials before me—& then I neither stir to the Right or to the Left, so help me God! till the Work is finished. Of it's Contents the Title will in part inform you—Consolations and Comforts from the exercise and right application of the Reason, the Imagination, and the moral Feelings, addressed especially to those in Sickness, Adversity, or Distress of mind, *from speculative Gloom*, &c. I put that last phrase, tho' barbarous, for your information / I have puzzled for hours together & could never hit off a phrase, to express that Idea, that is at once neat & terse—& yet good English.——The whole Plan of my literary Life I have now layed down——& the exact order, in which I shall execute them [it?], if God vouchsafe me Life & adequate Health—& I have sober tho' confident Expectations that I shall render a good Account of what may have appeared to you & others a distracting Manifoldness in my Objects & Attainments—.

You are nobly employed—most worthily of you / *you* are made to endear yourself to Mankind as an immediate Benefactor / I must throw my Bread on the Waters—you sow Corn & I plant the Olive. Different Evils beset us——you shall give me advice—& I will advise you—to look steadily at every thing & to see it as it is—to be willing to see a Thing to be evil even tho' you see at the same time that it is for the present an irremediable Evil—and not to overrate, either in the convictions of your Intellect or in the Feelings of your Heart, the Good, because it is present to you / &

in your power—and above all, not to be too hasty an Admirer of the Rich, who seem disposed to do good with their Wealth & Influence—but to make your Esteem strictly & severely proportionate to the *Worth* of the agent, not to the *value* of the action / & to refer the latter wholly to the Eternal Wisdom & Goodness, to God, upon whom it wholly depends, & in whom alone it has a moral Worth. I love & honor you, Poole! for many things—scarcely for any thing more than that, trusting firmly in the Rectitude & simplicity of your own Heart, and listening with faith to it's revealing Voice, you never suffered either my Subtlety or my Eloquence to proselyte you to the pernicious Doctrine of Necessity / all praise to the Great Being who has graciously enabled me to find my way out of that labyrinth-Den of Sophistry, &, I would fain believe, to bring with me a better clue than has hitherto been known, to enable others to do the same. I have convinced Southey —& Wordsworth / & W, you know, was even to Extravagance a Necessitarian—Southey never believed, & abhorred the Doctrine, yet thought the arguments for it unanswerable by human Reason. I have convinced both of them of the sophistry of the arguments, & wherein the Sophism consists—viz. that all have hitherto, both the Necessitarians & their Antagonists, confounded two essentially different Things under one name—& in consequence of *this* Mistake the Victory has been always hollow in favor of the Necessitarians.

God bless you | &<br>
S. T. Coleridge

P.S. If any Letter come to your Lodgings for me, of course you will take care of it.

### 537. To Mrs. S. T. Coleridge

*Address*: Mrs Coleridge | Greta Hall | Keswick | Cumberland
*MS.* Lord Latymer. *Pub.* E. L. G. i. 298.
*Postmark*: 25 January 1804.

No / 16, Abingdon Street, Westminster<br>
Wednesday Morning, Jan. 24 [25], 1804

My dear Sara

My right Hand is so swoln, that I cannot without pain and difficulty put the two fingers close enough to the Thumb to keep the Pen steady—my left hand is likewise swoln / & eke my knees and ancles. I am more and more convinced that it is not Gout—or at all events, that if my case be flying windy Gout, that flying windy Gout is not the same disease with regular Gout, but a something cutaneous—a something neither scrofulous nor scorbutic absolutely, & yet partaking of both. In my stomach, Heaven be praised! I am tolerably easy, and I draw my breath, if not freely, yet regularly / Let my mind remain in deep tranquillity, & I hope all good things of my Health / & having Health, I have a prideless steady Confidence, that I shall be active & perseverant to the full length, width, and depth of the faculties and acquirements, which Providence has entrusted to my Use and Keeping. So much of my Health, and State of Mind, the Things of main Interest to you, my dear Sara! believe me, hourly thro' the day I am planning or praying for your Comfort and Peace: nor is it possible, that any name can be more awfully affecting, or sink into my Heart, and my Heart's Heart, with a greater weight of Duty, than that of the virtuous Mother of my children. We will try hard, my dearest Friend! that the severest Judge shall be able to detect no other Evil in us, than the—misfortune, I trust, rather than Evil—of being unsuited to each other.

I arrived at the White Horse Cellar, Piccadilly, yester night, 7 o clock / and took myself & luggage in a Hackney Coach to 16, Abingdon Street; Poole (who last week had waited for me till past midnight at the Saracen's Head, Snow Hill) was at home / drest so *grand*!—& welcomed me with wonted cordiality / —he had prepared for me a very comfortable Bed at Waghorn's Coffee House, just at the head of the Street, next door to the House of Lords—a quiet domestic place, kept by Betsy Segur's Mother / Mrs Segur (who has the affection of a Mother to T. Poole with the reverence of one variously & deeply indebted to him, & who likewise had a Boy at Christ's Hospital, now dead, but to whom according to his own account I had been exceedingly kind when a Grecian) received me like a motherly affectionate open-hearted Woman / with her Poole & I breakfast, at ½ past 8—at 9 Poole goes to his Parliament Office, the WORSHIPFUL with his dozen Clarks!—& leaves me this nice Parlour till 4 o/clock.—I have so many Letters to write this morning . . .[1]

. . . to put a *Sock* over it on the pit of my Stomach.—God Almighty bless you in all things, my dear Sara! write to me as gladsomely, as you can: for O! my children, my children!—they & other things make me *so* sensitive & sore!—one who shrinks from a Touch, as feeling, that even a Touch might pass into agony / — but I shall grow firmer & manlier.—Tear off the latter Scrap below, & give it to Southey[2]— / Say all kind things to every body as if I had written them / . Again & again bless you, & S. T. Coleridge.——

[1] About six lines cut off the MS.    [2] See next letter.

### 538. To Robert Southey

MS. Lord Latymer. Hitherto unpublished.
Postmark: 25 January 1804.

[25 January 1804]

My dear Southey

At Dr Crompton's I read all the Reviews that I knew or guessed to be your's in the Annual Review, & if aught could reconcile me to the thought of reviewing at all, & of *you* as a Reviewer, those articles would have done it. I speak with quiet certainty, that if I had been a Stranger to you, or had never guessed that you were the Author, I should have felt *gratitude* to the Man, who had written the R. of the Baptist's Mission, Fischer's Travels, &c &c &c— / Reviews would be a Blessing, spite even of the necessary Evil involved in their Essence, of breeding a crumbliness of mind in the Readers, if they were executed as those were—.—I likewise read Mrs Barbauld's on Lamb / & if I do not cut her to the Heart, openly & with my name, never believe me again.——In your Review of Malthus be exceedingly temperate & courteous & guarded in your Language—W. Scott has reviewed Thalaba, I *hear*, in the Edingburgh Review / Thelwall has had a grand Rumpus with the Ed. Reviewers, written a pamphlet, of which a 1000 copies have already sold & is said to have laid them prostrate & flat.—Dr Crompton received a Letter from him which for honest-hearted drunken self-gloting Vanity in the delirium of Triumph surely never had it's like / 'I have left Edingburgh dismayed & contrite; Glasgow, it is believed, will rush forward eagerly to wipe off the stain, which, she deems, Edingburgh has brought on Scotland['] &c &c &c—& far worse—God bless you!— In less than a week I will write all the Gossip of London. Rickman left Town last night.

Bless you & S. T. C.

### 539. To Thomas Wedgwood

Address: T. Wedgwood Esqre | Cote House | Bristol
MS. Wedgwood Museum. Pub. Tom Wedgwood, 166.

16, Abingdon Street, Westminster
Wednesday afternoon, Jan. [25,] 1804

My dear Friend

Some divines hold, that with God to think & to create are one and the same act—if to think & even to compose had been the same as to write with me, I should have written as much too much as I have now written too little. The whole Truth of the matter is, that I have been very, very ill; your Letter remained four days unread, I was so ill / what effect it had upon me, I cannot express by words—it lay under my pillow day after day—I should have written 20 times—but as it often & often happens with me, my heart was too full—and I had so much to say, that I said nothing. I never received a delight that lasted longer upon me, 'brooded on my mind and made it pregnant,'[1] than the six last Sentences of your Letter—which I cannot apologize for not having answered / I should be canting calumnies against myself—for for the last six or seven weeks I have both thought & felt more concerning you & relatively to you, than of all other men put together. Somehow or other, whatever plan I determined to adopt, my fancy, good-natured Pandar of our wishes, always linked you on to it—or I made it your Plan, & linked myself on.—I left my home Dec. 20, 1803—intending to stay a day & a half at Grasmere, & then to walk to Kendal, whither I had sent all my Cloaths, and Viatica: from thence to go to London—& to see whether or no I could arrange my pecuniary matters so as leaving Mrs Coleridge all that was necessary to her comforts, to go myself to Madeira—having a persuasion strong as the Life within me, that one winter spent in a really warm genial climate would compleatly restore me—. Wordsworth had as I may truly say, *forced* on me a hundred Pound, in the event of my going to Madeira—& Stuart had kindly offered to befriend me——& during the days & affrightful nights of my Disease, when my Limbs were swoln, & my Stomach refused to retain the food taken in in sorrow, then I looked with pleasure on the scheme / but as soon as dry frosty weather came, or the rains & damps passed off, & I was filled with elastic Health from crown to Sole, then the Thought of the weight of pecuniary Obligation—having hitherto given no positive proof, that I was a fit moral object of so much exertion from so many people, revisited me—/—but I have broken off my Story—I stayed at Grasmere a month, $\frac{3}{4}$ths of the Time bed-ridden—& deeply do I feel the enthusiastic kindness of Wordsworth's Wife and Sister, who sate up by me, one or the other, in order to awaken me at the first symptoms of distressful Feeling—& when they went to rest, continued often & often to weep & watch for me even in their Dreams.——I left them Saturday, Jan. 14—have spent a very pleasant week at Dr Crompton's at Liverpool, & arrived at Poole's Lodgings last night, 8 o/ clock—. Tho' my right Hand is so much swoln, that I can scarcely keep my pen steady between my Thumb & Forefingers, yet my Stomach is easy, and my Breathing Comfortable / and I

---

[1] *Paradise Lost*, i. 21-22:

> Dove-like sat'st brooding on the vast abyss,
> And mad'st it pregnant.

am eager to hope all good things of my health—& that gained, I have a cheering, & I trust, prideless Confidence, that I shall make an active & perseverant use of the faculties & acquirements, that have been entrusted to my keeping, & a fair Trial of their Heighth, Depth, & Width. Indeed, I look back on the last 4 months with honest Pride, seeing how much I have done, with what steady attachment of mind to the same subject, and under what vexations & sorrows from without, and amid what inward Sufferings.—So much of myself. When I know more, I will tell y[ou] more.

I find that you are still at Cote—and Poole tells me, that you talk of Jamaica—as of a summer Excursion. If it were not for the Voyage, I would, that you would go to Madeira—for from the Hour, I get on board the vessel to the time that I once more feel England beneath my feet, I am as certain, as past & unvarying Experience can make me, that I shall be in Health, in high Health / & then I am sure not only that I should be a Comfort to you, but that I should be so without Diminution of my activity or professional usefulness.—Briefly, dear Wedgwood! I truly & at heart love you; & of course, it must add to my deeper & moral happiness to be with you, if I can be either assistance or alleviation. If I find myself so well—that I defer my Madeira Plan—I shall then go forthwith to Devonshire, to see my aged Mother once more before she dies—& stay two or three months with my Brothers—but where ever I am, I never suffer a day (except when I am travelling) to pass without doing something—Poole made me promise that I would leave a side for him / & preciously I have remembered it.— God bless him! he looks so worshipful in his office among his Clerks, that it would give a few minutes' good Spirits at least, to look in upon him.—I pray you, as soon as you can command your pen, give me half a score Lines: & now that I am *loose*, say whether or no I can be any Good to you. S. T. Coleridge

### 540. *To Thomas Poole*

*Address*: T. Poole Esqre | Parliament office
*MS. British Museum. Pub.* Letters, *ii. 454.*

My dearest Poole                          [January 2]6. 1804

I have called on Sir James Mackintosh who offered me his endeavors to procure me a place under him in India—of which endeavors he could not for a moment doubt the success—and assured me *on his Honor—on his Soul*!!! (N.B. his Honor!!) (N.B. his[1] Soul!!) that he was sincere.—Lillibullero—whoo! whoo! whoo!—Good Morning, Sir James.——

[1] Underlined four times in MS.

## To Thomas Poole

I next called on Davy who seems more and more determined to mould himself upon the Age in order to make the Age mould itself upon him—into this Language at least I have translated his conversation / o it is a dangerous business this Bowing of the Head in the Temple of Rammon / & such men I aptly christen *Theomammonists*, i.e. Those who at once worship God & Mammon/—However, God grant better Things of so noble a work of his!—And as I once before said, may that Serpent, the World, climb around the Club, which supports him, & be the symbol of Healing—even as if in Tooke's Pantheon[1] you may see the thing *done* to your eyes in the Picture of Esculapius.—Well! now for Business—I shall leave this note among the Schedules—they will wonder, plain sober People! what damn'd Mad-cap has got among them / or rather I will put it under the Letter just arrived for you, that at least it may perhaps be *under the Rose*[2] / —

Well—once again I will try to get at it—but I am landing on a surfy Shore, & am always driven back upon the open Sea of various Thoughts——

I dine with Davy at 5 o/clock this evening at the Prince of Wales's Coffee House, Leicester Square—& he can give us 3 hours of his Company—Now I beseech you *do* make a point & come—God bless you & may his Grace be as a [pair] of brimstone Gloves to guard against dirty diseases from such bad company as you are keeping—Rose & Thomas Poole!—!!!

S. T. Coleridge

### 541. To Thomas Wedgwood

*Address*: T. Wedgwood Esqre | Cote House | near | Bristol
*MS. Wedgwood Museum. Pub.* Tom Wedgwood, *169.*
*Postmark*: 28 January 1804.

16, Abingdon St. Westminster / Saturd. Jan. 28. 1804

My dear Friend

It is idle for me to say to you, that my Heart & very soul ache with the dull pain of one struck down & stunned / . I write to you / for my Letter cannot give you unmixed Pain / & I would fain say a few words to dissuade you. / What good can possibly come of your plan / will not the very chairs & furniture of your Room be shortly more, far more intolerable to you, than new & changing

---

[1] Andrew Tooke's famous work, *The Pantheon*, was first published in 1698.

[2] Coleridge refers to George Rose (1744–1818), the statesman. Rose had requested Rickman to gather statistical information concerning the poor by means of schedules sent to all parishes. Poole was working on these reports at this time.

Objects! Mere insufferable Reflectors of Pain & Wearisomeness of Spirit? O most certainly they will! You *must hope*, my dearest Wedgwood! you must act, as if you hoped! Despair itself has but that advice to give you. Have you ever thought of trying large doses of opium in a hot climate, keeping your Body open by Grapes & the Fruits of the Climate?—Is it impossible, that by drinking freely you might at last produce the *Gout*, and that a violent Pain & Inflammation in the Extremities might produce new trains of motion & feeling in your Stomach & the Organs connected with it, the Stomach, known & unknown? Worse than what you have decre'd for yourself cannot well happen.—Say but a word—& I will come to you—will be with you—will go with you—to Malta— to Madeira——to Jamaica—or (of the climate of which & it's strange effects I have heard wonders, true or not) to Egypt——.

At all events, and at the worst—even if you do indeed attempt to realize the scheme of going to & remaining at Gunville, for God's sake! my dear dear Friend! do keep up a correspondence with one or more, or if it were possible for you, with several. I know by a little what your sufferings are; and that to shut the eyes & stop up the ears is to give one's self up to storm & darkness and the lurid forms & horror of a Dream.—Poole goes off to night; but I shall send this Letter by the Post—I scarce know why—it is a feeling, I have & hardly understand—I could not endure to live, if I had not a firm Faith that the Life within you will pass forth out of the Furnace: for that you *have* borne what you have borne, & so acted beneath such Pressure, constitutes you an awful moral Being——I am not ashamed to pray aloud for you / .

Your most affectionate | Friend
S. T. Coleridge

Poole will call on you some time before Dinner on Monday, for an hour, unless he hear from you a wish to the contrary addressed to him at Mr King's, No / 2, Redcliff Parade.—

## 542. To Richard Sharp

*Address*: For | R. Sharpe, Esqre
*MS. Cornell University Lib. Hitherto unpublished.*

16, Abingdon St, Westminster.
Sunday Noon, Jan. 29. 1804

My dear Sir

In case, I should not be fortunate enough to find you at home, I will write half a dozen Lines to entreat you to be so good as to let me know by the Penny Post when I can see you, on what day you will be sufficiently disengaged to give me half an hour's conversation; & whether I shall wait upon you, or you will find it more convenient to take me in, in any one of your walks. To me it is perfectly indifferent—only I would wish to be certain to be at home—. I called on you the day after my arrival—nay, the second day—but it was the first day, I went out / & I wrote to you from Kendal, Sunday fortnight. I spent a pleasant week at Liverpool, & have all kind & respectful things to say to you from Dr Currie /

Yesterday I received an almost heart-breaking Letter from our Friend *T.W.* a tremendous Cloud of Gloom & Despondency—but I trust in God, that from the very restlessness of the misery, that induces it, it will soon be blown off, or dissolve /

T. Poole left Town last night for a week / —

Believe me, | my dear Sir, | with grateful & affectionate | Esteem | Your obliged Friend
S. T. Coleridge

## 543. *To Grosvenor Bedford*

*Address*: Grosvenor Bedford Esqre | Gerard St/
MS. New York Public Lib. *Hitherto unpublished.*

16, Abingdon St/   Sunday Noon, Jan. 29. 1804

Dear Sir

To one, who had known me intimately, I should not find it necessary to *apologize* for my non-appearance yester evening: he would know, that it is one of the *Counterpoises* to whatever is amiss in me—the never breaking of friendly engagements either forgetfully or with design. My explanation would have been forestalled: I should have had only the task of particularizing it.—— I was unwell all yestermorning, as I inevitably am, during wet & windy weather / about ½ past 2 I received a letter of tremendous gloom & darkest despondency from a very dear friend, a truly great & valuable man, but to whom ill health does not allow a day's Quiet throughout the year, following him, & driving him here & there & every where, as the Furies drove Orestes / . This Letter had *got into* me, more than I myself was conscious of—I walked (unwell indeed but seemingly no more so, than I always am sub Jove Pluviali) into the Strand to dine at 4 o clock with a Friend / I had not eaten half a dozen mouthfuls, when there burst out from all parts of my body a Sweat, like a tropical Rain / it literally *frightened* Stuart (with whom I was dining). I was obliged to leave the table very abruptly—suffered all the extremes of Joint Vomiting & Diarrhoea—& in short, could not stir—or scarcely think where I was, till the watchman was crying past 10 o clock / when I got myself conveyed home / I am tolerably well this morning—& shall walk to Gerard St, that if per accident you should be within, I may *tell* you in person, that I suffered a good deal of Pain (after I was so far recovered as to be in the way of thinking of it) from the expectation, &c &c, & of course, unpleasant speculations concerning me &c—. The Truth is, in the present most uncertain state of my Health, in this present entanglement & embranglement of my Destinies, I ought not to make any but *very conditional* Promises—Believe me, dear Sir,

respectfully your's,
S. T. Coleridge

## 544. To Thomas Poole

*Address*: T. Poole Esqre | N. Stowey | Bridgewater      *Single Sheet*
*MS. British Museum. Hitherto unpublished.*
*Postmark*: 1804.

Jan. 30. 1804. Monday Morning. / 16. Abingdon St /
My dear Poole

I promised Blake, that I would write to you to day. He met me in Parliament St yesterday morning, the queer pompous fool! & in a set discourse setting forth his extraordinary Qualifications (I am sure, that if I had been pleading for Davy or Southey, for some place to which they were fitted, I could not have spoken in a more romantic Strain than he of himself) he wished me to desire you to particularize the weekly Sum, at which you conceived his Scribe-and-Pharisee Extraordinariness purchaseable. 'What do you mean to allow him? He lives now near 4 miles from Abingdon St—consequently could not walk thither mornings, by 9 o/ clock / nor should like in all weather, to walk back at night / should therefore, if he accepted the Place, take a lodging room in the neighbourhood—all which he means to have considered in his *Price & Salary*.' I briefly told him, that you were chary of the public Money; & that if you could get a Clerk equally well fitted for your Business who did not live 4 miles off, & who did not require a double Lodging, it would be your Duty to take him; & that perhaps his extraordinary Talents might be as much out of place in the easy Drudgery of transcribing Letters & Schedules, & doing short sums in Addition, as the Sword Point of Alexander the Great in toasting cheese, &c &c &c.—However, if you have any occasion to write to me, the Homo will call here in 4 or 5 days; & I can give him your answer.—I dined with Stuart on Saturday—the first morsel

I put into my mouth, I burst all over me into a Sweat, that resembled a tropical Rain / it literally *frightened* Stuart / I hurried down to the Necessary—vomited a little, & was finally relieved by a violent Diarrhoea—& recovered, tho' I remain somewhat feeble—. I can refer it to no imprudence or excess—I had eat nothing since breakfast & a good deal less breakfast than usual, as Mrs S. remarked /—but this is ever the way with me / Rainy windy Weather diseases my Stomach: & if any thing happens to affect & harrass me, I have no other salvation from these or worse attacks, than to eat nothing / & how far that would answer, I cannot say / for to sleep is equally dangerous / but the first morsel of food that reaches my Stomach acts as poison /—But for a slight irregular Fluttering at the Heart, & a speck of *Coldness* felt there, I should not have known, that T. W's Letter had *got into me* / & even so it has been over & over & over again. In my vexations with Mrs C— I have believed, that I have been laughing or smiling at her Mistemper &c / & have been regularly undeceived at my Meal time / . It should seem, as if certain Trains of Feeling acted, *on me*, underneath my own *Consciousness*, which is all engrossed by vivid Ideas drawn from Nature & Books—& habitually applied to the purposes of Generalization / & so that all Feelings which particularly affect *myself*, *as* myself, connect & combine with my bodily sensations, especially the trains of motion in the digestive Organs, & therefore tho' I feel them *en masse*, I do not & cannot make them the objects of a distinct attention. Any one, who witnessed the effects of bad news &c &c on my body, would conclude that I was a creature of diseased Sensibility: & if I were to judge of myself by what takes place in my own consciousness after hearing or seeing any calamity or distressing occurrence, and by the freedom, I feel, to talk, chat, laugh, &c, I should think & often have thought myself utterly insensible / incapable of feeling deeply either for myself or for others.—This is an interesting Fact of Character.— Love to Ward. I have no other objections to G. Ward's publishing my Consolations & Comforts than these—first, if it should not succeed, I should be exceedingly agitated, as well knowing, how little he could bear such a loss—whereas, if Longman or Mawman published, I should not have a moment's fear before hand or distress afterwards—secondly, has he such influence as to be able to counteract any malignant opposition from Longman & Rees, & to give to the work those advantages of Sale, which Cadell or Mawman would give it?—/—Poole! if you have not already (as I so earnestly requested you) destroyed that Letter & all copy of that Letter, in which I wrote to you with dream-like imagination respecting Sir Isaac Newton, & my hope of optico-metaphysical discovery, I pray you do it now—& tell me, that it is done. I never was anxious about any Letter, saving that.——Have you seen T. W.?—O! Davy *did* talk hard-heartedly about him yesterday— but so have you of me—so do all who like you, are healthy & happy & prosperous, of the sickly &c, who are long sickly. S. T. C.

## 545. To William Godwin

*MS. Lord Abinger. Hitherto unpublished.*

Monday Morning, Jan. 30 1804

Dear Godwin

Poole left town on Saturday, & does not return for 7 or 8 days. If Mr Purkis, an intimate & dear friend of Poole's, & a man who has been attentive to me (he has been already introduced to you by me) should come to Town on Tuesday, in the hope of passing an hour or two with me, I shall take the liberty of leaving a Note here for him stating that I am sure you will welcome him if he will walk over & dine at ½ past 4 at Sommers' Town for his own sake, and as my friend. I found this morning your Packet on the Table / they are very careless here as to the delivery of Cards &c for me / I burnt the Letter after having read it—& will read over the M.S. this morning, if possible—for I must write two Letters of some length / at all events, I will return to it, early this evening. If it should be very bad weather tomorrow, you will not expect me till dinner Time / tho' indeed as even then I must take Coach, ill as I can afford these Scatterers of Cash, I may as well take it at 9 in the Morning as at 3 in the afternoon, & with more probability of getting a Coach.—I was sadly diseased by the rain & storm of Saturday—received a Letter of tremendous Gloom from T. W., which *got into me* unknown, *in the degree at least*, to my own consciousness—dined with Stuart, & had not swallowed half a dozen Morsels, when a Sweat, like a tropical Rain, burst out from all my Limbs, Head, Forehead, &c &c, so as to *frighten* Stuart—& this was instantly followed by a violent Diarrhoea not without vomiting—I soon recovered; but am still feeble.—This is always the case, when any distress occurs during wet, or damp weather— any thing that increases the sensations from the Stomach either directly as Food, or indirectly by withdrawing the counter action of the Senses, as Sleep, acts *then* inevitably like a dreadful Poison upon me.—And, what is strange, this Distress is often almost unknown to myself—nay, I have often accused myself of insensibility when smash! crash!——God bless you & S. T. C.

P.S. My kind respects to Mrs Godwin /

## 546. *To Sir George Beaumont*

*Address*: For | Sir George Beaumont, Bart | Dunmow Essex
*MS. Pierpont Morgan Lib. Pub. with omis.* Memorials of Coleorton, *i. 38.*
*Postmark*: 30 January 1804.

No/ 16, Abingdon St, Westminster. Jan. 30th, 1804

Dear Sir George

I could not endure to write to you, if in the permitting your Letters to remain unanswered I could attribute to myself any considerable portion of Blame. Some Divines have held, that with God to create and to think are one and the same act: if to compose Letters and to write them had been the same thing with me, you and dear Lady Beaumont would have each received a Volume. Indeed, I scarcely dare affront my own nature by a direct apology, as I am conscious that for the last three months I have thought more of you and relatively to you, than of any other person in the World, with the exception of Mr T. Wedgwood / the state of whose Health and Spirits has had perhaps some share in my own most miserable condition of Body. I am heart-sick and almost stomach-sick of speaking, writing, and thinking about myself.—It is enough, that I have been very, very ill; and have no chance of any succession of healthy Days while I remain in this Climate. Three Physicians of eminence, whom I have consulted separately, and two of whom are personally attached to me, have given it as their opinion, that a single Winter passed in a warm, even, and genial climate will entirely restore me / not perhaps to robust Health, but to that which alone I pray for, the power of exerting perseverantly & continuously those Faculties and Acquirements, which the Almighty has entrusted to my keeping. That this opinion is just, I have a persuasion strong as the Life within me: for a single Hour of dry frosty weather, or of dry air in summer Heat, *fills* me with elastic health, so that no one sensation reminds me that I have been or am again to be, ill & bedridden. One fact will explain the nature of my Complaint / About Friday Midnight the weather changed to wind and rain / it affected me in my sleep—and I awoke with a slight shock in my Stomach. All Saturday morning the bad weather continuing I was unable to breathe, except as one in an Asthma breathes, and unable to sit at the writing Desk for three minutes together. About one o/ clock I received a Letter of tremendous Gloom from T. Wedgwood / as usual, I read it without much conscious emotion—& some body coming in, I talked on general Subjects with ease, & had no suspicion that the Letter had *gotten* into me. I went out to dinner / and had not eat

3 morsels, before a Perspiration broke out upon me, like a Tropical Rain / followed by a bowel-seizure, &c &c—and in about an hour I was quite well.—In short, any harrassing thought instantly affects my Stomach; & any ungenial action upon the Skin does the same; & when these unite, the effect is a fearful one. Oftentimes when I have heard of or witnessed any calamity, my whole frame has gone *crash*, as it were, at the very moment that I have been accusing myself of insensibility. My Consciousness seems a faculty exclusively devoted to Love, and Pleasure, and general Thought; and Grief & Trouble link themselves on to those parts of my Being, which—as the blood & the secretions—are no parts of my Knowlege.—I left home on the 20th of December, meaning to spend one day at Grasmere—& thence to Kendal / at Grasmere I was taken ill, & literally imprisoned for more than a month / at length however I have reached London, with the resolution of going either to Madeira, or to Catania in Sicily, if I can by any proper way arrange the means of so doing, without injury or distress to Mrs Coleridge: and of this I have now little doubt. Wordsworth, after an obstinate refusal on my part for more than four months, has at length—I may almost say—*forced* me to accept the Loan of 100£: and tomorrow—after an interview with some merchants, from whom I am to receive all sort of distinct Information—I write to my Brothers, & request another 100£, which they are well able to spare, without even feeling the Loss—even if I should be deluded in my expectations of Health, & unable to repay the sums—and this is fully equal to all my wants both for the Voyage thither & back, my expences there for a year, & the leaving Mrs C. perfectly clear of all little Debts, &c. with my whole annuity.—Such are my Plans. That I write thus to you, you know enough of me, dear Sir George! to consider as a certain proof, how much & with what affectionate esteem my heart is attached to you. I anticipate exceeding comfort in becoming a regular correspondent; and henceforward you may *rely* on me that I shall be so, if I find & feel that my Letters will be that comfort & pleasure to you, which your's have been & ever will be to me. But as I *can* not, can*not*, endure to make up Letters of mere Thoughts & Generalizations, without hearing any thing directly & absolutely of & concerning you & dear Lady Beaumont, and without telling you any thing of my own self, however near my heart, I have prevailed on myself to write you what I am doing & how my affairs are situated now that all is settled, and I no longer risk that from your overflowing kindness, which would at once put a stop to my ever writing minutely of myself hereafter: whereas it is among my wishes to write my whole Life to you, including my Trials in a series of

546]     *To Sir George Beaumont*

Letters.—With grateful Love & m[ost devote]d Esteem, my honored Friends, I remain your's— . . .[1] S. T. Coleridge

P.S. Of my Poetry &c I write you, without fail, the day after Tomorrow. I stay in these rooms (an absent Acquaintance's Lodgings) for 8 or 9 days.—

### 547. *To Robert Southey*

*Address*: Mr Southey | Greta Hall | Keswick | Cumberland
*MS. Lord Latymer. Hitherto unpublished.*

Tuesday, Jan. 31. 1804. No/ 16, Abingdon St, Westminster

My dear Friend

If I were even an inveterate Dram Drinker, I verily believe, that I should make a Saint's Day on the morning, I received a Letter from you / You certainly write the most *spirit-filliping* Epistles of any man in the world / I sometimes have written spirit-rousing—— Sheets of Paper; but they have not been Letters. I received . . .[2]

### 548. *To George Bellas Greenough*

*Address*: G. B. Greenough Esqre | Parliament St
*Transcript Professor Edith J. Morley. Hitherto unpublished.*

16 Abingdon St. Westminster
Tuesday afternoon [31 January 1804][3]

Dear Greenough

I breakfasted with Sharp this morning & have resolved to go to Malta & thence to Sicily, according to your Suggestion. Pray, be so kind as to drop me a note informing me when you can make it convenient for us to breakfast together, either here or at your house, in order that I may hear your Journal & consult with you. If your cheek burnt about ½ past 8 on Sunday Night, it was owing to a spirited Eulogy of Davy on your Sicilian Tour & description of Ætna, which he declared to be in his opinion unrivalled—*a*—

[1] MS. torn.
[2] For Coleridge's reason for not completing this letter see Letter 549.
[3] This letter was written prior to Coleridge's arrival at Sir George Beaumont's on 7 Feb. 1804, for on his return he settled with Tobin in Barnard's Inn. Since Coleridge had seen Davy on Sunday, 29 Jan. (see Letter 544), and had written to Sharp the same day for an appointment (Letter 542), and since by 8 Feb. he had heard Greenough's 'admirable, because most minute, Journal of his Sights, Doings, and Done-untos in Sicily' (Letter 553), this letter must have been written 31 Jan. 1804.

nay—*the* Masterpiece, &c. Laudari a viro laudato[1] &c—but in earnest, it did give me great Pleasure without any surprize—

Your's | simply & truly,
S. T. Coleridge

### 549. To Robert Southey

MS. Lord Latymer. Pub. E. L. G. i. 300.

16, Ab. St. Westminster   Wednesday: Feb. 1. 1804. A Summer Day.

My dear Southey

An author [Godwin] has been inflicting a Tragedy upon me / & I have been all the morning in Durance & Endurance / when I received (about 1 o clock) a kind note from Rickman, in whose parcel this will go / went out under a promise of return in an Hour / in the meantime the Author locks up his Ms in my Cupboard / & takes the Key —& there was the Beginning of a Letter which I was writing yesterday when G. Bedford came & stayed out my ante-prandial Time /

I am tolerably well—only on Saturday in consequence of the bad weather & a Letter of tremendous Gloom of Despair from T. W. my Stomach was diseased, & on swallowing half a dozen morsels of my Dinner (at Stuart's) I burst out into a Sweat, like a tropical Rain / that literally *frightened Stuart*—after this one of the 4 or 5 most violent Bowel-scizures I have ever had—but in the evening I grew well again / —Yesterday was a day of hot Drizzle— & I was puffed & asthmatic the whole Day / & I doubt not, if any thing had happened to afflict me, I should have had another attack / .——I dined at Godwin's with Hamilton Rowan,[2] an excellent man / but I expect my author back, & have not time to say what I mean to say / so to night or tomorrow I will sit down & give you a Gossip-Journal of what I have done & whom seen—I received a cheering Letter from Sara—My Love to her, & she will send me in her next a little inventory of the Cloathes, I have with me / To day I dine at the beastly hour of ½ past 6 at General Hastings' to meet a man piping hot from France, an escaped Prisoner / —Here comes my Author / &

so God bless you, | &
S. T. Coleridge

---

[1] *Ciceronis Epis. ad Fam.* V. xii. 7; Naevius, *Hector's Departure*, Warm. Frag. 17 (Loeb).

[2] Archibald Hamilton Rowan (1751–1834), United Irishman, was imprisoned in the Dublin Newgate in 1794; he escaped three months later and went to France, where he met Mary Wollstonecraft. From 1795 to 1800 he was in the United States. After two years in Germany his pardon was effected and in 1803 he was allowed to return to England.

He is gone to the necessary—I will therefore only say, that Poole is gone out of Town, for a week, & Rickman returned / & that I dine with R. on Friday, & as much oftener as he will invite me, it being among my main wishes to be as much as possible with him.—

Lamb has left off drinking, & is unwell & low-spirited.—Tell Sara, that Miss Wakefield had arrived at Dr Crompton's only two days before I came thither / Every body loves her exceedingly. / She asked after Sara with fervent earnestness.—

I have not seen Longman / Some body at his Saturday meetings was discussing you & me, to the advantage of my Genius / Longman contrary to his custom could not bear it, & burst out, like a Flame / You may depend on it from *me*, Sir! who must know the two men / there is no comparison as to Genius / Let it be one sheet to two Volumes Mr Southey brings it or sends it to the *very hour* / whereas Mr Coleridge &c &c——God love you, my dear Southey, &c——

## 550. To Sir George Beaumont

*Addressed and franked*: London February second 1804 | Sir George Beaumont Bt. | Dunmore | Essex | Free J. N. Ley.
MS. Pierpont Morgan Lib. Pub. Memorials of Coleorton, *i. 43*.
*Postmark*: 2 February 1804.

No/16 Abingdon St, Westminster.
Wednesday, Feb. 2 [1]. 1804

Dear Sir George

I thank you for your kindness—& I hope, with no every day Thanks: yet if I know my own nature, twenty times an hundred Pound would not be as precious to me, as that (not unaffectionate) Esteem for me on your Part, which, I flatter myself, was the true Parent of your kindness. That I do not dare avail myself of your offer, becomes therefore a mere trifle: for the thing itself is but what an expressive motion of the Hand is to a generous Thought— the Symbol, and the Ornament, but not the Essence.—Thus much then in addition to my statement of my Case. Whatever affects my Stomach, diseases me; & my Stomach is affected either immediately—by disagreeing Food, or distressing Thoughts, which make all food disagree with me—or indirectly by any ungenial action upon *the Skin*, that terra incognita to Physicians & Metaphysicians / Now very cold dry weather, or very hot dry weather are alike benignant to me; it is Damp, Rain, Storm, Thaw, and Thaw-winds, in short, whatever makes the air heavy, that unfailingly deprive me of all power to be useful—excepting as far as the Contemplation of my own Being, & the Exercise & Increase of

Patience are useful—: which, assuredly, they are, regarded, as Causae Causarum.—This Winter therefore has been especially unfavorable to me / and it is seldom that even in Summer we have a month together of light dry weather—least of all at Bath, that sunless vapoury Bason among the Hills. I have *now* had the advice of *four* medical men, & the opinions of all the four coincide with the 3-years-old Persuasion of my own mind; namely, that I must hope for a Cure in such medicines only as can act continuously and regularly for many months together. Of these there are three— regulated Diet, Tranquillity, and an even & dry climate—. The old Schola Salernitana with a little alteration expresses the Thing exactly—& speaks to me oracularly:

> Si tibi deficiant Medici, Medici tibi fiant
> Haec tria, Mens aequa, Aer aequus, et aequa Diaeta.—

I persist therefore in going to Sicily: where I hope to find all three. I was hardly used from infancy to Boyhood; & from Boyhood to Youth most, MOST cruelly / yet 'the Joy within me', which is indeed my own Life and my very Self, was creating me anew to the first purpose of Nature, when other & deeper Distress supervened—which many have guessed, but Wordsworth alone knows to the full extent of the Calamity / Yet even this I shall master— if it please the Almighty to continue in me the Thoughts, that have been my Guides, Guardians, and Comforters for the last 5 months.—

I look back with honest pride on the latter months of my Life, when I review what I have accomplished under what sufferings. I have now completed my materials (and three months will enable me to send them to the Press) for a work, the contents of which you will conjecture from the Title—'Consolations & Comforts from the exercise & right application of the Reason, the Imagination, and the Moral Feelings.' The 'Consolations' are addressed to all in adversity, sickness, or distress of mind / the first part entirely practical—the second in which I consider distress of mind from gloomy Speculation will, of course, be speculative, & will contain a new Theodicee, & what will perhaps appear to many a new Basis of Morals / the 'Comforts' are addressed to the Happy & Prosperous, attempting to open to them new & perhaps better—at all events, more numerous & more various Sources of Enjoyment.— Of this work every page has & will come from my Heart's Heart— & I may venture, dear and honored Friends! to say to you, without dreading from you the Imputation of Vanity, that what I have written is to my own mind a pure Strain of Music.—While I am writing this work, I give one week in the 4 to poetry; and when I have finished it, I shall religiously *divide* my Time / one fortnight in each month I shall *then* devote to poetry, and the other Fortnight to Essays (7 in number, & of which the 3rd will be the first published) the first, on the Genius & Writings of Chaucer—2. The same, on Spencer. 3. Shakespere. 4. an Essay biographical & critical on Milton.—5. an Episodical Essay on the supposed Genius, Style, critical powers, & morals of Dr S. Johnson. 6. on Dryden & Pope. 7. On the sources of poetic Pleasure—in which without using the words bad or good, I simply endeavor to detect the causes & sources of the Pleasures, which different Styles &c have given in different ages, & then determining their comparative Worth, Permanency, & Compatibility with the nobler parts of our nature to establish in the utmost depths, to which I can delve, the characteristics of Good & Bad Poetry—& the intimate Connection of Taste & Morals.—In explaining what I shall do with Shakespere I explain the nature of the other five. Each scene of each play I read, as if it were the whole of Shakespere's Works—the sole thing extant. I ask myself what are the characteristics—the Diction, the Cadences, and Metre, the character, the passion, the moral or metaphysical Inherencies, & fitness for theatric effect, and in what sort of Theatres—all these I write down with great care & precision of Thought & Language— / and when I have gone thro' the whole, I then shall collect my papers, & observe, how often such & such Expressions recur / & thus shall not only know what the Characteristics of Shakespere's Plays are, but likewise what proportion they bear to each other. Then, not carelessly tho' of course with far less care I shall read thro' the old Plays, just before Shakespere's Time, Sir Phillip Sidney's Arcadia—Ben Johnson [*sic*], Beaumont & Fletcher, & Massinger / in the same way—so as to see & to be able to prove what of Shakespere belonged to his Age, & was common to all *the first-rate* men of that true Saeculum aureum of English Poetry, and what is his own, & his only—Thus I shall both exhibit the characteristics of the Plays—& of the mind—of Shakespere—and of almost every character at greater or less Length a philosophical Analysis & Justification, in the spirit of that analysis of the character of Hamlet, with which you were much pleased, and by being so, I solemnly assure, gave me Heart & Hope / and did me much good. For much as I loathe flattery from the bottom of my very *Stomach*, and much as I *wriggle* under the burthen & discomfort of the Praise of People, for whose Heads, Hearts, & specific Competence I have small respect, yet I own myself no self-subsisting Mind—I know, I feel, that I am weak—apt to faint away inwardly, self-deserted & bereft of the confidence in my own powers—and that the approbation & Sympathy of good & intelligent men is my Sea-breeze, without which I should languish from Morn to evening; a very Trade-wind to me, in which my Bark drives on regularly & lightly.—

An author of some Celebrity & more Notoriety was with me all yesterday, & inflicted on me 5 acts of a Tragedy—& all to day with aching Spirit I am to be employed in pencil-marking it's thousand flatnesses & incongruities of Diction & Sentiment / in addition to a conversation of two Hours yesterday in which I persuaded him to many essential alterations / & yet do all I can, I could as easily pray Caligula, or (within a month after his arrival in England) Buonaparte, out of Purgatory, as help this poor Devil of a Tragedy out of absolute Damnation. It will die the Death of a red hot Poker in water / all one Hiss.—But what can a decently good-natured man say to a Brother Bard who tells you that it is of importance to his Happiness & Pecuniary Circumstances?—But for this you would have received a large Sheet ful[l] of Verses in a Frank; & will do so in the course of a few Days—believe me, in no inconsiderable degree for the pleasure & relief which I myself shall have in the occupation.—Since the last Sentence I have been interrupted two hours. 1. by General Hastings. 2. by Godwin. 3 by the Poet Campbell, who stayed a most inordinate Time—this being the first time, I have ever *conversed* with him / —And now I must conclude half a sheet sooner than I expected.—Only this I must say, it being indeed one half of my purpose when I began the Letter. The more I have thought of the Translations from the Drawings, the more & more deeply am I persuaded of the excellence of the Idea / and no sooner am I any where settled, than I shall dedicate a certain portion of my Time to the realizing about 20— which I calculate, will be a small Volume, of 13 of which I have already the *leading Idea*—that is to say—whether I mean it as a moral Descriptive-poem, whether an Inscription, whether a Tale. But I had taken notes of 21 Drawings from the Blue Book—of which I retain a floating & general recollection of all, but an accurate & detailed Imagery only of three—& by no Industry of Search could I find the Paper of notes, which from some over care or other I have mislayed. I propose therefore, if it should be perfectly convenient to you, to pay you a visit for two or three days at Dunmow—you will, I am sure, be so good as not to suffer me to come if it be in the least degree inconvenient / but you will give me a few Lines, & if it be convenient, you will tell me, by what Coach to what Place I get the nearest to you——

Believe me, dear Sir | George & dear Lady Beaumont, | I remain | with grateful Respect & Affection | Your truly obliged Friend

S. T. Coleridge

P.S. I seem to feel uncomfortable in sending off this Letter, it is so wholly and exclusively all about *I myself I*; but really in the present moment I am of some anxiety to my own self—& your kindness, dear Sir George! forced me—at least, reduced me, into it.—

### 551. *To William Godwin*

*Address*: Mr Godwin | Polygon | Sommers Town.
*MS. Lord Abinger. Hitherto unpublished.*

Friday Morning, ½ past 8. Feb. 3. 1804

I am stunned and stupified by the disgraceful Scene of last night. Before *Mrs Godwin* I at once take to myself shame and sorrow: to her I have no defence, no excuse: simply and with eagerness I entreat her forgiveness. I dare believe, that her Resentment on your behalf, tho' it may exist more pure at present, was at the time not unmingled with grief & mortification on my account. It could not have happened, but for the circumstance that meaning fully to go away long before supper, & to sit up & finish the Tragedy, I had taken a large glass of Punch before Supper.—Yet still—whether the fume be not altogether passed off, I cannot say—yet still—with the exception of the one speech, for which I apologized to you at the time (O how shall I apologize for it to my own Heart?—) I cannot but think that I was spurred on, goaded, and stung to every thing, I said. Be this as it may, the Time, the Company, above all the Presence of Mrs Godwin afflicts & disquiets me.—I have at all times, (most unbelievable by those who only know the two or three first *Coatings* of my Being) a most intense Faith in my religious opinions, such as they are / this by the poisonous excitement of nervous Feeling & the Punch was made mad & extravagant—I felt & thought, as if the meanest man having such a Faith, & living under it, as his ultimate Principle of action, was as a God, compared with the most illustrious of those, who have disciplined their minds & hearts in disbelief. Yet even at that time—even during this Tirade of drunken Enthusiasm— upon my honor, I had not—for 3 minutes together—any passion of Self-conceit—or of contempt of *you*, as you—still less any the least wakings of Dislike to you.—I guess however, that the miserable Business was but the second Shock of the commotion that began before Supper respecting Southey & the Review—for I felt wounded by what I thought rash, harsh, & indelicate on your part, as I had proposed the Scheme, & mentioned Southey as ready to act upon it,— to stigmatize me, & him, as beings of gross & vulgar Egotism.—It is true, I was not conscious of this after supper; but I know, how

(1056)

subtly our Feelings are drawn out & continued, & how they rise up again magnified into monsters in our Dreams—& what is Drunkenness but a Dream?—I walked home fully persuaded that I was in the Right altogether—save only that my Nature is too gentle & innocent not to feel all the way little Taps at the Heart respecting Mrs Godwin's Presence, subtle anticipations of the tomorrow's compunction.—It is the part of vexation to criminate others / would that Lamb or his Sister, whose influence over me is uncontrolled, had but said—what is the matter with you, Coleridge?——Well, Godwin! I wish, you had but gone away when Mrs Godwin pressed you. An evil genius detained you.—I have written this Letter, because I cannot bear to see you till I hear from you / I am not a man to be much troubled about *Consequences*: it is the *Causes* of Things that sink deep into me. Yet still it would grieve me sorely, if I had left in your mind feelings & thoughts which you cannot do away—& which, tho' you may forgive outwardly & to the utmost of your power, yet leave you a different Being toward me—& me a different Being in you. Solemnly, I assure you that tho' I do think, you goaded me—as well as Mary Lamb respecting my Flattery—yet for myself I feel only sorrow & shame—toward you nothing but Love & Respect, even more if possible than before.—Give two or three Lines by the Bearer to say that I shall see you at ½ past 3—

S. T. Coleridge—

## 552. *To Mrs. S. T. Coleridge*

*Addressed and franked*: London fourth Feby 1804 | Mr Rt Southey | Greta Hall | Keswick    Free J. Ley.
MS. Lord Latymer. *Hitherto unpublished*. The first and second pages of the holograph are missing.
*Postmark*: 4 February 1804.

. . . deep into my Heart—& I am working for Godwin hours a thousandfold precious & wanted by me for my nearest & most pressing Interests, in order to prevent any involuntary Recurrence in his mind of the Feelings, I had planted there.—If however this Affair have the effect of making me infinitely jealous of myself in drinking, it will be some recompence / but never can I wholly forgive myself. Tho' undoubtedly Godwin had provoked, & deserved a moderate Dressing / Considering the endless Bustle I live in, I am well / but I think, I shall go on Tuesday to Dunmow / there I shall have quiet & will write both to you & to dear Southey—. I cannot recollect any thing about any sums of money / I am all in the dark / never mind—take what they send / & I will send you

## To Mrs. S. T. Coleridge

shortly enough to clear off every farthing, we owe at Keswick/.—Tell Southey, that I love & honor him from my heart / & I hope, that when I am abroad he will write affectionately to me: for then one needs it—in England amusing Letters are kind ones.—

Love to all—& I will write again, all & every thing, as soon as I have one evening's quiet. I dined & stayed till morning with Rickman yesterday / & dine again with him on Monday—he *is* a Talus with a Heart of Flesh & Blood—in very truth, a real, & alas! for that very reason—a wonderful man!—I bless you, my dear Sara! when I lie down, & when I rise up—O kiss all the darlings for their poor Father—& let your Letters be full of yourself & of them / no minutia will be too minute——. Hazlitt never meant Hartley for any but for me / he says / I *wish*, I *wish*, I could get a Portrait of myself for the Wordsworths—& give Hartley's to Mr Jackson & Mrs Wilson / I cannot bear to send it away from them /—You cannot conceive how much & often this is in my Thoughts—for without gratitude what would become of us—Tell Southey, I really *long* for a whole quiet Evening in order to be with him in Spirit by a spacious Letter—

Bless you again & again<br>S. T. Coleridge

Rickman yesterday sent a parcel per Coach to Penrith for Southey—in which I inclosed a Letter from me for S.—
Remember me affectionately to Mary Stamper.

### 553. To the Wordsworths

*Address*: Mr Wordsworth | Grasmere, near Ambleside, | Kendal | Westmoreland
*MS*. Dove Cottage. *Pub*. Letters, ii. 456.
*Postmark*: 10 February ⟨1804.⟩

Dunmow, Essex. Wednesday Night, ½ past 11<br>Feb. 8th, 1804

My dearest Friends

I must write, or I shall have delayed it till Delay has made the Thought painful as of a Duty neglected. I had meant to have kept a sort of Journal for you /; but I have not been calm enough; & if I had kept it, I should not have time to transcribe it, for nothing can exceed the Bustle, I have been in from the day of my arrival in Town. The only incident of any extr'ordinary Interest was a direful Quarrel between Godwin & me, in which to use his own phrase (unless Lamb suggested it to him) I 'thundered and lightened with frenzied Eloquence' at him for near an hour & a half. It ended in a reconciliation next day; but the affair itself, and the ferocious Spirit into which a Plusquam sufficit of Punch had betrayed me, has sunk deep into my Heart. Few events in my Life have grieved me more / tho' the fool's conduct richly merited a flogging, but not with a scourge of Scorpions. I wrote to Mrs Coleridge the next day, when my mind was full of it / & when you go into Keswick, she will detail the matter, if you have nothing better to talk of.—My Health has greatly improved / & rich & precious Wines (of several of which I had never before heard the names) agree admirably with me / & I fully believe, most dear William! they would with you—. But still I am as faithful a Barometer, and previously to & during all falling Weather am as asthmatic & stomach-twitched as when with you / I am a perfect Conjuror as to the state of the weather; & it is fact, that I detected myself in being somewhat flattered at finding the infallibility of my uncomfortable Feelings, as to falling weather either coming or come. What Sicily may do for me, I cannot tell / but Dalton,[1] the Lecturer on Natural Philosophy at the R. Institution, a man devoted to Keswick, convinced me, that there was five times the duration of falling weather at Keswick compared with the flat & midland Counties, & more than twice the gross quantity of water fallen.—I have as yet been able to *do* nothing for myself. My plans are to try to get such an introduction to the Captn of the War ship that shall next sail for Malta, as to be taken as his Friend—from Malta to Syracuse is but six hours' Passage in a Spallanieri[2]—at Syracuse I shall meet with a hearty Welcome from Mr Leaky [G. F. Leckie], the Consul—& I hope to be able to have a Letter from Lord Nelson to the Convent of Benedictines at Catania to receive & lodge me, for such time as I may chuse to stay—Catania is a pleasant Town with pleasant hospitable Inhabitants at the foot of Ætna, tho' 15 miles, alas! from the woody region. Greenough has read me an admirable, because most minute, Journal of his Sights, Doings, and Done-untos in Sicily——As to money, I shall avail myself of an 105£, to be repayed by you on the first of January, 1805[3]—and another 100£, to be employed in paying the Life Assurance, the Bills at Keswick, Mrs Fricker's next half year, & if any remain, to buy me comforts for my voyage, &c, Dante & a Dictionary, I shall borrow part from my Brothers, and part from Stuart—I can live a year at Catania, for I have no plan or desire of travelling except up & down Ætna, for 100£—&

---

[1] John Dalton (1766–1844), best known for his atomic theory.
[2] According to Professor J. A. Gengerelli, the word *spallaniere* (*barca con due veli*) is still used in Sicily.
[3] See Letter 569.

the getting back I shall trust to Chance. O my dear dear Friends! if Sicily should become a British Island—as all the Inhabitants intensely desire it to be—and if the Climate agreed with *you* as well as I doubt not, it will with me—& if it be as much cheaper than even Westmoreland, as Greenough reports—& if I could get a Vice-consulship, of which I have little doubt—O what a dream of Happiness could we not realize?—But Mortal Life seems destined for no continuous Happiness save that which results from the exact performance of Duty—and blessed are you, dear William! whose Path of Duty lies thro' vine-trellised Elm-groves, thro' Love and Joy & Grandeur—. 'O for one hour of Dundee!'[1]—— How often shall I sigh 'O! for one hour of the Recluse!'—I arrived at Dunmow on Tuesday, & shall stay till Tuesday Morning—you will direct No / 16, Abingdon St, Westminster. I was not received here with mere kindness—I was welcomed *almost* as you welcomed me when first I visited you at Racedown / And their solicitude of attention is enough to effeminate one. Indeed, indeed, they *are* kind & good people—& Old Lady Beaumont, now 86, is a sort of miracle for beauty, & clear understanding & chearfulness—The House is an old House by a Tan yard, with nothing remarkable but it's awkward Passages. We talk by the long Hour about you & Hartley, Derwent, Sara, and Johnnie—& few things, I am persuaded, would delight them more than to live near you—I wish, you would write out a Sheet of Verses for them / I almost promised for you, that you should send that delicious Poem on the Highland Girl at Inverslade.[2]—But of more importance incomparably is it, that Mary & Dorothy should begin to transcribe *all* William's MS poems *for me*. Think what they will be to me in Sicily!—They should be written in pages, & *lettered* up in parcels not exceeding two Ounces & a quarter each, including the Seal, and *three* Envelopes, one to the Speaker—under that one to John Rickman, *Esqre*, & under that one to *me*. Terrible mischief has happened from foolish people of R's acquaintance *neglecting* the middle Envelope, so that the Speaker opening his Letter finds himself made a Letter-smuggler to Nicholas Noddy / or some other unknown Gentleman. But I will send you the exact form. The weight is not of much importance; but better not exceed two Ounces & a quarter.—I will write again as soon as I hear from you—in the mean time, God bless you, dearest William, Dorothy, Mary!—and my Godchild!—S. T. Coleridge.

---

[1] Wordsworth's sonnet, *In the Pass of Killicranky*, line 11: 'O for a single hour of that Dundee.' *Poet. Works*, iii. 85.

[2] Ibid. 73. For *Inverslade* read *Inversneyde*.

## 554. To John Rickman

*Address*: J. Rickman Esqre | at his Office | House of Commons | London
*MS. Huntington Lib. Hitherto unpublished.*
*Postmark*: 13 February 1804.

Sunday, Feb. 13 [12]. 1804

My dear Sir

You will, I am sure, agree with me that I owe you an *explanation* rather than apology, for not being with you, tomorrow dinner, when I tell you, that on going out of town I was informed that the Coach went on Tuesdays, Thursdays, & Saturdays, & returned the *intermediate days*—accordingly, I had no doubt of being in London tomorrow afternoon, before 2 o/clock / but this morning the Servant, whom I had desired to secure a place for me for tomorrow, informs me that it does indeed go on the intermediate Days, only with the exception of Monday—because the Harlow Coach is always full on Mondays, of it's own Harlow Passengers—and the Dunmow Coach (which Dunmow has only a private Road) is a sort of Makeweight & *auxiliary* to the Harlow Coach—. This I could not possibly guess—and yet tho' I cannot but acquit myself morally, yet I am vexed whenever I am by whatever cause or necessity made to lose, (to appear to *break*) an engagement—Bitter Experience has taught me, how much pain a careless Man inflicts, how much respectability he loses with consequent Loss of Power.—

I am with good & pleasant people here; and Sir George Beaumont is a man of undoubted Genius.——
I remain | my dear Sir, | respectfully | your obliged | Friend & Servant,

S. T. Coleridge

If you should see Poole, will you be so good as to remind him to send immediately any Letter or Letters, there may be for me— Mr Coleridge, Sir George Beaumont's | Dunmow, Essex.—
I trouble you with paying postage for this Letter: for I am afraid to direct to you under cover to the Speaker, for fear I should make some Blunder in the Address.—

## 555. To Mrs. S. T. Coleridge

*Address*: Mrs Coleridge | Greta Hall | Keswick | Cumberland
*MS. Lord Latymer. Pub. E. L. G. i. 303.*
*Postmark*: 15 February ⟨1804.⟩  *Stamped*: Dunmow.

Tuesday, Feb. 15 [14]. 1804

My dear Sara

Dunmow, Essex.—I have no time to say with what glowing affection I was welcomed & have since been treated by Sir G. & Lady Beaumont / nor how often we have talked of you, of the children, & of Southey—who would meet in Sir G. Beaumont a man prepared to love *the person* as much as he now honors the *Man*. I am too late to write—yet will not let the Post go off—I return to London on Friday Morning—direct to the old place / I received your Letter this morning—my eyes are still red with crying over it, for Joy & tenderness & sorrow of absence / O my sweet Hartley! my darling—My own, very own Hartley!—& my Stump! my pretty affectionate Derwent!—You remember, I told you that he was just in the very same way on his first arrival at Grasmere, altho' I was then with him. My very Heart is still trembling—& my very heart thanks and loves you, my dear! for your Letter—Be as minute about the Children as you can / never let any thing escape /—

I thought to have been quite at leisure here & to have written a set of long Letters—but alas! Sir G. & Lady are bewitching Company—

My dear! I would have [you] draw as soon as you receive this Letter on Daniel Stuart, Esqre, Courier office, Strand, London, for 20£—payable to Mr Jackson, or order—. I shall apprize Stuart, & it will be duly honored—you may draw at six weeks' date, or even at a month's date. This will supply you with ready money, & pay off little Bills / & in a few weeks I will leave you debtless at Keswick, debts great & small, save that which we both owe to Southey for his Vice-fathership.

I have received another heart-withering Letter of absolute Despair from T. Wedgwood /

> May God Almighty bless you, | my dear Sara, | And your |
> ever faithful and anxious Friend,
>
> S. T. Coleridge

You told me nothing about sweet Sara / tell me every thing—send me the ve[ry] *Feel* of her sweet Flesh, the very Looks & Motions of that mouth / O I could drive myself mad about her!—...[1]

---
[1] Half a line inked out in MS.

*14 February 1804* [556

### 556. To Thomas Poole

*Address*: T. Poole, Esqre | Parliament Office | Abingdon St | Westminster
*MS. British Museum. Hitherto unpublished.*
*Postmark*: 15 February 1804.

Tuesday Afternoon / [14 February 1804]
on the point of Dinner

My dear Poole

To Longman, as far as I recollect, I made only a conditional promise—To Tobin none / I shall be in Town, God willing, on Friday afternoon, 2 o/ clock / of course shall be with you before 4——

I have no time to say with what kindness—I might without exaggeration [say]—glowing affection I was welcomed by Sir George & Lady Beaumont; & by Dowager Lady Beaumont, now 86 years of age, & chearful, active, intelligent, & with perfect senses.—The attention payed to me by the servants &c in obedience to their master & mistress would effeminate me, if I were long subject to their influences.

You[r's]
S. T. Coleridge

### 557. To John Rickman

*Address*: Jno/ Rickman Esqre
*MS. Huntington Lib. Pub. E. L. G. i. 301.*

[15 February 1804]

My dear Sir

I take the liberty of inclosing the Inclosed with a request, that you would have it franked—poetry being a poor Trade, which Buchanan assigns as a reason for the old maidship of the 9 Muses—they had no dowries. It gave me more pain than an event not attributable to my own neglect ought to have done, that I could not be with you on Monday—tho' that not being in my power, I was not sorry to remain a few days longer absent from the Bustle of London, with two such unaffectedly good people, as Sir George and Lady Beaumont / the more so, as I have learnt as much fr[om] Sir George respecting Pictures & Painting and Painte[rs as] I ever learnt on any subject from any man in the same Space of Time. A man may employ time far worse than in learning how to look at a picture judiciously.—I have been writing essays on the Volunteer, which will appear forthwith.[1] I am apprehensive, that you will

---

[1] No such contributions have been identified.

think them too favorable to the Ministers, too violent against their Opponents. I know full well, that you are not a man to return formal Thanks to—yet you will not be disgusted with any man for saying simply, what he feels really—and I have been much affected by the quiet promptness with which you have caused a Trial to be made of my Wife's Brother—. An earnest desire to do his Duty I am sure will not be wanting— / Your's sincerely,

S. T. Coleridge.

I return on Friday Noon / .—

### 558. To the Wordsworths

*Address*: [Mr W.] Wordsworth | [Grasm]ere, Ambleside, | Kendal | Westmoreland
*MS. Dove Cottage. Pub. with omis. E. L. G. i. 304.*

Wednesday. Feb. 16 [15]. Dunmow, Essex. 1804

My dearest Friends

O what a pen! I shall write as illegibly as dear Dorothy herself, whose darling Letter I received this morning / . I left the money for the payment of the Cradle with the Waiter of the King's Arms at Kendal—that same steady Fellow whom you know, & who knows you very well—I believe, that the King's Arms is the name of the Inn; but it is that from which the cheap Liverpool coach goes—it *is* the King's Arms; for I have it down in my pocket book—he could not tell me where the man lived; but promised me that he would be sure to find him out the next day, and pay him, & send *you* the receipt. You had better send the two lines which I will write at the end of the third page in to Mr Dun, and let him call at the King's Arms with it, & no doubt, the Waiter will pay him. I guess, that the Waiter has lost the Card & forgotten the name: for he seems a very honest Fellow. On my return to London I will immediately go about your watch Business. The Border Ballads[1] were left by Lamb at Richard's Rooms a year ago.[2]——O my darling Friends! I seem to see the Image of that Bridge as distinctly as if I were there / —*an* image of a very sweet

---

[1] The first two volumes of Scott's *Minstrelsy of the Scottish Border* appeared in 1802, the third volume in 1803.

[2] Coleridge refers to Richard Wordsworth, the poet's brother. On 2 June 1804 Lamb wrote that he had 'got from your brother Richard' the watch and the books and had forwarded them to the north (*Lamb Letters*, i. 370). On 29 Apr. 1804 Wordsworth thanked Sharp for 'your present of the *Minstrelsy of the Border*', but went on to say that he had not received the 'parcel' and that Dorothy would write to Lamb to have it forwarded with several other things. (*Early Letters*, 384–5.)

Bridge I most certainly do. Bless you all! my heart akes with Love of you.—You should have sent at once to the Cow pock Institution / Shall I go & get some, & send it down to you with ample directions / I can send any thing under two ounces free of postage when I am in London / and you may send *any weight* to me, only I would not have any one parcel exceed two ounces & a half: most carefully observing the following Directions—. Inclose the Packet in a cover directed to Mr Coleridge. 2. Inclose this in a Cover directed to Jno. Rickman, Esqre. 3. Inclose this in a Cover directed to The Right Honble | The Speaker | Palace Yard | Westminster. Be sure to be accurate in this. A correspondent of Poole's (T.W.) neglected the *second Cover*—& when the Speaker opened the Letter, he found a Letter for *T. Poole Esqre*—the *Speaker* made Letter-smuggler to an unknown *T. Poole Esqre*. But common Letters I would have you send as usual to *No / 16, Abingdon St*—but O! I conjure you, my dearest Dorothy & Mary! as you love me, as you value my utilities when absent from you, to set about making a Copy of *all* William's MS poems—. I solemnly promise that no English Eye shall behold a Line of them / either before or after my Sicilian Tour.—O I feel, I feel, what a treasure, what an inspiring Deity, they will be to me when I am absent / I would not talk thus warmly, if I did not know *how* much I am asking / therefore it is fit I should express, how great the good will be.—

I leave this place on Friday Morning.—I assure you, that Sir George Beaumont has often talked of William, his domestic Happiness, & his height & uniqueness of poetic Genius, till the Tears have been in his eyes, and on Lady Beaumont's Cheeks / who verily has a soul in point of quick enthusiastic Feeling, most like to Dorothy's—only not Dorothy's powers. Yet She has mentioned many things to me very very interesting concerning her early Life & Feelings.—

I am now going to ride. Last Friday I was dashed off my Horse in Lord Maynard's Park—& the Horse ran after, now feeding, now looking at & galloping after us—for Sir G. got off, & led his Horse—still as he came up to his [us?] kicking at & plunging at us—I thought, he was mad—for a mile & a half—at a Gate we caught him / & when remounted, as mild as a Lamb.—I shall quit these good people with regret for London / I fix my eye with unalterable steadiness on Sicily or Madeira / there is no change of weather in which I am not made to *feel* the necessity of it—The day before yesterday, nay, on Sunday I received a Letter which disturbed me / and bad weather accompanying it that night & the next I was attacked by my horrid Night-horrors—& last night I was not quite free / —but tho', my mind being pleasurably tranquil, I keep off these, yet every change of weather to wet or damp or heavy or boisterous makes me as asthmatic as ever—God bless you! I can write no more / —Th[is] Letter [s]hall cost you nothing —— it ought [not] indeed / —

Finally, initially & medially (a la mode W. Taylor of Norwich)...[1]

I cannot *read* the name of the Bridge-builder which D.W. calls *D*erwentian.[2]

## 559. To Robert Southey

*Address*: Mr Southey | Greta Hall | Keswick
*MS*. Lord Latymer. *Pub. with omis. E. L. G. i. 306.*
*Postmark*: 17 February 1804.

Friday afternoon [17 February 1804]

My dear Southey

I am this moment returned from Dunmow / the only place I have been at for a long long time, in which I have from my heart's heart wished you to have been with me. I have wished it indeed at Rickman's—but then you would have been in London, but then you would not have been with such divine Pictures, & Engravings as have made me almost an apostate to Music. I found your Letter on the Table. Poor Godwin implicated me in the same sort of disrespect as he uttered against you—quite in *his way*—without meaning any harm, but simple disclosing the unutterable Bluntness & Blindness of his Intellect—But I will write you concerning him—. As to myself, beyond all deniability I am a coward in giving pain; but what can you say to a man who comes & tells you, his pecuniary comforts will probably be greatly affected by your doing this or that?—I shall call on Longman tomorrow / —the King will certainly die[3]—Fox's Coalition with the Grenvilles is avowed— and the Prince's Life was last week despaired of from a frenzy fever, the consequence of three days' drinking / the two first, Claret & Port, did not affect him or his Rivals, the D. of Norfolk & E. of Guildford—on the third day they each drank 2 bottles of

---

[1] MS. cut off. Obviously the missing part of the letter contained the 'two lines' to the waiter at the King's Arms. See the first paragraph of this letter.

[2] Answering this letter on 6 Mar. 1804, Dorothy Wordsworth wrote: 'By the bye, I must write well and tell you that the Bridge builder was called Willy-good-Waller. I forgot to add that it was a sort of wonder in rural architecture, having been built without lime, and without a frame.' (*Early Letters*, 365.)

[3] In Jan. 1804 George III 'caught a severe cold, . . . his mind became again deranged, and for a while his life was in danger'. *D.N.B.*

Sherry, 2 of Madeira, and a bottle of Noyeau with several Glasses of Brandy—& the Hereditary Earl Marshall waved his flag triumphant over the prostrate Heir Apparent & the Earl—I expect to *write* to you tomorrow.——

Now for business. My kindest Love to *Sara Senior*, and desire her to draw upon Stuart, in whos[e] hands I shall deposit the mone[y] for a sum sufficient to pay *all* & *each* of all our Keswick Debts, with the exception of Mr. Edmondson's to whom I think it polite to write myself, & shall do it tomorrow / & for such a sum as will leave her about ten pound loose money—I would have the debts carried up to the present Day—I mean, Miss Crosthwaite's Bill—. George Fricker looks very well—I made a sort of a Bustle with Poole, which did not do *much* / and I went and told his Story plainly & simply to Rickman which did a great deal. For R. made Poole send for him / & I have great hopes, that he will do—& get forward / . I had made up my mind upon it—& if this does not do, I will strain every point of Interest, I have / for the young man is good & innocent / but I have great Hopes of this——Bless you

&

S. T. C.——

Don't be angry with poor G., who would fall prostrate & idolize you, if you would but let him.

I dine at Sharpe's with Poole—

### 560. *To John Rickman*

MS. *Huntington Lib. Pub. with omis.* Life and Letters of John Rickman, *Orlo Williams,* 1912, *p. 103.*

Feb. 18. 1804

My dear Sir

You were so kind as to express your intention of gaining some information for me from the Gentleman, whom I was so unlucky as to miss meeting: & I am not quite certain whether or not I distinctly stated the Desiderata—1. Are there any vessels likely to go for Malta, or Sicily? And when?—Is there a King's Ship going, with other, or by itself? And what chance have I of procuring a Passage on board it?—My object is to reach Catania as shortly & inexpensively, as I can / and I *suppose*, that my only, or best, way is to be landed at Malta, & thence to Syracuse in a (by me unspellable) Spallonieri, which is but six hours' voyage.——

I am at present lodged at Tobin's: & wholly disingaged, every day but Friday next, & so I shall keep myself. If you should happen to have even only an hour or two of any of the intervening Evenings, before we meet at Tobin's, it would be a pleasure to me to be with you—if you would let me know what time you are even *likely* to be at home, & really have the Time quite ad libitum. Of course, I should not take the Liberty of saying this but that it will not give me the least pain, if your time should be wholly pre-engaged / tho' it will give me pleasure, if it should be otherwise—and if I did not know enough of you, & hope that you know enough of me, to believe that you will use no sort of Ceremony whatsoever / indeed, if I do not hear from you, I shall take it for granted that your Time is anticipated / —

I met G. Burnet this morning. It made my heart feel almost as if it was going to ake, when I looked at his Eyes—they seemed so thoroughly those of an Opium-chewer—Heaven be praised, if I am mistaken—[b]ut he talked so nervously, & stated his plans so very, very helplessly— / He is going to Poland with no French in the power of his *Tongue*, & much less, than he himself supposes, in the power of his *Eyes*—and as to looking into a Sclavonic, or German Grammar—why, yes he had been *thinking* of it.——

Your's | my dear | Sir, | with unfeigned | Esteem
S. T. Coleridge

I had an excellent Letter yesterday from Southey. I know no instance of greater progress made in *vigor* of mind, in *robustness* of Understanding, than that made by our Friend in the last two or three years—O it *is* a delight to see any thing *grow* in a world where (if I may . . . [Remainder of manuscript missing.]

### 561. To Mrs. S. T. *Coleridge*

MS. Lord Latymer. Pub. with omis. Letters, ii. 460.

[Sunday, 19th February 1804]

J. Tobin, Esqre, No / 7, Barnard's Inn, Holborn. For Mr Coleridge. *So*: if you wish me to answer it by Return of Post; but if it be of no consequence, whether I receive it four hours sooner, or 4 h. later, then direct, Mr Lambe, East India House, London.—

Ten o' Clock o' the Morning   February the 19th,
Sunday / —To Thee I propos'd to write an hexameter Letter,
Thou of the Anakim fairest, beautiful Andandona!
Yes![1] in my Dreams I beheld thee: the Cawl of incarnate Osiris
Turban'd thy Head! thy Knees with profitless fury assailing[2]

---

[1] And [Cancelled word in line above.]
[2] and squealing with foul fury around thee [Cancelled words in line above.]

## 19 February 1804

Curly-tail'd Gruntlets accus'd thee, O false & immane to thy Guest-friend!
For lo! to those[1] Knees there depended the Hide of their grunnient Mother
Slain as she swill'd at thy Trough! save only this odorous She-shirt,
Other robe hadst thou none, O beautiful ANDANDONA!
Thus began I in Verse; but thinking that Prose will do better,
Fly, ye Hexameters! fly to William Taylor of Norwich
That so he once more may exclaim, O sav'd from Death and the Razor,
Welcome, dear pedlaring Jew, with the long white beard on thy Bosom.[2]

I did not receive your last Letter, written on the 'very, very windy, and very cold Sunday Night', till yesterday Afternoon, owing to Poole's neglect and forgetfulness. But Poole is one of those men who have one good quality, namely, that they always *do* one thing at a time, but who likewise have one defect, that they can seldom *think* but of one thing at a time. For instance, if Poole is intent on his matter, while he is speaking, he cannot give the least attention to his Language or Pronunciation, in consequence of which there is no one error in his Dialect which he has ever got rid of. My mind is in general of the contrary make / I too often *do* nothing in consequence of being impressed all at once (or so rapidly consecutive as to appear all at once) by a variety of Impressions. If there are a dozen people at Table, I hear & cannot help giving *some* attention, to what each one says—even tho' there should be 3 or 4 talking at once.——The Detail of the Good & the Bad of the two different *Makes* of Mind would form a not uninteresting Brace of Essays in a Spectator or Guardian.

You will of course repay Southey instantly all the money, you may have borrowed either for yourself or for Mr Jackson: & do not forget to remember, that a share of the *wine-bill* belonged to me. Likewise when you pay Mr Jackson, you will pay him just as if he had not had any money from you.—Is it half a year? or a year & a half's rent that we owe him? Did we pay him up to July last?— If we did, *then* were I you, I would now pay him the whole year's rent up to July next—and tell him, that you shall not want the

---

[1] For to thy [Cancelled words in line above.]
[2] These lines have not been published. The last line is adapted from William Taylor's
    O 'tis a pedlaring jew, by the long white hair on his bosom,
from 'The Show, an English Eclogue', published in the *Annual Anthology*, ii, 1800, p. 200, and signed Ryalto.

20£, which you have lent him, till the beginning of May. Remember me to him in the most affectionate manner; & say, how sincerely I condole with him on his Sprain.—Likewise, & as affectionately, remember me to Mrs Wilson.——

It gave me pain & a feeling of anxious concern, on our own account as well as on Mr Jackson's, to find him so distressed for money. I fear, that he will be soon induced to sell the House.— Now for our darling Hartley. I am myself not at all anxious or uneasy respecting his *Habits* of Idleness; but I should be very unhappy, if he were to go to the Town School, unless there were any steady Lad that Mr Jackson knew well & could rely on, who went to the same School regularly, and who would be easily induced by a half a crown, once in two or three months, to take care of him—let him always sit by him—& to whom you should instruct the Child to yield a certain degree of Obedience. If this can be done (& you will read what I say to Mr Jackson) I have no great Objection to his going to School & making a fair Trial of it. O may God vouchsafe me Health, that he may go to School to his own Father. I exceedingly wish, that there were any one in Keswick who would give him a little instruction in the elements of Drawing. I will go tomorrow, & enquire for some very elementary Book, if there be any, that proposes to teach it without the assistance of a Drawing-Master—and which you might make him *read to you* instead of his other Books. Sir G. Beaumont was very much pleased & interested by Hartley's promise of attachment to his darling Art. If I can find the Book, I will send it off instantly, together with the Spillĕkins (Spielchen, or Gamelet, I suppose) a German Refinement on our Jack Straw. You or some one of your Sisters will be so good as to play with Hartley, at first, that Derwent may learn it. Little Albert at Dr Crompton's, & indeed all the children, are quite Spillĕkin-mad. It is certainly an excellent Game to teach children steadiness of Hand & Quickness of eye, & a good opportunity to impress upon them the beauty of strict Truth, when it is against their own Interest, & to give them a pride in it, & habits of it——for the slightest perceptible motion produced in any of the Spillĕkins, except the one attempted to be *crooked* off the heap, destroys that Turn—& there is a good deal of foresight exerted in knowing when to give it a lusty Pull, so as to move the Spillĕkins under, if only you see that your Adversary, who will take advantage of this Pull, will himself not succeed, & yet by *his* or the second, Pull put the Spillĕkin easily in the Power of the third Pull—. Dorothy says—'It is very odd; but we saw nothing at all of this Rash (of Derwent's) all the while he was at Grasmere.' It *is* very odd: can it be the Air? or is his Diet less attended to?—I was

*19 February 1804* [561

exceedingly amused with his dear Prattle, even in a Letter—O bless him / & do not forget to write always a deal about him & Sara—& sweet Hartley.—But I own, it grieved me to find him almost immediately on his return to Keswick recommence his cry at washing; whereas at Grasmere he always took it like a little man, tho' it was plain, he did not much like it.—. . .[1] But I must not *scold*: or you will not write me *every* thing.—

I am now from [this point] writing in No / 44, upper Titchfield St / where I have (for the first time) [been] breakfasting with A. Welles, who seems a kind friendly man, & instead of recommending any more of his Medicine to me advises me to persevere in & expedite my voyage to a better climate / & has been very pressing with me to take up my home at his House—. To morrow I dine with Mr Rickman at his own House; on Wednesday I dine with him at Tobin's. I shall dine at Mr Welles to day, & thence by 8 o/clock to the Royal Institution to the Lecture / on Thursday afternoon 2 o clock to the Lecture / & on Saturday Night, 8 o-clock to the Lecture.—On Friday I spend the Day with Davy certainly; & I hope, with Mr Sotheby likewise.—Tomorrow or Wednesday I expect to know certainly what my plans are to be / *whither* to go, and *when* / and whether the intervening Space will make it worth my while to go to Ottery—or whether I shall go back to Dunmow, & return with Sir George & L.B. when they come to their House in Grosvenor Square. I cannot express to you how *very very* affectionate the Behaviour of these good people has been to me; & how they seem to love by anticipation those very few whom I love.

If Southey would but permit you to copy that divine passage of his Madoc, respecting the Harp of the Welch Bard & it's imagined Divinity with the two Savages[2]—or any other detachable Passage —or to transcribe his Kehama / I will pledge myself, that Sir George Beaumont & Lady B. will never suffer a single Individual to hear or see a single Line, you saying, that it is to be kept *sacred* to them, & not to be seen by any one else—you would be paying them . . . [Remainder of manuscript missing.]

### 562. *To Robert Southey*

*Address*: Mr Southey | Greta Hall | Keswick
MS. Lord Latymer. Pub. *with omis.* Letters, *ii.* 464.

Rickman's office, H. of Commons. Feb. 20. 1804. Monday Noon

Dear Southey

The affair with Godwin began thus: we were talking of Reviews, & bewailing their ill-effects—I detailed *my* plan for a Review viz.

[1] Three-fourths of a line inked out in MS.
[2] See *Madoc in Aztlan*, Book XI, Southey's *Poet. Works*, v. 274–5.

to occupy regularly the 4th side of an Evening paper &c &c—
adding that it had [been] a favorite scheme with me for two years
past.—Godwin very coolly observed—it was a plan which 'no man
who had a spark of honest pride' could join with—'no man, not
the slave of the grossest Egotism, could write in—.['] Cool and
civil!—I asked whether he & most others did not already do what
I proposed in *Prefaces*.—'Aye—in *prefaces*—that is quite a different
Thing.—['] I then adverted to the extreme rudeness of the Speech
with regard to myself, & added that it was not only a very rough,
but likewise a very mistaken opinion / for I was nearly if not quite
sure, that it had received the approbation both of you & of Words-
worth—'Yes—Sir! just so!—of Mr Southey—just what I said—[']
and so on mŏrĕ Godwiniānō—in language so ridiculously and
exclusively appropriate to himself, that it would have made you
merry—it was even as if he was looking into a sort of moral
Looking-Glass, without knowing what it was, & seeing his own
very very Godwinship, had by a merry conceit christened it in
your name, not without some annexment of me & Wordsworth.—
I replied by laughing in the first place at the capricious nature of
his nicety—that what was gross in folio, should become double-
refined in octavo fool's cap, or *pick-pocket* Quartos—blind slavish
Egotism in small pica, manly discriminating Self-respect in double
primer— / modest, as Maiden's blushes, between boards, or in
Calf's skin / & only not obscene in naked Sheets—and then in a
deep and somewhat sarcastic Tone tried to teach him to speak
more reverentially of his Betters by stating what & who they were,
by whom honored—& added that I would spare him the pain of
detailing, by whom depreciated.—Well! this Gust died away—I
was going home to look over his Duncity— he begged me to stay
till his return—about ½ an hour——I meaning to take nothing
more the whole evening took a crust of Bread, & Mary Lamb made
me a glass of punch of most deceitful Strength—. Instead of ½ an
hour Godwin stayed an hour & a half.—In came his Wife, Mrs Fen-
wick, and four young Ladies—& just as Godwin returned, Supper
came on and it was now useless to go—/—At Supper I was rather
a mirth-maker than merry—I was disgusted at Heart with the
grossness & vulgar Insanocaecity of this dim-headed Prig of a
Philosophicide—when after Supper his ill-stars impelled him to
renew the contest—I begged him for his own sake not to goad
me / for that I feared, my feelings would not long remain in his [my?]
power—he (to my wonder & indignation: for I had not decyphered
the cause) persisted—& then as he well said I did 'thunder &
lighten at him' with a vengeance, for more than an hour & a half—
every effort of self-defence only made him more ridiculous—If I

## 20 February 1804

had been Truth in person, I could not have spoken more accurately / but it was Truth in a war-chariot drawn by the Three Furies, & the Reins had slipped out of the Goddess's Hands; [as the Maid was somewhat inebriated—]¹ & yet he did not absolutely give way, till that stinging CONTRAST which I drew between him, as a Man, a writer, & a Benefactor of Society & those of whom he had spoken so irreverently. In short, I suspect, that I seldom at any time & for so great a length of time so continuously displayed so much power; & do hope & trust, that never never did I display one half the scorn & ferocity. The next morning the moment when I awoke / O mercy! I did feel like a very Wretch. I got up, & immediately wrote & sent off by a Porter, a Letter—I dare affirm, an affecting & eloquent Letter to him / & since then have been working for him / for I was heart-smitten with the recollection, that I had said all, all in the presence of his *Wife*.—But if I had known all I now know, I will not say that I should not have apologized; but most certainly I should not have made such an apology—for he confessed to Lamb that he should [not] have persisted in irritating me but that Mrs Godwin had twitted him for his prostration before me—as if he was afraid to say his Life was his own in my presence—. He admitted too, that altho' he never to the very last suspected, that I was tipsy—yet he saw clearly, that something unusual ailed me, and that I had not been my natural Self the whole evening. What a poor Creature! to attack a man who had been so kind to him, at the instigation of such a Woman! and what a woman to instigate him to quarrel with *me*, who with as much power as any, & more than most of his acquaintances had been perhaps the only one, who had never made a Butt of him—who had uniformly spoken respectfully to him——But it is past! and I trust will teach me Wisdom in future.—I have undoubtedly suffered a great deal from a cowardice in not daring to repel unassimilating acquaintances who press forward upon my friendship; but I dare aver, that if the circumstances of each particular Case were examined, they would prove on the whole honorable to me rather than otherwise. But I have had enough—& done enough. Hereafter, I shall shew a different Face; & calmly inform those who press upon me, that my Health, Spirits, and Occupation alike make it necessary for me to confine myself to the society [of] those, with whom I have the nearest & highest connection. So help me God! I will hereafter be quite sure that I do really & in the whole of my heart esteem & like a man before I permit him to call me friend.—

I am very anxious that you should go on with your Madoc. If

¹ Words in brackets inked out in MS.

the thought had happened to suggest itself to you originally, & with all those modifications & polypus Tendrils with which it would have caught hold of your Subject, I am assured that you would have made the first voyage *as* interesting at least as it ought to be, so as to preserve entire the fit proportions of Interest.—But go on!——

I shall call on Longman as soon as I receive an answer from him to a Note which I sent.—

This damp weather distresses me sorely—& last night I had two or three hours of horrible Dreams with screaming-fits.—

God bless you & S. T. Coleridge——

P. S. I have just received Sara's four Lines added to my Brother George's Letter: & cannot explain her not having received my Letters.—If I am not mistaken, I have written either three or four times—: upon an average I have written to Greta Hall once every five days since I left Liverpool / if you will divide the Letters, one to each five days—. I will write to my Brother immediately.—I wrote to Sara from Dunmow—to you instantly on my return / & now again. I do not deserve to be scolded at present.—I met G. Burnet the day before yesterday in Linc. Inn fields—so nervous, so helpless—with such opium-stupidly-wild eyes—O it made the place, one calls the Heart, feel as if it was going to [break.]

### 563. To John Rickman

*Address*: J. Rickman Esqre | Palace Yard | Westminster
MS. Huntington Lib. Pub. *with omis.* John Rickman, *104*.

Tuesday Morning [28 February 1804]

My dear Sir

I have been day after day about to answer your kind and to me very interesting Note. I had called on Mr Welles, long long before Southey's Letter—indeed as early as was necessary. But the general Remark has truth in it; but not as a shoot of my original nature / neither does there exist on earth a man more joyous, more various, in my enjoyments of retired Life, than I am / I have not been for some years without great objects—& my indolence &c has almost altogether arisen from my having been too too constantly forced off from these Objects—but enough! You will forgive me this little Escape of Feeling—I have felt in your society a feeling of confidence / which I never felt on so short an acquaintance, even in my younger Days—a feeling arising, no doubt, in great part from the familiarity of your name to my ears, from Lamb & Southey / the two men, whom next to Wordsworth, I love the best in the world.—I have said this even to *you* / fearless: indeed, I apprehend that we seldom fear to say any thing that we can say with the whole Heart.—I have sent you some Essays written at different times in the M. Post—but the best are unfortunately not there / especially, the character of Pitt—& one on Lord Grenville's Politics—which I have never been able to think meanly of / and (shame on me, if I speak with any affected humility) to think meanly of what I have written, almost immediately after the hot fit of composition, is ever a disease of my mind.—Those, I suppose, which will stand the best chance of interesting you are Mr Poole's Defence of Farmers—

As soon as my Volunteer Essays, and whatever of a Vindiciae Addingtonianae I can effect by simple attacks of the Antagonists of Ministers, are published, they shall be sent to you without fail.— If you have heard any thing of the Ship for Malta, you will be so good as to give me a Line—from 9 in the morning till 4 o clock, my best address is, Mr Coleridge, Courier office, Strand—after that time, No 7. Barnard's Inn, Holborn.

I have been very unwell for the last day or two—& rather roughly treated not by the Weather alone——

Mrs Wordsworth's Sister has sent off the poem for Lady Beaumont / & I should hope, that it would puzzle stupidity itself to mistake the directions, I gave, as to the 3 Covers.—

Believe me, | dear Sir, | Your's very sincerely
S. T. Coleridge—

I spent yesterevening with Lamb—& shall be there this evening sans fail—

### 564. *To Lady Beaumont*

*Address*: For | Lady Beaumont | Dunmow | Essex.
*MS. Pierpont Morgan Lib. Pub. with omis.* Memorials of Coleorton, *i.* 52.
*Postmark*: 5 March 1804.

Monday Afternoon March 5. 1804

Dear Madam

Within the last hour four Letters at once have been brought to me from Mr Lamb's—who has been ill, & prevented by illness from attending at the India House, & I too, alas! have been ill & in a sort of Stupor, & not knowing of Lamb's Illness took it for granted that there were no Letters for me— / These four all from Dunmow! I was so agitated at the sight, that I was incapable of opening either, for nearly three quarters of an hour / & there still remains one from your Ladyship unopened—and this I literally am as much afraid of, as a child of a dark room / at least, I must first assure your Ladyship & Sir George, that I will send the acid with the directions by tomorrow's Coach / and that I will devote the very first genial Half-hour, that I am favored with, to the attempt to translate into measured words the feelings of your Heart.——I have been as yet able to gain no certain intelligence respecting the Vessels for Malta; & think it unlikely that it will sail so soon as the 10th / for the King's Ship is not yet fixed on, for their Convoy.— As to my Christabel & some other Verses which are preparing for you, I am highly gratified that they are in your possession:[1] the thought, that you and Sir George will at times talk of the poem by your fire side, or in your summer evening walks, & sometimes wish for it's conclusion, will be one and a strong inducement to me, to finish it / I trust, I need not say to your Ladyship, that in a letter to Dunmow least of all correspondents should I dare to let my words outstrip my weighed meaning, my inmost Feeling.——

Now I think, I have gathered courage to open the Letter—. It is a kind Letter from Sir George—I will not fail to call on Mr Knight tomorrow before Noon.—

I have been advised by a very eminent Physician to try a very small drop of nitric acid (that is, VERY PURE aqua fortis) placed on the tumour by the point of a fine pen / & to continue this on the same place for some weeks, twice a day—. He says, he cannot positively answer for it's success—as he has only had occasion [to] advise it in two instances—; but that [in] both those it's success was compleat / & [if] it should answer equally well with me, it would be a very valuable discovery—as it leaves no scar, & spares all the danger that the surgical Lancet might occasion in places near or close upon the glands—especially, where there is S[crofula] in the constitut[ion.] . . .

. . . COURIER; but I doubt my interest in the Morning Post—— Your Ladyship's goodness will . . .[2]

Henceforward I shall be [certain] to receive my Letters re[gularly.]

P.S. On second thought I fear, that I can not get the acid prepared & sent to the Coach by tomorrow: if it be *possible*, it shall be done / but at latest, on the next Coach day.—Davy lectures to night: & I cannot see him till tomorrow.

---

[1] No such copy of *Christabel* has come to light.
[2] Four lines cut from pages 3 and 4 of the MS.

## 565. To Humphry Davy

*Address*: Humphry Davy, Esqre | Royal Institution | Albermarle St.
MS. *Royal Institution. Pub. with omis.* Frag. Remains, *93.*
*Postmark*: 6 March 1804.

Tuesday Morning [6 March 1804]
7. Barnard's Inn, | Holborn

My dear Davy

I trusted my cause last Sunday, I fear, to an unsympathizing Agent. To Mr Tuffin I can scarcely think myself bound to make a direct apology, as my promise was wholly conditional—viz, my Health & the Weather permitting. This I did—not only from general Foresight—but—from the possibility of hearing from you that you had not been able to untie your former engagement. To you therefore I owe the apology: & on you I expressly and earnestly desired Tobin to call, & to explain for me, that I had been in an utterly uncomfortable state of bodily feeling the whole Evening at Mr Pinny's, that I was much hurt by the walk home thro' the wet; instantly on my return had an attack in my bowels; that this had not wholly left me; & therefore that I could not come, unless the weather *altered.* By which I did not mean merely, it's *holding up* (tho' even this it did not do, at 4 o clock, at Barnard's Inn—the sleety rain was still falling, tho' slightly) but the drying up of the rawness and dampness, which would infallibly have diseased me, before I had reached the R. Institution—not to mention the effect of sitting a long evening in damp cloathes & Shoes on an Invalid scarcely recovered from a Diarrhoea.—I have thought it fit to explain at large, both as a mark of respect to you and because I have very unjustly acquired a character for breaking engagements, entirely from the non-sympathy of the Well with the Sick, the Robust with the Weakly. It must be difficult for most men to conceive the extreme reluctance with which I go at all into *company,* & the unceasing Depression which I am struggling up against, during the whole time, I am in it—which too often makes me drink more *during dinner* than I ought to do; and as often forces me into *efforts* of almost obtrusive conversation—*acting* the opposite of my real state of mind in order to arrive at a medium—as we roll paper the opposite way in order to smooth it out.——

Sir G. Beaumont, who has found himself benefited for a little while and in *some respects* by the occasional use of *vegetable* acids, wishes to try with caution the acid made by the Oxyg. Mur. of Potash & Vitriolic acid—I told him, when at Dun[mow] that it had had very pleasant effec[ts on] me for a little while: & I did not doubt, that by using it for a week or so, about ten drops a day he would find his stomach strengthened. Of course, I cannot ask you to have a small phial prepared for me to send to Dunmow on Thursday; but I should be much obliged to you if you would immediately send me a few lines by the Twopenny Post, containing such a recipe as will secure it's being made up accurately at Godfrey's—at the same time you will be so good as to tell me, what hour you expect Mr Sotheby on Thursday—

I am, my dear Davy, | with sincere & affectionate Esteem<br>your's ever, S. T. Coleridge

### 566. To Sir George Beaumont

*Address*: Sir George Beaumont Bart | Dunmow | Essex
*MS*. Pierpont Morgan Lib. *Pub. with omis.* Memorials of Coleorton, i. 55.

Thursday, ½ past 11.—March 8th 1804

Dear Sir George

I called on Mr Knight, on Tuesday Noon / he was engaged with a gentleman in looking over his collection. Bye the bye (whether it were that the sight of so many Bronzes all at once infected my eye, as by long looking at the setting Sun all objects become purple, or whether there really be a likeness) Mr Knight's own face represented to my fancy that of a living Bronze. It is the hardest countenance, I ever beheld, in a man of rank and letters, but the myrtle, no less than the yew-tree, starts up from the fissures of the crag, and the Vine, that rejoices the hearts of Gods and Men, spreads it's tendrils & ripens it's clusters on the naked rock.—In the following moment the likeness of his face to that Mask-portrait of Wordsworth at Keswick struck me with greater force; and till I had left the House, I did not recollect, that Lady Beaumont had observed the same.—I stayed not above three or four minutes—he appointed this day noon for my second call, when he is to give me whatever information & whatever assistance may be in his power.—Briefly, in *words* he was extremely civil, and this I regarded with complacency as the payment of a Debt of Attention to your name & recommendation / in tones, looks, and manners he was *embarrassing*—and this I was willing to consider as the effect of my own *unbellerophontic* countenance and mien. No doubt, I *like* a man the better for not being unfavorably impressed by my first appearance; but I never *think* the worse of him for the contrary.—However, I have breakfasted at Mr Greenough's some forty or fifty doors from Mr Knight's: & in a few minutes shall fulfil my engagement.—If my visit be brief, I shall send the oxygenated chalybeate Drops by to day's Coach—from the use of which (twice a day, an hour before dinner, & an hour before supper) I entertain sanguine expectations that you will derive an *Analogon* of Health at least, without the least after injury—& a good deal of Hope, that you will be actually & permanently benefited. You must begin with three drops in a small tumbler of tepid water—with milk & sugar (which, as far as I have seen, it does not curdle) it resembles apple juice—but better take it in simple water, as it is by no means unpleasant—something like the taste of a[n] unbaked baking-pear. Increase the dose one drop per day till you have brought it to eleven drops—there keep it for a week—& then decrease it a drop per day. This implies a three weeks' use of the medicine. Whether you will persevere so long, your own feelings must & will instruct you—if you find it increase your appetite & your cheerfulness, & induce no *increase* of Costiveness, you will do so, of course. Many hundreds have used it in stomach complaints—& I never heard of any one ill effect, immediate or remote from the use of it. I would take it at least three hours before bed time, lest, as you are no supper eater, the awakening of your Stomach might act, like Green Tea, & prevent you sleeping.—I could not get it made before 10 this morning—if therefore it does not accompany this Letter, the Letter will go without it—& you may be sure of it, together with a small Bottle of the Compound Acid of Davy, which I would *not* use at the same time——but if the other agreed with you, I would interpose a week, or month perhaps—& use the Compound acid exactly as you would lemon juice, adding from 8 to 12 drops to a large tumbler of water, well sugared—& drink it thro' a glass tube.—In the same parcel I include Daniel's Poems with the eminent Passages of the Hymen's Triumph (for which alone I have sent them) *marked*—& some trifles of my own.—But now I must wait on Mr Knight—which 'wait on' is a vile unenglish Phrase——& leave the Letter open, that I may finish it with the result.——

¼ after One. I have left Mr Knight, time enough, I hope, for the Coach. Mr Knight was extremely obliging, & no doubt, often seen would improve into a friendly man. He shewed me his views of Sicily chiefly by Hackart—from which I learnt what I knew before, that I shall see nothing in Sicily of half the *beauty* of Cumberland / and not one 100th part of the *number* of the grand and the impressive. My *Sole* Object is Health / I never even think of any thing else, even as an 'addamus lucro.['] Mr K. will procure me a Letter from Lady Hamilton to the Manager of Lord Nelson's Sicilian Domains—& shewed me all his Bronzes. I was *highly* delighted— and indeed much instructed. One figure which you have not seen, tho' imperfect, absolutely enamoured me—I have seldom in my

566]   *To Sir George Beaumont*

Life experienced such a *Burst* of pleasurable Sense of *Beauty* / it represents a Venus or Venus-like figure, as from the Bath, on one leg, putting on her Sandal on the upraised leg——I am not afraid of the charge of using violent language, when I say you will be enchanted——On Saturday I write without fail—to day I expect to meet and dine with Mr Sotheby at Davy's Room / With respectful remembrances to your Mother, I am, my dear Sir George,
most gratefully & affectionately your's,<br>S. T. Coleridge

### 567. To Sara Hutchinson

MS. *New York Public Lib. Pub. with omis. and without Sara Hutchinson's name*, Blackwood's Magazine, *November 1819, p. 197, and* Literary Remains of Samuel Taylor Coleridge, *ed. by H. N. Coleridge, 4 vols., 1836–9, ii. 413.* Coleridge's letter is written on the fly-leaves of a folio volume containing the third edition (1658) of Sir Thomas Browne's *Pseudodoxia Epidemica*, bound up with reprintings of *Religio Medici, Hydriotaphia,* and *The Garden of Cyrus*. The general title-page of this copy is missing; the volume was issued in 1659. Coleridge annotated the volume at various times between 1804 and 1824. The notes were published in *Literary Remains*, ii. 398–412.

At what time Sara Hutchinson received the volume is uncertain. Coleridge had it in his possession after his final departure from the north in 1810, for in a marginal note to the *Pseudodoxia* there is a reference to 'Sir H. Davy', who was not knighted until 1812. (In printing the notes to Browne, H. N. Coleridge omitted 'Sir H.' from Davy's name.) Likewise Coleridge must have had the volume at Highgate, since the letter to Sara Hutchinson was contributed to *Blackwood's* in 1819 by G. J. (presumably James Gillman's initials reversed), and since Coleridge added a marginal note clearly dated 'Tuesday 16 March 1824' at the end of the volume. As the Browne volume was sold, along with other books from Wordsworth's library, in June 1896, it must have been returned to Wordsworth, or to Sara Hutchinson, after Coleridge's death. The title-page of the *Pseudodoxia*, moreover, bears the autograph, 'M. Wordsworth Rydal Mount'.

In an unpublished note E. H. Coleridge comments on the letter and the Browne volume: 'This letter to S.H. . . . is the sole survivor of the correspondence between . . . [Coleridge and Sara Hutchinson.] Mrs Wordsworth, so her granddaughter Mrs Jane Kennedy told me, burnt all the rest of S.T.C.'s letters to Sara H. . . . The volume, which belonged to William Wordsworth the third (Bombay Bill), was sold in my presence at Sotheby's in 1896 for £30, I having bid £17.' Fortunately a few of Coleridge's letters to Sara Hutchinson escaped Mrs. Wordsworth's vigilance.

7. Barnard's Inn, Holborn, London<br>March 10th, 1804.[1] Saturday Night, 12 o/clock

My dear Sara!

Sir Thomas Brown is among my first Favorites. Rich in various Knowlege, exuberant in conceptions and conceits, contemplative,

[1] In one of the fly-leaves Lamb wrote: 'C Lamb 9th March 1804, bought

( 1080 )

imaginative, often truly great and magnificent in his style and diction, tho' doubtless too often big, stiff, and hyperlatinistic—: thus I might without admixture of falshood describe Sir T. Brown, and my description would have only this Fault, that it would be equally, or *almost* equally, applicable to half a dozen other Writers, from the beginning of the reign of Elizabeth to the end of the reign of Charles the second. He is indeed all this, & what he has more than all this peculiar to himself, I seem to convey to my own mind in some measure by saying, that he is a quiet and sublime Enthusiast with a strong tinge of the Fantast, the Humourist constantly mingling with & flashing across the Philosopher, as the darting colours in shot silk play upon the main dye! In short, he has brains in his Head, which is all the more interesting for a *little Twist* in the Brains——He sometimes reminds the reader of Montaigne but from no other than the general circumstance of an Egotism common to both, which in Montaigne is too often a mere amusing Gossip; a chit chat story of Whims & Peculiarities that lead to nothing, but which in Sir Thomas Brown is always the result of a feeling Heart conjoined with a mind of active curiosity—: the natural & becoming egotism of a man, who loving other men as himself, gains the habit & the privilege of talking about himself as familiarly as about other men. Fond of the Curious, and a Hunter of Oddities & Strangenesses, while he conceived himself with quaint & humorous Gravity a useful enquirer into physical Truth & fundamental Science, he loved to contemplate & discuss his own Thoughts & Feelings, because he found by comparison with other men's that *they* too were *curiosities*: & so with a perfectly graceful & interesting Ease he put *them* too into his Musaeum & Cabinet of Rarities—. In very truth, he was not mistaken—So compleatly does he see every thing in a light of his own, reading Nature neither by Sun, Moon, or Candle-Light, but by the Light of the faery Glory around his own Head, that you might say, that Nature had granted to him in perpetuity a Patent and Monopoly for all his Thoughts.—Read his Hydriotaphia above all—& in addition to the peculiarity, the exclusive *Sir Thomas Brown-ness* of all the Fancies & modes of Illustration, wonder at and admire his *entireness* in every subject, which is before him—he is totus in illo —he follows it, he never wanders from it—and he has no occasion to wander—for whatever happens to be his Subject, he meta-

for S T Coleridge.' Coleridge added below: 'N.B. It was on the 10th; on which day I dined & punched at Lamb's—& exulted in the having procured the Hydriotaphia, & all the rest lucro [ap]posita. S.T.C.' Between Lamb's note and Coleridge's is a note by Sara Hutchinson: 'Given by S. T. C. to S. Hutchinson March 1804.'

morphoses all nature into it.[1] In that Hydriotaphia or Treatise on some Urns dug up in Norfolk—how *earthy*, how redolent of graves & Sepulchres is every Line!—You have now dark mould, now a thigh-bone, now a Skull, then a bit of mouldered Coffin / a fragment of an old tombstone with moss in it's Hic Jacet—a ghost, or a winding Sheet, or the echo of a funeral Psalm wafted on a November wind—& the gayest thing you shall meet with shall be a silver nail or gilt Anno Domini from a perished Coffin Top.[2] The very same remark applies in the same force to the interesting, tho' far less interesting, Treatise on the Quincuncial Plantations of the Ancients—the same attention to oddities, to the remotenesses, & minutiae of vegetable forms—the same entireness of subject—Quincunxes in Heaven above, Quincunxes in Earth below, & Quincunxes in the Water beneath the Earth / Quincunxes in Deity, Quincunxes in the mind of Man / Quincunxes in bones, in optic nerves, in Roots of Trees, in leaves, in petals, in every thing! In short just turn to the last Leaf of this volume, & read out aloud to yourself the 7 last Paragraphs of Chap. V. beginning with the words—'More Considerables'—But it is time for me to be in bed / in the words of Sir Thomas, which will serve you, my darling Sara! as a fair specimen of his manner. [']But the Quincunx ‡ of Heaven (‡ the Hyades or 5 Stars about the Horizon at midnight at that time) runs low, and 'tis time, we close the five Ports of Knowlege: we are unwilling to spin out our waking Thoughts into the Phantasmes of Sleep, which often continueth praecogitations—making Cables of Cobwebs and wildernesses of handsome Groves—To keep our eyes open longer were to *act* our Antipodes. The Huntsmen are up in America, and they are already past their first Sleep in Persia.'—Think you, my dear Sara! that there ever was such a reason given before for going to bed at midnight / to wit, that if we did not, we should be acting the part

---

[1] For verbal echoes of this letter see Coleridge's lecture of 13 March 1818. *Literary Remains*, i. 235–6.

[2] Hazlitt's comment on this passage may be of interest: 'I do not think his account of the Urn-burial very happy. Sir Thomas can be said to be "wholly in his subject," only because he is *wholly out of it*. There is not a word in the *Hydriotaphia* about "a thigh-bone, or a skull, or a bit of moulded coffin, or a tombstone, or a ghost, or a winding-sheet, or an echo," nor is "a silver nail or a gilt *Anno Domini* the gayest thing you shall meet with." You do not meet with them at all in the text; nor is it possible, either from the nature of the subject, or of Sir T. Browne's mind, that you should! He chose the subject of Urn-burial, because it was "one of no mark or likelihood," totally free from the romantic prettiness and pleasing poetical common-places with which Mr. Coleridge has adorned it, and because, being "without form and void," it gave unlimited scope to his high-raised and shadowy imagination.' William Hazlitt, *Lectures on the Literature of the Age of Elizabeth*, 1901, p. 232.

of our ANTIPODES!!—and then 'The Huntsmen are up in America'!
—what Life, what Fancy!—Does the whimsical Knight give us
thus a dish of strong green Tea, & call it an *opiate*?—I trust, that
you *are* quietly asleep,

> And all the Stars hang bright above your Dwelling,
> Silent as tho' they watch'd the sleeping Earth!—[1]

S. T. Coleridge.

N.B. In page 48 of the 'Enquiries into common & vulgar Errors' there is a Plate of Urns & the figure of the Quincunx, ⋈ bound up by mistake, instead of being placed p. 48 of the Two last Treatises —which is the opening of the 'Cyrus Garden, &c[']—

N.B. In the marginal symbols, which I have made, ⊙ points out a profound or at least solid and judicious observation; = signifies that the sentence or passage in a line with it contains *majesty* of conception or Style; ∥ signifies *Sublimity*; ✵ *brilliance* or *ingenuity*; 2 signifies characteristic Quaintness; and ℱ, that it contains an *error* in fact or philosophy.[2] S. T. Coleridge.

### 568. To Robert Southey

*Address*: Robert Southey, Esqre | Greta Hall | Keswick | Cumberland
*MS. Lord Latymer. Hitherto unpublished.*
*Postmark*: 12 March 1804.

Mark Lane, 17.—March 12th, Monday Noon [1804]

My dear Southey

I am writing in Sharp's Library. I have been exceedingly anxious & harrassed in Mind & body for the last 8 or 9 days. Mr Rickman could give me no intelligence respecting the King's Ship appointed to convoy the Mediterranean Vessels: & yet I heard from good authority that they were certainly to go off in a few days. Mr Rickman advised me therefore not to trust to a King's Ship at all, as it would probably be fixed upon only a day or two before the day of Sailing—consequently too short a time for me to exert any *Interest* to go out in it.—Accordingly I came here; & Sharp very kindly sent out his Clerk who after some other enquiries that proved not to my purpose at length returned with a short well-bellied man, John Findlay, Commander of The Well

---

[1] *Dejection*, lines 130–1.
[2] These symbols occur only in the margins of pages 4, 13, 14, 18, 19, 20, and 25 of the *Pseudodoxia Epidemica*.

568]  *To Robert Southey*

Known Fast Sailing Brig, Speedwell, A.I. (that is to say, as Sharp informs [me], of the first class of Brigs in speed & condition) For Venice & Trieste with Liberty to touch at Malta / —It sails out of the River the latter end of this Week; but I need not be at Portsmouth before the end of 8 or 9 days from the date of this—but of this he will give me by Letter minute information tomorrow. I went on board to see the accomodations—to be sure, very neat but so small as to be literally a Box—There are already two Passengers, a Lady & a Gentleman / separate Concerns / I am a Third—& there can only be one more / —the Passage money 35 guineas, and I find my own Wine & Spirits; the Captn every thing else, as Porter, Ale, Provisions, Tea &c—but I have to buy a Mattrass, 3 Sheets, two blankets, a Pillow & Pillow Case—which the Captn is to buy for me, he says, he can get them much cheaper than I—& that the whole will not exceed £3 ‖ 10 ‖ 0—& these will be of use to me on my return, and on my passage perhaps from Malta to Sicily—. Accordingly, I engaged—& left him 20£ for a Deposit. As I was returning hither with him, I heard to my no small Surprize, & some little sudden Dip-down of the Heart, that the King's Ship had been fixed and known for a fortnight pass'd—the Lapwing Frigate!!—However, this is in great measure my own fault. If I had applied to Sharp, he knowing the Merchants engaged in the Mediterranean Trade would have heard of the Convoy the very Hour of it's Appointment—instead of which I relied wholly on Mr Rickman, who, *perforce*, relied wholly on a friend of his at the Admiralty who either forgot the application, or probably had himself not heard of the appointment. I have no reason to suppose that if I had heard of it, I could have made interest sufficient / Many People are going out to Malta from Government &c—& as many perhaps as there are accomodations for on board the Frigate / Still however it is *possible*; and the advantages would have been very great.

Be it as it will, I am heartily glad that the affair is settled / I could not have much longer endured the state of anxiety & suspense—at day I can do well enough; but at night my children, & other things & thoughts, lie hard & heavy upon me / & when they chance to combine with rain & damp, affect me wildly. Only last night I had a long hysterical weeping in my Sleep—long it must have been, from the wetness of the Pillow & my Shirt Collar.—What my Dream was, is not to tell; but when I awoke, the rain was beating against the Casement.—It is not *Cold* that hurts me—I am never better than in dry Frost—It is *Damp* without & anxiety, or Agitation, within that cause my Disease / and the former is often quite as predominant in our Summers as our

( 1084 )

winters—and I am resolved to be tranquil. Spite of every thing, I have certainly been, on a long Average, better & more tranquil for the last two months than before—and when I have once *set to*, I expect to be wholly tranquil. Our voyage will not be less than 9 weeks—as soon as I am on board, & have got over whatever Nausea or Sickness I may be attacked with (for I must not expect my former good Luck, with my present weaken'd Stomach) I shall systematize the day—& I shall be more my own Master on board the brig—and Mr Sharp, who is just come in says that for his part he would much rather go on board the Speedwell than the finest King's Ship, the company of the younger naval officers being generally oppressive.—The extreme Smallness of the Cabin, with 3 Bed holes in it, is no doubt a serious nuisance; but the people will most often be on the Deck / or I shall be.—

I have received the extracts from the Madoc, which I am re-transcribing—I shall send *my* Copy to Sir G.B.—which Sara must think a disrespect to her penmanship, but I wish to have a copy myself, & had rather have it in her Handwriting than in my own: whereas it is possible, that the Verses of the Poet Southey in the Handwriting of the ci devant Poet in rus & now Metaphysician, Coleridge, may be more of a *curiosity* with Sir G. & Lady Beaumont—/ I think it will be worth while to send off those silks & summerlets by Coach; if they can be sent so as to leave Keswick on the night of the receipt of this Letter—because Thursday is not a London Day, & Friday will be too late.

As soon as I am at leisure, I will write you again—and will then take all your Letters received by me since I have been in London, that of Monday Night 'συηκότατος Jερεμίας' among them, and answer them. To morrow or Wednesday at the farthest I will call on Rickman & Poole—& know something about George [Fricker]—that I may see what there is for me to do.—Poole has never once enquired of me concerning my affairs, or definite Plans—nay, seemed to *shy* it as if fearing that I might need his assistance—he wished me most mightily & almost by a demand of friendship to be with him in London / he knowing, that there were 2 places at least, at which I could be wholly free of expence / & no doubt, he was very fond of my *conversation* & the instruction he derived from it / but I had to pay for all my Lodgings, & 7 shillings every day for dinner—never once did he offer to pay for me / tho' he was manifestly vexed when I did not dine with him. Of course, I broke off—& went to Tobin's.—But I will say more of this, & give you my calm sum total as to Poole's present character——

God bless you, Southey!—&
S. T. Coleridge—

Stuart has no longer any influence with the M.P. He shall send you a *Courier*.——

### 569. To William Sotheby

Address: W. Sotheby, Esqre | No/ 47, Upper Seymour Street / | Portman Square | If Mr Sotheby should not be in town, or expected tomorrow, this to be *forwarded* to him.—.
MS. Colonel H. G. Sotheby. Pub. with omis. *E. L. G. i. 310.*
Postmark: 13 March 1804.

Tuesday Morning—March 13th, 1804

My dear Sir

Yesterday I engaged my passage for Malta on board a small—alas! too small—but neat & compact merchant-brig, 130 Tons, the Speedwell, John Findlay, Commander / the passage money, 35 guineas, exclusive of Bedding and Wine and Spirits. I had heard that no King's Ship had been fixed on as convoy, & that in all probability there might [be] none fixed till within a day or so of the Sailing, of course, too short a time to leave any rational hopes of my being able to make interest to be a passenger. But after all was settled, and I had left 20£ as a Deposit, I learnt by mere accident that a King's Ship had been appointed, Heaven knows how long since, namely, the Lapwing Frigate. However, I consoled myself that I have no real grounds of expectation that I could get a passage on board her—that in the Brig I shall be more independent, more my own Master—& that if it be small, the number of men is likewise small.—The Ship clears the River the end of this week; & my luggage must by that time be sent to the Brokers—but I need not be at Portsmouth till the 21st or 22nd of this month / I expect to know the very day before evening——I write now to intreat that you will be so good as to conciliate Sir Alexander Ball's[1] & Gen. Valette's[2] Protection to me / It has, at times, been a wandering wish of mine, (and I should perhaps have indulg'd it, but for my entire & utter want of Interest,) to get some small place in Malta or Sicily—I did not care if it occupied half my time: for I have no wish to receive what I have not earned—a place of course, for the performance of the Duties of which austere integrity & general information & sanity of mind were the chief Requisites——. If I should see any opening, when abroad, I shall not be prevented

---

[1] Sir Alexander Ball (1757–1809). After a distinguished record in the navy, Ball forced the capitulation of the French garrison at Malta in 1800, following a two-year blockade of the island. He became the first Governor of Malta and died there in 1809.

[2] General William Anne Villettes (1754–1808) was appointed in 1801 to the chief command of the troops in Malta.

from engaging your good offices in my Behalf, by my too deeply rooted dislike to call upon any man for any effort, still more on one, on whom I have no other claims than those derived from his own benevolence / . Mackintosh put this into my Head, by saying to me—that he thought, that if I had any sort of Interest with the Governor at Malta, I might probably without difficulty gain some little place or other that would at least liquidate my travelling or rather voyaging Expences.

I will make a little Book of half a dozen of mine & Wordsworth's poems for you by Thursday next, when I shall be at the Lecture in the Hope of seeing you.—

I shall direct this to Seymour St with a request that it may be forwarded. I heard from Wordsworth this morning; but the Letter was written before my last had reached him / I trust, you will have heard from him before I see you / as I cannot endure the thought of taking the Check out of it's Retirement till you have received the legal obligation for it's repayment in November—[1]

With best & kindest remembrances to Mrs and Miss Sotheby believe me, | my dear Sir, | with high not unaffectionate | Esteem | very sincerely your's

S. T. Coleridge.—

### 570. To John Rickman

*Address*: Jno. Rickman, Esqre | at his Office | H. of Commons
*MS. Huntington Lib. Pub. with omis. E. L. G. i. 307.*

Tuesday, March 13. ½ past I. [1804]

My dear Sir

I have left my name at your House—& finding no one here at the office I take the liberty of playing Scribe solo in it—just to inform you, that hopeless since our last conversation on the Subject

---

[1] Sotheby had given Coleridge a check for £100, Wordsworth standing as security. On 12 Mar. 1804 Wordsworth wrote to Sotheby: 'Agreeable to a request of Mr. Coleridge I take the liberty of sending you enclosed a promissory note for 100£ which he informs me you have been so good as to advance for him: I have taken the liberty of drawing the note payable at *ten* months, which is two months later than the latest time mentioned by Mr. Coleridge; but Mr. Coleridge did not know that it would be full as easy for me to advance the money at present as at any time earlier than ten months from this date.' The promissory note accompanying this letter reads as follows:

I promise to pay Wm. Sotheby Esq., ten months after date, the Principal, and legal Interest of one hundred Pounds advanced by him to S. T. Coleridge on my account.

W. Wordsworth.

*Early Letters*, 371–3.

of getting my passage on board a King's Ship—hearing nothing of
the appointment of any one—&c I went to Sharp's yesterday &
from thence went on the River to examine the accomodations of
the Speedwell, a merchant brig of only 130 Tons.—The Cabin,
a common room for the Captn & three Passengers, myself, a Gentleman, & a Lady, is a perfect *Bobadillo* / however, I had previously
made enquiry after two much larger Vessels, but they could not
*engage* to touch at Malta, tho' they thought it highly probable that
they should—they were for Smyrna—whither I did not wish to
go—for why? It would be out of my way: & having kept clear of
all p minus x Buboes[1] I have no fancy at all for Plague Buboes.
So weary of anxiety which already had been at work upon me for
a week past, I engaged with the man, leaving 20£ as a Deposit.
The fare is very high / 35 guineas exclusive of Wine & Spirits, and
of Bedding—which will be 7 or 8£ more! As we were going on
board, I asked the Captn (John Findlay) whether he knew who
the Captn was appointed to convoy them / he said, he did not know
*as yet*. This I took as a full confirmation of what I had indeed never
doubted—namely, that no King's Ship had as yet been fixed upon.
But on my return with him on Tower Hill I heard to my surprize
and (momentary) consternation, that tho' he did not know the
commanding officer's name, yet there had been a ship of War
appointed, heaven knows how long—the Lapwing Frigate, to
wit.—I felt instantly & still feel that this Miss is absolutely &
entirely my own fault—that I ought to [have] considered, that the
merchants & Captns in the Mediterranean Trade must know the
appointment as soon as it [is] known at all—& of course that I
ought to have desired some one or more of *them* to apprize me
thereof—which I might easily have done / whereas a Gentleman in
the Navy Office, or Admiralty, might easily *miss* the Information,
& in the multiplicity of official Business easily & venially forget
a thing not in the track of his daily Concerns.—I feel myself rash
& blameable; but I console myself by thinking, that if I had known
of it, I have no rational data of Hope as to my having or procuring
sufficient Interest to get on board her / that I have no positive
reason for supposing, that I should not have had as much money
to pay for my passage on board the one, as on board the other / &
if it were otherwise, that yet I shall be more my own Master on
board the Brig—which if it be small, has proportionally a small
number of men—The voyage will be 8 or 9 weeks!!! a week of
these at Gibraltar.—The vessel leaves the *River* the latter end of
this week—& before that time my Luggage (which is no great

---

[1] Formerly a slip of paper, now removed, was pasted over the words 'having
kept clear of all p minus x Buboes'.

matter,) must be sent on board; but that more troublesome Luggage, my poor crazy whimsical Carcase, need not be at Portsmouth, IN *all probability*, till the 22nd of this month. But I shall be informed before evening of the exact Day—

I hope, I shall have an opportunity of spending an hour or two with you tete a tete—or with Lamb, at least—which will be the same Thing unless it be a better one. Unless I pass any evening at your House, I shall be at Lamb's *every evening* till the Time of my Departure from ½ past 8 or 9 to 12—or whatever hour later or earlier, the Genius of Comfort & Health may inspire or command.——

I shall leave a Letter or two here tomorrow to be franked / & I own, I feel a sudden Dip-down of old Indefatigable (the Heart, to wit) at the thought, that it will be [the] last for years—may be the last for ever.—I have only a choice of Evils—had I stayed at home, my children would soon have been Orphans.

S. T. Coleridge

P.S. If my heart had been as easy as my mind is active, I could have filled up those Latin Words right quaintly.—[1]

Tobin is this moment come in / to beg you to dine with him on Saturday (is not that Speak: Din: Day?) or Monday, letting him know by to morrow which day will be the more convenient.——

### 571. *To George Bellas Greenough*

*Address*: G. B. Greenough Esqre
*Transcript Professor Edith J. Morley. Hitherto unpublished.*

Tuesday afternoon, 2 o'clock<br>March 13, 1804

Dear Greenough

O the pen is better than I thought—and I make you a present of the making therefore, which to the Quill is as a House to a Ground Property—a very neat writing Pen on my Word!—

Yesterday morning, weary of suspense & hearing nothing of a King's Ship, I engaged my Passage on board the Speedwell Brig, John Findlay, Commander—of only 130 Tons Burthen, 35 guineas the Passage money, exclusive of Wine, Spirits, & Bedding!—Jesus Christ!—Well, I left a deposit of 20£—& then heard that a King's Ship, the Lapwing Frigate, to wit—had been appointed, heaven knows how long—however all things are for the best, I hope, tho'

---

[1] Someone had written the following Latin words on the paper Coleridge used for his letter: Se quoque fu[git] | Suspicor | Suspicor | illum futurum | esse.

if taken prisoner by an Algerian or Frenchman I might be a little puzzled to develope the optimism on this side the Grave. I must be at Portsmouth about the 21st of this month / but all other luggage save that worst and most troublesome Luggage, my crazy Carcase, must be on board by Friday. Remember Leaky, Syracusa, Catania, if you can—& the Pictures, Drawings, I mean—where are they? I am a bit downish hearted—however sick or well, sad or merry, at home or abroad, landed or stranded, I am & shall remain, I trust, your well-wisher & with affectionate esteem

S. T. Coleridge.

## 572. To John Rickman

*Address*: Jno. Rickman, Esqre | At his Office | H. of Commons
*MS.* Huntington Lib. *Pub. with omis.* E. L. G. *i.* 311.

Wednesday, March 14. 1804

My dear Sir

I thank you for your kind note / I received the letters duly. Tomorrow I must *dine* with Stuart / as I shall be at his office arranging my own concerns till the very hour of dinner; but I will be with you by a quarter before 7 infallibly; and the Virgin Mary with the uncrucified[1] Lamb will come with me.—I have written the direction for the inclosed Letter below—lest it *should* be overweight with an envelope / tho' I believe, it would not.— The East India House has very politely made me a present thro' Mr Charles Lamb, an EMINENT in the India Service, of a hundred or so of Pens: & if the H. of Commons would do the same, with a stick or two of Wax, in short, any little additament that might be made instrumental in the service of G. Britain by spreading & increasing it's literary Action upon the world, I should consider as a flattering mark of respect from that Honorable Assembly— and should prize it considerably more than even a Vote of Thanks & recommendation for a Title—unless a good warm Salary or Estate were the gilt Lace to my *Coat* of Arms.—

Your's, my dear Sir, | with affectionate well-wishing | & sincere esteem

S. T. Coleridge

[1] Formerly a slip of paper, now removed, was pasted over the words 'the Virgin' and 'the uncrucified'.

## 573. *To George Dyer*

*Address*: Mr G. Dyer
MS. Mr. G. Whitmore. Hitherto unpublished. In his *Privileges of the University of Cambridge*, 1824, Dyer says that in the *Monthly Magazine* for November 1802 he began a series of articles entitled 'Cantabrigiana', and on 1 March 1804 he published the anecdote referred to in Coleridge's letter: 'The poetical abilities of Mr. Coleridge, formerly of Jesus College, are well known. He obtained one of the prizes at Cambridge, and but one, for a Greek ode. Being once in company with a person who had gained two prizes, the latter carried himself with an air of superiority and triumph, and seemed to estimate his own abilities above Coleridge's, in the ratio of at least two to one. A person in company growing, at length, indignant at the vaunting airs of the conceited young fellow, exclaimed, "Why zounds, Sir, a man's leg may as easily be too big for the boot, as your's just fitted it."'

Thursday Morning [15 March 1804]

Dear Sir

If you *knew* me, you would know that I am not of the genus irritabile; and must resign all claim to the poetic inspiration, if irritability be an essential character of it. I felt no resentment or offence on my own account; nor as much concern as a tolerably careful man ought to feel. This you will readily admit if you reflect that the person who could have won 2 prizes, when *I* had won only one, might be immediately detected by referring to the University Book / —Luckily no such person then existed—tho' it is not unlikely that either Mr Butler or Mr Frere would apply it to themselves, & consider it as a calumny.—However, I repeat to you that my concern was *for you* not for *myself*—on *general* principles, not the consequence of a particular Feeling. Good Heavens, my dear Sir! who would dare open their mouths in your presence, if it were generally known that you would without their knowlege or consent *publish* any anecdote of them and with their names—tho' the anecdote might have been possibly an escape of venial Vanity in the Flush of Wine, probably tho' strictly Truth yet Truth, of such a nature, that publicity would make it more mischievous than falshood—besides the reluctance to be named in a public journal is a valuable characteristic of an Englishman, & should neither be invaded nor on light grounds given up.——But these are all reflections that have no doubt occurred to yourself—as likewise that the intending a civility by the infliction of an injury criminates a man's general Habit of *Mind*, & *Understanding*, more than it exculpates his immediate state of Feeling.—As I never felt, so it is not possible that I can retain, the least offence; but *one demand I must make*, & I will take the liberty of stating it to you with unmistakeable Plainness—to wit, that you *do not* correct the account *at all, nor*

## To George Dyer

*in any way re-peat my name, nor in any way attempt to draw back the attention & recollection of the Readers of the Dyerhoea Cantabrigiensis to that anecdote. Let it perish / stirring up a ——— never yet lessened* the Stench. These things die of their own inanity if not industriously kept alive—like a soap-bubble that if left to itself would soon alight on the ground or drive against the wall, & break & dissipate / but which may be blown now here, now there, with proper care, & made the stare & play thing of children for ten times the length of it's natural Life—I must INTREAT you to give your attention to the Lines in this Letter under marked; & in full reliance of your kind acquiescence in this respect I remain,

Dear Sir, | your's with sincere good wishes,

S. T. Coleridge

P.S. I find but 3 epigrams worth your having which I inclose. If printed at all, they must be printed without my name—and may be said to be by a Student[1] of Jesus College, Cambridge.[2]—

[1] For 'Student' Coleridge originally wrote but crossed out 'ci-devant Member'.

[2] The epigrams are no longer with this manuscript letter, but undoubtedly were the ones attributed to 'A Student of Jesus College' in Dyer's 'Cantabrigiana'. The first two appeared in the *Monthly Magazine* for Apr. 1804, the third in June.

From off that delicate fair cheek,
Oh Maid, too fair, I did but seek
To steal a kiss, and lo! your face,
   With anger or with shame it glows;
What have I done, my gentle Grace,
   But change a lily to a rose?

At once your cheek and brow were flush'd,
Your neck and ev'n your bosom blushed;
And shame may claim the larger part,
   In that smooth neck, and all above:
But the blush so near the heart,
   Oh! let it be a blush of love.
Pygmalion thus lit up with life
The statue that became his wife.

### Epigram—

Dear Anne, a wond'rous Trinity
Hath made thee a Divinity,
The being strangely beautiful,
And strangely chaste and dutiful,
And what is more than either,
The being each together.

### Balsamum in vitro.

Charity's a balsam—woman's but a glass—
That, alas! how costly!—how fragile, this, alas!

( 1092 )

*17 March 1804* [574

574. To William Sotheby

*Address*: W. Sotheby, Esqre | Fair Mead Lodge | Loughton | Essex.
*MS. Colonel H. G. Sotheby. Hitherto unpublished.*
*Postmark*: 17 March 1804.

Saturday, March 17. 1804

My dear Sir

On Thursday from 10 in the morning to 4 in the afternoon I was stretched on the Sopha in distempered Dosing, or hurried off from the Sopha thither quo mortalia Viscera cogunt, to return & fall back to the same Dose. Something had deranged my Stomach & Bowels; & the sensations from Within were too strong, of course, & abstracted the attention due to outward Impressions—the general Theory, no doubt, of all Dosing from Poison or Disease.——
Yet I am not certain that I should not have made an effort to see you, or attempt to realize it, if I had not received a note that morning from Mr Sharp, containing an invitation from Mr Boddington[1] to meet *you* at his House on Sunday, with Courtney,[2] Rogers, and such like (to me very uninteresting) Et Ceteras of your name.—
I am deeply—what am I about to say? *obliged* to you for your Letters—& other acts of zealous Friendship?—Nay! if what you know & believe of me does not convey to your heart other intuitions of what I feel toward you, Mr Sotheby! and what I think of you, these commonplace phrases can do [no]thing—& if it *has* made you partaker of the Soul that is in me, professions will but dilute & degrade the Feeling. That which I presumed to say to you at the commencement of my correspondence, I must again repeat— namely, that it is delightful to me in my best & noblest moments to contemplate you as a man possessing the moral advantages of a high rank in Society with plainness, simple Honesty, and the virtues that seem to thrive best in the Shade—& as a Poet—pardon me, pardon me, my dear Sir! if in the fullness & suddenness of the Feeling that has overshadowed me, I offer the semblance of an Insult by seeming to praise you thro' the Detraction of another— but upon my Life I could not help thinking of poor Rogers.—It arose, I believe, from the circumstance that his Friend, Sharp, has just left me—a truly friendly man I have found him / of his Understanding & powers of giving intellectual feasts all are agreed; and I should be a sad fellow if I did not think of his Heart something very like the opposite of what some of his 'good friends' would fain have prepossessed me with. I ought to make an apology

---

[1] Samuel Boddington, Richard Sharp's business partner. See P. W. Clayden, *The Early Life of Samuel Rogers*, 1887, pp. 121–2.
[2] Probably John Courtenay (1741–1816), politician.

to you for having again mentioned the Loan after what had passed between us. In these cases, Explanation is always the *best*, tho' often an insufficient, Apology. I have a diseased Restlessness in things of this kind / & too careless of my own perhaps I touch the gold & silver of others, as if my very Touch with a sort of anti-Midas, or rather Mosaic, power would instantly transmute them into serpents and Scorpions. Excess of Delicacy agitates me; & agitation hurries me into Indelicacies: so awfully true is it, that no Virtue can have dividual Being from Reason—and Reason dwells only in Temperate Zones, & perishes in Extremes. Present my kind & respectful Remembrances to Mrs and Miss Sotheby: for their sakes I will endeavor to finish Christabel & the Dark Ladie before I reach Malta: & be assured, they shall have the very first fair Copy.——I will send you on Monday the poems, you wished, if I should not see you tomorrow, as your Letter makes me fear, I shall not.

Excuse this Scrap of Paper.——Tobin is out, & I can find no other——with grateful & affectionate
                    Esteem I remain, my dear Sir, most truly your's,
                                                S. T. Coleridge.

Sir G. Beaumont & Lady came to Town last night: I dine there to day.—


## 575. To John Rickman

*Address*: Jno. Rickman, Esqre | Palace Yard | Westminster.
*MS. Huntington Lib. Pub. with omis. E. L. G. i. 312.* The text of the second part of this letter, which is missing from the manuscript, is taken from a transcript in the possession of the Coleridge family.

                    Saturday Night, ½ past 10. March 17. [1804]
My dear Sir

So little notion had I that the Papers, you gave me last night on parting from you, had any reference to *me*, so fully persuaded that they were public papers and in some way connected with the conversation of the evening which had deeply impressed me, that being extremely busy all the morning I never looked at them, reserving them for my return from Sir G. Beaumont's, which I knew would be at an early Hour, & when I should be alone and quiet. This afternoon at 4 o/clock on emptying my pockets in order to *lighten* myself I glanced with my eye on the direction for the first time / & I am unable to express to you the odd feeling of great Pleasure, & stinging Vexation, that (now one, now the other) worked to and fro upon me, when I found that they contained all

## 17 March 1804

Wordsworth's Manuscript Poems for me—& SENT THRO' YOU. Be assured, my dear Sir! I never meant, never gave permission, that any thing should be sent thro' you, save only that Copy of my Christabel for Lady Beaumont / and which I did not do merely to save myself any expence, but to do the thing in a handsome way to her Ladyship. So far the contrary, I had desired them long ago to be sent me by the Coach; and on Monday last receiving a Letter from Wordsworth directed Abingdon Street, I instantly wrote to him, pressing him to send these poems (Heaven knows, the best & deepest Comfort, & companiable Support I shall have during my long dreary Absence) but to direct them not to 16, Abingdon St/ (I suppose, he must have missed a Letter or blundered—or he could not have done *that*) but to direct them to me at the Porter's Lodge, Barnard's Inn.—It is as compleat a γλυκύπικρον, as I have had for some time / ——As it is the first, so it shall be the last—Lamb can tell you, how reluctantly & *corn*-treading[ly] I ever avail myself of any privilege of a Friend or Acquaintance, as well knowing the Indelicacy with which many will use it, & the painful situations, it may involve & often has done.—I shall have impressed you very scurvily if you could believe me insincere, or not deeply sincere, when I say, that this circumstance disturbed in no small degree the recollection of as instructive & *abiding* an Evening, as I have passed these many many months / From the kind manner in which you gave them me, I trust, that nothing painful to yourself has happened—& believe me, dear Sir, with unfeigned esteem & kindest remembrances Your Friend & Servant
S. T. Coleridge

Saturday Night—12 o'Clock
My Dear Sir /

I break open my Letter / for Tobin has just come in from Captn. Burney's and delivered me Southey's Letter in an Envelope with a few words from you. I certainly do feel a comfort that I had written to you before. My dear Sir! I never gave any person hint or notion to write to me thro' you save only that one for which I had your direct permission / tho' I can very easily allow that I might have foreseen that one branch of a family having sent one pacquet; some other might avail himself of the same mode / yet I cannot blame myself—as I had *expressly* desired that the Poems might be sent to me by Coach / As to private or common Letters I have received none thro' you save from Southey & as he never was desired by me thus to send his letters, and as he has sent two or three by the regular post what could I do other than suppose that he had inclosed the letters, I have received from him thro' you, in a Letter to you, & that this had been an understood Privilege between you and the Poet? It is a strange thing & yet no uncommon one to be conscious of perfect innocence, and yet feel a pang of shame with vexation & to find in the former, not a removal but only a lame comforter of the latter.—Do not think, my dear Sir! that I write frettedly—I am far from feeling so, nay the very contrary, for considering the 3 Pacquets I have reason to acknowledge and thank you for the gentleness of your Hint & Delicacy of your Reproof.—

> Yours truly
> S. T. Coleridge.

## 576. To John Rickman

*Address*: John Rickman, Esqre | Palace Yard | Westminster
*MS. Huntington Lib. Hitherto unpublished.*

> Sunday Afternoon. 7. Barn. Inn
> March 18th, 1804

My dear Sir

I will forgive you tho' you should suspect me of having caught the *Dyer*hoea explanatoria, sive morbus hyperbotheratorius symptomaticus, scilicet Luti in Cerebrum—a disease not quite so bad to the *Patient* as *Water* on the Brain, but more troublesome to his Friends.—As I returned from Greenough's this morning (by whose Man I sent you a double Note) I cast my eye again on your Notula that accompanied Southey's Letter last night: & found that in my confusion I had read the word 'prohibition' as 'permission'. Strange & ridiculous as this must appear to you, it is literally true: & produced my second note *opossum*ed in the belly of the Former.—This mistake arose however, in good part, from my never having received (consciously, at least) any 'prohibition' from you, written or verbal. On opening the papers yesterday afternoon my own instant Feelings, God knows! were 'a prohibition' with a vengeance. I guess that some note or communication from you must have missed me / or that I have been guilty of a Cataleptical Fit of Absence of mind at the time of your speaking to me, which appears incredible to myself, & almost impossible.——
I write now simply to say that from half a dozen Lines in one of the Envelopes from Miss Wordsworth (which I did not see till now, within 5 minutes of my sitting down to write to you, & saw in consequence of searching the Envelopes for any Pencil'd or written Lines from you, that might explain the Affair to me) I fear, it is not

*impossible* that one other may have been sent in the same way; tho' no human words tho' written with Light instead of Ink could have been clearer than mine: for I wrote out my Address, 'Mr Coleridge, No. 7. Barnard's Inn, Holborn: to be left at the Porter's Lodge'—& specified too the Coach it was to go by, & how they were to send it to the Coach. This Letter went off last Monday—: & was written merely to prevent their sending them to 1[6] Abingdon St/ for I had no notion or suspicion of *their* being sent thro' you / . I hope, that my Letter will have prevented it. Unless the *Pacquet* (I shall hate the word as long as I live) has been sent off before this second Letter came, it *must* do so, I should suppose. But if any cross accident should have prevented their receipt of my Letter in Time (for they receive Letters only 3 times a week, & are three miles from the House where their Letters are left) I beseech you to call up to your mind, that I shall be more than sufficiently wounded by the Thing itself, & shall not need, even tho' I could conceive myself as deserving, any additional Pain from the Thought of your being offended with me was well as chagrined at the Event.——Excess of Delicacy agitates me / agitation make me act abruptly & hurryingly—and this too often ends in some palpable Indelicacy—so true is it that no Virtue can live apart from Reason, and Reason perishes in Extremes—& to die of a Plethora is as common for a virtue as for real Flesh & Blood. I fear, I may have been illustrating per exemplum my own remark / However this may be, here & every where, I always have, however I may miss in shewing, sincere respect & esteem & am truly your's,

S. T. Coleridge.

### 577. To Robert Southey

*Address*: Mr Southey | Greta Hall | Keswick.
*MS.* Lord Latymer. *Hitherto unpublished.*
*Postmark*: 20 March 1804.

Tuesday, March 20th 1804

My dear Southey

God Almighty bless you / & for your two kind Letters!—I have been seriously, alarmingly ill—a Diarrhoea of incessant fury for 10 hours—I was afraid to take opiates lest the stimulus acted on inflamed Bowels should produce mortification / At length finding a semblance of fainting fits come on every time, I went to the Stool, I saw that I could not get over it *without*/ so I sent for some Laudanum, & took it drop by drop as it were—& by this extreme caution succeeded at length, & without injury. But O! I *am* weak indeed. I dare not trust myself with any thing the least affecting

## To Robert Southey

—Only this. Your presence at Keswick is beyond all Compare my greatest *Comfort*.—

Luckily, Tuffin had taken me to sleep at his House: for I had dined at Boddington's, in his Palace, in Upper Brook St, where I met Rogers & Courtney, two Contemptibles—& Campbell, the WRETCH! the hateful bad-hearted Coxcomb!—I was to breakfast the next morning with Sir G. Beaumont, who arrived in Town on Friday Night—.—O Heaven! what a night!—I was conveyed by my own crawling Limbs to Sir G. B's on Monday Noon / where I have been ever since, tended most affectionately.

I *expect* to leave Town on Friday Morning for Portsmouth / the Ship left the River on Monday.—I will take up all your Letters, e novo / as soon as I get strong enough——

I cannot write to Sara now / but will & to Hartley too, before I leave Town.—

O dear dear Southey! old days crowd in upon me—I love & honor you from my Soul.—You will go on as you have gone / — Love & Blessing to all of you!

S. T. Coleridge

Direct *if* you write again, Post Office, Portsmouth /


### 578. To J. G. Ridout

*Address*: Mr Ridout | Louk [Lark?] hall Lane | Clapham
MS. Mr. R. N. Carew Hunt. *Hitherto unpublished.*
*Postmark*: 23 March 1804.

March 23, 1804. Sir G. Beaumont's, Grosvenor Square

My very dear Sir

Judging my own feelings I think any pain of sympathy however severe better incomparably than the pain which must accompany the suspicion of a Friend's neglect or want of due Feeling. With less reluctance therefore than I otherwise could have done it, you being in your present weak state, I inform you, that the second day from the day, I saw you, I was strangely unwell—& kept myself at home / was however almost obliged to go out on Sunday, tho' carefully wrapt up & in a coach—that that night I had a most alarming attack of cholera morbus, which is now going about, and of which a friend of an acquaintance of mine died the very hour, that my Fit was in it's Height of Fury. Most PROVIDENTIALLY I went home with Mr Tuffin, close by Mr Boddington's where I had dined—had I walked to Barnard's Inn thro' that bitter parching wind & damp air with it, & there been as I should have been, quite *alone* (for Mr Tobin slept out) without fire, or medicine, or attendance, I must have owed my Life to a miracle. The Diarrhoea raged after the first *painful* fit for ten hours, & gradually abated—this being the first day in which I can call myself recovered—or consider myself as wholly in Sunshine, and out of the Shadow of the wings of the destroying Angel. But in consequence of the Abrasion of the mucous Covering my Bowels *tremble* (especially just under my Navel) at every *loud* sound, I hear—almost at every sound, I myself utter.—

I was moved hither on Monday: & no Parents, no Brother or Sister could have behaved with more anxious kindness to me than Sir G. & Lady Beaumont.—I leave Town in two or three days at the farthest for Portsmouth / . O little, I trust, need I say, my dear Sir! how I rejoice at your Convalescence—I will offer up a solemn Prayer for you with a fervent Heart, among the names of my Children & Wife & Friends even as I mount the Ship, that may carry me perhaps to a Burial in a foreign Land. But if we have made God our Father, the whole Universe must be our Home!— May the Spirit of God aid us both so to do——

Your's with affectionate esteem, | dear Mr Ridout,
your's most truly, S. T. Coleridge

## 579. To William Sotheby

*Address*: W. Sotheby, Esqre | Lodge | Loughton | Essex
*MS. Colonel H. G. Sotheby. Pub. E. L. G. i. 314.*
*Postmark*: 24 March 1804.

Saturday Afternoon, March 24th 1804

My dear Sir

½ past 2. Consequently not 20 minutes since I quitted you; but it would be needle-hunting in a Hay-load to attempt to find you. This moment (I have not yet read the whole of the Note) I have heard from Mr Sharp—'My dear Sir! I have seen Captn Findlay— The Speedwell is gone to Gravesend and will be at Portsmouth if the present wind continues on Tuesday—The Captain says, you must go hence on Tuesday Morning or Evening, and therefore you *must secure immediately a place* at the Angel Inn behind St Clement's Church in the Strand—The Tuesday Morning Coach goes very early—the Mail at 7 in the Evening—&c.'—So perish the smaller and even so the larger Schemes of human Hope & human Foresight!—This Night before I lay my head on the pillow, I will send you, that one Poem at least / —

I am somewhat agitated / but let us have faith, that as not even a Sparrow's feather falls to the ground without a calculated

579]                    To William Sotheby

Purpose—a purpose existent from eternity, so likewise the lesser Gains & Losses, Disappointments & Sudden Pleasures, of the moral World begin motions that propagate themselves to infinity—and the unfelt agitation of the Air from the falling Feather is as necessary & therefore as important to an Omniscient mind, as the Storm that shatters a Continent into an Archipelago / —

I would still spend a day with you, if there were only *the Time* to be considered / but two days having been cut off, I must husband my Spirits—& from Sunday Afternoon, 4 o/ clock, at which time I hope to have done all that Respect, Civility, & my own Business require of me, I shall stay within doors, yea; and keep my mind & faculties *within their doors too*, or at farthest allow them only a ticklish Convalescent's Walk in the Garden or on the House-leads, till the hour of my departure from [London?]. I will not now bid you fa[rewell] or address aught to your Wife and Daughter, for whom I entertain a respect which, I trust, suffers no diminution or alloy of depreciation from the pleasurable Affection, which *will* interfuse itself / ——for I know that I should again repeat it / & I have again to write /

                                                    S. T. Coleridge

Will it not be making my self of far too much consequence to suppose that this Accident breaks up your Engagement on Wednesday?—You must write & let me know what I am to say to Sir G. & Lady Beaumont.

## 580. *To Thomas Wedgwood*

*Address*: T. Wedgwood, Esqre | Eastbury | near | Blandford
*MS*. Wedgwood Museum. *Pub. with omis.* Tom Wedgwood, *170*.
*Postmark*: 24 March 1804.

My dear Friend

Tho' fearful of breaking in upon you, after what you had written to me, I yet *could* not have left England without having written both to you and your Brother.—I received your Letter at the very moment, I received a Note from Sharp informing [me] that I must instantly secure a place in the Portsmouth Mail for Tuesday—& if I could not, that I must do so in the Light Coach for Tuesday early-morning.—I am agitated by many Things—& only write now because you desired an answer by return of Post.—I have been dangerously ill—but the illness is going about, & [is] not connected with my immediate ill-health however it may be with my general Constitution. It was the cholera morbus—but for a series of the merest accidents I should have been seized in the

*From a portrait painted by James Northcote in March 1804 and now in
the possession of Jesus College, Cambridge*

Streets, in a bitter East wind with cold rain—at all events, have walked thro' it struggling with the seizure / —it was Sunday Night—& have suffered it at Tobin's, Tobin sleeping out at Woolwich, no fire, no wine or spirit or medicine of any kind, & no human Being within call—but luckily, perhaps the occasion would better suit the word *providentially,* Tuffin took me home with him / —after the first painful Fit the Diarrhoea *raged* for 10 Hours —& gradually abating ceased on Thursday Afternoon / my Bowels from the Abrasion of their mucous covering tremble at every *loud* sound, I hear, almost at *every* sound, I myself utter—but however this is rather a History of the past than of the present—I have now only enough for memento—and already on Wednesday I considered myself in clear sunshine, out of the Shadow of the Wings of the Destroying Angel.—What else relates to myself I will write on Monday— / Would to Heaven, you were going with me—if it were not for the Voyage—for all other Things I could make the prayer with an unwavering mind, not without chearings of Hope. Let me mention one thing—Lord Cadogan was brought to absolute Despair & Hatred of Life by a Stomach Complaint, being now an old man. The Symptoms as stated [to me], were strikingly like your's—[consi]dering the enormous difference of the two characters —the same flitting Fevers, dire Costiveness with Diarrhœa, Dejection, compelled Changes, &c—. He was advised to reduce lean Beef to a pure Jelly by Papin's Digester with as little water as would secure it from burning—& of this to take half a wine glass from 10 to 14 times a day—this & *nothing else* / He did so—Sir G. Beaumont saw within a few weeks a letter from himself to Lord St Asaph, in which he states the circumstance, his perseverance in it, rapid amelioration & final recovery—I am now, he says, in real good Health / as good, & in as chearful spirits, as I ever was when a young man.—Minjay, the Medical man of Thetford, was his attendant, & could give you all particulars—

May God bless you, even *here* /
S. T. Coleridge.

### 581. *To Humphry Davy*

*Transcript Royal Institution. Pub.* Frag. Remains, *95.*

Sunday. March 25. 1804

My dear Davy,

I returned from Mr Northcote's[1] having been diseased by the change of weather too grievously to permit me to continue sitting:

[1] 'March 26 . . . Northcote shewed us a Head of Coleridge which He began

for in these moods of body brisk motion alone can prevent me from falling into distempered sleep. I came in, meditating a letter to you, or rather the writing of the letter which I had meditated yesterday, even while you were yet sitting with us. But it would be the merest confusion of my mind to force it into activity at present. Yours of this morning must have sunken down first, & have found its abiding resting place—O dear friend! blessed are the moments, and if not moments of humility, yet as distant from whatever is opposite to humility, as Humility itself, when I am able to hope of myself as you have dared hope of and for me. Alas! they are neither many, nor of quick recurrence. There *is* a something, an essential something wanting in me. I feel it, I *know* it—tho' what it is, I can but guess. I have read somewhere that in the tropical climates there are Annuals [as lofty] and of as ample girth as forest trees. So by a very dim likeness, I seem to myself to distinguish power from strength & to have only the power. But of this I will speak again: for if it be no reality, if it be no more than a disease of my mind, it is yet deeply rooted & of long standing & requires help from one who loves me in the Light of knowledge. I have written these lines with a compelled understanding, my feelings other where at work: and I fear, unwell as I am, to indulge any deep emotion however ennobled or endeared. Dear Davy! I have always loved, always honoured, always had faith in you, in every part of my being that lies below the Surface, & whatever changes may have now & then *rippled* even upon the surface, have been only jealousies concerning you in behalf of all men, and fears from exceeding great hope. I cannot be prevented from uttering & manifesting the strongest convictions & best feelings of my nature by the accident, that they of whom I think so highly, esteem me in return & entertain reciprocal hopes.—No! I would to God I thought of myself, even as you think of me but——

So far had I written my dear Davy, yesterday afternoon,[1] with all my faculties beclouded, writing mostly about myself, but Heaven knows! thinking wholly about you. I am too sad, too much dejected to write what I could wish. Of course, I shall see you this evening here at ¼ after nine. When I mentioned it to Sir George, 'Too late'! said he: 'no if it were 12 o'clock, it would be better than his not coming.' They are really kind & good, Sir G. & Lady Beaumont. Sir G. is a remarkably *sensible* man which I mention because it *is* somewhat REMARKABLE in a Painter of Genius, who

yesterday & finished today. It is for Sir G. Beaumont, & is very like.' *The Farington Diary*, ed. by James Greig, 8 vols., 1922–4, ii. 210.

[1] This letter, which was begun on Sunday afternoon, was completed on Monday morning and delivered by Lady Beaumont's servant. See next letter.

is at the same time a man of rank, & an exceedingly amusing Companion.

I am still but very indifferent—but this is so old a story that it affects me but little. To see *you* look so very unwell on Saturday was a new thing to me, and I want a word something short of affright, & a little beyond anxiety to express the feeling that haunted me in consequence.—

I trust that I shall have time & the gifted Spirit to write to you from Portsmouth, a part at least of what is in & upon me in my more genial moments.—

> But always | I am & shall be | My dear Davy! | with hope & esteem & affection, the | Aggregate of many Davys, | your sincere friend
>
> S. T. Coleridge.[1]

---

[1] Davy's farewell letter to Coleridge is included in part:

> 12 o'clock—Monday [Sunday?]
>
> My dear Coleridge
>
> My mind is disturbed and my body harrassed by many labours, yet I cannot suffer you to depart without endeavoring to express to you some of the unbroken and higher feelings of my spirit, which have you at once for their cause, and object.——
>
> Years have passed away since we first met, and your presence, and recollections with regard to you have afforded me continual sources of enjoyment. Some of the better feelings of my nature have been elevated by your converse; and thoughts which you have nursed, have been to me an eternal source of consolation.—
>
> In whatever part of the World you are, you will often live with me, not as a fleeting idea but as a *recollection* possessed of creative energy, as an *Imagination* winged with fire inspiriting and rejoicing.—
>
> You must not live much longer without giving to *all men* the *proof of power*, which those who know you feel in admiration. Perhaps at a distance from the applauding and censuring murmurs of the world, you will be best able to execute those great works which are justly expected from you; you are to be the historian of the Philosophy of feeling—Do not in any way dissipate your noble nature / Do not give up your birth-right.——
>
> May you soon recover perfect health; the health of strength and happiness! May you soon return to us confirmed in all the powers essential to the exertion of *genius*——You were born for your Country and your native land must be the scene of your activity. I shall expect the time when *your spirit* bursting through the clouds of ill health will appear to *all men* not as an uncertain and brilliant *flame* but as a fair and permanent *light*, fixed though constantly in motion, as a sun which gives its fire not only to its attendant *Planets*; but which sends *beams* from all its *parts* into all worlds. . . . [Transcript Royal Institution.]

## 581 A. To Lady Beaumont

*Address*: Lady Beaumont.
*MS. Pierpont Morgan Lib. Pub.* Memorials of Coleorton, *ii. 124.*

Monday Morning   March 26 1804[1]

I have left your Ladyship the two first Parts of the biographical, or philosophico-biographical Poem to be prefixed or annexed to the Recluse:[2] your Ladyship may perhaps wish to *look* them over. When I gave your Ladyship Davy's Letter to me,[3] I *trust*, that I need not say, how wholly my consciousness was taken up with Davy, & with the Letter as a proof of his Tenderness & Seriousness of mind / Of the subject of the Letter I thought as little as of the man in the Moon / the Sentiments expressed concerning me are so very widely [different] from the habitual Thoughts of my own mind & Heart / in simple truth, I have long layed the whole affair to sleep, having repeatedly & SOLEMNLY assured both Davy and Wordsworth, that I knew myself better than they could—& that I *knew*, that they had grossly over-rated me—. I would, I could think otherwise. Tho' an error, yet being joyous & *stimulant* it might do me great good; & I should have wit enough to keep it to myself.—

Yet after I had given you the Letter, the Indelicacy of the *Semblance* of the Thing struck & pained me—tho' I in the next moment blamed myself for the Feeling: for 'if I suppose that Sir George and Lady B. know so little of my heart & habits of Feeling as this fear implies, how dare I imagine that I know them / & what would become of all the Emotions & Feelings that hang upon that supposed knowlege'——

S. T. Coleridge

Shall I request your Ladyship to be so good as to let one of the servants take the accompanying Letter to Mr Davy?—[4]

## 582. To John Rickman

*Address*: Jno. Rickman, Esqre | at his Office | House of Commons.
*MS. Huntington Lib. Pub. with omis.* John Rickman, *106.*

7, Barnard's Inn, Tobin's   Monday, March 26, 1804
My dear Sir
I have crawled hither, and having crawled on to the Strand, to Stuart's, I must be *carried* back. I have again been miserably ill——

---

[1] In publishing this letter, William Knight dated it 16 Mar. 1811 at the beginning and 25 Mar. 1811 at the conclusion.
[2] Referring, of course, to Books I and II of *The Prelude*.
[3] For Davy's letter see note to the preceding letter.   [4] Letter 581.

## 26 March 1804

the Diarrhoea——but I am literally *sick* of thinking, talking, & writing about my own miserable Carcase.—I have received *orders* from the Captain instantly to take my place for Portsmouth / at the latest to be at Portsmouth by Wednesday early-morning. Accordingly, I have taken my place by the Tuesday Evening's Mail.—So much of myself.—As to the *pacquets* the greatest part by far of my suffering arose from my imagination having conjured up very livelily the possibility of *your* having been placed in an uneasy situation—an indelicate one for *you* / & there seemed such a dreadful unappropriateness in your character to the very picture of such a Thing, that I at first & till I received your Letter, *fretted* about it.—

My dear Sir! I am on the point of leaving my Friends, children, Country—& in a very weak state of Health / & that my mind is rather in a sad & somewhat *solemn* mood, will appear to most people no other than natural.—Whether I return is to my own feelings uncertain / If I had stayed, I *know* that I should have had your Friendship / if not in the highest, yet assuredly not in the common-place Sense of the word / for I should have appeared to you finally as *I am* / & of the *sum total* of that I am not ashamed.—Of yourself let me say a few words to you—at a moment, when I am incapable of even thinking a thought not accorded to by my earnest conviction / I had been taught to form a high opinion of you by two men, whom I love & honor / & I leave you with a far higher. All your habits both of action & feeling—your whole code of Self-government—would to God I could but imitate them as entirely as I approve of them! / If I had written, admire them, you ought not to have been disgusted / for approbation accompanied by a sense of the Difficulty would make no very bad definition of Admiration / —But I am as weak at heart as in body—& must have done / ——If I see any thing in Malta or Sicily likely to interest you, be assured, that all my habits of Indolence will not be strong enough to prevent me from communicating them to you.—

I re-inclose W. Taylor's Letter. It is in[deed] a very sensible one—every one must have his Prepossessions. My coolest retrospects do not furnish me with any thing decisive in favor of Mr Fox, either as a wise or a good man—/

God bless you, my dear Sir! | I shall ever remain | with affectionate Esteem | Your Friend & fervent Well-wisher

S. T. Coleridge

## 583. To William Sotheby

*Address*: W. Sotheby, Esqre | Lodge | Loughton | Essex
*MS*. Colonel H. G. Sotheby. *Hitherto unpublished.*
*Postmark*: 27 March 1804.

Sir G. Beaumont's—Monday Night   March 26, 1804

My honored Friend

I will fill up the Letter from Portsmouth to you with the Poem—I am not at present sufficiently collected.—Davy dines here on Wednesday, 4 o/ clock; & with him the Poet, Crow,[1] who is even now arrived at the Royal Institution. Sir G. and Lady Beaumont bade me express their Compliments; & that they expect you, as before.——

Dear Sotheby! if I return, we shall be Friends: if I die, as I believe I shall, you will remember me. Such Remembrances do us all good.—

I pray fervently for you and your's—your Wife, your Daughter, for all your children. Again and again may our Almighty Father bless you and

your gratefully affectionate
S. T. Coleridge

## 584. To Sir George and Lady Beaumont

*Address*: Sir G. Beaumont /
*MS*. Pierpont Morgan Lib. *Pub. with omis*. Memorials of Coleorton, *ii. 164*.

[27 March 1804]

My dear and honored Friends

Having left this House I shall have small Heart to return hither merely to leave it again. It will not be easy for me to forget the sudden and impetuous transition of Feeling, which I experienced last night, when having bade you good night—almost our last words a mirthful Story—I opened the second Green Door: & when I was at length left alone in my bed room—o dear & heart-honored Sir George & Lady Beaumont! I sate by the fire, a world of confused Images of Keswick, Dunmow, London passing before my very eyes, till the waters dropt from them, & the walls of the Room brought me back to more serious, and deeper, o far deeper emotion. I knelt and prayed for you. May Almighty God preserve & bless you! If I did not in my heart's heart cherish you, and (abstracting that Hue of Respect to the difference of your Rank, which is with

---

[1] William Crowe (1745–1829), author of *Lewesdon Hill*.

me a business not of Force or of Habit but of deliberate moral Election) feel toward you, dear Sir George and dear Lady Beaumont, even as tho'

> We had been rear'd upon the self-same Hills,
> Fed the same flocks by Fountains, Shades, and Rills,[1]

I should find in the consciousness of your affectionate & zealous Esteem of me a burthen which my Spirit could not support. Wherever I am, and whatever, yet sick or well, on this or on the other Side of the world of waters, yea, be it my faith, that—alike on this or on the other side of the Grave, I shall

> remain, dear Friends! with gratitude, esteem & with many affections blended in one Your Friend
> S. T. Coleridge[2]

I have inclosed Taylor's Letter—the fair Woman's Verses shall be sent to you.

## 585. To George Bellas Greenough

*Address*: G. B. Greenough Esqre | Corner of Charles Street | Parliament Street
*Transcript Professor Edith J. Morley. Hitherto unpublished.*
*Postmark*: 27 March ⟨1804⟩.

Courier office    Tuesday, March 27, 1804

My dear Greenough

I cannot with truth express my regret for not having seen you: for I am perilously weak, & have endeavoured to see none that are not necessary for business—& most avoided those from whom I should part with any emotion. If you think it worth while, the Brandy might be sent by one of the heavy Coaches tomorrow morning, either from Golden Cross or the Bell Savage, directed to me, at Mr Mottley, Bookseller, Portsmouth.

But however this may be, do not forget to leave the two Draw-

---

[1] *Lycidas*, 23–24.
[2] 'If good wishes innumerable', wrote Sir George Beaumont in a farewell letter, 'can accelerate a passage yours will be the shortest that ever was made to Malta—Never again mention obligations to us—believe me, and from my soul I speak it, the advantages Lady Beaumont and myself have gained from you and Wordsworth more than a million times repay the trifling attentions we had it in our power to shew you both.' Lady Beaumont added: 'In the portmanteau you will find as portable a dictionary and grammar as could be procured, and do not forget there is a packet of James's powders in the drawer of the writing desk, the middle part contains all the manuscripts of Wordsworth and I flatter myself the convenience will reconcile you to the use of it. . . . I shall not easily forget the sensations I felt at parting, but I can only say Adieu.' MS. Dove Cottage.

ings at John's for I am very anxious that they should go into Cumberland. Farewell! If I return, I will remember you: if I die, you will remember me. For I have been & remain
affectionately yours
[Signature cut off.]

### 586. To Richard Sharp

*Address*: R. Sharp, Esqre | 17. Mark Lane
*MS. Cornell University Lib. Hitherto unpublished.*
*Postmark*: 27 March 1804.

My dear Sir

Need I say, that Illness has prevented our meeting / at the time of your calling I was at Northcote's, the Painter, on my way cityward, & there was seized—O me!—I am not sorry, in my present exceedingly effeminate & untranquil State of Feeling that I shall have left the Kingdom without any formal Parting from you—If Gratitude consist in repaying Love by Love, merited Esteem by merited Esteem, & good services by earnest dispositions akin to them, I am, & shall ever be, your grateful Friend
S. T. Coleridge.

P.S. If I draw at all, I shall draw on Mr Stuart according to your Letter. Present my respectful remembrances to Mr Boddington: & tell Mr Tuffin, that the Time may come when I shall, in a way unwished by him, call to mind his House, & the Shelter it afforded me & my infirmities.—S.T.C.

### 587. To Thomas Poole

*Address*: T. Poole Esqre | Parliament Office | Abingdon St | Westminster.
*MS. British Museum. Pub.* Thomas Poole, *ii. 138.*

Tuesday, March 27, 1804

Dear Poole

I will write to you from Portsmouth. At present, weak as I am & daily tottering into relapses, it would not be wise—scarcely safe—for me either to write to you at full & [or?] to take leave of you in person.—May the Almighty guide you onward where ever & when ever the Road leads to Happiness & that sole Virtue which is in FAITH not in the OUTWARD WORKS.
S. T. Coleridge

## 588. To Mrs. S. T. Coleridge

*Address*: Mrs Coleridge | Greta Hall | Keswick
*MS.* Lord Latymer. *Pub. E.L.G. i. 315.*
*Postmark*: 27 March 1804.

Courier office, Tuesday Afternoon, ½ past 2. March 27, 1804
My dear Sara

I *have* been very ill, having had a relapse; but am now pretty well, only weak. I have taken my place in the Portsmouth Mail for tonight—& expect to sail on the 30th / —but of this there is small certainty. Of course, I shall inform you of my arrival, & with it convey all I can learn. Sir G. and Lady Beaumont have been, in strict & moderate words, exceedingly good & kind to me during my Indisposition / but of this in detail hereafter.—I have advised, 'Davison, Noel, Templer, Middleton, Johnson, & Wedgwood, Bankers, 34. Pall Mall, London' that your Drafts are to be honored to whatever amount I am entitled to draw—& that you will advise them thereof when you draw—. You have an 100£ to draw this year—which you will draw whenever you like it or want it / — Perhaps, it would be as well to draw for 50£ a time, at least / as it will be right for you to post pay your Letter of Advice—'Gentlemen, I have drawn on you a draft payable to Mr —— or order, so many days after date, in the name and in the account of S. T. Coleridge. Sara Coleridge— To | Messrs Davison, Noel, Templer, | & Co | Bankers, | Pall Mall | London.[']

You may make your note what date you like, a month, 5, 6, 8 weeks after date—in short what you like——5 or 6 is as good as ready money.

A small Parcel will come for Hartley soon, & in it a Letter from me.—

You must not draw for more than the 60£ on Stuart / as I have been obliged to take up the 20£—so many petty expences have accumulated / for example—a pair of green Spectacles & Case, 21 Shillings, a Hat, 26S, Boots, 36S, Medicines, Spirits, Servants, &c &c——

My Love to all. I will write from Portsmouth; God speeding me thither.

Heaven bless you, & our | darlings—&
S. T. Coleridge

Do not be uneasy about money. If you want more, you shall have more.

## 589. To Robert Southey

*Address*: R. Southey, Esqre | Greta Hall | Keswick | Cumberland
*MS*. Lord Latymer. *Pub. E.L.G. i. 316.*
*Postmark*: 30 March 1804. *Stamped*: Portsmouth.

Crown Inn, Portsmouth: Wednesday Morning, 10 o clock.
March 28th, 1804

My dear Southey

I arrived here this morning between 7 and 8. My Ship, it seems, is not yet in sight; but is confidently expected in the course of the Day. Where my Captain is, I cannot tell; but the Convoy is expected to sail tomorrow. So much the better for me. This is a noisy dirty Inn: & if any accident should put off the Convoy, a very improbable Event, I should take the first Passage-boat for Upper Ride in the Isle of Wight, & stay there. I hope, I shall know the whens & hows before the Post goes out to day: if not, I shall delay the Letter.—

Sir G. Beaumont continues in Town about a month or five weeks. When you come to town, be sure [to] call on him / Corner of South Audley Street, Grosvenor Square / the Corner that is in the Square. He himself mentioned it twice—that if you came to town during his Sojourn there, he hoped you would call on him. He & his Lady are worth going a good way to see for their own Sakes: & the Pictures in his Picture Room are most exquisite.—The famous Rubens, two Claudes, a Gaspar Poussin!! & yet Sir George's own Landscapes hang by them undishonored / while the Niobe of Wilson, which in poetic Conception & *form* is a first-rate & sublime Landscape, with the exception of the Sharp-shooters in the Clouds—yet in colouring looks quite *mealy* and *pastey* by comparison.—I have no doubt that he will shew you, or procure you to see, the two or three famous collections, Lord Ashburnham's, Angerstein's,[1] &c. But however this may be, do not forget to call on Northcote & beg to see the portrait of Lorenzo de Medici's, imagined to be by Bronzino / & on Commyns, the Picture Cleaner in Pall Mall (Sir G. would give you a note to him) to see the Landscape by Salvator Rosa, if he still have it in his keeping, and above all the picture of St Helena dreaming the vision of the Cross, designed by Raphael & painted by Paul Veronese. That is a POEM indeed!——

(My Address—S. T. Coleridge, *Esqre*, Dr Stoddart's, Malta.)

[1] The collection of paintings belonging to John Julius Angerstein (1735–1823) was purchased by the British government in 1824 and formed the nucleus of the National Gallery.

## 28 March 1804

As for myself, I am somewhat better; but still weak, & stupid— & probably should be all the better for a few Hours' sound Sleep.— I will therefore defer the remainder of the Letter, until something to say to you comes from without, or rises up within.—God love you, dear Friend!——

While I was writing, Mottley, a dashing Bookseller, a booted buckskin-breeched Jockey—to whom Stuart gave me a Letter of most urgent recommendation (he is their Portsmouth Correspondent) called / he is a man of wealth & influence here, & a knowing Fellow. He took me thro' the Dock-yards / & I was lucky enough to be present at a HEAT, i.e. at the welding a huge *faggot* of small *laths* of red hot Iron into the Shaft of the Anchor of a Man of War. It was truly sublime—the enormous Blaze, the regular yet complex intertwisted Strokes of between 20 & 30 men, with their huge Flail-hammers——the astonishment how they could throw them about with such seeming wildness without dashing out each other's Brains—& how they saved their Eyes amidst the Shower of Sparks / the Iron *dripping* like a Mill-wheel from the intense white Heat / —verily it was an unforgettable Scene!—The poor men are pitiable Slaves—from 4 in the morning they work till 9 at night, & yet are payed less than any other in the yard. They all become old men in the prime of manhood. So do the Rope-makers / who yet only work from 7 till noon. The Rope room is a VERY LOW broad room, of a length far too great for the Eye to see from one end to the other— / it gave me a grand idea of an Hindostan Cavern.—A pin machine has been lately introduced, after a rebellion among the men / & but for the same deplorable Delusion 2 thirds of that Labor might be done by machines, which now eats up the Rope-men, like a Giant in a fairy tale.

On my return I took an early dinner—or rather attempted to take it / my stomach bad, & it is possible, that a wretched Steak was too abrupt a Transition from the dinners, I have lately been almost habituated to: tho' I have never once since I left Keswick broke thro' my Rule of eating only of one thing that has had Life. If I eat Fish, I eat neither fowl nor flesh—& so on. And all this afternoon I have been sleeping on the chairs; & have caught a cold in my Head.—No news of the Convoy. Tomorrow I dine with Mottley, who was engaged in the Country to day. He is really a civil Fellow without any professions, or shew.—Yesterday, as I was returning with Stuart from Hammersley's (the Banker's) we met & I was introduced to Sheridan, whose manners are startlingly like those of Hatfield / & like him, his very first words were a Compliment—his next a Promise / his last united both. I could take that man in; but, I'll be damn'd, if he could take me in.—

Inter nos, Stuart, who knows him well, says, that he really did intend to take & introduce me to Addington.—But of this say NO WORD.—

It would have affected you deeply to have seen the manner in which Sir George parted from me.—His Valet packed up every thing—sent off every thing, & did not leave me till I entered the Mail.—They stocked me with Wines in stout bottles & lock-up Cases, with Medicine, Portable Soup, an elegant Thing to lock up my Letters, Papers, &c &c—& when I was at Dunmow, Sir George thrice intreated me to accept of an 100£—the which I mildly but firmly refused / —but on the morning, I left Dunmow, as I was going into the Coach, the Servant delivered me a Letter from Sir George, with the 100£ inclosed—& the Letter itself for it's delicacy, deliberate Affection, and elevated good sense was 'worth twice the Sum', to use a very vulgar phrase.—Stuart has been equally kind & zealous—that man has a real Friendship for me. It may seem madness in me to wish more Friends: yet who can know Rickman, that STERLING MAN, & not desire to be something more than an acquaintance? Mine is a severely moral Wish. I shall think of him at Malta, whenever the Sea-breeze blows upon and braces me. He does not *altogether* like me: & as I live, I have one pleasure in it—for I know the sincerity, the bottomness of my own Feelings. Too often have I mistaken in myself Sympathy for Friendship.

P.S.—I will write again to YOU; but to Sara I shall not write till I reach Gibraltar—*if* I reach it.——O Southey! from Oxford to Greta Hall—a spiritual map with our tracks, as of two Ships that left Port in Company——It is not for either of us to do it; but a Poet might make a divine Allegory of it.—I have said nothing of Edith; but that which you let no one know of in the bottom of your Heart, that same anxiety & hope & fear flutters at the bottom of mine. S. T. C.

### 590. To Daniel Stuart

*Address*: D. Stuart, Esqre | Courier office | Strand | London
*MS*. British Museum. *Pub*. Letters from the Lake Poets, 27.
*Postmark*: 30 March 1804. *Stamped*: Portsmouth.

Thursday, March 29th, 1804. Crown Inn, Portsmouth

My dear Stuart

I arrived here yesterday morning between 7 & 8, tolerably well, I was going to say; but perhaps endurably unwell would come nearer the Truth. I called on Boddington's & Sharp's Agent

## 29 March 1804

(having left your Letter at Mottley's Shop) / he made a very brisk & dexterous Riddance of me. Shortly after my return to my Inn, having gained no other intelligence but the important one of the non-arrival of the Speedwell, I had a call from Mottley—who expressed his Regret that he was absolutely engaged on a party into the country that day; but he would give the morning to me / & the whole of the tomorrow, when he hoped I would dine with him. Accordingly, he took me all round the Dock-yard—& tho' I take but little pleasure in these Sights, yet I felt myself interested & that I had spent a remarkably instructive morning. The evening I wrote a very long Letter to you, which was no doubt a great Relief to myself; but on reperusing it this morning I felt, that it would be oppressive to you, & tho' I will not destroy it, yet I shall not send it—at present, at least.—I cannot however help saying, how very much I was touched this morning by the tenderness & unaffected goodness of your Letter to me.—Mr Mottley called, took me in his Boat to the huge Hospital, and to Gosport &c / became very communicative, pleasant, & very very civil & attentive. It is not possible, that a Man could do more honor to a Letter of Recommendation. I dine with him in about half an hour—. My Ship is not yet arrived; & the wind is against her. Yet it is thought, that she will come to night—& it is possible, that we may sail on Saturday.

I have confident Hopes, that I shall not find myself under the necessity of drawing for any thing more than I have already done; much less, to exceed your first kind offer. One thing only I have ventured to do. Northcote told me, that he could get his Portrait of me admirably *copied* for 4 or 5 guineas:[1] & I being exceedingly desirous that my Friends in the North should possess a Likeness of me, in case of my Death, have authorized him to have it copied, if it continues to be admired as much as it has been / & if he in his conscience can rely on the Artist for a Copy strictly honorable to the original, even tho' the original should be lost.—If he does it, he is to give a check on you for £5, 5S—the last Liberty of this Kind, that I shall ever take.

Lord St Vincent is unpopular here, as every man must be who detects & punishes Jobs & Abuses.[2] No man can deny, that Reforms were wanting—& that he has made them. And tho' the fortiter in re, et suaviter in modo make a very pleasant Punch,

---

[1] No such copy is known, but Beaumont had prints made of the Northcote portrait for Wordsworth and Southey. See *Early Letters*, 496–7, and *Southey Letters*, i. 321.

[2] John Jervis (1735–1823), Earl of St. Vincent, was First Lord of the Admiralty from 1801 to 1804.

yet when we cannot get it, we must put up with the *naked Spirit*. A strong Potion was wanting.

I am more *curious* than interested about Sheridan.—But here comes Mottley.—I shall write again tomorrow.——I am much better both in Health & cheerfulness to day than yesterday—

Believe me, dear Stuart! if I did not find in the very bottom of my Soul thorough Esteem & habitual Affection for you, your multiplied Love & Kindness to me would be a Burthen which my Spirit could not endure—; but these Things are not thrown away, if I deserve to be, & am,

what I trust, I am | Your sincere Friend,
S. T. Coleridge.

## 591. To Mrs. S. T. Coleridge

*Address*: Mrs Coleridge | Greta Hall | Keswick | Cumberland
*MS*. Lord Latymer. *Pub. with omis*. Letters, ii. 467.
*Postmark*: 2 April 1804. *Stamped*: Portsmouth.

Mr. J. C. Mottley's, Thomas St, Portsmouth
Sunday, April 1. 1804

My dear Sara

I am waiting here with great anxiety for the arrival of the Speedwell. The Leviathan Man of war, our Convoy, has orders to sail with the first fair wind: & whatever wind can bring in the Speedwell will carry out the Leviathan unless she have other orders than those generally known. I have [left] the Inn, and it's crumena-molga [*sic*] natio:[1] & am only at the expence of a Lodging, at ½ a guinea a week / for I have all my meals at Mr Mottley's, to whom a Letter from Stuart introduced me, & who has done most especial Honor to the Introduction. Indeed he could not well help / for Stuart in his Letter called me his very very particular Friend, & that every attention would sink more into his Heart than one offered to himself or to his Brother. Besides, you know, it is no new thing for people to take sudden & hot Likings to me. How different Sir G.B.!—He disliked me at first / & when I am in better spirits & less flurried, I will transcribe his last Letter. It breathed the very soul of calm, and manly, yet deep Affection!——Hartley will receive his & Derwent's Spillekins with a Letter from me by the first Waggon that leaves London after Wednesday next—

My dear Sara! the mother, the attentive and excellent Mother of my children must needs be always more than the word friend can express when applied to a woman / I pray you, use no word

[1] Cf. *Anatomy of Melancholy*, Pt. I, Sect. 2, Memb. 3, Subs. 15: 'such a purse-milking nation'. Burton is quoting from Dousa.

that you use with reluctance / . Yet what we have been to each other, our understandings will not permit our Hearts to forget!—God knows, I weep Tears of Blood, that so it is!—For I greatly esteem & honor you / Heaven knows, if I can leave you really comfortable in your circumstances, I shall meet Death with a face, which I feel at the moment I say it, it would rather shock than comfort you to hear.

Thank Southey for his Letter of this morning / if he & you direct your Letters to me to Mr J. C. Mottley, Portsmouth, they will be carefully forwarded to me without any additional expence——

My Health is indifferent / I am rather endurably unwell, than tolerably well.

I will write Southey tomorrow or next day—tho' Mottley rides & drives me about, sight-seeing, so as to leave me but little Time. I am not sure that I shall see the Isle of White [sic] /

Write to Wordsworth / inform him that I have received all & every thing—& will write him very soon—as soon as I command Spirits / Time—I could *command*. [Tell] him where I am & how I am situated, & how to direct to me both now & when I am sailed / for Mottley can send off all Letters to Malta under Government Covers—you direct therefore at all times merely—to me at Mr J. C. Mottley's, Portsmouth /

My very dear Sara, | May God Almighty bless you | & your
affectionate
S. T. Coleridge

I mourn for poor Mary.—

## 592. *To the Wordsworths*

*Address*: Mr Wordsworth | Grasmere, near | Ambleside | Kendal | Westmoreland
*MS.* Dove Cottage. *Pub. Chambers*, Life, *342*.
*Postmark*: 6 April 1804. *Stamped*: Portsmouth.

Mr J. C. Mottley's, Portsmouth.—Wednesday Morning, April 4th
1804

My dearest Friends

I have this moment read your Letter, Dorothy's & William's: which I received about an hour ago: for the sight of Dorothy's Handwriting on the directions of your Letter move[s] me so deeply, that my heart fails me—I dread the emotion from the opening of it—. O dearest & most revered William! I seem to grow weaker & weaker in my moral feelings / and every thing, that forcibly awakes me to Person & Contingency, strikes fear into me, sinkings and misgivings, alienation from the Spirit of Hope, obscure withdrawings out of Life, and something that you have given to Mortimer,[1] I believe in your Tragedy, a wish to retire into stoniness & to stir not, or to be diffused upon the winds & have no individual Existence. But all will become better when once I can sit down, & work: when my Time is my own, I shall be myself again. These Hauntings and Self-desertions are, no doubt, connected with the irritable state of my Bowels & the feebleness of my Stomach; but both they & these, their bodily causes, are exasperated by the rapid Changes, I have undergone—not only from one face to another in an endless detail of Change—; but in the abrupt & violent Transitions from Grasmere and dear you to Liverpool, to London, to Drinkings & Discussings—again from these to compleat quietness at Dunmow—& from Sir G. & Lady Beaumont back again to London Parties——then a few soothing & comfortable Days, & very instructive ones, with those good & (in a most appropriate sense) *elegant* people in town / & now at Portsmouth, from the quietest House & the most select & innocent conversation in London, & merely to particularize the whole of this contrast, from the House of a truly great Painter, a descendant of Beaumont, the Poet (& glorying in it more than in being, as he likewise is, a descendant of Kings, and one of the 4 or 5 most ancient noble families in Europe) to the company of Sailors & Portsmouth Shop-keepers, many of them good-natured & prompt to serve me, but all of them loose livers & loose talkers, smoking & drinking regularly to intoxication—& I in the midst of them with Oaths & Curses flying about me & whizzing by my ears, like Bullets!——This morning, however, my Captain presented himself to me—he arrived last night; he says that the Leviathan, of 74 guns, which is to convoy us, has as yet not received her orders, but probably will have them to day, namely, orders to sail with the first fair wind; but that the Wind at present (S.W.) is point blank against us, and in an obstinate corner.—The Captain seems a good sea man, and dines here to day.—I am at no expence here, except Lodging & Washing—which together does not exceed 13 Shillings a week—I have been 4 days at the Crown, with a private room, one dinner, one Tea, 3 breakfasts, one pint of wine, and one glass of Punch; & Mottley *congratulated* me, that I got off so cheap as a guinea & a half including Waiter, Boots, & Chambermaid. The last Landlord payed 10,000£ for the Inn to his Predecessor, besides the Rent to the House-owner, & made so large a fortune in six years, that he has retired & built a grand House

---

[1] The name Mortimer appears for Marmaduke in MS. B of *The Borderers.* Cf. *Poet. Works*, i. 343.

10 miles from Portsmouth, that cost him 8000£ / & this present Landlord, paying the same sum for the Trade, is making money, they say, still faster—& there are two other Inns in the Town, the one quite as lucrative, and the other nearly so.——You will direct all your Letters, in the first instance, to Mr Lambe, India House, London (remember to annex the e)—Lamb will carry them to Mr Rickman, who will have them frank'd to me to Mr J. C. Mottley's, Portsmouth / and Mottley will then forward them to me, not only with far greater regularity, than I should get them by the Post, but entirely free of all expence. He is a sort of agent, I believe, to Sir Alexander Ball, the Governor of the Island. In short, *you* have nothing to do but to direct your Letters Mr Lambe, &c— / & write on a large single Sheet, and send two single Letters rather than one double one.—But of all things I most eagerly wish to have my beloved Dorothy's Tour / Southey goes to London a week after his Wife's Confinement, if she do well. He could take it, & Rickman could get it franked; if you made it up in *Letters* (not like your last in *pacquets*, but more in the form & size of a common double Letter) each Letter, including the weight of the Seal not to exceed an Ounce & a Half—so as to allow for an envelope & large official Seal. The whole weight allowed to be franked by the Clerks of the H. of Commons is two Ounces—you may therefore exceed the ounce & a half, but take care—that no one Letter is so much as an Ounce & 3 quarters.—If however Southey should not go, or you should not have it ready, then send it, exactly in the same *Letter-form*, & in Letters, each *short* of an Ounce & 3 quarters, inclusive of the two Envelopes—directed. 1. S. T. Coleridge, Esqre, Mr J. C. Mottley's, Portsmouth. 2. Inclose this in an Envelope, directed simply, Jno. Rickman, Esqre. 3. Inclose this in another Cover, & direct it to, The Right Honor[a]ble, The Speaker, Palace Yard, Westminster. N.B.—Whatever you do, do not forget the 2nd Cover to Rickman, lest the Speaker should find himself Letter-smuggler to Squire Coleridge: and secondly, send them not all together, nor even day after day; but interpose four or five days between each Letter.—And after this once every month or six weeks, if dear William have written any Verses, more than will go in a single sheet to Lam*be*, you will send an Ounce & 3 quarters to me at Mottley's, under cover to Jno. Rickman, Esqre, under Cover to the Speaker.—I hope, you will write once every ten days at least, to Lambe / & these with one containing the poetry of six weeks—O dear dear Friends! I love you, even to anguish love you: & I know no difference, I feel no difference, between my Love of little Sara, & dear little John. Being equally with me, I could not but love them equally: how could I—the child

of the man, for whom I must find another name than Friend, if I call any others but him by the name of Friend—Mary & Dorothy's own Darling—the first *free* Hope of you all!—

I meant this merely as a Letter of Instructions & mere Intelligen[ce.] Your Le[tter] of this morning, as is too often the case with your Lette[rs,] was not dated. Take care of this, my dear Friends!—I shall feel need to say, God forgive me! if I suffer any two nights to pass without adding a few Lines to my Journal to you / & if any Vessels leave Malta, & no Letter come to you, the Vessel must be lost. I *hope,* I shall be able to send them free of expence.—J. C. Mottley is a Bookseller, & Proprietor of a successful Provincial Paper—he has a large Business, & supplies several Public offices with Stationery—. He has 3 Brothers all high in different public Offices here. To me he has been exceedingly civil / & is now, to oblige me & on my representation, using his utmost Interest to procure a place of 100£ & some thing more, in the Sick & Hurt Office for Mrs Coleridge's Brother. I have almost *expectations* that he will succeed: the person, in whose patronage those places are, has *promised* him the first Vacancy. Five minutes after I had mentioned to him how anxious I was to get him a place, & how deserving a youth he was, he *wrote* to the gentleman / in order that I might see the Answer before my Departure. He had been asking my Advice about one of his own Clerks, a fine young man who had in a very modest way asked for an increase of Salary. I advised Mottley to advance it somewhat beyond his Request: & to promise him in case of perseverant Industry & Fidelity a small Share in the Business, as soon as he was [of] age / He is now between 18 & 19 —& the whole of Mottley's Shop Business rests on him, for Mottley is a man of *Pleasure* / I grounded my advice on his (Mottley's) character, & the necessity, as a mere man of Prudence, that he should have some one bound to him by other than common Ties. Mottley stood like one lost in Thought / then said, you are *right*! you are quite in the Right, Sir!—I will do it, by God!—Then I mentioned to him poor George Fricker / &c. Mottley has just been in here: tells me, he has done exactly as I advised him—& left the young man in such agitation of Joy & Gratitude, (in great measure on account of a Mother to whom he is devoted & who is in extreme Distress) that he begged leave to retire to his Lodgings for a couple of Hours.—I have told this Story on account of an anecdote that affected me & will affect you.—I told him, says Mottley to me, that it was *you* in great measure, to whom he was indebted for it—the gentleman, who talked to him about the Lyrical Ballads. (The young man happened to be reading the Tintern Abbey, & apparently with due Emotion & an intelligent Face). 'As I live, Sir!

(replied he to Mottley) I felt I don't know how—as I never felt before, at that man's Face when first he spoke to me.'—Curious accidents!—Probably, very probably, that young man will some time or other be one of the richest Tradesmen in Portsmouth / & he himself will not be able to say, how much of it he will have owed to the accident of his reading your Tintern Abbey.—Mottley has a number of excellent Qualities about him; but he is a sad loose Liver. Drinks hard, smokes hard, cannot bear to be alone; & tho' exceedingly prosperous, & with a nice sweet-tempered Wife & six fine Children, the two youngest exquisitely beautiful in the petite style, nevertheless, alas! alas! addicted to almost promiscuous Intercourse with women of all Classes. At first, he was actually *astonished* at my principles & practice / but now he evidently looks up to me for them / I never looked or spoke severely or austerely to him / & I have some hopes of him from one circumstance—he did not doubt a moment that I had told him the Truth respecting myself.—If you speak of him at all in your Letters, mention him by the name of Poecilus (Ποικίλος).—Letters here are sometimes opened by order of Government / & his Brother is high in office. I will send off this lest I should be too late for the Post.—S. T. C.

### 593. To Daniel Stuart

*Address*: D. Stuart Esqre | Courier Office | No/ 348 | Strand | London
*MS*. British Museum. *Pub. with omis.* Letters from the Lake Poets, *30*.
*Postmark*: 6 April 1804. *Stamped*: Portsmouth.

Thursday, April 5th, 1804

My dear Stuart

I have no other Fear except that your Friendship may urge you farther than it ought to do. I never permit myself to form an *expectation* in any thing of this kind, consequently I suffer no disappointment: and as to Sheridan's promises, I should as soon expect my Dreams to realize themselves. Both may do so, by CHANCE. Indeed, and indeed, my dear Sir! the only strong feeling, I have, or ever have had, on this Subject, is that of your kindness in exerting yourself in a Way, that neither you nor I would do for ourselves.—The wind pipes loud, & is point-blank against us: & my Captain has just called here to let me know, that we cannot reach the Ship with this Gale / Else I was to have gone aboard this Afternoon. To morrow I go—& may even sail—if the wind blows a puff that makes it possible, it will be attempted.—Mottley continues most assiduously kind & attentive. He has indeed a number of *excellent* Qualities; but (in confidence I can say so to *you*) he is a man of pleasure, & the worst of all is that with a nice sweet-tempered Wife & six or 7 very sweet Children he assuredly addicts himself to low & promiscuous Intercourse / & if he does not take care in time, he will drink & smoke off a portion of his Liver, before ever a single Stitch in the Side gives him warning of it.—He is a man of much influence, & very much & generally liked.—I have every reason to remember him with respect & sense of obligation, even abstracting all that goes to your account, & striking off all the transferable Debt.—I am in much better bodily Health than when I left you, notwithstanding that I live in a Cloud of Smoke, among loose Livers & loose Talkers, with volleys of oaths rattling about my ears, like Grape-Shot, or whizzing by, like so many Bullets with holes in them.—They are a kind-hearted people, prompt & hospitable; but from the constant Influx of Sailors the Inhabitants are all Mock-tars, & the whole Town is a huge Man of War of Brick & Mortar.—

I was much pleased with the leading Paragraph on D'Enghien.[1] It was well written & with good feeling.—

I probably shall write again: but if I should be hurried off & prevented, I shall only be deprived of that which, be assured, is painful to me even in a Letter, the bidding you a last Farewell: for I am, my dear Stuart, most unfeignedly

Your sincere Friend<br>S. T. Coleridge

My direction even after I have sailed will be—Mr J. C. Mottley's, | Portsmouth.
You need not add Bookseller, if you prefix J. C. to the Sir name. Mottley will forward them to me free of expence & regularly.

### 594. To John Rickman

*Address*: Jno. Rickman, Esqre.
*MS. Huntington Lib. Pub. E.L.G. i. 320.*

Portsmouth.— Friday, April 6th. Noon. [1804]
My dear Sir

I am off—pray, write to Southey & tell him that I am off, am well, & bless them all!—Let me say one thing—the only severe pang, I suffered, on account of the pacquets, I suffered at the time

---

[1] The Duc d'Enghien was charged with complicity in the conspiracy of Cadoudal against the life of Napoleon. This charge was false; he was then hastily tried for bearing arms against France and executed at Vincennes on 21 Mar. 1804.

of opening them, before I knew that you had written or would write / You could have written nothing but what you did write / & if you had written nothing, I should have suffered much much more / This on my *Honor*! The only thing I shall request of you will be this—to suffer two or three double Letters to be inclosed to you, each at an interval of six or seven days—& to have them franked—S. T. Coleridge, Esqre, at J. C. Mottley's, Esqre, Portsmouth—/—& the same *one once* in *5* or *6* weeks, during my absence / viz. whatever Poetry Wordsworth writes in that space of time, which cannot make a large Letter. Mr Mottley, who has been exceedingly kind, will forward them to Malta, free of expence.—

Tell George Fricker to write to Keswick to his Sisters—& that I have been trying to do some thing for him. I meant to have written him:—as to the means of *de ignorancing* himself.——I have been trying to get him a place in the Sick & Wounded office (but this I would not mention to him). Mottley will write if it succeeds: & the Lad will take your advice.——I will write by the first opportunity—

My dear Sir!—different Constitutions breed different manners—we must judge by actions / There are HATFIELDS[1]—& likewise there are IAGOS—Whatever shape Virtue can assume, Vice will counterfeit——You *do* judge by actions—I will try to do so—and not to love in haste / Wherever I am, I shall remember you: for in simple nakedness of Heart I respect you & with a feeling of affection /

S. T. Coleridge

## 595. *To Sir George Beaumont*

*Address*: Sir George Beaumont, Bart | Grosvenor Square | London
*MS*. Pierpont Morgan Lib. *Pub*. Memorials of Coleorton, *i. 58.*
*Postmark*: 8 April 1804. *Stamped*: Portsmouth.

Friday Night, April 6th / 1804. Spithead, on board the Speedwell
My dear Sir George

What I feel deeply, why should I fear to say plainly? And what is there worthy to accompany the reward of a quiet conscience, if it be not the approbation & Sympathy of those, whom we honestly esteem? It is perhaps no compliment to the World, we live in, that I hesitated to say, that your anxiety for my Health would be a

---

[1] The fraudulent marriage of John Hatfield and Mary Robinson, the 'Buttermere Beauty', excited considerable attention. Coleridge reported on the affair in three contributions to the *Morning Post*, 11 and 22 Oct. and 5 Nov. 1802. Hatfield was hanged for forgery in Sept. 1803.

## To Sir George Beaumont

strong Inducement to me to take care of it.—I am often afraid of giving way to my best feelings, lest they should appear as mere *Heat* of manner / an overboiling, that puts out the miserable pittance of Fire, that made it boil. But different Constitutions breed different modes of manifestation / if there are HATFIELDS in abundance, there is likewise no lack of Iagos: Virtue can exhibit itself in no Shape, which Vice will not learn to counterfeit: and you, & I, my honored Friend! will judge by actions, as far as they go—and, where they fail us, by a tact, that makes us *feel* differences in things, which we should be puzzled to explain by words.

I was hurried off this morning to my Vessel—but the Wind has again wester'd—but our Commodore, Captn H. W. Bayntun,[1] of the Leviathan, (I wonder, whether Mr or Captn Sotheby knows him?) is to sail with the first Puff that wins a point & a half on the hither Side of Impossibility. We *hope* to go tomorrow: we may be here this day fortnight: it is hard to say, which is the more probable.—I am better, than I was. My Spirits are low: and I suffer too often sinkings & misgivings, alienations from the Spirit of Hope, strange withdrawings out of the Life that manifests itself by existence—morbid yearnings condemn'd by me, almost despis'd, and yet perhaps at times almost cherish'd, to concenter my Being into Stoniness, or to be diffused as among the winds, and lose all individual existence. But all this I well know is a symptom of bodily disease, and no part of sentiment or intellect / closely connected with the excessively irritable State of my Stomach and the Viscera, & beyond doubt greatly exasperated by the abruptness & suddenness of my late Transitions from one state to another. Mercy on me! from Grasmere and the Wordsworths, to London, to drinkings, talkings, discussings, vain & noisy Exhibition / thence another Grasmere (quite another & yet essentially the same) at Dunmow / again to London—& again a few happy days with you & Lady Beaumont / & whither then? To Portsmouth, among men, kind-hearted indeed, & absolutely eager to serve me, & to express a Liking to me that from such men quite astonished me—but among Loose Livers & loose Talkers, with Oaths & Dirt rattling about my Ears, like Grape Shot, & whistling by me, like so many perforated Bullets. For at Portsmouth all are mock tars—the whole Town is one huge Man of War of Brick & Mortar.—Positively, this Night, that Star so very bright over the mast of a noble Vessel—& the sound of the water breaking against the

---

[1] Henry William Bayntun (1766–1840) had recently returned from ten years' service in the West Indies. His ship, the *Leviathan*, then on her way to join the fleet under Nelson in the blockade of Toulon, was to play a prominent role in the Battle of Trafalgar.

## 6 April 1804 [595

Ship Side—it seems quite a *Home* to me.—Our Captain is a mild good sort of man / a Scotchman / prudent, well-meaning, unprofessing & plain as the best Englishman, & with every appearance of a good Sailor. There are two Passengers besides me / the one a half pay Lieutenant, turned small Merchant, who with a bright eye over a yellow-purple face that betrays to me that half his Liver is gone or going, has said 4 or 5 times aloud, that good wine never did any man any harm / & an unconscientiously fat Woman, who would have wanted Elbow Room on Salisbury Plain / a body that might have been in a less spendthrift mood of Nature sliced into a company, & a reasonable Slice allotted to her as Corporal! I think, I never saw so large a woman, such a monopolist, patentee, abstract, of superfluous Flesh!—*Enough of her*—in a double sense of the Phrase.—My Direction continues to be, simply, at Mr J. C. Mottley's, Portsmouth. Mr Mottley will have them forwarded to me with more regularity than by the post, & free of expence. The man has been really kind to me: & I hope, I have done him some *good*, in the best sense of the World.—I shall lose no opportunity to write to you: & Lady Beaumont will do me the justice to believe, that I have never forgotten her wish respecting the Epitaph. I have waited for the Time.—I will suppose it possible, that I may yet again write to you before I lose sight of my native Shores—for even in a Letter it is painful to me to bid you & your dear Lady a last Farewell. Nay! that I trust, never can be the case / never, never! if I, and you, honored Friends, are what I believe we are, & continue to be so. Then Death *itself* will be only a Voyage—a Voyage not *from*, but to our native Country. [F]ervently I bless, & pray for you! and am, dear Sir G. & dear Lady [Bea]umont, your grateful & most affectionate Friend,

S. T. Coleridge.—

### 596. To Robert Southey

*Address*: R. Southey Esqre | Greta Hall | Keswick
*MS*. Lord Latymer. *Hitherto unpublished.*
*Postmark*: 9 April 1804. *Stamped*: Portsmouth.

Saturday, April 7th, 1804

My dear Southey

I came on shore this morning with the Captn / it being a calm, & the sailors said the[y] smelt a West wind / but they are deceived / since I have been on Shore, it has turned favorable & we shall assuredly sail tomorrow, if it continue. I write now, merely to say, that I have been anxious about George Fricker, and meant

( 1123 )

to have written to him as to the means of *dëignorancing* himself. When you see him, give him an English Grammar / & a Lesson or two yourself concerning Punctuation to which Rickman says he is strangely a stranger. I have interested Mottley about him / he has written one pressing Letter / & I was in great Hopes, I should have heard the Result before I sailed—It is for a Clerk's place in the Sick & Wounded office here, worth more than an 100£ a year now, & prospects of rising with good behaviour & industry. Mottley says, his not hearing is a GOOD OMEN / it is a *new Clerk* & his existence not yet agreed to / if, says M., Mr Stuart had given it away already, he would have written immediately / for he *offered it me* for any young man, I would recommend—so I suppose, he is making application to the Board.——If he misses this, I will try for another—& yet for another / & perhaps I may get him a better place abroad than at home / if I cannot succeed in the Latter. Rickman has written me a very kind Letter which moved me greatly—so manly & so kind!—I congratulate you on the possession of such a Friend.—*Never let him know*, that I knew or had mentioned to you that he & Poole had had any unpleasant feelings towards [ea]ch other respecting a Blunder of Poole & T. Wedgwood, which must have placed Rickman in a very awkward situation with the Speaker.—

Poole wrote me a Letter / Good God! to believe & to profess that I have been so & so to him, & yet to have behaved as he has done—denied me once a Loan of 50£ when I was on a Sickbed—I never dreamt of asking him. Wordsworth did it without my knowlege—& it would have been against my Consent. Poole *answered* not *W* but me, and proposed to have a subscription of 50£ raised for me, to which *he* would contribute 5£; but wondered, that I had not applied to my Brothers!!![1]—and 3 years long did I give my mind to this man / exclusive of introductions &c &c——. Southey! I write of myself, but I am exceedingly anxious with your anxiety.—Write instantly, franked or unfranked, S. T. Coleridge, Esqre, Mr J. C. Mottley's, Portsmouth—just as if I was really th[ere. God b]less you, DEAR Southey!

S. T. Coleridge

[1] See Letter 411.

*16 April 1804*

597. To Robert Southey

*Address*: Robert Southey, Esqre. | Greta Hall | *Keswick* | Cumberland | England
*MS*. Lord Latymer. *Pub. with omis*. Letters, *ii. 469*.
*Postmark*: Foreign Office, 23 May 1804.

Monday Noon. April 16th 1804.—Off Oporto, & the Coast of Portugal

My dear Southey

I was thinking long before day light this morning, that I ought, spite of Toss & Tumble & cruel Rocking, to write a few Letters in the course of this & the 3 following days; at the end of which, if the North West Wind ["]Still blows behind"[1] we may hope to be at Gibraltar. I have 2 or 3 very unpleasant Letters to write: & I was planning whether I should not begin with *these*, have them off my hands & thoughts, in short whistle them down into the Sea / & then take up the paper, &c, a *whole* man / when, lo! I heard the Captn above deck talking of Oporto, slipt on my great Coat, & went shoeless up to have a Look / & a beautiful Scene verily it was!—& *is*!—The High land of Portugal, & the Mountain land behind it, & behind that fair Mountains with blue Pyramids & Cones. By the Glass I could distinguish the larger Buildings in Oporto / a scrambling City, part of it seemingly walls washed by the Sea, part of it upon Hills / at first view, it looked much like a vast Brick kilnery in a sandy clayey Country, on a hot summer afternoon / seen more distinctly, it gave the nobler idea of a ruined City in a Wilderness, it's Houses & Streets lying low in ruins under it's ruined walls, & a few Temples & Palaces standing untouched.— But over all the Sea between us & the Land, short of a stone throw on the left of the Vessel, there is such a delicious warm olive green, almost yellow, on the water / & now it has taken in the Vessel, & it's boundary is a gun shot to my right, & one fine Vessel exactly on it's edge / —This tho' occasioned by the Impurity of the nigh Shore & the disemboguing Rivers, forms a *home* scene / it is warm & land-like.—The air is balmy & genial; & all, that the fresh Breeze can do, can scarcely keep under it's vernal Warmth.—The Country round about Oporto seems darkly wooded: and in the distant Gap far behind & below it, on the *curve* of that High Ridge forming a Gap, I count 17 Conical & Pyramidal Summits; below that the high Hills are saddle-backed. In picturesque Cant, I ought to have said; BUT, below that &c.—To me the Saddle-back is a pleasant form, which it never would have occurred to me to

[1] *Ancient Mariner*, line 87.

christen by that name / Tents & Marquees, with little points & summits made by the Tent-poles suggest a more striking Likeness.—Well! I need not say, that the Sight of the Coast of Portugal made it impossible for me to write to any one before I had written to you, I now seeing for the first time a country, you love so dearly. But you perhaps are not among my Mountains!—God Almighty grant that you may not. Yes! you are in London: all is well, & Hartley has a younger Sister than tiny Sally. If it be so, call her Edith—Edith by itself Edith / but somehow or other I would rather, it were a Boy—*then* let nothing, I conjure you, no false compliment to another, no false feeling indulged in yourself, deprive your eldest Son of his Father's name. Such was ever the manner of our Forefathers: & there is a dignity, a self-respect or an aweful pre-eminently self-referring Event, in the custom that makes it well worthy of our Imitation. I would have done; but that from my earliest years I have had a feeling of Dislike & Disgust connected with my own Christian Names: such a vile short plumpness, such a dull abortive smartness, in [the] first Syllable, & this so harshly contrasted by the obscurity & indefiniteness of the syllabic Vowel, & the feebleness of the uncovered liquid, with which it ends—the wabble it makes, & staggering between a diss- & a trisyllable—& the whole name sounding as if you were abeeceeing. S. M. U. L.—altogether it is perhaps the worst combination, of which vowels & consonants are susceptible.—While I am writing, we are in 10.41m. Latitude: & are almost 3 leagues from Land— at one time we were scarcely one League from it: and about a quarter of an hour ago the whole country looked so very like the country from Hutton moor to Saddleback & the adjoining part of Skiddaw!—I cannot help some anxious Feelings respecting you: nor some superstitious Twitches within, as if it were wrong at this distance to write so prospectively & with such particularization of that which is contingent, which may be all otherwise—but God forbid! and surely, Hope is less ominous than Fear.

We set sail from St Helen's, April 9th, Monday Morning; have dropt down thither from Spithead on Sunday Evening. We lost 26 hours of fair wind before our Commodore gave the signal.— Our Brig a most excellent, a first-rate Sailor; but laden deep with heavy Goods (84 large Cannon for Trieste in the Hold) which makes it rock most cruelly. I can only

—Wedn. April 18th.—I was going to say, I can only compare it to a Wench kept at home on some gay Day to nurse a fretful infant, and who having long rocked it in vain, at length rocks it in spite.—But the Rain came suddenly on: & (this too is the second time) brought on almost instantly a stomach & bowel attack / a

## 16 April 1804

boil came out in the fork of the right Thigh, and the Lid of my left eye is still swoln & red—& both Monday & yester night were nights of Dejection & Discomfort, while & whenever I was awake, and of Horror when I slept. This morning just at day light I found a pleasant, indeed highly pleasurable Sleepiness, wrap round my whole being: & at breakfast I was better. After breakfast I found that the two preceding Days had accumulated some sordes in my Stomach; & I drank three half pints of Salt water—delivered myself of a great deal of mucous stuff with green & yellow Bile—& really eat a better dinner to day than I have done these six weeks: tho' I have taken since I have been at sea no animal food in the Solid.—I was not at all sea-sick / for the first two or three hours I was hot-eyed with fever-smells in my nose—& 4 or 5 times since in very gusty weather, when my stomach has been weak, I have thrown my food in a jerk off my Stomach; but it was by an action seemingly as mechanical as that by which one's glass or tea cup is emptied by a thwart blow of the Sea: preceded by no sense of sickness, accompanied with no nausea, no straining, indeed by no sort of sensation, & followed by permanent comfortable feeling—according to the state of my Health. But tho' the rough weather & the incessant Rocking does not disease me, yet this damned Rocking depresses me inconceivably—like Hiccups, or Itching, it is troublesome & impertinent & forces you away from your Thoughts—like the presence & gossip of an old Aunt or long staying Visitor to two Lovers.—O with what envy have I gazed at our Commodore, the Leviathan of 74 guns, the majestic & beautiful Creature / sailing right before us, sometimes a half a mile, oftener a furlong, (for we are always first) with two or at most three Topsails, that just bisect the naked masts, as much naked masts above as below, upright, motionless, as a church with it's Steeple—as tho' it moved by it's will, as tho' it's speed were spiritual—the being & essence without the body of motion, or as tho' the distance passed away by it, & the objects of it's pursuit hurried onward to it.—In all other respects I could not be better off—except perhaps the two passengers—one a gross worldly minded fellow, not deficient in sense or judgment, but inert to every thing except Gain & eating / —the other, a woman once housekeeper in Gen. Fox's Family, a creature with a horrible Superfluity of Envelope, a Monopolist & patentee of flabby Flesh: or rather *Fish*. Indeed she is at once Fish, Flesh, & *Foul*: tho' no chicken. And so unutterably feeble in her mind & Thought, tho' she has been in all parts of the World, & seen all sorts of people. O Christ! for a sea sick woman [man?] to see the man eat, & this Mrs Carnosity talk about it. She eats every thing by a choice / 'I must have that little potatoe'—

(baked in grease under the meat) 'it looks so smilingly at one.'—
'Do cut me if you please['] (for she is so fat, she cannot help herself)
'that small bit—just there, Sir!—a leettle tiny bit *below*, if you
please.'—'Well! I have brought plenty of pickles, I *always* think
&c' / 'I have always three or four jars of brandy cherries with me;
for with boil'd rice now &c for I always think &c'—and true
enough, if it can be called thinking, she does always think upon
some little damned article of eating that belongs to the House-
keeper's Cupboards & Locker. And then her plaintive Yawns / such
a mixture of moan & petted Child's dry *Cry*, or *Try* at a Cry, in
them / And she said to me this morning, 'how unhappy, I always
think, one always is, when there is nothing & nobody, as one may
say, about *one* to amuse *one*. It makes me so *nervou*[*s.*]' She eats,
drinks, snores—& simply the being stupid & silly & vacant the
learned Body calls nervous.—Shame on me for talking about her /
the S[un] is setting so exactly behind my back, that a Ball from it
would strike the stern of the Vessel against which my Back rests.
But Sunsets are not so beautiful, I think, at Sea as at Land.—I am
sitting at *my* Desk, namely, the Rudder Case, on the Duck Coop;
the Ducks quacking at my Legs. The Chicken & Duck Coops run
thus *c* [sketch] *c* and so inclose on three sides the Rudder case—But
now immediately as the Sun has sunk, the Sea runs
high, & the Vessel begins it's old trick of Rocking, which it had
intermitted the whole Day—the second Intermission only since
our Voyage. O how glad I was to see Cape Mondego—& then
yesterday the Rock of Lisbon, and the fine mountain at it's
interior extremity which I conceited to be Cintra / it's outline from
the Sea something like this—and just at

[sketch]

A where the fine stony M with a C lying on it's Back, begins, is
a Village or Villages—and before we came abreast of this, we saw
far inland, seemingly close by several breasted Peaks two Towers,
& by the glass 3, of a very large Building, be it Convent or Palace—
However, I knew you had seen all these places, over & over again /
the *Dome*-shaped Mountain or Cape Espeichel between Lisbon &
Cape St Vincent is one of the finest, I ever saw—indeed all the
mountains have a noble outline / We sail on at a wonderful rate, &
considering that we are in Convoy, shall have made a most lucky
Voyage to Gibraltar, if we are not becalmed, & taken in the Gut /
for we shall be there tomorrow afternoon, if the wind hold—&

have gone it in ten Days!—It is unlucky to prophesy good Things; but if we have as good fortune in the Mediterranean, instead of 9 or 11 weeks, we may reach Malta in a month or 5 weeks, including the week which we must probably stay at Gibraltar.—I shall keep the Letter open till we arrive there, simply put two strokes under the word 'GIBRALTAR', and close up the Letter, as I may gain thereby a fortnight's post.—You will not expect to hear from me again till we get to Malta. I had hoped to have done something during my Voyage; at all events to have written some Letters, &c. But what with the Rains, the incessant Rocking, & my consequent ill-health or Stupefaction, I have done little else than read thro' the Italian Grammar.—I took out with me some of the finest Wine & the oldest in the Kingdom; some marvellous Brandy, & Rum 20 years old—& excepting a pint of Wine which I had mulled at two different times, & instantly ejected again, I have touched nothing but Lemonade from the day, we set sail, to the present Hour. So very little does any thing grow into a Habit with me. This I should say to poor Tobin, who continued *advising* and *advising* to the last moment. O God! he is a good fellow, but this rage of *advising*, & of *discussing characters*, and (as almost all men of strong habitual health have the trick of doing) of finding out the cause of every body's ill health in some one malpractice or other— this & the self-conceit & presumption necessarily generated by it, added to his own marvellous Genius at utterly misunderstanding what he hears / transposing words often in a manner that would be ludicrous if one did not suspect that his Blindness had a share in producing it—all this renders him a sad Mischief-maker, & with the best intentions a manufacturer & propagator of Calumnies. I had no notion of the extent of the mischief till I was last in town. I was low even to sinking when I was at the Inn / Stuart, best kindest man to me! was with me, & Lamb, & Sir G. B.'s Valet— but Tobin fastened upon me, and advised & reproved, & just before I stepped into the Coach reminded me of a Debt of 10£, which I had borrowed of him for another person, an intimate Friend of his, on the condition that I was not to repay him till I could do it out of my own purse, not borrowing of another, & not embarrassing myself—in his very words 'till he wanted it more than I.'—I was calling to Stuart, in order to pay the sum; but he stopped me with fervor, & fully convinced that he did it only in the *rage* of Admonition, I was vexed that it had angered me. Therefore say you nothing of it: for really he is at bottom a good man. I dare say nothing of home. I will write to Sara from Malta, the moment of my arrival—if I have not time to write from Gibraltar. One of you write to me by the regular Post, S. T. Coleridge, Esqre, Dr Stoddart's, Malta: the other to me at Mr J. C. Mottley's, Portsmouth / that I may see whether Mottley was right or no, & which comes first.—

God bless you all, and S. T. Coleridge

Remember me kindly to Mr Jackson, Mrs Wilson—to the Calverts, & to Mr & Mrs Wilkinson:—& to Mary Stamper I beg to be remembered.—My heart has ached for Mrs Lovell: tho' *out of herself* I am persuaded there is nothing deplorable in her situation. Bless my soul! if she had Spirits & a contented mind with activity, she would have been, or soon would be, a happy Wife—with her manners, sense, & person!—

Gibraltar
½ past 4,
The Afternoon
April 19th 1804

If Mr S. be absent, Mrs Coleridge will open the Letter.
April 23rd.—if wind serves, we set sail tomorrow.—

## 598. *To James Webbe Tobin*

MS. British Museum. Pub. Anima Poetae, ed. by E. H. Coleridge, 1895, p. 68.
The letter sent to Tobin has not come to light, but Coleridge made a copy of it in one of his note-books. Tobin answered Coleridge's letter on 14 Aug. 1804, saying among other things: 'A Letter of yours fraught with advice against advising & other censorious matters was duly received by me.'

April 19th, 1804

Men who habitually enjoy robust Health, have too generally the trick, and a very cruel one it is, of imagining that they discover the secret of all their Acquaintances' Ill health in some Malpractice or other: and sometimes by gravely asserting this here & there & every where (as who likes his Penetration under a Bushel?) they not only do all, they can, without intending it, to deprive the poor Sufferer of that Sympathy which is always a Comfort, and in some degree a Support to human Nature, but likewise too often implant serious alarm & uneasiness in the minds of the person's Relatives, & his dearest and nearest connections. Indeed but that I have known it's inutility, that I should be ridiculously sinning against my own Law while I was propounding, and that those who are most fond of advising are the least able to bear advice from others (as the passion to command makes men disobedient), I should often have been on the point of advising you against the two fold rage of Advising, and of discussing characters, both the one & the other of which infallibly generates Presumption, and

Blindness to our own Faults. Nay—more particularly where from whatever cause there exists a slowness to understand or an aptitude to mishear & consequently misunderstand what has been said—it too often renders an otherwise truly good man a Mischief-maker to an Extent, of which he is little aware. Our Friend's Reputation should be a Religion to us: & when it is lightly sacrificed to what Self-Adulation calls a Love of telling the Truth—[(]in reality, a Lust of talking something seasoned with the Cayenne & Capsicum of Personality) depend upon it, something in the Heart is warped, or warping: more or less according to the greater or lesser power of the counteracting Causes. I confess to you, that being exceedingly low & heart-fallen, I should have almost sunk under the Operation of Reproof and Admonition (—the whole too in my own conviction grounded on utter mistake—) at the moment I was quitting, perhaps forever! my dear Country, and all that makes it so dear—But the high Esteem, I cherish toward you, and my Sense of your Integrity, and the Reality and Worth of your Attachment and Concern, blows upon me refreshingly, as the Sea Breeze on the tropic Islander.—Shew me any one made better by blunt Advice, and I may abate of my Dislike to it. But I have experienced the good effects of the contrary in Wordsworth's conduct to me; & in Poole & others have witnessed enough of *it's* ill-effects to be convinced that it does little else but harm both to the Adviser & Advisee.—

## 599. *To Daniel Stuart*

*Address*: D. Stuart, Esqre | Courier Office | Strand | London.
*MS. British Museum. Pub. with omis.* Letters, *ii. 475.*
*Postmark*: Foreign Office, 23 May 1804. *Stamped*: Lisbon.

On board the Speedwell, at anchor in the Bay of Gibraltar:
Sat. Night, April 21, 1804

My dear Stuart

We dropped anchor half a mile from the Landing Place of the Rock of Gibraltar on Thursday afternoon, between 4 and 5: a most prosperous Voyage of eleven Days. And every day too, once always, often twice, we were obliged to counterpoise our Sails (in seaman's phrase, which I avoided because I was not sure of the Spelling, to lay (or lie) by) for the Laggards of our Flock. We set sail on Monday Morning, 9 o/clock, April the 9th—with convoy, and no rough Weather (we have never once shipped a wave) this is one of the quickest Passages, that the Captains remember. You will recollect, that I wrote to you with some anxiety respecting the non-arrival of my Vessel from the Downs—& I confess, that I felt some discontent at our detention, when the West India Convoy set sail, 5 days before us—the day after the arrival of the Speedwell at Spithead. That Convoy was driven by stress of weather &, as it is said, by some error in the Commodore's Compasses—half the Ships wrecked, & among the rest the Commodore's, & he & great part of his crew lost. It is impossible not to *feel* events like these, as something *providential*: & tho' the Reason denounces the notion as *superstitious*, & indeed arrogant (for who are we, that we should be *favorites* with Heaven to the exclusion of the W. India Ships?) yet the feeling remains—neither greater or less—common to all men, whatever their opinions may be, and amid all difference of knowlege & understanding. It must therefore be right at the bottom; & probably needs only a wiser interpretation to appear so.—To cut short my *sermon*, what a number of sad accidents in the navy have occurred in the last 4 or 5 months!—The day before yesterday I saw a Letter from Barcelona, giving an account that the Swift Cutter with Dispatches to Lord Nelson had been boarded by a French Privateer & the Dispatches taken, her Captain having been killed in the first moments of the Engagement: and the same Letter conveyed the still more melancholy tidings of the utter loss of the Hindostan by Fire off the coast of Spain, between this place & Toulon. All the crew were saved but 4, lost. I repeated this Intelligence at Griffith's Hotel on the Rock—a naval officer was present, who appeared thunderstruck, evidently much affected. He had come to Gibraltar in the Hindostan / told me, that the Captain had shewn him her Invoice, chiefly of naval Stores of all kinds for Malta with an hundred Artificers—& that they were valued at something more than 300,000£. So valuable was she, & so very deeply laden, that tho' she mounted 40 or 50 guns, she was not suffered to proceed hence by herself; but had a frigate appointed to convoy her. Another Gentleman late from Malta informed me too, that they are in great Distress for these naval Stores at Malta.— It is *possible*, that you may not have heard this by a shorter channel: therefore I have given so much of my paper to it. And now of myself. I have not been *sea*-sick; tho' 4 or 5 times a thwart Blow of the Sea has jerked a dish of Tea out of my stomach by an action as merely mechanical, as it has more often jerked the Tea out of the cup—no nausea preceding, no effect or even sensation accompanying, & no uncomfortableness following it. But yet I have been far from well: our Vessel, tho' of the first Class, & by far the best Sailor of any merchantman in the convoy, and always in the Wake or abreast of the Commodore, yet being deeply laden with heavy goods (84 large Cannon in the Hold for Trieste) rocked almost incessantly—the two last days, & one day in the early part of our Voyage the only exceptions, the wind then bearing *abeam*, or on the side of the Ship, steadied it. The remaining eight days it was scarcely endurable. I can only compare it to a Wench kept at home on some Fair day or great Holiday to nurse a fretful Infant, & who having rocked it in vain rocks it at length in Spite. It was to the last degree wearisome; & acted upon me, just as the Hiccough does—it is no great pain in itself, but it is vexatious from it's impertinence, permitting one to think of nothing but it's own villainous Self. I had hoped that I should have written a good deal: & wrote out with much pomp of promise a plan for the employment of my Time—to write in the morning, to fag Italian after dinner (we always dine at one) & to try to finish my Christabel in the quiet hours between that & bed time—but alas! alas! I have scarcely been able even to write a Letter: and all my reading has been confined to half a dozen Dialogues at the end of the Italian Grammar. The cruel Rocking took away from my hard Bed—one hard Mattrass upon boards—all sense of support: I seemed to lie on a wave / and tho' it did not make me sea-sick, yet it evidently diseased my Stomach / for I eat no morsel of solid animal Food till Wednesday last. The Rocking ceased—the weather was heavenly; & my natural Appetite returned. I took out with me some of the finest Wine, & of the oldest Rum & Brandy in the Kingdom; but excepting a single pint of Wine *mulled* at two different times, & both doses ejected or rather *ejaculated* instantly in statu quo, I tasted nothing stronger than Lemonade during our whole Voyage, till the last Day.—But for the last 4 days I have been uncommonly well; & as is always the case with [me w]hen I feel well, I have not the slightest Inclination to drink any thing but a tumbler or two of Beer—I am indifferent to wine, & absolutely dislike Spirits. Since we anchored, I have passed nearly the whole of each day in scrambling about on the back of the Rock among the Monkeys: I am a match for them in climbing, but in Hops & flying Leaps they beat me. You sometimes see 30 or 40 together of these our poor Relations: & you may be a month on the Rock, & go to the back every day & not see one.—O my dear Friend! it is a most interesting place this—a Rock, which thins as it rises up so that you can sit astraddle on almost any part of it's summit—between two & three miles from North to South; rude as this Line [is], it gives you the outline of it's appearance from the Sea, close to it, tolerably accurately—only in nature it gives you very much the idea of a rude statue of a Lion couchant, like that in the Picture of

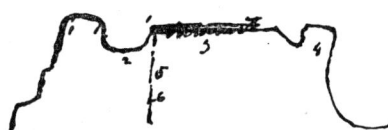

the Lion & Gnat in the common Spelling Books—or of some Animal with a great dip in the Neck. The lion's Head toward the Spanish, his stiffened Tail (4) to the African—At 5 a range of Moorish Towers & wall begins, & at 6 the Town begins, the Moorish wall running strait down by the side of it. Above the Town little gardens & neat small Houses are scattered here & there, wherever they can force a bit of gardenable ground; & in these are Poplars, with a profusion of Geraniums, & other Flowers unknown to me: & their fences are most commonly that strange vegetable Monster, the prickly Aloe, it's leaves resembling the head of a Battledore, or the wooden wings of a church Cherub, & one Leaf growing out of another—Under the Lion's Tail is Europa Point, which is full of Gardens & pleasant Trees / —but the highest Third of the mountain is a *Heap* of Rocks, with the Palmitoes growing in vast quantities in their Interstices—with many flowering weeds, very often peeping out of the small Holes or Slits in the body of the Rock, just as if they were growing in a bottle.—To have left England only eleven days ago, with two flannel waistcoats on, & 2 others over them with 2 flannel Drawers under cloth Pantaloons—& a thick pair of yarn Stockings—to have had no temptation to lay any part of these aside during the whole of the Voyage—& now to find myself in the Heat of an English Summer, among Flowers & seeking Shade & courting the Sea breezes, all the Trees in rich foliage, & the Corn knee-high & so exquisitely green & to find myself forced to retain only one flannel waistcoat, & roam about with a pair of silk Stockings & Nankeen Pantaloons, is a delightful Transition—How I shall bear the intensity of [a] Maltese or even Sicilian Summer, I cannot guess; but if I get over it, I am confident from what I have experienced, the last 4 days, that their late Autumn & Winter will almost re-*create* me. I could fill a fresh Sheet with a description of the singular faces, dresses, manners, &c &c of the Spaniards, Moors, Jews (who have here a peculiar Dress, resembling a College Dress), Greeks, Italians, English &c, that meet in the hot crowded Streets of the Town; or walk under the Aspen Poplars which form an *Exchange* in the very center. But words would do nothing. I am sure, that any young man, who has a Turn for character-painting might pass a year on the Rock with infinite advantage / A dozen Plates by Hogarth from this Town!—We are told that we shall set sail tomorrow Evening. The Leviathan leaves us & goes to join the Fleet; and the Maidstone Frigate is to convoy us to Malta. When you write, send one Letter to me, at Mr J. C. Mottley's, Portsmouth / & another by the Post, to me at Dr Stoddart's, Malta, that I may see which comes first. God grant that my present Health may continue / and then

## 21 April 1804

my After Letters will be better worth the postage. But even this Scrawl will not be unwelcome to you, since it tells you that I am safe, improving in my Health, & ever, ever, my dear Stuart, with true Affection and willing Gratitude, your s[ince]re Friend, S. T. Coleridge /

P.S.—I should like very much to have Cobbett & the Courier sent to me. Mr J. C. Mottley will convey them by every opportunity free of expence, if they are sent to him for that purpose—You may be sure that Curiosity has a very small share in the formation of this Wish.

### 600. *To Mrs. S. T. Coleridge*

*Address*: For England. | Mrs Coleridge | Greta Hall | Keswick | Cumberland | England    *Single Sheet* | per *Germania* | *e Londra*
MS. Lord Latymer. Pub. *with omis.* Letters, *ii. 480*. The top and bottom of pages 1 and 2 have been cut from the holograph. The opening lines of this letter are supplied from a passage quoted by Wordsworth in a letter to Sir George Beaumont. *Early Letters*, 407.
*Postmark*: 27 August 1804.

June 5. 1804,[1] Tuesday noon; Dr Stoddart's, Malta

I landed in more than usual health in the harbour of Valetta, about four o'clock, Friday afternoon, April [May] 18. Since then I have been waiting day after day for the departure of Mr. Laing, tutor of the only child of Sir A. Ball, our civil governor who is to return to England with young Ball by the very first opportunity, means to make Keswick on his way to Scotland, and will take for me Letters to Greeta Hall, Grasmere, and for Sir George Beaumont and Lady B.—but an opportunity offers of sending these overland by Messina and Naples, and I gladly avail myself of it, and shall send off this Letter with fervent prayers for its safe arrival, chiefly because a report spread through our Convoy, that the Gentleman the Passenger on board the Speedwell had died, Wednesday[2] April [May] 9th! I wrote to Southey from Gibraltar, directing you to open the Letter in case Southey should be in town. You received it, I trust, & learnt from it, that I had been pretty well, & that we had had a famous quick Passage. At Gibraltar we stayed 5 days, & so lost our fair wind—& our after voyage to Malta was storm, that carried away our Main yard &c, long dead calms, every

---

[1] Mrs. Coleridge in writing to Mrs. George Coleridge summarizes Coleridge's letter and gives the date as 11 June 1804; Coleridge himself near the conclusion reports that Mrs. Stoddart's little girl 'died on Tuesday, June 5th /.' It is obvious, therefore, that the letter was begun, as Wordsworth writes, on 5 June and completed on 11 June.

[2] From this point on the text of this letter is from the manuscript.

rope of the whole Ship reflected in the bright soft blue Sea—& light winds, often varying every quarter of an hour, & more often against us than for us. We were the best sailing Vessel in the whole convoy; but every day we had to lie by, & wait for the Laggards. This is very disheartening—likewise the frequent danger in light winds or calms, or in foggy weather, of running foul of each other is another heavy inconvenience of convoy—& in case of a deep calm in a narrow sea, as in the Gut of Gibraltar, in the Archipelago, &c, where Calms are most common a privateering or piratical Row boat might board you & make slaves of you, under the very nose of the Man of War, which would lie a lifeless Hulk on the smooth water. For these Row boats mounting from one to four or 5 guns could instantly sink a man of war's boat—& one of these last even had very nearly made a British Frigate *strike*.—I mention these facts, because it is a common notion that going under Convoy you are as snug as a bug in a rug—If I had gone without convoy on board the Speedwell I should have reached Malta in 20 days from the day I left Portsmouth—but however we were congratulated on having had a VERY GOOD passage, for the Time of the year, having been only 40 days including our stay at Gibraltar—& if there be inconveniences in a Convoy, I have reason to know, & to be grateful for, it's advantages. The whole of the voyage from Gibraltar to Malta, excepting the last 4 or 5 days I was wretchedly unwell; oppressed, uncomfortable, incapable of the least exertion of mind or attention, tho' not *sick*, in the intervals of eating; and the moment, I eat any thing, I became sick and rejected it——at length, my appetite wholly deserted me; I *loathed* the sight of Food; & for 3 days preceding the 8th of May I had not taken half an ounce of Food—which made me neglectful of taking an opening medicine—.—O merciful God! what days of Horror were not that[1] ... Body & Being.—The next day I was comfortable, only a little feverish—; on the Friday till Saturday Dawn [12 May] the Fever ran high; but on Saturday I bettered rapidly—& the remainder of the Voyage enjoyed a lightness, health, & appetite, unknown to me for months before.[2]—

[1] In summarizing Coleridge's account of his illness, Wordsworth supplies some of the details missing from the mutilated manuscript: 'a languor and oppression, and rejection of food, accompanied with a dangerous constipation, which compelled the Captain to hang out signals of distress to the Commodore for a surgeon to come on board. He was relieved from this at last after undergoing the most excruciating agonies, with the utmost danger of an inflammation in the bowels. ... It is manifest that the obstruction in the bowels, which would, as it seems, have cost him his life but for the timely aid of the surgeon was entirely owing to a want of proper opening medicines.' *Early Letters*, 408.

[2] Here Coleridge wrote and then crossed out, 'I have been thus minute

Whoever makes a sea voyage, should above all things provide themselves with aloetic pills, castor oil, & several other purgatives —as sometimes one will answer when others disagree—& every thing depends on keeping the Body regularly open.—

The Harbour at Valetta is narrow as the neck of a Bottle in the entrance; but instantly opens out into a Lake with tongues of Land, capes, one little Island, &c &c, where the whole Navy of England might lie as in a Dock in the worst of weathers—all around it's banks in the form of an amphitheatre rise the magnificent Houses of Valetta, and it's two over-the-water Towns Bormola & Floriana (which are to Valetta what the Borough is to London)—the Houses all lofty & built of fine white free-stone, something like Bath, only still whiter & *newer*-looking, yet the windows from the prodigious Thickness of the walls being all out of sight, the whole appeared to me as Carthage to Æneas, a proud City well nigh but not quite finished / —. I walked up a long street of good breadth, all a flight of Stairs / no place for beast or carriage —each broad Stair composed of a cement (Sand & Terra Pozzolana) hard & smooth, as the hardest pavement of smooth rock by the Sea side—& very like it.—I soon found out Dr Stoddart's House, which seemed a large Pile of Building—. He was not at home; but I stayed for him / & about 2 hours [later] he came in, & received me with an explosion of surprize & welcome, more *fun* than *affection* in the manner; but just as I wished it. More than this would have made me uncomfortable from my incapability . . .

['The first week after his landing he was uncommonly well, but was afterwards seized with a fever which left him very low.'][1] . . . Limb—(I was dining out)—hurried home—got to bed—& remained in a raging Fever from 4 till 10 o/clock / Stoddart did not know that I had returned—for I came in & went to bed without any one seeing me / & I supposed, that I was scarcely in my right senses. At 10 o/clock the servant came in & found me, & of course call'd down Stoddart / —this brought me to myself—I desired Stoddart to give me 30 drops of Laudanum in a large Tumbler of warm Lemonade—& in about 20 minutes I was manifestly & greatly better—& soon after fell into perspiration & a gentle Sleep.— Yesterday & to day I have been pretty well.—These accidents I think nothing of. In a hot climate, now that the Glass is high as

because one report spread thro'', apparently recalling that he had already mentioned in the first paragraph of this letter the false report, which spread through the Convoy, of his death aboard the *Speedwell* on Wednesday, 9 May.

[1] This sentence from Wordsworth's letter to Sir George Beaumont supplies information missing from the mutilated manuscript and concerns an illness which Coleridge suffered shortly after his arrival at Malta. Cf. *Early Letters*, 408.

80 in the Shade, the healthiest persons are liable to fever on the least disagreement of Food with the first passages—& my general Health is, I would fain believe, better *on the whole*. My appetite is languid, except at breakfast; & unfortunately they dine very late at this House—I shall make my meal therefore at 2 o/clock on cold meat, & eat no more till Tea time / this I have done twice, & it has answered very well.—But the worst of all, & the only thing at all alarming in my case, is the now constant oppression in my breathing—so that I walk up and down, like a Leopard in his Den. The immediate cause is flatulence; as likewise of the sudden Doses with twitches & starts, into which I fall if I sit down to read for any length of Time.—I live however in Hope—I will try the most scrupulous regimen of Diet—& Exercise— / and I rejoice to find that the Heat, great as it is, does not at all annoy me. In about a fortnight I shall probably take a Trip to Sicily, & spend the next 2 or 3 months in some cooler & less dreary Place; & return in September. For 8 months in the year the Climate of Malta is delightful; but a drearier Place Eye never saw. No stream in the whole Island / only one Place of Springs, which are conveyed by aqueducts & supply the Island with about one third of it's water / the other 2 thirds they depend for on the rain / & the Reservoirs under the Houses, Walls, &c &c, to preserve the Rain are *stupendous!*—The Tops of all the Houses are flat, & covered with that smooth hard composition; & there and every where, where Rain can fall, are channels—& pipes to conduct it to the Reservoirs—. Malta is about 20 miles by 12—a mere rock of free stone / in digging out this they find large quantities of vegetable soil—they separate it / with the stones build their Houses, & garden & field walls— all of an enormous thickness—the fields seldom so much as half an acre ☐, one above another in that form / so that every thing grows as in huge garden Pots, & the whole Island looks like one monstrous fortification / —Nothing *green* meets your eye—one dreary grey-white / —& all the country Towns from the retirement & invisibility of the windows look like Towns burnt out & desolate.—Yet the fertility is marvellous—you almost see things grow—& the population I suppose unexampled. The Town of Valetta itself contains about 110 Streets, all at right angles to each other, each having from 12 to 50 houses—but very many of them very steep—a few *staired* all across—& almost all in some part or other, if not the whole, having the Footway on each side so staired— / The Houses lofty, all looking new / the good Houses are built with a court in the center—& the rooms large & lofty— from 16 to 20 feet high, & walls enormously thick / all necessary for coolness.—The fortifications of Valetta are endless—when I first

walked about them, I was struck all of a heap with their Strangeness, and when I came to understand a little of their purpose, I was overwhelmed with wonder / Such *vast masses*—bulky mountain-breasted Heights—gardens with pomegrana[te] Trees & the prickly Pear in the Fosses—& the Caper (the most beautiful of Flowers) growing profusely in the interstices of the high walls & on the battlements. The Maltese a dark, light limbed people—the women $\frac{5}{10}$ths ugly—of the remainder $\frac{4}{5}$ths would be ordinary but that they look *so quaint*—and $\frac{1}{10}$th perhaps may be called quaint-pretty. The prettiest resemble pretty Jewesses in England.—They are the noisiest race under Heaven, & Valetta the noisiest place—/ sudden shot-up explosive *Bellows*—no cries you ever heard in London would give you the faintest Idea of it—. Even when you pass by a fruit stall, the fellow will put his Hand like a speaking Trumpet to his mouth & shoot such a Thunder bolt of Sound full at you / — then the endless Jangling of these cursed Bells &c &c.—Sir Alexander Ball[1] & General Valette (the civil & military Commanders[)] have been markedly attentive—Sir A. B. even friendly & confidential to me—.——Poor Mrs Stoddart was brought to bed of a little Girl on the 24th of May—& it died on Tuesday, June 5th/. On the night of it's Birth, poor little Lamb!—I had such a lively vision of my little Sara, that it brought on a sort of hysterical Fit on me—. O Merciful God! how I tremble at the thought of Letters from England—I should be most miserable *without* them, & yet I shall receive them like a sentence of Death / so terribly has Fear got the upper hand in my habitual Feelings from my long destitution of Hope & Joy.—Hartley, Derwent! my sweet children! a father's blessings on you /! With tears & clasped hands I bless you—O I must write no more of this.——

I have been haunted by the Thought that I have lost a box of Books, containing Shakespere (Stockdale's) the 4 or 5 first Volumes of the British Poets, Young's Syllabus (a red-paper Book), Condilliac's Logic, Thornton on Public Credit &c—. Be sure, you inform me whether or no I did take these Books from Keswick—.—I will write to Southey by the next opportunity. You recollect that I went away without knowing the result of Edith's Confinement; not a day in which I do not think of it. My Love to dear Southey—

[1] The warm friendship between Coleridge and Ball, based as it was on mutual admiration, began shortly after Coleridge's arrival at Malta on 18 May 1804, and the two men were intimately associated until Coleridge's departure in Sept. 1805. After Ball's death in Oct. 1809 Coleridge wrote an apotheosis of him in *The Friend*. 'Ah! how could I be otherwise than deeply affected, by whatever reminded me of that daily and familiar intercourse with him, which made . . . [my residence at Malta] in many respects, the most memorable and instructive period of my life?' *The Friend*, No. 19, 28 Dec. 1809.

## To Mrs. S. T. Coleridge

& remember me to Mr Jackson, & Mrs Wilson with the kindest words—& to Mary Stamper—/—My kind remembrances to Mr & Mrs Wilkinson & the Calverts.—. How is your Sister Mary in her Spirits?—My wishes & prayers attend her. I am anxious to hear about poor George & shall write about him to Portsmouth in the course of a week—for by that time a Convoy will be going to England, as we expect.—I hope, that in the course of three weeks or a month I may be able to give a more promising account of my Health—as it is, I have reason to be satisfied. The effect of years cannot be done away in a few weeks—I am tranquil & resigned—and even if I should not bring back Health, I shall at least bring back experience, & suffer with patience & in silence. Again & again God bless you, my dear Sara!—Let me know every thing of your Health &c &c. O the Letters are on the Sea for me—& what tidings may they not bring me!—

S. T. Coleridge.

### 601. To William Sotheby

*Address*: W. Sotheby Esqre | 47. | U. Seymour St, | London   To be forwarded, if | Mr Sotheby be out | of Town.
*MS.* Colonel H. G. Sotheby. *Pub.* E.L.G. i. 321.
*Postmark*: 19 September 1804. Ship Letter Portsmouth.

July 5, 1804. Malta

My dear Sir

I hope, that Mr Laing who returns to England with young Ball, will find you out. Mr L. is a truly amiable well informed young Clergyman who has in fact been Sir Alexander's Secretary as well as Tutor of his Son. From him you will hear every thing of Malta—and as soon as I get to Sicily, I shall write to you. Your Letters to Sir A. B. and General Villette produced every effect that Letters possibly could do—my extreme low Spirits & Languor has prevented me from hitherto cultivating the General's acquaintance as much [as] I ought & wished to have done / for he was very attentive & polite, & I have no doubt would do any thing to serve a man so introduced by you—. I have hitherto lived with Dr Stoddart, but tomorrow shall take up my residence at the Palace, in a suite of delightfully cool & commanding Rooms which Sir Alexander was so kind as not merely to offer me but to make me feel that he wished me to accept the Offer—I have been writing for him to the last moment / an excuse for this brief Scrawl than which there might be a hundred worse, I am sure, in your opinion. I had from

Gibraltar to Malta a most distressful Passage of almost continual
Illness—& at one time I expected to die—& God be praised! that
time was far enough from the most unhappy, I have lately passed.
Since my arrival I have never had those sharp illnesses, I used to
have in England—& since I have revolutionized my system, that
is to say, forced myself to eat my meals & to take a few glasses of
Port wine after dinner, bathed regularly at or before sun rise, read
very little, brooded less, & tried not to be idle a moment, but
always either to be actually writing, or taking exercise, or in
company, I have been perceptibly better—my breathing less
smothered—& I am less apt to sink at once into nervous dosings,
with twitches &c—. I cannot expect that greatly as something or
other within me, Stomach, or Liver, or mesentery, is deranged,
I can establish my Health otherwise than very slowly; but it is
greatly in my favor that this very hot weather (the Thermometer
86 in the Shade) agrees with me—I am not at all oppressed or
*discomfortized* by it—& I believe, I am the only Englishman in the
Island that can say this. When I write from Sicily, I hope I shall
be able to send a yet more chearful account, & to tell you not only
how I am, but likewise what I have done. Mean time remember me
with respectful affection to Mrs Sotheby, and Miss Sotheby, and
believe me, my dear Sir! whether sick or well, in Malta or in
England I remember your kindnesses with pleasure as well as
gratitude for I feel that I am not unworthy of them—With very
affectionate esteem your obliged & attached Friend

S. T. Coleridge

Sir A. Ball is a very extraordinary man—indeed a great man.
And he is really the abstract Idea of a wise & good Governor. The
Ministers were in luck. Merciful Heaven! what wretches they send
out as Consuls to the States of Barbary—the seat & bustle-place
of French [Intr]igue—& thither they send to check the picked
Agents of the French Government—a Mr Langford—whose
Brawls with his Wife, & notorious Follies drove every servant out
of his House—a man, the laughing-stock of all Malta!—'O he is
only a Barbary Consul!'—These 'onlies' threaten our country
terribly, my dear Sir! and if you have any influence with any
persons about Government, you would act the part of a true
Patriot in pressing on them the necessity of sending out men of
Talents & Character to all the Coasts of [the] Mediterranean—
Fools that *are* to be provided for had far better be pensioned at
once; the Nation would save millions by the scheme.

P.S. Sir A. has repeatedly told [me], that if any place should
be vacant, he would give it me / & has offered me the Salary of the

under Secretary during his Absence,[1] which may be about 2 months including his Quarantine—& indeed has given me the power to draw for 2 months' Salary—that is to say, 50£. But this I do not intend doing.

## 602. To Mrs. S. T. Coleridge

Address: Mrs Coleridge | Greta Hall | Keswick | Cumberland    By favor | of the Rev'd | Mr Laing
MS. Lord Latymer. Pub. with omis. Ill. London News, *10 June 1893, p. 698.*

Valette, Malta. Thursd. Afternoon, July 5, 1804. ½ past I

My dear Sara

I have been at work for the Governor since 5 o/clock this morning / and now I have about half a dozen hours only before the convoy sets sail, to write all my Letters in. My procrastination is not here to blame, as usual: for I have been employed ever since the arrival of the Agincourt. I can barely therefore tell you, to whom I write the first, that this Letter will be conveyed to England by Mr Laing, & young Mr Ball, Sir Alexander's only Son, who is going to spend two years with a Professor at Glasgow—that Mr Laing was Sir A.'s private secretary in reality as well as his Son's Tutor—the Son of an Architect of high character at Edingburgh—himself of Oxford, of the same College with Robert Southey, a little his Junior / a truly amiable, well-informed man (a Clergyman) and only too modest. His kindness to me has been very great / as well as Sir Alexander, the Governor's—Young Ball is an amiable young man. Of course, my dear, you will welcome them in some sort as my representatives—& insist on their sleeping at Greta Hall & staying as long as they can when they come to Keswick—this Letter will be sent you from London—.—

[1] By 6 July 1804 Coleridge had already prepared certain reports which Sir Alexander Ball dispatched to the Ministry in London; and it seems certain that not long after his arrival in Malta he assumed the title of private secretary, a post he retained until Jan. 1805, at a salary of £25 a month. Actually Coleridge's services were much needed, Mr. Macaulay, the Public Secretary, being 80 years old and 'effete and superannuated', and E. T. Chapman, the Under-Secretary, being absent from the island. Even during the three months Coleridge was in Sicily (early August to 6 Nov. 1804), he was engaged in semi-official work for Ball. (See Letters 602, 604, 609, 610, 612, and 636.)

On the death of Macaulay, 18 Jan. 1805, Coleridge became Public Secretary to Sir Alexander Ball. He held this appointment until Sept. 1805, when Chapman, the newly appointed Public Secretary, returned to Malta. Despite the arduous nature of his duties, Coleridge was entitled to only half the secretary's salary of £1,200 per annum, since, as he himself says, he preferred not to be involved 'in the responsibility of the Treasurer'. (See Campbell, *Life*, 149, and Letters 614, 616, 618, and 636.)

## 5 July 1804

I wrote to you over land many weeks ago, & can only *hope* that you received it—all our communications with England are so uncertain. It informed you that I arrived safe & well after a very painful Passage, in which I was miserably ill—since then I have never had such sharp illnesses as in England—but dreadful Languor, weight on my breathing, & a sort of sudden fits of Sleep with nervous Twitches in my Stomach and Limbs on sitting down for a quarter of an hour unemployed or reading. I scarcely eat or drank any thing—but since the very hot weather has commenced, (and the officers here who have been in the E. & W. Indies say that it is hotter now in Valette than it is at Calcutta, or Kingston in Jamaica) I—a single exception—have been much better. For the last 8 or 10 days I have altered my whole System—risen every morning & bathed before the Sun rise, lived more freely, & forced myself to dine regularly—& find my whole Salvation in never suffering myself to be idle ten minutes together; but either to be actually *composing*, or walking, or in Company—for the moment I begin to think, my feelings drive me almost to agony & madness: & then comes on the dreadful *Smothering* upon my chest &c. I shall be much happier by living at the Palace instead of staying with Dr Stoddart, who has behaved *well enough* to me, but &c.—At the Palace I have the pleasantest & coolest suite of Rooms, I have seen in Malta—and with a view from the windows that you would wonder any view could be so impressive having neither River, Trees, nor grassy Field in Sight / but the Harbour & main Sea, & Buildings &c make altogether a glorious Sight.—I shall stay here a fortnight longer at least—perhaps a month—& then go to Sicily, take the Tour of that Island—then to Naples—& then back to Malta in the fall of the Year. Stoddart & his wife & Sister are at St Julian's, about 4 miles from Valette—& have left me this huge House to myself—but I breakfast, dine, & take Coffee at the Governor's—. I shall write to Southey as soon as ever I arrive in Sicily—tho' I shall probably linger on day after day in hopes of a Convoy from England with Letters. Malta furnishes little indeed to write about—the dreariest of all dreary Islands—and I described Valette to you in my former Letter—& besides, Mr Laing will tell you all & every thing, about it and me.—

Sir Alex. Ball, the Governor, has been very kind to me—and I believe, thinks highly of me—but I have never been my right Self a single Hour from the time, I arrived on the Island. My stomach indeed is very weak—the mesenteric Glands are certainly affected by the habit of suppressed painful Thought—yet still I live in hopes that gradually I shall bring myself round. It is a great Thing in my favor that this very hot weather agrees with me. Not having heard from England I scarcely dare mention the Chi[ldren,] but the Thought that Laing is going—I hope to see *them*—going to Keswick at all events has made it a struggle with me several times to preserve the common decencies of Manliness.—How you go on with regard to money, &c &c &c &c &c, you will write of course—I trust, I shall not have occasion to draw on Mr Stuart—at least, not before my final Quitting of the Mediterranean. My only expences here are my washing, a few Pounds' worth of summer Cloathes, & perhaps 4 Shillings a week in bathing & ice creams.— May God Almighty preserve you well and happy. While I live, your comforts will be always thought of by me as my first Duties. Again & again may God bless you, and our dear Children,

&

S. T. Coleridge

Of course, say the kindest things for me to Mr Jackson & Mrs Wilson.

P.S. My sole Reason for not writing to Southey at present, hurried as I am, is my ignorance respecting the result of Edith's Confinement—& the heart-damps of Fear which that Ignorance occasions in my exceeding low-spiritedness. May God bless him, and all whom he loves & who are thereby necessary to his Happiness.—Of course you will say what you ought for me to your Sisters.—

### 603. *To Robert Southey*

*Address*: Robert Southey, Esqre | Greta Hall | Keswick    By favor of the Revd F. Laing.
*MS. Lord Latymer. Hitherto unpublished.*

Malta, July 6th, 1804

My dear Southey

This will, I hope, introduce to you a fellow-Collegiate of your's, tho' a little your junior, the Revd F. Laing—of whom I have written in a Letter to Mrs C. which he will forward by the Post—. I have there told you, how kind he has been to me / & that besides this he is a modest, sensible, & every way amiable man. With him is Sir A. Ball's Son / —I need say no more to you—I should have written to you if I had received any intelligence from England of our families, and of Edith. May God bless you! I think of you ever yearningly & with habitual affection /

S. T. Coleridge

*6 July 1804* [604

### 604. To Daniel Stuart

*Address*: D. Stuart, Esqre | Courier Office | Strand
*MS. British Museum. Pub.* Letters from the Lake Poets, *41.*

July 6th, 1804. Malta

My dear Stuart

I wrote to you from Gibraltar—from thence to Malta I had a miserable voyage indeed, with the exception of the last 4 or 5 days. For two days I was so ill that I expected to die. [We] left Gibraltar April 25th and after a tedious series of Calms and Light winds and Storm that drove us out of our course, dropt anchor in the grand Harbour of Valette, in the afternoon of May 18th.—Since then I have never had those sharp Illnesses; but have nevertheless been in a pit[i]able state of Hopelessness & Heartlessness, increased probably by my having no opportunity of either writing home or receiving Letters from thence.—But within the last fortnight I have been much better—and have at last, I hope & trust, learnt to manage myself. I rise every morning & bathe at or before Sun rise—force myself to regular meals—breakfast at the Palace at 8 o/clock in the Morning, and dine there at 4 in the afternoon—& tho' I am as temperate as a man need be, I no longer live so abstinently as I had done before / but above all things, I find my whole salvation depends on being always either at *work*—(not *reading*: for in half an hour my Stomach begins to be *twitchy*; my breathing smothered; my eyes close in spite of my will; and I fall into diseased & painful Doses; but) actual [wri]ting & composition / or in company—. It is greatly in [my] favor that the hot weather agrees with me—I have never [fe]lt a moment's inconvenience from the heat, tho' it has been hotter for the last fortnight than at Calcutta, or Kingston / & the Thermometer at 86 in the Shade / — and tomorrow I shall get into the coolest & incomparably the pleasantest Apartments in the whole Island—close under the Observatory at the Palace, & commanding from one or other of the windows the main Sea and the Harbour with all it's Thumb and Finger Coves & the whole of the Towns of Valette, Floriana, Victoria, Sanglia, Bormola—& Civita Vecchia in the distance. Sir A. Ball is indeed in every respect as kind and attentive to me as possible so that on the whole I am perfectly satisfied with the wisdom of the Plan—if I had recovered my Health all at once, I never could have believed there had been any occasion for my leaving England. Now I *know* that a change of climate, and an absence from [England] & inward Distractions were necessary for me / [After being near death, I hope I shall return] in Spirit a regenerated Creature. [I am yet more confident of maintaining myself here & I flatter myself that I shall have] no occasion to draw on your kindness for any money till the time of my Return / and perhaps not then. . . .[1] I have inclosed some Sybilline Leaves, which I wrote for Sir A. B. who has sent them home to the Ministry—they will give you *my Ideas* on the Importance of the Island / i.e. if you can read the Scrawl. If they appear just to you, & there should be any which you have not anticipated, you will, of course, take them—only not in the same words. I am hurried now, having been kept hard at work at the Palace / but by the next opportunity I trust, I shall have received Letters from you, & that I shall send you in return something worth Reading. It often soothes me to imagine that you have spent or are spending your Summer at Keswick in Greta Hall— / wherever you are, may God bless you—a kind and true Friend have you been to me—and [if] at this distance from you I could [think of] you without emotion and a flow of affectionate feeling, I should be ashamed of [myself.]                                                                 S. T. Coleridge.

P.S. If I live, I shall be made a perfect [man of busin]ess: I consider my[self] already as a sort of diplomatic Understrapper Hid in Sir Alexander's [Palace]. But this you will speak of to no one, of course / . I shall soon be able both to speak & write both F[rench?] and Italian. The Maltese talk Arabic mixed with Italian. O how I long for a letter from you—to know your opinion of the Change of Ministry—&c &c—

### 605. *To Sir George and Lady Beaumont*

*Address*: For England. | Sir G. Beaumont, Bart | Dunmow | Essex
*MS*. Pierpont Morgan Lib. *Pub*. Memorials of Coleorton, *i. 69.*
*Postmark*: Foreign Office, 17 September 1804.

                                                     August 1. 1804. Malta
My dear Friends

Lady Beaumont once told me, that, when she was young, as a means of awakening devotional feelings she often imaged to herself a mountain, or sea shore, or something great in Nature. O be assured, dear Sir George & dear Lady Beaumont, that affectionate & grateful Feelings never visit me of their own accord, but they bring your remembrance along with them; & that I never in any mood think of you but there commences a new Going-on in

---

[1] Two and two-thirds lines entirely faded. The passages in brackets represent conjectural readings.

my Heart. But I have but a few minutes to write to you / I must therefore make haste to say, that Major Adye goes thro' Sicily to Naples, & from thence makes the best of his way to Gibraltar: and that he has in trust, and will expedite by the first safe opportunity a series of Letters to you—containing my few very few adventures, & my topographical & political Information. Not knowing exactly where to direct to you, I have addressed the outward Cover to D. Stuart Esqre, Courier office—who will take care of it till sent for. I shall go to Syracuse, Catania, Etna, Messina, & perhaps to Naples with Major Adye, & two other Gibraltar Gentlemen; & of course shall add to my pacquet the Journal of my hasty Tour— From thence I shall return to Syracuse, & probably spend six weeks there—thence back again to Malta, & there winter. I am as comfortable here as a man can be: & as happy as *I* can be absent from England, and from all that make England so dear to me. I live at the Palace of St Antonio in the country, four miles from La Vallette, & when in town, in the Palace at La Vallette. A Parent could scarcely be kinder to me than Sir A. Ball, the Governor / — Great as the Heat has been on the Thermometer, 85 to 87 degrees, yet there is always a free Air here, & I have never once felt the Heat oppressive. I take care not to expose myself—& take my exercise from 5 to 7 in the morning, & not till after 7 in the Evening. The Climate *to me* appears heavenly: & the Sirocco a mere Joke compared with our close *drizzly* weather, in England. On the whole, my Health is, I hope, better. I am scarcely ever ill, & very seldom am tormented with distressful Dreams; but tho' exceedingly careful & temperate, my appetite is languid, my stomach faint, & I have reason to know that I rather enjoy a Reprieve in consequence of the absence of the diseasing Causes, than have acquired Strength to bear up against them. But I have only tried the season of inclement Heat: & have every thing to hope from late Autumn, Winter, and early Spring.—Sir A.B. will send this Letter among his—Dear & honored Friends! daily do I think of you, and often often have I prayed for you both—Alike in Malta, and in England I am,

    dear Sir George | and | dear Lady Beaumont, | with heartfelt
        Respect | Your grateful & most devoted | Friend,
                      S. T. Coleridge

I arrived here, as you will have heard, on the 18th of May—since then we have had three showery Forenoons; & this is deemed an uncommonly wet Summer. We have had an Earthquake or two. I have received only one very short Letter from England—and that compleatly unintelligible to me from allusions to others, which evil chance has taken to the Fleet. The disappointment was so great, as [to] make me seriously ill for two days.

## 606. To the Wordsworths

*Pub.* Early Letters, *413*. The text of this extract is taken from a letter of Dorothy Wordsworth to Lady Beaumont, dated 23 September 1804. The quotation is thus introduced: 'I have now to speak of poor Coleridge, from whom we have ourselves received a short letter. It is the first that has reached us, but alas! the third he had sent off so we may guess that he has written more than once to you and others of his Friends. The letter is mainly filled with lamentations that he had received no letters from *any Body*—a trunk had arrived which he had opened with the full confidence of finding packets from us all, and it contained nothing but a parcel of German Almanacks!!! What he says upon the state of his health is on the whole very favourable, though he adds that he seems to be well rather from the absence of diseasing causes than from an increase of constitutional strength. He was living as comfortably as possible in such a desart as Malta; (at Sir Alexander Ball's country house) and his expenses were very small, (no inconsiderable source of comfort to him, anxious as he always is about working and doing something when expenses stare him in the face). He intended going to Sicily the week after he wrote— (his letter is dated the fourth of August) and might probably stay till the first week in October. I will give you one extract—after speaking of the heat he says:'

Fourth of August, 1804

... Still, however, though I bear these summer months so well any cool, clouded, blowing day gives me manifest strength and spirits, and I have therefore much to hope and with much reason, from the late autumn and winter, when the weather is by confession of all perfectly divine. O that it were only a more beautiful country!— ...

## 607. *To Robert Southey*

*Address*: For England | Robert Southey Esqre | Greta Hall | Keswick | Cumberland

Mrs Coleridge will open this, if Mr S. be absent.

*MS.* Lord Latymer. *Pub.* E.L.G. *i. 323.*
*Postmark*: Foreign Office, 17 September 1804.

Malta, August 4th, 1804

My dear Southey

General Oakes sets off, almost without notice, for England / part of the way over land. I have only time to say that I am and have been most anxious to hear from you and concerning you and *your's*; that I have received NO LETTERS, some evil chance having intercepted them or sent them to the Fleet off Toulon / I received the Box with the German Pocket books—& O! bitter disappointment not even a Scrawl on a single bit of Paper in it—& I kept it unopened almost a whole day, my heart beat so violently with expectation that I feared to see the Letters, of which I doubted not to find many, for I supposed the Box to have been put up by Mottley—I continue free from Disease, but I have reason to know that it is because the diseasing causes are absent, and not that I have as yet gained any strength to bear up against them.— The violent Heat does not disagree with me—I know what [it] is by the Thermometer, but I do not feel it—and no doubt I have better things to hope for from the late Autumn & Winter / I go to Sicily next week / have been for the last six weeks or so domesticated with Sir A. Ball, who is exceedingly kind to me. I live when in the Country (which I am 9 days out of 10) at the Palace of St Antonio 4 miles from La Vallette; when in la Vallette at the Palace there / and if living in lofty & splendid Rooms be a pleasure, I have it.—

I hope to have an opportunity of writing to Sara in the course of the next week, but I must not let this slip by. O my sweet Children! and I know nothing of them / May God Almighty bless you

and
S. T. Coleridge

### 608. To Daniel Stuart

*Address*: For England | D. Stuart, Esqre | Courier office | Strand | London
*MS*. British Museum. *Pub*. Letters, *ii*. 485.
*Postmark*: 3 February 1805. *Stamped*: Ship letter, Plymouth.

Oct. 22. 1804. Syracuse

My dear Stuart

I have written to you a long letter this morning by way of Messina; and from other causes am so done up and brain-weary that I must put you to the expence of this as almost a Blank, except that you will be pleased to observe my attention to business in having written two Letters of advice, as well as transmitted first and second of exchange, for 50£ which I have drawn upon you, payable to order of Dr Stoddart at usance. I shall want no more for my Return. I shall stay a month at Messina; and in that time visit Naples.—Supposing the Letter of this morning to miss, I ought to repeat to you, that I leave the publication of the Pacquet, which is waiting for Convoy at Malta for you, to your own opinion— If the information appear new or valuable to you, & the letters themselves entertaining, &c publish them / only do not sell the

Copy right of more than the right of two Editions to the Bookseller—he will not give more, or much more, for the Copy right of the whole.—

May God bless you! | I am & shall be as long as I exist | Your truly grateful and | affectionate Friend,

S. T. Coleridge

### 609. To Sir Alexander Ball

Address: To | his Excellency | Sir A Ball, Bart | &c &c | Malta
From a transcript of the original letter made by a sister of Henry Lushington, chief secretary to the government of Malta from 1847 to 1855. Pub. E.L.G. i. 324. The originals of this and the following letter were found in the archives of the Malta secretariat during Lushington's incumbency; the copies were transmitted to E. H. Coleridge by F. Lushington in 1897.

A search of the Maltese archives in 1931 and a recent investigation by a Maltese official have failed to uncover any Coleridge manuscripts, and confirm information that the early records of the chief secretary's office were burnt. Campbell, Life, 147, and E.L.G. i. 324 n.

Monday Night Nov. 5. 1804. Syracuse

Dear Sir

On Saturday noon I saw from the Ramparts a small French Privateer bring into this harbour a merchant vessel under British Colors. The Captn and the Crew of the Privateer appeared both in looks and manners as ill-conditioned Ruffians, as could have been well brought together in one open Boat. I could not learn either on that day or on the next by any Inquiry, which I had a right to make, that the legality of the Capture as far as it depended on the real character of the Captors had been at all examined into, any questions asked whether the acting Commander of the Privateer was or was not commissioned by any belligerent Government, or any of those precautions taken, which (perhaps from my ignorance of the usages of Neutral Ports) I had supposed to have been customary, both from the respect which every civilized Government owes to itself, and as a check upon Piracy, the common object of detestation with all Governments not absolutely barbarous. This morning I heard that the merchantman had been ransomed in a manner that seemed to imply no great confidence in the Captors themselves as to the lawfulness of the Prize.

Three or four American Officers dined at Mr Leckie's[1] at an unusually late Hour; and from one of them (Captn Decatur)[2] I

[1] Gould Francis Leckie was the English representative at Syracuse. (Campbell, Life, 146.) In 1808 he published his Historical Survey of the Foreign Affairs of Great Britain, which Coleridge recommended to his readers in The Friend, No. 26, 1 Mar. 1810.

[2] Stephen Decatur (1779–1820), American naval officer and hero of the Tripolitan war.

## 5 November 1804

heard, that there was some disturbance on the Marina, that an English Cutter was placed alongside of the French Privateer, the Crew of which had fled to the Ramparts. Between 7 and 8 o'clock, (immediately after our dinner) an officer came with the Governor's Carriage intreating Mr Leckie's presence instantly on the Marina. He went, & I with him, and on stepping out of the Carriage I found by the Torches that about 300 Soldiers were drawn up on the Shore opposite the English Cutter, and that the walls &c were manned: Mr Skinner and two of his Officers were on the rampart, and the Governor and a crowd of Syracusan Nobles with him at the distance of two or three yards from Mr Skinner. After some conversation with Mr Leckie, the Governor desired to know if Mr Skinner had received a Letter (See PA the paper inclosed in this Letter.)[1] from him. Mr Skinner acknowleged the receipt; but in consequence of his not understanding Italian it had been left unread. The Letter (in answer to Captn Sk's first letter, marked A) was sent for; smoked &c, & then interpreted by Mr L. to Mr Skinner. This Letter Mr Skinner will of course deliver to your Excellency; it appeared to me a Letter of mere Evasion, with no definite meaning. Mr Skinner then thro' Mr Leckie demanded of the Governor that the Crew of the Privateer should be given up to him, as Pirates, if they had acted without lawful authority; or if the Privateer had acted with lawful authority, that authenticated Copies of the Commission and other Papers appertaining should be delivered to him, for the British Government at Malta. The Governor promised, that early tomorrow morning such examination should be made; that if the men were found guilty, they should be delivered up: if not, Copies of the Papers on which their acquittal had been founded. It was then asked by Mr Leckie whether or no the Governor meant to consider a pretended Commission given by a French General in a Neutral Port as a legal Commission. The Privateer pretended to no other: and as Letters of Marque could not be legally given from a Neutral Port, either the Kingdom of Naples &c must be at war with G. Britain, or this could be no Commission. This question though repeatedly pressed and argued on, the Governor would not answer, but he would send instantly to Palermo, that it might be decided by the Government there: and it would be at least a month, before any answer could be expected. Mr Skinner then demanded whether the Governor would secure the Crew of the Privateer till such time as a definite decision should be received. This the Governor refused. For this night they should be placed in the Lazaretto under a Guard; and

[1] The documents originally included in this and the following letter have not come to light.

on the morning the Papers should be examined. Further, he neither promised or said anything definite. He talked, or rather screamed, indeed incessantly. I never witnessed a more pitiable scene of confusion, & weakness, & manifest determination to let the French Escape, and of ridiculous attempts to do it with some shew of Reason. Mr Skinner then complained of want of respect to himself as a Commander of a British Vessel of War, no flag having been raised to him or return made to his Port signal on his Entrance into the Harbour. For this the Governor promised compleat satisfaction. He was wholly ignorant of it; and would put the man in irons, to whose neglect of Duty this omission had been owing. So the Scene ended, for the Night. It is but justice however to notice the coolness, dignity and good sense, with which Mr Skinner acted throughout the whole of the Business, and which formed an interesting Contrast to the noisy Imbecillity of the Governor, and the brutal Insolence of the Commander of the Privateer, who in a very indecent manner leapt from the Rampart on which he had been standing with his Crew, and threatened the Governor flinging back his own words upon him with tones and gestures of personal Insult, which drew from the Governor no other mark of resentment or word of animadversion, but a very timid 'Basta! basta!' to which the Privateer (who spoke Italian) answered '*Basta! basta! basta! Non* basta!' and then remounted the wall.

How the affair will end, as far as the Governor is concerned in it, it is easy to foresee. The Commander of the Privateer will produce a real or forged Paper from a French General at Taranto, on which—tho' without deciding that the same is a *legal* commission, he will acquit the Crew of Piracy, and suffer them to escape, and probably make a complaint against Mr Skinner, if he should pursue them within the 24 hours &c &c. The policy of the Governor consists wholly in this—he says to himself, whatever is done to offend the French, however rightfully, the French are nigh at hand to punish, and certain to resent, / whatever is done against the English by the Neapolitan Government he believes that the English Cabinet never will resent—'from the kind regard (I use his own words as nearly as I can render them) the good Sovereign of England has for our poor King.' Whenever an argument is pressed, which cannot be answered, the substitute for an Answer is a Shrug of the Shoulders and 'nostro povero Re!'

The same conduct is pursued with regard to the Americans, between whom & the English the most mortifying distinctions are made. For instance, Captn Craycroft was put in Quarantine because he came from Malta—the Americans from the same place have all Prattic instantly. I was surprized to see Mr Millar yesterday, till I found that he had come with Captn Chauncey. It is said that the Americans give false accounts of themselves; but this is not true. No questions are asked that can draw out a true account, and even when by some accident the Truth is said, the Prattic Master is deaf to all but the answers to the previously concerted questions.

At the time that the Americans were permitted to come on shore instantly on their arrival from Malta, the Governor was hourly expecting an order to put all Vessels from Malta under a Quarantine of 29 days instead of eight—so great an alarm had the accounts of the Fever at Gibraltar spread. But of all this I shall write to your Excellency more at length by the first safe opportunity from Messina, whither I am going tomorrow morning in company with Mr Ricaud—if I can see this affair settled before noon. For Mr Leckie is obliged to go into the country to attend his sowing; and it will be a satisfaction to Mr Skinner if I see the original Papers, of which he is to have Copies for me. Tomorrow morning early I go to the Marina, & shall give this Letter to Mr Skinner, and if anything else occur, I will write a second. Dear Sir! I have not wholly deserved all that you must necessarily have thought of me; this is at least the 5th Letter which I have written to you. But from Messina I hope to convince [you] that I have neither been forgetful of you or of my Duty—as far as my Health & state of Spirits has permitted. I hesitate to go to Naples, for which place you have been so good as to furnish me with a Letter; but I will explain myself at length from Messina. With my most respectful & grateful Remembrances to Lady Ball, I

remain, dear Sir, | with respectful attachment | your obliged and grateful | humb. Serv.

S T Coleridge.

To be read first.

### 610. *To Sir Alexander Ball*

*Address*: To his Excellency | Sir A. Ball Bart | &c &c | Malta
*Transcript* Miss Lushington. *Pub. E.L.G. i. 328.*

L'Hirondelle, Quarantine Harbour, Malta
Thursday Morning Nov. 8. 1804

As we cannot go on shore, & Captn Skinner has not had time to prepare his papers so as to be able to send them to your Excellency sufficiently clear without the aid of explanation by word of mouth, I have thought it best to finish the account of the affair which I had begun on Monday Night, & carried on as far as the affair itself had extended. On Tuesday Morning Mr Leckie feeling the delicacy of his situation as a Sicilian subject and a man under especial obligations to the King of Naples declined further interference in the business, unless he should be directly desired by the Governor and as an interpreter merely. I waited therefore on the Governor myself; & found him & his Counsellors in extreme confusion, three out of four talking at once. The Governor speaks very pure Italian, and his enunciation, however rapid from passion and impatience of mind, is yet always unusually distinct. I had therefore no difficulty in understanding him. From him, though with great difficulty, in consequence of his passionate gestures, ejaculations, digressions, long stories about Lieutenant *Spencer* &c I learnt at last, that the Board of Health had wished to remove the Privateer & the Crew to another part of the Harbour, whither Captn Skynner could not follow, and that Captn Skynner had positively refused to permit them; but from the time of his landing to that very moment had kept his Guns, with the Tompions out, directly pointed at the Privateer, almost as it were within Pistol shot of the Batteries. At the same time the Officer, who acts as the Governor's Secretary and who is comparatively at least a man of sense, shewed me Captn Skynner's first Letter—which at first a little surprized me, as in this the only demand made was the liberation of the two Vessels taken by the Privateer—to which it appeared certainly a sufficient answer, that the two Vessels were not in that Harbour, nor in any place within the authority or indeed knowlege of the Governor of Syracuse. I saw however the grounds on which Captn Skynner had proceeded. He knew, that tho' the Vessels were not in the Harbour, yet that large sums of money as well as valuable stores extorted & pillaged from the two Vessels were on board the Privateer: and thought it his Duty therefore to prevent their escape till such time as their conduct should be examined into. I knew too myself, from good authority, that the Privateer had no other commission, but a pretended one, from Gouvion St Cyr, issued from the Neutral Port of Taranto—I had called on Commodore Prebbell, & seen five other American Captains, and they all, separately, as well as the American Consul, had assured me that this was no legal commission, & that the Privateer Crew were mere Pirates. Likewise, it was known to many that this very commission had been recalled by the French Consul at Palermo in consequence of a general order from Buonaparte not to issue Letters of Marque to Vessels under 50 Ton, and to recall all such as had been previously issued. I thought it prudent therefore to turn the whole attention as much as possible on the utter want of legitimate character in the Privateer. The Governor desired me at last to go to Captn Skynner & to desire him to communicate to him in writing his wishes and demands respecting the Crew & Vessel.

I accordingly went, & having consulted with Captn Skynner wrote the Demands, of which I enclose the copy, marked AA. I read them to Captn Skynner, & asked him if the words conveyed his full meaning, & not mine, & it being what he wished he signed it, & after some useless time wasted at the Governor's I went home. Mr Leckie translated it; I transcribed the translation fairly, & took a Copy of the original, & sent it & the Translation to the Governor. I found him himself in the Health office on the Marina, complaining bitterly, that he had brought down the originals of the Privateer's Papers (See F, G, H, & I.) & copies, & that Captn Skynner was still dissatisfied. On speaking however to Captn S. I found that this was a mistake originating in the Governor & Captn S. not understanding each other—I therefore at the Captn's desire examined the Original Papers, & collated them line for line with the Copies— & delivered them with the Letter which had been sent to me for Captn S. in answer to his Demands. (See Answer *B*.) I knew beforehand that the assessor, a man of the very worst character & notoriously the creature of the French, would declare the Papers regular, & the commission good, though without assigning any one reason; & upon this opinion of the Assessor the Governor would found his detention or non-detention of the Privateer. Accordingly, I advised Captn Skynner to restate his reasons for his full belief of the piratical character of the Privateer, & the little claim it had to protection from any neutral or even civilized Port / For to fix the attention upon this, I saw, was the only way to place the measures of the British Cutter in a point of view, from which they would appear justifiable. The Assessor, on whose opinion all was to depend, I had conversed with in the morning; & so had Leckie— who came in about Noon—It is strictly fact, that he had not even heard the names of any one of the Books, which are allowed to contain the principles of the public maritime Laws of Europe— nor could he say, on what principles he meant to decide on the regularity or irregularity of the Papers of the Privateer.—The opinion of the Assessor (see Papers *C. D.*) was at length obtained, just as Mr Skynner's last Letter was sent off—& with the opinion the Governor's refusal to detain even for an hour the Privateer or the crew. / Of course nothing further was to be done / and as soon as I had taken a copy of the Letter &c, (see Paper *E.*) I put up my Things hastily, & instead of going to Messina have returned to Malta, thinking, that I might be of some service perhaps to

610]  To Sir Alexander Ball

Captn Skynner in the explanation of the Business, & that if adviseable, I might as easily get to Messina from La Valette as from Syracuse. We left the Port of Syracuse about 11 o clock on Tuesday Night—& with the Maltese Vessels that were ready to accept Convoy—one of which had been ransomed for 400 dollars an hour before Captn Skynner's arrival at Syracuse. We arrived before Valette at 8 o clock, & were instantly put in Quarantine——

    I remain with usual devotion, dear Sir | Your obliged & grateful humb. Serv.

S. T. Coleridge.

I have mentioned and inclosed all the papers, excepting the *Petition* delivered by your Excellency to Captn Skynner, which was read by the Governor & of which he took a Copy. This Captn Skynner will redeliver to your Excellency——

P.S. I have now inclosed that Petition (Pap. L.) and likewise the Governor's Letter to your Excellency.

*To be read second*

### 611. *To Robert Southey* [ ? ]

*Transcript Coleridge family. Hitherto unpublished.* E. H. Coleridge in a note appended to this fragment says that it was 'transcribed by an unknown female hand and sent to J. H. Green, Esq.'.

Malta.  Nov. 10. 1804

. . . I was blasted in my only absolute wish, having married for honor & not for love! Southey! that I think & feel so kindly & lovingly of *you*, who were [the] sole cause of my marriage,[1] this is a proof to me that my nature is not ignoble—& that if Life survive Death, I may yet *be*—the actual part of me defecated from my exceeding great unworthiness!

S T Coleridge.

### 612. *To Mrs. S. T. Coleridge*

*Address*: For England. | Mrs Coleridge | Keswick | Cumberland
*MS*. Lord Latymer. *Pub. E.L.G. i. 332.*
*Postmark*: Foreign Office, 11 February 1805.

Malta, 12 Decembr, 1804
Dear Sara

  I will not occupy much of the short Letter, I have time to write, in expressing what anguish even to bodily disease I have suffered

---

[1] See Letters 60, 63, 65, 73, 77, and 79.

## 12 December 1804 [612

by the almost total failure of my Letters from England, the *certain* Loss of *one* large pacquet sent by me homeward from Sicily, which was taken by an Algerine & my papers not improbably at Paris at this time / & no certainty of the other. A convoy will leave this place in less than a fortnight, when I shall write at full / this Letter I send to the fleet, in *hope* that it may come to hand, by a Russian officer of my acquaintance / I returned or rather was abruptly recalled from Syracuse, Nov. 7th, just as the Carriage was at the door in which I was going to Messina, & thence to circle the Island / I was there about 3 months, chiefly at Syracuse or within forty miles of it / but I have been twice on the Top of Mount Etna, & if I had gone on to Messina, I should have been just in time to have seen the Eruption of Vesuvius. The fatigue of ascending Etna is the only thing that has not been exaggerated in it—& of Sicily in general all is exaggerated grossly except the abominableness of the Government, & the vice & abject wretchedness of the people. I have been strenuous in awakening our Government to the true character & views of the Court of Naples, for the last 4 months;[1] yet still I have reason to fear, that the cowardice & ignorance of Ministers, their improper choice of foreign agents, & a sort of stupid personal feeling for the King & Queen of Naples will throw Sicily into the hands of France / if even *at this moment* it is not done.— My Health is *very greatly* improved in this heavenly climate / the Trees are loaded with Oranges, now in the state for plucking—&

[1] There survives in the British Museum a letter from Ball to Leckie which shows not only that Coleridge did not exaggerate in saying Ball's confidence in him was unlimited, but also that Ball commissioned him to prepare reports to be dispatched to the ministry in London.

Sir Alexander Ball to Gould Francis Leckie
Naples 24th August 1804

Dear Leckie

You have admirably described the leading features of my friend Coleridge whose company will be a delightful feast to your Mind—We must prevail on him to draw up a Political Paper on the Revenue and resources of Sicily with the few advantages which His Sicn. Majesty derives from it, and the danger he is in of having it seized from him by the French. We should then propose to His Majesty to transfer his right of that Island to Great Britain upon condition that she shall pay him annually the amount of the present Revenue which he receives from thence—she must further engage to enter into a Treaty offensive and defensive against the Barbary Powers—It would not be a bad thing to seize upon the Papal Dominions and annex them to those of Naples as an Indemnity for Sicily and by going a step further Tuscany might be added. This would create a strong Balance against France in the Mediterranean which could be supported by us from the strong Port of Sicily—Our late Ministers were too timid as well as ignorant of Foreign Politics to undertake any great enterprize—Lord Melville is the boldest of the present Ministers and possesses the most comprehensive Mind. Coleridge's Paper should be presented to him— . .

## To Mrs. S. T. Coleridge

La Vallette echoes with the cries of Green Peas / G. Peas cried in *Arabic* in December!—The last week was very cold & rainy, & I suffered from it / but now it is exactly like our pleasantest days in Autumn / Were I happy, I should grow stout; but tho' I am tranquil, I do not know what it is to have one *happy* moment, or *one* genial Feeling! Not one—so help me God!—No visitations of mind or of fancy—but only the same dull gnawing pain at the heart, sometimes indeed, tho' seldom, relieved by a flood of tears when I can say aloud to myself—My Children! my children!

I am still an Inmate of the Palace, tho' I sleep & study in a sort of Garrets in the Treasury, commanding a most magnificent view of open Sea, & lake-like Harbours; as grand & impressive as a view can be without Trees, river, or green fields. I only however stay here till a suite of rooms can be fitted up for me at the Palace / my old ones were given in my absence to Commissioner Otway.— What I am to receive, I scarcely know / I have had 50£; but my various expences in Sicily, bedding, 2 pair of Sheets, mosquito curtain, &c & for clothes (as I dine at the Palace as confidential Secretary of the Government every day)—as well as for the little comforts I must have in my own rooms, & the expence of my servant—&c &c obliged [me] to draw upon Stuart for 50£; which however I hope to replace by the next convoy / at all events I shall send you 50£ to pay my Life-assurance, & your Mother.—Out of this 100£ however which I have spent, you must understand that I have payed Dr Stoddart an old debt of 25£; which reduces it to 75£. I guess that in [a] few days I shall have to receive a 100£, as four m[onths'] Salary—I am constantly & even laboriously emplo[yed] & the confidence placed in me by Sir A. Ball is un-limi[ted.] I am—if I do not cry off myself—to go into Greece in the beginning of January, on a corn-commission for the Island, & from thence thro' Albania along the North[ern] Shore of the Archipelago to Constantinople, then up the Black Sea to the mouth of the Dnieper & into the Crimea / & possibly into the Heart of Russia. Captn Leake is to be with me, if he is not called off by other Duties;[1] but it will be a most anxious business—as I shall have the trust & management of 70, or 80 thousand £, while I shall not have for my toils, & perils more than 3 or 4 hundred £, exclusive

---

[1] As early as 26 Nov. 1804 Sir Alexander Ball notified the Earl of Camden, the Secretary of War, that Captain Leake was to be sent to the Black Sea to purchase corn, and added: 'He takes with him a Mr Coleridge, that in the Event of his not being able to remain as long as may be requisite, this Gentleman may be on the Spot to act as his Substitute.' [MS. Public Record Office.] Coleridge did not go on this commission. Possibly the death on 18 Jan. 1805 of Mr. Macauley led Ball instead to offer Coleridge an interim appointment pending the arrival of Mr. Chapman, the new Public Secretary.

of all my expences in travelling &c—On the whole, if I could get off with honor, I would—& shall make the attempt / I undertook it in a fit of Despair, when Life was a burthen to me. If I could make up my mind to stay here, or to follow Sir A.B. in case that circumstances & changes in the political world should lead him to Sardinia, no doubt, I might have about 500£ a year, & live mainly at the Palace / but O God! O God! if that, Sara! which we both know too well, were not unalterably my Lot, how gladly would I prefer the mere necessaries of Life in England, & these obtained by daily Effort! But since my Health has been restored to me, I have felt more than ever how unalterable it is!—Whatever & where ever I am; be assured that my first anxiety & prominent Duty will be to contribute every thing in my power to make you as happy as I can, compatibly with the existence of that Health & Tranquillity (joyless indeed both) on which the very power of doing any thing for you must depend. I hope however to see more clearly the way before me in less than a fortnight.—How I long for Letters from Southey & from Grasmere. O my children! my children! I cannot write their names / even to speak of them thus is an effort of courage. Remember me, of course, to Mr Jackson & Mrs Wilson / &c / —. May God Almighty preserve your Health & Life, for your own Happiness, & for the sake of our dear Children.— I remain faithful to you and to my own Honor in all things; and am most anxiously and affectionately

your Friend & more than Friend, S. T. Coleridge

### 613. *To the Wordsworths*

*Pub.* Early Letters, *478*. This fragment, which is quoted by Dorothy Wordsworth in a letter to Lady Beaumont, is all that survives of Coleridge's letter.

Malta 19th January, [1805]

... I send this to you by way of Gibraltar (ah! with what faint hopes of its arrival!) That good Man Major Adye! he is dead—and all his papers burnt as plague-papers,[1] and there perished my fine

---

[1] These papers contained Coleridge's ideas on the *Recluse* (see Letter 617), and Wordsworth must have deeply deplored the loss. As early as 6 Mar. 1804 he had urged Coleridge to send his notes: 'I cannot say how much importance I attach to this; if it should please God that I survive you, I should reproach myself forever in writing the work if I had neglected to procure this help.' Three weeks later, just before Coleridge left for Malta, he was even more insistent. Having learned that Coleridge had been dangerously ill, he wrote: 'I cannot help saying that I would gladly have given 3 fourths of my possessions for your letter on *The Recluse*. ... I cannot say what a load it would be to me, should I survive you and you die without this memorial left behind. Do, for heaven's sake, put this out of the reach of accident immediately.' With

613]  *To the Wordsworths*

Travels addressed to Sir George Beaumont. But enough of the melancholy. First then, I am in good health. Secondly, it is my fixed determination to leave this place in March, but whether by the Convoy, or overland through Trieste I must be decided by circumstances. . . .

### 614. *To Robert Southey*

*Address*: For England. *Per Inghilterra* | Robert Southey, Esqre | Greta Hall Keswick | Cumberland[1] | Single Sheet.
*MS.* Lord Latymer. *Pub.* Letters, *ii.* 487.
*Postmark*: 22 March 1805.

2nd Feby. 1805. Sat. Morning, 4 o/clock. Treasury, Malta.

Dear Southey

A Privateer is to leave this Port to day at Noon, for Gibraltar / and it chancing that an Officer of Rank takes his passage in her, Sir A. Ball trusts his Dispatches, with due precautions, to this unusual mode of conveyance, and I must inclose a Letter to you in the government parcel. I pray, that the Lead attached to it will not be ominous of it's tardy voyage, much less of it's making a diving-tour whither the spirit of Shakespere went under the name of the dreaming Clarence.[2] Certain it is, that I awoke about some half hour ago, from so vivid a dream, that the work of Sleep had completely destroyed all Sleepiness—I got up, went to my Office-room, rekindled the wood-fire, for the purpose of writing to you, having been so employed from morn to eve in writing public Letters, some as long as memorials, from the hour that this opportunity was first announced to me, that, for once in my life at least, I can with strict truth affirm that I have had *no time* to write to you / if by time be understood the moments of Life, in which our powers are alive.—I am well—at least, till within the last fortnight. I wAs perfectly so—till the news of the Sale of my blessed House played the 'foe intestine' with me.[3] But of that

his usual dilatoriness, Coleridge delayed preparing his notes until after his arrival in Malta, and they were destroyed *en route* to England. *Early Letters*, 368, 379–80; and E. L. Griggs, 'Wordsworth through Coleridge's Eyes', *Wordsworth*, ed. by G. T. Dunklin, 1951, pp. 51–53, 65–68, and 82–83.

[1] This and other letters from Malta in 1805 were sealed with a signet bearing the imprint:

[2] *Richard III*, I. iv.
[3] William Jackson, the owner of Greta Hall, had unsuccessfully tried to arrange for the sale of the house. See *Early Letters*, 433 and 436–7.

( 1160 )

hereafter.——My dear Southey! the longer I live, and the more I see, know, and think, the more deeply do I seem to feel your Goodness / and why at this distance may I not allow myself to utter forth my whole thought by adding—your greatness. 'Thy Kingdom come' will have been a petition already granted, when in the minds and hearts of all men both words mean the same—or (to shake off a state of feeling deeper than may be serviceable to me) when, gulielmosartorially speaking (i.e. Williamtaylorice̱) the latter word shall have become an incurable Synonime, a lumberly Duplicate, thrown into the kennel of the Lethe-lapping Chronos Anubioeides, as a carriony bare-ribbed Tautology. O me! it will not do! You, my children, the Wordsworths, are at Keswick and Grasmere—and I am at Malta—and it is silly hypocrisy to *pretend* to joke, when I am heavy at heart. By the accident of the sale of a dead Colonel's Effects, who arrived in this healing Climate too late to be healed, I procured the perusal of the second Volume of the Annual Review.[1] I was suddenly and strangely affected by the marked attention, which you had payed to my few Hints, by the insertion of my Joke on Booker, but more, far more than all, by the affection for me which peeped forth in that 'William Brown of Ottery.' I knew, you stopt, before, and after, you had written the words. But I am to speak of your Reviews in general. I am confident, for I have carefully reperused almost the whole Volume, & what I knew or detected to be your's, I have read over and over again, with as much quiet care and as little Warping of Partiality, as if it had been a manuscript of my own, going to the Press / I can say confidently, that in my best judgment they are models of good sense, and correct style—of high and honest feeling intermingled with a sort of Wit, which (I now translate as truly, tho' not as verbally as I can the sense of an observation, which a literary Venetian who resides here as the editor of a political Journal, made to me after having read your review of Clarke's Mar. Dis.)[2] unites that happy *turn* of words, which is the essence of French Wit, with those comic picture-making combinations of Fancy, that characterizes the old wit of old England. If I can find time to copy off what in the hurry of the moment I wrote on loose papers that cannot be made up into a letter without subjecting you to an expence utterly disproportionate to their value, I shall prove to you that I have been watchful in marking what appeared to me false, or *better-not*, or *better-otherwise*, parts, no less than what I felt to be excellent. It is enough to say at present, that seldom in

---

[1] Southey contributed eighteen reviews to the *Annual Review*, ii. 1803. Cf. *Life and Corres.* vi. 398–9.

[2] James Stanier Clarke, *The Progress of Maritime Discovery*, 1803.

my course of reading have I been more deeply impressed than by the sense of the diffused Good, they were likely to effect. At the same time I could not help feeling, to how many false and pernicious principles both in Taste and in Politics they were likely by their excellence to give a non-natural circulation. W. Taylor grows worse and worse. As to his political dogmata, concerning Egypt &c, God forgive him! he knows not what he does! But as to his Spawn about Milton, and Tasso—nay, Heaven forbid! it should be *Spawn* / it is pure Toad's spit, not as Toad spit is, but as it is vulgarly believ'd to be. *See too his Art: in the Crit. Rev.*

Now for your feelings respecting Madoc, I regard them as all nerve- and stomach-work, you having too recently quitted the business—Genius too has it's intoxication, which however divine, leaves it's headaches and it's nauseas. Of the very best of the few bad, good, and indifferent things I have written, I have had the same sensations.—Concerning the immediate *chrysopoetic* powers of Madoc I can only fear somewhat and hope somewhat—Midas and Apollo are as little Cronies as Marsyas and Apollo, but of it's great and lasting effects on your Fame, if I doubted, I should then doubt all things, in which I had hitherto had firm faith / neither am I without cheerful Belief respecting it's *ultimate* effects on your worldly Fortune. O dear Southey! when I see *this* Booby with his ten pound a day, as Mr Commissary X, and *that* thorough-Rogue two doors off him, with his 15£ a day, as Mr General Pay Master YZ, it stirs up a little Bile from the Liver, & gives my poor stomach a pinch, when I hear you talk of having to look forward for an 100 or 150£. But cheerily! what do we complain of? would *we* be either of those men? O had I domestic Happiness, and an Assurance even of the Health, I now possess, continuing to me in England, what a blessed Creature should I be, tho' I found it necessary to feed me and mine on roast Potatoes for 2 days in each week in order to make ends meet, and to awake my Beloved with a Kiss on the first of every Janry—Well, my best Darling! we owe nobody a farthing!—and I have you, my children, two or three friends, and a thousand Books!——

I have written very lately to Mrs Coleridge. If my Letter reach her, as I have quoted in it a part of your's of Oct. 19th, she will wonder that I took no notice of the House and the *Bellygerent*. / From Mrs C. I have received no letter by the last Convoy. In truth, I am, and have reason to be, ashamed to own to what a diseased excess my sensibility has worsened into. I was so agitated by the receipt of Letters, that I did not bring myself to open them for 2 or 3 days, half-dreaming that from there being no Letter from Mrs C., some one of the Children had died, or that she herself had

## 2 February 1805 [614

been ill or—— for so help me God! most ill-starred as our marriage has been, there is perhaps nothing that would so frightfully affect me as any change respecting her Health or Life. And when I had read about a 3rd of your Letter, I walked up & down, & then out, & much business intervening, I wrote to her before I had read the remainder, or my other Letters. I grieve exceedingly at the event, & my having foreseen it does not diminish the Shock. My dear Study! and that House in which such persons have been! where my Hartley has made his first love-commune with Nature / to belong to White! Oh how could Mr Jackson have the heart to do it! As to the Climate, I am fully convinced, that to an Invalid all parts of England are so much alike, that no disadvantages on that score can overbalance any marked Advantages from other causes. Mr J. well knows that but for my absolute confidence in him I should have taken the House for a long Lease—but, poor Man! I am rather to soothe than to reproach him. When will he ever again have lovi[ng] Friends & Housemates like to us—? and dear good Mrs Wilson! Surely M[rs] Coleridge must have written to me tho' no Letter has arrived.

Now for myself—I am anxiously expecting the arrival of Mr Chapman from Smyrna, who is (by the last ministry, if that should hold valid) appointed Successor to Mr Macauley, as Public Secretary of Malta, the second in rank to the Governor. Mr M. an old man of 80, died on the 18th of last month, calm as a sleeping Baby, in a tremendous Thunder & Lightning Storm / In the interim, I am and some 50 times a day subscribe myself, Segretario Publico dell' Isole di Malta, Gozo, e delle loro dipendenze. I live in a perfect Palace, & have all my meals with the Governor; but my profits will be much less, than if I had employed my time & efforts in my own literary pursuits. However, I gain new Insights / & if (as I doubt not, I shall) I return, having expended nothing, having paid all my prior debts as well as interim expences, [(] of the which debts I consider the 100£ borrowed by me from Sotheby, on the firm of W. Wordsworth, the heaviest) with Health, & some additional Knowlege both in Things & Languages, I surely shall not have lost a year. My intention is assuredly to leave this place at the farthest in the latter end of next month, whether by the Convoy, or overland by Trieste, Vienna, Berlin, Embden, & Denmark, I must be guided by circumstances—At all events it will be well if a Letter should be left for me, at the Courier office in London, by the first of May, informing me of all which is necessary for me to know / But of one thing I am most anxious, namely, that my Assurance-money should be paid—I pray you, look to that / You will have heard long before this Letter reaches you that the

French Fleet have escaped from Toulon / I have no Heart for Politics—Else I could tell you how for the last 9 months I have been working in memorials concerning Egypt, Sicily, & the Coast of Africa / Could France once possess these, she would be in a far grander sense than the Roman, an Empire of the World—& what would remain to England? England & that which our miserable Diplomatists affect, now to despise, & now to consider as a misfortune, our language & institutions in America?—France is blest by nature / for in possessing Africa she would have a magnificent Outlet for her Population as near her own Coasts as Ireland to our's—an America, that must forever be an integral part of the Mother Country. Egypt is eager for France—only more, far more eager for G. Britain. The universal cry there / I have seen translations of 20 at least mercantile Letters in the Court of Admiralty here, (in which I have made a speech with a Wig & Gown, a true Jack of all Trades) all stating that the vox populi is—English, English, if we can! But *Hats*, at all events!—('*Hats*' means Europeans in contradistinction to Turbans!)—God bless you, Southey!—I wish earnestly to kiss your child—and all whom you love, I love, as far as I can, for your sake——

S. T. C.

## 615. To Daniel Stuart

*Address*: D. Stuart, Esqre | Courier Office | Strand
*MS. British Museum. Pub. with omis. Letters, ii. 493.* The letter is preceded by the following order, in Coleridge's handwriting and signed by both Coleridge and Stoddart:

Malta 27 April 1805

Dr Stoddart requests that Mr Burrell will repay to D. Stuart, Esqre. the fifty pounds received by him on account of a Bill drawn on Mr D. Stuart by S. T. Coleridge, Syracuse Oct. 23, 1804, in favor of Dr Stoddart, and indorsed to Mr Burrell by the latter—Or if by any accident the fifty pound should not be payed by Mr Stuart, Mr Burrell is to withdraw the Bill, the account having been settled at Malta.

between us { J *Stoddart*
{ S. T. Coleridge

N.B. The above Bill has also been counterordered by Dr S's letters to Mr Burrell of Jany. 1. & March 4. 1805.

April 30th, 1805.

*Read the last paragraph of this Letter first*

Favored by Captn Maxwell, of the Artillery—N.B. an amiable mild man, who is prepared to give you any information

Dear Stuart

The above is a Duplicate, or rather a *sex-* or *septem*-plicate of an order sent off within three weeks after my Draft on you had

## 30 April 1805

been given by me. And very anxious I have been, knowing that all or almost all, my letters have failed. It seems like a Judgement on me. Formerly, when I had the sure means of conveying Letters, I neglected my Duty thro' Indolence, or Procrastination / For the last year when—having *all* my Heart, *all* my Hope in England—I found no other gratification than that of writing to Wordsworth, and his Family, his Wife, Sister, & Wife's Sister, to Southey, to you, to T. Wedgwood, Sir G. Beaumont, &c. Indeed I have been supererogatory in some instances.—But an evil destiny has dogged them. One large, and (forgive my vanity!) rather important, set of Letters to you on Sicily and Egypt, were destroyed at Gibraltar among the papers of the most excellent man, Major Adye, to whom I had entrusted them on his departure from Sicily, and who died of the Plague *four days* after his arrival at Gibraltar. But still was I afflicted (shame on me, even to violent weeping) when all my many many Letters were thrown over board from the Arrow, the Acheron, and a merchant Vessel—to all which I had entrusted them / —the last thro' my own over-care. For I delivered them to the Captn with great pomp of Seriousness, in my official character as Public Secretary of the Islands / he took them, & considering them as public papers, on being close chaced & expected to be boarded threw them overboard / and he however escaped steering for Africa, & returned to Malta.—But regrets are idle things.—

In my letter which will accompany this I have detailed my Health, and all that relates to me / in case however that Letter should not arrive, I will simply say, that till within the last two months or ten weeks my Health had improved to the utmost of my Hopes, tho' not without some intrusions of Sickness—but latterly the loss of my Letters to England, the almost entire non-arrival of Letters from England / not a single one from Mrs Coleridge, or Southey, or you, and only one from the Wordsworths—& that dated Septembr, 1804!—my consequent heart-sad'ning anxieties, and still still more the depths which Captn John Wordsworth's Death sunk into my Heart, & which I heard abruptly & in the very painfullest way possible in a public Company[1]—all these joined to my disappointment in my expectations of returning to England by this Convoy, and the quantity and variety of my public occupations from 8 o/clock in the morning to 5 in the afternoon, having besides the most anxious duty of writing public Letters & Memorials, which belongs to my Talents rather than to my pro-tempore Office—these and some other causes, that I cannot mention, relative to my affairs in England, have produced a sad change indeed in my Health / but however I hope, all will

[1] John Wordsworth perished in the wreck of the *Abergavenny* on 5 Feb. 1805.

be well—I have had a fever, & it has brought out Boils on my Body, which has greatly weakened my Stomach, but I hope for the best, & it is my present inten[tion] to return home over land by Naples, Ancona, Trieste, &c on or about the 20th of next month——

The Gentleman who will deliver this to you is Captn Maxwell of the Royal Artillery, a well informed and very amiable Countryman of your's—he will give you any information, you wish, concerning Malta. An intelligent Friend of his, an officer of Sense and Science, has entrusted to him an Essay on Lampedosa,[1] which I have advised him to publish in a Newspaper, leaving it to the Editor to divide it / It may perhaps need a little *softening*, but it is an accurate & well-reasoned Memorial. He only wishes to give it *publicity*, & to have not only his name concealed but every circumstance that could lead to a suspicion / —If after reading it you approve of it, you would greatly oblige him by giving it a place in the Courier—he is a sensible independent man—For all else, to my other Letter—I am,

dear Stuart, | with faithful recollections | your much obliged & truly grateful | Friend and Servant,

S. T. Coleridge

### 616. To Daniel Stuart

*Address*: D. Stuart, Esqre | Courier Office | Strand | London
*MS*. British Museum. *Pub*. E.L.G. *i. 335*. This letter is preceded by a copy in Stoddart's handwriting of the order included in the headnote to Letter 615.
*Postmark*: 10 July 1805.   *Stamped*: Ship letter Plymouth.

May 1. 1805

My dear Stuart

I have had three weeks & more, notice of the Convoy for England / the first ten days or so I have been occupied with public Letters and Memorials, so much so as to be at night almost too tired, my spirits too exhausted, to undress myself—the last eleven or 12 days I have been very ill—worse than I have been since my arrival in Malta, with the exception of a few days in Sicily—The fever has ended in a number of Boils, which have at length broke, and from being Torture are now only troublesome; but under all this my Stomach has been so injured, that I have taken no solid food for a fortnight past—& it is well for me if once a day I can keep a little Broth on my Stomach. However, I am plainly tho' very slowly convalescent—Among several causes of my illness duly following, or crowding on each other, the loss of my whole store of Papers in

---

[1] i.e. Lampedusa, a small island midway between Malta and Tunis.

## 1 May 1805

the Arrow, Acheron, and a Merchant Vessel may be counted as not the least / having had another not unimportant packet respecting Sicily, Egypt, and Africa, directed to you, & after your perusal, to Sir G. Beaumont, burnt at Gibraltar, among Major Adye's Papers. But of the last parcel (i.e. in the Arrow) I had written the greater part in times stolen from Sleep / but enough!

In the last Letter, which I received from you, I was affected and alarmed by the state of my accompts—Mr White's assurance, £61₁₁11₁₁5—I never dreamt of it's exceeding £34.—I immediately retracted my Bill for 50£ on you; and it never would have been presented but for the unfortunate Loss of Letter after Letter. I have sent a duplicate of the Order at the Top of this Letter in another which will be, I hope, delivered to you by Captn Maxwell, of the Royal Artillery, an amiable & intelligent young man. Not less than 5 or 6 of similar orders have been sent—so exceedingly anxious have I been not to appear to make free with you in pecuniary matters.—I meant to have sent 90£ to Mrs Coleridge by this Convoy / & have the Money all ready / but the violence of my fever, with the almost continual Sickness at Stomach, rendered me incapable of taking the proper means of procuring a right Bill. I have sent out even now, having only a few minutes to spare and if I succeed, will inclose it / which you will be so good as to remit to Mrs Coleridge. If not, I will send it tomorrow‡ viâ Naples—by which I shall at all events send the duplicate / Should this Letter not arrive, you will greatly oblige me by at least remitting 50£ to Mrs Coleridge / as I shall by means of Sir A. Ball, and by availing myself of every communication place the arrival of a good Bill out of all common Chance / I have scraped up, by hard and slavish Labor, about a hundred and fifty Pound, Maltese Currency; or 130£ English / but would to Heaven! I had never accepted my office as Public Secretary, or the former of Private Secretary—Even in a pecuniary Point of View I might have gained twice as much, & improved my reputation—But regrets are idle!

Pray, write to Mrs Coleridge—and say, that my Constitution is, I hope, improved by my Abode here; but that accidents, partly of an excess of official Labor and anxiety, partly from distress of mind at my not hearing from my friends & knowlege that they could not have heard from me, &c &c &c has produced sad alteration in me for the worse; but that [I] dedicate the next three works [weeks?] to an unceas[ing] effort to recover ground; & sometime about the [end] of May (dependent of course on Vessels & the

‡ Sir A. Ball has been here and tells me that it must not be sent overland; but that an imperial Man of war goes in 3 days & will overtake the Convoy. [Note by S. T. C.]

state of politics) I have resolved to return home over land by Naples, Ancona, Trieste, & Germany—that my Heart is almost broken that I could not go home this Convoy—all was resolved that I should / but the Gentleman, who is to be Public Secretary here, still delays his arrival, & may probably not come till July / but I have resolved, let the struggle cost what it may, & even at the forfeiture of Sir A. Ball's Good will, to return home at the latter end of May—I have the Title, and the Palace of the Public Secretary; but not half the Salary—tho' I had a Promise of the whole / But the Promises of men in office are what every one knows them to be / & Sir A. B. behaves to me with really personal fondness, and with almost fatherly attention—I am one of his Family, whenever my Health permits me to leave my own House—/

My dear Stuart! I thank you for the Couriers——they have (such as have arrived) amused me greatly, and indeed instructed me.— For a long long space of Time I have received no Letters from you. Indeed, greatly as I am delighted by any proof of your remembering me, I have no need of them as remembrances of you / for I know, that till I die, or at least untill my Reason and Memory die, I shall always feel all your kindness to me, & be with firm & grateful attachment

your affectionate Friend, S. T. Coleridge

<h3 style="text-align:center">617. To the Wordsworths</h3>

*Pub.* Early Letters, *508.* This fragment, which is quoted by Dorothy Wordsworth in a letter to Lady Beaumont, is all that survives of Coleridge's letter.

May 1st, [1805]

. . . Should this letter arrive alone, do not be uneasy. I have indeed been so ill, the effect of a variety of causes, as to be unable to write by this convoy; the multitude and importance of the public letters, joined with events that I dare not at present speak of—but which have wrenched my very heart. O dear Friends! Death has come among us!—I have but a few minutes, as the convoy is off a day before the time given out. I mean to return in the latter end of May at all events, and have wept like a child that the convoy is off without me, but my office of public Secretary makes it impossible —but I am resolved, let it cost what it may, that in May go I will. Till within the last month my health was delightfully improved, with the exception of one nervous fever in Sicily.

I have only time to say that I hope all will yet be well—that an Imperial Vessel of War sails three days hence, and will overtake

1 May 1805                                [617

the Convoy—that I shall employ the whole of the intermediate time in writing to you. . . .

My Ideas respecting your Recluse were burnt as a Plague-garment, and all my long letters to you and Sir George Beaumont sunk to the bottom of the Sea!


618. *To Mrs. S. T. Coleridge*

*Address*: For England | Mrs Coleridge | Keswick | Cumberland
*MS. Lord Latymer. Pub. with omis.* Letters, *ii. 496.*
*Postmark*: 8 September 1805.   *Stamped*: Ship letter, Portsmouth.

Malta, 21 July 1805

Dear Sara

The Niger is ordered off for Gibraltar at a moment's warning; and the Hall is crowded with officers, and Merchants whose Oaths I am to take, and accompts to sign / I will not however suffer it to go without a line, & including a draft for 110£ / another opportunity will offer in a week or ten days, & I will inclose a Duplicate in a Letter at large—/ Now for the most important articles / My Health *had* greatly improved; but latterly it has been very, very bad / in great measure owing to dejection of Spirits / my Letters having failed, the greater part of those to me, and almost all mine home-ward—as if I were to be punished for former neglect by writing industriously to no purpose / My Letters to you—my Letters, & the duplicates of them, written with so much care & minuteness to Sir George Beaumont / those to Wedgewood—to the Wordsworths —to Southey—/ Major Adye's sudden Death /—and then the loss of the two frigates / the capture of a Merchant's Privateer—all have seemed to spite /— No one not absent on a dreary Island so many leagues of sea from England can conceive the effect of these Accidents on the Spirits & inmost soul / So help me Heaven! they have nearly broken my Heart / And added to this, I have been hoping and expecting to get away for England for 5 months past, and Mr Chapman not arriving, Sir Alexander's Importunities have always overpowered me / tho' my gloom has encreased at each disappointment / I am determined however to go in less than a month / My office, as Public Secretary, the next civil dignity to the Governor, is a very very busy one / & not to involve myself in the responsibility of the Treasur[er] I have but half the Salary—I often times subscribe my name 150 times a day—S. T. Coleridge, Pub. Sec. t. h. M. Civ. Commissr or (if in Italian) Seg. Pub. del Commisso. Regio / & administer half as many Oaths / besides which I

( 1169 )

have the public Memorials to write / & worse than all constant matters of Arbitration / / ——

Sir A. Ball is indeed exceedingly kind to me—The officers will be impatient / I would, I could write a more chearful account of my Health / all I can say is that I am better than I have been—and that I was very much better before so many circumstances of dejection happened / I should overset myself compleatly, if I ventured to mention a *single name* / How deeply I love / O God!—it is agony at Morning & evening /                                S. T. Coleridge /

On being told abruptly by Lady Ball of John Wordsworth's fate I attempted to stagger out of the room (the great Saloon of the Palace with 50 people present) and before I could reach the door fell down on the ground in a convulsive hysteric Fit /— I was confined to my room for a fortnight after /—and now I am afraid to open a Letter / & I never dare ask a question of any newcomer.

The night before last I was much affected by the sudden entrance of poor *Reynell* (our inmate at Stowey)—more of him in my next. May God Almighty bless you and——

### 619. To Mrs. S. T. Coleridge

*Address*: Mrs Coleridge | Keswick | Cumberland | England
*MS. Lord Latymer. Pub. E.L.G. i. 337.*
*Postmark*: 5 December 1805.  *Stamped*: Plymouth.

21 Aug. 1805.   Treasury-House, Malta.
With the second Bill of Exchange for 110£

My dear Sara

Having written to you at full by the Juno Frigate, tho' from it's not being absolutely certain that she will touch directly at Gibraltar I did not choose to inclose the second Bill of Exchange, I now write merely as an Envelope for that Bill, by Colonel Smith who goes to day to Naples, from thence over Land to England with Dispatches. I had flattered myself that I should have gone with him: as indeed I have been flattering myself every week for the last six months that I should have permission and opportunity to go / but Sir Alexander has still contrived, in one way or another, to prevent it. Now however he has given me his solemn promise that as soon as I have written six public Letters, & examined into the Law-forms of the Island (which cannot take me more than a week altogether) he will forward me immediately to Naples, and will use his best interest with Mr Elliot, our Ambassador at Naples, to send me home with Dispatches—which, of course, would *frank me home*. As this however is an uncertainty I am obliged to retain about 120£ by me / but whatever money I am obliged to spend in travelling over Land, will be amply repaid to me by the Booksellers.—It has injured my Health very considerably, this continued Disappointment both in my Return, and in my Letters—and the well-grounded Suspicions, that the Letters sent by me have not been more fortunate than those sent from England to me. The Weather has been dreadfully hot for the last month / sometimes as high as 95° in Fahrenheit, seldom lower than 85°/—It has brought out Boils & Prickly Heat on my body, and variously annoyed me. On the 27th of July last, an Earthquake took place in the Kingdom of Naples which destroyed three Towns and about 8000 people in Abruzzo, & so shook the City of Naples that the calculated Damage is 20 per cent on the whole value of the whole city, about eight million Ducats. Scarce a single House remains uncracked. The Commissioners entered one House to examine it the next morning; the Master of the Family answered, that it had received a little crack in the ceiling; but would last as long as their time. The Commissioners examined it, ordered the Family out of the House that instant; and in 16 minutes the whole fell in!—

We had about a month before a smart Earthquake in Malta, which shook my bed and me in it as with a Giant's Ar[m] but did no mischief. Ships 60 leagues distant from [Lan]d felt it: and it appeared as [if they had] suddenly struck on a rough shore, & were *raking* the stones.

Sir Alexander Ball's Kindness to & Confidence in me is unlimited / he told a Gentleman a few days ago, that were he a man of Fortune he would gladly give me 500£ a year to dine with him twice a week for the mere advantage, which he received from my Conversation / and for a long time past he has been offering me different places to induce me to return / he would give me a handsome House, Garden, Country House, & a place of 600£ a year certain / I thank him cordially—but neither accept nor refuse. I had lately a fine Opening in America, which I was much inclined to accept; but my knowlege of Wordsworth's aversion to America stood in my way.—

My Health is by no means what I could wish it / the quantity and variety of my public Business confine me, & I cannot take enough Exercise / & Malta, alas! it is a barren Rock / the Sky, the Sea, the Bays, the Buildings are all beautiful / but no rivers, no brooks, no Hedges, no green fields, almost no Trees, & the few that are are unlovely.—It might have been better for me if I had remained wholly independent / for the living in a huge Palace all to myself, like a mouse in a Cathedral on a Fair or Market Day, and the being

619]  *To Mrs. S. T. Coleridge*

hail'd 'Most illustrious Lord, the Public Secretary' are no pleasures to me who have no ambition, & having no *curiosity*, the deal, I see of men & things only tends to tinge my mind with melancholy.—However, I trust, that the first of September will be the latest time I shall stay here[1] / of all tender recollections I have spoken in my last—& do not wonder if with people about me craving dispatch of Business, I cannot bring myself to write down names that make my inmost Heart as often bleed tears as dissolve with tenderness: all whom I loved in England I seem to love tenfold in Malta /—My dear Sara! may God bless you / be assured, I shall never, never cease to do every thing that can make you happy
—S. T. Coleridge

### 620. To Washington Allston[2]

*Address*: Al Signre | Signre Allston | Pittore Americano | Caffe Greco | Strada de' Condotti | Roma
MS. *Washington Allston Trust. Pub. with omis.* The Life and Letters of Washington Allston, *by J. B. Flagg, 1893, p. 76, and* Letters, *ii. 498.*

[Florence.][3]  Tuesday, June 17th, 1806
My dear Alston

No want of affection has occasioned my silence.—Day after day I expected Mr Wallis[4]— Benvenuti[5] received me with almost insulting coldness, not even asking me to sit down / neither could I by any enquiry find that he ever returned my call / and even in answer to a very polite note enquiring for Letters sent a verbal message, that there was one and I might call for it.—However, within the last 7 or 8 days he has called and made this amende honorable / he says, he forgot the name of my Inn, & called at two or three *in vain* / *whoo!* I did not tell him, that within 5 days I sent him a note, in which the Inn was mentioned, & that he sent me a message in consequence / & yet never called for 10 days afterwards. However, yesterevening the Truth came out / he had been bored by Letters of recommendation, & till he received a Letter from Mr Migliorini looked upon me as a *Bore* / which however he

[1] Coleridge left Malta for Syracuse, presumably on Monday, 23 Sept. 1805.
[2] Washington Allston (1779–1843), the American painter. He and Coleridge had become acquainted in Rome.
[3] Coleridge had left Rome for Florence in the company of Thomas Russell of Exeter, who was studying art. See Letter 636. An unpublished letter from Russell to Coleridge is preserved in Dove Cottage.
[4] George Augustus Wallis (1770–1847), the painter. Later in the letter Coleridge mentions Wallis's son Trajan and daughter Emilie.
[5] Probably Pietro Benvenuti (1769–1844), the painter, who was made professor of the Florentine Academy in 1803.

( 1172 )

might & ought to have got rid of in a more gentlemanly manner / Nothing more was necessary than the day after my arrival to have sent his Card by his Servant. But I forgive him from my Heart / It should however be a Lesson to Mr Wallis, to whom & for whom he gives Letters of *Rec.*/—

I have been dangerously ill—for the last fortnight / & unwell enough, Heaven knows, previously—but about 10 days ago on rising from my bed I had a manifest stroke of Palsy along my right side, and right arm / My Head felt like another man's Head—so dead was it, that I seemed to know it only by my left hand, and a strange sense of Numbness—violent attempts to vomit, each effort accompanied by involuntary & terrific Screams—Enough of it / continual vexations & preyings upon the Spirit / I gave Life to my Children / and they have repeatedly given it to me / for by the Maker of all things, but for them I would try my chance. But they pluck out the wing-feathers from the mind——I have not entirely recovered the *sense* of my side or hand / but have recovered the use. I am harrassed by local & partial Fevers.

This day at Noon we set off for Leghorn / all passage thro' the Italian States & Germany is little other than impossible for an Englishman / & Heavens knows, whether Leghorn may not be blockaded / However we go thither & shall go to England in an American Ship / Inform Mr Wallis of this & urge him to make his way——assure him of my anxious thoughts & fervent wishes respecting him / and of my Love for Trajan & his Family—Tell Mr Migliorini that I should have written him long ago but for my ill-health; but will not fail to do it on my arrival at Pisa / from thence too I will write a Letter to you / for this I do not consider as a Letter.—Nothing can surpass Mr Russell's Kindness & tender-heartedness to me: and his understanding is far superior to what it appears on first acquaintance / I will write likewise to Mr Wallis / O *conjure* him not to leave Amelia behind!——

I have heard in Leghorn a sad sad character of one of those, whom you call acquaintance—but who call you their dear Friend /—

My dear Alston! somewhat from increasing age, but much more from calamity & intense pre-affections my heart is not open to more than kind good wishes in general; to you & to you alone since I have left England, I have felt more / and had I not known the Wordsworths, should have loved & esteemed you *first* and *most* / and as [it] is, next to them I love & honor you / Heaven knows, a part of such a Wreck as my Head & Heart is scarcely worth your acceptance——

S. T. Coleridge

Direct to me, at Mr Degen's, Leghorn / God bless you!——

## 621. To Daniel Stuart

*Address*: D. Stuart, Esqre | 348, | Strand | to be delivered immediately | S. T. C.
MS. British Museum. *Pub. with omis.* Letters, *ii. 501.*

Bell Inn, Friday Street / Monday Morning
August 18th, 1806

My dear Sir

I arrived here from Stangate Creek last night, a little after ten: and have found myself so unusually better ever since I leaped on land, yesterafternoon, that I am glad that neither my strength or spirits enabled me to write to you on my arrival in Quarantine, on the eleventh. Both the Captain and my fellow-passenger[1] were seriously alarmed for my Life—and indeed such have been my unremitting Sufferings from pain, sleeplessness, costiveness, loathing of food, & spirits wholly despondent, that no motive on earth short of an awful duty would ever prevail on me to take any sea-voyage likely to be longer than three or four days. I had rather starve in [a ho]vel; and if Life thro' disease become worthless, will choose a Roman Death.—It is true, I was very low before I embarked—your kind Letter concluding with the Sums, I stand indebted to you, never for an hour ceased to prey on my mind. To have been working so hard for 18 months in a business, I detested —to have been flattered and to have flattered myself, that I should on striking the balance have payed all my debts, & maintained both myself and family during my exile, out of my savings—and earnings, including my travels thro' Germany, thro' which I had to the very last hoped to have passed—& find myself—but enough!
—I cannot charge my conscience with a single extravagance, nor even my Judgement with any other imprudences than that of suffering one good and great man to over-persuade me from month to month to a delay, which was gnawing away my very vitals—and of being duped in disobedience to my first feelings & previous Ideas by another diplomatic minister, who is a rascal. I sent one Bill & a duplicate for 110£ to Mrs C— & actually had entrusted another for 100£ to Mr Noble at Naples for the same purpose, & discovered the dupery scarcely time enough to withdraw it, which I did with an aking heart—had I not done it, tho' at that time, it was merely for the convenience of not drawing on England, I should have been left starving in a foreign country / for a gentleman offered to take me without expence to Rome, which I accep[ted] with the full intention of staying only a fortnight & then returning to Naples to pass the winter at Noble's House, which Mr Noble

---
[1] Thomas Russell.

## 18 August 1806

offered me partly out of compassion for the wretched state of my finances, which were but barely sufficient for my intended Journey in the Spring—and partly out of gratitude for my many attentions, and one or two serious services to his Brother & Partner at Malta, while I was the Public Secretary.—By Mr Noble's advice I left every thing (but a good suit of cloathes, & my shirts &c)—all my letters of credit, manuscripts, &c &c—with him.—I had not been ten days in Rome before the French Torrent rolled down on Naples—all return was impossible, all transmission of Papers not only insecure, but being English & many of them political, highly dangerous both to the Sender and Sendee—After two months sickening anxiety I received certain tidings that Mr N. had decamped (having admirably out-maneuvred the French) with all my papers & effects; but whether to Malta, or Sardinia was not known. /[1] But this is only a fragment of a Chapter of Contents /— and I am too much agitated to write the Detail, but will call on you as soon as my two or three remaining [guineas] shall have put a decent Hat upon my [head], & Shoes on my feet.—I am literally afraid even to cowardice to ask for any person [or] of any person —Including the Quarantine, we had 55 days of Ship-board, working up against head winds, rotting & sweating in calms, or running under hard gales, with the dead lights secured / & from the Captain and my fellow-passenger I received every possible Tenderness— only when I was very ill, they layed their wise heads together, & the Latter in a Letter to his Father begged him to inform my Family, that I had arrived & he trusted, that they would soon see me, in better health & spirits than I had quitted them, a Letter which must have alarmed if they saw into it, & wounded if they did not. I was not informed of it till this morning.—God bless you, my dear Sir! I have yet chearful Hopes that Heaven will not suffer me to die degraded by any other Debts, than those which it ever has been & ever will be, my joy & pride still to pay & still to owe, those of a truly grateful Heart—& to you among the first of those to whom they are due.                                              S. T. Coleridge.—

[1] Stoddart reported to the Wordsworths that Coleridge, on his withdrawal from Naples to Rome, 'sent a box of papers and other things to Mr. G. Noble, who with his family escaped to Messina, and took the box with him soon after the French entered Naples in February'. *The Letters of William and Dorothy Wordsworth: the Middle Years*, ed. by E. de Selincourt, 2 vols., 1937, i. 37.

## 622. To Robert Southey

*Address*: Robert Southey, Esqre | Keswick | Cumberland | To be opened, if Mr S. be not at home | by the family—
MS. Lord Latymer. *Pub. with omis. E.L.G. i. 340.*
*Postmark*: 20 ⟨August⟩ 1806.

Wednesday, Aug. 19 [20], 1806

My dear Southey

I write to you rather than to Mrs Coleridge because I can write more tranquilly—indeed, it agitates me so much that if I could have settled any rational plan to have set off tomorrow or to night, I should not have written at all—but have let the information sent to Grasmere suffice—After as sore a heartwasting as I believe ever poor creature underwent / and which commenced at, & continued without interval, from April, 1805[1] I landed at lower Haslow [Halstow] in Kent on Sunday afternoon last—a few hundred yards from a curious little Chapel, which being open and no one in it I hurried to—& offered, I trust, as deep a prayer as ever without words or thoughts was sent up by a human Being—Very, very ill I was at my setting off from Leghorn / not one meal in ten, little as I eat, could I retain on my stomach / and we had 55 days aboard ship / & what I suffered even to the last day, may the worst of men only ever feel. Had not the Captain loved me as he often said better than a Brother, & performed all the offices of a Nurse, I could not have survived—so obstinate was my costiveness, & so alarming the effect of purgative medicines / No doubt, my silly horror of having an Enēma performed on me, greatly increased the sum of my sufferings; perhaps, if I had consented to have had one or even two every day, I might have suffered but little / whereas, I own with shame, but in part this was owing to the exceeding despondency of my mind, I had it not above a dozen times / I had had the fore-thought to purchase an instrument, & was assured that I could administer it myself—but partly owing to the instrument, and partly to the Nature of the obstruction—tho' the Captain was the strongest man on board—it used to take all the force of his arm, & bring the blood up in his face before he could finish / once I brought off more than a pint of blood—& three times he clearly saved my Life.—I detail these shocking circumstances to you & my wife in order that you may feel part of the gratitude which I am ever to do.—Tho' as proud and Jealous an American as ever even America produced, he would come and even with tears in his eyes beg and pray me to have an enēma / & strange it is!—but tho' the pain is so trifling that it is almost a

[1] Presumably, Coleridge refers to the time when he first learned of John Wordsworth's death, i.e. 31 Mar. 1805.

( 1176 )

misnomer to call it pain, yet my dread of and antipathy increased every time /—However, almost immediately after my landing Health seemed to flow in upon me, like the mountain waters upon the dry stones of a vale-stream after Rains. And I can safely say, that for 16 months I have never enjoyed four *days* of such Health, as I have had since Sunday Afternoon—& my nights have been unusually good.—My body is quite open—& tho' I do not respire freely, yet I respire with comparative ease.—One night indeed I was awakened with the old *knock* of the Head, & was very bad indeed for three Hours with hysterical Wind—but I attribute this to a little imprudence in drinking off—from thirst I did not perceive it—some stale beer instead of Porter——& it's long continuance was entirely to my being without assistance without hot water, or ether, or indeed any thing but the water in the wash-bason ——With great care, meat, potatoes, porter—& dissolved meat once an hour so as always to keep off faintness, I shall do—But whether it does, I live or die at home—I am now going to Lamb's—Stuart is at Margate / all are out of town / I have no one to advise me—I am shirtless, & almost penniless—but money I can get immediately—My *MSS* are all—excepting two pocket-books—either in the Sea, or (as is the case with $\frac{9}{10}$ths) carried back to Malta—I will try to write again before night—I will come as soon as I can come.

S. T. Coleridge

## 623. *To Daniel Stuart*

*Address*: D. Stuart Esqre. | Mrs Humble's | [Bo]arding House | Margate
*MS. British Museum. Pub. with omis.* Letters from the Lake Poets, *57.* The bottom of pages 3 and 4 of the holograph is cut off.
*Postmark*: 22 August 1806.

Friday Morning [22 August 1806]

My dear Stuart

Your Letter of this morning is not [to] be answered by *words.* There are acts of friendship where it is better not to give birth even to the whole of the inward *feelings* appropriate to them / what does not pass forth, remains within, and it's own stillness sinks more securely into us, & becomes one with our habitual Being. I shall avail myself of your kind offer of your House at Brompton tomorrow—chiefly for fear that Wordsworth may come up to town, after me. Otherwise I should not hesitate to come down to you without delay—for indeed, indeed, I sorely want counsel in many things—but in some I want counsel which none but you, of my friends, *can* give me.——Fortunately, I had perused with attention the few political papers, which I had with me aboard ship, the very day before the Spanish Privateer Ruffian boarded us—& which occasioned & indeed necessitated the Captain to throw overboard his & my papers promiscuously—so that the contents, tho' not the language, are fresh in my memory—I likewise contrived to preserve two pocket-books, full of memoranda, each as large as a large duodecimo Volume, and a valuable paper on the present state of Egypt much fuller of facts & more sober reasoning, than the one written for Sir A. B. to be sent to the ministry—I collected every fact from respectable Eye-witnesses, & not a few from Selim Effendi, the Mamaluke Minister at Malta, with whom I was very intimate—For the rest of my papers I must wait, till they come from Malta, & ought to be thankful, that Noble made his escape with him [them?], & that they are not now (mangled & distorted) brought to birth in the Moniteur bit by bit by the forceps of some literary Accoucheur in Paris—My Health improves wonderfully. My Captain to whom I owe my Life, and who saw me this morning, could scarcely believe his eyes—Almost immediately on my Landing Health seemed to flow in upon me like mountain waters upon the dusty pebbles of a Vale-stream after long-wanted Rains. In short, tho' no emolument could ever force me again to the business, intrigue, form and pomp of a public situation, yet beyond all doubt I have acquired a great variety of useful knowlege, quickness in discovering men's characters, and adroitness in dealing with them / I have learnt the *inside* character of many eminent living men / & know by heart the awkward & wicked machinery, by which all our affairs *abroad* are carried on / In short, if I recover a steady tho' imperfect Health, I perhaps should have no reason to regret my long Absence, not even my perilous detention in Italy—for by my regula[r atten]tion to the best of the good things in Rom[e,] and associating almost wholly with the Artists of acknowleged highest reputation I acquired more insight into the fine arts in the three months, than I could have done in England in 20 years.

. . . This, this perpetual Struggle, and endless *heart-wasting*, was at the bottom of all my irresolution, procrastination, languor, and former detestable habit of poison-taking—: this turned me away so long from political and moral disquisition, poetry, and all the flowers & herbs that grow in the Light and Sunshine—to be meanwhile a Delver in the unwholesome quick-silver mines of abstruse Metaphysics. . . .[1]

I am, my dear Stuart, gratefully, as I ought to be,

S. T. Coleridge[2]

[1] Stuart's endorsement on the manuscript, 'Coleridge 1806 wife', indicates the subject-matter of the missing parts of this letter.

[2] The last sentence and the signature no longer appear on the holograph and are drawn from *Letters from the Lake Poets*, 60.

15 September 1806

## 624. To Daniel Stuart

*Address*: D. Stuart, Esqre | Post-Office | Margate
*MS*. British Museum. *Pub. with omis*. Letters, ii. 505.
*Postmark*: 15 September 1806.

Monday [15 September 1806]

My dear Stuart

I arrived in town safe; but so tired by the next evening, that I went to bed at 9 and slept till past 12, on Sunday.—I cannot keep off my mind from the last subject, we were talking about; tho' I have brought my notions concerning it to hang so well on the Balance, that I have in my own judgment few doubts as to the relative weight of the arguments persuasive and dissuasive. But of this 'face to face'. I sleep at the Courier Office: and shall institute & carry on the enquiry into the characters of Mr Pitt and Mr Fox; and having carried it to the Treaty of Amiens, or rather to the recommencement of the war, I propose to give a full and severe critique of 'the enquiry into the state of the Nation'—taking it for granted that this Work does on the whole contain Mr Fox's latest political creed / and this for the purpose of answering the M. Chronicle's assertions, that Mr Fox was the greatest & wisest Statesman/ that Mr Pitt was no Statesman—/ I shall endeavor to shew, that both were undeserving of that high character; but that Mr Pitt was the better / that the evils, which befel him, were undoubtedly produced in great measure, by blunders and wickedness on the continent, which it was almost impossible to foresee / while the effects of Mr Fox's measures must in and of themselves produce calamity and degradation.[1]—

To confess the Truth I am by no means pleased with Mr Street's[2] character of Mr Fox, as a Speaker and man of Intellect / As a piece of panegyric, it falls woefully short of the article in the M. Chronicle in style and selection of thoughts; and runs at least equally far beyond the bounds of Truth.—Persons who write in a hurry are very liable to contract a sort of snipt convulsive style, that moves forward by short repeated *Pushes*, with isochronous asthmatic Pants. He:— He:— He:— He: or the like, beginning a dozen short sentences, each making a period. In this way a man can get rid of all that happens at any one time to be in his memory, with very little choice in the arrangement, and no expenditure of Logic in the Connection.—However, it is the matter more than the

---

[1] No prose contributions to the *Courier* for this period have been identified. Charles James Fox died 13 Sept. 1806; William Pitt, the younger, had died on 23 Jan. of the same year.

[2] T. J. Street was joint proprietor of the *Courier* with Daniel Stuart.

manner, that displeased me—for fear, that what I shall write for tomorrow's Courier, may involve a kind of Contradiction. To one outrageous passage I persuaded him to add a note of amendment: as it was too late to alter the article itself. It was impossible for me, seeing him satisfied with the article himself, to say more—than that he appeared to me to have exceeded in eulogy. But beyond doubt in the political position occupied by the Courier, with so little danger of being anticipated by the other papers in any thing which it *ought* to say, except some obvious points which being common to all the papers can give credit to none—it would have been better to have announced his Death and simply led [the] way for an after disquisition, by a sort of shy disclosure, with an appearance of *suppression*, of the Spirit, with which it would be conducted.

There are Letters at the Post-office, Margate, for me. Be so good, as to send them to me directed to the Courier Office. I think of going to Mr Smith's[1] to morrow or not at all. Whether Mr Fox's Death will keep Mr S. in town, or call him there, I do not know.—— At all events, I shall return by the time of your arrival.

May God bless you. I am ever, my dear Sir! as your obliged, so your affectionately grateful Friend

S. T. Coleridge

P.S. My respectful Compliments to your Sister.—

### 625. *To Mrs. S. T. Coleridge*

*Address*: Mrs Coleridge | Keswick | Cumberland    *Single Sheet*
MS. Lord Latymer. *Pub. with omis.* Letters, ii. 507.
*Postmark*: 16 September 1806.

16 Sept. 1806

My dear Sara

I had determined on my arrival in town to write to you at full, the moment I could settle my affairs, and speak decisively of myself. Unfortunately, Mr Stuart was at Margate / and what with my Journeys to & fro, day has passed on after day—Heaven knows, counted by me in sickness of heart. I am now obliged to return to Parndon to Mr W. Smith's—at whose house Mr & Mrs Clarkson are, & where I spent 3 or 4 days a fortnight ago. The reason at present is that Lord Howick[2] has sent a very polite message to me thro' Mr Smith, expressing his desire to make my

---

[1] William Smith (1756–1835), M.P. for Norwich, lived at Parndon, Essex.
[2] Charles Grey (1764–1845), Lord Howick, became First Lord of the Admiralty in Jan. 1806, and not long after Fox's death, Secretary for Foreign Affairs. See Letter 627.

*16 September 1806*

acquaintance. To this I have many objections: which I want to discuss with Mr S. / and at all events, I had rather go with him to his Lordship's than by myself. Likewise, I have had an application from the R. Institution for a Course of Lectures,[1] which I am much disposed to accept, both for money and reputation.—In short, I must stay in Town till Friday Sen'night: for Mr Stuart returns to Town on Monday next, and he relies on my being there for a very interesting private concern of his own, in which he needs both my council and assistance.—But on Friday Sennight, please God! I shall quit Town / and trust to be at Keswick on Monday, Sept. 29th. If I finally accept the Lectures, I must return by the midst of November; but propose to take you and Hartley with me, as we may be sure of Rooms either in Mr Stuart's House at Knight's Bridge, or in the Strand.—My purpose is to divide my time steadily between my [']Reflections moral and political grounded on Information obtained during two years resident in Italy and the Mediterranean': and the Lectures on the Principles common to all the Fine Arts. It is a terrible misfortune that so many important papers are not in my power, and that I must wait for Stoddart's care & alertness: which I am sorry to say, is not to be relied on. However, it is well that they are not at Paris.

My heart akes so cruelly that I do not dare trust myself to the writing of any tenderness either to you, my dear![2] or to our dear children. Be assured, I feel with deep tho' sad affection toward you;

---

[1] Coleridge did not begin his lectures at the Royal Institution until 15 Jan. 1808, and the subject was shifted from 'Principles common to the Fine Arts' to 'the Principles of Poetry'.

[2] Whatever Coleridge was writing to Mrs. Coleridge, and his letters seem affectionate enough, he wrote far differently to others. The Wordsworths were busy with letters concerning his domestic problems, and the Lambs, too, had become involved. (See *Middle Years*, i. 63, 65–67, and *Lamb Letters*, ii. 19–22.) 'Yesterday I wrote', said Mary Lamb to Dorothy Wordsworth on 29 Aug. 1806, 'anxiously longing for Mr. Wordsworth and Mr. Southey to endeavour to bring Mrs. C. to consent to a separation and to day I think of the letter I received from Mrs. Coleridge, telling me, as joyful news, that her husband is arrived, and I feel it very wrong in me even in the remotest degree to do anything to prevent her seeing that husband—she and her husband being the only people who ought to be concerned in the affair.' And Wordsworth, writing to Sir George Beaumont in Sept. 1806, had this to say: 'In fact, he dare not go home, he recoils so much from the thought of domesticating with Mrs. Coleridge, with whom, though on many accounts he much respects her, he is so miserable that he dare not encounter it. What a deplorable thing!'

Coleridge's letter to Mrs. Coleridge was apparently written at Mary Lamb's insistence. 'You must positively must write to Mrs. Coleridge this day, and you must write here, that I may know you write, or you must come and dictate a letter for me to write to her. . . . A letter from me or you *shall go today*.' Mary Lamb to Coleridge, Sept. 1806.

& hold your character in general in more than mere esteem, in reverence. My Health continues pretty good; but so dreadful were the oppressions, evacuations & loss of Blood on board Ship, and so regular the rejection of my food with discolored Bile, that both my Stomach and Bowels are excessively *sore*—and any thing that affects and saddens makes my poor inside *ake* with the oddest sensation of bodily and mental pain blended. I do not gather strength so fast as I had expected; but this I attribute to my very great anxiety. I am indeed *very feeble*; but after 55 days of such horrors following the dreary heart-wasting of a year & more, it is a wonder that I am as I am.

I sent you from Malta 110£ / and a duplicate in a second Letter. If you have not received it, the Triplicate is either at Malta or on it's way from thence. I *had sent* another 100£; but by Elliot's villainous treatment of me was obliged to recall it. But these are trifles.

Mr Clarkson is come; & is about to take me down to Parndon (Mr S.'s Country Seat in Essex, about 20 miles from Town)—I shall return by Sunday or Monday / & my address, S. T. Coleridge, Esqre. No/ 348, Strand, London.

My grateful Love to Southey: and blessings on his little one.——
And May God Almighty preserve you, my dear!

And your faithful, tho' long
absent, Husband
S. T. Coleridge

### 626. To Mrs. S. T. Coleridge

*Address*: Mrs Coleridge | Keswick | Cumberland
*MS. Lord Latymer. Hitherto unpublished.*
*Postmark*: ⟨26⟩ September ⟨1806⟩.

Friday Afternoon / [26 September 1806]
My dear Love

Now that it wants but a few minutes of 5, I have just found your Letter—& can only say, that in consequence of having been disappointed in seeing Lord Howick on the day appointed, I am *obliged* to stay over Monday——and that I entreat you not to expect me by the Hour or the day—I hope & *expect* to leave London on Monday Night—in the Mail——but I greatly dread travelling two nights, my legs and ancles swell so.—God bless you all,

for ever and ever /
S. T. Coleridge

I have just received a letter from Lord & Lady Holland[1]—but this will not detain me an hour——Lord Howick's is so far a business of importance that I can not neglect it without offending both him & Mr Smith.—

## 627. To Mrs. S. T. Coleridge

*Address*: Mrs Coleridge | Keswick | Cumberland
*MS. Lord Latymer. Pub. E.L.G. i. 341.*
*Postmark*: 29 September 1806.

Monday afternoon—[29 September 1806]

My dear Sara

I am fretted almost out of all patience. But that we are to meet so soon, I would detail to you my disappointment in calling on Lord Howick; and the circumstances which have almost compelled me not to abandon the attempt, tho' it was always against my inclinations, & tho' I never expected any thing from it.[2] As to Sine Cure Places, or Pensions, they are out of the question, for any but noblemen's Sons, or the relations of men with great Parliamentary Interest / and as to active secretaryships, and all those situations which imply the continual subjection of one's own intellect to the views & purposes of another, I know them too well already / and 500 or even 1000£ a year would be a poor Compensation.—However, I had made up my mind that I had done all that Mr Smith could expect of me; & had prepared every thing for departure, when another accursed Rub has intervened——the American Captain with unaccountable Delay & Breach of Promise has not sent my Books, & *MSS*—with other trifles—and if I go out of town without them, I am almost sure to lose them / which would be absolutely irreparable—

Be assured, that to leave London is the strongest wish, of which a mind and body so enfeebled as mine, is capable—I intreat you not to be depressed or agitated by Delays, which I cannot avoid. Indeed, it has so much deranged my Health, & disquieted my Sleep, that—unless I am to come to you with sick Stomach and swoln Limbs, I must stay on the Road—I intend therefore to go to Parndon tomorrow morning, to stay there one day; from thence to go to Cambridge, and from thence to the great North Road—

[1] Lord Holland (1773–1840), Fox's nephew, became a member of the Privy Council on 27 Aug. 1806, and entered the Cabinet as Lord Privy Seal on 15 Oct.

[2] Coleridge later wrote to Josiah Wedgwood that he was 'sent for by Lord Howick in consequence of my conversations with Mr W. Smith; but his Lordship's Porter repelled me from his door with gross Insult, and took my Letter even with a broad Hint, that he should not deliver it'.

and to contrive matters so that I may not have to sit up more than one night in the Coach—

I cannot express to you, what a dreadful Damp your account of the Children's ages threw on my Spirits—I could scarcely breath for more than an Hour after. But may the Almighty look down on them, & make their years a blessing to them. I love them so, that I retire back from the sense of the exceeding love, I bear them, like a coward—I seem to myself too weak to bear the burthen of my own Heart. But let me hope that the evils of Life are passing off— and that I shall have blue Sky in among the moving Clouds.

I should have called on George [Fricker] to day; but it has rained incessantly, and I am not quite as well even as usual. I hear a very good account of him.

I would to God, I could tell you positively the day when I shall be at Keswick. Be assured, nothing will detain me even an hour short of ill-consequences that would cast a gloom over my arrival. For however declining I may feel myself *within*, I very much wish to present an outward appearance of Health & Strength / I visit no body in London; but C. and M. Lamb—and have not been to one public Place.—

Let me intreat you, my dear Wife! again and again not to fret yourself at these delays more than you can help. If the Books were not absolutely necessary to me, I should leave the business to C. Lamb—altho' I could not even then do it with prudence, for Charles is a very bad negociator, and an impatient Commissary. My grateful Love to Southey—and kind remembrances to Mr Jackson & Mrs Wilson. O my dear Hartley!——Affectionately your Husband,

S. T. Coleridge.

### 628. *To Captain Derkheim*

*Address*: Captn Derkheim | of the American Ship, Gosport, | off | *Deal*
MS. Lord Latymer. Pub. *E.L.G. i. 344.* This letter did not reach Captain Derkheim of the *Gosport.* See next letter.

30 Septr 1806   348, Strand, London

Dear Sir

I am so much affected by your setting sail without leaving either my books, or a single Line to direct me concerning the trunk that was put in Quarantine, that it is with a heart of anguish that I attempt to congratulate you on your marriage: tho' I most sincerely wish you all happiness. Indeed grievous as the loss of the books is to me—of books that can be neither useful nor amusing to you—and tho' this loss will entirely deprive me of the power of giving my intended Lectures, to the loss of 150£ at least—yet still I seem to suffer more than all from the perplexed and distracted state of mind, into which I have been thrown. When I recall your kindness to me on board the Gosport, and your constant promises / & then again think of my urgent and almost *begging* Letters to you—& that you never could take the trouble even of letting me know definitely where my Books & other little things were—my hearts sinks within me!—I cannot bear to express indignation, lest I should accuse myself as ungrateful—I can not bear to think of my gratitude, lest I should rouse up a sense of your cruelty.

I have little hope that this will find you—or that, if it does, you will give me an answer.—Yet I conjure you by your own peace of mind to write me one Line—just to let me know where the Trunk is—& where the loose Books. Any thing else—as the Attar of Roses—you are welcome to / but these can be of no use to you and are invaluable to me. I called by advice of the good woman of the Coffee House on Mr Busher, 7 Catherine St; did not see him but saw his Wife; who seemed to enjoy my loss as a *good thing.*—I cannot but persuade myself that you have left them somewhere or other for me / I shall therefore call with Mr Sharp or some other merchant of character on Mr Le Mesurier or Anderson to make enquiry.

However it be, I wish nevertheless that Heaven may protect you, and that those, of whom you think highly & affectionately, may never treat you with neglect & injury.

S. T. Coleridge

## 629. *To Mrs. S. T. Coleridge*

*Address*: Mrs Coleridge | Keswick | Cumberland
*MS. Lord Latymer. Pub. E.L.G. i. 345.*

[2 October 1806][1]

My dear Love

I have been sitting in a thorough *mope* for the whole day, not knowing what to do; and every now and then resolving that I would go & seek a place in the Mail for to night, spite of all that Prudence or the state of my Health could suggest to the Contrary. The idea of so frequently disappointing you harrasses me insufferably. But alas! I have a doleful tale to relate. I have acquainted you with what tenderness Captn Derkheim treated me during my long Voyage from Leghorn, and that I have reason to believe that

---

[1] This date is established by the reference in the next letter to 'my Letter of yesterday'. The postmark is illegible.

I owe my Life to him / When I quitted his Ship at Stangate Creek, with a prejudice against Smuggling almost peculiar to Americans & arising out of the happy state of a new Country under a republican Government, he persuaded me not to take my loose Books (some 40 volumes) nor my trunk of books & other valuables, on shore with me, which by connivance of the Custom-house Officers, whom we had bribed, I could easily have done—as my Companion actually did, without the slightest difficulty. These of course were to be first quarantined, and then sent to the Custom-house. The Captain repeatedly entreated me not to take the least concern / that it was altogether unsuited to my exceeding weakness, both of body and spirits—that he would do the whole—the loose books he would himself bring out of the Ship, by 4s and fives at a time—& that he would see me every day—and as soon as the Trunk could be got out of the Custom House, he would get it, settle for it, & send it to the Courier Office.—Among my scanty property there were about a dozen pieces of Roman Pearls—each sufficient for two large double necklaces & a pair of Bracelets—and 5 bottles of Ottar of White Roses, which were presented to me by the Minister of the Dey of Tunis, as a mark of acknowlegement for my having pleaded for the Dey in the Court of Admiralty at Malta.—These of course I had designed for you—not indeed for your own use—but that you might make little presents of them / especially, I meant you to have sent all the Ottar of Roses—except one bottle—to Lady Beaumont / for the Ottar of WHITE Roses is more than tenfold the value of the other, dear & scarce as both are, when genuine / & indeed is not to get once in 20 years in this country. However, observing that the Captn often admired the Roman Pearls, & be[ing] wholly penniless, I thought, that my shewing myself grateful to a man, who had preserved my Life, would give you more pleasure, than the giving away the Pearls yourself—I therefore begged him to accept of them / but reserved the Attar of Roses, which (I know) he got out of the Ship. It irks me to tell you the sequel—instead of calling on me, every day—he only dined with me once—I was always fagging after him in vain, & have written no less than four letters of almost passionate entreaty, for my *books* as I could not give my lectures without them / I received two strange evasive answers—the last acknowleging but excusing his neglect by the fact, that he had been courting a Lady & was married—but all things he would settle with me, face to face—I waited three or four days, anxiously expecting to see him / at length, over borne with anxiety & suspense I went after him on Tuesday—& lo! he had *sailed* on the Sunday Morning, without leaving a Line for me, or speaking a word concerning my property to his Wife or Wife's relations. I sent a Letter to him inclosed by Mr Street in one to his Correspondent at Deal—the Cor: found that the Ship had passed that very morning with a fair wind / but after met his wife—who knew nothing of the business, & only said—Good God! Mr Coleridge is an intimate friend of Captain Derkheim's—

The anxiety, fatigue, walking in wet shoes to Tower Hill & back, & above all the shocking Struggle between Indignation & Gratitude proved too much for me/ and I was obliged to keep my bed till yester evening—& am still quite a bewildered man. The loss is very serious to me in many respects—and I can only explain it by supposing, that he had given away the Attar of Roses to his mistress, & was ashamed to see me afterwards. I have only one chance, that of searching the Custom House for my Books—but I am wholly unable to do it myself, & can find no friend to do it for me / Likewise, more than half my Cloathes are at Parndon, so that I have not now even a clean Shirt—What can I do, my Love?— Be assured, nothing you can suffer, is one 4th of what I suffer in consequence of this Delay.—I will write again to morrow. God bless you, my dear Love! & your Husband

S. T. C.

### 630. To Mrs. S. T. Coleridge

*Address*: Mrs Coleridge | Keswick | Cumberland
*MS. Lord Latymer. Pub. E.L.G. i. 347.*
*Postmark*: 3 October 1806.

Friday Afternoon [3 October 1806]

My dear Love

Tho' the state of my Health in addition to the unfortunate, indeed distressing, accident which I detailed to you in my Letter of yesterday, must I am sure appear to you not merely justifying, but even necessitating, causes of mine & your disappointment, yet I am anxious that you should know the whole of my plans. Davy had been for many days urging me, with an eagerness and importunity not common to him, to go with him to Mr Bernard's[1] at Roehampton, as to day. This I had as firmly refused, stating the impropriety of so frequently vexing & disappointing you—& my own eagerness to be with you, & my Children. Since however I have been absolutely prevented from going off at the time proposed, [and] as the business is really important—no less indeed than that of laying a plan of my giving Lectures every winter both

---

[1] Thomas Bernard (1750–1818), the philanthropist, set on foot the plan of the Royal Institution in 1799. He succeeded to the baronetcy in 1810 on the death of his brother.

at the Royal and London Institutions, & mainly assisting in a work to be published at the latter, from all which it seems probable that I [shall] make a respectable annuity of perhaps 400£ a year, I at length consented—shall return on Sunday Morning—on Monday shall go certainly (if I can move at all) to Parndon, where I have left almost all my cloathes / & having in respect to common politeness stayed one day, shall go to Cambridge & from thence make the best of my way to Keswick. Of course, it is impossible to state the day or hour of my arrival; and I do trust, that it is not necessary for me to add, that I will not make a minute's unnecessary Delay. —This Shock both to my plans & feelings from the misconduct of the American has done my poor Health serious Injury—I still feel like a bewildered man—Tobin informed [me] two days ago that he had received (if I mistake not) a letter from dear Southey, strongly disapproving of my scheme of giving Lectures.[1] I wish, he had written to me, & let me know his reasons. Something (he knows) I must do, & that immediately, to get money—& this seems both the most respectable, & the least unconnected with my more serious literary plans / if —which I should be glad to be less sceptical concerning—Providence enable me to live long enough. And if I should die, as soon as I feel probable, it seems the most likely mode of distinguishing myself so as to leave Patrons for you & my Children.

But when I arrive, we can talk this over. A single course can do me no great harm.——Stuart (who is indeed and indeed a kind and earnest Friend to me) strongly & warmly

The Coach—
S. T. Coleridge

## 631. *To George Fricker*

Pub. Rem. *337.*

Saturday afternoon. [4 October 1806][2]

My dear young friend,

I am sorry that you should have felt any delicacy in disclosing to me your religious feelings, as rendering it inconsistent with your tranquillity of mind to spend the Sunday evening with me. Though

---

[1] Wordsworth was equally opposed to Coleridge's plan to lecture. In a letter to Coleridge dated 7 Nov. 1806, he writes: 'I write now to entreat that you would not on any account entangle yourself with any engagement to give Lectures in London, and to recommend your coming hither [to Coleorton] where you may sit down at leisure and look about you before you decide.' From a transcript of Wordsworth's letter made by E. H. Coleridge.

[2] Although Cottle suggests 1807 as the date of this letter, Letter 633 settles the matter.

I do not find in that book, which we both equally revere, any command, either express, or which I can infer, which leads me to attach any criminality to cheerful and innocent social intercourse on the Lord's day; though I do not find that it was in the least degree forbidden to the Jews on their Sabbath; and though I have been taught by Luther, and the great founders of the Church of England, that the Sabbath was a part of the ceremonial and transitory parts of the law given by heaven to Moses; and that our Sunday is binding on our consciences, chiefly from its manifest and most awful usefulness, and indeed moral necessity; yet I highly commend your firmness in what you think right, and assure you solemnly, that I esteem you greatly for it. I would much rather that you should have too much, than an atom too little. I am far from surprised that, having seen what you have seen, and suffered what you have suffered, you should have opened your soul to a sense of our fallen nature; and the incapability of man to heal himself. My opinions may not be in all points the same as yours; but I have experienced a similar alteration. I was for many years a Socinian; and at times almost a Naturalist, but sorrow, and ill health, and disappointment in the only deep wish I had ever cherished, forced me to look into myself; I read the New Testament again, and I became fully convinced, that Socinianism was not only not the doctrine of the New Testament, but that it scarcely deserved the name of a religion in any sense. An extract from a letter which I wrote a few months ago to a sceptical friend, who had been a Socinian, and of course rested all the evidences of Christianity on miracles, to the exclusion of grace and inward faith, will perhaps, surprise you, as showing you how much nearer our opinions are than what you must have supposed. 'I fear that the mode of defending Christianity, adopted by Grotius first; and latterly, among many others, by Dr. Paley, has increased the number of infidels;—never could it have been so great, if thinking men had been habitually led to look into their own souls, instead of always looking out, both of themselves, and of their nature. If to curb attack, such as yours on miracles, it had been answered:—Well, brother! but granting these miracles to have been in part the growth of delusion at the time, and of exaggeration afterward, yet still all the doctrines will remain untouched by this circumstance, and binding on thee. Still must thou repent and be regenerated, and be crucified to the flesh; and this not by thy own mere power; but by a mysterious action of the moral Governor on thee; of the Ordo-ordinians, the Logos, or Word. Still will the eternal filiation, or Sonship of the Word from the Father; still will the Trinity of the Deity, the redemption, and the thereto necessary assumption of humanity by the Word, "who is with God, and is God," remain truths: and still will the vital head-and-heart FAITH in these truths, be the living and only fountain of all true virtue. Believe all these, and with the grace of the spirit consult your own heart, in quietness and humility, they will furnish you with proofs, that surpass all understanding, because they are felt and known; believe all these I say, so as that thy faith shall be not merely real in the acquiescence of the intellect; but actual, in the thereto assimilated affections; then shalt thou KNOW from God, whether or not Christ be of God. But take notice, I only say, the miracles are extra essential; I by no means deny their importance, much less hold them useless, or superfluous. Even as Christ did, so would I teach; that is, build the miracle on the faith, not the faith on the miracle.'

May heaven bless you, my dear George, and | Your affectionate friend,

S. T. C.

## 632. *To Mrs. S. T. Coleridge*

*Address*: Mrs Coleridge | Keswick | Cumberland
*MS. Lord Latymer. Pub. E.L.G. i. 349.*
*Postmark*: 9 October 1806.

Thursday [9 October 1806]

My dear Sara

Tho' still disappointed with regard to the portion of Books, which I have happily recovered from my Loss, by their having been in a Trunk containing property of Mr Russel and which Trunk was marked with his name / I am resolved to delay no longer—but to act by Letters. I came from Parndon this morning, in order to receive & send off by the waggon all I had recovered & whatever was not immediately necessary to me / in this I have been *vexatiously* disappointed / for 2 or 3 of the Books & a collection of Prints from the Fresco Works of Raphael I shall want *instantly*—however spite of it I am about to return to Parndon this same afternoon / & tomorrow leave it with poor dear Mrs Clarkson, whom I shall leave at Bury on Saturday—& thence take the very first stage to Awkenbury [Alconbury?] Hill—& thence to Keswick—My own Health makes an interrupted Journey almost necessary / & common humanity of common friendship would find in Mrs Clarkson's state a motive to go out of my road twenty miles—Her husband & Child cannot go with her / & she so earnestly entreated me that I neither *could* nor *dared* refuse her.

This continual off & on has injured my Health, & almost drain'd my purse.—I have at length agreed to lecture at the Royal Institution on the Principles common to the Fine Arts; & am to receive 120£ for the course—I am in some hopes that (if not now) yet in another year I may be able to join on to this a Lectureship of more Importance at the London Institution. The opportunity of giving Hartley opportunities of Instruction, he would not otherwise have, weighs a great deal with me—

Your Brother is a very good young man / & I am very much pleased with him indeed. He is not a whit the worse for his Methodism—

Our sweet Children! God bless them & us! | Your faithful Husband,
S. T. Coleridge

I ought to have seen Mr Sharp / but I cannot endure any more to disappoint you & myself—

Never forget to tell Southey, that I never suspend my affectionate Remembrance of him / & that I enjoy his fair fame like a breeze on my own feverish Forehead. Indeed, his reputation is so high as to deserve the name of Fame / Malthus has just published an appendix in answer to his Review—he told Mrs Smith, that he had attributed the Review to Mrs Bare-bald, but now found it was Mr Southey. He praised the power of the Review, but abominated it's temper. —Did S. find any likeness in W. Scott's Lay of the l. M. to Christabel?[1] I have not read the L. myself; but at least half a dozen (among others Davy, Lamb, Mrs Clarkson, Miss Smith) have mentioned it to me.[2] I do not believe it.

[1] Speaking of Scott's *Lay*, which appeared early in 1805, Southey wrote to Wynn: 'The beginning of the story is too like Coleridge's Christobell, which he [Scott] had seen; the very line, "Jesu Maria, shield her well!" is caught from it. When you see the Christobell, you will not doubt that Scott has imitated it; I do not think designedly, but the echo was in his ear, not for emulation, but *propter amorem*. This only refers to the beginning, which you will perceive attributes more of magic to the lady than seems in character with the rest of the story.' *Life and Corres.* ii. 316.

[2] Dorothy Wordsworth, too, felt that 'the resemblance between certain parts of the *Lay of the last Minstrel* and *Christabel* must strike everyone who is acquainted with the two poems'; and she added: 'My Brother and Sister think that the Lay being published first, it will tarnish the freshness of *Christabel*, and considerably injure the first effect of it.' *Early Letters*, 533–4.

Coleridge gave Stoddart a copy of *Christabel*, presumably in 1801. Subsequently, in 1802 Stoddart recited the poem to Scott, who was so taken with it that in 1803, when the Wordsworths called on him in Scotland, he told them he could repeat much of the poem himself and that at the time he heard Stoddart recite *Christabel*, 'he had begun his poem and was much delighted to meet with so happy a specimen of the same kind of irregular metre which he had adopted'. The Wordsworths 'were struck with the resemblance' to *Christabel*, and Wordsworth was later to blame himself for not mentioning to Scott 'that the style of his Poem had been, and would be in its future progress, influenced by this acquaintance with *Christabel*'. It was not until 1830 that Scott himself

## 633. To George Fricker

*Address*: Mr G. Fricker | No/ 4 Castle Court | Budge Row—
MS. Lord Latymer. Pub. E.L.G. i. 351.
*Postmark*: 9 October 1806.

My dear George                    Thursday Afternoon, [9 October 1806]

Mr Russel's Friend / a Mr Austwick, who is Clerk at Russel's Waggon Office at the Bell (*or Bull*?) in Friday Street, Cheapside, had undertaken to get out the Trunk—& Mr R. promised most positively Monday afternoon that it should be left here the next day or Wednesday at the farthest—And lo! it is not here.—I wish, you would call on Mr Austwick—there will be no money to pay—& giving my best compliments in a respectful manner (I mean, so as to imply *my* respect for him, which he really deserves, as well as that which you always & of your own nature pay to every man) entreat him to send it with all convenient speed by the *Kendal* Waggon to me, at Keswick: above all, not forgetting the engravings from Rafael, which Mr Russel promised to leave for me, as well as a *List* of his other Things.

I fear, you rather misunderstood one part of my Letter. I by no means gave that extract, as containing the whole of my Christian Faith; but as comprising such doctrines, as a clear Head & honest Heart assisted by divine Grace might in part discover by self-examination and the light of natural conscience, & which *efficiently* and *practically* believed would prepare the way for the *peculiar Doctrine* of Christianity, namely, Salvation by the Cross of Christ. I meant these doctrines as the Skeleton, to which the death & Mediation of Christ with the supervention of the Holy Ghost were to add the Flesh, and Blood, Muscles, nerves, & vitality.——God of his goodness grant, that I may arrive at a more living Faith in these last, than I now feel. What I now feel is only a very strong *presentiment* of their Truth and Importance aided by a thorough conviction of the hollowness of all other Systems. Alas! my moral being is too untranquil, too deeply possessed by one lingering passion after an earthly good withheld— & probably withheld by divine goodness —from me, to be capable of being that, which it's own 'still small voice' tells me, even in my dreams, that it ought to be, yet of itse[lf] cannot be. Indeed, I am at times on the brink of obdurate despair

---

'openly announced, that the metre of *Christabel* suggested and determined the metre of the *Lay*, and that he was "bound to make the acknowledgment due from the pupil to his master"'. Ibid. 533, and *Christabel*, ed. by E. H. Coleridge, 1907, pp. 44–45.

## 9 October 1806

—& am kept from it often by the wish of warning others.—I hope to converse with you shortly—if God spare my Life——

I pray you, never talk of your obligations to me. Solemnly, I know of none. The Lambs are always happy to see you—& if you have indeed no other objection to visiting them often, besides that mentioned by you, *that*, my dear George, is alike unworthy of yourself, & of their kind & open nature. I am never ashamed to accept of that, which (circumstances reversed) I am conscious, I should find it my *duty* to give. Your affect: Friend,

S. T. Coleridge

P.S. I leave Parndon (to which I now hasten) tomorrow, & go by slow journeys to Keswick.

I have opened the letter to beg you, on second thoughts, not to do any thing unless you hear from me again.

### 634. *To Thomas Clarkson*

*Address*: For | T. Clarkson, Esqre | Mr. Wm. Allen's | Plough Court | Lombard Street | London
*MS. John Crerar Lib. Pub. E.L.G. i. 352.*
*Postmark*: 16 October 18⟨06⟩. *Stamped*: Bury.

13 Oct. 1806.[1] Bury St Edmonds

My dear Sir

You have proposed to me questions not more awful than difficult of Solution. What metaphysically the Spirit of God *is*? What the Soul? What the difference between the Reason, and the Understanding ($νοῦς\ καὶ\ ἐπιστήμη$: Vernunft, und Verstand) and how metaphysically we may explain St Paul's assertion, that the Spirit of God bears witness to the Spirit of man?—In the first place I must reduce the two first questions to the *form* of the 3rd and fourth. What the Spirit of God *is*, and what the Soul *is*, I dare not suppose myself capable of *conceiving*: according to my religious and philosophical creed they are *known* by those, to whom they are revealed, even (tho' in a higher and deeper degree) as color (blue for instance); or motion; or the difference between the Spirals of the Hop-plant and the Scarlet Bean. *Datur*, non intelligitur. They can only be explained by images, that themselves require the same explanation, as in the latter Instance, that the one turns to the right, the other to the Left, the one is with, the other against the Sun: i.e. by relative & dependent, not positive and fundamental, notions. The only reasonable form of question appears to me to be, under what

[1] As the last paragraph shows, this letter was completed on Wednesday, 15 Oct. 1806.

connection of ideas we may so conceive and express ourselves concerning them, as that there shall be no inconsistency to be detected in our definitions, and no falsehood felt during their enunciation, which might war with our internal sense of their actuality. And in this sense these definitions are not without their use—they remove the stumbling-block out of the way of honest Infidels, that we are either Enthusiasts or Fanatics, that is, that our faith is built wholly either on blind bodily feelings arising in ourselves, or caught contagiously by sympathy with the agitations of a supersti[ti]ous crowd around the Fanes. (*Fanatici*.) And further, Seraphs and purified Spirits may burn unextinguishably in the pure elementary fire of direct knowlege, which has it's life and all the conditions of it's power in itself—but our Faith resembles sublunary Fire, that needs the Fuel of congruous, tho' perhaps perishable, notions to call it into actuality, and maintain it in clearness and the flame that rises heaven-ward, thus raising and glorifying the thick Vapor of our earthly Being. This premised, I venture—(most unfeignedly not without trembling and religious awe—) to proceed in an attempt to answer your first question:

First, then what is the difference or distinction between THING and THOUGHT? (or between those two experiences of our nature, which in the unphilosophical jargon of Mr Hume and his Followers, in *opposition* say rather, in direct contrariety, to the original and natural sense of the words, it is now fashionable to misname, IMPRESSIONS and IDEAS—) In other words, what do we mean by REALITY?—I answer—that there exist a class of notices which have all a ratio of vividness each with the other, so that tho' the one may be more vivid than the other, yet in the sane and ordinary course of our nature, they are all alike contra-distinguishable to another class of notices, which are felt and conceived as dependent on the former, and to be to them in some sort as a stamp on paper is to a seal sharp-cut in hard Stone. The first class we call *Things & Realities*; and find in them—not indeed absolutely, but in a sense which we all *understand*—(and I am not now disputing with a quibbler in mock-logic, but addressing myself to a Reasoner, who *seeks* to understand, and looks into himself for a sense, which my words may excite in him, not *to* my words for a sense, which they must against his own will *force* on him) we find, I say, in this first class a *permanency*, and *expectability* so great, as to be capable of being contra-distinguished both by these, and by their *vividness* to the second class, that is our Thoughts, which therefore as appearing posterior & faint we deem the Images & imperfect Shadows of the former. Language seems to mark this process of our minds / *Res*—Reor. So Thought is the participle of the Past: *Thing*, derived from the Participle present, or actuality in full and immediate action.—Consequently, all *our* Thoughts are in the language of the old Logicians *inadequate*: i.e. no *thought*, which I have, of any *thing* comprizes the whole of that Thing. I have a distinct Thought of a Rose-Tree; but what countless properties and goings-on of that plant are there, not included in my *Thought* of it?—But the Thoughts of God, in the strict nomenclature of Plato, are all IDEAS, archetypal, and anterior to all but himself alone: therefore consummately *adequate*: and therefore according to our common habits of conception and expression, incomparably more *real* than all things besides, & which do all depend on and proceed from them in some sort perhaps as our Thoughts from those *Things*; but in a more philosophical language we dare with less hesitation to say, that they are more intensely *actual* / inasmuch as the human understanding never took an higher or more honorable flight, than when it defined the Deity to be—Actus purissimus sine *potentialitate*: and Eternity, the incommunicable Attribute, and may we not say, the Synonime of God, to be the simultaneous possession of all equally.——These considerations, my dear Sir! appear to me absolutely necessary, as pioneers, to cut a way thro' to the direct solution (*See the latter Half of the first, and the first half of the second, page of this Letter*)[1] of your first Question—What is (i.e. what can we without detectible incongruity conceive of) the Spirit of God? Answer.—God's Thoughts are all consummately adequate Ideas, which are all incomparably more *real* than what we call *Things*. God is the sole self-comprehending Being, i.e. he has an Idea of himself, and that Idea is consummately adequate, & superlatively real—or as great men have said in the throes and strivings of deep and holy meditation, not only substantial or essential, but super-substantial, super-essential. This Idea therefore from all eternity co-existing with, & yet filiated, by the absolute Being (for as OUR purest Thoughts are *conceived*, so are God's not first conceived, but *begotten*: & thence is he verily and eminently *the* FATHER) is the same, as the Father in all things, but the impossible one, of self-origination. He is the substantial Image of God, in whom the Father beholds well-pleased his whole Being—and being substantial (ὁμοού-σιος) he of divine and permanent Will, and a necessity which is the absolute opposite of compulsion, as delightedly & with as intense LOVE contemplates the Father in the Father, and the Father in himself, and himself in the Father. But all the actions of the Deity are intensely real or substantial / therefore the action of Love, by which the Father contemplates the Son, and the Son the Father, is equally real with the Father and the Son; & proceeds

[1] i.e. the last sentence p. 1193 to end of first paragraph, p. 1194.

co-eternally both from the Father and the Son—& neither of these Three *can* be conceived *apart*, nor *confusedly*—so that the Idea of God involves that of a Tri-unity; and as that Unity or Indivisibility is the intensest, and the Archetype, yea, the very substance and element of all other Unity and Union, so is that Distinction the most manifest, and indestructible of all distinctions—and Being, Intellect, and Action, which in their absoluteness are the Father, the Word, and the Spirit will and must for ever be and remain the 'genera generalissima' of all knowlege. Unitarianism in it's immediate intelligential (the Spirit of Love forbid, that I should say or think, in it's intentional and actual) consequences, is Atheism or Spinosism—God becomes a mere power in darkness, even as Gravitation, and instead of a moral Religion of practical Influence we shall have only a physical Theory to gratify ideal curiosity—no Sun, no Light with vivifying Warmth, but a cold and dull moonshine, or rather star-light, which shews itself but shews nothing else— Hence too, the Heresy of the Greek Church in affirming, that the Holy Spirit proceeds only from the Father, renders the thrice sacred doctrine of the Tri-unity not only above, but against, Reason. Hence too, the doctrine of the Creation assumes it's intelligibility—for the Deity in all it's three distinctions being absolutely perfect, neither susceptible of addition or diminution, the Father *in* his Son as the Image of himself surveying the Possibility of all things possible, and *with* that Love, which is the Spirit of holy Action ($\tau\grave{o}$ ἅγιον πνεῦμα, as the air $+$ motion $=$ a wind) exerted that Love *in* that Intelligence, & that Intelligence *with* that Love, (as nothing new could be affected on the divine Nature, in it's whole Self) therefore in giving to all possible Things contemplated in and thro' the Son that degree of Reality, of which it's nature was susceptible. And this leads me directly to your Second Question, namely—

2. What is (that is, what can we congruously conceive of) the Soul?—

As the Father by and for the Word, and with and thro' the Holy Spirit has given to all possible Existences all susceptible perfection, it is in the highest degree probable that all things, susceptible of Progression, are progressive; and as Intelligence involves the notion of *order*, it follows necessarily, that as we can have no notion of desirable Progression (i.e. desirable for the Progressor, as well as for all others) but what supposes a growth of consciousness—or the image of that incommunicable attribute of self-comprehension, to which all creatures make approaches such as the Geometricians figure to us in the demonstration of Asymptot[e]s. Now from those Possibilities, which exist only in the consciousness of others (and

## 13 October 1806

hence the absolutely inanimate is called by the Platonists, τὰ μὴ ὄντα) to the highest consciousness short of Deity there must subsist infinite orderly degrees—1. those who exist to themselves only in *moments*, and whose continuousness exists in higher minds. 2. those who are conscious of *a* continuousness, but not only not of their whole continuousness, but who do not make that consciousness of *a* continuousness an object of a secondary consciousness—i.e. who are not endued with reflex Faculties. 3. Those who tho' not conscious of the whole of their continuousness, are yet both conscious of *a* continuousness, & make that the object of a reflex consciousness—And of this third Class the Species are infinite; and the first or lowest, as far as we know, is Man, or the human Soul. For Reflexion seems the first approach to, & shadow of, the divine Permanency; the first effort of divine working in us to bind the Past and Future with the Present, and thereby to let in upon us some faint glimmering of that State in which Past, Present, and Future are co-adunated in the adorable I AM. But this state & growth of reflex consciousness (my Time will not permit me to supply all the Links; but by a short meditation you will convince yourself) is not conceivable without the action of kindred souls on each other, i.e. the modification of each by each, and of each by the Whole. A male & female Tyger is neither more or less whether you suppose them only existing in their appropriate wilderness, or whether you suppose a thousand Pairs. But Man is truly altered by the co-existence of other men; his faculties cannot be developed in himself alone, & only by himself. Therefore the human race not by a bold metaphor, but in a sublime reality, approach to, & might become, one body whose Head is Christ (the Logos). Hence with a certain degree of satisfaction to my own mind I can define the human Soul to be that class of Being, as far as we are permitted to know, the first and lowest of that Class, which is endued with a reflex consciousness of it's own continuousness, and the great end and purpose of all it's energies & sufferings is the growth of that reflex consciousness: that class of Being too, in which the Individual is capable of being itself contemplated as a Species of itself, namely, by it's conscious continuousness moving on in an unbroken Line, while at the same time the whole Species is capable of being regarded as one Individual. Now as the very idea of consciousness implies a recollection of the last Links, and the growth of it an extension of that retrospect, Immortality—or a recollection after the Sleep and Change (probably and by strict analogy the growth) of Death (for growth of body and the conditional causes of intellectual growth are found all to take place during Sleep, and Sleep is the Term repeatedly and as it were fondly used by the inspired

Writers as the Exponent of Death, and without it the aweful and undoubtedly taught, Doctrine of the Resurrection has no possible meaning)—the very idea of such a consciousness, permit me to repeat, implies a recollection after the Sleep of Death of all material circumstances that were at least immediately previous to it. A spacious field here opens itself for moral reflection, both for Faith, and for Consolation, when we consider the growth of consciousness (and of what kind our's is, our *conscience* sufficiently reveals to us: for of what use or meaning could *Conscience* be to a Being, who in any state of it's Existence should become to itself utterly lost, and entirely new?) as the end of our earthly Being—when we reflect too, how habits of Vice of all Kinds tend to retard this growth, and how all our sufferings tend to extend & open it out, and how all our Virtues & virtuous and loving Affections tend to bind it, and as it were to inclose the fleeting Retrospect as within a wall!—And again, what sublime motives to Self-respect with humble Hope does not the Idea give, that each Soul is a Species in itself; and what Impulses to more than brotherly Love of our fellow-creatures, the Idea that all men form as it were, one Soul!—

Your third Question admits—in consequence of the preceding—of a briefer and more immediate Answer. What is the difference between the Reason, and the Understanding?—I would reply, that that Faculty of the Soul which apprehends and retains the mere notices of Experience, as for instance that such an object has a triangular figure, that it is of such or such a magnitude, and of such and such a color, and consistency, with the anticipation of meeting the same under the same circumstances, in other words, all the mere φαινόμενα of our nature, we may call the Understanding. But all such notices, as are characterized by UNIVERSALITY and NECESSITY, as that every Triangle *must* in all places and at all times have it's two sides greater than it's third—and which are evidently not the effect of any Experience, but the condition of all Experience, & that indeed without which Experience itself would be inconceivable, we may call Reason—and this class of knowlege was called by the Ancients Νοούμενα in distinction from the former, or φαινόμενα. Reason is therefore most eminently the Revelation of an immortal soul, and it's best Synonime—it is the forma formans, which contains in itself the law of it's own conceptions. Nay, it is highly probable, that the contemplation of essential Form as remaining the same thro' all varieties of color and magnitude and developement, as in the acorn even as in the Oak, first gave to the Mind the ideas, by which it explained to itself those notices of it's Immortality revealed to it by it's conscience.

## 13 October 1806

Your fourth Question appears to me to receive a full answer from the preceding Data / For if God with the Spirit of God created the Soul of Man as far as it was possible according to his own Likeness, and if he be an omnipresent Influence, it necessarily follows, that his action on the Soul of Man must awake in it a conscience of actions within itself analogous to the divine action / and that therefore the Spirit of God truly bears witness to the Spirit of man, even as vice versâ the awakened Spirit will bear witness to the Spirit of God. Suppose a dull impression from a Seal pressed anew by that Seal—it's recovered Characters bear witness to the Seal, even as the Seal has born witness to the latest yet existing Impression.——

Accept my thanks for your trouble about my Trunk; it was impossible for you to have done otherwise than you did, acting with your habitual kindness & avoidal of procrastination. Mrs Clarkson bore her journey well; & has continued remarkably well till this Day (i.e. Wednesday)—This afternoon she has been in pain; but I trust it will be transient. I leave Bury to morrow,[1] God permitting—I need not say, I shall be glad to hear of & from you at Keswick: for I am with unfeigned Esteem your affect.

Friend    S. T. Coleridge

### 635. To the Wordsworths

*Pub.* Middle Years, *i. 84.* These fragments are all that survive of Coleridge's letter, which the Wordsworths received on 23 November. They are quoted by Dorothy in a letter to Mrs. Clarkson.

When Coleridge, after a delay of more than two months following his return to England on 17 August 1806, finally arrived in the lake country, he went first not to Keswick but to Penrith, where he hoped to see Sara Hutchinson. She, however, had left little more than half an hour earlier for Kendal, to join the Wordsworths, who were on their way to spend the winter at Coleorton. Learning of her departure, Coleridge set off for Kendal, arriving there on Sunday evening, 26 October 1806. Three days later Wordsworth and Sara Hutchinson left by coach for Coleorton, but not before Coleridge gave them a 'promise' to join them within a month, and after they left he went on to Keswick.

According to an unpublished note transcribed by E. H. Coleridge, he arrived at Greta Hall on 30 October 1806. To this note Derwent Coleridge added an explanatory comment: 'I well remember his expected arrival. My mother had taken my pillow for my father's bed, who required several. In her telling me this, I exclaimed—"Oh! by all means. I would lie on straw for my father", greatly to my mother's delight & amusement. How well does this speak for my mother. I was then just at the close of my sixth year.'

[Circa 19 November 1806]

. . . I am very glad, deeply conscious as I am of my own weakness,

[1] A notebook entry shows that Coleridge was in Cambridge on Thursday, 16 Oct., 'after 12 years' absence'; he did not arrive in Keswick until 30 Oct.

that I had seen you before I came to Keswick; indeed the excess of my anguish occasioned by the information given me at Penrith was a sort of oracle to me of the necessity of seeing you. Every attack that could be made on human weakness has been made; but, fortunately for so weak a moral being as I am, there was an indelicacy and artifice in these which tho' they did not perceptibly lessen my anguish, yet made my shame continually on the watch, made me see always, and without the possibility of a doubt, that mere selfish desire to have a *rank* in life and not to be believed to be that which she really was, without the slightest wish that what was should be otherwise, was at the bottom of all. Her temper, and selfishness, her manifest dislike of me (as far as her nature is capable of a *positive* feeling) and her self-encouraged admiration of Southey as a vindictive feeling in which she delights herself as satirizing me &c. &c. . . .

We have *determined* to part absolutely and finally; Hartley and Derwent to be with me but to visit their Mother as they would do if at a publick school. . . .

I think it probable I shall leave this place for your mansion of sojourn before an answer can reach me[1]. . . .

### 636. To George Coleridge

*Address*: Revd G. Coleridge | Ottery St Mary | Devon
MS. *Lady Cave. Pub. E.L.G. i. 360.*
*Postmark*: 3 December ⟨1806⟩. *Stamped*: Keswick.

Sunday Evening, 30 November, 1806

My dearest Brother

As I indeed deserve much blame for my silence and general suspension of brotherly Intercourse, so I suffer your gentle and therefore more painful reproof, to sink into my heart unresisted; tho' the cause of my neglect and apparent lack of Love toward you is not only *different* from that, to which you attribute it, but the very opposite. It is not, my earliest and most honored friend! th[at] a wide range of Intercourse with men has placed me above the need of those comforts, which result from filial or fraternal Intercommunion; but that the same wretchedness of Body and fluctuation of Mind (which sorely against my will dragged me from Solitude or at least the most confined society and afterwards

[1] The Wordsworths were now settled at Coleorton in Leicestershire, in a farm-house lent by Sir George Beaumont, and on 7 Nov. Wordsworth had written to Coleridge: 'You might bring Hartley with you and live here as long as you liked free of all expense but washing.' From a transcript of Wordsworth's letter made by E. H. Coleridge.

## 30 November 1806

by accident and equally against my inclination whirled me about among many faces in many countries) had placed me so far below those comforts, that all the affections, for which my nature seemed to have been *made*, became it's crown of Thorns, and I could find tranquillity, or a stupor that counterfeited tranquillity, only in absolute Abstraction:

> For not to *think* of what I needs must *feel*,
> But to be still and patient all I can;
> And haply by abstruse Research to steal
> From my own Nature all the natural Man;
> This was my sole Resource, my only Plan!
> And that which suits a Part infects the Whole,
> And now is almost grown the Habit of my Soul.

The last Letter, which I wrote before the Ship left Portsmouth Harbour for Malta, was addressed to you. By neglect either of my Captain or his Portsmouth Boatman, it was not sent: and is still in my Desk. In this Letter I had stated to you my real state of Mind, Body, and Estate: and that not having gone, I was always planning another, but had never fortitude to set about it in good Earnest.——Shortly after my arrival in Malta Sir A. Ball begged me to accept of the office of Private Secretary to him *nominally*, during the time of Mr Chapman's Absence, who was then on a Corn-Mission in the Black Sea; and would certainly not return in less than two months. This was stated to be meant as a compliment to my general Talents, and as a return for a political Memorial which I had written. The Salary too (it was stated) would pay the expences of my intended Sicilian Tour &c.——My mind misgave me; but at length I accepted of the offer. I then removed to the Palace; and so far from finding it *nominal*, I had no small difficulty in realizing my Sicilian Project—However I did this in the fall of the year; and did not return to Malta till the close of it.

Mr Chapman was not yet returned; and Mr Macauley, the Public Secretary, was perfectly *effete* and superannuated. For Sir A. Ball *personally* I had a great affection, and respect—indeed, admiration / and he on the other hand had treated me with the most unbounded respect in public, which I valued only for the motive, and with a fatherly tenderness and confidence in private. Always a facile Being, I could not resist his intreaties to take upon me the office first of assistant and afterwards on the Death of Mr Macauley which took place in a few weeks, of Public Secretary, still looking forward with anxious Hopes to the arrival of Mr Chapman. At all events, I had determined to return to England in [the] Spring —my Object had failed—whatever benefit the *climate* of Malta afforded, it was but a poor counter-balance to the utter dreariness of that white rock, the removal from all the ordinary pleasurable actions on my mind of Books, or Prospects, or familiar Faces, and the round of official Splendor and official Employments: things which were not made for me.—However, April came; but Mr Chapman had not returned, & it was as uncertain as ever, when he *would.* Sir A. Ball *intreated* me not to leave him: I could not say, *no*! I did not *say, yes*! but I sullenly complied with him, and from that month lost all the little Spirits and Activity of mind, which I had hitherto retained. I will not tire you with the Detail. Suffice, that I was detained from Month to Month, till on my arrival in Sicily in November [September], meaning to pass from Messina to Trieste, & so thro' Germany to England (for a long sea-voyage I dreaded more than Death, & with abundant Reason) I soon discovered, that I had been detained too long: and that I must winter either in Sicily or Naples.—By the inducements of Elliot, our Minister at Naples, I was at length persuaded to go to Naples; discovered Elliot to be—every thing, that Sir A. Ball was not, & nothing that he was. I went from thence to Rome, meaning to return to Naples, and leaving almost all my little property, Papers, &c in the care of Mr Noble, an English Resident—before I had been in Rome a fortnight, the French Torrent poured [down] on that devoted Country, the natural and necessary consequence [of] the mad & profligate, if not traitorous, plans of [our] Minister.[1]—I still hoped to have made interest [by] means of the artists & to have been permitted to go thro' Milanese into Germany; but it was impossible.—Besides, my Finances were exhausted; and my Letters of Credit I had left at Naples. Had I left Malta in the April, I should have been in point of money neither loser or gainer to any considerable amount—as it was, my employments have cost me at least 200£, besides loss of Time, and of that literary reputation, which to me is (my maker knows) no [more] desirable, than as it is a duty of Gratitude in me to *aim* at it, and as the attainment of it might procure friends for my little ones after my decease, which I less than most men have any right to consider as a distant Event.

From Rome by the friendship of young Russell I passed to Florence, [ju]st in time to escape an arrest from the French—and after long Delays at Florence & Pisa and Leghorn, I at length embarked as an American in an American Vessel; and after 55 days of literal Horror, almost daily expecting and wishing to die, I at last trod again on my native Land.——I will assuredly continue this Letter to morrow—the to night's Post will not permit me to

[1] The conduct of Hugh Elliot (1752–1830) as minister to Naples was such that he was recalled from his post.

write farther, either of myself or of you.—Of Edward [I] read with pain, but without Surprize.[1] For the last six or seven years I have been more and more convinced, tho' I pretend not to *understand* much less *explain* the fact, that our *moral nature* is a power of itself; and not a mere modification of our common Intellect / so that a man may have wit, prudence, sense, &c &c, & yet be utterly destitute of a true *moral* sense. And when I observe the impotence of this moral sense, however highly possessed, unassisted by something still higher, &, if I may so express myself, still more extranatural, I own, it seems to me, as if the goodness of God had occasionally *added* it to our nature, as an intermediate or connecting Link between that nature and a state of Grace. My love to *William*: I will write him soon.—Till tomorrow, farewell!—S. T. Coleridge.

## 637. *To the Wordsworths*

*MS. Pierpont Morgan Lib. Pub.* Middle Years, *i. 81–82, but misdated 16 November.* This fragment, which is quoted by Dorothy Wordsworth in a letter to Lady Beaumont, is all that survives of Coleridge's letter.

Dorothy Wordsworth's letter, postmarked 10 December 1806, and written on 7 December, reads in part: 'Poor Coleridge—We have had four letters from him, & in all he speaks with the same steadiness of his resolution to separate from Mrs C; & she has fully agreed to it, & consented that he should take Hartley & Derwent & superintend their education, she being allowed to have them at the holidays; . . . but in a letter which we have received tonight he tells us, that she breaks out into outrageous passions, & urges continually that one argument (in fact the only one which has the least effect upon her mind) that this person, & that person & every body will talk. He would have been with us here before this time, but for the chance of giving H and D the hooping cough, &, on that account, he is miserably perplexed for he has no other place to carry them to. . . . My Brother has written to advise him to bring the Boys to us, thinking it very doubtful whether our children's cough . . . is the *hooping* cough or not.'

[*Circa* 3 December 1806]

. . . If I go away without them [Hartley and Derwent] I am a Bird who has struggled himself from off a Bird-lime twig, & then finds a string round his leg pulling him back. . . .

. . . I cannot therefore deny that I both have suffered, & am suffering hourly, to the great injury of my health, which at times alarms me, as *dropsical*—. . .

---

[1] Edward Coleridge had apparently left his post as assistant master in the King's School at Ottery St. Mary, where George Coleridge was headmaster. Coleridge later offered to assist his brother, but nothing came of the plan.

## 638. To Mrs. S. T. Coleridge

*Address*: Mrs Coleridge | Greta Hall | Keswick | Cumberland
*MS*. Lord Latymer. *Pub. with omis.* Letters, ii. 509.
*Stamped*: Ashby de la Zouch.

[25 December 1806]

My dear Sara

By my letter from Derby you will have been satisfied of our safety so far. We had however been grossly deceived as to the equi-distance of Derby & Loughborough. The expence was nearly double. Still however I was in such tortures, and my Boils bled, throbbed, and *stabbed* so con furia, that perhaps I have no reason for regret. At Coleorton we found them dining, Sunday, ½ past One o clock.—To day is Xmas Day. Of course, we were welcomed with an uproar of sincere Joy: and Hartley[1] hung suspended between the Ladies for a long minute. The Children, too, jubilated at Hartley's arrival.—He has behaved very well indeed—only that when he could get out of the Coach, at dinner or to make water, I was obliged to be on incessant watch to prevent him from rambling off into the fields—instead of doing what he wanted by the Coach, he twice ran into the field, and to the very further end of it—and once after the dinner was on Table, I was out 5 minutes seeking him in great alarm, & found him at the further end of a wet meadow, on the marge of a river. After dinner, fearful of losing our places by the window (of the long Coach) I ordered him to go into the Coach & sit in the place where he was before: and I would follow. In about 5 minutes I followed: no Hartley!—Halloing—in vain!—At length, where should I discover him! In the same meadow, only at a greater distance, & close down on the very edge of the Water. I was angry from downright Fright! And what, think you, was Cataphract's excuse!—'It was a misunderstanding, Father! I thought, you see, that you bid me go to the very same place, in the meadow, where I was.'——I told him, that he had interpreted the Text by the suggestions of the Flesh, not the Inspiration of the Spirit: and *his Wish* the naughty Father of the base-born Thought.—However, saving and excepting his passion for field-truantry, & his hatred of confinement (in which his fancy at least

---

[1] Coleridge took only Hartley with him to Coleorton, Derwent remaining with his mother at Keswick. Coleridge wrote to the Wordsworths that Mrs. Coleridge intended to meet him in London in the spring, and he later told his brother that she wished to accompany him to Ottery 'that our separation may appear free from all shadow of suspicion of any other cause than that of unfitness & unconquerable difference of Temper'. MS. Lady Cave.

## 25 December 1806

Doth sing a doleful song about green fields,
How sweet it were in Woods and wild Savannas
To hunt for Food and be a naked man
And wander up and down at Liberty)[1]

he is a very good, and sweet child—of strict honor & truth, from which he never deviates except in the form of sophism when he sports his logical false dice in the game of Excuses. This however is the mere effect of his activity of Thought, & his aiming at being clever & ingenious. He is exceedingly amiable toward Children. All here love him most dearly: and your name sake[2] takes upon her all the duties of his Mother & darling Friend, with all the Mother's love & fondness. He is very fond of *her*—; but it is very pretty to hear how, without any one set declaration of his attachment to Mrs Wilson and Mr Jackson his love for them continually breaks out—so many things remind him of them, & in the Coach he talked to the Strangers of them just as if every body *must* know Mr J. & Mrs W.——His Letter is only half-written: so cannot go to day.—We all wish you a merry Christmas / & many following ones.—Concerning the London Lectures, we are to discuss it, William & I, this Evening—and I shall write you at full the day after tomorrow—tomorrow there is no Post—but this Letter I mean merely as bearer of the tidings of our safe arrival. I am better than usual. Hartley has coughed a little every morning, since he left Greta Hall; but only such a little cough, as you heard from him at the door. He is in high Health. All the Children have the hooping Cough; but in an exceedingly mild degree. Neither Sara nor I, ever remember to have had it / Hartley is made to keep at a distance from them; & only to play with Johnny in the open ai[r].

I found my Spice-megs; but many papers I miss.
The Post boy waits—
My Love to Mrs Lovell, to Southey & Edith,—
    & believe me anxiously & for ever | Your sincere Friend,
                      S. T. Coleridge.

[1] *The Foster-Mother's Tale*, lines 61–64, *Poems*, i. 184.
[2] Sara Hutchinson.

# INDEX

Aaron, R. I., 677 n.
Adams, Dr. Joseph, 1021, 1023.
Addington, Henry, Viscount Sidmouth, 771, 1075, 1112.
Addison, Isabella, *Letter to*, 753.
Adye, Major, 1147, 1159, 1165, 1167, 1169.
Aikin, Arthur, 392–3.
Aikin, John, 201.
Akenside, Mark, 215, 230, 279, 289, 307.
Allen family, 359 n., 883, 885, 888, 890–2, 898, 900, 932.
Allen, Robert, 33, 35, 48, 51, 70–71, 82 n., 85, 101, 104, 146, 181 n., 192 n., 234, 265, 336–7.
Allston, Washington, *Letter to*, 1172.
Anacreon, 17, 28.
*Analytical Review*, 201, 224, 227.
Andrews, J. P., 554.
*Annual Anthology*, 419 n., 532, 540, 545–6, 549–50, 552, 554, 562–3, 573, 576, 589, 924.
Aquinas, Thomas, 681, 787 n., 903.
Aristotle, 213, 585, 675, 680–2, 684, 692–3, 696, 707, 768, 864, 947, 954.

Bacon, Francis, 530, 535, 682 n., 685–6, 700, 927, 947.
Bacon, Roger, 703.
Baillie, Joanna, 621.
Ball, Sir Alexander, *Letters to*, 1150, 1153; 1086, 1117, 1135, 1139–49, 1157 n., 1158, 1160, 1163, 1167–71, 1178, 1201–2.
Bampfylde, J. C., 533, 540.
Banks, Sir Joseph, 869, 919, 933.
Barbauld, Mrs. Anna L., 197, 201, 341 n., 393, 420, 577–8, 654, 1039, 1191.
Barclay, Robert, 893.
Barrow, Isaac, 1017.
Bartram, William, 613.
Baxter, Richard, 245, 956.
Beaumont and Fletcher, 1054.
Beaumont, Sir George and Lady, *Letters to*, 964, 966, 993, 998, 1016, 1048, 1052, 1075, 1078, 1104, 1106, 1121, 1146; 957–8, 980, 1006, 1061–3, 1065, 1070–1, 1075, 1077, 1085, 1094–5, 1098–1102, 1106, 1109–10, 1112, 1114, 1116, 1135, 1160, 1165, 1167, 1169, 1186, 1200 n.
Beaumont, John, 1116.
*Beauties of the Anti-Jacobin*, 552.

Beddoes, Thomas, 174, 195, 201, 203, 214, 222, 226, 254, 256–7, 294, 349, 382, 401 n., 413, 435, 548 n., 557, 590, 606, 632, 726–7, 771, 852, 861, 878, 896, 930, 937, 975–7, 991, 994.
Bedford, Grosvenor, *Letter to*, 1044; 98, 1051.
Beireis, G. C., 521–2.
Berkeley, George, 245, 278, 335 n., 681 n., 699, 703, 1032.
Bernard, Thomas, 1187.
Bethell, Christopher, 45.
Biddle, John, 956.
Biggs and Cottle, *Letters to*, 592, 594, 616, 617, 637, 659; 190, 194, 202, 297, 300, 368, 387, 556, 611, 623.
Bloomfield, Robert, 623, 716, 829, 847, 913.
Blumenbach, J. F., 472, 477, 494, 497, 590–1.
Bolingbroke, Lord, 652.
Bonaparte, *see* Napoleon.
Bowdon family, 1–3, 10, 302, 388.
Bowles, William Lisle, *Letters to*, 317, 355; 29, 32, 35 n., 71 n., 86, 90 n., 94, 101, 133, 139, 203, 230, 252, 259, 278–9, 286–7, 294, 304, 327, 344, 384, 812, 829, 855, 864, 865 n.
Boyer, James, 2, 15–16, 64 n., 65, 137.
*British Critic*, 201, 227, 708, 735, 820, 829, 860.
Browne, Sir Thomas, 1080–3.
Brucker, J. J., 321 n., 323, 324 n., 554.
Brun, Friederike, 865 n.
Bruno, Giordano, 809.
Brunton, Ann, 109–10, 113, 117.
Brunton, Elizabeth (Mrs. Merry), 107–8.
Brunton, John, 107 n., 109, 112.
Buchan, Earl of, 151, 164.
Buchanan, George, 390 n., 1063.
Buller, James and Francis (Judge), 303, 388.
Bürger, G. A., 438, 565–6.
Burke, Edmund, 195, 198 n., 199, 221, 252, 738, 954.
Burnett, George, 84, 150, 154, 162, 165–6, 168–73, 186, 188–9, 192, 194, 321–2, 420, 570, 578, 787, 910, 1031, 1068, 1074.
Burnett, James, Lord Monboddo, 679.
Burns, Robert, 278, 286, 607, 747, 829.
Burton, Robert, 961, 1114.

( 1207 )

## Index

Butler, Joseph, 385–6, 703.
Butler, Samuel (author of *Hudibras*), 919.
Butler, Samuel (Bishop of Lichfield), *Letter to*, 82; 45, 47, 1091.

Caldwell, George, 21, 24, 46, 80, 103, 105, 110–11, 120, 568.
Calvert, Raisley and William, 567 n., 670–2, 849, 939, 1130, 1140.
Campbell, Thomas, 714, 829, 1055, 1098.
Canning, George, 34 n., 112.
Carlisle, Anthony, 648.
Carlyon, Clement, 497, 520, 523.
Casimir (Sarbiewski), 76–77, 97.
Castle, Michael, 194.
Catcott, G., *Letter to*, 323; 324.
Chapman, E. T., 1142 n., 1158 n., 1163, 1169, 1201–2.
Chatterton, Thomas, 332–3, 585, 826.
Chaucer, 951, 955, 960, 1054.
Chester, John, 415 n., 416, 418–20, 428, 431, 433–4, 440, 445, 448, 453, 456–7, 459, 472, 476, 489, 495, 497, 510, 514, 519–21, 523, 572, 618, 634, 651, 676, 708, 713.
Christensen, Prof. Francis, 466 n.
Chubb, John, *Letter to*, 341; 343.
Cicero, 682, 809, 1051.
Clarkson, Thomas and Mrs., *Letters to*, 944, 1193; 674, 749, 774, 857, 886, 889, 894, 898, 995, 1017, 1020, 1180, 1182, 1190–1.
Claudianus, 68.
Coates, John, 180, 182, 189.
Coates, Matthew, *Letter to*, 1020; 606.
Coates, William, 186, 606, 740.
Coleridge, Ann, 1, 102, 311.
Coleridge, Berkeley, 394 n., 407–9, 418, 446, 449 n., 453, 459, 476, 478–9, 481–5, 490, 575, 656, 895.
Coleridge, Derwent, 622–3, 626–7, 632, 634, 646–7, 650–1, 653, 656, 662, 668–9, 673, 676, 713, 715, 728, 733, 738, 746, 776, 785–6, 789, 802, 804, 827, 844, 846–7, 850, 859, 871–2, 884–6, 889, 891, 902, 909, 917, 943, 958, 960, 964–5, 975, 977, 979, 1004, 1009; described by Coleridge, 1014–15, 1022; 1017, 1024, 1026–7, 1031, 1060, 1062, 1070, 1114, 1139, 1199 n., 1200, 1203.
Coleridge, Edward, 18, 36–37, 39–41, 53–54, 57–58, 69, 310–11, 409, 528, 532, 803, 895, 898, 1009, 1023.
Coleridge, Francis S., 39–41, 53, 55, 311, 347–8, 352–3, 355.
Coleridge, George, *Letters to*, 5, 6, 7, 9, 11, 15, 16, 17, 19, 34, 36, 37, 38, 42, 43, 45, 53, 55, 57, 59, 63, 64, 66, 69, 70, 73, 74, 75, 77, 78, 79, 80, 81, 125, 383, 394, 409, 531, 802, 805, 1005, 1200; 3, 64 n., 72, 113 n., 118, 123, 131 n., 164, 201, 232, 234, 311, 324 n., 331, 348, 418, 528, 540, 570, 607, 724, 756, 778, 895, 897–8, 1074.
Coleridge, Hartley, 192 n., 236, 240, 243, 245–7, 251, 254, 257, 260–1, 263–4, 269, 271–3, 275, 285, 293, 296, 301, 308, 317, 320, 339–40, 352, 382, 384–5, 398, 408–9, 117–18, 446, 476, 485, 489–90, 495, 503, 523, 528, 530, 532, 534, 536, 550, 553, 563, 572, 574–7, 579, 584, 588, 609; described by Coleridge, 612, 615, 625, 668, 1014, 1022, 1204–5; 614, 621–3, 644–5, 649–50, 653, 656, 662, 673–4, 676, 713, 728, 738, 740, 746, 763, 774, 776, 780, 785–6, 789, 802, 804, 827–8, 844, 847, 850, 871–2, 884–5, 889, 891, 902, 909, 917, 935, 941, 943, 958, 960, 964, 975, 979, 1024–5, 1031, 1058, 1060, 1062, 1070–1, 1098, 1109, 1114, 1126, 1139, 1163, 1181, 1184, 1191, 1200, 1203.
Coleridge, James, *Letters to*, 65, 894; 10, 18, 36–38, 40, 42–43, 53–54, 57, 59–60, 65, 69, 72, 75 n., 310, 385, 409, 528, 756, 802–3, 805, 880, 1009.
Coleridge, John (brother), 310.
Coleridge, John (father), 1 n., 302–3, 310, 347–8, 353–5, 387–8, 528.
Coleridge, Mrs. John (mother), *Letter to*, 1; 10, 21, 37–38, 40–41, 47, 57, 59, 61, 63, 69, 123, 232, 303, 310, 347–8, 352–5, 385, 388, 398, 409, 531, 803, 895, 898, 1009, 1041.
Coleridge, Luke H., *Letter to*, 1; 2 n., 57 n., 59 n., 311.
Coleridge, Samuel Taylor: autobiographical fragments concerning ancestry, family, and early childhood, 302–3, 310–12, 346–8, 352–5, 387–9; at Christ's Hospital, 1–14, 388–9, 1038; at Jesus College, Cambridge, 15–36, 42–57; holds Christ's Hospital Exhibition, 15–16, 21, 64 n., 81 n., 132 n.; obtains Rustat Scholarship, 16–17, 20–21, 34, 46, 64 n., 75 n., 80, 81 n.; candidate for Browne Medal, 17, 34, 45 n., 56, 330, 1091 n.; appointed Librarian and Chapel Clerk, 40–41, 46, 53; summers in Devonshire, 36–41, 57–61; fails to gain University Craven Scholarship, 42–45, 47, 59 n., 67–68; proposes *Imitations from the Modern Latin Poets* (unrealized), 46, 70, 76–77, 82 n., 101, 116–17,

( 1208 )

*Index*

152, 154, 161; experiences in the 15th Light Dragoons: enlistment, service, and discharge, 61–79, 265, 337, 359 n., 404; returns to Cambridge, 64 n., 65, 79–82; manifests penchant for self-analysis, 71, 78, 125–7, 259–60, 349–50, 354, 398, 454–5, 628–9, 714, 761–2, 782–4, 814–15, 831, 916, 959, 1102; meets Southey at Oxford, 82 n.; Pantisocracy, 84, 88, 96–99, 101, 103, 112–16, 119–23, 132, 138, 146, 149–51, 155, 158–9, 163–72, 710; Welsh tour, 85–95; encounters Mary Evans, 87–88, 92; at Bristol, 96; engaged to Sara Fricker, 99 n.; returns to Cambridge *via* London, 97–129; in London, 129–49; last appeal to Mary Evans and his feelings on losing her, 129–31, 144–5, 164, 170; returns to Bristol with Southey and settles there, 149–295; early political lectures, 152, 155, 164, 172, 296 n.; working on *Poems* (1796), see under *Works*; quarrels with Southey, 157–9, 161, 163–73, 294; marriage and brief residence at Clevedon, 159–63; plans and issues the *Watchman*, 174–84, 188–203, 207–12; preaches in Unitarian chapels, 176, 179–80, 182, 230, 232–3, 326, 370, 373, 375, 381, 384, 407, 409, 413 n.; poverty and plans for earning a livelihood, 185, 192, 194, 203, 208–12, 218–20, 222, 226–37, 240–2, 249–51, 255–7, 263–6, 269–77, 287–8, 318; resorts to opium, 188, 249–52, 276, 349 n., 394; early association with Wordsworth, 215–16, 297, 319–20; birth of Hartley Coleridge, 236; plans second edition of *Poems* (1797), see under *Works;* residence at Nether Stowey, 296–413; composes *Osorio*, see under *Works*; intimacy with Wordsworth at Stowey, 325–32, 334–412 *passim*; composes *Kubla Khan*, 348 n.; composes *Ancient Mariner*, 357, 368, 379 n., 387, 412; misunderstanding with Southey, Lamb, and Lloyd, 357–9, 390, 399–400, 403–7, 410, 489 n., 524–5, 541–2; accepts and then returns gift of £100 from the Wedgwoods, 360–9; candidate for Unitarian pastorate at Shrewsbury, 361–73; accepts annuity from the Wedgwoods, 370–5 (*see also under* Wedgwood annuity); proposal for 3rd edition of poems develops into plan for *Lyrical Ballads*, 387, 390–1, 399–403, 411–12; composition of *Christabel* interrupted, 407 n.; birth of Berkeley Coleridge, 407; visit to Germany, 413–523; projected *Life of Lessing*, 454–5, 480–1, 484, 516, 518–19, 553, 559, 563, 610, 623, 632; death of Berkeley Coleridge, 478–9, 481–3; returns to England, 523; journey to Sockburn and tour of the Lakes with Wordsworth, 542–6; first meeting with Sara Hutchinson, 546 n.; in London writing for *Morning Post*, 547–85; foreshadowing of domestic discord, 562, 571; translates Schiller's *Wallenstein*, 574 (see also under *Works*); visits Wordsworth at Grasmere, 585–7; determines to settle at Keswick, 588, 590–1; assists Wordsworth in second edition of *Lyrical Ballads* (1800), *see separate entry*; at Greta Hall, Keswick, 607–744, 755–75; birth of Derwent Coleridge, 622; views on baptism, 624–5, 626 n.; composes Part II of *Christabel*, 623, 631–2, 634–5, 643, 728; breakdown in health, 647–51, 653, 655, 667–72, 721–33, 735–43; preoccupation with philosophy during illness, 671–2, 675–703, 706–9; opium habit established, 731, 787, 884, 888–9, 897, 915, 917, 919, 930, 934, 942, 979, 982, 984 n., 1019, 1027, 1029, 1043, 1097, 1137, 1178; visits Durham and the Hutchinsons at Bishop Middleham and Gallow Hill, 744–55; financial difficulties, 755–7, 760, 765–6, 770–1; domestic discord, 762, 767, 774–5, 778, 784–6; visits London and Stowey, 775–89; writing for *Morning Post*, 776, 787; revisits Gallow Hill, 788 and note; at Keswick, 790–879; composes *Dejection*, a revealing autobiographical document, 790–8; 'two discordant Wills': abortive attempts at reconciliation with Mrs. Coleridge, 796, 832–3, 875–6, 879–82, 886–8, 894, 901, 908, 929, 975 n., 985, 1015, 1038, 1053, 1115; changing religious views, 803, 805–7, 821–4, 860–2, 893; dissatisfaction with Wordsworth's poetic creed, 811–12, 830–1; proposes to 'lay down Canons' of Criticism respecting Poetry', 829–30, 847, 877; contributes to *Morning Post*, 856–7, 865, 874, 876, 892; distinguishes between imagination and fancy, 865–6, 1034; travels in Wales with Tom Wedgwood, 878–901; birth of Sara

( 1209 )

## Index

Coleridge, Samuel Taylor (*cont.*)
Coleridge (daughter), 902; returns to Keswick, 902–18; visits Bristol, Stowey, Gunville, and London, 918–42; insures life in anticipation of journey abroad, 926, 941–5; returns to Keswick, 942; outlines his proposed *Instrument of Practical Reasoning*, 946–8, 952; increasing ill health, 974–82, 989–93, 1019–21, 1027–9,1032,*fol.*; Scottish tour, 975, 977–90; at Keswick, 990–1024; retrospective account of early political views, 999–1003; plans residence abroad, 1021; financial arrangements, 1023, 1040, 1049, 1059, 1062, 1067, 1069–70, 1087, 1109, 1113, 1129; at Grasmere, 1024–31, 1040; in London settling plans for journey abroad, 1037–1109; determines to sail in the *Speedwell* for Malta, 1083–6, 1088–90; at Portsmouth, 1110–24; en route to Malta, 1125–35; illness aboard the *Speedwell* and death rumoured, 1135–6; at Malta, 1135–49; Private and later Public Secretary to Sir A. Ball, 1140–72, 1201–2; in Sicily, 1149–53, 1157; returns to Malta, 1153–72; proposed as assistant commissary on mission to Black Sea, 1158; leaves Malta for Sicily, 1172 n., 1202; in Italy, 1172–3, 1202; arrives in England 'shirtless & almost penniless', 1174–7; plans for earning a livelihood, 1177–91; depressed anew over his 'ill-starred' marriage, 1178, 1181–2; reveals religious views, 1188–90, 1192–9; reunion with the Wordsworths and Sara Hutchinson at Kendal, 1199 n.; arrives at Greta Hall, Keswick, 1199 n.; determines on separation from Mrs. Coleridge, 1199–1200, 1203, 1204 n.; joins the Wordsworths at Coleorton, 1204–5.

Works: *Absence*, 128–9; *Addison, To Miss Isabella and Miss Joanna Hutchinson*, 753–5; *Addressed to a Young Man of Fortune*, 268, 286–7; *Anacreon, An Ode in the Manner of*, 28; *Ancient Mariner, The*, 357, 368, 379 n., 387, 412, 592 n., 593, 594 n., 598–602, 631 n., 720, 1125; *Answer to a Child's Question*, 998; *Answer to 'A Letter to Edward Long Fox, M.D.'*, 254 n.; *Author of Poems, To the*, 186–7, 552; *Ballad of the Dark Ladié* (fragment), 550, 812, 1094; *Before Gleim's Cottage*, 856 n.; *Betham, To Matilda*, 864; *Bowles, To the Rev. W. L.*, 136; *Brunton, To Miss*, 108–9; *Burke*, 142; *Chatterton, Monody on the death of*, 104 n., 195 n., 203, 299, 333, 381, 399, 826; *Christabel*, 379 n., 407 n., 540, 545, 549, 592 n., 623, 627, 631–2, 634–5, 643, 649, 662, 707, 716, 728, 782, 941, 982 n., 1024, 1076, 1094–5, 1133, 1191; *Christmas Carol, A*, 552, 554–5; *Coleridge, To the Rev. George*, 210 n., 298 n., 324 n., 329, 334; *Complaint of Ninathóma, The*, 52; *Concert-Room, Lines composed in a*, 550; *Conciones ad Populum*, 152, 155, 196, 201, 221, 867 n.; *Connubial Rupture, On a late*, 223–4; *Day-Dream, A*, 792 n., 793 n.; *Day-Dream, The*, 857 n.; *Dejection: an Ode*, 669 n., 788 n., 790–8, 815–19, 831–2, 857 n., 875, 901, 966 n., 970–2, 1008, 1083, 1201; *Departing Year, Ode to the*, 268, 288–9, 292–3, 297–300, 307, 309, 313, 315, 318, 320, 325, 329, 497; *Destiny of Nations, The*, 243 n., 275, 285, 297, 309, 329–30, 387, 391; *Devil's Thoughts, The*, 550; *Disappointment, To*, 23; *Discovery made too Late, On a*, 115–16, 121 n., 129 n.; *Dungeon, The*, 387 n., 593–4, 631 n.; *Easter Holidays*, 3–4; *Elbingerode, Lines written in the Album at*, 504–5; *Eolian Harp, The*, 294; *Epigrams*, 536, 552, 1092 n.; *Epitaph*, 992; *Epitaph for Howard's Tomb, An*, 35–36; *Faded Flower, The*, 95; *Fall of Robespierre, The*, 90 n., 97–98, 101, 104, 106, 110, 117, 121, 125–6; *Fears in Solitude*, 409, 417 n., 550, 552, 573; *Fire, Famine, and Slaughter*, 573; *Fortune, To*, 61, 129 n.; *Foster-Mother's Tale, The*, 387 n., 593–4, 631 n., 804, 1205; *Fox and Statesman, The*, 185; *Fragment Found in a Lecture-Room, A*, 34–35; *France: an Ode*, 418 n., 550 n., 912; *Friend, Lines on a*, 124 n., 127–8; *Friend, To a*, 147–8, 286; *Frost at Midnight*, 418 n., 550 n., 791 n.; *Genevieve*, 128–9; *Gentle Look, The*, 136; *Georgiana, Ode to*, 552, 554; *Godwin, To William*, 141, 221; *Greek Ode on Astronomy*, 56, 330; *Greek Prize Ode on the Slave Trade*, 34, 330, 1091; *Happiness*, 11–14, 85–86; *Hexameters*, 451–2; *Hexameters: Paraphrase of Psalm XLVI*, 532–3; *Home-Sick*, 493; *Honos Alit Artes*, 6; *Hymn before Sun-rise, in the Vale of Chamouni*, 854 n., 857 n.,

( 1210 )

## Index

864–5, 995–7, 1004; *Imitated from the Welsh*, 137; *Infant, On an*, 483; *Inscription for a Fountain*, 1004; *In stale blank verse*, 406; *Introduction to the Tale of the Dark Ladie*, 550 n. (see also *Love*); *Jeu d'esprit*, 1068–9; *Joan of Arc*, 172, 207, 243, 297 (see also *Destiny of Nations*); *Kisses*, 60; *Koskiusko*, 140; *Kubla Khan*, 335 n., 348 n., 394 n.; *Life*, 14; *Lime-Tree Bower my Prison, This*, 334–6, 349–50; *Linley, Lines to W.*, 352 n.; *Love*, 550 n., 592–7, 631 n., 676 n.; *Lover's Complaint, A*, 29; *Mad Monk, The*, 904 n.; *Mathematical Problem, A*, 7–9; *Melancholy*, 855–6; *Nightingale, The*, 406, 489 n., 490, 593–4, 631 n., 676 n.; *Nil Pejus est Caelibe Vitâ*, 4–5; *O'er her pil'd grave*, 669; *Osorio*, 304, 313, 316, 318, 320, 324–7, 344–5, 349 n., 350–2, 355–8, 360 n., 384–5, 387, 400–2, 409, 412, 479, 585, 589, 603–4, 606, 608, 611, 624, 653, 662, 745, 764 n., 958; *Pains of Sleep, The*, 982–4, 991, 1009–10; *Pantisocracy*, 104, 134; *Perspiration*, 84; *Pity*, 134, 254; *Pixies, Songs of the*, 299, 333, 399; *Plot Discovered, The*, 152, 155, 196 and note, 205; *Poems on Various Subjects* (1796), 153 n., 156 n., 157, 162–3, 173, 186–7, 190–1, 193, 195–7, 201, 204–5, 219, 220 n., 243; *Poems* (1797), 153 n., 237 n., 241–3, 247, 252 n., 275, 278, 297–300, 309, 312–16, 324–5, 328–34, 356, 382, 390; *Poems* (1803), 745, 799, 950 n.; *Poole, Lines to Thomas*, 163 n., 295; *Poole, To T.*, 296; *Priestley*, 140; *Rain, An Ode to the*, 857 n., 876; *Raven, The*, 391–2; *Recantation (The Mad Ox)*, 573; *Religious Musings*, 91 n., 147, 162–3, 187, 195 n., 197, 203, 205, 207, 215–16, 223–4, 243, 247, 293, 309, 329, 331, 391; *Remorse*, 764 n.; '*Robbers, The*', *To the Author of*, 122 n., 243; *Rose, The*, 58; *Ross, Lines written at the King's Arms*, 87, 95; *Sea-Shore, On revisiting the*, 752; *Sheridan, To R. B.*, 141–2; *Sigh, The*, 124; *Silver Thimble, The*, 187; *Snow-Drop, The*, 639–42; *Something Childish*, 488–9; *Sonnet composed on a Journey Homeward*, 246, 260–1, 277–8; *Sonnet on receiving a Letter*, 245–6; *Sonnet to a Friend*, 246–7, 261, 429; *Sonnet to Earl Stanhope*, 156 n., 242; *Sonnets attempted in the Manner of Contemporary Writers*, 357–9, 404; *Sonnets from Various Authors*, 252, 285, 287, 571 n.; *Sonnets on Eminent Characters*, 131, 137, 143, 156; *Southey, To Robert*, 143; *Stranger Minstrel, A*, 563 n., 904; *Talleyrand to Lord Grenville*, 560–1; *Three Graves, The*, 883; *Tooke, Verses addressed to J. Horne*, 224–5; *Tranquillity, Ode to*, 997–8, 1004; *Translation*, 107–8; *Triumph of Loyalty, The*, 650, 662, 663 n.; *Two Round Spaces on the Tombstone, The*, 628 n., 632–3; *Unfortunate Woman, To an*, 314; *Unfortunate Woman at the Theatre, To an*, 313–14; *Vivit sed mihi non vivit*, 87–88, 92; *Wallenstein*, 574–5, 577, 579, 581, 583, 587, 610, 621, 626, 643, 648, 863; *Watchman, The*, 174–84, 188–203, 207–13, 268; *Wills of the Wisp, The*, 769; *Wish, A*, 28–29; *Written after a Walk*, 37–38, 242 n.; *Young Ass, To a*, 142–3; *Young Lady, To a*, 117–18; *Zapolya*, 466 n.

Coleridge, Sara (*née* Fricker), *Letters to*, 415, 420, 428, 435, 445, 449, 458, 470, 477, 481, 484, 496, 503, 776, 779, 785, 788, 879, 881, 882, 885, 886, 889, 891, 893, 898, 907, 939, 940, 977, 980, 984, 1024, 1025, 1037, 1057, 1062, 1068, 1109, 1114, 1135, 1142, 1156, 1169, 1170, 1180, 1182, 1183, 1185, 1187, 1190, 1204; 99, 103–5, 109, 113, 115, 132, 143, 145, 149 n., 150–1, 159–62, 164, 168–9, 171–3, 180, 185–6, 188, 190–2, 194, 203, 208–9, 211–12, 218, 220 n., 222, 226, 228, 231, 233–6, 241, 247, 251, 254, 257, 260, 263–6, 269–75, 285, 288, 292, 295–7, 301, 306, 308, 317, 320, 322, 326, 334, 336, 338–9, 349, 356, 358, 382, 384–5, 398, 401, 407–9, 414, 419, 441, 455, 458, 478, 489 n., 490–1, 510, 514, 516, 525, 530–4, 536, 540, 542, 545, 547, 550, 559, 562–3, 569–77, 579, 581–2, 584, 589, 609, 612, 615–16, 618–19, 621–3, 625–7, 632, 634, 645, 647, 651, 655–6, 662, 668, 673, 676, 705, 713, 724–6, 729, 733, 738, 741, 746, 757, 760, 762 n., 765–7, 770, 774, 780, 784, 799–800, 802, 804, 807, 812, 827, 830, 832–5, 847–8, 850, 859–60, 867, 875–6, 878, 899, 902–3, 906, 911, 914, 917, 919, 925–6, 928–9, 938, 944–5, 965, 975, 982, 990, 995, 1006–7, 1010, 1015, 1017–18, 1022–3, 1027, 1031, 1040, 1046, 1049, 1051–2, 1059, 1067, 1074,

## Index

Coleridge, Sara (*née* Fricker) (*cont.*) 1085, 1098, 1112, 1129–30, 1149, 1156, 1162–3, 1165, 1167, 1174, 1176, 1200.

Coleridge, Sara (daughter), 902, 906, 911, 919, 943, 945, 958, 960, 975; described by Coleridge, 977, 1014–15, 1022; 979, 1004, 1017, 1031, 1060, 1062, 1071, 1117, 1126, 1139.

Coleridge, William (brother), 310–11.

Coleridge, William Hart (nephew), 59, 311, 1009, 1203.

Coleridge, William, 279, 444, 550.

Collins, William, 279, 444, 550.

Colson, John, *Letters to*, 234, 264; 202–3, 254.

Condillac, 675, 947, 1139.

Cooper, Thomas, 115.

Cornish, George, *Letter to*, 72; 39 n., 73.

Cottle, Amos, 324, 330, 551, 826.

Cottle, Joseph, *Letters to*, 153, 156, 157, 159, 160, 162, 173, 174, 185, 186, 187, 189, 190, 193, 201, 204, 205, 217, 241, 248, 296, 309, 312, 315, 319, 321, 324, 325, 328, 329, 330, 340, 344, 356, 380, 386, 390, 399, 400, 402, 411, 546; 152, 153 n., 161, 168, 183, 190, 210, 222, 226, 270, 272, 274–5, 323, 358, 382–3, 385, 405 n., 414, 542 n., 543, 551, 586, 645–6, 746, 749, 826, 829, 847, 959.

*Courier*, 351, 582, 1076, 1086, 1135, 1163, 1166, 1168, 1179–80, 1186.

Cowper, William, 279, 396, 829, 965.

*Critical Review*, 224, 227, 263, 265 n., 270, 273, 318, 489 n., 1162.

Croft, Herbert, 340, 585 n.

Crompton, Peter, 179, 229, 231, 233–4, 240, 242, 305–6, 607, 746, 786, 934, 1021, 1039–40, 1052, 1070.

Cruikshank, John and family, 161, 210 n., 218, 242, 251, 257, 265, 269, 272, 297, 301, 415, 417, 455, 458, 480, 526–7, 541, 574, 670, 788, 800.

Curran, John P., 612, 619–20, 624.

Currie, James, 607–8, 746, 1044.

Dalton, John, 1059.

Daniel, Samuel, 1079.

Dante, 951, 1059.

Danvers, Charles, 168, 175, 222, 226, 549, 746, 748, 750, 913.

Darwin, Erasmus, 177–8, 214, 216, 294, 305, 320 n., 412, 574, 647, 695, 738, 829–30.

Davy, Humphry, *Letters to*, 556, 589, 604, 611, 630, 637, 648, 662, 670, 726, 733, 773, 1077, 1101; 548–9, 553, 559, 564, 571, 576, 588–9, 592 n., 613, 617, 623, 651, 668, 708, 715–16, 725, 744–5, 748, 751, 758, 767–8, 771, 777–9, 782, 787, 789, 861, 927, 938–9, 1012, 1028, 1032, 1042, 1045, 1047, 1050, 1071, 1076, 1079–80, 1104, 1106, 1187, 1191.

Decatur, Stephen, 1150.

Defoe, Daniel, 347, 653.

Dennis, John, 1007.

Derkheim, Capt., *Letter to*, 1184; 1174–6, 1178, 1183, 1185–8.

Descartes, R., 672, 675; discussion of, 677–703; 708, 947.

Diogenes Laërtius, 682–4.

Disney, John, 101, 153, 223, 293, 577–8, 821.

Drayton, Michael, 617 n., 811.

Dryden, John, 702, 743, 955, 1054.

Duns, J. Scotus, 681, 746, 787 n., 944 n., 1020.

Dupuis, C. F., 260.

Dyer, George, *Letters to*, 100, 151, 154, 218, 1091; 97–98, 101, 105, 117, 211, 252, 324, 393, 540, 549, 749, 941, 959, 1096.

Dyer, Gilbert, 530–1, 535.

*Edinburgh Review*, 912, 936, 953, 1039.

Edmondson, Mr., 774, 973–4, 981, 999, 1017, 1067.

Edwards, John, *Letters to*, 178, 181, 188, 191; 230.

Edwards, Templer, & Co., *Letter to*, 819.

Edwards, Thomas, 118–19.

Eichhorn, J. G., 477, 494, 861–2.

Elliot, Hugh, 1170, 1182, 1202.

Emmet, Robert, 999, 1002–3.

Erigena, J. Scotus, 903, 949, 954.

Estlin, John Prior, *Letters to*, 222, 232, 292, 301, 326, 327, 337, 361, 367, 369, 370, 385, 407, 410, 576, 820, 892; 162, 178, 189, 193, 201, 210 n., 226, 257, 270, 274, 312 n., 358, 369, 375, 387, 391–2, 413, 426, 476, 483, 829, 860–1, 880, 886, 902.

Evans, Anne, *Letters to*, 29, 54; 22, 24–25, 29, 33, 48.

Evans, Mrs. Charlotte, *Letters to*, 21, 32, 47; 19–20, 54.

Evans, Elizabeth, 22, 31, 49, 87, 92.

Evans, Mrs. Elizabeth, of Darley, 227–9, 231–4, 306, 351–2, 789.

Evans, Mary, *Letters to*, 24, 31, 49, 129, 144; 19 n., 22, 61 n., 77 n., 87–88, 92, 112–13, 121, 123–4, 145, 164, 170.

Evans, Tom, 5 n., 19 n., 22.

Evanson, Edward, 822.

Favell, Samuel, 99–100, 104 n., 109, 137, 336.

# Index

Feder, J. G. H., 679.
Fellows, John, *Letters to*, 211, 219, 227; 178–80.
Fichte, J. G., 673–4, 768.
Ficino, M., 682.
Fielding, Henry, 725, 955.
Findlay, Capt. John, 1083–4, 1086, 1088–9, 1099, 1105, 1110, 1116, 1119, 1123, 1125, 1136 n., 1201.
Flower, Benjamin, *Letters to*, 196, 247, 266; 98 n., 116, 288.
Fox, Charles, 325, 551.
Fox, Charles James, 51, 178, 565, 568, 573, 665, 676, 771, 892, 912, 954, 1066, 1105, 1179–80.
Fox, Edward Long, 254.
Fox, George, 893, 956.
Freeling, Francis, *Letter to*, 945.
Frend, William, 20, 153, 156, 293.
Frere, John Hookham, 34 n., 630, 1091.
Fricker, Edith, *see* Southey, Edith.
Fricker, Eliza and Martha, 99, 143, 464, 530–1, 536, 748.
Fricker, George, *Letters to*, 1188, 1192; 119, 192, 273, 548–9, 786, 1064, 1067, 1085, 1118, 1121, 1123, 1140, 1184, 1191.
Fricker, Mrs., 114, 123, 162, 171, 192, 207–8, 220 n., 273, 326, 365, 368, 387, 464, 483, 573, 590, 662, 739, 748, 891, 903, 926, 953, 1023, 1059, 1158.
Fricker, Sara, *see* Coleridge, Sara.

Gassendi, Pierre, 680, 701.
Gerrald, Joseph, 214–15, 221.
Gessner, Salomon, 808–11, 813–14, 856–7, 863–4, 874.
Gibbon, Edward, 619, 644, 877.
Godwin, William: *Letters to*, 560, 579, 587, 619, 621, 624, 635, 652, 656, 706, 713, 724, 735, 742, 761, 775, 781, 782, 941, 946, 950, 1047, 1056; 102, 138–9, 141; *Political Justice*, 115, 198–200, 213, 247, 253, 267, 293, 320, 736; 214–15, 221, 269, 306, 413, 433, 517, 529, 549, 553, 557; *St. Leon*, 559, 570; 590, 612; *Antonio*, 621, 624, 652–3, 656–8, 714; 628; *Abbas*, 713–14, 742–3; *Thoughts*, 736, 751, 761; 784; *Life of Chaucer*, 951; 1026, 1051, 1055, 1057–9, 1066–7, 1071–3.
Goethe, 435.
Goldsmith, Oliver, 332.
Gracchus, Caius, *Letter to*, 197.
Gray, Thomas, 18, 27–28, 116, 133, 278, 309, 444.
Greenough, G. B., *Letters to*, 520, 718, 784, 1050, 1089, 1107; 497, 708, 713, 1059–60, 1078, 1096.

Grenville, William W., Lord, 560–1, 1066, 1075.
Grey, Charles, Lord Howick, 1180, 1182–3.
Grotius, 861, 1189.
Gwyn, General, 63, 66, 72, 75 n.

Hall, Joseph, 870, 877.
Hall, Robert, 197, 247–8.
Hamilton, Anthony, 464 n., 476, 517, 519.
Harrington, James, 870.
Harris, James, 679.
Harris, John, 657.
Hart family, 57, 310–11, 355, 531–2.
Hartley, David, 126, 137, 200, 209, 215, 245, 280, 371, 647, 686, 689, 695, 703, 706, 768, 947, 949, 961.
Hawkes, Thomas, 230, 232–3, 235 n.
Hayley, William, 829, 847, 963.
Hays, Mary, 550, 563, 734.
Hazlitt, William, 394, 411 n., 413 n., 800, 949, 957–8, 960; characterized by Coleridge, 990–1; amatory escapade, 990 n., 1024 n.; 1004, 1025 n., 1058, 1082 n.
Heath, Charles, *Letter to*, 96.
Herbert, Edward, 681–2.
Herder, J. G., 535, 861–2.
Herschel, William, 727, 919.
Heyne, C. G., 472, 475, 477.
Hobbes, Thomas, 675–6, 680, 683, 685–6, 691, 701, 707, 746.
Hobhouse, Benjamin, 219, 223, 368, 474, 476.
Hogarth, William, 507, 1134.
Holcroft, Thomas, 138–9, 215.
Holland, Philemon, 943.
Homer, 40, 258, 348, 546, 934.
Hooker, Richard, 956.
Horace, 444, 646, 653, 700, 867 n., 939.
Horsley, Samuel, 102, 265, 318 n., 821, 829.
Howell, Mr., of Bridgwater, 301, 326, 341, 368, 372, 377.
Howell, Mr., of London, 776 n., 777–8, 780, 787, 880.
Hucks, Joseph, 82 n., 83–85, 87, 90, 92–93, 528, 540.
Hume, David, 197, 385, 538, 578, 588, 644, 672, 679, 681, 701, 703, 707, 743, 746, 768, 927–8, 1194.
Hutchinson, George, 746–7, 750, 753–4.
Hutchinson, Joanna, *Letter to*, 753; 850, 1012.
Hutchinson, Mary, *see* Wordsworth, Mary.
Hutchinson, Sara, *Letters to*, 779, 790, 804, 825, 834, 841, 848, 851, 852,

( 1213 )

# Index

Hutchinson, Sara, *Letters to (cont.)* 1023, 1080; 546 n., 613 n., 672–3, 746 n., 747–8, 760, 762 n., 785, 788, 879 n., 892, 894, 908–9, 917, 1025, 1075, 1165, 1199 n., 1205.
Hutchinson, Thomas, 746 n., 748, 753–4, 825–6, 850, 852.
Hutton, James, 177, 222.

Iamblichus, 262, 682.
Inchbald, Mrs. Elizabeth, 589, 743–4.
Ireland, Samuel and W. H., 286, 386, 391, 585.

Jackson, William, of Exeter, 533, 539.
Jackson, William, of Greta Hall, 614, 618–19, 644, 661, 673, 717, 740, 780, 786, 789, 819, 827, 833–4, 836, 846–7, 849, 860, 891, 898–9, 929, 940, 979, 1025, 1058, 1062, 1140, 1144, 1159, 1163, 1184, 1205.
Jennings, James, 106, 290, 959.
Johnson, Joseph, 417–18, 420, 432, 550, 552, 632.
Johnson, Samuel, 619, 628–9, 644, 767, 877, 1054.
Jonson, Ben, 1054.
Jordan, Dorothea, 51, 654, 665.
Jortin, John, 807.
Josephus, 861, 867.
Juvenal, 685.

Kant, Immanuel, 209, 284 n., 444, 675–6, 707, 768, 936.
Keate, John, 45, 56 n.
Kemble, J. P., 318, 357, 423, 621, 635, 657.
King, John (surgeon), 650, 852, 931, 937.
King, Mr. and Mrs. (Sarah Poole), 218, 250–1, 266, 270–1, 276, 358, 662, 733, 739, 907, 1043.
Klopstock, F. G., 420, 435, 437, 441–5, 811.
Kotzebue, A. F. F., 378, 435.

Laing, F., 1135, 1140, 1142–4.
Lamb, Charles: *Letters to*, 238, 403; 136, 146–7, 262, 267, 286, 297; poems printed with Coleridge's and Lloyd's (1797), 299, 313, 324, 330–1; 309; visits Stowey, 328–9, 330 n., 334–6; misunderstanding with Coleridge, 357–9, 390 n., 400 n., 403–7, 419 n., 489 n., 542; 540, 552 n., 563, 574, 579–83; described by Coleridge, 588; on *The Ancient Mariner*, 602 n.; 612, 624, 645–6, 653–4, 662, 775; visits Keswick, 846 n., 852 n., 855; 940–3, 946, 950 n., 960, 1039, 1052, 1057–8,
1064, 1068, 1073–5, 1080 n., 1089–90, 1095, 1117, 1129, 1177, 1184, 1191, 1193.
Lamb, Mary, 147, 267, 580, 588 n., 846 n., 852 n., 941–2, 1057, 1072, 1090, 1181 n., 1184.
Lambert, J. H., 675.
Landor, W. S., 540, 573.
Lardner, Nathaniel, 195, 197, 371, 554, 821–4, 867.
Law, Edmund, 807.
Lawson, Sirs Gilfrid and Wilfrid, 455, 610, 614–15, 618–19, 645, 717, 834, 868–9, 871.
Leckie, G. F., 1059, 1090, 1150–1, 1153–5, 1157 n.
Le Grice, C. V., 2, 16–17, 20, 51, 70, 135, 336.
Le Grice, Samuel, 99–100, 102.
Leibnitz, G. W., 472, 590, 676, 702, 747.
Leslie, John, 876–77, 923, 1011–12.
Lessing, G. E., 197, 437, 443, 455, 480, 516, 518–19, 523, 553, 559, 563, 610, 632, 861.
Lewis, M. G., 318 n., 378–9, 905.
Lindsey, Theophilus, 101, 821.
Linley, William, 304, 352 n., 355, 357–8, 384, 603.
Literary Fund, the Committee of, *Letter to*, 220.
Lloyd, Charles (poet), 235–8, 240, 243–4, 251, 252 n., 256–7, 263–4, 266, 270, 273–5, 285–6, 301, 313, 315–16, 318, 320 n., 324, 330, 334 n., 345 n., 357–9, 390, 399–400, 403–7, 410, 489 n., 524 n., 525, 541–2, 563, 620, 651, 654, 846, 850.
Lloyd, Charles, Sr., *Letters to*, 240, 255, 263; 235–7, 270, 273, 320.
Locke, John, 126, 200, 209, 280, 675–6; discussion of, 677–703, 708–9; 707, 746, 927.
Longman, T. N., *Letters to*, 654, 715; 551, 553, 556, 570, 579–80, 583, 590, 592 n., 605, 617 n., 626, 646, 648, 665, 668–9, 707, 711, 733, 736, 739, 745, 750, 760, 863, 948–9, 950 n., 955 n., 960, 963, 1046, 1052, 1063, 1066, 1074.
Lonsdale, Earl of, *see* Lowther, Sir James.
Losh, James, 308, 786.
Lovell, Mary (*née* Fricker), 96 n., 99, 101, 143, 150, 207–8, 211, 553, 786, 789, 833–4, 859–60, 924–5, 929, 934, 937, 992, 1015, 1115, 1130, 1140.
Lovell, Robert, *Letter to*, 96; 85, 90, 99, 101, 104–5, 129, 134, 138–9, 149 n., 150, 156, 164, 170, 173, 207–8, 215.

( 1214 )

# Index

Lovell, Robert (son), 207, 211, 789, 943.
Lowth, Robert, 521, 974.
Lowther, Sir James, Lord Lonsdale, 828, 837.
Lowther, Lord, 874, 958, 973.
Lucretius, 205, 674, 810.
Luff, Charles, 890, 894, 898, 911, 913, 918.
Lully, Raymond, 947.
Luther, Martin, 703, 1189.
*Lyrical Ballads* (1798), 216 n., 387 n., 399–400, 402–3, 411–12, 489 n., 592 n.
*Lyrical Ballads* (1800), 585, 592–603, 606, 611, 616–18, 620–1, 623, 627, 631–2, 634–5, 637, 643, 646, 648–9, 651, 654, 658–9, 663–8, 676, 707–8, 714, 737–8, 745, 784, 804.
*Lyrical Ballads* (1802), 811–12, 827, 830–1, 1013, 1118.

Macaulay, Alexander, 1142 n., 1158 n., 1163, 1201.
Mackintosh, James, 359 and note, 567, 569, 588, 628 n., 633, 636, 675–6, 681, 695, 736–7, 770–1, 780, 783, 787, 870, 931–2, 1016, 1041, 1087.
Maclaurin, C., 702.
Malebranche, N., 679, 695, 703.
Malthus, T. R., 417, 517–18, 1026–7, 1039, 1191.
Martin, Henry, *Letters to*, 90, 106.
Massinger, Philip, 1054.
Mawman, Joseph, 788, 949, 1046.
Meanley, Astley, 182, 191.
Mendelssohn, Moses, 284 n.
Middleton, T. F., 15, 17–18, 21, 26, 46, 112.
Milton, John, 122, 170, 216, 223, 258, 275, 279, 281, 313, 319–20, 437, 442–5, 513, 530, 542, 557, 575, 582, 584, 658, 679, 709, 723, 738, 751, 791, 809, 830, 858, 864, 866–7, 869–71, 877, 899, 910, 955, 960, 1018, 1022, 1033–4, 1040, 1054, 1107, 1162.
Montagu, Basil, *Letter to*, 870; 361–3, 527, 567–8, 757, 763.
Montgomery, James, 182–4.
*Monthly Magazine, Letter to* editor of, 381; 248, 259, 263, 268, 270, 273, 279, 312, 315, 357 n., 369, 549.
*Monthly Review, Letter to* editor of, 647; 224, 227, 320.
Moore, Col. Nathaniel, 889–90, 957 n.
Moore, Thomas, 905.
Morgan, Mrs., 168–9, 171.
*Morning Chronicle, Letters to* editor of, 61, 131; 129, 138, 146, 155–6, 200, 214, 221–2, 226–7, 1179.

*Morning Post, Letters to* editor of, 391, 550, 560, 639; 359, 363, 365, 381, 386, 417, 419, 541, 545 n., 554, 559 and note, 564, 568–9, 572–5, 581–2, 594 n., 612, 618–19, 623, 626–31, 634, 657, 759, 762, 776, 790 n., 813, 815 n., 855–7, 865, 869, 874, 875 n., 876, 892, 912, 946, 950–1, 954, 1007, 1013, 1016, 1075–6, 1086.
Mottley, J. C., 1107, 1111, 1113–21, 1123–4, 1130, 1134–5, 1149.

Napoleon, 436, 533, 539, 554, 557–8, 561, 583, 603, 626–9, 701, 781, 912, 1006–7, 1010, 1017, 1033, 1055, 1154.
Nelson, Horatio, Viscount, 420, 430, 442, 768, 1059, 1079, 1132.
Nesbitt, Fanny, 57 n., 60.
Newton, Isaac, 280, 679, 686, 702–3, 709, 751, 866, 1014, 1046.
Noble, G., 1174–5, 1178, 1202.
Northcote, James, 958 n., 1101, 1108, 1110, 1113.
Northmore, Thomas, 528–9, 540, 861.

Ogle, Nathaniel, 71, 76 n.
Ovid, 858.
Owen, William (later Pughe), 955.

Paine, Thomas, 39–40, 193, 197, 327, 386, 540.
Paley, William, 48, 200, 720, 807, 822, 949, 954, 1189.
Palma, C. F., 466.
Parr, Samuel, 101, 331, 494, 585, 736, 771.
Parry, Charles and Frederick, *Letters to*, 496, 520; 474, 476, 497, 507, 520, 523.
Pascal, 478, 994.
Peach, Mr., 780, 898.
Pearce, William, 15, 17–18, 20, 46, 53, 74, 79–80.
Perry, James, 138, 222, 226–7.
Phillips, Richard, 368, 549, 552 n., 570, 573, 592 n., 618, 661, 665–6, 670, 948–9, 952.
Pilling, Robert H., 1020 n.
Pindar, 17, 864.
Pinney, John Frederick and Azariah, 216 n., 399 n., 567–8, 613, 747–8, 757, 762, 765, 770, 772, 1077.
Pitt, William, 10, 203, 322, 432, 510, 528, 539, 568, 573–5, 581, 583, 603, 626–7, 1007, 1075, 1179.
Plampin, James, 15, 59 n., 64 n., 80–81.
Planck, G. J., 862.
Platner, E., 679.

( 1215 )

## Index

Plato, 261, 295, 554, 675, 680, 682, 684, 693, 776 n., 866, 872, 947, 954, 1195, 1197.
Pliny, 805.
Plutarch, 681, 861, 943.
Poole, Richard, 207, 217, 408, 411, 609.
Poole, Thomas, *Letters to*, 160, 194, 202, 204, 207, 210, 217, 226, 228, 230, 235, 242, 249, 251, 257, 263, 266, 269, 271, 287, 288, 296, 302, 310, 332, 338, 345, 346, 352, 358, 374, 380, 387, 408, 411, 413, 414, 415, 418, 430, 441, 453, 478, 490, 510, 526, 527, 556, 562, 571, 574, 581, 584, 607, 617, 634, 650, 661, 664, 668, 674, 706, 708, 710, 719, 730, 738, 755, 758, 763, 769, 771, 776, 777, 787, 799, 899, 906, 920, 938, 944, 1009, 1011, 1035, 1041, 1045, 1063, 1108; 162 n., 163, 217, 234, 265, 297, 301, 308, 312, 315, 317, 319 n., 320, 324–6, 329, 331, 334, 339, 342–4, 363, 369, 373 n., 385, 387, 391, 403, 417–18, 419 n., 427, 446, 449, 459, 464, 472, 476, 483–4, 489, 496, 509, 519, 524–5, 530, 532, 534–6, 539, 569, 591, 609–10, 615, 622 n., 643, 677 n., 779–82, 788, 848, 876, 920–4, 926–8, 930–4, 1038, 1040–1, 1043–4, 1047, 1052, 1061, 1065, 1067, 1069, 1075, 1085, 1124, 1131.
Pope, Alexander, 50, 412, 545, 873, 955, 1007, 1054.
Porphyry, 947.
Porson, Richard, 44, 45 n., 138–9, 494.
Pretyman, George, 540.
Priestley, Joseph, 89 n., 91, 98, 192–3, 215, 217, 372, 443, 482, 675, 710, 806, 821, 829.
Purkis, Samuel, *Letters to*, 580, 583, 614, 918, 926; 413, 559, 571, 933, 938–9, 1047.
Pye, H. J., 829.
Pythagoras, 680, 691.

Ramus, Petrus, 947.
Rathbone, William, 607–8.
Rees, Abraham, 675.
Reid, Thomas, 947.
Remnant, William, 417, 432, 446.
Reynell, Richard, 326, 341 n., 1170.
Richardson, Samuel, 955.
Rickman, John, *Letters to*, 1061, 1063, 1067, 1074, 1087, 1090, 1094, 1096, 1104, 1120; 768, 941, 943–4, 960, 1011, 1036, 1039, 1051–2, 1058, 1060, 1065–7, 1071, 1083–5, 1112, 1117, 1124.

Ridout, J. G., *Letters to*, 942, 1098; 787, 941.
Ritson, Joseph, 936.
Robertson, William, 619.
Robinson, Mary E., *Letter to*, 903.
Robinson, Mrs. Mary, 318 n., 550, 562–3, 575–6, 589, 621 n., 629, 639, 669, 904–6.
Rogers, Samuel, 333, 412, 676, 737, 744, 829, 913, 964–5, 1093, 1098.
Roscoe, William, 230, 607–8, 615, 746.
Rose, George, 1042.
Roskilly, Mr., *Letter to*, 450; 440, 449, 455, 570, 578 n.
Rossiter, A. P., 854 n., 865 n.
Rousseau, J. J., 214, 245, 563.
Rowe, John, 361–2, 368, 370, 373, 375 379.
Rowe, Nicholas, 743.
Rumford, Count, 195, 203, 206, 210, 288.
Rush, Sir William and Lady, 757, 763, 786, 789, 850, 889.
Russell, Thomas, 1172 n., 1173–5, 1190, 1192, 1202.
Russell, William, 554.

Saint Augustine, 542, 812, 1004.
Schiller, J. C. F., 122, 209, 279, 294 n., 304, 325, 378, 435, 444, 574–5, 577, 587, 628, 648.
Scott, Walter, 956, 989, 1039, 1064, 1191.
Scotus, Duns, *see* Duns, J. Scotus.
Scotus, Erigena, *see* Erigena, J. Scotus.
Search, Edward, *see* Tucker, Abraham.
Selden, John, 617 n.
Sennertus, Daniel, 531, 683–4.
Shaftesbury, Earl of, 214, 701.
Shakespeare, 50, 135, 279, 304, 313, 325, 386, 391, 412, 439, 444, 507, 557, 585, 653, 672, 709, 738, 751, 810, 847, 858, 919, 951, 955, 960, 1022, 1034, 1054, 1139, 1160.
Sharp, Granville, 820–1, 829.
Sharp, Richard, *Letters to*, 1031, 1043, 1108; 675–6, 737, 744, 783, 907, 913, 954, 990, 1050, 1067, 1083, 1085, 1093, 1099–1100, 1112, 1185, 1191.
Sheridan, Richard Brinsley, *Letter to*, 304; 313, 316, 327, 356–8, 384–5, 409, 564, 603–4, 606, 608, 611, 621, 623–4, 646, 652–4, 1111, 1114, 1119.
Shuter, W., 412 n.
Siddons, Mrs. Sarah, 51, 318, 423.
Sidney, Sir Philip, 1054.
Skinner, Capt., 1151–6.
Smerdon, Fulwood, 1, 37–40, 60, 123–4, 127.

( 1216 )

# Index

Smith, Adam, 799.
Smith, Charlotte, 252 n., 571, 589, 829.
Smith, John, *Letter to*, 196; 182–3.
Smith, R. P., 34.
Smith, William, 1180–3.
Sotheby, William: *Letters to*, 808, 813, 855, 862, 868, 871, 873, 1086, 1093, 1099, 1106, 1140; *Georgics*, 812; *Orestes*, 855, 857, 863, 872–4; *Tour through Parts of Wales*, 855; 941, 1033, 1071, 1078, 1080, 1122, 1163.
South, Robert, 701.
Southey, Edith (*née* Fricker), *Letter to*, 102; 99, 103, 115, 132, 143, 150, 158, 173, 191, 336, 489, 530–1, 553, 571, 717, 745–6, 750, 757, 760, 767, 786, 828, 833–4, 848, 859–60, 911, 925–6, 928–9, 975, 984, 992, 994, 1006, 1010, 1015, 1017, 1027, 1112, 1117, 1139, 1144.
Southey, Robert: *Letters to*, 82, 85, 97, 101, 103, 105, 109, 112, 118, 121, 132, 133, 138, 145, 148, 149, 157, 163, 248, 290, 332, 345, 358, 523, 524, 530, 533, 538, 545, 547, 551, 553, 562, 569, 572, 575, 585, 716, 727, 744, 747, 748, 750, 766, 774, 778, 828, 846, 851, 859, 902, 910, 923, 928, 934, 935, 942, 953, 955, 959, 960, 974, 982, 988, 1026, 1028, 1039, 1050, 1051, 1066, 1071, 1083, 1097, 1110, 1123, 1125, 1144, 1148, 1156, 1160, 1176; first meeting with Coleridge, 82 n., 163; 95–96, 144 n., 152–3, 155; first quarrel with Coleridge, 157–9, 161, 163–73, 294; journey to Portugal, 173, 208 n., 217; 175, 185, 243–5, 258, 279, 286, 300, 313, 344, 356–7; second quarrel with Coleridge, 358–9, 390 n., 403 n., 404, 405 n., 410, 489 n.; 447; reconciliation with Coleridge, 523–5, 541 n.; 528–9, 556–8, 565; second journey to Portugal, 585, 588; 623, 726, 735; returns to England, 745; 750, 757, 759–60, 766, 774–5, 785–9, 800, 806, 826, 829 n., 932, 958 n., 965, 985, 992–4, 1001, 1004, 1006, 1010–11, 1014–15, 1017, 1019–22, 1024–5, 1037–8, 1045, 1056–8, 1062, 1068–9, 1074, 1095–6, 1115, 1117, 1120, 1135, 1139, 1142–4, 1159, 1165, 1182, 1184, 1188, 1191, 1200.
  *Works: Amadis of Gaul*, 829; *Annual Anthology*, see separate entry; *Curse of Kehama*, 1071; *Joan of Arc*, 166, 172, 183, 196, 201, 203, 247, 258, 285–6, 293, 300, 313, 412, 551; *Madoc*, 546, 646, 745, 750, 831, 913, 1004, 1024, 1030–1, 1071, 1073, 1085, 1162; *Poems* (1795), 95 n., 133–5, 139, 300; *Poems* (1797), 133 n., 134–5, 144 n., 275, 290, 297, 300, 320, 333–4, 551; *Thalaba*, 533, 546, 551–2, 570, 646, 745, 759–60, 912 n., 1039.
Southey, Thomas, 539, 859–60, 924–5, 929.
Spallanzani, L., 649, 651.
Sparrow, Mr. and Mrs., 16–18, 20, 35–38, 43, 532.
Spenser, Edmund, 391, 431, 769 n., 951, 955, 960, 1054.
Spinoza, 534, 551, 590, 768, 1196.
Stanhope, Charles, Lord, 156, 242, 787.
Statius, 289.
Stedman, J. G., 535.
Sterne, Laurence, 955.
Stillingfleet, Edward, Bishop of Worcester, 679, 683.
Stoddart, John, 643, 662, 744, 825, 911, 965, 977, 1110, 1129, 1134, 1137, 1139–40, 1143, 1149, 1158, 1164 n., 1166 n., 1175 n., 1181, 1191 n.
Stolberg, F. L., Count, 443, 511, 769, 865 n.
Street, T. J., 629, 1179, 1187.
Strutt, Jedediah, and sons, 177–9, 227, 306, 789.
Stuart, Daniel, *Letters to*, 561, 578, 581, 603, 626, 627, 628, 729, 759, 763, 777, 780, 1112, 1119, 1131, 1145, 1149, 1164, 1166, 1174, 1177, 1179; 359, 386, 417, 420, 535, 541, 545 n., 547, 552–4, 559, 564, 568, 573–4, 581–2, 591, 618, 624, 631, 634, 637, 657, 736, 751, 774, 787–8, 876, 880, 885, 912, 945, 950, 1007, 1016, 1040, 1044–7, 1051, 1059, 1062, 1067, 1086, 1090, 1104, 1108–9, 1111–12, 1124, 1129, 1144, 1147, 1158, 1177, 1180–1, 1188.
Süssmilch, J. P., 518.
Swift, Jonathan, 260, 955.

Taylor, Jeremy, 245, 487, 530, 807, 870, 877, 955, 960.
Taylor, Thomas, 260, 608, 987.
Taylor, William, *Letter to*, 564; 530, 535, 540, 576, 860–2, 955, 1066, 1069, 1105, 1161–2.
*Telegraph*, 150, 152, 433.
Thelwall, John and Mrs., *Letters to*, 204, 212, 220, 253, 258, 276, 287, 293, 305, 340, 343, 348, 382, 655, 667, 722, 1017, 1019; 339–42, 414 n., 1039.
Thomson, James, 154–5.

( 1217 )

*Index*

Tillotson, John, 807.
Tobin, James Webbe, *Letters to*, 612, 622, 1130; 345, 550, 556, 634, 650, 726–7, 735, 739, 744, 782, 930, 937, 942, 1012, 1063, 1067–8, 1071, 1077, 1085, 1089, 1094–5, 1099, 1101, 1129, 1188.
Tobin, John, 345 n., 942.
Tomkins, P. W., 808 n., 813, 856, 863–4, 874.
Tomkins, Thomas, 10–11, 24.
Tooke, J. Horne, 224–5, 254, 307, 417, 494, 559–60, 625, 720.
Toulmin, Joshua, 301, 326, 372, 377, 407–9.
Tourdes, J., 649, 651.
Trollope, A. W., 6.
Tucker, Abraham, 949, 952.
Tuckett, G. L., *Letter to*, 61; 42–43, 46, 64 n., 70, 77 n., 192 n.
Turner, Sharon, 955.
Tyschen, T. C., 494.

Underwood, T. R., 733–4, 744, 786, 938, 939 n.
Unknown Correspondents, *Letters to*, 128, 208 n.

Vallon, Annette and Caroline, 788 n., 849.
Vane, Sir Frederick, 490.
Villettes, W. A., 1086, 1139–40.
Virgil, 139, 546, 672, 722, 743, 811.
Voltaire, 78, 197, 702.
Von Axens, 431–2, 457, 517.
Voss, J. H., 283 n., 834, 856.

Wade, Josiah, *Letters to*, 175, 176, 180, 184, 190, 229, 316, 321, 338, 369, 401, 704; 100, 168, 174 n., 179, 222–3, 226, 228, 232, 270, 274, 358, 368, 380, 414, 426, 483, 828–9.
Wakefield, Gilbert, 101, 153, 156, 201, 528, 803.
Wallis, G. A., 1172–3.
Warburton, William, 803, 821.
Ward, George, 1046.
Ward, Thomas, *Letters to*, 536, 537; 238, 243, 251, 358, 375, 381, 417, 420, 435, 458, 476, 489, 495, 529, 572, 574, 583, 608, 618, 635, 651, 665, 669, 676, 733, 757, 777, 787, 800, 901, 907, 923, 934, 939, 945, 1011, 1014, 1046.
Warner, Richard, 826–7.
Warton, Thomas, Jr., 382.
Washington, George, 89.
Watson, Richard, Bishop of Llandaff, 193, 196 n., 197, 740.
Wedgwood annuity, 359 n., 360 n., 370–5, 377, 380–1, 383–5, 387, 412, 457, 496, 519, 552–3, 559, 583, 586, 591, 611, 646–7, 661–2, 665, 669–70, 710, 730, 739–41, 770, 819, 874, 926, 1023, 1049, 1109.
Wedgwood family, 359 n., 370, 383, 413, 883, 898, 900, 920, 932.
Wedgwood, Josiah, *Letters to*, 360, 364, 373, 464, 517, 567, 586, 591, 609, 642, 647, 677, 685, 691, 697; gift of £100 to Coleridge, 360–9, 383–4; 370–5, 377, 380, 383–4, 413–15, 417–18, 419 n., 431–2, 454, 457, 539 n., 579, 675, 708, 739–40, 744, 765, 767, 771–2, 788, 878–9, 890, 898, 900, 912, 920, 924–5, 927, 930–1, 934, 936–9, 1100.
Wedgwood, Thomas, *Letters to*, 380, 558, 874, 878, 913, 915, 921, 922, 931, 932, 990, 1039, 1042, 1100; 345 n., 360 n., 361, 363, 370, 373 n., 377, 380–5, 413, 519, 563, 567, 591, 609, 622 n., 642, 646–7, 650, 675–6, 733 n., 755 n., 756, 765, 776, 780, 787 n., 883–5, 889–92, 894, 897–902, 906–7, 909–12, 919–20, 923, 927–8, 930–1, 936, 938–9, 1011–12, 1032–4, 1044, 1046–8, 1051, 1062, 1065, 1124, 1165, 1169.
Weekes, Shadrach, 100, 103, 114, 122.
Weld, Isaac, 530.
Welles, A., *Letter to*, 986; 976, 989, 993–4, 1071, 1074.
White, James, 265, 286.
Wicksteed, John, *Letter to*, 392.
Wieland, C. M., 435, 444.
Wilberforce, William, 196, 654, 665–7.
Wilkinson, Thomas, 786, 789, 827, 939, 978–9, 981, 1130, 1140.
Wilson, Mrs., 644, 740, 786, 827–8, 884, 898, 1025, 1029, 1058, 1163, 1205.
Wolcot, John (Peter Pindar), 829, 905–6.
Wolff, Christian, 679.
Wollstonecraft (Godwin), Mary, 549, 553.
Wood, Isaac, *Letter to*, 375; 361, 363, 368.
Wordsworth, Christopher (brother), 541, 543, 820, 829.
Wordsworth, Dorothy: *Letters to*, 542, 672, 1058, 1064, 1115, 1148, 1159, 1168, 1199, 1203; 327; described by Coleridge, 330–1; 334, 336, 352, 379, 399 n., 403, 414, 416, 419, 421, 425–6, 431, 433, 440–1, 444–5, 451, 459, 479, 484, 490, 582, 592 n., 594 n., 613 n., 616 n., 617 n., 637 n., 664 n., 670, 718, 726, 737, 748, 762 n., 775, 788, 794, 811, 828, 848–9, 859–60, 870–1, 880 n., 894, 908–

( 1218 )

# Index

9, 911, 958, 964–5, 975, 978, 994, 1010, 1025, 1031–2, 1035, 1040, 1070, 1096, 1165, 1191 n.
Wordsworth, John (brother), 543–4, 732, 827, 880, 909 n., 921–2, 932, 939, 1165, 1168, 1170.
Wordsworth, John (son), 957, 975, 1012, 1060, 1117, 1205.
Wordsworth, Mary (née Hutchinson), 542 n., 545, 746 n., 753–4, 788, 792, 794, 828, 850, 852, 892, 894, 908, 958, 964, 975, 1031–2, 1035, 1040, 1060, 1065, 1118, 1165.
Wordsworth, Richard, *Letter to*, 525; 526–7, 942, 1064.
Wordsworth, William: *Letters to*, 377, 406, 440, 450, 452, 453, 527, 538, 547, 575, 957, 1058, 1064, 1115, 1148, 1159, 1168, 1199, 1203; 154 n.; early acquaintance with Coleridge, 215–16, 297; visit to Stowey, 319–20, 325 n.; Coleridge at Racedown, 325–9; Coleridge's estimate of, 325, 334, 391, 410, 491, 582, 584, 658, 714, 811, 957, 1032–4; 330, 331; settles at Alfoxden, 332 and note, 334, 336; 340; 'caballed against', 341–4, 403; 352, 359 n., 361 n., 399; proposal for volume of poems, see *Lyrical Ballads* (1798); 402, 410–12, 414; German tour, 415 n., 416, 419, 421, 426, 431, 433–4, 436, 440–6, 450–6, 458–60, 479, 484, 490–1; 519, 525–7, 543–5; settles at Grasmere, 544 n.; 546 n., 556, 565–8, 574; proposes new edition of *Lyrical Ballads*, see separate entry, 585–6, 588, 592; criticism of *Ancient Mariner*, 592 n., 602 n., 631 n.; 603, 606, 608, 610–14, 618, 620, 622–3, 627–8, 630–2, 635, 643, 654, 656–8, 661, 666, 670–1, 673, 676, 705, 707, 709–10, 715, 717–18, 726, 737, 739, 741 n., 742, 748–50, 755–7, 760, 762 n., 763, 765–6, 768, 771, 775; marriage, 788, 790 n., 874; 794, 799, 809, 811, 814, 817; visits Annette and Caroline Vallon in France, 825, 849, 851, 858; 827–9, 839, 859–60, 880 n., 894, 908–9, 911, 913, 937–9, 945, 950, 954, 960–1, 964–5, 972–4; visits Scotland, 975, 977–9, 985, 994, 1010; 977, 1012–13, 1018, 1020–3, 1025, 1031, 1037, 1040, 1049, 1053, 1058, 1072, 1074, 1078, 1087, 1095, 1104, 1115, 1121–2, 1124, 1131, 1161, 1163, 1165, 1171, 1173, 1177, 1181 n., 1188 n., 1191 n.; at Coleorton, 1199 n., 1200 n., 1203, 1205.
  *Works: Alcaeus to Sappho*, 628 n., 629; *A slumber did my spirit seal*, 480; *Borderers, The*, 325, 332, 345 n., 358, 400–2, 412, 415, 417, 547, 603, 623–4, 1116; *Brothers, The*, 611, 616, 676 n., 714, 738; *Butterfly, To a*, 800; *Character, A*, 784; *Convict, The*, 593, 595; *Excursion, The*, 327–8, 397–8, 631; *Guilt and Sorrow*, 216 n., 400, 411; *H.C., To Six Years Old*, 1014; *Her Eyes are Wild*, 652, 676 n.; *Highland Girl, To a*, 1060; *Intimations Ode*, 793, 797; *It was an April morning*, 637; *Joanna, To*, 827, 844; *Leech Gatherer*, see *Resolution and Independence*; *Lucy Gray*, 795; *Lyrical Ballads*, see separate entry; *Michael*, 649, 659, 663–4, 676 n., 707, 714, 738; *Pedlar, The*, see *Excursion*; *Peter Bell*, 411, 547, 791, 816, 978; *Poems on the Naming of Places*, 631 n., 637, 957; *Prelude, The*, 538, 1104; *Recluse, The*, 391, 527, 538, 575, 646, 1012–13, 1034, 1060, 1104, 1159 n., 1169; *Resolution and Independence*, 965–70; *Ruth*, 623, 632, 714, 830; *Sonnets*, 869, 1013, 1060; *Sparrow's Nest, The*, 801; *There was a Boy*, 452; *Three years she grew*, 632; *Tintern Abbey*, 489 n., 649, 1118–19.
Wrangham, Francis, *Letters to*, 107, 110, 120, 657, 750; 19 n., 201, 749.
Wright, Joseph, 177–8.
Wynn, C. W. W., 148, 169 n.

Young, Edward, 3, 864.

Zeno, 213, 554, 768.
Zimmermann, E. A. W., 535.
Zimmermann, J. G., 535.

PRINTED IN
GREAT BRITAIN
AT THE
UNIVERSITY PRESS
OXFORD
BY
CHARLES BATEY
PRINTER
TO THE
UNIVERSITY